# The New Century Hymnal

# The New Century Hymnal

*Jesus Christ is the same yesterday and today and forever.*
*Hebrews 13:8*

## The Pilgrim Press
*Cleveland, Ohio*

# The New Century Hymnal

# CONTENTS

vi

# FOREWORD

The praise of God proclaimed through music begins in scripture with the song of Miriam and Moses at the Exodus and culminates in a reprise of their anthem by an apocalyptic choir of the saints at the close of history. For Jews and Christians the faithful people of God at worship are preeminently a community of song.

The psalmist calls us to celebrate our living faith not only in hymns from the past but in every "new song" inspired by the marvelous deeds of God across all time. The Christian story itself was sung by Mary, by the angelic choir at Bethlehem, at the gathering in the Upper Room, and throughout the churches of the New Testament. Hymns that touched the hearts of the faithful in enduring ways became part of the memory of the church. Today we sing the poetry of Ambrose of Milan and Hildegard of Bingen with fresh language made possible by new understandings of their words. We also sing the testimony of contemporary hymnwriters who remind us that God is not without witnesses in any age.

In the metaphor of centuries of hymnody, ancient and modern, we discern that God is always more than our human words are able to express. Our reverence for the mystery of God's being invites humility as we seek language that opens human hearts to the good news of God's love for all creation. We acknowledge the limitations of our words while we confess that in Jesus Christ the Word of God became flesh and lived within history.

Where language fails us, we live with confidence that the Holy Spirit intercedes for us with sighs too deep for words. Our hymns are a testimony to this ministry of the Holy Spirit. Hymns are more than the sum of their parts. They become for us a language that transcends human speech. They are the poetry of eternity within time. They are signs of grace that comes from beyond ourselves.

*The New Century Hymnal* does not claim to reach the heights of this vision of hymnody. It is, at best, the contribution of the United Church of Christ to the larger quest of the universal church to praise God faithfully in each generation. It is, however, a hymnal boldly committed to a spirit of inclusiveness. It welcomes and celebrates the diversity of all the people of God as surely as it confesses the mystery of diversity within God the Holy Trinity.

Thousands of people have participated in the preparation of this hymnal. One among them, however, with indefatigable courage and conviction, inspired the vision that has resulted in the pages that follow. We are indebted to Ansley Coe Throckmorton for her deep faith, scholarly gifts, and pastoral heart, without which this hymnal would not have been possible.

Thomas E. Dipko
*Executive Vice President*
*United Church Board for Homeland Ministries*

# PREFACE

"Jesus Christ is the same yesterday and today and forever." *The New Century Hymnal* is rooted in that conviction, in the conviction that the unchanging Jesus Christ, whose story is told through the centuries, in many images and languages, is the same Jesus Christ of the gospels and epistles. Seers and saints, poets and prophets of many ages have told of the unchanging Jesus Christ in their own ways. This hymnbook, following the common lectionary, also tells that same story in many ways.

Believers know that images of Christ have always preceded Christology, and that those images of Christ lie behind the confessions and creeds of the church. This book retains not only the images of other periods of history—images of shepherd, sovereign, healer, teacher, liberator, and so on—but it also contains the images of poets, prophets, and saints of our time who sing of the changeless Jesus Christ in images of our own age and for the new century now upon us.

Bernard of Clairvaux once observed that we must drink from our own wells. And the South American pastor and theologian Gustavo Gutiérrez brought that observation to bear on the lives of his people. So likewise Hildegard of Bingen, Martin Luther, Charles Wesley, Isaac Watts, Sarah Flower Adams, Madeleine Marshall, and Brian Wren—and each of us does the same. To drink from one's own well in this matter is to live, sing, and pray in the spirit of the unchanging Jesus Christ, as each of us has encountered Christ, to discern the mysterious connection between that life and our lives.

One of the great gifts to our time is the spirit now moving among us calling us to affirm the fullness of God, the goodness of creation, and the value of every person. The search for language and metaphor to express that breadth and richness marks this book.

In doing these things this hymnbook preserves much of the best hymnody of the past, and of the present, and it leads to a future we begin dimly to see. We have shaped a book that expresses the faith of the church in the unchanging Jesus Christ in words and images of our time. In whatsoever way it is faithful to these high standards, it is offered *Deo Gloria*.

Ansley Coe Throckmorton
*General Secretary for Education and Publication*
*United Church Board for Homeland Ministries*

# INTRODUCTION

In 1977, General Synod XI of the United Church of Christ directed the Executive Council to create a new official hymnal using language that is inclusive. In October 1989 the United Church Board for Homeland Ministries set aside resources to develop the hymnal. The project was completed in three phases. First, the Board of Directors of the United Church Board for Homeland Ministries appointed an advisory Hymnal Committee of thirteen members to function within its Division of Education and Publication, which provided appropriate staffing, research tools, and logistical support. The committee consisted of men and women from various geographical regions and traditions within the United Church of Christ. Each member brought liturgical sensibility, professional skill, cultural perspective, theological acumen, and particular musical erudition. As a result, the committee proved far greater than the sum of its parts.

The committee met between February 1990 and January 1993 in churches all across the continental United States, in Hawaii, and at the national offices in Cleveland. At its meetings and at thirty-five public forums the committee, in conversation with United Church of Christ local church members, considered hymns celebrating a diversity of liturgical, mission-oriented, and topical emphases. They invited and tested hymns from communities of Asian Americans, Native Americans, African Americans, and Latinos/Latinas. A significant portion of this hymnal can be credited to the probing questions and insightful observations of United Church of Christ members and others.

As a corollary to the hymnal forums, a churchwide research project that ran from the summer of 1990 through the summer of 1991 sought information from every local church in the denomination: "What do you sing? What do you want to sing? In a new hymnal, what might be a help or a hindrance?" From thousands of responses, two major findings surfaced: the majority of congregations that would buy hymnals in the next decade seek, first, new music, and second, inclusive metaphors for God and the human community. These findings confirmed the vision of General Synod in 1977 for an inclusive-language hymnal, and they were the foundation for the work of the advisory Hymnal Committee as it sought to design a hymnal for current and future worshipers in the United Church of Christ. In April 1993 the committee completed the first phase of the development process. It had reviewed more than ten thousand hymns, designed the contents, selected the repertory, and wrestled with every imaginable nuance, subtlety, and challenge of the language of love, justice, and worship of God.

For the second phase, the Hymnal Committee was succeeded by an Editorial Panel appointed by the Board of Directors of the United Church Board for Homeland Ministries. The board charged the panel with refining and completing the vast work submitted by the Hymnal Committee. The panel set about the delicate work of balancing hymnal components, texts and tunes included, and reviewing the language of all texts. The panel's work concluded in the fall of 1994.

In the final phase, the editors and the hymnal office staff prepared the hymnal layout, edited the manuscript, garnered the copyrights, monitored the typesetting, and pursued everything necessary to produce a hymn collection suited for the ecumenical church.

Within the historic Protestant traditions that shape the United Church of Christ, the hymnbook serves as a primary vehicle to nurture the faith of church members. All who worked on this project were guided by the affirmation that *The New Century Hymnal* should provide rich, varied metaphors for singing about God, and language to sing about people that excludes no one—words that all people can sing.

This work was done amid what can only be called a new reformation. It recognized that its task was to do more than select six hundred historic and familiar hymns. It was also asked to consider hundreds of submitted manuscripts and new hymns that emerged from a wide variety of global traditions. The committee also reviewed newly published hymnals within the ecumenical community that presented even more possibilities. Each religious and cultural tradition presented its own treasured core hymnody. The Board for Homeland Ministries, the Hymnal Committee, and the Editorial Panel, in concert with the stated convictions of General Synod, believe the fullness of God is greater than exclusively masculine words and images. Thus the Hymnal Committee sought to broaden the traditional divine references so that they included the feminine. It searched for hymns containing similes, parables, analogies, and metaphors that point to the fullness of God.

In addition to this broad process of selection, every text underwent careful scrutiny of its metaphors and pronouns that refer to God, Christ, and the Spirit. Why the scrutiny? Because for nearly two millennia these words have tended toward exclusively masculine characterization, bearing painful consequences, especially for women. Every effort was made to ensure that all hymns spoke to and for all God's people, equally. This resulted in the examination of language from racial, ethnic, and sociocultural perspectives, and the review of language that could be diminishing to people with physical disabilities. Consideration was also given to imagery to assure that it relate to the scientific understandings of a coming generation.

For the required text revisions, contemporary poets and hymn lyricists explored the scriptures, the prophets, mystics, and seers to forge fresh forms to address the living God and describe our world. Just as translators have rendered scriptures in present-day language, the poets were asked to revise language, yet maintain the nuance and intent of the original. In fact, numerous Latin and German hymns were newly translated for this hymnal. As a result, in the next century, as in preceding centuries, the church will be able to worship in the common language of the day.

It is the hope of all who labored on *The New Century Hymnal* that the church will discover a language that stretches the dimensions of justice and helps reveal the unfathomable depths of the God of biblical faith. It represents an attempt to embody a faith and joyous hope to sustain the church in a new millennium. May it serve as a transforming witness to the church of Jesus Christ as it celebrates public worship and sings gratefully—buoyantly—with the psalmist, "Praise God! Praise God from the heavens; Praise God in the heights; Praise God all the angels; Praise God, all you Host! Let everything that breathes, praise the living God! Praise God."

James W. Crawford
*Chair, Hymnal Committee*

# Acknowledgments

## Hymnal Committee

Janet Satre Ahrend, James W. Crawford (Chair), Daniel L. Johnson, Joyce Finch Johnson, Dorothy Lester *(ex officio, Office of Church Life and Leadership)*, Luis Olivieri, Jeffrey Radford, Linda Jambor Robinson, A. Knighton Stanley, Catherine Thiedt, and Stephen Wayles

## Editorial Panel

Stephen W. Camp, Cesar A. Coloma, James W. Crawford, Martha S. Due *(Chair)*, and Miriam Therese Winter

## United Church Board for Homeland Ministries Staff

Charles Shelby Rooks, *Executive Vice President, 1984–1992\**
Thomas E. Dipko, *Executive Vice President from 1992\*+*
Ansley Coe Throckmorton, *General Secretary, Division of Education and Publication\*+*
Arthur G. Clyde, *Hymnal Editor+*
Kristen Lundstrom Forman, *Assistant Editor*
Jonathan B. McNair, *Assistant Editor, Music*
Sylvia Penny, *Copyright Specialist*
Lynne M. Deming, *Publisher*
*(\*members ex officio of the Hymnal Committee)*
*(+members ex officio of the Editorial Panel)*

## Grateful Appreciation to

Gene Paul Strayer, *who was succeeded on the committee by* Stephen Wayles.

Lavon Bayler, Dosia Carlson, Carl P. Daw Jr., Ruth Duck, Sylvia G. Dunstan, Marty Haugen, Carolyn Jennings, Madeleine Forell Marshall, Elizabeth C. Ragan, Thomas H. Troeger, and Miriam Therese Winter, *who assisted in the revision of hymn texts.*

Bede Kotlinski, O.S.B., *who consulted on the Latin texts.*

Jon Michael Spencer, Marilyn K. Stulken, and Mary Louise VanDyke, *who assisted in the preparation of historical notes.*

Burton H. Throckmorton Jr., *who was consulted on the versification and language of the psalms.*

June Christine Goudey and Robert D. Witham, *who helped compile the worship resources.*

Jo Shelnutt Melendy and Howard H. Tobak, *who assisted in the preparation of scriptural references.*

Joan Menocal, *who designed the divider pages.*

# EDITOR'S NOTES

As worshipers begin to use the hymn section of this book, they will find a pattern throughout the pages. Preceding each hymn are the first line, scriptural references, and source(s) of the text. As is customary, *alt.* indicates that the original text has been altered; *adapt.* indicates more extensive revision. There are three noteworthy elements of style. First, in many instances, a non-English text precedes the English translation in recognition of the culture of origin. Second, poetic capitalization has been dealt with uniformly by using capitals at musical cadence points to achieve consistency in appearance. Third, in verses outside the music score, hyphens have been added for singing ease.

The historical notes following the hymns provide background, however brief, on the circumstances of origin. The composer, tune name, meter, and other information pertaining to the music also follow the hymn, making a clear distinction between music and text information. Dates appearing in the citations indicate, for the most part, the year of creation or first publication. Birth and death dates are located in the index. Users will find extensive indexes to aid in selecting hymns for the lectionary year. In addition, traditional topical and scriptural indexing have been provided.

Much care has been taken to present music that most congregations will find within their abilities. At the same time, the hymnal provides an occasional challenge that may require some practice and effort. The majority of settings are harmonized to allow for part singing. When unison settings appear, it is often because they were conceived that way, and usually it indicates a strong, vigorous melody. Performance directives are few, since worship tradition, occasion, architecture, instrumentation, and other factors can greatly alter the choice of tempo or dynamic. The collection allows for experimentation, and enthusiastic participation will sometimes be preferred to absolute "correctness" of style. All are encouraged to try the many languages and styles that have been included in the book to gain a sense of the church's diversity. This can provide opportunities to invite those who know this music to introduce it.

*The New Century Hymnal* was compiled with anticipation of the joy it will bring. It was also prepared with the hope that its musical and poetic offerings will be true both to past traditions and to the desire of the church to renew its worship. As in every age, texts have been changed to provide for worship in the vernacular. The wisdom of using skilled hymnwriters to perform this task should be evident as the hymns are sung. Many classic texts are reclaimed through new translations, which in some instances restore verses that had fallen into disuse. Throughout, the goal has been not to achieve the perfect or ultimate version, but to make the hymns live in our own time to be passed into the hands of coming generations, for their use and adaptations.

Arthur G. Clyde
*Editor*, The New Century Hymnal

# ORDERS FOR WORSHIP

*In the Orders for Worship that follow, the word "Sovereign" may be said instead of the word "Lord."*

# SERVICE OF WORD AND SACRAMENT I

## PRELUDE

*The service may begin with music as the congregation gathers. The greeting and sentences of adoration or the hymn may follow, according to local custom.*

## GREETING

*All may be invited to stand for one of these or another greeting informed by scripture.*

**A** LEADER
In the name of the triune God: the Creator, the Christ, and the Holy Spirit.

ALL
**Amen.**

**B** LEADER
The grace of our Lord Jesus Christ and the love of God and the communion of the Holy Spirit be with you all.[1]

PEOPLE
**And also with you.**

**C** *for use except during Lent*

LEADER
Alleluia! Christ is risen.

PEOPLE
**Christ is risen indeed. Alleluia!**

## SENTENCES OF ADORATION

*All may be invited to stand. One or more of the following sentences or others appropriate for the day or season are said.*

**A** LEADER
Our help is in the name of the Holy One, who made heaven and earth.[2]

**B** LEADER
Christ, our paschal lamb, has been offered for us. Let us, therefore, celebrate the festival.[3]

**C** LEADER
In the beginning was the Word, and the Word was with God, and the Word was God.[4]

**D** LEADER
God's love has been poured into our hearts through the Holy Spirit which has been given to us.[5]

**E** LEADER
God has brought the people of the covenant from the land of bondage into freedom.

**F** LEADER
Jesus came to preach good news to the poor, to proclaim release to the captives and recovery of sight to the blind, to liberate those who are oppressed, and to proclaim the year of God's favor.[6]

## HYMN OF ADORATION

*All may be invited to stand. This may be a processional hymn.*

1

## CONFESSION OF SIN

*The people may be seated. A leader may offer one of these prayers or one in his or her own words.*

**A** LEADER
We are called to examine our faithfulness to God's covenant with us. God, in whose presence we gather, promises us grace and pardon when we acknowledge our weakness and shame. Let us confess our sin to almighty God.

ALL
**Eternal God, whose Word is a lamp for our feet and a light for our path, we recognize and confess that we have failed to respond fully to your gracious presence in our lives. Through Jesus Christ you have offered us new life, fulfillment, and the freedom to serve you. We confess that we are captive to sin, that our sin binds us with false pride, and that the wrong we do is made worse by the good we leave undone. Reconcile us to you and to all people. God of mercy, forgive all our sin and strengthen us anew for life as you intend it; through Jesus Christ our Savior. Amen.**

**B** LEADER
If we say we have no sin, we deceive ourselves, and the truth is not in us.

PEOPLE
**But if we confess our sins, God, who is faithful and just, will forgive our sins and cleanse us from all unrighteousness.[7]**

LEADER
Let us confess our sins before God and one another.

ALL
**Most merciful God, we confess that we are in bondage to sin and cannot free ourselves. We have sinned against you in thought, word, and deed, by what we have done and by what we have left undone. We have not loved you with our whole heart. We have not loved our neighbors as ourselves. For the sake of Jesus Christ, have mercy on us. Forgive us, renew us, and lead us, so that we may delight in your will and follow in your ways, to the glory of your name. Amen.[8]**

## SILENCE

*Silence may be observed for reflection and prayer.*

## PRAYER FOR MERCY

*The* Kyrie, Trisagion, *or other words may be said or sung. Musical settings, 745–753.*

**A** LEADER
Lord, have mercy.

PEOPLE
**Christ, have mercy.**

LEADER
Lord, have mercy.

**B** LEADER
Holy God, Holy and mighty, Holy Immortal One,

ALL
**Have mercy upon us.**

## ASSURANCE OF PARDON

*A leader may speak of God's pardon and mercy, using one of the following or her or his own words.*

**A** LEADER

God hears the confession of our hearts and lips. Through Jesus Christ we are forgiven all our sins, and by the Holy Spirit we are empowered for new life.

ALL

**We believe the good news of Jesus Christ. Amen.**

**B** LEADER

Anyone in Christ becomes a new person altogether; the past is finished and gone, everything has become fresh and new. Friends, believe the good news of the gospel:

ALL

**In Jesus Christ, we are forgiven.**[9]

## PASSING THE PEACE

*As a sign of their reconciliation with God and each other, all may greet those around them with an embrace or a handshake, accompanied by such words as: "The peace of God be with you," and the response: "And also with you." All may be invited to rise for the passing of the peace. Leaders of the service may move among the congregation to share the signs of peace.*

## ACT OF PRAISE

*All may be invited to stand for a call to praise and a hymn, psalm, or gloria.*

LEADER

Let us sing praise to God.

ALL

**We will continually praise God's holy name.**

**A** *A hymn, psalm, or gloria such as the following may be read or sung. Musical settings, 754–760.*
ALL

**Glory to God in the highest, and peace to God's people on earth.**

**Holy One, heavenly God, sovereign God and Creator, we worship you, we give you thanks, we praise you for your glory.**

**Lord Jesus Christ, God's only begotten one, Lord God, Lamb of God, you take away the sin of the world: have mercy on us; you are seated at the right hand of Majesty: receive our prayer.**

**For you alone are the Messiah, you alone are the Lord, you alone are the Most High, Jesus Christ, with the Holy Spirit, in the glory of the triune God. Amen.**

**B** *This gloria may be said or sung. Musical settings, 754, 755.*
ALL

**Glory to God the Creator, and to the Christ, and to the Holy Spirit: as it was in the beginning, is now, and will be for ever. Amen.**

## READING OF SCRIPTURE

## OLD TESTAMENT LESSON

READER *before the lesson*

Listen for the word of God in _____.

*After the lesson, a psalm may be said or sung, followed by a gloria, unless one has been said or sung earlier, or the following or a similar announcement may be made.*

READER
Here ends the Old Testament lesson.

## EPISTLE LESSON

READER  *before the lesson*
Listen for the word of God in _____.

READER  *following the lesson*
Here ends the Epistle lesson.

## GOSPEL LESSON

*In some local churches, standing, by those who are able, for the reading of the Gospel is customary as it is a sign of respect for Jesus Christ, who addresses the congregation. Responses before and after this lesson may be said or sung. (See 761–764.)*

READER  *before the lesson*
Listen to the Gospel of Jesus Christ according to _____.

PEOPLE
**Glory to you, O Christ.**

READER  *following the lesson*
This is the good news.

PEOPLE
**Praise to you, O Christ.**

## SERMON

## AFFIRMATION OF FAITH

*All may be invited to stand for a form of the Statement of Faith of the United Church of Christ, a creed, or a church covenant. (See 881–887.)*

## HYMN, ANTHEM, OR OTHER MUSIC

## PRAYERS OF THE PEOPLE

*The people may be seated. Leaders may announce special concerns for prayers and invite the people to indicate needs or to name causes for thanksgiving. Intercessions may include prayers for:*

- *The church universal, including ecumenical councils, specific churches in other places, the United Church of Christ and its leaders, and this local church.*
- *The nations and all in authority.*
- *Justice and peace in all the world.*
- *The health of those who suffer in body, mind, or spirit.*
- *The needs of families, single people, and the lonely.*
- *Reconciliation with adversaries.*
- *The local community and all other communities.*
- *All who are oppressed or in prison.*

*A litany of prayers and responses, with silences, may be used; a pastoral prayer may be offered; petitions may be offered by anyone present, ending with a phrase to which all may respond, such as those below. A longer period of silence may precede or follow the prayers.*

**A** LEADER
Christ, in your mercy,

**B** LEADER
Holy Spirit, our Comforter,

PEOPLE
**Hear our prayer.**

PEOPLE
**Receive our prayer.**

## Concerns of the Church

*Leaders and people may announce information concerning the program, ministry, and people of the church.*

## Offertory

*A leader may introduce the offertory and give an invitation to Holy Communion, using his or her own words or the following:*

**A** LEADER

Through Christ let us continually praise God and share what we have, for such sacrifices are pleasing to God.

**B** LEADER

Let us present with joy our offerings of commitment and support for the work of Christ's church.

PEOPLE

**Let us prepare Christ's table with the offerings of our life and labor.**

*Music may be offered to God's glory while the tithes and offerings are being received. Silence is also appropriate. The people may express their dedication and thanksgiving to God through music, prayers, dance, and other acts. The congregation may be invited to stand as representatives bring the gifts to the table. The communion elements may be brought to the table with the other gifts.*

**A** *A doxology, such as the following to the tune "Old Hundredth," may be sung. (See also 776–782.)*

ALL

**Praise God from whom all blessings flow; Praise Christ the Word in flesh born low; Praise Holy Spirit evermore; One God, Triune, whom we adore. Amen.**

**B** *This doxology may be sung. Musical setting, 777.*

ALL

**Praise God from whom all blessings flow; Praise Christ, all creatures here below; Praise Holy Spirit the Comforter; One God, Triune, whom we adore. Amen.**

AND

*A prayer of dedication may be said.*

**If there is to be no celebration of Holy Communion, the service may be concluded with the Prayer of Our Savior, a hymn, a benediction, and a postlude.**

## Invitation

*All may be invited to stand. A leader may use these or other words informed by scripture. The people respond.*

LEADER

Beloved in Christ, the Gospel tells us that on the first day of the week Jesus Christ was raised from death, appeared to Mary Magdalene, on that same day sat at the table with two disciples, and was made known to them in the breaking of the bread.

*The people may sing or say the following. Musical settings, 786, 787.*

ALL

**This is the joyful feast of the people of God. Men and women, youth and children, come from the east and the west, from the north and the south, and gather about Christ's table.[10]**

LEADER

This table is for all Christians who wish to know the presence of Christ and to share in the community of God's people.

# Communion Prayer

*All may be invited to stand.*

PASTOR
God be with you.

PEOPLE
**And also with you.**

PASTOR
Lift up your hearts.

PEOPLE
**We lift them to God.**

PASTOR
Let us give thanks to God Most High.

PEOPLE
**It is right to give God thanks and praise.**

*The pastor leads in thankfully recalling God's great acts of salvation, using the outline in C on page 8 or one of these.*

**A** PASTOR
We give you thanks, God of majesty and mercy, for calling forth the creation and raising us from dust by the breath of your being.

We bless you for the beauty and bounty of the earth and for the vision of the day when sharing by all will mean scarcity for none.

We remember the covenant you made with your people Israel, and we give you thanks for all our ancestors in faith. We rejoice that you call us to reconciliation with you and all people everywhere and that you remain faithful to your covenant even when we are faithless.

We rejoice that you call the entire human family to this table of sacrifice and victory. We come in remembrance and celebration of the gift of Jesus Christ, whom you sent, in the fullness of time, to be the good news. Born of Mary, our sister in faith, Christ lived among us to reveal the mystery of your Word, to suffer and die on the cross for us, to be raised from death on the third day, and then to live in glory.

*A seasonal preface may be said here.*

We bless you, gracious God, for the presence of your Holy Spirit in the church you have gathered. With your sons and daughters of faith in all places and times, we praise you with joy.

**B** PASTOR
We give you thanks, Holy One, almighty and eternal God, always and everywhere, through Jesus Christ, the only one begotten by you before all time, by whom you made the world and all things.

We bless you for your continual love and care for every creature. We praise you for forming us in your image and for calling us to be your people.

Although we rebelled against your love, you did not abandon us in our sin, but sent to us prophets and teachers to lead us into the way of salvation.

Above all, we give you thanks for the gift of Jesus, our only Savior, who is the way, the truth, and the life.

In the fullness of time you came to us and received our nature in the person of Jesus, who, in obedience to you, by suffering on the cross, and being raised from the dead, delivered us from the way of sin and death.

We praise you that Jesus now reigns with you in glory and ever lives to pray for us.

We thank you for the Holy Spirit who leads us into truth, defends us in adversity, and gathers us from every people to unite us in one holy church.

Therefore, with the entire company of saints in heaven and on earth, we worship and glorify you, God Most Holy.

*All may sing or say the following. Musical settings, 789, 790. (See also 791–795.)*

ALL
**Holy, holy, holy God
of love and majesty,
the whole universe speaks of your glory,
O God Most High.**

**Blessed is the one
who comes in the name of our God!
Hosanna in the highest!**

*The people may be seated as the prayer continues. As the following words are spoken, the pastor may indicate the communion elements.*

**A** PASTOR
We remember that on the night of betrayal and desertion, and on the eve of death, Jesus gathered the disciples for the feast of Passover.

Jesus took bread, and after giving thanks to you, broke it, and gave it to the disciples, saying: "This is my body which is for you. Do this in remembrance of me."

In the same way also the cup, after supper, saying: "This cup is the new covenant in my blood. Do this, as often as you drink it, in remembrance of me."[11]

Therefore we proclaim the mystery of our faith.

**B** PASTOR
For in the night of betrayal Jesus took bread, and after giving thanks to you, broke the bread, and gave it to the disciples, and said: "Take, eat: This is my body which is given for you. Do this in remembrance of me."

In the same way also after supper, Jesus took the cup, and after giving you thanks, gave it to them and said: "Drink this, all of you: This is my blood of the new covenant, which is poured out for you and many, for the forgiveness of sins. Do this, as often as you drink it, in remembrance of me."[12]

*Either of these may be said or sung with option A or option B of the prayer. Musical settings, 796–799.*

**A** ALL

**Christ's death, O God,
we proclaim. Christ's resurrection
we declare.
Christ's coming we await.
Glory be to you, O God.**

**B** ALL

**Christ has died.
Christ is risen.
Christ will come again.**

*Option A or B of the prayer continues.*

PASTOR

Eternal God, we unite in this covenant of faith, recalling Christ's suffering and death, rejoicing in Christ's resurrection, and awaiting Christ's return in victory.

We spread your table with these gifts of the earth and of our labor. We present to you our very lives, committed to your service in behalf of all people.

We ask you to send your Holy Spirit on this bread and wine, on our gifts, and on us. Strengthen your universal church that it may be the champion of peace and justice in all the world. Restore the earth with your grace that is able to make all things new.

ALL

**Be present with us as we share this meal, and throughout all our lives, that we may know you as the Holy One, who with Christ and the Holy Spirit, lives for ever. Amen.**

PASTOR

Holy One, show forth among us the presence of your life-giving Word and Holy Spirit, to sanctify us and your entire church through these holy mysteries. Grant that all who share the communion of the body and blood of our risen Savior may be one in Jesus Christ.

May we remain faithful in love and hope, until the perfect feast with our exalted Savior in the eternal joy of your heavenly realm.

ALL

**Gracious God, accept with favor this our sacrifice of praise, which we now present with these holy gifts. We offer to you ourselves, giving you thanks for the perfect offering of the only one begotten by you, Jesus Christ our Savior:**

**By whom and with whom and in whom, in the unity of the Holy Spirit, all honor and glory be to you, eternal God, now and for ever. Amen.**

*If option A or B of the communion prayer has been used, the service continues with the Prayer of Our Savior.*

**C** *The pastor, following this or a similar outline, may offer the prayer of great thanksgiving in her or his own words.*

- *Give thanks for God's goodness to us shown in the creation of the world and in the events of history.*
- *Remember people of faith through whom God has spoken to the human family as witnessed in scripture.*
- *Give thanks for the birth, life, death, and resurrection of Jesus Christ.*
- *Recall Jesus' words at the institution of the supper in the upper room.*
- *Remind us that our participation in Holy Communion is a sacrifice of praise which includes the offering of our lives to God.*
- *Briefly proclaim faith in Christ who has died, is raised, and will return at the close of history.*
- *Give thanks for the gift of the Holy Spirit whose presence is invoked.*

## PRAYER OF OUR SAVIOR

*Standing, sitting, or kneeling, all may sing or say the prayer received from Jesus Christ.*

LEADER

Let us pray as Christ our Savior has taught us.

**A** ALL
**Our Father in heaven, hallowed be your name, your kingdom come, your will be done, on earth as in heaven. Give us today our daily bread. Forgive us our sins as we forgive those who sin against us. Save us from the time of trial and deliver us from evil. For the kingdom, the power, and the glory are yours now and for ever. Amen.**[13]

**B** ALL
**Our Father, who art in heaven, hallowed be thy name. Thy kingdom come. Thy will be done on earth as it is in heaven. Give us this day our daily bread. And forgive us our trespasses, as we forgive those who trespass against us. And lead us not into temptation, but deliver us from evil. For thine is the kingdom, and the power, and the glory, for ever and ever. Amen.**

**C** ALL
**Our Father, who art in heaven, hallowed be thy name. Thy kingdom come. Thy will be done on earth as it is in heaven. Give us this day our daily bread. And forgive us our debts, as we forgive our debtors. And lead us not into temptation, but deliver us from evil. For thine is the kingdom, and the power, and the glory, for ever. Amen.**

## BREAKING BREAD AND POURING WINE

*The bread is broken and the wine is poured as visible and audible reminders of the sacrificial self-giving of Jesus Christ. These actions call to mind the cost as well as the joy of Christian discipleship.*

PASTOR *while taking the bread and breaking it*
The bread which we break is the communion of the body of Christ.

PASTOR *while pouring the wine and raising the cup*
The cup of blessing which we bless is the communion of the blood of Christ.

## LAMB OF GOD

*Either version of the ancient* Agnus Dei[14] *may be said or sung by all. Musical settings, 800, 801. (See also 802–804.)*

**A** ALL
**Lamb of God, you take away the sins of the world: have mercy on us.**

**Lamb of God, you take away the sins of the world: have mercy on us.**

**Lamb of God, you take away the sins of the world: grant us peace.**

**B** ALL
**Jesus, Lamb of God: have mercy on us. Jesus, bearer of our sins: have mercy on us. Jesus, redeemer of the world: give us your peace.**

9

## CALL TO THE SUPPER

**A** PASTOR

The gifts of God for the people of God. Come, for all things are ready.

**B** PASTOR

The gifts of God for the people of God. Take them in remembrance that Christ died and was raised for you.

## SHARING THE ELEMENTS

*In giving the bread and cup, the pastor and those assisting may use their own words or the following, and the people respond.*

**A** PASTOR *while giving the bread*

Take and eat, this is the body of Christ, broken for you.

PEOPLE
**Amen!**

PASTOR *while giving the cup*

Take and drink, this is the cup of the new covenant, poured out for you.

PEOPLE
**Amen!**

**B** PASTOR *while giving the bread*

The body of Christ, the bread of heaven.

PEOPLE
**Amen!**

PASTOR *while giving the cup*

The blood of Christ, the cup of salvation.

PEOPLE
**Amen!**

*After the distribution of the bread and cup, the elements may be covered, according to local custom. Words of dismissal may precede the prayer of thanksgiving if people have moved from their seats to receive communion.*

## PRAYER OF THANKSGIVING

*All may be invited to stand. A leader may give thanks in her or his own words or may use the following:*

LEADER
Let us pray.

**A** ALL

**Almighty God, we give you thanks for the gift of our Savior's presence in the simplicity and splendor of this holy meal. Unite us with all who are fed by Christ's body and blood that we may faithfully proclaim the good news of your love and that your universal church may be a rainbow of hope in an uncertain world; through Jesus Christ our Redeemer. Amen.**

**B** ALL

**Bountiful God, we give you thanks that you have refreshed us at your table by granting us the presence of Christ. Strengthen our faith, increase our love for one another, and send us forth into the world in courage and peace, rejoicing in the power of the Holy Spirit. Amen.**[15]

## HYMN OF PARTING

*All may be invited to stand. Depending on local custom, the commissioning and benediction, with or without the "Song of Simeon," may precede the hymn.*

## SONG OF SIMEON

*All may sing or say the ancient* Nunc Dimittis. *Musical settings, 805–808.*

ALL

**Holy One, now let your servant go in peace; your word has been fulfilled: my own eyes have seen the salvation which you have prepared in the sight of every people: a light to reveal you to the nations and the glory of your people Israel.**[16]

## COMMISSIONING

*All may be invited to stand as a leader says these or other words of commissioning.*

LEADER

Go forth into the world to serve God with gladness; be of good courage; hold fast to that which is good; render to no one evil for evil; strengthen the faint-hearted; support the weak; help the afflicted; honor all people; love and serve God, rejoicing in the power of the Holy Spirit.[17]

## BENEDICTION

*A leader may offer one of the following or another blessing.*

**A** LEADER
The blessing of God Almighty: the Creator, the Redeemer, and the Sanctifier, be with you all.

PEOPLE
**Amen.**

**B** LEADER
Now may the God of peace who brought again from the dead our Savior Jesus, the great shepherd of the sheep, by the blood of the eternal covenant, equip you with everything good that you may do God's will, working in you that which is pleasing in God's sight; through Jesus Christ, to whom be glory for ever and ever.

PEOPLE
**Amen.**[18]

## POSTLUDE

*The congregation may be seated and remain until the postlude is concluded.*

# Service of Word and Sacrament II

## Concerns of the Church

*Leaders and people may announce information concerning the program, ministries, and people of the church here or at the offertory.*

## Prelude

*Music may be played as the congregation gathers.*

## Hymn of Adoration

*All may be invited to stand. According to local custom, the hymn may follow the prelude or the greeting.*

## Greeting

*All may be invited to stand as a leader offers one of these greetings or another informed by scripture.*

**A** LEADER
The grace of our Lord Jesus Christ and the love of God and the communion of the Holy Spirit be with you all.[19]

PEOPLE
**And also with you.**

**B** LEADER
Dear friends, let us love one another, because love comes from God. Whoever loves is a child of God and knows God.

PEOPLE
**Whoever does not love does not know God, for God is love.[20]**

**C** LEADER
With what shall we come before the Holy One, and bow ourselves before God on high?

PEOPLE
**Shall we come before God with burnt offerings, with calves a year old?**

LEADER
God has showed you, O people, what is good; and what does the Holy One require of you?

PEOPLE
**To do justice, and to love kindness, and to walk humbly with our God.[21]**

## Invocation

*All may be invited to stand.*

**A** LEADER
Christ is with us.

PEOPLE
**Christ is in our midst.**

LEADER
Let us pray.

**B** LEADER
God be with you.

PEOPLE
**And also with you.**

LEADER
Let us pray.

*One of these prayers or one in a leader's own words may be offered, asking for the congregation to be made responsive to the presence of God.*

**A** ALL

**Eternal God, companion of all who seek you, and seeker of all who turn away from you, draw near to us that we may draw near to you, and grant us the grace to love and to serve you that we may find in your will our true freedom; through Jesus Christ, the way, the truth, and the life. Amen.**

**B** ALL

**Gracious God, gentle in your power and strong in your tenderness, you have brought us forth from the womb of your being and breathed into us the breath of life. We know that we do not live by bread alone but by every word that comes from you. Feed our deep hungers with the living bread that you give us in Jesus Christ. May Jesus' promise, "Where two or three are gathered in my name, there am I in the midst of them,"[22] be fulfilled in us. Make us a joyful company of your people so that with the faithful in every place and time we may praise and honor you, God Most High. Amen.**

## ACT OF PRAISE

*All may be invited to stand as a gloria, a hymn such as "From All That Dwell below the Skies," or a psalm is read or sung. This may be a responsive reading. During Lent, it is appropriate to omit hymns that contain the alleluia.*

## READING OF SCRIPTURE

*The people may be seated as the scripture lessons are introduced. It is recommended that the schedule of readings found in the ecumenical lectionary be used. If it is not, care should be taken to maintain a balance in readings from the Old Testament, the Epistles, and the Gospels.*

*A collect for illumination, a seasonal collect, or an extemporaneous prayer asking for attentive hearts may precede the first reading. A brief introduction to the theme of each lesson may be offered. In order to distinguish the lesson from the commentary, the reader may announce: "A reading from _____" and may conclude: "Here ends the lesson."*

## OLD TESTAMENT LESSON

*After the Old Testament lesson, a psalm may be said or sung, followed by a gloria.*

## EPISTLE LESSON

## GOSPEL LESSON

*In some local churches, standing, by those who are able, for the reading of the Gospel is customary as it is a sign of respect for Jesus Christ, who addresses the congregation in words remembered by the early church.*

## SERMON

## AFFIRMATION OF FAITH

*All may be invited to stand for a form of the Statement of Faith of the United Church of Christ, a creed, or a church covenant. (See 881–887.)*

# Hymn, Anthem, or Other Music

## Prayers of the People

*The people may be seated. Leaders may announce special concerns for prayers and invite the people to indicate needs or to name causes for thanksgiving. See page 4 for topics for intercessions. A litany of prayers and responses, with silences, may be used; a pastoral prayer may be offered; petitions may be offered by anyone present, ending with a phrase to which all may respond, such as those below. A longer period of silence may precede or follow the prayers.*

**A** LEADER
God, in your mercy,
PEOPLE
**Hear our prayer.**

**B** LEADER
O God, hear our prayer.
PEOPLE
**Let our cry come unto you.**

## Confession of Sin

**A** LEADER
Let us confess our sin against God and each other.

ALL
**Merciful God, we know that you love us and that you call us to fullness of life, but around us and within us we see the brokenness of the world and of our ways. Our successes leave us empty; our progress does not satisfy. Our prosperous land is not the promised land of our longing. Forgive our willful neglect of your word, our insensitivity to the needs of others, and our failure to feed the spirit that is within us; through Jesus Christ our Redeemer. Amen.**

**B** *An introduction and prayer from scripture may be used, such as the following paraphrased verses from 1 John and Psalm 51.*

LEADER
If we say we have no sin, we deceive ourselves, and the truth is not in us.
PEOPLE
**If we confess our sins, God is faithful and just and will forgive our sins and cleanse us from all unrighteousness.**[23]

LEADER
Sisters and brothers, in the words of the psalmist, let us ask for the forgiveness we need.

ALL
**Have mercy on us, O God, according to your steadfast love; according to your abundant mercy blot out our transgressions. Wash us thoroughly from our iniquity, and cleanse us from our sin. Create in us a clean heart, O God, and put a new and right spirit within us. Cast us not away from your presence, and take not your Holy Spirit from us. Restore to us the joy of your salvation, and uphold us with a willing spirit.**[24] **Amen.**

## Silence

*Silence may be observed for reflection and prayer.*

14

## Assurance of Pardon

*A leader may speak of God's pardon and mercy in his or her own words or may use one of these, and the people respond.*

**A** LEADER

Almighty God has forgiven you all your sins and has promised to bring you to everlasting life.

PEOPLE

**Amen. Almighty God has forgiven you all your sins and has promised to bring you to everlasting life.**

LEADER

Amen.

**B** LEADER

Since we are justified by faith, we have peace with God through our Lord Jesus Christ.

PEOPLE

**Through Jesus Christ we have obtained access to this grace in which we stand, and we rejoice in our hope of sharing the glory of God.**[25]

## Passing the Peace

*In preparation for the offertory and Holy Communion, all may greet those around them as a sign of their desire to be at peace with all people. This sign of peace may be expressed by a handshake or an embrace, accompanied by such words as: "The peace of God be with you," and the response: "And also with you."*

*The people may be invited to rise for the passing of the peace. The following words paraphrased from Matthew or other words may be used to introduce this act of reconciliation.*

LEADER

So if you are about to offer your gift to God at the altar and there remember that your sister or brother has something against you, leave your gift in front of the altar, go at once and make peace with your brother or sister, and then come back and offer your gift.[26]

PEOPLE

**In response to Christ's command, we reach out to each other in love.**

*Leaders of the service may move among the congregation to share the signs of peace. During this period, an opportunity may be given to those present to make their commitment to Christian discipleship or to renew their commitment to the Christian life.*

## Offertory

*The people may be seated. As part of the offering of life and labor, significant announcements concerning the mission of the church may be made at this time. A leader may introduce the offertory and give an invitation to Holy Communion, using her or his own words or one of the following.*

**A** LEADER

We shall bring to Christ's table with our offerings the bread and wine for the supper. Christ invites to this table all who profess the Christian faith, who endeavor to be at peace with their neighbors, and who seek the mercy of God.

**B** LEADER

As we prepare the table for Christ's supper, let us recall the words of the apostle Paul: So then, my sisters and brothers, because of God's great mercy to us I appeal to you: Offer yourselves as a living sacrifice to God, dedicated to God's service and pleasing to God.

PEOPLE

**This is the true worship that we should offer.**[27]

15

*Music may be offered to God's glory while the tithes and offerings are being received. Silence is also appropriate. The people may express their dedication and thanksgiving to God through music, prayers, dance, and other acts.*

*The people may be invited to stand as representatives bring the gifts to the table. The communion elements may be brought to the table with the other gifts. A doxology may be sung, and a prayer of dedication may be said. Musical settings, 776–785.*

## LORD'S PRAYER

LEADER
Let us pray as Christ our Savior has taught us.
*Standing, sitting, or kneeling, all may sing or say the prayer received from Jesus Christ.*
**If Holy Communion is not to be celebrated, the service may be concluded with a hymn, a benediction, and a postlude.**

## INVITATION

*All may be invited to stand. In these or other words informed by scripture, a leader may remind the congregation that Christ is the host, and they are guests at the table.*

**A** LEADER
Jesus said: I am the bread of life. You who come to me shall not hunger; you who believe in me shall never thirst.[28]

PEOPLE
**In company with all who hunger for spiritual food, we come to this table to know the risen Christ in the sharing of this life-giving bread.**

**B** LEADER
Luke, the evangelist, wrote of our risen Savior, who at the table with two of the disciples took bread and blessed and broke it and gave it to them. Their eyes were opened, and they recognized the risen Christ in the breaking of the bread.

PEOPLE
**In company with all believers in every time and beyond time, we come to this table to know the risen Christ in the breaking of the bread.**

## COMMUNION PRAYER

*All may be invited to stand.*

PASTOR
God be with you.

PEOPLE
**And also with you.**

PASTOR
Lift up your hearts.

PEOPLE
**We lift them to God.**

PASTOR
Let us give thanks to God Most High.

PEOPLE
**It is right to give God thanks and praise.**

*The pastor leads the congregation in thankfully recalling God's great acts of salvation, using the outline on page 8 or one of these prayers.*

**A** PASTOR

Eternal God, who has created the heavens and the earth, giving breath to every living thing, we thank you for all the gifts of creation and for the gift of life itself. We thank you for making us in your own image, for forgiving us when we act as though you have no claim on us, and for keeping us in your steadfast care.

We rejoice in Jesus Christ, the only one eternally begotten by you, who was born of your servant Mary and shared the joys and sorrows of life as we know it.

We remember Christ's death, we celebrate Christ's resurrection, and, in the beloved community of your church, we await Christ's return at the end of history.

We take courage from the abiding presence of your Holy Spirit in our midst.

We offer you our praise for women and men of faith in every age who stand as witnesses to your love and justice. With all the prophets, martyrs, and saints, and all the company of heaven, we glorify you:

*Musical settings, 789, 790. (See also 791–795.) All may say or sing:*

ALL

**Holy, holy, holy God of love and majesty, the whole universe speaks of your glory, O God Most High.**

**Blessed is the one who comes in the name of our God! Hosanna in the highest!**

*The people may be seated or kneel. As the following words are spoken, the pastor may indicate the communion elements.*

PASTOR

We remember that on the night of betrayal and desertion, Jesus took bread, gave you thanks, broke the bread, and gave it to the disciples, saying: "This is my body which is broken for you. Do this in remembrance of me."

In the same way, Jesus also took the cup, after supper, saying: "This cup is the new covenant in my blood. Do this, as often as you drink it, in remembrance of me."

By eating this bread and drinking this cup, we proclaim Christ's death, celebrate Christ's resurrection, and await Christ's coming again.[29]

PEOPLE
**Amen. Come, Christ Jesus!**

PASTOR

Gracious God, we ask you to bless this bread and cup and all of us with the outpouring of your Holy Spirit. Through this meal, make us the body of Christ, the church, your servant people, that we may be salt, and light, and leaven for the furtherance of your will in all the world.

PEOPLE
**Amen. Come, Holy Spirit.**

**B** PASTOR

Holy God, our loving Creator, close to us as breathing and distant as the farthest star, we thank you for your constant love for all you have made. We thank you for all that sustains life, for all people of faith in every generation who have given themselves to your will, and especially for Jesus Christ, whom you have sent from your own being as our Savior. We praise you for Christ's birth, life, death, and resurrection, and for the calling forth of your church for its mission in the world. Gifted by the presence of your Holy Spirit, we offer ourselves to you as we unite our voices with the entire family of your faithful people everywhere:

*Musical settings, 789, 790. (See also 791–795.) All may say or sing:*

ALL

**Holy, holy, holy God of love and majesty, the whole universe speaks of your glory, O God Most High.**

**Blessed is the one who comes in the name of our God! Hosanna in the highest!**

*The people may be seated or kneel. As the following words are spoken, the pastor may indicate the communion elements.*

PASTOR

Merciful God, as sisters and brothers in faith, we recall anew these words and acts of Jesus Christ. Now as they were eating, Jesus took bread, and blessed, and broke it, and gave it to the disciples and said: "Take, eat: This is my body." Jesus took a cup, and after giving thanks, gave it to the disciples and said: "Drink of it, all of you; for this is my blood of the covenant, which is poured out for many for the forgiveness of sins."[30] We remember Christ's promise not to drink of the fruit of the vine again until the heavenly banquet at the close of history, and we say boldly what we believe:

*All may say or sing: (See 799.)*

ALL

**Christ has died. Christ is risen. Christ will come again.**

PASTOR

Come, Holy Spirit, come. Bless this bread, and bless this fruit of the vine. Bless all of us in our eating and drinking at this table that our eyes may be opened, and we may recognize the risen Christ in our midst, in each other, and in all for whom Christ died.

PEOPLE

**Amen.**

*If option A or B of the communion prayer has been used, the service continues with breaking bread and pouring wine.*

**C** *The pastor may offer the prayer of great thanksgiving in his or her own words, using the outline on page 8 or a similar one.*

## BREAKING BREAD AND POURING WINE

*The bread is broken and the wine is poured as visible and audible reminders of the sacrificial self-giving of Jesus Christ. These actions call to mind the cost as well as the joy of Christian discipleship.*

PASTOR *while taking the bread and breaking it*

Through the broken bread we participate in the body of Christ.

PASTOR *while pouring the wine and raising the cup*

Through the cup of blessing we participate in the new life Christ gives.

## Resurrection Acclamation

*Because Holy Communion is the memorial feast of the risen Christ, not a fast held for a deceased Jesus, the following words may be said immediately before the people receive the bread and cup. During the season of Lent, the alleluia may be omitted. The pastor may speak of the presence of Christ in her or his own words.*

**A** PASTOR

[Alleluia!]
Fear not, I am the first and the last, and the living one.

PEOPLE
**I died, and behold I am alive for evermore.**[31]
**[Alleluia!]**

**B** PASTOR

[Alleluia!]
Christ our Passover is offered for us.

PEOPLE
**Therefore let us keep the feast.**
**[Alleluia!]**

## Sharing the Elements

PASTOR

The gifts of God for the people of God. Come, for all things are ready.

*In giving the bread and cup, the pastor and those assisting may use their own words or one of these, and the people respond.*

**A** PASTOR *while giving the bread*

The body of Christ, the living bread.

PEOPLE
**Amen!**

PASTOR *while giving the cup*

The blood of Christ, the saving cup.

PEOPLE
**Amen!**

**B** PASTOR *while giving the bread*

Eat this, for it is the body of Christ, broken for you.

PEOPLE
**Amen!**

PASTOR *while giving the cup*

Drink this, for it is the blood of Christ, shed for you.

PEOPLE
**Amen!**[32]

*After the distribution of the bread and cup, the elements may be covered, according to local custom. Words of dismissal may precede the prayer of thanksgiving if people have moved from their seats to receive communion.*

## Prayer of Thanksgiving

*All may be invited to stand. A leader may give thanks in his or her own words or may use one of the following.*

**A** LEADER

Let us pray.

ALL

**Eternal God, you have called your people from east and west and north and south to feast at the table of Jesus Christ. We thank you for Christ's presence and for the spiritual food of Christ's body and blood. By the power of your Holy Spirit, keep us faithful to your will. Go with us to the streets, to our homes, and to our places of labor and leisure that whether we are gathered or scattered, we may be the servant church of the servant Christ, in whose name we rejoice to pray. Amen.**

**B** ALL

**We give thanks, almighty God, that you have refreshed us at your table by granting us the presence of Jesus Christ. Strengthen our faith, increase our love for one another, and send us forth into the world in courage and peace, rejoicing in the power of the Holy Spirit; through Jesus Christ our Savior. Amen.**[33]

*The benediction and recessional hymn may follow, or, if there is no recessional by the choir, the hymn of parting may precede the benediction.*

## BENEDICTION

*All may be invited to stand. A leader may use one of these or may dismiss the congregation with other words of comfort and challenge and with a blessing in words informed by scripture, and the people respond.*

**A** LEADER
May God bless you and keep you.

PEOPLE
**Amen.**

LEADER
May God's face shine upon you and be gracious to you.

PEOPLE
**Amen.**

LEADER
May God look upon you with kindness and give you peace.[34]

PEOPLE
**Amen.**

LEADER
Let us go forth into the world, rejoicing in the power of the Holy Spirit.

PEOPLE
**Thanks be to God!**

**B** LEADER
Holy One, now let your servant go in peace; your word has been fulfilled:

PEOPLE
**My own eyes have seen the salvation which you have prepared in the sight of every people:**

LEADER
A light to reveal you to the nations;

PEOPLE
**And the glory of your people Israel.**[35]

## HYMN OF PARTING

## POSTLUDE

*The congregation may be seated and remain until the postlude is concluded.*

# SERVICE OF THE WORD I

## PRELUDE

*The service may begin with music as the congregation gathers. The hymn or introit may follow, according to local custom.*

## CALL TO WORSHIP

*A leader may use one of the following or may offer other words appropriate to the season.*

**A** LEADER
Morning has broken. Let us give thanks for the gift of life and for the presence of the Holy One among us. Let us worship God together.

**B** LEADER
Our help is in the name of God, who made heaven and earth. Let us worship God.

PEOPLE
**Thanks be to God!**

## HYMN OF ADORATION

*All may be invited to stand. This may be a processional.*

## INTROIT

*An introit related to the season may be said or sung.*

## PRAYER OF CONFESSION

*All may be seated. A leader may offer a prayer based on scripture, may use his or her own words, or may use one of the following prayers.*

LEADER
Let us confess our sins before God and one another.

**A** ALL
**Almighty and merciful God, you created and are creating still. In your presence our limits lie stark before us. We confess our unclean lips, our cold hearts, our turning away from neighbors, our broken promises, and our unrepentant hours. Forgive us, O Holy One. We confess that we have squandered the gifts you have given. We have neglected the land. We have grasped for goods. We have used each other. We have loved power more than people. Forgive us, O Holy One. Cleanse from us the illusion of innocence. Come into our hearts, and make us new again. We pray in the name of Jesus. Amen.**

**B** ALL
**Most merciful God, we confess that we are in bondage to sin and cannot free ourselves. We have sinned against you in thought, word, and deed, by what we have done and by what we have left undone. We have not loved you with our whole heart. We have not loved our neighbors as ourselves. For the sake of Jesus Christ, have mercy on us. Forgive us, renew us, and lead us, so that we may delight in your will and follow in your ways, to the glory of your holy name. Amen.**[36]

## SILENCE

*Silence may be observed for reflection and prayer.*

## ASSURANCE OF PARDON

*A leader may speak of God's pardon or mercy in her or his own words or may use one of the following.*

**A** LEADER

In Jesus Christ, God knows and receives us as we are. Listen, give thanks, and live.

**B** LEADER

Almighty God, who is great in mercy and promises forgiveness of sin to all who truly repent and are sincere in faith, have mercy on you, pardon and deliver you from all sin, confirm and strengthen you in all goodness, and bring you to everlasting life.

PEOPLE

**Amen.**

**Thanks be to God.**

## PASSING THE PEACE

*As a sign of their reconciliation with God and each other, all may greet those around them with an embrace or a handshake, accompanied by such words as: "The peace of God be with you," and the response: "And also with you."*

*All may be invited to stand for the passing of the peace. Leaders of the service may move among the congregation to share the signs of peace.*

## PSALM OR RESPONSIVE READING

*A psalm may be sung or read responsively or in unison.*

## GLORIA

*All may be invited to stand for a gloria or another hymn of praise. Musical settings, 754–760.*

## READING OF SCRIPTURE

*The people may be seated as the scripture lessons are introduced. It is recommended that the schedule of readings found in the ecumenical lectionary be used. If it is not, care should be taken to maintain a balance in readings from the Old Testament, the Epistles, and the Gospels.*

*A collect for illumination, a seasonal collect, or an extemporaneous prayer asking for attentive hearts may precede the first reading. A brief introduction to the theme of each lesson may be offered. In order to distinguish the lesson from the commentary, the leader may announce the lesson.*

## OLD TESTAMENT LESSON

READER *before the lesson*

Listen for the word of God in _____.

*After the lesson, a psalm may be said or sung, followed by a gloria, unless one has been said or sung earlier, or the following or a similar announcement may be made.*

READER

Here ends the Old Testament lesson.

# EPISTLE LESSON

READER *before the lesson*
Listen for the word of God in _____.

READER *following the lesson*
Here ends the Epistle lesson.

# GOSPEL LESSON

*In some local churches, standing, for those who are able, for the reading of the Gospel is customary as it is a sign of respect for Jesus Christ, who addresses the congregation in words remembered by the early church. The responses before and after this lesson may be said or sung. (See 761–764.)*

READER *before the lesson*
Listen to the Gospel of Jesus Christ according to _____.

PEOPLE
**Glory to you, O Christ.**

READER *following the lesson*
This is the good news.

PEOPLE
**Praise to you, O Christ.**

# SERMON

# AFFIRMATION OF FAITH

*All may be invited to stand for a form of the Statement of Faith of the United Church of Christ, a creed, or a church covenant. (See 881–887.)*

# HYMN, ANTHEM, OR OTHER MUSIC

# PRAYERS OF THE PEOPLE

*The people may be seated. Leaders may announce special concerns for prayers and invite the people to indicate needs or to name causes for thanksgiving. See page 4 for topics for intercessions. A litany of prayers and responses, with silences, may be used; a pastoral prayer may be offered; petitions may be offered by anyone present, ending with a phrase to which all may respond, such as those below. A longer period of silence may precede or follow the prayers.*

**A** LEADER
Christ, in your mercy,

PEOPLE
**Hear our prayer.**

**B** LEADER
Holy Spirit, our Comforter,

PEOPLE
**Receive our prayer.**

# LORD'S PRAYER

*Standing, sitting, or kneeling, all may sing or say the prayer received from Jesus Christ.*

# CONCERNS OF THE CHURCH

*The people may be seated. A leader and the people may announce information concerning the program, ministry, and people of the church.*

## Offertory

*A leader may use his or her own words or one of the following to introduce the offertory.*

**A** LEADER
Let everyone give, not grudgingly or of necessity, but from the fullness of our gratitude to God.

**B** LEADER
Let us give, as each is able, according to the blessings God has given each of us.

*Music may be offered to God's glory while the tithes and offerings are being received. Silence is also appropriate. The people may express their dedication and thanksgiving to God through music, prayers, dance, and other acts. The people may be invited to stand as representatives bring the gifts to the table. A doxology may be sung, and a prayer of dedication may be said. Musical settings, 776–782, 784, 785.*

## Hymn

### Commissioning and Benediction

**A** LEADER
The blessing of the God of Sarah and of Abraham; the blessing of Jesus Christ, born of Mary; the blessing of the Holy Spirit, who broods over us as a mother over her children; be with you all. Amen.[37]

**B** LEADER
Go forth into the world to serve God with gladness; be of good courage; hold fast to that which is good; render to no one evil for evil; strengthen the fainthearted; support the weak; help the afflicted; honor all people; love and serve God, rejoicing in the power of the Holy Spirit.[38]

The grace of Jesus Christ, the love of God, and the communion of the Holy Spirit, be with you all.[39] Amen.

## Postlude

*The congregation may be seated and remain until the postlude is concluded.*

# Service of the Word II

## Concerns of the Church

*Leaders and the people may announce information concerning the program, ministry, and people of the church now or at the offertory.*

## Prelude

*The service may begin with music as the congregation gathers. The call to worship or hymn may follow, according to local custom.*

## Call to Worship

*All may be invited to stand. A leader may offer one of the following or other words appropriate to the season.*

**A** LEADER

Rejoice, for God is among us. Give thanks, for in Christ we are a new people. Sing praise, for we come to worship God.

**B** LEADER

Come from the east and the west, the north and the south, and worship the God of our fathers and mothers, the God of Jesus Christ. Amen. The grace of Jesus Christ and the love of God and the communion of the Holy Spirit be with us all.[40]

PEOPLE
**Amen.**

## Hymn of Adoration

*All may be invited to stand. This may be a processional hymn.*

## Invocation

*All may be invited to stand. A leader may offer a prayer in her or his own words or may use one of these, asking for the worshipers to be made responsive to the presence of God.*

**A** LEADER
Christ is with us.

PEOPLE
**Christ is in our midst.**

LEADER
Let us pray.

**B** LEADER
God be with you.

PEOPLE
**And also with you.**

LEADER
Let us pray.

### AND

**A** ALL
**O God, distant yet near, we gather as witnesses to your promise that if we seek you with all our hearts, we will find you. Be among us this day. Hear the confessions of our mouths and the yearnings of our hearts. Help us**

**B** ALL
**Gracious God, gentle in your power and strong in your tenderness, you have brought us forth from the womb of your being and breathed into us the breath of life. We know that we do not live by bread alone**

change the narrowness of our vision and the pettiness of our living. Make us new again with your holy grace. Grant us the maturity to accept your many gifts in humility and to use them with faithfulness. Grant to us your spirit that our worship may have integrity and energy, ever witnessing to your holy presence in our lives. We praise and give thanks to you, Eternal Presence; through Jesus Christ we pray. Amen.

but by every word that comes from you. Feed our deep hungers with the living bread that you give us in Jesus Christ. May Jesus' promise, "Where two or three are gathered in my name, there am I in the midst of them,"[41] be fulfilled in us. Make us a joyful company of your people so that with the faithful in every place and time we may praise and honor you, God Most High. Amen.

## PRAYER OF OUR SAVIOR

LEADER
Let us pray as Christ our Savior has taught us.
*Standing, sitting, or kneeling, all may sing or say the prayer received from Jesus Christ.*

## PSALM OR RESPONSIVE READING

*A psalm may be sung or read responsively or in unison.*

## GLORIA

*All may be invited to stand for a gloria or another hymn of praise. Musical settings, 754–760.*

## PRAYER FOR ILLUMINATION
## OR COLLECT FOR THE DAY

*The people may be seated. A leader may offer a prayer for illumination in her or his own words asking for open hearts and attentive minds, may use a seasonal collect, or may use one of these.*

**A** LEADER
Eternal God, in the reading of the scripture, may your word be heard; in the meditations of our hearts, may your word be known; and in the faithfulness of our lives, may your word be shown. Amen.

**B** LEADER
Almighty God, you have revealed yourself to us as one God; give us grace to continue steadfast in the living of our faith and constant in our worship of you, for you live and reign, one God, now and for ever. Amen.

## READING OF SCRIPTURE

*It is recommended that the schedule of readings found in the ecumenical lectionary be used. If it is not, care should be taken to maintain a balance in readings from the Old Testament, the Epistles, and the Gospels.*

*A brief introduction to the theme of each lesson may be offered. In order to distinguish the lesson from the commentary, the reader may announce: "A reading from _____" and may conclude: "Here ends the lesson."*

## SERMON

## Hymn, Anthem, or Other Music

## Prayers of the People

*The people may be seated. Leaders may announce special concerns for prayers and invite the people to indicate needs or to name causes for thanksgiving. See page 4 for topics for intercessions. A litany of prayers and responses, with silences, may be used; a pastoral prayer may be offered; petitions may be offered by anyone present, ending with a phrase to which all may respond, such as those below. A longer period of silence may precede or follow the prayers.*

**A** LEADER
Merciful God,

PEOPLE
**Hear our prayer.**

**B** LEADER
Healing Spirit,

PEOPLE
**Receive our prayer.**

## Passing the Peace

*As a sign of their reconciliation with God and each other, all may greet those around them with an embrace or a handshake, accompanied by such words as: "The peace of God be with you," and the response: "And also with you." All who are able may rise for the passing of the peace. Leaders of the service may move among the congregation to share the signs of peace.*

## Offertory

*As part of the offering of life and labor, significant announcements concerning the mission of the church may be made. Music may be offered to God's glory while the tithes and offerings are being received. Silence is also appropriate. The people may express their dedication and thanksgiving to God through music, prayers, dance, and other acts. Upon presentation of the offerings, a leader may offer a prayer of dedication, and a doxology may be sung. Musical settings, 776–782, 784, 785.*

## Hymn

## Commissioning and Benediction

**A** LEADER
Let us go forth into the new seasons of our lives.

PEOPLE
**We go forth into growing and changing and living.**

LEADER
Let us go with caring awareness for the world and all that is in it.

PEOPLE
**We go to discover the needs and opportunities around us.**

LEADER
Let us go forth in peace and be led out in joy.

ALL
**We go in God's continuing presence, with the power to love and the strength to serve. Amen.**[42]

**B** LEADER
God's peace go with you into the worlds in which you live; be nurtured by the time of gathering, be faithful in the time apart. Love and serve each other in the name of the faithful God, who calls us to be God's people; and the blessing of God, Creator, Redeemer, and Sanctifier, be with us always. Amen.

## Postlude

*The congregation may be seated and remain until the postlude is concluded.*

# SERVICE OF THE WORD III

## CONCERNS OF THE CHURCH

*Leaders and the people may announce information concerning the program, ministry, and people of the church now or at the offertory.*

## PRELUDE

*The service may begin with music as the congregation gathers. The hymn or call to worship may follow, according to local custom.*

## HYMN OF ADORATION

*All may be invited to stand. This may be a processional hymn.*

## CALL TO WORSHIP

*All may be invited to stand. A leader may use words appropriate for the season or may use one of these.*

**A** LEADER
God knows us and our hungers. God loves us like a father and nurtures us like a mother. God draws us to each other and claims us as the people of God. Knowing this, let us worship God.

**B** LEADER
The Holy One bends low at home with the humble, taking up residence in the contrite heart and forming all people in God's image. Come, let us worship. Let us offer thanksgiving and praise to God.

## INVOCATION

*All may be invited to stand. A leader may offer a prayer in her or his own words or may use one of the following, asking for the worshipers to be made responsive to the presence of God.*

**A** ALL
**O God of the morning and of the evening hours, let your Spirit come on us here gathered. This is the holy place where we, your people, call on you in faith, joining heart and voice in thanksgiving and praise to your name. Amen.**

**B** *for use in the morning*

ALL
**We come before you, O God, and wait for the kindling flame of your Holy Spirit, calling us into fuller and richer lives. You have blessed us by the night's rest and by morning's light. Open us to your claim on us. Show us your way. Let us live in the spirit of Jesus Christ our Savior. Amen.**

## SENTENCES OF PRAISE

*All may be invited to stand as one or more of these sentences are said, or other sentences appropriate for the day or liturgical season are offered.*

**A** LEADER
Blessed is God, who reveals to us the presence of the Christ, and who incorporates us into divine love.

**B** LEADER
God has brought the people of the covenant from the land of bondage into freedom.

**C** LEADER
In the beginning was the Word, and the Word was with God, and the Word was God.[43]

## PSALM OR RESPONSIVE READING

*A psalm may be sung or read responsively or in unison.*

## GLORIA

*All may be invited to stand for a gloria or another hymn of praise. Musical settings, 754–760.*

## READING OF SCRIPTURE

*The people may be seated. It is recommended that the schedule of readings found in the ecumenical lectionary be used. If it is not, care should be taken to maintain a balance in readings from the Old Testament, the Epistles, and the Gospels.*

*A brief introduction to the theme of each lesson may be offered. In order to distinguish the lesson from the commentary, the reader may announce: "A reading from_____" and may conclude: "Here ends the lesson."*

*The reading of scripture may begin with the following or other words of preparation.*

LEADER

God offers to us, through prophets and apostles, words of life which through faith become the word of life. Listen then for that word in these lessons.

## PRAYERS OF THE PEOPLE

*The people may be seated for the prayers. Leaders may announce special concerns for prayers and invite the people to indicate needs or to name causes for thanksgiving. See page 4 for topics for intercessions. A litany of prayers and responses, with silences, may be used; a pastoral prayer may be offered; petitions may be offered by anyone present, ending with a phrase to which all may respond, such as those below. A longer period of silence may precede or follow the prayers.*

**A** LEADER
Holy Spirit,

PEOPLE
**Be with us as we pray.**

**B** LEADER
Healing Spirit,

PEOPLE
**Receive our prayer.**

## OFFERTORY

*As part of the offering of life and labor, significant announcements concerning the mission of the church may be made. Music may be offered to God's glory while the gifts are being received. Silence is also appropriate. The people may express their dedication and thanksgiving to God through music, prayers, dance, and other acts.*

*The people may be invited to stand as representatives bring the gifts to the table. A doxology may be sung. A leader may offer a prayer of dedication, using one of these or his or her own words. Musical settings, 776–782, 784, 785.*

**A** LEADER
Bless these tithes and offerings, O God, returned to you. Multiply and use them to bring the word and the touch of Jesus to this place and throughout the world, in the name of Jesus Christ. Amen.

**B** LEADER
Holy One, blessed are you, who entrust to our care and use the richness of creation. Through our tithes and offerings, we return to you a portion of that which you have given us. May they be a means of serving you in the mission to which you have called us; through Jesus Christ. Amen.

# HYMN

## SERMON

## PRAYER OF THANKSGIVING

*A leader may offer a prayer of thanksgiving for the opportunity to hear and understand God's word in her or his own words or may use this prayer.*

LEADER

Thanks be to you, O God, for from the beginning you have entrusted us with your word and have called us to give heart, mind, voice, and love to serving its truth, even as Jesus Christ brought it to life among us. Amen.

## LORD'S PRAYER

LEADER

Let us pray as Christ our Savior has taught us.

*Standing, sitting, or kneeling, all may sing or say the prayer received from Jesus Christ.*

## HYMN

## BENEDICTION

*A leader may use one of the following or may dismiss the congregation with other words of comfort and challenge and with a blessing informed by scripture.*

**A** LEADER

May God's Holy Spirit lead you. May God's strength protect you. May God's peace be with you. Go now in the name of God, by the grace of Christ, and with the presence of the Holy Spirit. Amen.

**B** LEADER

Let us go and meet the world which God loves and for which Christ died. Let us proclaim that God is worthy of our trust and Christ of our discipleship. Let us live as heirs of Christ and as the people of God in the midst of God's world. Amen.

## POSTLUDE

*The congregation may be seated and remain until the postlude is concluded.*

# ORDER FOR BAPTISM

*Water in adequate supply may be in the baptistry, a font, a bowl, or a pitcher, depending upon local custom. If it is the practice of the local church to use a paschal candle, it may stand near the place of baptism and be lighted.*

## INVITATION

*The pastor and others who will lead the baptismal service may invite those who desire baptism for themselves or their children to come to the place where baptism will be celebrated. They may go out into the congregation to escort the candidates to the place for baptism. The invitation may be given informally, in words that reflect the growing relationship between the local church and the candidates.*

*As an expression of a special ministry of hospitality to children to be baptized, all children present may be invited to stand near children who are to be baptized.*

*A baptismal hymn may be sung.*

## WELCOME

*The pastor and people may introduce the baptismal service, using one of these statements or similar words.*

**A** PASTOR

Members and friends in Christ, we gather now to celebrate the gift of grace in the sacrament of baptism.

PEOPLE

**There is one body and one Spirit. There is one hope in God's call to us.**

PASTOR

There is one Lord, one faith, one baptism, one God and Creator of us all.[44]

**B** PASTOR

Dear friends, as we come to this font of living water, let us recall the meaning of baptism. For just as the body is one and has many members, and all the members of the body, though many, are one body, so it is with Christ.

PEOPLE

**For by one Spirit we were all baptized into one body—Jews or Greeks, slaves or free—and all were made to drink of one Spirit.**

PASTOR

Now you are the body of Christ and individually members of it.[45]

**C** *for use when children are baptized*

PASTOR

They were bringing children to Jesus that Jesus might touch them; and the disciples rebuked them. But when Jesus saw it, Jesus was indignant, and said to them,

PEOPLE

**"Let the children come to me, do not hinder them; for to such belongs the realm of God. Truly, I say to you, whoever does not receive the realm of God like a child shall not enter it."**

PASTOR

And Jesus took them in his arms and blessed them, laying his hands upon them.[46]

# ADDRESS

*The pastor may address those gathered, using one of these options or other words based on scripture.*

**A** PASTOR

Jesus came to John to be baptized by him. But John tried to make him change his mind. "I ought to be baptized by you," John said, "yet you have come to me!"

PEOPLE

**Jesus said, "Let it be so for now. For in this way, we shall do all that God requires." So John agreed.**

PASTOR

As soon as Jesus was baptized, he came up out of the water. Then heaven was opened to him, and he saw the Spirit of God coming down like a dove and lighting on him.

PEOPLE

**Then a voice said from heaven, "This is my own dear Son, with whom I am well pleased."**[47]

PASTOR

At another time Jesus said: Go and make disciples of all nations, baptizing them in the name of the Father and of the Son and of the Holy Spirit.[48]

**B** PASTOR

Jesus said: Unless we are born anew, we cannot see the reign of God; unless we are born of water and the Spirit, we cannot enter God's new order.[49]

Paul the apostle said: All of us who have been baptized into Christ Jesus were baptized into Christ's death. We were buried therefore with Christ by baptism into death, so that as Christ was raised from the dead, to the glory of God, we too might walk in newness of life.[50]

AND

**A** *for baptism of infants and young children*

PASTOR

The sacrament of baptism is an outward and visible sign of the grace of God. Inasmuch as the promise of the gospel is not only to us but also to our children, baptism with water and the Holy Spirit is the mark of their acceptance into the care of Christ's church, the sign and seal of their participation in God's forgiveness, and the beginning of their growth into full Christian faith and discipleship.[51]

**B** *for baptism of older children, youth, and adults*

PASTOR

Baptism is the sacrament through which we are united to Jesus Christ and given part in Christ's ministry of reconciliation. Baptism is the visible sign of an invisible event: the reconciliation of people to God. It shows the death of self and the rising to a life of obedience and praise. It shows also the pouring out of the Holy Spirit on those whom God has chosen. In baptism, God works in us the power of forgiveness, the renewal of the Spirit, and the knowledge of the call to be God's people always.[52]

*This response may follow either option.*

PEOPLE

**This is the water of baptism. Out of this water we rise with new life, forgiven of sin and one in Christ, members of Christ's body.**

## Questions of the Candidates

*If there are no infants or young children to be baptized, continue with the questions for older children and adults on page 34.*

### Infants and Young Children

*These questions may be used when the candidates are unable to speak for themselves. If more than one child is to be baptized, all parents and sponsors may respond in unison.*

PASTOR *addressing the parent(s)*

Do you desire to have your child(ren) baptized into the faith and family of Jesus Christ?

PARENT(S)
*I/We* **do.**

PASTOR *addressing the parent(s) and sponsor(s), if any*

Will you encourage *this child/these children* to renounce the powers of evil and to receive the freedom of new life in Christ?

PARENT(S) AND SPONSOR(S)
*I/We* **will, with the help of God.**

PASTOR

Will you teach *this child/these children* that *he/she/they* may be led to profess Jesus Christ as Lord and Savior?

PARENT(S) AND SPONSOR(S)
*I/We* **will, with the help of God.**

PASTOR

Do you promise, by the grace of God, to be Christ's disciple(s), to follow in the way of our Savior, to resist oppression and evil, to show love and justice, and to witness to the work and word of Jesus Christ as best you are able?

PARENT(S) AND SPONSOR(S)
*I/We* **do, with the help of God.**

PASTOR

Do you promise, according to the grace given you, to grow with *this child/these children* in the Christian faith, to help *this child/these children* to be *a faithful member/faithful members* of the church of Jesus Christ, by celebrating Christ's presence, by furthering Christ's mission in all the world, and by offering the nurture of the Christian church so that *she/he/they* may affirm *her/his/their* baptism?

PARENT(S) AND SPONSOR(S)
*I/We* **do, with the help of God.**

*If there are no older children or adults to be baptized, continue with the congregational assent on page 35.*

## OLDER CHILDREN AND ADULTS

*These questions may be used when the candidates are able to speak for themselves. If more than one person is to be baptized, they may respond to the questions in unison.*

PASTOR *addressing the candidate(s)*

<u>Name(s)</u>, do you desire to be baptized into the faith and family of Jesus Christ?

CANDIDATE(S)

**I do.**

> PASTOR *addressing the sponsor(s), if any*
>
> Are you ready with God's help to guide and encourage <u>name(s)</u>, by counsel and example, in prayer and with love, to follow the way of Jesus Christ?
>
> SPONSOR(S)
> **I am.**

PASTOR *addressing the candidate(s)*

Do you renounce the powers of evil and desire the freedom of new life in Christ?

CANDIDATE(S)

**I do.**

PASTOR

Do you profess Jesus Christ as Lord and Savior?

CANDIDATE(S)

**I do.**

PASTOR

Do you promise, by the grace of God, to be Christ's disciple, to follow in the way of our Savior, to resist oppression and evil, to show love and justice, and to witness to the work and word of Jesus Christ as best you are able?

CANDIDATE(S)

**I promise, with the help of God.**

PASTOR

Do you promise, according to the grace given you, to grow in the Christian faith and to be a faithful member of the church of Jesus Christ, celebrating Christ's presence and furthering Christ's mission in all the world?

CANDIDATE(S)

**I promise, with the help of God.**

## CONGREGATIONAL ASSENT

*All may be invited to stand as the congregation is asked to make promises.*

PASTOR

Jesus Christ calls us to make disciples of all nations and to offer them the gift of grace in baptism.

Do you, who witness and celebrate this sacrament, promise your love, support, and care to the one(s) about to be baptized, as *he/she/they* live(s) and grow(s) in Christ?

PEOPLE

**We promise our love, support, and care.**

## AFFIRMATION OF FAITH

*All may be invited to stand. Responses are made in unison by each worshiper, including the candidate(s) for baptism.*

PASTOR

Let us unite with the church in all times and places in confessing our faith in the triune God.

**A** PASTOR

Do you believe in God?

PEOPLE

**I believe in God.**

PASTOR

Do you believe in Jesus Christ?

PEOPLE

**I believe in Jesus Christ.**

PASTOR

Do you believe in the Holy Spirit?

PEOPLE

**I believe in the Holy Spirit.**

**B** *An ancient baptismal creed, another creed, a statement of faith, or the local church covenant may be used in full or in an abbreviated version. (See 881–887.)*

*When incorporating baptism and confirmation or reception of members, begin the Order for Baptism here.*

## PRAYER OF BAPTISM

*The congregation may be seated. A prayer may be offered, using the pastor's own words, option A with B, or B alone.*

PASTOR

Christ be with you.

PEOPLE

**And also with you.**

PASTOR

Let us pray.

**A** PASTOR

We thank you, God, for the gift of creation called forth by your saving Word. Before the world had shape and form, your Spirit moved over the waters. Out of the waters of the deep, you formed the firmament and brought forth the earth to sustain all life.

In the time of Noah, you washed the earth with the waters of the flood, and your ark of salvation bore a new beginning.

In the time of Moses, your people Israel passed through the Red Sea waters from slavery to freedom and crossed the flowing Jordan to enter the promised land.

In the fullness of time, you sent Jesus Christ, who was nurtured in the water of Mary's womb.

Jesus was baptized by John in the water of the Jordan, became living water to a woman at the Samaritan well, washed the feet of the disciples, and sent them forth to baptize all the nations by water and the Holy Spirit.

*The water may be visibly poured.*

**B** *may be used alone or with option A*

PASTOR
Bless by your Holy Spirit, gracious God, this water. By your Holy Spirit save those who confess the name of Jesus Christ that sin may have no power over them. Create new life in *the one/all* baptized this day that *she/he/they* may rise in Christ. Glory to you, eternal God, the one who was, and is, and shall always be, world without end. Amen.

## ACT OF BAPTISM

> ### NAMING OF A CHILD
> *When a child is baptized, as each child is handed into the arms of the pastor, the parent(s) may be asked to name the child.*
>
> PASTOR
> By what name will your child be called?
>
> PARENT(S)
> *Name.*

*The pastor, administering the water by pouring, sprinkling, or immersion, says one of these.*

**A** PASTOR
*Name*, you are baptized in the name of the Father, and of the Son, and of the Holy Spirit.

PEOPLE
**Amen.**

**B** PASTOR
*Name*, I baptize you in the name of the Father, and of the Son, and of the Holy Spirit.

PEOPLE
**Amen.**

*The pastor may lay hands on the head of the baptized and say these or similar words.*

PASTOR
The Holy Spirit be upon you, *name*, child of God, disciple of Christ, member of the church.

## ACT OF PRAISE

*A doxology or another act of praise may follow the baptism.*

*If this order is being used in conjunction with one of the Orders for Affirmation of Baptism, return to the Order for Confirmation at the prayer on page 40 or the Order for Reception of Members at the address on page 46.*

## PRAYER FOR THE BAPTIZED

*A prayer for the baptized may be said, using one of the following or the pastor's own words.*

**A** PASTOR

We give you thanks, O Holy One, mother and father of all the faithful, for *this your child/these your children* and for the grace acknowledged here today in water and the Holy Spirit. Embrace us all as sons and daughters in the one household of your love. Grant us grace to receive, nurture, and befriend *this new member/these new members* of the body of Christ.

ALL

**Give to the newly baptized: strength for life's journey, courage in time of suffering, the joy of faith, the freedom of love, and the hope of new life; through Jesus Christ, who makes us one. Amen.**

**B** *includes optional words for use when a child is baptized.*

PASTOR

Let us pray for *the one/those* baptized today.

Gracious God, you have filled the world with joy by giving us the gift of Jesus. Bless *this newly baptized person/these newly baptized people.* May *she/he/they* be filled with joy; may *he/she/they* never be ashamed to confess a personal faith in you.

> Bless the parent(s) [and sponsor(s)] of *this child/these children.* May *she/he/they* always show *her/his/their* gratitude for the life you have given by loving and caring for <u>*name(s)*</u>.

Bless these your faithful people. Unite them in the peace of Christ and the company of the Holy Spirit.

PEOPLE

**Amen.**

## BENEDICTION

*Those leading the service may greet the newly baptized, the parents, and the sponsors informally. A lighted candle or another gift signifying discipleship may be given to each newly baptized person. The pastor, sponsors, or others may move through the congregation with the newly baptized and introduce the person(s) as a sign of entry and incorporation into the living community of faith.*

PASTOR

Go in the peace of Christ.

ALL

**Thanks be to God.**

*Those who have participated in the Order for Baptism may return to their places in the congregation.*

*A Service of Word and Sacrament or a Service of the Word continues, omitting the affirmation of faith.*

# ORDER FOR CONFIRMATION: AFFIRMATION OF BAPTISM

## INVITATION

*After the sermon has been preached, appointed representatives and the pastor may gather in the chancel for confirmation. An elected leader of the church may invite all who have indicated willingness to affirm their baptism by confirmation to come forward, using the following or similar words.*

LEADER

We invite to come forward *the one/those* who wish(es) to affirm *his/her/their* baptism by being confirmed.

*The name(s) of individual(s) may be read, and the candidate(s) may be invited to come forward and stand.*

LEADER

Friends in Christ, we all are received into the church through the sacrament of baptism. *This person has/These people have* found nurture and support in the midst of the family of Christ. Through prayer and study *she/he/they has/have* been led by the Holy Spirit to affirm *her/his/their* baptism and to claim in our presence *her/his/their* covenantal relationship with Christ and the members of the church. *He/She/They is/are* here for service to Jesus Christ, using the gifts which the Holy Spirit bestows.

## SENTENCES

*One of the following or other passages from scripture may be read.*

**A** LEADER

Hear the words of Jesus: I am the vine, you are the branches. Anyone who abides in me, and I in that person, is the one who bears much fruit. If you abide in me, and my words abide in you, ask whatever you will, and it shall be done for you. If you keep my commandments, you will abide in my love. These things I have spoken to you, that my joy may be in you, and that your joy may be full.[53]

**B** LEADER

God's message is near you, on your lips and in your heart, that is, the word of faith that we preach. If you confess with your lips that Jesus is Lord and believe that God raised Jesus from the dead, you will be saved. For it is by our faith that we are put right with God; it is by our confession that we are saved.[54]

**C** LEADER

You are no longer strangers and sojourners, but you are equally citizens with the saints and members of the household of God, built upon the foundation of the apostles and prophets, Christ Jesus alone being the cornerstone, in whom the whole structure is joined together and grows into a holy temple in Christ; in whom you also are built into it for a dwelling place of God in the Spirit.[55]

## QUESTIONS OF THE CANDIDATES

*These questions parallel the questions asked of candidates for baptism. If there is more than one candidate, they may be asked together to respond in unison.*

*The first question includes words for candidate(s) being baptized as well as one(s) affirming baptism. With more than one candidate, it may be necessary to address the question using each set of words.*

PASTOR
<u>Name(s)</u>, do you desire to *affirm your baptism/be baptized* into the faith and family of Jesus Christ?

CANDIDATE(S)
**I do.**

PASTOR
Do you renounce the powers of evil and desire the freedom of new life in Christ?

CANDIDATE(S)
**I do.**

PASTOR
Do you profess Jesus Christ as Lord and Savior?

CANDIDATE(S)
**I do.**

PASTOR
Do you promise, by the grace of God, to be Christ's disciple, to follow in the way of our Savior, to resist oppression and evil, to show love and justice, and to witness to the work and word of Jesus Christ as best you are able?

CANDIDATE(S)
**I promise, with the help of God.**

PASTOR
Do you promise, according to the grace given you, to grow in the Christian faith and to be a faithful member of the church of Jesus Christ, celebrating Christ's presence and furthering Christ's mission in all the world?

CANDIDATE(S)
**I promise, with the help of God.**

## AFFIRMATION OF FAITH

*The congregation may be invited to stand. The responses are made in unison by each worshiper, including the candidate(s).*

PASTOR
Let us unite with the church in all times and places in confessing our faith in the triune God.

**A** PASTOR
Do you believe in God?

PEOPLE
**I believe in God.**

**B** *An ancient baptismal creed, another creed, a statement of faith, or the local church covenant may be used in full or in an abbreviated version. (See 881–887.)*

PASTOR
Do you believe in Jesus Christ?

PEOPLE
**I believe in Jesus Christ.**

PASTOR
Do you believe in the Holy Spirit?

PEOPLE
**I believe in the Holy Spirit.**

*The congregation may be seated.*

*If there is a candidate for baptism, use the Order for Baptism, beginning with the prayer of baptism on page 35. Following the act of praise on page 36, return to this point of the Order for Confirmation.*

*If no one is to be baptized, the service continues with the prayer of the candidates which follows.*

## PRAYER OF THE CANDIDATE(S)

*The candidates may be invited to stand or kneel.*

PASTOR AND CANDIDATE(S)
**O God, my God, known to me in Jesus Christ, I give myself to you as your own, to love and serve you faithfully all the days of my life. Amen.**[56]

## PRAYERS OF THE CONGREGATION

PASTOR
Let us pray in silence.
*A period of silent prayer follows.*

PASTOR
Let us pray together.

ALL
**Almighty God, who in baptism received these your servants into the church, forgave their sins, and promised them eternal life, increase in them the gifts of your Holy Spirit. Grant love for others, joy in serving you, peace in disagreement, patience in suffering, kindness toward all people, goodness in evil times, faithfulness in temptation, gentleness in the face of opposition, self-control in all things. Thereby strengthen them for their ministry in the world; through Jesus Christ our Savior. Amen.**

*If the Lord's Prayer is not to be said elsewhere in the service, it may be said at this time.*

## ACT OF CONFIRMATION

*Parents and baptismal and/or confirmation sponsors, if any, may come forward and stand near the confirmands. Candidates may be invited to kneel. The pastor and other leaders of the local church may place hands upon each candidate individually. One of the following or similar words may be said.*

**A** PASTOR
*Name*, the God of peace sanctify you.
I pray that you will be preserved

**B** PASTOR
*Name*, the God of mercies multiply
grace and peace in you, enable you

40

blameless to the coming of our Savior Jesus Christ.

CANDIDATE(S) AND PEOPLE

**Amen.**

**C** PASTOR

Strengthen, O God, this your servant *name* with your heavenly grace that *he/she* may continue yours for ever; and daily increase in *him/her* your Holy Spirit, until you receive *him/her* at last in your eternal home.

CANDIDATE(S) AND PEOPLE

**Amen.**

truly and faithfully to keep your vows, defend you in every time of danger, preserve you to the end, and finally bring you to rest with all the saints in glory everlasting.

CANDIDATE(S) AND PEOPLE

**Amen.**

**D** PASTOR

O God, in the grace of Jesus Christ you have accepted this your servant *name* through the water of baptism. Nourish in *her/him* the power of your Holy Spirit that *she/he* may serve you in the world.

CANDIDATE(S) AND PEOPLE

**Amen.**

## PRAYER OF CONFIRMATION

PASTOR

We rejoice, O merciful God, with *this person/these people* in the gift of the Holy Spirit, and in the Spirit's power to awaken us to new truth and to inspire us to venture into fullness of life.

We give you thanks that *she/he/they has/have* been moved to affirm *her/his/their* baptism. Help *him/her/them* to live not for *himself/herself/themselves* but for Christ and those whom Christ loves. Keep *her/him/them* steady and abounding in hope, never giving up, pressing toward the goal of life with you in Jesus Christ.

CANDIDATE(S) AND PEOPLE

**Amen.**

*The newly confirmed individual(s) may rise and stand in place.*

## ADDRESS

PASTOR

By your baptism you were made one with us in the body of Christ, the church. Today we rejoice in your pilgrimage of faith which has brought you to this time and place. We celebrate your presence in this household of faith.

## QUESTION ABOUT PARTICIPATION

PASTOR

Do you promise to participate in the life and mission of this family of God's people, sharing regularly in the worship of God and enlisting in the work of this local church as it serves this community and the world?

CANDIDATE(S)

**I promise, with the help of God.**

## WELCOME

*Members of the local church may be invited to stand and say the following or other words of welcome.*

PASTOR

Let us, the members of *local church*, express our welcome and affirm our mutual ministry in Christ.

PEOPLE

**We promise you our continuing friendship and prayers as we share the hopes and labors of the church of Jesus Christ. By the power of the Holy Spirit may we continue to grow together in God's knowledge and love and be witnesses of our risen Savior.**

## GREETING OF CHRISTIAN LOVE

*The congregation may be seated. The pastor and representatives of the local church may greet each newly confirmed person individually with these or other words and may offer the hand of Christian love.*

PASTOR AND REPRESENTATIVES

**In the name of Jesus Christ, and on behalf of *local church*, we extend to you the hand of Christian love.**

## PRAYER

PASTOR

Let us pray.

**A** PASTOR

Eternal God, we praise you for calling us to be your servant people and for gathering us into the body of Christ. We thank you for sending to us *this believer/ these believers* that we may work together in serving the needs of others. Confirm in us the power of your covenant that we may live in your Spirit, share regularly in worship, and so love each other that we may have among us the same mind which was in Christ Jesus, to whom be all honor and glory.

ALL

**Amen.**[57]

**B** PASTOR

Almighty and ever-living God, may your hand ever be over your servant(s) confirmed today. May your Holy Spirit ever be with *her/him/them.* So lead *him/her/them* in the knowledge and obedience of your Word that *he/she/they* may serve you in this life and dwell with you in the life to come; through Jesus Christ.

ALL

**Amen.**[58]

**C** PASTOR

O God, we praise you for calling us to faith and for gathering us into the church, the body of Christ. We thank you for your people gathered in this local church and rejoice that you have increased our community of faith. Together may we live in the Spirit, building one another up in love, sharing in the life and worship of the church, and serving the world for the sake of Jesus Christ.

ALL

**Amen.**[59]

## BENEDICTION

PASTOR

Go in the peace of Christ.

PEOPLE

**Thanks be to God.**

*Those who have participated in the Order for Confirmation may return to their places in the congregation.*

**At the conclusion of this order, a Service of Word and Sacrament or a Service of the Word continues, omitting the affirmation of faith.**

# ORDER FOR RECEPTION OF MEMBERS: AFFIRMATION OF BAPTISM

## INVITATION

*After the sermon has been preached, appointed representatives and the pastor may gather in the chancel. An elected leader of the church may invite all who have indicated willingness to affirm their baptism by joining this local church to come forward, using the following or similar words.*

LEADER

We invite to come forward *the one/those* who wish(es) to affirm *his/her/their* baptism by uniting with us in this household of faith.

*The name(s) of the individual(s) may be read and the candidate(s) may come forward and stand, if able. If member(s) are being received from other churches by letter of transfer, that information may be presented.*

LEADER

Friends in Christ, we all are received into the church through the sacrament of baptism. *This person has/These people have* found nurture and support in the midst of the family of Christ. Through prayer and study *she/he/they has/have* been led by the Holy Spirit to affirm *her/his/their* baptism and to claim in our presence *her/his/their* covenantal relationship with Christ and the members of the church. *He/She/They is/are* here for service to Jesus Christ, using the gifts which the Holy Spirit bestows.

## SENTENCES

*One of the following or other passages from scripture may be read.*

**A** LEADER

Hear the words of Jesus: I am the vine, you are the branches. Anyone who abides in me, and I in that person, is the one who bears much fruit. If you abide in me, and my words abide in you, ask whatever you will, and it shall be done for you. If you keep my commandments, you will abide in my love. These things I have spoken to you, that my joy may be in you, and that your joy may be full.[60]

**B** LEADER

God's message is near you, on your lips and in your heart, that is, the word of faith that we preach. If you confess with your lips that Jesus is Lord and believe that God raised Jesus from the dead, you will be saved. For it is by our faith that we are put right with God; it is by our confession that we are saved.[61]

**C** LEADER

You are no longer strangers and sojourners, but you are equally citizens with the saints and members of the household of God, built upon the foundation of the apostles and prophets, Christ Jesus alone being the cornerstone, in whom the whole structure is joined together and grows into a holy temple in Christ; in whom you also are built into it for a dwelling place of God in the Spirit.[62]

## QUESTIONS OF THE CANDIDATES

*These questions parallel the questions asked of candidates for baptism. If there is more than one candidate, they may be asked together and respond in unison.*

*The first question includes words for candidate(s) being baptized as well as one(s) affirming baptism. With more than one candidate, it may be necessary to address the question using each set of words.*

PASTOR

*Name(s)*, do you desire to *affirm your baptism/be baptized* into the faith and family of Jesus Christ?

CANDIDATE(S)

**I do.**

PASTOR

Do you renounce the powers of evil and desire the freedom of new life in Christ?

CANDIDATE(S)

**I do.**

PASTOR

Do you profess Jesus Christ as Lord and Savior?

CANDIDATE(S)

**I do.**

PASTOR

Do you promise, by the grace of God, to be Christ's disciple, to follow in the way of our Savior, to resist oppression and evil, to show love and justice, and to witness to the work and word of Jesus Christ as best you are able?

CANDIDATE(S)

**I promise, with the help of God.**

PASTOR

Do you promise, according to the grace given you, to grow in the Christian faith and to be a faithful member of the church of Jesus Christ, celebrating Christ's presence and furthering Christ's mission in all the world?

CANDIDATE(S)

**I promise, with the help of God.**

## AFFIRMATION OF FAITH

*The people may be invited to stand. The responses are made in unison by each worshiper, including the candidate(s).*

PASTOR

Let us unite with the church in all times and places in confessing our faith in the triune God.

**A** PASTOR

Do you believe in God?

PEOPLE

**I believe in God.**

**B** *An ancient baptismal creed, another creed, a statement of faith (see 881–887), or the local church covenant may be used in full or in an abbreviated version.*

45

PASTOR
Do you believe in Jesus Christ?

PEOPLE
**I believe in Jesus Christ.**

PASTOR
Do you believe in the Holy Spirit?

PEOPLE
**I believe in the Holy Spirit.**

*The congregation may be seated.*

*If there is a candidate for baptism, use the Order for Baptism, beginning with the prayer of baptism on page 35. Following the act of praise on page 36, return to this point of the Order for Reception of Members.*

*If no one is to be baptized, the service continues here.*

## ADDRESS

*The following or similar words may be addressed to all people uniting with the church by baptism, reaffirmation or re-profession of faith, or by transfer or certification from other Christian churches.*

PASTOR
By your baptism you were made one with us in the body of Christ, the church. Today we rejoice in your pilgrimage of faith which has brought you to this time and place. We give thanks for every community of faith that has been your spiritual home, and we celebrate your presence in this household of faith.

## QUESTION ABOUT PARTICIPATION

PASTOR
Do you promise to participate in the life and mission of this family of God's people, sharing regularly in the worship of God and enlisting in the work of this local church as it serves this community and the world?

CANDIDATE(S)
**I promise, with the help of God.**

## WELCOME AND RECEPTION

*Members of the local church may be invited to stand and say the following or other words of welcome.*

PASTOR
Let us, the members of *local church*, express our welcome and affirm our mutual ministry in Christ.

PEOPLE
**We welcome you with joy in the common life of this church. We promise you our friendship and prayers as we share the hopes and labors of the church of Jesus Christ. By the power of the Holy Spirit may we continue to grow together in God's knowledge and love and be witnesses of our risen Savior.**

## GREETING OF CHRISTIAN LOVE

*The congregation may be seated. The pastor and representatives of the local church may greet each new member personally with these or other words and may offer the hand of Christian love.*

PASTOR AND REPRESENTATIVES

**In the name of Jesus Christ, and on behalf of <u>*local church*</u>, we extend to you the hand of Christian love, welcoming you into the company of this local church.**

PRAYER

PASTOR

Let us pray.

**A** PASTOR

Eternal God, we praise you for calling us to be your servant people and for gathering us into the body of Christ. We thank you for sending to us *this believer/these believers* that we may work together in serving the needs of others. Confirm in us the power of your covenant that we may live in your Spirit, share regularly in worship, and so love each other that we may have among us the same mind which was in Christ Jesus, to whom be all honor and glory.

ALL

**Amen.**[63]

**B** PASTOR

Almighty and everliving God, may your hand ever be over your servant(s) who made a commitment to membership here today. May your Holy Spirit ever be with *her/him/them*. So lead *him/her/them* in the knowledge and obedience of your Word that *he/she/they* may serve you in this life and dwell with you in the life to come; through Jesus Christ.

ALL

**Amen.**[64]

**C** PASTOR

O God, we praise you for calling us to faith and for gathering us into the church, the body of Christ. We thank you for your people gathered in this local church and rejoice that you have increased our community of faith. Together may we live in the Spirit, building one another up in love, sharing in the life and worship of the church, and serving the world for the sake of Jesus Christ.

ALL

**Amen.**[65]

BENEDICTION

PASTOR

Go in the peace of Christ.

PEOPLE

**Thanks be to God.**

*Those who have participated in the Order for Reception of Members may return to their seats.*

**At the conclusion of this order, a Service of Word and Sacrament or a Service of the Word continues, omitting the affirmation of faith.**

# ORDER FOR THANKSGIVING FOR ONE WHO HAS DIED

## PRELUDE

*This service may begin with music for a service of the resurrection. If the coffin is set in place before the people arrive or is not present at all, the service may continue with the opening hymn or the greeting.*

## PROCESSION AND SENTENCES

*If the coffin is brought into the church in a procession, a leader may meet it at the entrance and say any of the following sentences as she or he precedes the coffin and family up the aisle to the chancel. If there is no procession, the sentences may be used following the greeting. The congregation may be invited to stand for the procession. The one presiding may say one or more sentences.*

LEADER
Hear the promises of God.

**A** LEADER
God is near to all who call, who call from their hearts. The desires of those who fear God are fulfilled; their cries are heard; they are saved.[66]

**B** LEADER
I am the resurrection and the life; all who believe in me, though they die, yet shall they live, and whoever lives and believes in me shall never die.[67]

**C** LEADER
Fear not, I am the first and the last, and the living one; I died, and behold I am alive for evermore.[68]

**D** LEADER
Fear not, for I am with you, be not dismayed, for I am your God; I will strengthen you, I will help you, I will uphold you with my victorious hand.[69]

**E** LEADER
When we were baptized into Christ Jesus, we were baptized into Christ's death. By our baptism, then, we were buried with Christ and shared Christ's death, in order that, just as Christ was raised from death by the glorious power of God, so too we might live a new life.[70] For if we have been united with Christ in a death like Christ's, we shall certainly be united with Christ in a resurrection like Christ's.[71]

**F** LEADER
Blessed are the dead who die in Christ. "Blessed indeed," says the Spirit, "that they may rest from their labors, for their deeds follow them!"[72]

## HYMN OF ADORATION

*As the procession nears the chancel, a hymn may be sung. If there is no procession, the people may rise for the opening hymn as a leader enters; or a leader may enter during the prelude and open with the greeting and/or the sentences. Then the service may continue with the hymn.*

## Greeting

*All may be invited to stand. A leader may greet the people informally, name the person for whom they gather in thanksgiving, and interpret briefly the meaning of the service. One or more of the following may be used.*

**A** LEADER

The grace of our Lord Jesus Christ and the love of God and the communion of the Holy Spirit be with you all.[73]

PEOPLE

**And also with you.**

**B** LEADER

Friends, we gather here in the protective shelter of God's healing love. We are free to pour out our grief, release our anger, face our emptiness, and know that God cares. We gather here as God's people, conscious of others who have died and of the frailty of our own existence on earth. We come to comfort and to support one another in our common loss. We gather to hear God's word of hope that can drive away our despair and move us to offer God our praise. We gather to commend to God with thanksgiving the life of _name_ as we celebrate the good news of Christ's resurrection. For whether we live or whether we die, we belong to Christ who is Lord both of the dead and of the living.[74]

**C** LEADER

Gracious is our God and righteous; our God is full of compassion.

PEOPLE

**I will walk in the presence of God in the land of the living.**

LEADER

I will fulfill my vows to God in the presence of all God's people.

PEOPLE

**Precious in the sight of God is the death of those who die in faithfulness.**[75]

## Prayer

*The people may be seated. The service may continue with a confession of sin and an assurance of pardon or a collect or a prayer of thanksgiving for the communion of saints.*

**A** LEADER

The peace of Christ be with you.

PEOPLE

**And also with you.**

LEADER

Let us pray.

ALL

**Almighty God, whose will is sovereign and whose mercy is boundless, look upon us in our sorrow and enable us to hear your word. Help us hear so that, through patience and**

**B** ALL

**Holy God, whose ways are not our ways and whose thoughts are not our thoughts, grant that your Holy Spirit may intercede for us with sighs too deep for human words. Heal our wounded hearts made heavy by our sorrow. Through the veil of our tears and the silence of our emptiness, assure us again that ear has not heard, nor eye seen, nor human imagination envisioned, what you have prepared for those**

the encouragement of the scriptures, we may hold fast to the assurance of your favor and the hope of life eternal; through Jesus Christ our risen Savior. Amen.

who love you; through Jesus Christ, the firstborn from the dead. Amen.

## READING OF SCRIPTURE

*The psalms, read responsively or antiphonally or sung, may be used before and/or after the lessons. It is appropriate to include at least one Gospel lesson. Where it is the custom, all may be invited to stand for the Gospel reading. Members of the family of the deceased and other lay persons may be readers. A gloria may be said or sung at the conclusion of the final psalm. Suggested readings include the following.*

### PSALMS

Psalms 23; 27:7-14; 42:1-5; 46; 90:1-4, 12-17; 121; 130; 139:1-18, 23-24

### OLD TESTAMENT

Job 19:25-27; Isaiah 25:6-9, 61:1-3; Lamentations 3:22-26, 31-33

### EPISTLES

Acts 10:34-43; Romans 8:9-11, 31-39; 1 Corinthians 13, 15:12-20, 15:35-50; 2 Corinthians 4:7-11, 16; 5:1-5; Ephesians 3:14-21; 1 Thessalonians 4:13-18; 2 Timothy 1:8-13; Revelation 21:1-6

### GOSPELS

Matthew 5:3-10, 11:28-30; Luke 23:33, 39-43; John 6:37-40; 11:17-27; 12:24-26; 14:1-3, 18-19, 25-27

### SERMON

*The people may be seated for a sermon.*

### WORDS OF REMEMBRANCE

*A leader or a friend or member of the family of the deceased may offer thanksgiving for the one who has died and recall the individual's uniqueness if this is desired and has not been done during the sermon.*

### AFFIRMATION OF FAITH

*All may be invited to stand and affirm the resurrection faith by saying a creed, statement of faith, or other affirmation, such as the following from Romans.*

LEADER

Let us say again what we believe.

ALL

**We believe there is no condemnation for those who are in Christ Jesus, and we know that in everything God works for good with those who love God, who are called according to God's purpose. We are sure that neither death, nor life, nor angels, nor principalities, nor things present, nor things to come, nor powers, nor height, nor depth, nor anything else in all creation, will be able to separate us from the love of God in Christ Jesus our Lord. Amen.**[76]

# Hymn, Anthem, or Other Music

*Music may be offered in God's praise.*

## Prayers of Thanksgiving and Intercession

*These or other similar prayers may be offered. A litany may be used. The prayers may be used individually or together, with or without each "Amen" said by the pastor or people. Prayers to be offered at the death of a child follow the general prayers.*

LEADER
Let us pray.

**A** LEADER
Merciful God, we thank you for your word; it is a lamp for our feet, a light for our path. We thank you especially that in the night of our grief and in the shadows of our sorrow, we are not left to ourselves. We have the light of your promises to sustain and comfort us. Through our tears, give us vision to see in faith the consolation you intend for us. In your mercy, grant us the unfailing guidance of your saving Word, both in life and in death; through Jesus Christ our risen Savior.

PEOPLE
**Amen.**

**B** LEADER
O God, our strength and our redeemer, giver of life and conqueror of death, we praise you with humble hearts. With faith in your great mercy and wisdom, we entrust *name* to your eternal care. We praise you for your steadfast love for *her/him* all the days of *her/his* earthly life. We thank you for all that *he/she* was to those who loved *him/her* [and for *his/her* faithfulness to the church of Jesus Christ]. *Mention may be made of the person's Christian life and service.*

We thank you that for *name* [all sickness and sorrow are ended, and] death itself is past and that *she/he* has entered the home where all your people gather in peace. Keep us all in communion with your faithful people in every time and place, that at last we may rejoice together in the heavenly family where Jesus Christ reigns with you and the Holy Spirit, one God, for ever.

PEOPLE
**Amen.**

**C** LEADER
God of all mercies and all comfort, in tender love and compassion, embrace your sorrowing servants. Be their refuge and strength, and ever present help in trouble. Show them again the love of Christ that passes all human under-standing; for by death Christ has conquered death, and by rising Christ has opened to all of us the gates of everlasting life. Thanks be to you, O God.

PEOPLE
**Amen.**

**D** LEADER
Let us pray for ourselves.

PEOPLE

**O God, whose days are without end and whose mercies cannot be counted, awaken us to the shortness and uncertainty of human life. By your Holy Spirit, lead us in faithfulness all our days. When we have served you in our generation, may we be gathered with those who have gone before, having the testimony of a good conscience, in the communion of your holy church, in the confidence of a certain faith, in the comfort of a saving hope, in favor with you, our God, and at perfect peace with the world; through Jesus Christ our Redeemer. Amen.**

*At the death of a child, the following prayers or others in the leader's own words may be offered.*

**E** LEADER

Gentle God, born an infant in Jesus Christ in the family of Joseph and Mary, we give you thanks for _name_ born among us full of hope and promise. We remember that Jesus Christ lifted children into loving arms to embrace and bless them. We ask you to embrace and bless _name_ as part of your heavenly family where by your grace, our lives are brought to fullness in the peace of your eternal home. We ask this through Jesus Christ, your beloved child, and our risen Savior.

PEOPLE

**Amen.**

**F** *for parents*

LEADER

God of all mercies, whose heart aches with our human hurting, we commend to your love the parent(s) of this child, _name(s) of parent(s)_, [and all his/her/their children who mourn]. Sustain the family in this loss and in their loneliness. Kindle anew the ashes of joy. Grant the peace of knowing that this child is with you, the Mother and Father of us all, both in this life and in the life that is to come; through Jesus Christ our Savior.

PEOPLE

**Amen.**

*If Holy Communion is not to be celebrated, the service may be concluded with silence, the Prayer of Our Savior, the commendation, and the closing acts that follow.*

*If Holy Communion is to be celebrated, the service continues with the offertory of the bread and wine from a service of word and sacrament, especially the "Brief Order" in Book of Worship, United Church of Christ. Members of the family or friends of the deceased may bring the bread and wine to the table. All Christians present may be invited to receive. After the post-communion prayer of thanksgiving, the Order for Thanksgiving for One Who Has Died may continue with the commendation on page 53 and the closing acts which follow it.*

## SILENCE

*Silence may be observed for reflection and prayer.*

## PRAYER OF OUR SAVIOR

LEADER

Let us pray as Christ our Savior has taught us.

*Standing, sitting, or kneeling, all may sing or say the prayer received from Jesus Christ.*

## COMMENDATION

*All may be invited to stand. The leader may go to the coffin for one of the following or another commendation. The words are also appropriate if no coffin is present.*

**A** LEADER

Holy God, by your mighty power you gave us life, and in your love you have given us new life in Jesus Christ. We now entrust *name* to your merciful care. We do this in the faith of Christ Jesus, who died and rose again to save us and is now alive and reigns with you and the Holy Spirit in glory for ever.

PEOPLE

**Amen.**

**B** LEADER

Into your hands, O merciful Savior, we commend your servant *name*. Acknowledge, we humbly pray, a sheep of your own fold, a lamb of your own flock, and a *daughter/son* of your own redeeming. Receive *her/him* into the arms of your mercy, into the blessed rest of everlasting peace, and into the company of the saints in light.[77]

PEOPLE

**Amen.**

## SONG OF SIMEON

*All may be invited to stand and sing or say the ancient* Nunc Dimittis. *See pages 805–808.*

ALL

**Holy One, now let your servant go in peace; your word has been fulfilled: my own eyes have seen the salvation which you have prepared in the sight of every people: a light to reveal you to the nations and the glory of your people Israel.[78]**

*At the request of the family of the deceased or in the case of cremation, an Order for Committal may take place.*

## BENEDICTION

*The congregation may be invited to stand. A leader may give the benediction. According to local custom, the hymn may precede the benediction.*

**A** LEADER

Now may the God of peace who brought again from the dead our Savior Jesus, the great shepherd of the sheep, by the blood of the eternal covenant, equip you with everything good that you may do God's will, working in you that which is pleasing in God's sight, through Jesus Christ; to whom be glory for ever and ever.

ALL

**Amen.**[79]

**B** LEADER

May God bless you and keep you.

PEOPLE

**Amen.**

LEADER

May God's face shine upon you and be gracious to you.

PEOPLE

**Amen.**

LEADER

May God look upon you with kindness and give you peace.[80]

PEOPLE
**Amen.**

*[for use, except during Lent]*
LEADER
Alleluia. Christ is risen.

PEOPLE
**Christ is risen indeed.**
**Alleluia.**

LEADER
Let us go forth in the name of Christ.

PEOPLE
**Thanks be to God.**

## HYMN

*All may be invited to stand for a hymn. If there is to be a recessional, the leader(s) may precede the coffin and the family to the door.*

## POSTLUDE

# Morning Prayer

*The practice of Christian morning prayer came from our Jewish heritage. This suggested service of prayer is based on traditions of early Christian daily public worship. Appropriate for any gathering for morning worship, morning prayer can be adapted for use in the home by family or for individual devotions. A daily lectionary may be used to provide scripture and psalm selections.*

## Opening Sentence

*All may stand or, if desired, remain seated throughout.*

O God, open my lips.
**And my mouth shall proclaim your praise.**

## Doxology

*The following or other praise of the Trinity may be said or sung. (See also 776–782.) Alleluia is omitted in the season of Lent.*

Praise to the holy and undivided Trinity, one God:
**as it was in the beginning, is now, and will be forever. Amen.**

|  | *Throughout Lent* |
|---|---|
| Alleluia!<br>**Alleluia!** | Praise to you, O Christ,<br>**Sovereign of eternal Glory.** |

## Morning Hymn or Canticle (Optional)

*A morning hymn or canticle may be sung. See Morning hymns; "Canticle of the Three," 738.*

## Morning Psalm

*One of the following psalms, or others, may be used: Psalm 51, 63, 67, or 95. (See Psalter section, pp. 621–731.) Following the morning psalm, the people may be seated.*

## Psalms

*An additional psalm for the day or other psalms may be sung or said. Following each psalm is a period of silence for reflection.*

## Reading from Scripture

*One or more readings from scripture are announced and read, followed by*

**A**

The word of truth.
**Thanks be to God.**

**B** *following a Gospel reading*

This is the good news.
**Praise to you, O Christ.**

*After a silence for reflection following the reading of scripture, an appropriate meditation or a reading other than scripture may be offered. Silence may follow.*

## Canticle of Zechariah

*May be sung or spoken. A hymn version, 110, may be used, or the pointed version in the Psalter, p. 733.*

Blessed be the Sovereign God of Israel,
> **who has looked favorably on the people and redeemed them.**
God has raised up a mighty savior for us
> **in the house of God's servant David;**
as God spoke through the mouth of the holy prophets from of old,
> **that we would be saved from our enemies and from the hand of all who hate us.**
Thus God has shown the mercy
> **promised to our ancestors,**

and has remembered God's holy covenant,

**the oath that God swore to our ancestor Abraham,**

to grant us that we, being rescued from the hands of our enemies,

**might serve God without fear, in holiness and righteousness**
**before God all our days.**

And you, child, will be called the prophet of the Most High,

**for you will go before God to prepare God's ways;**
**to give knowledge of salvation to the people**
**by the forgiveness of their sins.**

By the tender mercy of our God,

**the dawn from on high will break upon us,**

to give light to those who sit in night and in the shadow of death,

**to guide our feet into the way of peace.**

## PRAYERS

*One of the following prayers for mercy may be said. (Musical settings, 745–753.)*

**A**

God be with you.
**And also with you.**
(Let us pray, saying "Christ have mercy.")
That there may be purpose and fulfillment, O God, in all that we do,
**Christ have mercy.**
That we may show others this day the love that you have taught us,
**Christ have mercy.**
That the church throughout the world may respond to your call for peace and justice,
**Christ have mercy.**
That those who are in need be helped and comforted,
**Christ have mercy.**
*(Other intercessions may be added.)*
That we may be strengthened by your grace for the tasks of this day,
**Christ have mercy.**

| **B** | **C** | **D** |
|---|---|---|
| Holy God, | Lord, have mercy. | Sovereign, have mercy. |
| Holy and Mighty One, | **Christ, have mercy.** | **Christ, have mercy.** |
| Holy Immortal One, | Lord, have mercy. | Sovereign, have mercy. |
| **Have mercy upon us.** | | |

## PRAYER OF OUR SAVIOR

*One of the following versions or another version may be said.*

| **A** | **B** |
|---|---|
| **Our Father in heaven,** | **Our Father-Mother, who is in the heavens,** |
| **hallowed be your name,** | **may your name be made holy,** |
| **your kingdom come,** | **may your dominion come,** |
| **your will be done,** | **may your will be done,** |
| **on earth as in heaven.** | **on the earth as it is in heaven.** |

| | |
|---|---|
| Give us today our daily bread. | Give us today the bread we need; |
| Forgive us our sins | and forgive us our debts, |
| as we forgive those who sin against us. | as we have forgiven our debtors; |
| Save us from the time of trial | and do not put us to the test, |
| and deliver us from evil. | but rescue us from evil. |
| For the kingdom, the power, | For yours is the dominion, and the power, |
| and the glory are yours, | and the glory forever. Amen. |
| now and for ever. Amen. | |

## COLLECT

God be with you.
**And also with you.**

*One of the following prayers or another may be used.*

### General

Almighty God, give us faith to live this day not knowing where it will lead, but with the assurance that your love and guidance are with us always; through Jesus Christ. **Amen.**

### Advent

Stir up our hearts, O God, to prepare the way for the coming of the Promised One. Help us to spend our days open to the presence of Christ in our lives. **Amen.**

### Christmastide

Almighty God, you have given us the Word in flesh. Let the Word be the wisdom for all that we do in our lives; through Jesus Christ, this Word, who reigns with you and the Holy Spirit, one God, now and forever. **Amen.**

### Epiphany

Almighty God, as you have led us to your Child by a star, lead us to seek faithfully your presence in our lives this day; through Jesus Christ, the light of the world. **Amen.**

### Lent

Most merciful God, all have sinned and fall short of your glory; but you have given us your only begotten Child that we may have eternal life. Keep us ever mindful of this gift that we may gratefully serve you all of our days. **Amen.**

### Eastertide

Almighty God, in Christ you have embraced all of life through the one who is the way, the truth, and the life. Pour out your grace upon us that we may love all of life as you have loved us. **Amen.**

*A concluding hymn may be sung (optional).*

May the God of hope fill you with all joy and peace in believing, so that you may abound in hope by the power of the Holy Spirit.

Let us bless God.
**Thanks be to God.**

# EVENING PRAYER

*The practice of Christian evening prayer came from our Jewish heritage. This suggested service of prayer is based on traditions of early Christian daily public worship. Appropriate for any gathering for evening worship, this order for prayer can be adapted for use in the home by family or for individual devotions. In the earliest tradition, lamps are lighted as the hymn of praise is sung to Christ, the radiant light. If evening prayer is the final prayer of the night, a penitential prayer may be said following the opening sentence. A daily lectionary may be used to provide scripture and psalm selections.*

## SERVICE OF LIGHT

*For the lighting of candles or lamps (optional).*

Jesus Christ is the light of the world.
**The light shines in the deepest night,**
**and the night cannot overcome it.**
Stay with us now, for it is evening,
**and the day is almost over.**
Let your light disperse the shadows
**and shine within us here.**

## EVENING HYMN

*A hymn is sung when the candles or lamps have been lit. "O Holy Radiance," 739, "O Wisdom," 740, "Christ, Mighty Savior,"93, or another evening hymn may be used. If the preceding Service of Light is not used, Evening Prayer may begin with the Opening Sentence and Doxology, and an evening hymn may be inserted before the Evening Psalm.*

## OPENING SENTENCE

*All may stand or, if desired, remain seated throughout.*

O God, come to my aid.
**Hear my voice when I cry to you.**

## DOXOLOGY

*The following or other praise of the Trinity may be said or sung. (See also 776–782.) Alleluia is omitted in the season of Lent.*

Praise to the holy and undivided Trinity, one God:
**as it was in the beginning, is now, and will be forever. Amen.**

|  | *Throughout Lent* |
| --- | --- |
| Alleluia! | Praise to you, O Christ, |
| **Alleluia!** | **Sovereign of eternal Glory.** |

## EVENING PSALM

*Psalm 141 is said or sung. (See Psalter, pp. 716, 730, 731.) In keeping with the intention of Psalm 141, incense may be used. Following the psalm, the people may be seated.*

## PSALM

*Following the evening psalm, one or more psalms may be said or sung, especially Psalms 110–117; 120–133; 135–147. Following each psalm is a period of silence for reflection.*

## READING FROM SCRIPTURE

*One or more readings from scripture are announced and read, followed by*

| **A** | **B** | **C** *following a Gospel reading* |
| --- | --- | --- |
| God have mercy on us. | The word of truth. | This is the good news. |
| **Thanks be to God.** | **Thanks be to God.** | **Praise to you, O Christ.** |

*After a silence for reflection following the reading of scripture, an appropriate meditation or a reading other than scripture may be offered. Silence may follow.*

# THE SONG OF MARY

*May be sung or spoken. Hymn versions, 106, 119, may be used, or the pointed version in the Psalter, p. 732.*

My soul magnifies the Sovereign,
> **and my spirit rejoices in God my Savior;**

for God has looked with favor on the lowliness of God's servant.
> **Surely, from now on all generations will call me blessed;**

for the Mighty One has done great things for me,
> **the Mighty One whose name is holy.**

God's mercy is for those who fear God
> **from generation to generation.**

God has shown great strength;
> **and has scattered the proud in the thoughts of their hearts.**

God has brought down the powerful from their thrones,
> **and lifted up the lowly;**

God has filled the hungry with good things,
> **and sent the rich away empty.**

God has helped God's servant Israel,
> **in remembrance of God's mercy,**

according to the promise made to our ancestors,
> **to Abraham and Sarah and to their descendants forever.**

## PRAYERS

*One of the following prayers for mercy may be said. (Musical settings, 745–753.)*

**A**

God be with you.
**And also with you.**

(Let us pray, saying "O God, hear our prayer.")
For the peace from on high and for our salvation, let us pray,
**O God, hear our prayer.**

For the welfare of all churches, and for those who lead us in the faith,
**O God, hear our prayer.**

For our nation and our community, and for those who preside in public offices,
**O God, hear our prayer.**

For all who hunger, are sick, and in pain,
**O God, hear our prayer.**

(Other intercessions may be added.)
For a peaceful evening and safety this night,
**O God, hear our prayer.**

| **B** | **C** | **D** |
|---|---|---|
| Holy God, | Lord, have mercy. | Sovereign, have mercy. |
| Holy and Mighty One, | **Christ, have mercy.** | **Christ, have mercy.** |
| Holy Immortal One, | Lord, have mercy. | Sovereign, have mercy. |
| **Have mercy upon us.** | | |

# Prayer of Our Savior

*One of the following versions or another version may be said.*

**A**

Our Father in heaven,
    hallowed be your name,
    your kingdom come,
    your will be done,
    on earth as in heaven.
Give us today our daily bread.
Forgive us our sins
    as we forgive those who sin against us.
Save us from the time of trial
    and deliver us from evil.
For the kingdom, the power,
    and the glory are yours,
    now and for ever. Amen.

**B**

Our Father-Mother, who is in the heavens,
    may your name be made holy.
    may your dominion come,
    may your will be done,
    on the earth as it is in heaven.
Give us today the bread we need;
    and forgive us our debts,
    as we have forgiven our debtors;
    and do not put us to the test,
    but rescue us from evil.
For yours is the dominion, and the power,
    and the glory forever. Amen.

## Collect

God be with you.
**And also with you.**

*The following or others may be used.*

### General

Almighty God, you have brought us to the ending of this day; release us from all chains of strife and draw us close with your gentle bands of peace. **Amen.**

### Advent

Almighty God, as you have sent the Word to be the light of the world, let that light shine in our hearts that we may be filled with the joy and peace that you alone can provide. **Amen.**

### Christmastide

Almighty God, may the light that shines from the cradle in Bethlehem be the light in our hearts that guides us and protects us; we pray in the name of the Christ, who is the way, the truth, and the light. **Amen.**

### Epiphany

Eternal Light, you have shone your glory upon us in Christ, the Word made flesh. May our lives ever be a reflection of your gift of salvation to us. **Amen.**

### Lent

O Jesus, Sun of Salvation, shine in our inmost beings this night; be the lamp to our way, and our beacon of hope. We pray in the name of Christ, the light of the world. **Amen.**

### Eastertide

Almighty God, you have given us the gift of eternal life in the risen Christ. May the glory light of the resurrection shine within us forevermore, through Jesus Christ we pray. **Amen.**

*A concluding hymn may be sung (optional).*

**A**

Let us bless God.
**Thanks be to God.**

**B**

May God bless us and protect us.
**May God bring us to everlasting light.**
**Amen.**

[37] Source unknown, quoted in *Jesus Christ–The Life of the World* (Geneva: World Council of Churches, 1983).

[38] Adapted by permission from *Services of the Church #1*. Copyright © 1966 and 1969 United Church Press.

[39] 2 Corinthians 13:14, adapted.

[40] 2 Corinthians 13:14, adapted.

[41] Matthew 18:20.

[42] Mary Ann Neevel in *Bread for the Journey: Resources for Worship*, ed. Ruth C. Duck. Copyright ©1981 The Pilgrim Press. Used by permission.

[43] John 1:1.

[44] Ephesians 4:4-6, adapted.

[45] 1 Corinthians 12:12-13, 27.

[46] Mark 10:13-16, adapted.

[47] Matthew 3:13-17, *Good News Bible*, adapted.

[48] Matthew 28:19, adapted.

[49] John 3:3, 5, adapted.

[50] Romans 6:3-4, adapted.

[51] Adapted by permission from *Services of the Church #3*. Copyright 1969 United Church Press.

[52] Adapted by permission from *Services of the Church #3*. Copyright 1969 United Church Press.

[53] John 15:5, 7,10,11, adapted.

[54] Romans 10:8-10, *Good News Bible*, adapted.

[55] Ephesians 2:19-22, adapted.

[56] Adapted from *Book of Common Worship*, Church of South India. Copyright 1963 Oxford University Press. Used by permission.

[57] Adapted by permission from *Services of the Church #3*. Copyright 1969 United Church Press.

[58] Adapted from The Episcopal Church, *The Book of Common Prayer* (Boston: Seabury Press, 1979).

[59] Adapted by permission from *Uniting Church Worship Services: Baptism and Related Services*. Copyright 1981 The Uniting Church in Australia Assembly Commission on Liturgy.

[60] John 15:5, 7, 10, 11, adapted.

[61] Romans 10:8-10, *Good News Bible*, adapted.

[62] Ephesians 2:19-22, adapted.

[63] Adapted by permission from *Services of the Church #3*. Copyright 1969 United Church Press.

[64] Adapted from The Episcopal Church, *The Book of Common Prayer* (Boston: Seabury Press, 1979).

[65] Adapted by permission from *Uniting Church Worship Services: Baptism and Related Services*. Copyright 1981 The Uniting Church in Australia Assembly Commission on Liturgy.

[66] Psalm 145:18-19, adapted.

[67] John 11:25-26, adapted.

[68] Revelation 1:17-18.

[69] Isaiah 41:10, adapted.

[70] Romans 6:3-4, *Good News Bible*, adapted.

[71] Romans 6:5, adapted.

[72] Revelation 14:13, adapted.

[73] 2 Corinthians 13:14, adapted.

[74] Romans 14:8-9, adapted.

[75] Psalm 116:4, 8, 12-13, adapted and reprinted from *Lutheran Book of Worship*, copyright © 1978 *Lutheran Book of Worship*. Used by permission of Augsburg Publishing House.

[76] Romans 8:1, 28, 38-39, adapted.

[77] The Episcopal Church, *The Book of Common Prayer* (Boston: Seabury Press, 1979).

[78] International Consultation on English Texts, adapted.

[79] Hebrews 13:20-21, adapted.

[80] Numbers 6:24-26, adapted.

# HYMNS

# Immortal, Invisible, God Only Wise

1

*Walter C. Smith, 1867; alt.*

*1 Tim. 1:17; Ps. 36:6*

1 Im - mor - tal, in - vis - i - ble, God on - ly wise,
2 Un - rest - ing, un - hast - ing, and si - lent as light,
3 Your life is life - giv - ing— to both great and small;
4 So per - fect your glo - ry, so bril - liant your light,

in light in - ac - ces - si - ble hid from our eyes,
not want - ing, not wast - ing, but rul - ing in might;
in all life you're liv - ing, the true life of all;
your an - gels a - dore you, all veil - ing their sight;

Most bless - ed, most glo - rious, the An - cient of Days,
Your jus - tice like moun - tains high soar - ing a - bove,
We blos - som and flour - ish as leaves and as flowers,
All praise we now ren - der as your an - gels do:

al - might - y, vic - to - rious, your great name we praise.
your clouds which are foun - tains of good - ness and love.
then with - er and per - ish— but naught dims your powers.
in awe at the splen - dor of light hid - ing you.

*Walter C. Smith, minister of the Free Church of Scotland and later moderator of the Assembly, wrote poetry as a retreat from work and to say what could not be fully expressed in the pulpit.*

Tune: ST. DENIO 11.11.11.11.
*Adapt. from a Welsh ballad in John Roberts'*
Caniadaeth y Cysegr, *1839*

# Glory, Glory Hallelujah

2

*Exod. 15:20; Gen. 28:12; Ps. 81:6*

*African-American spiritual*

1 Glo - ry, glo - ry hal - le - lu - jah, since I
2 I feel bet - ter, so much bet - ter, since I
3 Feel like shout - ing "Hal - le - lu - jah!" since I
4 I am danc - ing Mir - iam's dance now, since I
5 I am climb - ing Ja - cob's lad - der, since I
6 Ev - ery round goes higher and high - er, since I

laid my bur - dens down. Glo - ry, glo - ry hal - le -
laid my bur - dens down. I feel bet - ter, so much
laid my bur - dens down. Feel like shout - ing "Hal - le -
laid my bur - dens down. I am danc - ing Mir - iam's
laid my bur - dens down. I am climb - ing Ja - cob's
laid my bur - dens down. Ev - ery round goes higher and

lu - jah, since I laid my bur - dens down.
bet - ter, since I laid my bur - dens down.
lu - jah!" since I laid my bur - dens down.
dance now, since I laid my bur - dens down.
lad - der, since I laid my bur - dens down.
high - er, since I laid my bur - dens down.

*Despite their physical captivity, the enslaved of antebellum
America often found an inward freedom through their faith in
Jesus the liberator. This liberation, which permitted them to sing
rejoicingly, anticipated their eventual physical emancipation.*

Tune: GLORY, GLORY 8.7.8.7.
*African-American spiritual
Arr. Joyce Finch Johnson, 1992*

# Wakantanka Taku Nitawa
## (Many and Great, O God, Are Your Works)

**3**

*Dakota hymn, Joseph R. Renville, 1842*
*Paraphr. by R. Philip Frazier, 1929; alt.*
*For another translation, see 341*

Ps. 104:24–25; Jer. 10:12–13; 2 Esd. 16:56–60

*Optional hand-drum rhythm:*

1 Wa - kan - tan - ka    ta - ku    ni - ta - wa        tan - ka - ya
2 Wo - eh - da - ku    ni - ta - wa kin    he        mi - na - gi
1 Man - y and    great,    O    God,    are your    works,    Mak - er    of
2 Grant un - to    us    com - mu - nion with    you,        O    star a -

qa    o - ta;    Ma - hpi - ya    kin    e - ya - hna - ke    ca,
kin    qu    wo;    Ma - hpi - ya    kin    i - wan - kam ya - ti,
earth and    sky;    Your hands have    set    the    heav - ens with    stars,
bid - ing    One;    Come un - to    us    and    dwell with        us:

ma - ka kin    he    du - o - wan - ca,    Mni - o - wan -
wi - co - wa - śte    yu - ha nan - ka,    Wi - co - ni
your fin - gers spread    the    moun - tains and    plains.    Lo,    at your
with you are    found    the    gifts    of    life.    Bless    us with

ca    śbe - ya    wan - ke    cin,    he - na    o - ya - ki - hi.
kin    he    ma - ya - qu    nun,    o - wi - han - ke    wa - nin.
word    the    wa - ters were formed;    deep seas o - bey your    voice.
life    that    has    no    end,    e - ter - nal    life with    you.

Probably the best-known Native American hymn, "Many and
Great" is sung with great reverence by the Dakota people in
worship, at communion, and for births, funerals, and burials.
Renville helped establish the Lac qui Parle mission in Minnesota.
Frazier, a Native American, was a Congregational minister.

Tune: LACQUIPARLE 9.6.9.9.9.6.
*Native American melody (Dakota)*
*Adapt. Joseph R. Renville, 1842*
*Harm. James R. Murray, 1877*

# 4 Joyful, Joyful, We Adore You

Ps. 145:10; Isa. 49:13

*Henry van Dyke, 1907; alt.*

1 Joy-ful, joy-ful, we a-dore you, God of glo-ry, God of love;
2 All your works with joy sur-round you, earth and heaven re - flect your rays,
3 You are giv-ing and for-giv-ing, ev - er bless-ing, ev - er blessed,
4 Mor-tals, join the might-y cho-rus which the morn-ing stars be - gan;

Hearts un-fold like flowers be-fore you, open-ing to the sun a - bove.
Stars and an-gels sing a-round you, cen-ter of un - bro-ken praise.
Well-spring of the joy of liv-ing, o - cean depth of hap - py rest!
Bound-less love is reign-ing o'er us, re-con-cil-ing race and clan.

Melt the clouds of sin and sad-ness, drive the storms of doubt a - way;
Field and for-est, vale and moun-tain, flower-y mead-ow, flash-ing sea,
Lov-ing Spir-it, Fa-ther, Moth-er, all who love be - long to you;
Ev-er sing-ing, move we for-ward, faith-ful in the midst of strife,

Giv-er of im - mor-tal glad-ness, fill us with the light of day.
Chant-ing bird and flow-ing foun-tain, teach us what our praise should be.
Teach us how to love each oth - er, by that love our joy re - new.
Joy-ful mu-sic leads us on-ward in the tri-umph song of life.

Henry van Dyke was a noted church leader, U.S. ambassador,
Navy chaplain, and prolific writer. Many people associate this
hymn with Beethoven's ninth symphony, but few are aware
of the original poem by the German classicist F. Schiller
(1759–1805) that inspired Beethoven.

Tune: HYMN TO JOY 8.7.8.7.D.
*Ludwig van Beethoven, 1824*
*Adapt. and harm. Edward Hodges, 1846*

# Praise to God

*Nobuaki Hanaoka, 1980; alt.*

*Rom. 14:11; John 3:16; Eph. 5:16–20; Ps. 68:4, 32*

1 Praise to God, praise to God, for the green-ness of the trees, for the beau-ty of the flowers, for the bless-ing of the sky, for the great-ness of the sea. Praise to God, praise to God, now and for-ev-er-more.

2 Thanks to God, thanks to God, for the gift of friends in Christ, for the church, our house of faith, for the gift of won-drous love, for the gift of end-less grace. Thanks to God, thanks to God, now and for-ev-er-more.

3 Sing to God, sing to God, for the grace of Je-sus Christ, for the love of par-ent God, for the com-fort and the strength of the Spir-it, ho-ly God. Sing to God, sing to God, now and for-ev-er-more.

*Nobuaki Hanaoka was born in Japan and has earned degrees in theology from Japanese and American schools. Hanaoka has served as a pastor in Sacramento, California, and has published articles in both Japanese and English. He is the author of* Nihilism and Nothingness, *1968.*

Tune: SAKURA 6.7.7.7.7.6.6.
*Traditional Japanese melody*
*Harm. Jonathan McNair, 1993*

# 6 Sing Praise to God, Our Highest Good

*Ps. 105; 1 Chron. 16:9; 1 Pet. 1:3–7*

*Johann J. Schütz, 1675*
*Transl. Madeleine Forell Marshall, 1993*

1 Sing praise to God, our high-est good, pro - found re - spect ex -
2 Cre - a - tion thanks you, Ho - ly One: you made us and re -
3 What God has made, God will pre-serve, with righ-teous-ness un -
4 I cry to God, in pain and grief, "Please, God of mer - cy,

press - ing. God gives us health, life, live - li - hood, with ev - ery
new us. De - light-ed at what you have done, you show your
fail - ing. Re - gard-less what we may de - serve, we see this
hear me!" My cer - tain help pro - vides re - lief, faith, hope, and

need - ed bless - ing. To God, who won-drous works per-forms, cre -
great - ness through us. So may all liv - ing things pro-claim the
good pre - vail - ing. To God who gov - erns ev - er - more with
love to cheer me. So let me sing, joy - ful and free: ah,

a - ting life and calm-ing storms, to God give praise and glo - ry!
won-ders of their Mak-er's name: to God give praise and glo - ry!
jus - tice serv - ing rich and poor, to God give praise and glo - ry!
thank-ful Chris-tians, sing with me: to God give praise and glo - ry!

5  For-ev-er with us, God is here,
     Nor ev-er will de-sert us.
   So dear-ly loved, we shall not fear:
     there's noth-ing that can hurt us.
   We place our trust in God's com-mand,
     who leads us with a moth-er's hand:
   to God give praise and glo-ry!

6  Dear Chris-tian friends, we bear the name
     of Christ, our sure sal-va-tion.
   Let us re-call Christ Je-sus came,
     most ho-ly in-car-na-tion,
   Came from the one God we a-dore,
     came with new life for-ev-er-more:
   to God give praise and glo-ry!

*Johann Jakob Schütz practiced both civil and canon law in*
*Frankfurt, Germany, throughout his life. He had an interest in the*
*company that purchased land in Germantown, Pennsylvania, from*
*William Penn in 1683. Schütz published two collections of hymns.*

Tune:  MIT FREUDEN ZART  8.7.8.7.8.8.7.
*Bohemian Brethren's* Kirchengesäng, *1566*
Harm. The English Hymnal, *1906; adapt.*

# All People That on Earth Do Dwell                                     7

*William Kethe, 1561*
*Adapt. Thomas H. Troeger, 1992*

*Ps. 100*

1  All      peo - ple  that   on    earth   do    dwell,  sing
2  Know     that  there  is   one    God,   in  - deed,   who
3  En  - ter  the   sa - cred  gates  with   praise, with
4  Pro - claim  a - gain  that  God   is     good,   whose

out   your  faith  with   cheer - ful   voice;  De - light  in   God whose
fash - ions  us   with - out   our     aid,   Who  claims us,  gives us
joy   ap - proach the   tem - ple     walls.  Ex - tol  and  bless our
mer - cy  is   for - ev - er     sure,   Whose  truth  at   all  times

praise  you   tell,  whose   pres - ence calls  you   to    re - joice.
all    we    need,  whose   ten - der  care  will   nev - er   fade.
God    al - ways  as     peo - ple whom the  Spir - it   calls.
firm - ly   stood, and    shall from age  to   age   en - dure.

*Old Hundredth is perhaps the best known and most widely used*
*of all psalm tunes. It came into English use in 1561 with Kethe's*
*paraphrase of Psalm 100 and has been associated with it ever since.*

Tune:  OLD HUNDREDTH  L.M.
*Attrib. to Louis Bourgeois (c. 1510–c. 1561)*
Trente quatre Pseaumes, *Geneva, 1551*

8

# Praise to the Living God

Ps. 84:1–2

Curtis Beach, 1966; alt.

1 Praise to the liv - ing God, the God of love and light, Whose
2 Praise to the liv - ing God, from whom all things de - rive, Whose
3 Praise to the liv - ing God, who knows our joy and pain, Who
4 Praise to the liv - ing God, a - round, with - in, a - bove, Be -

word brought forth the myr - iad suns and set the worlds in flight;
Spir - it formed up - on this sphere the first faint seeds of life;
shares with us our com - mon life, the sa - cred and pro - fane.
yond the grasp of hu - man mind, but whom we know as love.

Whose in - fi - nite de - sign, which we but dim - ly see, Per -
Who caused them to e - volve, un - wit - ting, toward God's goal, Till
God toils wher-e'er we toil, in home and mart and mill; And
In these tu - mul-tuous days, so full of hope and strife, May

vades all na - ture, mak - ing all a cos - mic u - ni - ty.
hu - man-kind stood on the earth, as liv - ing, think - ing souls.
deep with - in the hu - man heart God leads us for - ward still.
we bear wit - ness to the Way, O Source and Goal of life.

Curtis Beach, born into a family of several generations of
ministers, was educated at Harvard University, the Boston
University School of Theology, and the University of Southern
California. A minister in the United Church of Christ, Beach
authored The Gospel of Mark: Its Making and Meaning.

Tune: DIADEMATA S.M.D.
George J. Elvey, 1868

# We Sing to You, O God

## 9

*Gracia Grindal, 1985, 1989*

1 We sing to you, O God, the Rock who gave us birth, let
2 We wan-dered far from home out in a des-ert land, you
3 You bear us through the world, an ea-gle to her young, who
4 O God, e-ter-nal God, we hide with-in your wings, the

our re-joic-ing sing your name in all the earth. To you, O
shield-ed with your love our fear-ful pil - grim band. You kept us
ris - es on her wings and bears us toward the sun. We ride the
ev - er-last-ing arms to whom our prais - es ring. Your word is

God, let songs be raised, in joy - ful hymns, our feast of praise.
safe with - in your arms and shel - tered us a - gainst the storm.
vaults of light and air and trust in your un - fail - ing care.
true, your way is just, you are the God in whom we trust.

Poet, author, and teacher of poetry and writing, Gracia Grindal
has held editorial and consultant positions for several hymnic
publications. She has served as professor of pastoral theology
and ministry communication at Luther Northwestern
Theological Seminary, Minneapolis.

Tune: CAMANO 6.6.6.6.4.4.4.4.
*Richard Proulx, 1979*
Alternate tune: DARWALL'S 148TH

# 10

# Maoz Tsur Y'shuati
## (Rock of Ages)

*Jewish traditional*
*Transl. Marcus Jastrow and Gustave Gottheil, 20th century*

1 Ma - oz tsur y' - shu - a - ti l'cha na - eh l'-sha - bei - ach,
1 Rock of a - ges, let our song praise your sav - ing pow - er;
2 Chil-dren of the Ho - ly God, wheth - er free or fet - tered,

ti - kon beit t' - fi - la - ti v'-sham to - dah n' - za - bei - ach.
you, a - mid the rag - ing foe, were our shel - tering tow - er.
wake the ech - oes of that song where you may be scat - tered.

L'-eit ta - chin mat - bei - ach mi - tzar ham'-na - bei - ach,
Fu - rious it as - sailed us, but your arm a - vailed us,
Yours the mes - sage cheer - ing that the time is near - ing

az eg - mor b'shir miz - mor cha - na - kat ha miz bei - ach.
and your word broke its sword when our own strength failed us.
which will see all set free, ty - rants no more fear - ing.

This traditional Jewish hymn and its tune are sung during
Hanukkah. Instituted by Judas Maccabeus and the congregation
of Israel in 165 B.C.E., Hanukkah commemorates the
rededication of the Jerusalem temple after the victory that year
over Antiochus Epiphanes.

Tune: MAOZ TSUR 7.6.7.6.6.6.3.3.6.
(ROCK OF AGES)
*Traditional Hebrew melody*

# Bring Many Names

**11**

*Brian Wren, 1989*

*Gen. 1:27*

Unison

1 Bring man-y names, beau-ti-ful and good, cel-e-brate, in
2 Strong moth-er God, work-ing night and day, plan-ning all the
3 Warm fa-ther God, hug-ging ev-ery child, feel-ing all the
4 Old, ach-ing God, grey with end-less care, calm-ly pierc-ing

par-a-ble and sto-ry, ho-li-ness in glo-ry, liv-ing, lov-ing God.
won-ders of cre-a-tion, set-ting each e-qua-tion, gen-i-us at play:
strains of hu-man liv-ing, car-ing and for-giv-ing till we're rec-on-ciled:
e-vil's new dis-guis-es, glad of good sur-pris-es, wis-er than de-spair:

1-5 |||| 6

Hail and Ho-san-na! bring man-y names! great, liv-ing God!
Hail and Ho-san-na, strong moth-er God!
Hail and Ho-san-na, warm fa-ther God!
Hail and Ho-san-na, old, ach-ing God!

5 Young, grow-ing God, ea-ger,
on the move,
say-ing no to false-hood and
un-kind-ness,
cry-ing out for jus-tice,
giv-ing all you have:
Hail and Ho-san-na,
young, grow-ing God!

6 Great, liv-ing God, nev-er ful-ly known,
joy-ful dark-ness far be-yond our see-ing,
clos-er yet than breath-ing,
ev-er-last-ing home:
Hail and Ho-san-na,
great, liv-ing God!

*The author states that aspects of the divine are revealed in our maleness, femaleness, youth, and age in a moving, growing matrix of life in God. The tune Westchase was composed especially for this text.*

Tune: WESTCHASE 9.10.11.9.
*Carlton Young, 1989*

# 12  I Sing the Mighty Power of God

*Ps. 136:5–9; James 1:17*

*Isaac Watts, 1715; alt.*

Descant

3 On earth there's not a plant or flower but makes your glo - ry known.

1 I sing the might-y power of God that made the moun-tains rise,
2 I sing the good-ness of our God that filled the earth with food;
3 On earth there's not a plant or flower but makes your glo - ry known.

The clouds a - rise and spread their showers by or - der from your throne.

That spread the flow-ing seas a - broad, and built the loft - y skies.
God formed the crea-tures with a word, and then pro - nounced them good.
The clouds a - rise and spread their showers by or - der from your throne.

All life is but a gift from you and ev - er in your care;

I sing the wis-dom that or - dained the sun to rule the day;
Oh, how your won-ders are dis-played, wher - e'er I turn my eye:
All life is but a gift from you and ev - er in your care;

*The tune Ellacombe was named for a place in Devonshire, England. It was first published in a collection of tunes used in the private chapel of the Duke of Wirtemberg, and was possibly sung with the text "Ave Maria, klärer."*

Tune: ELLACOMBE C.M.D.
Gesangbuch der herzoglichen
Wirtembergischen katholischen Hofkapelle, *1784*
Descant, The New Century Hymnal, *1993*

Wher - ev - er peo-ple gath - er, you, O God, are pres - ent there.

The moon shines full at God's com-mand, and all the stars o - bey.
If I sur - vey the ground I tread, or gaze up - on the sky!
Wher - ev - er peo-ple gath - er, you, O God, are pres-ent there.

# O My Soul, Bless Your Creator

**13**

*Anon.*
United Presbyterian Book of Psalms, *1871; alt.*

*Ps. 103*

1 O my soul, bless your Cre - a - tor; all with-in me bless God's name;
2 God for-gives all your trans-gres-sions, all who suf - fer, gen - tly heals;
3 Far as east from west is dis - tant, God has put a - way our sin;
4 As it was with - out be - gin - ning, so it lasts with - out an end;
5 Un - to all who keep God's cov-enant and are stead-fast in God's way;

Bless your Mak - er, and for-get not all God's mer - cies to pro-claim.
God re - deems you from de-struc-tion, and with you so kind-ly deals.
Like a moth - er and a fa - ther, God com - pas - sion - ate has been.
To their chil - dren's chil-dren ev - er shall God's righ - teous - ness ex - tend:
Un - to all who still re-mem-ber God's com-mand-ments and o - bey.

*Psalm 103, a beautiful psalm of thanksgiving for God's*
*forgiveness and steadfast love, is summed up in the lines of this*
*hymn. The author of the paraphrase is unknown.*

Tune: STUTTGART 8.7.8.7.
*Attrib. to Christian F. Witt*
Psalmodia Sacra, *Gotha, 1715*

# 14

# How Can I Say Thanks

*Ps. 115:1*

*Andraé Crouch, 1971; alt.*

How can I say thanks for the things you have done for me?

Things so un-de-served, yet you gave to prove your love for me; the

voic-es of a mil-lion an-gels could not ex-press my grat-i-tude. All that I

am, and ev-er hope to be; I owe it all to you.

To God be the glo-ry, to God be the glo-ry, to

God be the glo - ry for the things you have done.

*Refrain*

With your blood you have saved me; with your power you have raised me;

*Second time, end*

to God be the glo - ry for the things you have done.

Just let me live my life— let it be pleas-ing un-to you;

*to Refrain*

And if I gain an - y praise, let it go to glo - ri - fy you.

*Andraé Crouch, the son of a bishop in the Church of God in Christ, belongs to the contemporary gospel era. Beginning in 1969 this new gospel music was made to "rock" with the help of electronic instrumentation.*

Tune: MY TRIBUTE Irr. with refrain
*Andraé Crouch, 1971*

# My Heart Is Overflowing
## (The Song of Hannah)

1 Sam. 2:1–10

Miriam Therese Winter, 1993

**Unison**

1 My heart is ov-er-flow-ing with glad-ness and with praise.
2 The liv-ing God has spo-ken. Earth an-swers with a song.
3 All who are poor and low-ly will have a heaven-ly home.
4 The pow-er of com-pas-sion can turn the world a-round.
5 The One who once cre-a-ted and now sus-tains the earth,

The God who guards my go-ing gives mean-ing to my days.
Weap-ons of war are bro-ken, the weak are feel-ing strong.
The hum-ble and the ho-ly shall sure-ly know sha-lom.
The firm in faith will fash-ion gar-dens from bar-ren ground.
Bold-ly an-ti-ci-pat-ed we too would bring to birth.

Ho-ly the Rock of A-ges known in word and deed,
See, we no long-er hun-ger, cry-ing out for bread.
God lifts the need-y from the ash-es of de-spair,
Ech-oes of joy are found re-sound-ing from the tomb.
Love con-quers e-vil, set-ting all the cap-tives free.

*In this song, Hannah, after many childless years, celebrates the birth of Samuel with gratitude for God's faithfulness and concern for the oppressed. This canticle is echoed later in the New Testament "Song of Mary" or "Magnificat."*

Tune: TOLLEFSON 7.6.7.6.6.6.7.6.
Paulette Tollefson, 1971

Giv - ing the vic - to - ry, ful - fill - ing my ev - ery need.
Our God re-stores to life and rais - es us from the dead.
Fav - ors the out - cast and the down-trod - den ev - ery - where.
Cheer-ful the child-less wom-an: Life stirs with-in her womb.
Praise God for life be - get-ting life for e - ter - ni - ty.

## Let Us with a Joyful Mind

**16**

*John Milton, 1624*
*Adapt. Thomas H. Troeger, 1993*

*Ps. 136*

1 Let us with a joy - ful mind praise our God for - ev - er kind,
2 New-made earth was filled with light through God's all com - mand - ing might,
3 Daz - zling bright the sun o - beys God who shines with bright - er rays,
4 Stars and moon that span - gle night all de - pend on heav - en's light,

*Refrain*

Rich with mer-cies that en - dure, ev - er faith-ful, ev - er sure.

5 Crea-tures of the sea and land
   all are fed by God's own hand,
  Rich with mer-cies that en-dure,
  ev-er faith-ful, ev-er sure.

6 There-fore with a joy-ful mind,
   praise our God for-ev-er kind,
  Rich with mer-cies that en-dure
  ev-er faith-ful, ev-er sure.

*As a youth of fifteen, John Milton composed a lengthy, elaborate*
*paraphrase of Psalm 136 from which these lines have been*
*selected. Milton, an English Puritan and Congregationalist, is*
*best known for* Paradise Lost.

Tune: INNOCENTS 7.7.7.7.
The Parish Choir, *1850*

# 17 To You, O God, All Creatures Sing

*Ps. 148*

St. Francis of Assisi, 1225
Adapt. Miriam Therese Winter, 1993

**Descant**

4 To you,     God,     day af-ter day,     earth     in

**Unison**

1 To you, O God, all crea-tures sing,     and     all     cre - a - tion, ev - ery-
2 Your wind that blows the tem - pest by,     your     clouds that sail a - cross the
3 Your flow - ing wa - ters, crys - tal clear,     make     mel - o - dies for you to
4 To     you, O God, day af - ter     day,     your     plan - et earth in ev - ery

ev - ery way sings your prais - es, al - le - lu - ia! As     fruit,     fra - grant

*(Harmony)*     *(Unison)*

thing     sings your prais - es, al - le - lu - ia! Your     burn - ing sun with gold - en
sky     sing your prais - es, al - le - lu - ia! Your     morn - ing ris - es with a
hear,     sing your prais - es, al - le - lu - ia! Your     fire, . . . boun - ti - ful and
way,     sings your prais - es, al - le - lu - ia, As     sa - vory fruit and fra - grant

*Miriam Therese Winter described her thoughts about adapting this text: "As I entered into communion with the word and spirit of the hymn, I felt called to enable that unknown-to-me poet's wisdom to live on into the future, a moving commission, and also felt a bond with the one who had gone before."*

Tune: LASST UNS ERFREUEN
8.8.4.4.8.8. with alleluias
*Geistliche Kirchengesäng, Cologne, 1623*
*Harm. Ralph Vaughan Williams, 1906*
*Descant, The New Century Hymnal, 1993*

flower show forth glo - ry and power, sing - ing prais - es, al - le -

(Harmony)

beam, your sil - ver moon with soft - er gleam sing your prais-es,
song, and lights of eve - ning sing a - long, sing your prais-es, al-le -
bright, re - mem - bering your warmth and light, sings your prais-es,
flower show forth your glo - ry and your power, sing - ing prais-es,

lu - ia, al-le - lu - ia, al-le - lu - ia, al - le - lu - ia!

(Unison)

lu - ia, al-le - lu - ia, al-le - lu - ia, al - le - lu - ia.

5 Now we who are of ten-der heart,
for-giv-ing oth-ers, take our part,
sing your prais-es, al-le-lu-ia!
To you we lift our pain and care,
re-ceive the bur-dens that we bear,
sing-ing prais-es, al-le-lu-ia,
al-le-lu-ia, al-le-lu-ia, al-le-lu-ia.

6 In you, a kind and gen-tle death
pre-pares to hush our fi-nal breath,
sing-ing prais-es, al-le-lu-ia!
Christ goes be-fore us to re-new
the way that leads us home to you.
Hear our prais-es, al-le-lu-ia,
al-le-lu-ia, al-le-lu-ia, al-le-lu-ia.

# 18 Guide Me, O My Great Redeemer

Exod. 13:21; 16:4; 17:6; Ps. 105:39–44; Rev. 22:1–2

*William Williams, 1745*
*St. 1, transl. Peter Williams, 1771; alt.*
*St. 2–3, transl. William Williams, 1772; alt.*

1 Guide me, O my great Re - deem - er, pil - grim through this
2 O - pen now the crys - tal foun - tain, where the heal - ing
3 When I reach the Riv - er Jor - dan, bid my anx - ious

bar - ren land; I am weak, but you are might - y;
wa - ters flow. Let the fire and cloud - y pil - lar
fears sub - side. Death of death, and hell's de - struc - tion,

hold me with your power-ful hand. Bread of heav - en, bread of heav - en,
lead me all my jour - ney through. Strong de - liv - erer, strong de - liv - erer,
land me safe on heav-en's side. Songs of prais - es, songs of prais - es

feed me till I want no more, feed me till I want no more.
ev - er be my strength and shield, ev - er be my strength and shield.
I will ev - er sing to you, I will ev - er sing to you.

*John Hughes, a railroad official by trade, composed this tune for the 1907 anniversary of Capel Rhondda, Pontypridd, Wales. Cwm Rhondda refers to the "low valley" area surrounding the urban district of Rhondda in southern Wales.*

Tune: CWM RHONDDA 8.7.8.7.8.7.7.
*John Hughes, 1907*
*Alternate setting: ZION*

# Guide Me, O My Great Redeemer

**19**

William Williams, 1745
St. 1, transl. Peter Williams, 1771; alt.
St. 2–3, transl. William Williams, 1772; alt.

Exod. 13:21; 16:4; 17:6; Ps. 105:39–44; Rev. 22:1–2

1 Guide me, O my great Re - deem - er, pil - grim through this bar - ren
2 O - pen now the crys - tal foun - tain, where the heal - ing wa - ters
3 When I reach the Riv - er Jor - dan, bid my anx - ious fears sub -

land; I am weak, but you are might - y; hold me with your power - ful
flow. Let the fire and cloud - y pil - lar lead me all my jour - ney
side. Death of death, and hell's de - struc - tion, land me safe on heav - en's

hand. Bread of heav - en, feed me till I want no more,
through. Strong de - liv - erer, ev - er be my strength and shield,
side. Songs of prais - es I will ev - er sing to you,

bread of heav - en, feed me till I want no more.
strong de - liv - erer, ev - er be my strength and shield.
songs of prais - es I will ev - er sing to you.

*The Thomas Hastings tune for this text is popular in the United
States. A self-taught musician, Hastings was a colleague of Lowell
Mason in New York City, where they worked together to raise the
standard of worship music.*

Tune: ZION 8.7.8.7.4.7.4.7.
*Thomas Hastings, 1830*
*Alternate setting: CWM RHONDDA*

# God of Abraham and Sarah

*James Gertmenian, 1986; alt.*

1 God of A-bra-ham and Sar-ah, God of Mo-ses, Mir-iam's Guide;
2 God who danc-es in cre-a-tion, spin-ning stars a-bove our heads;
3 God who loves the poor in spir-it, God who com-forts those who mourn;
4 In our lives from birth to dy-ing, depth of sor-row, height of joy;

God of Da-vid and the proph-ets, God in Je-sus glo-ri-fied:
God whose face is scribed in mu-sic, by whose hand the earth is fed:
Balm for wounds, the friend of sin-ners, tak-ing the side of earth's for-lorn:
Prais-ing God in ev-ery sea-son, let ev-ery key our hearts em-ploy.

Up from the dust you raise a peo-ple, breathe in the breath of life, of soul;
Up from the ground you raise the moun-tains, raise our spir-its, lift our eyes;
Up from the depths you raise your peo-ple, giv-ing them cour-age for the day;
Praise is the heal-ing, praise, the glo-ry, praise is the fin-al mys-ter-y;

Down through the years the peo-ple praise you till al-le-lu-ias make them whole!
Down through the years your peo-ple praise you till al-le-lu-ias flood the skies!
Down through the years the peo-ple praise you till al-le-lu-ias light their way!
Down through the years let peo-ple praise you till al-le-lu-ias set them free!

*The healing power of praise and the history of God's dealings
with humankind are the themes of this hymn, written by a United
Church of Christ minister who is the grandson of Armenian
immigrants. The tune is named for his father.*

Tune: CONSTANTINE 8.7.8.7.D.
*Melody by James Gertmenian, 1986
Harm. Ronald Huntington, 1986; alt.*

# God Reigns o'er All the Earth

*Jane Parker Huber, 1981*

**21**

*Isa. 52:7–10*

1 God reigns o'er all the earth! Green hills and val-leys low, the
2 God reigns o'er hu-man life! Through youth and ag-ing years, in
3 God reigns o'er time and space! In his-tory's by-gone days, Christ's
4 God reigns! Em-man-u - el! God with us ev-ery day, in

farms and towns in golds and browns God's grace and beau-ty show.
death, in birth, in grief, in mirth, in all our hopes and fears.
faith-ful folk in rev-erence spoke to bring God earn-est praise.
all our past and to the last, our com-fort and our stay.

God reigns o'er all the earth! Stone banks and spread-ing plains, in
God reigns o'er hu-man life! Our in - spi - ra - tion still. Through
God reigns o'er time and space! O'er gal - ax - y and sun, through
God reigns! Em-man-u - el! Let praise to Christ be sung! God's

rain-bow hues— reds, yel-lows, blues— of streams and coun-try lanes.
all our schemes, in all our dreams, we see God's reign-ing will.
time-less years the cos-mos hears the heaven-ly mu - sic run.
pres-ence here makes all things dear. Let joy - ful bells be rung!

*The author's notes on this text describe it as a progression of
awareness of God's reign among us—in physical surroundings,
in the various stages of life, in time and space, and supremely in
Christ, God with us.*

Tune: TERRA BEATA S.M.D.
*Traditional English melody
Adapt. Franklin L. Sheppard, 1915*

# 22 Sing Praise to God, Who Has Shaped

Ps. 68:4, 32; Ps. 105

*Joachim Neander, 1680*
*Transl. Madeleine Forell Marshall, 1993*

1 Sing praise to God, who has shaped and sus - tains all cre - a - tion! Sing praise, my soul, in pro - found and com - plete ad - o - ra - tion! Glad-some re - joice— or - gan and trum - pet and voice— join - ing God's great con-gre - ga - tion.

2 Praise God, our guard - ian, who lov - ing - ly of - fers cor - rec - tion, Who, as on ea - gle's wings, saves us from sin - ful de - jec - tion. Have you ob - served, how we are al - ways pre - served by God's pa - ren - tal af - fec - tion?

3 Sing praise to God, with sin - cere thanks for all your suc - cess - es. Mer - ci - ful God ev - er loves to en - cour - age and bless us. On - ly con - ceive, what god - ly strength can a - chieve: strength that would touch and car - ess us.

4 Sing praise, my soul, the great name of your high God com - mend - ing. All that have life and breath join you, their notes sweet-ly blend - ing. God is your light! Soul, ev - er keep this in sight: a - men, a - men nev - er end - ing.

*Joachim Neander was a dedicated, caring pastor of the Reformed Church in Düsseldorf, Germany. This was the most familiar of his fifty-six hymn texts, which were published along with many of his original tunes in 1680, the year of his death.*

Tune: LOBE DEN HERREN 14.14.4.7.8.
Erneuerten Gesangbuch, *Stralsund, 1665*
Adapt. and harm. William S. Bennett, 1863

# There's a Wideness in God's Mercy

*Frederick William Faber, 1854; alt.*

1 There's a wide-ness in God's mer-cy, like the wide-ness of the sea;
2 For the love of God is broad-er than the mea-sures of our minds;

there's a kind-ness in God's jus-tice, which is more than lib-er-ty.
and the heart of the E-ter-nal is most won-der-ful-ly kind.

There's no place where earth-ly sor-rows are more felt than in God's heaven;
If our love were but more faith-ful, we would glad-ly trust God's word;

there's no place where earth-ly fail-ings have such kind-ly judg-ment given.
and our lives would show thanks-giv-ing for the good-ness of our God.

*Of Huguenot Protestant ancestry, Frederick William Faber was influenced by the Oxford Movement and eventually became a Catholic priest. He wrote 150 hymns to correspond to the number of psalms.*

Tune: IN BABILONE 8.7.8.7.D.
*Dutch melody*
*Arr. Julius Röntgen, 1906*
*Alternate tune: HOLY MANNA*

# Yigdal Elohim Chai
## (The God of Abraham Praise)

*Gen. 12:1; 17:15–16; Exod. 3:14; Isa. 44:6; Rev. 4:8*

*Moses Maimonides, 12th century*
*Versification attrib. to Daniel ben Judah, c. 1400*
*Transl. Max Landsberg and Newton Mann, 1884; alt.*

1 Yig - dal e - lo - him chai v' - yish - ta - bach,
1 The God of A - braham praise, all prais - es to God's name,
2 God's spir - it free - ly flows, high surg - ing where it will;
3 God has e - ter - nal life im - plant - ed in the soul;
4 The God of Sar - ah praise, all prais - es to God's name,

nim - tza v' - ein eit el m' - tzi - u - to
who was and is and is to be, for - e'er the same!
God spoke of old in proph - et's word; that word speaks still.
God's love shall be our strength and stay, while a - ges roll.
who was and is and is to be, for - e'er the same!

E - chad v' - ein ya - chid k' - yi - chu - do,
The one e - ter - nal God, be - fore what now ap - pears;
Es - tab - lished is God's law, and change - less it shall stand,
All praise the liv - ing God! Ex - tol that hal - lowed name,
The one e - ter - nal God, be - fore what now ap - pears;

*The twelfth-century scholar Moses Maimonides drew up the thirteen articles of the Hebrew creed, which were subsequently cast in metrical form (the Yigdal). This translation represents an ecumenical collaboration between Rabbi Landsberg and Unitarian minister Mann.*

Tune: LEONI 6.6.8.4.D.
*Traditional Yigdal melody*
*Adapt. Meyer Lyon, 1770*

ne - lam v'-gam ein sof l' - ach - du - to.
the First, the Last: be - yond all thought through time - less years!
deep writ - ten on the hu - man heart, in ev - ery land.
who was, and is, and ev - er shall be still the same!
the First, the Last: be - yond all thought through time - less years!

## O God, Our Help in Ages Past    25

*Isaac Watts, 1719; alt.*                                    *Ps. 90:1–2, 4–5*

1 O God, our help in a - ges past, our hope for years to come,
2 Un - der the shad-ow of your throne your saints have dwelt se - cure;
3 Be - fore the hills in or - der stood or earth re - ceived its frame,
4 A thou - sand a - ges in your sight are like an eve - ning gone,

Our shel - ter from the storm-y blast, and our e - ter - nal home:
Suf - fi - cient is your arm a - lone, and our de - fense is sure.
From ev - er - last - ing you are God, to end - less years the same.
Short as the watch that ends the night be - fore the ris - ing sun.

5 Time, like an ev-er-roll-ing stream,
  soon bears us all away;
  We fly for-got-ten, as a dream
  fades at the o-pening day.

6 O God, our help in a-ges past,
  our hope for years to come,
  Still be our God while trou-bles last,
  and our e-ter-nal home!

*Watts, minister of a Congregational church in London, wrote theological and philosophical works and hundreds of "hymns of human composure" (everyday language). He augmented the congregational singing of psalms with a new style of hymnody.*

Tune: ST. ANNE C.M.
*William Croft, 1708*

# 26 We Worship You, God

Ps. 104:2–6, 10–13

Robert Grant, 1833; alt.

1 We wor - ship you, God; your power and your love
2 We tell of your might, we sing of your grace,
3 The earth, with its store of won - ders un - told,
4 Your boun - ti - ful care, what tongue can re - cite?
5 Frail chil - dren of dust, and fee - ble as frail,

are bla - zoned a - broad, a - round, and a - bove:
whose robe is the light, whose can - o - py space;
Al - might - y, your power has found - ed of old,
It breathes in the air, it shines in the light;
in you do we trust, nor find you to fail;

Our Shield and De - fend - er, the An - cient of Days,
Your char - iots of wrath the deep thun - der - clouds form,
Es - tab - lished it fast by a change-less de - cree,
It streams from the hills, it de - scends to the plain,
Your mer - cies how ten - der, how firm to the end,

pa - vil - ioned in splen - dor, and gird - ed with praise.
and broad is your path on the wings of the storm.
and round it you cast, like a man - tle, the sea.
and sweet - ly dis - tills in the dew and the rain.
our Mak - er, De - fend - er, Re - deem - er, and Friend!

*Born in Bengal, India, Robert Grant became a lawyer
in England, a member of Parliament, and for the last
four years of his life was governor of Bombay. This text
was inspired by William Kethe's paraphrase of Psalm 104.*

Tune: LYONS 10.10.11.11.
*Attrib. to J. Michael Haydn (1737–1806)*
*Alternate tune: HANOVER*

# From All That Dwell below the Skies

*Isaac Watts, 1719; alt.*

*Ps. 117*

1 From all that dwell be-low the skies let the Cre-a-tor's praise a-
2 E-ter-nal are your mer-cies, God; your truth stands ev-er high and

rise; Al-le-lu-ia! Al-le-lu-ia! Let the Re-deem-er's name be
broad: Al-le-lu-ia! Al-le-lu-ia! Your praise shall sound from shore to

sung through ev-ery land, by ev-ery tongue. Al-le-lu-ia, al-le-
shore till suns shall rise and set no more.

lu-ia, al-le-lu-ia, al-le-lu-ia, al-le-lu-ia!

*Isaac Watts, author of more than 600 hymns, paraphrased the
two verses of Psalm 117 into this two-stanza hymn, which was
included in his* Psalms of David, *1719. The tune originated
in a German Catholic hymnal.*

Tune: LASST UNS ERFREUEN
8.8.4.4.8.8. with alleluias
Geistliche Kirchengesäng, *Cologne, 1623*
*Harm. Ralph Vaughan Williams, 1906*

28

# For the Beauty of the Earth

*St. 1–3, Folliott S. Pierpoint, 1864; alt.*
*St. 4, Miriam Therese Winter, 1993*

1 For the beau-ty of the earth, for the splen-dor of the skies,
2 For the won-der of each hour of the day and of the night,
3 For the joy of hu-man love, broth-er, sis-ter, par-ent, child,
4 For the good that love in-spires, for a world where none ex-clude,

For the love which from our birth o-ver and a-round us lies,
Hill and vale, and tree and flower, sun and moon, and stars of light,
Friends on earth, and friends a-bove, for all gen-tle thoughts and mild,
For a faith that nev-er tires, and for ev-ery heart re-newed,

*Refrain*

God of all, to you we raise this our hymn of grate-ful praise.

*Folliott S. Pierpoint, author of numerous hymns, penned these verses near his native city of Bath, England, on a late spring day when flowers were in full bloom and all the earth seemed to rejoice.*

Tune: DIX 7.7.7.7. with refrain
*Conrad Kocher, 1838*
*Adapt. William H. Monk, 1861*

29

# Let Heaven Your Wonders Proclaim

*Ps. 89:1–2, 8–17*

*English transl., The Iona Community, 1991*
*Original Spanish text, Salvador T. Martinez*

*Refrain, in unison*

Let heav-en your won-ders pro-claim, let an-gels your faith-ful-ness praise, for who in the heights or the depths can e-qual your maj-es-ty, O God?

*In harmony (Melody in tenor)*

1 Your strength rules the rage of the sea, your
2 The heav-ens are yours and the earth: you
3 All tough-ness and val-or are yours, and
4 So glad are the peo-ple who praise you, who

*(Melody in tenor)*

*(Basses, hum)*

faith-ful-ness calms its wild waves, you quell ev-ery fear of the
found-ed the world and its wealth; The north and the south show your
strong is your hand lift-ed high; Yet jus-tice is found at your
live in the light of your love; In you, God a-lone, is their

*(all sing)*

deep, and scat-ter your en-e-mies a-far.
skill, the east and the west at-test your fame.
throne, and love is for-ev-er by your side.
strength, their hon-or, their jus-tice, and their joy.

*This beautiful and simple melody, composed by Salvador Martinez, is in the style of a Philippine folk tune. It may be sung with a simple guitar accompaniment.*

Tune: MARTINEZ 8.8.8.9. with refrain
*Salvador T. Martinez, 1989*
*Arr. The Iona Community, 1991*

30

# Colorful Creator

Ruth Duck, 1992

*Unison*

1 Col-or-ful Cre - a - tor, God of mys-ter - y,
2 Har-mo-ny of a - ges, God of lis-tening ear,
3 Au-thor of our jour - ney, God of near and far,
4 God of truth and beau - ty, Po-et of the Word,

thank you for the art - ist teach-ing us to see glimps-es of the
thank you for com - pos-ers tun - ing us to hear ech - oes of the
praise for tale and dra-ma tell - ing who we are, strip-ping to the
may we be cre - a-tors by the Spir - it stirred, o - pen to your

mean - ing of the com - mon - place, vi - sions of the
Gos - pel in the songs we sing, sounds of love and
es - sence strug-gles of our day, times of change and
pres - ence in our joy and strife, ves - sels of the

*1–3*
ho - ly in each hu - man face.
long - ing from the deep - est spring.
con - flict when we choose our way.

*4*
ho - ly cours-ing through our life.

*This hymn was written for the 1992 installation of Linda Clark as Houghton Scholar of Sacred Music at Boston University, where Ruth Duck earned her Th.D. degree. It praises the Artist who inspires our creativity.*

Tune: HOUGHTON 11.11.11.11.
*Carlton R. Young, 1992*

# All Things Bright and Beautiful

*Cecil F. Alexander, 1848; alt.*

*Unison*
*Refrain*

All things bright and beau-ti - ful, all crea-tures great and small,

*Last time, end*

All things wise and won - der - ful, our dear God made them all.

1 Each lit - tle flower that o - pens, each lit - tle bird that sings,
2 The pur - ple-head - ed moun-tain, the riv - er run - ning by,
3 The cold wind in the win - ter, the pleas-ant sum - mer sun,

*to Refrain*

God made their glow-ing col - ors, and made their ti - ny wings.
The sun - set, and the morn - ing that bright-ens up the sky.
The ripe fruits in the gar - den, God made them ev - ery one.

*This hymn for children is based on the first article of the
Apostles' Creed: "Maker of heaven and earth." The English
hymnwriter Cecil Frances Alexander was married to William
Alexander, who became bishop of Ireland.*

Tune: ROYAL OAK 7.6.7.6. with refrain
*English melody
Adapt. Martin Shaw, 1915*

# 32 God of the Sparrow God of the Whale

*1 Thess. 5: 18; Ps. 136*

*Jaroslav J. Vajda, 1983*

1 God of the spar-row God of the whale
2 God of the earth-quake God of the storm
3 God of the rain-bow God of the cross
4 God of the hun-gry God of the sick
5 God of the neigh-bor God of the foe
6 God of the a-ges God near at hand

God of the swirl-ing stars How does the crea-ture say
God of the trum-pet blast How does the crea-ture cry
God of the emp-ty grave How does the crea-ture say
God of the prod-i-gal How does the crea-ture say
God of the prun-ing hook How does the crea-ture say
God of the lov-ing heart How do your chil-dren say

Awe How does the crea-ture say Praise
Woe How does the crea-ture cry Save
Grace How does the crea-ture say Thanks
Care How does the crea-ture say Life
Love How does the crea-ture say Peace
Joy How do your chil-dren say Home.

*After forty years in the ministry, Jaroslav Vajda wrote this text
to provoke answers to how and why we serve God. By creating
new poetic forms and adapting ageless ideas and expressions,
Vajda speaks in the language of his time.*

Tune: ROEDER 5.4.6.7.7.
*Carl F. Schalk, 1983*

# God Created Heaven and Earth

*Taiwanese hymn*
*Transl. Boris and Clare Anderson, 1981*

*Ps. 148; Gen. 1:1–5*

1 God cre - a - ted heaven and earth, all things per - fect
2 Let us praise God's mer - cy great, all our needs that
3 God is one, will ev - er be: i - dols are mere
4 But God's grace be - yond com - pare saves us all from

brought to birth; God's great power made
love a - wait; God, who fash - ions
van - i - ty; Hand-made gods of
death's de - spair; So earth's crea - tures

dark and light, earth re - volv-ing day and night.
all that lives, to each one a bless - ing gives.
wood and clay can - not help us when we pray.
small and great give thanks for that bless - ed state.

*This popular Taiwanese hymn speaks in symbols that*
*are universal. I-to Loh is a professor of church music*
*and ethnomusicology and is a leader in the development*
*of indigenous Christian hymnody in Asia.*

Tune: TŌA-SĪA 7.7.7.7.
*Pi-po melody*
*Harm. I-to Loh, 1963; rev. 1982*

# Alabanza
## (As the Rain Is Falling)

Ps. 96

*Pablo Fernández Badillo, 1977*
*Transl. Roberto Escamilla and Elise S. Eslinger, 1983*

1 Al ca - er la llu - via re - sur - ge con ver - dor
2 El "co - quí" se a - le - gra, se sien - te muy fe - liz.
1 As the rain is fall - ing, the flow - ers start to bloom.
2 The co - quí is hap - py, is hap - py sing - ing praise;

to - da la flo - res - ta. ¡Re - nue - va la crea - ción!
Can - ta en su a - la - ban - za: "co - quí, co - quí, co - quí."
All of God's cre - a - tion be - gins to be re - newed.
sing - ing joy - ful prais - es, "co - quí, co - quí, co - quí,"

Mi - ra el ro - jo li - rio; el duen - de ya bro - tó.
El pi - ti - rre can - ta y tri - na el rui - se - ñor.
See the red, red lil - y; the tu - lips have come up.
Sings the mock - ing - bird, and sings the night - in - gale;

¡Be - lla pri - ma - ve - ra que a - nun - cia su ful - gor!
¡Cuán a - le - gre - men - te a - la - ban al Crea - dor!
It is love - ly spring-time, in glo - ry prais - ing God.
hap - pi - ly their prais - es re - flect cre - a - tion's joy.

Estribillo (Refrain)

To - da flor sil - ves - tre, la ma - ya, el cun-dea - mor.
¡Có - mo se te a - la - ba en to - da la cre - a - ción!
All God's great cre - a - tion is sing - ing songs of love,
How all of cre - a - tion has joined in prais - ing God.

1. ¡To - do ma - ni - fies - ta la glo - ria de mi Dios!
in beau-ty is shown the glo - ry of our God!

2. Yo qui-sie-ra ha - cer - lo en for - ma i - gual, mi Dios.
I al - so shall of - fer my songs of praise to you.

*Coquí: a small frog-like creature, found only in Puerto Rico, that "sings." Duende: a small, purple flower.*

Tune: ALABANZA 6.6.6.6.D. with refrain
*Pablo Fernández Badillo, 1977*

*Pablo Fernández Badillo, a Presbyterian musician from Puerto Rico, writes in both traditional and contemporary hymnic styles, often incorporating elements of folk or popular music. This was one of 104 of his hymns published in "Himnario Criollo" (1977).*

# 35 O Mighty God, When I Survey in Wonder

*Carl Boberg, 1885*
*Transl.* The New Century Hymnal, *1994*

1 O might-y God, when I sur-vey in won-der the world that
2 When your voice speaks in rolls of thun-der peal-ing, your light-ning
3 The Bi-ble tells the sto-ry of your bless-ing so free-ly
4 And when, at last, the clouds of doubt dis-pers-ing, you will re-

formed when once the word you said, The strands of life all wo-ven close to-
pow-er bursts in bright sur-prise; When cool-ing rain, your gen-tle love re-
shed up-on all hu-man life; Your con-stant mer-cy, ev-ery care ad-
veal what we but dim-ly see; With trum-pet call, our great re-birth an-

*Refrain*

geth-er, the whole cre-a-tion at your ta-ble fed,
veal-ing, re-flects your prom-ise, arc-ing through the skies, (1–3) My soul cries
dress-ing, re-liev-ing bur-dened souls from sin and strife.
nounc-ing, we shall re-join you for e-ter-ni-ty, (4) Then we will

out in songs of praise to you, O might-y God! O might-y God! My soul cries
sing your praise for-ev-er more, O might-y God! O might-y God! Then we will

out in songs of praise to you, O might-y God! O might-y God!
sing your praise for-ev-er-more, O might-y God! O might-y God!

*Carl Boberg, a popular evangelical minister and teacher in Sweden, wrote his poem "O Store Gud" in the summer of 1885. Several years later, he was surprised to hear it sung with this old Swedish melody, with which it has been associated ever since. The first literal English translation by E. Gustav Johnson was published in the United States in 1925. The hymn also became known in Germany and Russia, where the British missionary Stuart K. Hine was inspired to create his English paraphrase known as "How great thou art." This translation and arrangement were created for* The New Century Hymnal *to restore the meaning and flavor of Boberg's original hymn.*

Tune: O STORE GUD
11.10.11.10. with refrain
*Swedish folk melody*
Harm. The New Century Hymnal, *1994*

# To God Compose a Song of Joy 36

*Ruth Duck, 1986*

Ps. 98

1 To God com-pose a song of joy; to God make mel-o-dy,
2 Be-fore the na-tions God re-veals a just and righ-teous will,
3 In ev-ery cor-ner of the earth, God comes to save and free;
4 With trum-pet, with the sound of horns, with strings, yes, with the lyre,

Whose arm of strength does won-drous things, whose hand brings vic-to-ry!
Re-mem-ber-ing in faith-ful love the house of Is-ra-el.
Break forth with shouts of ho-ly joy; all lands, make mel-o-dy.
With voic-es praise the sov-ereign God, a lust-y, joy-ous choir.

5 Let seas in all their full-ness roar;
   sing, peo-ple of all lands;
   Let moun-tains join and sing for joy;
   let riv-ers clap their hands.

6 The God of jus-tice comes to save;
   let earth make mel-o-dy;
   For God will judge with righ-teous-ness
   and rule with eq-ui-ty.

*Ruth Duck is associate professor of worship and dean of the chapel at Garrett Evangelical Theological Seminary in Evanston, Illinois. A minister in the United Church of Christ, she has edited several books of worship resources and hymns.*

Tune: RICHMOND C.M.
*Thomas Haweis, 1792*

# Our God, to Whom We Turn

Edward Grubb, 1925; alt.

1 Our God, to whom we turn when wea-ry with il - lu - sion,
2 You are in - deed the truth; though we, who deign to find you,
3 All beau-ty your de - cree: the moun-tains and the riv - ers,
4 O hid - den fount of truth, of love, and peace, and beau-ty,

whose stars se - rene-ly burn a - bove this earth's con - fu - sion,
have tried, with thought un - couth, in fee - ble words to bind you.
the line of lift - ed sea, where spread-ing moon-light quiv-ers.
in - spire us from our youth with joy and strength for du - ty.

Yours is the might - y plan, the stead-fast or - der sure,
It is be - cause you are we're driv - en to the quest;
The deep-toned or - gan blast that rolls through arch - es dim,
May your fresh light a - rise with - in each heart ob - scure,

in which the world be - gan, en - dures, and shall en - dure.
till truth from false-hood part, our souls can find no rest.
hints of the mu - sic vast of heaven's e - ter - nal hymn.
till, bar - ing all dis - guise, we know you true and sure!

*The English Quaker Edward Grubb was owner and editor of a monthly periodical,* The British Friend. *He also wrote and lectured on biblical and religious history and related subjects.*

Tune: STEADFAST 6.7.6.7.6.6.6.6.
(O GOTT, DU FROMMER GOTT, *Hanover, 1646*)
Neu Ordentlich Gesangbuch, *1646*
*Harm. from J. S. Bach (1685–1750)*
*Alternate tune: DARMSTADT*

# "Lift Up Your Hearts!"

Henry M. Butler, 1881; alt.

*Unison*

1 "Lift up your hearts!" We lift them up to you,
2 A-bove the lev - el of the for-mer years,
3 Lift ev - ery gift that God to us has given;
4 Then as the trum - pet call, in af - ter years,

for in your pres - ence it is right to do;
the mire of sin, the weight of guilt - y fears,
low lies the best till blessed by God in heaven;
"Lift up your hearts!" rings peal - ing in our ears,

"Lift up your hearts!" In joy to - geth - er laud,
The mist of doubt, the blight of love's de - cay,
Low lie the bound - ing heart, the teem - ing brain,
With spir - its one, with hearts in - spired and awed,

"We lift them up, we lift them up to God."
O God of life, lift all our hearts to - day!
till, once more, they re - turn to God a - gain.
"We lift them up, we lift them up to God!"

*This text is a meditation written for students at Harrow School, England. It is based on a liturgical dialogue, Sursum Corda, used since the third century in the Eastern and Western church to introduce the eucharisteō or prayer of consecration.*

Tune: WOODLANDS 10.10.10.10.
*Walter Greatorex, 1916*

Music Copyright ©, Oxford University Press

# 39

# Cantemos al Creador
## (Creator God We Sing)

Ps. 68:4, 32

Carlos Rosas, 1976; alt.
Transl. Dimas Planas-Belfort; alt.

**Dm / F / Gm / A**

1 Can - te - mos al Crea - dor   un him - no de a - le - grí - a,
2 Can - te - mos al Crea - dor   un him - no de a - la - ban - za
1 Cre - a - tor God we sing,   a hymn of joy we're mak - ing;
2 Cre - a - tor God we sing,   your power and wis-dom bless-ing;

**A7 / Gm / A7 / Dm**

de a - gra - de - ci - do a-mor   al na - cer el nue - vo dí - a. Pues
que ex-pre-se a d-mi - ra - ción,   ma - ra - vi - lla y es - pe - ran - za, Pues
our grate-ful love we bring,   as the new day's light is break-ing. God
our hope and won-der bring,   ad-mir - a - tion now ex - press-ing. The

**F / Gm / A / A7**

hi - zo el cie - lo, el mar,   el sol y las es - tre - llas,   y en e - llos vio bon-
to - da la crea-ción   pre-go - na su gran - de - za:   a - sí nues-tro can-
made the sea and land;   the sun and stars came roll - ing   from God's own lov - ing
u - ni-verse main-tains   that God in might is dwell-ing;   and we, in hum-ble

**Gm / A7 / Dm**

dad,   pues sus o - bras e - ran be - llas.
tar   va a-nun - cian-do su be - lle - za.
hand,   their Cre - a - tor's love ex - tol - ling.
strains,   of God's beau-ty here are tell-ing.

*Estribillo (Refrain)*

**Dm / F**

¡A - le - lu-ya;
Al - le - lu-ia,

a - le - lu - ya! ¡Can - te-mos al Crea-dor: A - le - lu - ya!
al - le - lu - ia! Cre - a - tor God we sing: Al - le - lu - ia!

*This processional hymn by Mexican composer and hymnwriter Carlos Rosas was originally the second movement in his mass setting "Rosas Del Tepeyac." Rosas has served as director of the Mexican-American Cultural Center in San Antonio, Texas.*

Tune: ROSAS 6.7.6.8.D. with refrain
*Carlos Rosas, 1976*
Harm. The New Century Hymnal, *1993*

# You Are the Way

**40**

*George W. Doane, 1824; alt.*

*John 14:6*

1 You are the way; through you a - lone can we the true God find;
2 You are the truth; your word a - lone true wis - dom can im - part;
3 You are the life; the o - pen tomb pro-claims God's love a - new;
4 You are the way, the truth, the life; grant us that way to know,

In you, O Christ, is now re-vealed God's heart and will and mind.
You on - ly can in - form the mind and pur - i - fy the heart.
And God will ne'er for - sake the one who trusts, O Christ, in you.
That truth to keep, that life to win, whose joys e - ter - nal flow.

*Jesus' words to Thomas, "I am the way, and the truth, and the life," inspired this hymn. George W. Doane, a powerful leader in the Episcopal church in the United States, served as parish priest, professor, and bishop of New Jersey.*

Tune: NUN DANKET ALL' C.M.
(GRÄFENBERG)
*Johann Crüger, 1647, in*
Praxis Pietatis Melica

# 41

# I Thank You, Jesus

*Kenneth Morris, 1948*

*This is one of countless hymns of African-American worship that are known as "testimony hymns." Such congregational songs emphasize personal experiences with God, especially the way God has delivered people from the tribulations of life.*

Tune: THANK YOU, JESUS Irr.
*Kenneth Morris, 1948*
*Adapt. and arr. Joyce Finch Johnson, 1992*

thank you, Je-sus, my Sav-ior God, for you brought me, yes, you
been my sis-ter, my broth-er, too, for you brought me, yes, you

brought me from a might-y, a might-y long way, a might-y long way.
brought me from a might-y, a might-y long way, a might-y long way.

## O for a Thousand Tongues to Sing 42

*Charles Wesley, 1740; alt.*

1 O for a thou-sand tongues to sing my great Re-deem-er's praise,
2 My gra-cious Sav-ior and my God, as-sist me to pro-claim,
3 Je-sus! the name that calms our fears, that bids our sor-rows cease
4 Glo-ry to God, and love and praise be ev-er, ev-er given

The glo-ries ev-er ech-o-ing the tri-umphs of God's grace!
To spread through all the earth a-broad the hon-ors of your name.
Is mu-sic in the sin-ner's ears, is life, and health, and peace!
By all the saints in ev-ery age, the church in earth and heaven.

*The hymn is a cento from a longer poem of eighteen stanzas
written by Charles Wesley on the first anniversary of his
conversion. The present form of the hymn is one edited by John
Wesley for The Wesleyan Hymn Book, 1780.*

Tune: AZMON C.M.
*Carl G. Gläser, 1828*
*Adapt. in L. Mason's* Modern Psalmody, *1839*
*Alternate tune: RICHMOND*

# 43      Love Divine, All Loves Excelling

*Mal. 3:1; 2 Cor. 3:18; 5:17; Eph. 5:27*          *Charles Wesley, 1747; alt.*

1 Love di-vine, all loves ex-cel-ling, joy of heaven, on earth be found,
2 Breathe, O breathe your lov-ing Spir-it in-to ev-ery trou-bled breast;
3 Come, al-might-y to de-liv-er, let us all your life re-ceive;
4 Fin-ish, then, your new cre-a-tion; pure and spot-less may we prove;

Fix in us a hum-ble dwell-ing, all your faith-ful mer-cies crown;
Let us all in you in-her-it, let us find your prom-ised rest;
Sud-den-ly re-turn, and ne-ver, ne-ver-more your tem-ples leave.
Let us see your great sal-va-tion per-fect-ly re-stored in you;

Je-sus, you are all com-pas-sion; pure, un-bound-ed love im-part.
Take a-way our love of sin-ning; Al-pha and O-me-ga be;
You we would be al-ways bless-ing, love you as your an-gels love,
Changed from glo-ry in-to glo-ry, till in heaven we take our place,

Vis-it us with your sal-va-tion, en-ter ev-ery trem-bling heart.
End of faith, as its be-gin-ning, set our hearts at lib-er-ty.
Pray and praise for your un-fail-ing, wound-ed arms out-stretched a-bove.
Crowned as saints, we ev-er shall be lost in won-der, love, and praise.

*This hymn is said to have been suggested by a "Song of Venus"
from Dryden's* King Arthur. *It is one of 6,500 written by Charles
Wesley, the "sweet singer of Methodism," who was skilled at
interweaving literary and scriptural images.*

Tune: BEECHER 8.7.8.7.D.
*John Zundel, 1855*
*Alternate tune: HYFRYDOL*
*For another harmonization, see 368, 495*

# Beautiful Jesus

## 44

Münster Gesangbuch, *1677*
*Transl. Madeleine Forell Marshall, 1993*

1 Beau - ti - ful Je - sus, Head of all cre - a - tion,
2 Beau - ti - ful spring - time, love - ly, green, and hope - ful,
3 Beau - ti - ful sun - shine, clear, so love - ly, moon - light,
4 All earth - ly beau - ty, all ce - les - tial ra - diance

God and the bless - ed Mar - y's child: I want to love you,
all earth ex - hales its sweet per - fume: Je - sus is sweet - er,
stars shine like an - gels, ranked through space: Je - sus shines bright - er,
fade when com - pared to Je - sus' face. Let me not cher - ish

praise and a - dore you, joy of my soul, so long de - sired.
Je - sus is pur - er, sad hearts at this, re - joice and bloom.
Je - sus shines clear - er, in per - fect beau - ty, love, and grace.
beau - ties that per - ish; let me this love - ly good em - brace.

*This text, which has also been translated as "Fairest Lord Jesus"*
*and "Beautiful Savior," was included in a German Catholic*
*hymnal published in Münster. The melody, known by various*
*names, is thought to be a Silesian folk tune.*

Tune: SCHÖNSTER HERR JESU 5.6.8.5.5.8.
*Silesian folk melody*
*Harm. Richard S. Willis, 1850*

# 45

# Cristo es la peña de Horeb
## (Christ Is the Mountain of Horeb)

*Exod. 17:6; Song of Sol. 2:1–2; John 4:7–14*

*Anonymous; alt.*
*Transl. The New Century Hymnal, 1993*

1 Cris-to es la pe - ña de Ho - reb, que es-tá bro - tan - do,
2 Cris-to es el li - rio del va - lle de las flo - res,
1 Christ is the Moun - tain of Ho - reb which is flow - ing:
2 Flow-er of flow - ers, the Lil - y of the Val - ley,

a - gua de vi - da sa - lu - da-ble pa - ra ti.
Cris-to es la ro-sa her-mo-sa y pu - ra de Sa - rón.
wa - ter of life pour forth to heal, to make us whole.
the Rose of Shar-on, bloom-ing pure and free for you.

Cris-to es la pe - ña de Ho - reb, que es-tá bro - tan - do,
Cris-to es la vi - da y a - mor de los a - mo - res,
Christ is the Moun - tain of Ho - reb which is flow - ing:
O Christ, the path - way of love a - bove all loves,

a - gua de vi - da sa - lu - da-ble pa - ra ti.
Cris - to es la e - ter - na fuen-te de la sal - va - ción.
wa - ter of life pour forth to heal, to make us whole.
E - ter - nal Foun-tain of sal - va - tion flow-ing free.

*This anonymous hymn has been sung since the 1930s and is especially popular among the pentecostal churches of Puerto Rico. The arrangement, in the "pasodoble" rhythm, captures the style in which it is most often performed in its country of origin.*

Tune: CRISTO ES LA PEÑA 12.12.12.12.D.
*Puerto Rican melody*
*Arr. Luis Olivieri, 1993*

# Beautiful Jesus

Ven, a to - mar - la que_es más  dul - ce  que  la  miel,
Ven, a bus - car - la cuan - do  en  tris - te - za_es - tés,
Sweet - er than  hon - ey  is  the  stream, come taste and  see—
Come seek the  One who un - der - stands your grief and  pain,

Re - fres - ca_el  al -  ma, re - fres - ca  to - do tu  ser.
Re - fres - ca_el  al -  ma, re - fres - ca  to - do tu  ser.
Re - fresh your  be -  ing, re - fresh your  heart  and  mind.
Re - fresh your  be -  ing, re - fresh your  heart  and  mind.

Cris - to_es la  pe -  ña de_Ho - reb, que_es-tá  bro - tan -  do,
Cris - to_es el  li -  rio del  va - lle  de  las  flo -  res,
Christ  is  the  Moun - tain of  Ho - reb which is  flow -  ing:
Flow - er  of  flow - ers, the  Lil - y  of the  Val -  ley,

a - gua de  vi - da sa - lu - da - ble pa - ra  ti.
Cris - to_es la  ro-sa_her - mo - sa_y  pu - ra de Sa - rón.
wa - ter of  life pour forth  to  heal, to make us  whole.
the  Rose of  Shar - on, bloom-ing  pure and free for  you.

# 46

# Hope of the World

*Georgia Harkness, 1954; alt.*

1 Hope of the world, O Christ of great com-pas - sion,
2 Hope of the world, God's gift of our re-demp - tion,
3 Hope of the world, who by the cross did save us
4 Hope of the world, O Christ, o'er death vic-to - rious,

speak to our fear - ful hearts by con - flict torn.
bring - ing to hun - gry souls the bread of life,
from death and sad de - spair, from sin and guilt,
who by this sign did con - quer grief and pain,

Save us your peo - ple from con-sum-ing pas - sion,
Still let your Spir - it un - to us be giv - en
We ren - der back the love your mer - cy gave us;
We would be faith - ful to your gos - pel glo - rious;

from false pur - suits through which our lives are worn.
to heal earth's wounds and end its bit - ter strife.
take back our lives and use them as you will.
our Sov - ereign who for - ev - er more shall reign!

*Author of many books in her field and an internationally recognized teacher, Georgia Harkness was one of the leading women theologians of her generation. This text was written for the Second General Assembly of the World Council of Churches.*

Tune: ANCIENT OF DAYS 11.10.11.10
*J. Albert Jeffrey, 1886*
*Adapt. The New Century Hymnal, 1992*

# O Christ Jesus, Sent from Heaven

**47**

*James W. Crawford, 1994*

*John 17:17–23*

1 O Christ Je - sus, sent from heav-en, Love E - ter - nal,
2 O Christ Je - sus, our sal - va - tion, Shep-herd kind, life's
3 O Christ Je - sus, Fa - ther - Moth-er, Spir - it, Tri - une
4 O Christ Je - sus, preached down a - ges, in the womb of

cru - ci - fied, wel - come Sav - ior, mis - sion bear - ing,
Bread and Wine, Word Made Flesh, God's Bless - ed Ser - vant,
Source of all, claim our wound-ed, halt - ing wit - ness;
God be - gun, pray re - store your bro - ken Bod - y,

dwell a - mong us, now re - side. Al - le - lu - ia!
wash - ing feet shows your de - sign. Al - le - lu - ia!
we sur - ren - der to your thrall. Al - le - lu - ia!
born when Cal - vary's work was done. Al - le - lu - ia!

Way of An - guish, sow your peace, with us a - bide.
Liv - ing Wa - ter, slake our hearts with grace di - vine.
Truth In - car - nate, stir us with your ser - vant call.
Life for Oth - ers, hear our plea: "May all be one!"

*James W. Crawford served as minister of the Old South Church in Boston for more than twenty years. His text uses imagery from the Gospel of John to indicate that the church's unity lies in the risk and hope of loving service.*

Tune: WESTMINSTER ABBEY 8.7.8.7.8.7.
*Henry Purcell, c. 1680*
*Arr. Ernest Hawkins, 1842*
*Alternate tune: REGENT SQUARE*

# 48

# Jesus the Christ Says

*John 6:48; 14:6; 11:25; 8:12; 9:5*

*Urdu, anon.; alt.*

This anonymous hymn, both text and tune, originated in
Pakistan or northern India and has been sung around the world
since its publication by the East Asia Christian Council and the
World Council of Churches.

Tune: YISU NE KAHA  9.9.9.9.9.9.
*Urdu melody*
*Arr. Francis B. Westbrook, 1950*

# Ask Me What Great Thing I Know

*Johann C. Schwedler, 1741*
*Transl. Benjamin H. Kennedy, 1863; alt.*

*1 Cor. 2:2; Gal. 6:14*

1 Ask me what great thing I know that de-lights and stirs me so,
2 Who de-feats my fierc-est foes? Who con-soles my sad-dest woes?
3 Who is life in life to me? Who the death of death will be?
4 This is that great thing I know; this de-lights and stirs me so:

What the high re - ward I win, whose the name I
Who re - vives my faint - ing heart, heal - ing all that
Who holds all my days se - cure, in God's heart where
Faith in Christ who died to save, Christ who tri - umphed

glo - ry in: Je - sus Christ, the cru - ci - fied.
grief im - parts? Je - sus Christ, the cru - ci - fied.
love is sure? Je - sus Christ, the cru - ci - fied.
o'er the grave, Je - sus Christ, the cru - ci - fied.

*Johann Christoph Schwedler, one of the most powerful preachers of Germany, was author of more than 450 hymns. This hymn was frequently used at funerals in Schwedler's native Silesia.*

Tune: HENDON 7.7.7.7.7.
H. A. César Malan, 1827

# 50 I Sing the Praise of Love Almighty

*Gerhard Tersteegen, 1757*
*Transl. Madeleine Forell Marshall, 1993*

1 I sing the praise of Love al - might - y, which shines re - vealed in
2 How lov - ing - kind you are, how gen - tle, how your heart reach - es
3 Se - cure my heart and all my be - ing, in you, my Sav - ior,
4 May my heart bear the deep im - pres - sion of love that Je - sus

Je - sus' face. I of - fer up all that de - lights me,
af - ter mine! My heart re - sponds in el - e - men - tal
cru - ci - fied. You gave your life to work my heal - ing,
shares with me, My life be - come a pure ex - pres - sion

all mean de - sires, each fond em - brace, Turn from my - self, in
sym - pa - thy, beat - ing per - fect time. This mu - tual love, this
bleed-ing for me, you groaned and died. Be - lov - ed Je - sus,
of all that Chris - tian love can be: Each word, each act, a

pure de - vo - tion, and ea - ger plunge in love's vast o - cean.
strong at - trac - tion, I know no oth - er sat - is - fac - tion.
my sal - va - tion, you have, through love, re - stored cre - a - tion.
bright re - flec - tion of joy in Love's own res - ur - rec - tion.

*Gerhard Tersteegen was an eighteenth-century hymnwriter and mystic, nurtured in the German Reformed Church. The four stanzas that comprise "Ich bete an die Macht der Liebe" were drawn from a longer poem and became popular in this form when published by Pastor Johannes Evangelist Gossner in his* Choralbuch *of 1825.*

Tune: ST. PETERSBURG 9.8.9.8.9.9.
*Dimitri Bortniansky, 1825*

# O Sing a Song of Bethlehem

51

Louis F. Benson, 1899; alt.

Luke 2:8–20, 25–32; Matt. 14:22–33; Mark 4:39; 6:47–52;
John 6:16–21; Acts 5:30–31; 10:39–43

1 O sing a song of Beth-le-hem, of shep-herds watch-ing there,
2 O sing a song of Naz-a-reth, of days of joy and sun,
3 O sing a song of Gal-i-lee, of lake and woods and hill,
4 O sing a song of Cal-va-ry, its glo-ry and dis-may,

and of the news that came to them from an-gels in the air:
O sing of fra-grant flo-wers' breath, and of the sin-less One:
of One who walked up-on the sea and bade its waves be still:
of One who hung up-on the tree, and took our sins a-way:

The light that shone on Beth-le-hem fills all the world to-day;
For now the flowers of Naz-a-reth in ev-ery heart may grow;
For though, like waves on Gal-i-lee, rough seas of trou-ble roll,
For Christ who died on Cal-va-ry is ris-en from the grave;

of Je-sus' birth and peace on earth the an-gels sing al-way.
now spreads the fame of Je-sus' name on all the winds that blow.
when faith has heard the Sav-ior's word, falls peace up-on the soul.
God's sov-ereign Child, who rec-on-ciled, is might-y now to save.

Using four biblical locations important to the story, the American
hymnwriter Louis F. Benson has summarized the life of Jesus and
related it to the present. Benson edited several Presbyterian
hymnals and wrote a number of books on hymnody.

Tune: KINGSFOLD C.M.D.
Traditional English melody
Arr. Ralph Vaughan Williams, 1906

# 52

# There Is a Name I Love to Hear
## (O How I Love Jesus)

*Frederick Whitfield, 1855; alt.*

1 There is a name I love to hear, I love to sing its worth;
2 It tells my Sav-ior's love for all; Christ died to set us free;
3 It bids me serve a - mid the wrath God's peo - ple face each day,

It sounds like mu - sic to my ear, the sweet - est name on earth.
What - ev - er prob - lems may be - fall, we'll live in dig - ni - ty.
And sheds a - long life's trou - bled path bright sun - shine on my way.

*Refrain*

O how I love Je - sus, O how I love Je - sus,

O how I love Je - sus, whose love has first found me.

*Frederick Whitfield was ordained in the Church of England and served several English parishes. This hymn is a combination of Whitfield's stanzas and a refrain by an unknown author, both set to an existing nineteenth-century tune. The text was published in a leaflet in 1855.*

Tune: O HOW I LOVE JESUS C.M. with refrain
*United States, 19th century*

# Glorious Is Your Name, O Jesus

53

*Robert J. Fryson, 1982; alt.*

Glo-rious is your name, O Je-sus, prais-es to your name. Oh, glo-ri-ous and

righ-teous and ho - ly is your name. Oh, glo - ri-ous is your name.

I feel your pres-ence in this place, your Spir - it makes me whole; I can

feel your warm em - brace and all the joy with-in my soul, Oh, glo - ri-ous

is your name, Oh, glo - ri-ous is your name.

*Composer Robert J. Fryson served as minister of music for the Amistad United Church of Christ, as well as choral director for several other Washington, D.C., churches. Fryson also was active as a soloist and recording artist with his sacred music group, "The Voices-Supreme."*

Tune: GLORIOUS IS YOUR NAME  Irr.
*Robert J. Fryson, 1982*

# 54

# O Praise the Gracious Power

*Eph. 2:11–22*

*Thomas H. Troeger, 1984*

1 O praise the gra-cious power that tum - bles walls of fear And
2 O praise per - sis - tent truth that o - pens fist - ed minds And
3 O praise in - clu-sive love, en - cir - cling ev - ery race, Ob -
4 O praise the word of faith that claims us as God's own, A
5 O praise the tide of grace that laps at ev - ery shore With

gath - ers in one house of faith all stran - gers far and near:
eas - es from their anx - ious clutch the prej - u - dice that binds:
liv - i - ous to gen - der, wealth, to so - cial rank or place:
liv - ing tem - ple built on Christ, our rock and cor - ner - stone:
vi - sions of a world at peace, no long - er bled by war:

*Refrain*

We praise you, Christ! Your cross has made us one!

*Thomas H. Troeger and Carol Doran have collaborated on several collections of new hymnody that utilize selected lectionary readings as their inspiration. This text focuses on the unifying power of Christ, to which Paul attests in the letter to the Ephesians.*

Tune: CHRISTPRAISE RAY S.M. with refrain
*Carol Doran, 1984*
*Alternate tune: MARION*

Copyright © 1985, Oxford University Press, Inc.

6 O praise the power, the truth,
   the love, the word, the tide,
   Yet more than these, O praise their source,
   praise Christ the cru-ci-fied:
   We praise you, Christ!
   Your cross has made us one!

7 O praise the liv-ing Christ
   with faith's bright song-ful voice!
   An-nounce the gos-pel to the world
   and with these words re-joice:
   We praise you, Christ!
   Your cross has made us one!

# Rejoice, You Pure in Heart

**55**

*Edward H. Plumptre, 1865; alt.*

*Ps. 20:5; Phil. 4:4*

1 Re - joice, you pure in heart; lift prais - es to the sky;
2 Bright youth and sea - soned age, strong souls and spir - its meek,
3 With voice as full and strong as o - cean's surg - ing praise,
4 Yes, on through life's long path, still chant-ing as you go,
5 Praise God who rules all worlds, the ris - en Christ a - dore,

Your fes - tal ban - ner wave with joy, the cross of Christ raise high!
Raise high your free, ex - ult - ing song, God's won-drous prais - es speak.
Send forth the hymns the saints have loved, the psalms of an - cient days.
From youth to age, by night and day, in glad-ness and in woe:
Praise God the Spir - it, Ho - ly Fire, one God for ev - er - more!

*Refrain*

Re - joice, re - joice, re - joice, give thanks and sing.
Re - joice Re - joice

*This hymn, inspired by Philippians 4:4, was written for the Choral Festival held at Peterborough Cathedral in England. The author was an Anglican priest and a professor of theology at Oxford University.*

Tune: MARION S.M. with refrain
*Arthur H. Messiter, 1883*
*For an alternate setting, see 71*
*Alternate tune: CHRISTPRAISE RAY*

# Soplo de Dios viviente
## (Breath of the Living God)

56

*Osvaldo Catena; alt.*
*Transl. The New Century Hymnal, 1993*

This text by the contemporary Argentinian hymnwriter and composer
Osvaldo Catena utilizes a traditional melody from Norway. The
hymn was published in Cancionero Abierto IV in 1979.

Tune: FLORINDEZ Irr. with refrain
Norwegian traditional melody
Arr. Lorraine Floríndez, 1991

3  So-plo de Dios vi-vien-te
    por quien na-ce-mos en el bau-tis-mo;
   So-plo de Dios vi-vien-te
    que con-sa-gras-te la cre-a-ción.
    *(Estribillo)*

3  Breath of the liv-ing God,
    source of life a-new
    through our ho-ly Bap-tism,
   Breath of the liv-ing God,
    by whom all cre-a-tion is sanc-ti-fied:
    *(Refrain)*

# O Holy Spirit, Root of Life

**57**

*Jean Janzen, 1991; based on writings by*
*Hildegard, Abbess of Bingen, 12th century*

1 O   Ho - ly   Spir - it,   Root   of   life,   Cre - a - tor,
2 E - ter - nal   Vig - or,   Sav - ing   One,   you   free   us
3 O   Ho - ly   Wis - dom,   Soar - ing   Power,   en - com - pass

cleans - er   of   all   things,   a - noint   our   wounds, a -
by   your   liv - ing   Word,   be - com - ing   flesh   to
us   with   wings   un - furled,   and   car - ry   us,   en -

wak - en   us   with   lus - trous   move - ment   of   your   wings.
wear   our   pain,   and   all   cre - a - tion   is   re - stored.
cir - cling   all,   a - bove,   be - low,   and   through   the   world.

*Hildegard of Bingen (1098–1179) was a "woman for all*
*seasons." A German abbess, she was a prolific liturgical*
*composer and poet, artist and mystic, and scientist and*
*theologian whose works exhibit deep spirituality. This new text*
*combines rich images from Hildegard's songs "De Spiritu*
*Sancto," "O Virtus Sapientiae," and "O Vis Aeternitatis."*

Tune:  PUER NOBIS NASCITUR  L.M.
*Melody from "Piae Cantiones," 1582*
*Adapt. Michael Praetorius, 1609*

# 58

# Spirit of Love

*Shirley Erena Murray, 1992*

1 Spir - it of love, you move with - in cre - a - tion,
2 Though we have frayed the fab - ric of your mak - ing,
3 Great loom of God, where his - to - ry is wo - ven,

draw - ing the threads to col - or and de - sign:
tear - ing a - way from all that you in - tend,
you are the frame that holds us to the truth,

Life in - to life, you knit our true sal - va - tion,
Yet, to be whole, hu - man - i - ty is ach - ing—
Christ is the theme, the pat - tern you have giv - en—

come, work with us, and weave us in - to one.
come, work with us, and weave us in - to one.
come, work with us, and weave us in - to one.

*Originally titled "Weaver Spirit," this text was written for the World Council of Churches Assembly at Canberra. It addressed one of the themes of that meeting—"Come, Holy Spirit, Reconcile Your People."*

Tune: PERFECT LOVE 11.10.11.10.
*Joseph Barnby, 1889*

# Holy Spirit, Ever Dwelling

**59**

*Timothy Rees, 1922; alt.*

1 Ho-ly Spir-it, ev-er dwell-ing in the ho-liest realms of light;
2 Ho-ly Spir-it, ev-er breath-ing on the church the breath of life;
3 Ho-ly Spir-it, ev-er work-ing through the church's min-is-try—

Ho-ly Spir-it, ev-er brood-ing o'er a world of gloom and
Ho-ly Spir-it, ev-er striv-ing through your peo-ple's cease-less
Quick-ening, strength-ening, and ab-solv-ing, set-ting cap-tive sin-ners

blight; Ho-ly Spir-it, ev-er rais-ing earth-bound souls to glo-ry
strife; Ho-ly Spir-it, ev-er form-ing in the church the mind of
free; Ho-ly Spir-it, ev-er bind-ing age to age and soul to

high; Liv-ing, life-im-part-ing Spir-it; you we praise and mag-ni-fy.
Christ: In our wor-ship we will praise you for your fruit and gifts un-priced.
soul, In com-mu-ni-ty un-end-ing you we wor-ship and ex-tol.

*Timothy Rees, Welsh curate, lecturer, chaplain, and winner of*
*the Military Cross in World War I, was appointed Bishop of*
*Llandaff in 1931. These words were written for the Anglican*
*Community of Mirfield, Yorkshire, of which he was a member.*

Tune: NETTLETON 8.7.8.7.D.
*John Wyeth's Repository of Sacred Music, 1813*

# 60

# O Spirit of God

*Rom. 8:1–2, 9–17*

*Johann Niedling, c. 1650*
*Transl. Madeleine Forell Marshall, 1993*

1 O Spir-it of God, O life-giv-ing breath! You com-fort
2 O Spir-it of God, O ho-li-est flame! Ig-nite our
3 O Spir-it of God, O life-giv-ing power! In-crease our
4 O Spir-it of God, O ho-li-est light! Il-lu-mine,
5 O Spir-it of God, our com-fort and guide, In life, in

us in life and death. When hu-mans gasp in
love, our hearts re-claim, That we, a blessed com-
faith, bring it to flower. With-out that strength which
by your Word, our night. Our Mak-er's power and
death, close by our side: For this, we hon-or

pain and grief, you breathe as-sur-ance and re-lief:
mu-ni-ty, may lov-ing Chris-tian ser-vants be:
you sup-ply, our life in Christ will fade and die:
glo-ry show, and Je-sus, whom we joy to know:
you with song, ex-press-ing thanks our whole life long:

*The German hymnwriter Johann Niedling taught school in*
*Altenburg, Saxony. Among the six collections he compiled*
*was the popular* Lutherische Handbüchlein.

Tune: O HEILIGER GEIST 10.8.8.8.10.
(O JESULEIN SÜSS)
Geistliche Kirchengesäng, *1623*
*Harm. adapt. from J. S. Bach, 1993*

O Spir - it of God, O life - giv - ing breath!
O Spir - it of God, O ho - li - est flame!
O Spir - it of God, O life - giv - ing power!
O Spir - it of God, O ho - li - est light!
O Spir - it of God, our com - fort and guide!

# Gracious Spirit, Holy Ghost

*Christopher Wordsworth, 1862; alt.*

**61**

*1 Cor. 13:1–14*

Unison

1 Gra-cious Spir - it, Ho - ly Ghost, taught by you, we cov - et most
2 Love is kind, and suf-fers long; love is meek, and thinks no wrong;
3 Proph-e - cy will fade a - way, melt - ing in the light of day;
4 Faith and hope and love we see, join - ing hand in hand a - gree;

Of your gifts at Pen - te - cost, ho - ly, heaven-ly love.
Love than death it - self more strong; there-fore, give us love.
Love will ev - er with us stay; there-fore, give us love.
But the great - est of the three, and the best, is love.

*The author, a nephew of poet William Wordsworth and a celebrated*
*Greek scholar, served as Bishop of London. Jane Marshall is known*
*as a church music composer, educator, and editor.*

Tune: ANDERSON 7.7.7.5.
*Jane Marshall, 1985*

# 62

# Come, Share the Spirit

*Luke 4:18–19; Isa. 61*

Vicki Vogel Schmidt, 1987; alt.

*With a happy, driving beat*
Unison

1 Come, share the Spir - it, mov - ing a - mong us, weav - ing
2 Come, Rush - ing Wa - ters, let jus - tice roll like an
3 Come, Gen - tle Breez - es, breath of all lov - ing, giv - en

in and through this place; break - ing down the walls that
ev - er - flow - ing stream; till the poor find strength as they
to God's cho - sen band; let us dance and feast with the

split and di - vide, bring - ing whole - ness to em - brace.
hear the good news, and the rich a - dopt new dreams.
bro - ken ones, bring com - pas - sion to our land.

Come, Liv - ing Spir - it, bloom in our hearts as when the
Come, Blaz - ing Fire, a - noint our tongues with the
Come! Lift our hands in joy - ful ap - plause to the

*Vicki Vogel Schmidt wrote this hymn for a meeting of the Northwest Minnesota Synod of the Evangelical Lutheran Church in America. It utilizes the theme for the merger of Lutheran denominations in 1987—"Come, share the Spirit."*

Tune: SHARE THE SPIRIT  Irr.
*Vicki Vogel Schmidt, 1987*
Arr. The New Century Hymnal, *1993*

des - ert bursts with life; take thirst - y souls, fill
mes - sag - es of peace; till, though blind, we see, and
Mak - er of the earth; for our Fa - ther who lifts us

them with your love, and re - move all greed and strife.
deaf, we hear, and im - pris - oned, find re - lease.
when we fall, and our Moth - er who gives us birth!

## Holy Spirit, Truth Divine 63

*Samuel Longfellow, 1864; alt.*

1 Ho - ly Spir - it, truth di - vine, dawn up - on this soul of mine.
2 Ho - ly Spir - it, love di - vine, glow with - in this heart of mine.
3 Ho - ly Spir - it, power di - vine, fill and nerve this will of mine.
4 Ho - ly Spir - it, law di - vine, reign with - in this soul of mine.

Voice of God and in - ward light, wake my spir - it from its night.
Kin - dle ev - ery high de - sire, pu - ri - fy me with your fire.
Bold - ly may I al - ways live, brave - ly serve, and glad - ly give.
Be my law, and I shall be firm - ly bound, for - ev - er free.

*Louis Moreau Gottschalk was the first American musician to be acclaimed at home and abroad as a virtuoso pianist and gifted composer, often incorporating folk and popular tunes into his own concert music. Mercy was arranged from his piano composition, "The Last Hope."*

Tune: MERCY 7.7.7.7.
*Louis Moreau Gottschalk, 1867.*
*Arr. Edwin Parker, 1888*

# 64

# Fire of God, Undying Flame

Acts 2:1–21

Albert F. Bayly (1901–1984); alt.

1 Fire of God, un - dy - ing Flame, Spir - it who in splen-dor came,
2 Breath of God, that swept in power in the Pen - te - cos - tal hour,
3 Strength of God, your might with - in con - quers sor - row, pain, and sin.
4 Truth of God, your pierc - ing rays pen - e - trate my se - cret ways.
5 Love of God, your grace pro-found knows not ei - ther age or bound.

Let your heat my soul re - fine, till it glows with love di - vine.
Ho - ly Breath, be now in me source of vi - tal en - er - gy.
For - ti - fy from e - vil's art all the gate - ways of my heart.
May the light that shames my sin guide me ho - lier paths to win.
Come, my heart's own guest to be; dwell for - ev - er - more in me.

Albert F. Bayly, an English Congregational minister, wrote his
first hymn after age forty and subsequently published several
collections of hymnody. Most hymnals published since 1950
have included at least one of his hymns.

Words Copyright © 1988 Oxford University Press.

Tune: NUN KOMM DER HEIDEN HEILAND
7.7.7.7.
Plainsong melody; adapt. Johann Walther in
Geistliche Gesangbuchlein, Wittenberg, 1524
Harm. Melchior Vulpius (c. 1560–1616)

# 65

# Este es el día
## (This Is the Day)

Ps. 118:19–29

Pablo D. Sosa, 1983; alt.
Transl. Roberto Escamilla and Elise S. Eslinger, 1983

¡Es - te es el dí - a! ¡Es - te es el dí - a! ¡Es - te es el dí - a
This is the day, yes! This is the day, yes! This is the day . . . .

que hi - zo Dios!

that God has made!

1  A-bran-me las puer-tas  de  la  jus - ti - cia,
2  Te a-la - ba - ré  por-que  tú me has o - í - do,

1  O-pen the doors of  true  jus - tice and mer - cy.
2  I  will sing prais-es  to  you, our  Re-deem-er,

y  en - tra - ré  a - la - ban-do al Crea - dor.  Es - ta es la puer - ta  que
y  por - que  fuis - te  mi  gran sal - va - ción.  La  pie-dra que  to - dos

I  shall now,  I  shall now  en - ter those gates.  This  is the door that  our
since you have heard me  I  sing  a  new song.  Know that the rock which once

Dios nos ha  da - do,  to - dos los  jus - tos  por  e - lla en-tra - rán.
han des-pre - cia - do,  re - sul-ta a - ho - ra  ser  fun - da - men - tal.

God  is pro-claim - ing,  on - ly  the righ-teous shall  en - ter there-in.
had  been re - ject - ed  has  be-come for  us  the  true cor - ner-stone.

*Estribillo (to Refrain)*

3  Es el Crea-dor quien ha he-cho
      to-do es-to;
   ¡qué ma-ra-vi-lla po-der ver-lo hoy!
   Es-te es el dí-a que Dios ha he-cho,
      con a-le-grí-a go-ce-mos en él.
   *(Estribillo)*

3  God now has en-tered in, God our Cre-a-tor.
      Won-der-ful, won-der-ful is our great God.
   This is the day that our Mak-er has of-fered.
   Let us re-joice and be glad and sing praise.
      *(Refrain)*

*The refrain of this psalm setting from Argentina was inspired by the echoing voices of gauchos (cowboys) calling to greet each other as they rode through the fields.*

Tune: ESTE ES EL DIA  11.10.11.10. with refrain
*Pablo D. Sosa, 1983*
*Arr. Roberto Milano, 1984*

66

# O Day of Radiant Gladness

*St. 1-2, Christopher Wordsworth, 1862; alt.*
*St. 3, Charles P. Price, 1980; alt.*
*St. 4, The Hymnal 1982; alt.*

1 O day of ra-diant glad - ness, O day of joy and light;
2 This day at the cre - a - tion the light first had its birth;
3 This day God's peo-ple, meet - ing, the Ho - ly Scrip-ture hear;
4 That light our hope sus - tain - ing, up - on the pil - grim way,

O balm of care and sad - ness, most beau - ti - ful, most bright;
this day for our sal - va - tion Christ rose from depths of earth;
Christ's liv - ing pres-ence greet - ing, through bread and cup made near.
at length our rest at - tain - ing, our end - less Sab-bath day.

This day the high and low - ly, through a - ges joined in tune,
This day our God vic - to - rious the Spir - it sent from heaven,
We jour-ney on, be - liev - ing, re - newed with heaven-ly might,
We sing to you our prais - es, our Hope, our Joy, our Sun:

sing "Ho - ly, ho - ly, ho - ly" to the great God tri - une.
and thus this day most glo - rious a tri - ple light was given.
from grace more grace re - ceiv - ing on this blessed day of light.
the church its voice up - rais - es to you, blessed Three in One.

*Christopher Wordsworth, Anglican priest, wrote voluminously*
*on the Bible and church history in addition to his hymn writing.*
*This hymn is from his Holy Year, 1862.*

Tune: ES FLOG EIN KLEINS WALDVÖGELEIN
7.6.7.6.D.
*Memmingen manuscript, 17th century*
*Harm. George R. Woodward, 1904*

# Let Me Enter God's Own Dwelling

*Benjamin Schmolck, 1732*
*Transl. Madeleine Forell Marshall, 1993*

1 Let me en - ter God's own dwell-ing, o - pen wide the love - ly door!
2 I have come to church to meet you: con - de - scend to come to me!
3 Make my mind and bod - y ho - ly, sanc - ti - fy my ears and lips.
4 In this hour of Gos - pel sow - ing, let my earth be fruit-ful ground.

Here, all earth - ly powers ex - cel - ling, God re - ceives the sick and poor.
Anx - ious, need - y, I en - treat you, come in - side, and wel - come be—
Lift my spir - it, poor and low - ly, all bright van - i - ties e - clipse.
In - tel - lec - tual light be - stow - ing, raise my green faith, sweet and sound.

Joy, my heart, in this dear place: here I see God face to face.
Here at home, with - in my breast— I, your tem - ple, rich - ly blessed.
Take my praise, how - ev - er flawed, as an of - fering, wor - thy God.
Let me prove a stalk of wheat, when your har - vest is com - plete.

5 Re-in-force me, weak and fail-ing,
  mak-ing sure your pre-cious word—
(Thieves and e-vil un-a-vail-ing)—
  lives with-in my heart se-cured.
Shin-ing word, my star-ry guide,
  plant-ed for me, deep in-side.

6 Let me hear when you com-mand me,
  let me leap to do your will.
When I wan-der, rep-ri-mand me,
  com-fort me when I lie ill.
In the hour of si-lent dread,
  feed me with your heaven-ly bread.

*A native of Silesia, Benjamin Schmolck was ordained a Lutheran
pastor. Although he was one of only three clergy serving thirty-six
villages, he wrote more than 1,000 hymns, Joachim Neander, an
important Reformed musician, wrote the music.*

Tune: UNSER HERRSCHER 8.7.8.7.7.7.
*Joachim Neander, 1680*

# 68 God Is Truly with Us

Matt. 1:23; 2 Cor. 9:8; Rev. 4:8–11

*Gerhard Tersteegen, 1729*
*Transl. Frederick W. Foster and others; alt.*

1 God is tru-ly with us; sing we and a-dore now: praise the One we come be-fore now. Here with-in this tem-ple, here in sound and si-lence, wor-ship God in deep-est rev-erence. You a-lone, God, we own, you, our God and Sav-ior; praise to you for-ev-er.

2 God is tru-ly with us; loud our praise re-sound-ing! Ech-oes of the saints sur-round-ing! "Ho-ly, ho-ly, ho-ly," hear the hymn as-cend-ing, an-gels, saints, their voic-es blend-ing! Bow your ear to us here; hear, O Christ, the prais-es that your Church now rais-es.

3 Source of ev-ery bless-ing, bless the ones who name you, let our words and deeds pro-claim you. Like the saints and an-gels prais-ing you in glo-ry, may your ser-vants sing your sto-ry. And in all, great and small, may we do most near-ly what you love most dear-ly.

*Gerhard Tersteegen, an important German hymnwriter of the Reformed Church, began preaching at prayer meetings and gained a considerable following. He devoted his life to praying, preaching, visiting the poor, and writing and translating devotional material.*

Tune: WUNDERBARER KÖNIG 6.6.8.6.6.8.3.3.6.6.
*Joachim Neander, in A und Ω,*
Glaubund Liebesübung, Bremen, 1680

# Come, God, Creator, Be Our Shield

**69**

*Marion M. Meyer, 1990*

*Ps. 84:8–12*

1 Come, God, Cre - a - tor, be our shield, the
2 Come, gra - cious Je - sus, be our guest, our
3 Come, Ho - ly Spir - it, be our guide, our

One to whom our cares we yield;
morn - ing joy, our eve - ning rest;
strength to risk a - gainst the tide,

And in our wor - ship, faith im - part, your
And in our dai - ly lives im - part your
That in God's world we shall im - part your

grace and calm to ev - ery heart.
love and peace to ev - ery heart.
light and hope to ev - ery heart.

*After serving as a teacher in Baghdad, Iraq, Marion Meyer joined the staff of The Pilgrim Press and United Church Press in 1958. She retired thirty years later as senior editor. Her tune, named for Old First Reformed Church, U.C.C., in Philadelphia, was composed as a setting for the traditional table grace she adapted in stanza two.*

Tune: OLD FIRST L.M.
*Marion M. Meyer, 1990*
*Harm. The New Century Hymnal, 1994*

70

# God Is Here! As We Your People Meet

*Fred Pratt Green, 1978; alt.*

1 God is here! As we your peo-ple meet to of - fer praise and prayer,
2 Here are sym-bols to re - mind us of our life - long need of grace;
3 Here our chil-dren find a wel-come in the Shep-herd's flock and fold;
4 Sov - ereign God, of earth and heav-en, in an age of change and doubt

May we find in full - er mea-sure what it is in Christ we share.
Here are ta - ble, font, and pul - pit, here the cross has cen - tral place.
Here as bread and wine are tak - en, Christ sus - tains us as of old.
Keep us faith - ful to the gos - pel, help us work your pur - pose out.

Here, as in the world a - round us, all our var - ied skills and arts
Here in hon - es - ty of preach-ing, here in si - lence, as in speech,
Here the ser - vants of the Ser - vant seek in wor-ship to ex - plore
Here, in this day's ded - i - ca - tion, all we have to give, re - ceive;

wait the com - ing of the Spir - it in - to o - pen minds and hearts.
here, in new-ness and re - new-al, God the Spir - it comes to each.
what it means in dai - ly liv - ing to be - lieve and to a - dore.
we, who can - not live with-out you, we a - dore you! We be - lieve!

*Though he retired in 1969, this distinguished British poet has continued
to write hymns. In addition to administering several circuits and local
congregations, Fred Pratt Green published plays, translations, and
poems. Emory University in Atlanta awarded him an honorary doctorate.*

Tune: ABBOT'S LEIGH 8.7.8.7.D.
*Cyril V. Taylor, 1941*

# Rejoice, You Pure in Heart

**71**

*Edward H. Plumptre, 1865; alt.*

*Ps. 20:5; Phil. 4:4*

1 Re - joice, you pure in heart; lift prais-es to the
2 Bright youth and sea-soned age, strong souls and spir-its
3 With voice as full and strong as o-cean's surg-ing
4 Yes, on through life's long path, still chant-ing as you
5 Praise God who rules all worlds, the ris-en Christ a -

sky; Your fes - tal ban - ner wave with joy, the
meek, Raise high your free, ex - ult - ing song, God's
praise, Send forth the hymns the saints have loved, the
go, From youth to age, by night and day, in
dore, Praise God the Spir - it, Ho - ly Fire, one

*Refrain*

cross of Christ raise high!
won-drous prais - es speak.
psalms of an - cient days.    Ho - san - na!    Ho -
glad - ness and in woe:
God for ev - er - more!

san - na!    Re - joice, give thanks and sing.

*Richard Wayne Dirksen served on the musical staff of the Washington Cathedral for more than forty years, and was the first layperson in an American cathedral to be appointed precentor. Dirksen composed this tune for the installation of John M. Allin as presiding bishop of the Episcopal church.*

Tune: VINEYARD HAVEN S.M. with refrain
*Richard Wayne Dirksen, 1974*
*For an alternate setting, see 55*

# 72

# Sekai no Tomo
## (Here, O God, Your Servants Gather)

*John 14:6; Rom. 10:12–13; Eph. 1:7–14*

*Tokuo Yamaguchi, 1958; alt.*
*Phonetic transcription, I-to Loh, 1958*
*Transl. Everett M. Stowe, 1958; alt.*

1 Se - ka - i no to - mo to te o tsu - na - gi,
1 Here, O God, your ser - vants gath - er, hand we link in hand;
2 Man - y are the tongues we speak, scat-tered are the lands,
3 Na - ture's se - crets o - pen wide, chan-ges nev - er cease;
4 Grant, O God, an age re - newed, show us how love thrives,

Jyu - ji - ka no mo - to ni ta - tsu wa - re - ra,
look - ing toward our Sav - ior's cross, joined in love we stand.
yet our hearts are one in God, one in love's de - mands.
where, O where, can wea - ry souls find the source of peace?
help us as we work and pray, send us for our lives

Ka - mi no mi - ku - ni o me - a - te to - shi,
As we seek the realm of God, we u - nite to pray:
In de - spair our hope ap - pears, call - ing age and youth:
Un - to all those sore dis - tressed, torn by end - less strife:
Truth and cour - age, faith and power need-ed in our strife:

Shu Ye - su no mi - chi o su - su - mi - yu - kan.
Je - sus, Sav - ior, guide our steps, for you are the Way.
Je - sus, Teach-er, dwell with us, for you are the Truth.
Je - sus, Heal - er, bring your balm, for you are the Life.
Je - sus, Lead - er, be our Way, be our Truth, our Life.

*This hymn was composed for the fourteenth World Council of
Christian Education, 1958. Tokuo Yamaguchi has served many
Japanese parishes and since 1979 has been pastor emeritus of
Toyohashi Church, Aichi Prefecture. His translation of* The
Journal of John Wesley *won official commendation.*

Tune: TOKYO 7.5.7.5.D.
*Japanese gagaku mode
Arr. Isao Koizumi, 1958*

# Enter, Rejoice, and Come In 73

*Louise Ruspini; alt.* *Ps. 100*

1 En - ter, re - joice, and come in. En - ter, re - joice, and come in.
2 O - pen your-self to the song. O - pen your-self to the song.
3 O - pen your hearts ev - ery - one. O - pen your hearts ev - ery - one.
4 Don't be a - fraid of some change. Don't be a - fraid of some change.
5 En - ter, re - joice, and come in. En - ter, re - joice, and come in.

To - day will be a joy - ful day; en-ter, re-joice, and come in.

*This song, based on Psalm 100, became popular in the 1970s in
the United States. It works equally well with organ, piano, or
guitar accompaniment.*

Tune: ENTER, REJOICE 7.7.8.7.
*Louise Ruspini*
Harm. The New Century Hymnal, *1993*

## 74 We Have Gathered, Jesus Dear

*Tobias Clausnitzer, 1663*
*Transl. Madeleine Forell Marshall, 1993*

1 We have gath - ered, Je - sus dear, we have come to
2 All our in - tel - lec - tual dreams come to noth - ing,
3 Born of God, true light of light, Ho - ly Spir - it,

watch and lis - ten. Fix our minds, our sens - es clear,
fade at day - break. All our hope - ful plots and schemes,
pure, un - fail - ing: All our fac - ul - ties ex - cite,

to re - ceive your heaven-ly les - son. Please im - prove our
start in pre - tense, end in heart - ache. Thought-ful speech, and
ears and heart and mouth un - seal - ing: Then, through Je - sus'

con - cen - tra - tion: draw us in - to con - tem - pla - tion.
ac - tive jus - tice, you ac - com - plish these with - in us.
me - di - a - tion, God will hear our sup - pli - ca - tion.

*Written to precede the sermon, this hymn briefly reflects the Nicene Creed in the third stanza. Tobias Clausnitzer, a German Lutheran pastor, served for a time as a chaplain to a Swedish regiment and later as a parish pastor.*

Tune: LIEBSTER JESU  7.8.7.8.8.8.
*Johann R. Ahle, 1664*
*Harm. Das grosse Cantional, Darmstadt, 1687*

# Lord, Make Me More Holy

## 75

*African-American spiritual*

1 Lord, make me more ho - ly. Lord, make me more ho - ly.
Lord, make me more ho - ly, un - til we meet a - gain.
Ho - ly, ho - ly, ho - ly un - til we meet a - gain.

2 Lord, make me more faith-ful, . . . Faith-ful, . . . un-til we meet a-gain.
3 Lord, make me more hum-ble, . . . Hum-ble, . . . un-til we meet a-gain.
4 Lord, make me more right-teous, . . . Right-teous, . . . un-til we meet a-gain.

*The origins of this African-American spiritual have been traced to the area of Charleston, South Carolina, where it may have been sung as a closing hymn for worship. It is one of a number of devotional songs expressing the desire to attain the spiritual character of Jesus.*

Tune: LORD, MAKE ME MORE HOLY
6.6.6.6.6.6.
*African-American spiritual*

# 76  Sent Forth by God's Blessing

*Omer Westendorf, 1964*

**Descant**

2 With praise and thanks - giv - ing to God ev - er liv - ing, the

**Unison**

1 Sent forth by God's bless-ing, our true faith con - fess-ing, the
2 With praise and thanks - giv - ing to God ev - er liv - ing, the

tasks of our ev - ery-day life we will face. Our faith ev - er

peo - ple of God from this dwell-ing take leave. The ser - vice is
tasks of our ev - ery-day life we will face. Our faith ev - er

shar - ing, in love ev - er car - ing, em - brac - ing God's chil-dren of

end - ed, O now be ex - tend-ed the fruits of our wor-ship in
shar - ing, in love ev - er car - ing, em - brac - ing God's chil-dren of

*Omer Westendorf, author of numerous hymns, compiler of several hymnals, and founder of World Library Publications, included this hymn in* People's Mass Book, *1964, the first vernacular Roman Catholic hymn and service book to implement the decrees of Vatican II.*

Tune: THE ASH GROVE  6.6.11.6.6.11.D.
*Welsh folk melody*
*Harm. Leland Sateren, 1972*
*Descant,* The New Century Hymnal, *1993*

# Lord, Make Me More Holy

*African-American spiritual*

# 77 Lord, Dismiss Us with Your Blessing

*Luke 2:29; Rom. 1:16*

*Attrib. to John Fawcett, 1773; alt.*

1 Lord, dis-miss us with your bless-ing; fill our hearts with
2 We give thanks and ad-o-ra-tion for your gos-pel's
3 So that when your love shall call us, Sav-ior, from the

joy and peace; Let us each your love pos-sess-ing,
joy-ful sound; May the fruits of your sal-va-tion
world a-way, Fear of death shall not ap-pall us,

tri-umph in re-deem-ing grace: Oh, re-fresh us,
in our hearts and lives a-bound: Ev-er faith-ful,
glad your sum-mons to o-bey: May we ev-er,

oh, re-fresh us, trav-eling through this wil-der-ness.
ev-er faith-ful, to the truth may we be found.
may we ev-er live with you in end-less day.

*Influenced by George Whitefield's preaching, John Fawcett joined the Baptist church, and served as minister in Wainsgate, England, for fifty-four years. Yielding to the persuasion of his parishioners, he declined invitations to move elsewhere. He wrote more than 160 hymns.*

Tune: SICILIAN MARINERS 8.7.8.7.8.7.
*Sicilian melody, 18th century*
The European Magazine and Review, *1792*

# Part in Peace

**78**

*Sarah Flower Adams (1805–1848); alt.*

1 Part in peace! the day be-fore us, prais-es sing for life and light.
2 Part in peace! with deep thanks-giv-ing, ren-dering as we home-ward tread,
3 Part in peace! our voic-es rais-ing, in God's pres-ence al-ways be.

Are the shad-ows length-ening o'er us? Bless God's care who guards the night.
Love and ser-vice to the liv-ing, gen-tle mem-ory to the dead.
This the wor-ship and the prais-ing, bring-ing peace to you and me.

*Daughter of an editor, Sarah Flower Adams gave up a successful
acting career in London to continue writing poems and hymns.
One of her best-known texts is "Nearer, my God, to thee."*

Tune: CHARLESTOWN 8.7.8.7.
*Southern Harmony, 1835*
*Harm. Carlton R. Young, 1964*

# May the Sending One Defend You

**79**

*Brian Wren, 1989; rev. 1993*

1 May the Send-ing One de-fend you, may the Seek-ing One a-mend you,
2 May the Giv-en One re-trieve you, may the Gift-ed One re-lieve you,
3 May the Bind-ing One u-nite you—may the One Be-loved in-vite you—

May the Keep-ing One be-friend you, in your glad-ness and in your griev-ing.
May the Giv-ing One re-ceive you, in your fall-ing and your re-stor-ing.
May the Lov-ing One de-light you— Three-in-One, joy in life un-end-ing.

*Brian Wren wrote this text during a visit with composer Mikkel
Thompson on Bainbridge Island, Washington. When he first
heard the tune, Wren said, "It cried out for a text, and suggested
the style of ancient Celtic blessings."*

Tune: ROLLINGBAY 8.8.8.9.
*Mikkel Thompson, 1989*

80 Savior, Again to Your Dear Name

Ps. 141:3–4a; 139:11–12; John 14:27

John Ellerton, 1866; alt.

1 Sav - ior, a - gain to your dear name we raise
2 Grant us your peace up - on our home-ward way;
3 Grant us your peace, as day turns in - to night;
4 Grant us your peace through - out our earth - ly life,

with one ac - cord our part - ing hymn of praise;
with you be - gan, with you shall end the day;
stay with us till the com - ing of the light;
our balm in sor - row, and our stay in strife;

We join to bless you ere our wor - ship cease,
Guard all the lips from sin, the hearts from shame,
Keep safe all those who call up - on your name,
Then, when your voice shall bid our con - flict cease,

then, in the si - lence, wait your word of peace.
that in this house have called up - on your name.
for dark and light to you are both the same.
call us, O God, to your e - ter - nal peace.

John Ellerton, a priest of the Church of England, wrote this hymn
for a choral association festival. The final stanza was sung at his
funeral. Ellerton edited and contributed to numerous hymnals.

Tune: ELLERS 10.10.10.10.
Edward J. Hopkins, 1869

# God Be with You

**81**

*Jeremiah E. Rankin, 1880; alt.*

1 God be with you till we meet a-gain; By good coun-sel guide, up-hold you,
2 God be with you till we meet a-gain; Wings of shel-ter safe-ly hide you,
3 God be with you till we meet a-gain; When life's per-ils thick con-found you,
4 God be with you till we meet a-gain; Keep love's ban-ner float-ing o'er you,

With a shep-herd's care en-fold you: God be with you till we meet a-gain.
Dai-ly man-na still pro-vide you: God be with you till we meet a-gain.
Put un-fail-ing arms a-round you: God be with you till we meet a-gain.
Smite death's threat-ening wave be-fore you: God be with you till we meet a-gain.

*Refrain*

Till we meet, till we meet, till we meet at Je-sus' feet;
till we meet, till we meet a-gain, till we meet,

till we meet, till we meet, God be with you till we meet a-gain.
till we meet, till we meet a-gain,

*Written during his last pastorate, at First Congregational Church in Washington, D.C., Jeremiah Rankin's hymn spread quickly throughout America and England by way of Moody and Sankey's revival meetings. Rankin later served as the seventh president of Howard University.*

Tune: GOD BE WITH YOU 9.8.8.9. with refrain
*William G. Tomer, 1880*

## 82      Go, My Children, with My Blessing

*Jaroslav J. Vajda, 1983, 1990; alt.*

1 Go, my chil-dren, with my bless-ing, nev - er a - lone;
2 Go, my chil-dren, fed and nour-ished, clos - er to me;

Wak - ing, sleep-ing, I am with you, you are my own;
Grow in love and love by serv-ing, joy - ful and free.

In my love's bap - tis-mal riv - er I have made you mine for-ev - er,
Here my Spir - it's pow-er filled you, here with ten - der com-fort stilled you;

Go, my chil-dren, with my bless-ing, you are my own.
Go, my chil-dren, fed and nour-ished, joy - ful and free.

*For marriage services, this stanza may be sung between stanzas 1 and 2 above.*

In this un-ion I have joined you hus-band and wife,
Now, my chil-dren, live to-geth-er as heirs of life:
Each the oth-er's glad-ness shar-ing,
each the oth-er's bur-dens bear-ing,
Now, my chil-dren, live to-geth-er as heirs of life.

*American hymnwriter and translator Jaroslav Vajda crafted this benediction text as though God were "dismissing the congregation after worship, while drawing together a review of the events that transpired during the service." The wedding stanza was a later addition.*

Tune: AR HYD Y NOS 8.4.8.4.8.8.8.4.
*Traditional Welsh melody*
*For another harmonization, see 425*

# I Sing as I Arise Today

*Attrib. to St. Patrick (372–466)*
*Transl. anon.*

1 I sing as I a - rise to - day! I call on my Cre - a - tor's might: The will of God to be my guide, The eye of God to be my sight,

2 The word of God to be my speech, The hand of God to be my stay, The shield of God to be my strength, The path of God to be my way.

3 Al - le - lu - ia, al - le - lu - ia, Al - le - lu - ia, al - le - lu - ia, Al - le - lu - ia, Al - le - lu - ia, al - le - lu - ia.

*The prayer known as "Breastplate" has been traditionally ascribed to St. Patrick, who is said to have brought Christianity to Ireland. It appears in many versions, including this anonymous morning hymn.*

Tune: SEED OF LIFE L.M.
*William P. Rowan, 1986*

# 84

# This Is the Day

Ps. 118:24; Luke 24:1–7; Acts 2:1–4

St. 1 paraphr. by Les Garrett, 1967; alt.
St. 2–3, traditional; alt.

1 This is the day, this is the day that our God has made, that our
2 This is the day, this is the day Je-sus rose a-gain, Je-sus
3 This is the day, this is the day when the Spir-it came, when the

God has made; we will re-joice, we will re-joice and be glad in it, and be
rose a-gain; we will re-joice, we will re-joice and be glad in it, and be
Spir-it came; we will re-joice, we will re-joice and be glad in it, and be

glad in it. This is the day that our God has made, we will re-joice and be
glad in it. This is the day Je-sus rose a-gain, we will re-joice and be
glad in it. This is the day when the Spir-it came, we will re-joice and be

glad in it; This is the day, this is the day that our God has made.
glad in it; This is the day, this is the day Je-sus rose a-gain.
glad in it; This is the day, this is the day when the Spir-it came.

*The first stanza of this hymn was written by Leslie Garrett, who was born in New Zealand and served as pastor of a church in western Australia. The other two stanzas are anonymous.*

Tune: THIS IS THE DAY Irr.
Les Garrett, 1967

# I Woke Up This Morning

*African-American traditional*

The spiritual lyrics:

1. I woke up this morn-ing with my mind  stayed on

2. Sing-ing and pray-ing with my mind  stayed on

Hal-le-lu - jah,

Je - sus,  Woke up this morn-ing with my mind  stayed on  Je - sus,

Je - sus,  Sing-ing and pray-ing with my mind  stayed on  Je - sus,

Woke up this morn-ing with my mind  stayed on  Je - sus,

Sing-ing and pray-ing with my mind  stayed on  Je - sus,

Hal-le-lu - jah,

Hal-le - lu,  hal-le - lu,  hal-le - lu - jah.

Hal-le,  hal-le - lu - jah.

*The spirituals that were passed down through the African-American oral tradition were not only enduring but also adaptable. During the civil rights movement of the 1960s this spiritual was sung as "Woke up this morning with my mind on freedom."*

Tune: WOKE UP THIS MORNING  Irr.
*African-American spiritual*
*Arr. Jeffrey Radford, 1993*

# 86 When Morning Gilds the Skies

Ps. 5:3; 59:16–17

Katholisches Gesangbuch, *1828*
*Transl. Edward Caswall, 1854; alt.*

1 When morn - ing gilds the skies, my heart a - wak-ing cries,
2 New strength comes night or day when from the heart we say,
3 Dis - cor - dant hu - man - kind, in this your con-cord find,
4 Be this, while life is mine, my can - ti - cle di - vine,

may Je - sus Christ be praised! A - like at work and prayer,
may Je - sus Christ be praised! Let sin and e - vil fear,
may Je - sus Christ be praised! Let all the earth a - round
may Je - sus Christ be praised! Be this the e - ter - nal song,

one pur-pose I de - clare: may Je - sus Christ be praised!
when this sweet chant they hear: may Je - sus Christ be praised!
ring joy-ous with the sound: may Je - sus Christ be praised!
through all the a - ges long: may Je - sus Christ be praised!

*This anonymous German Catholic hymn was translated to English by Edward Caswall, an Anglican—and later, Roman Catholic—priest. Among the scripture references is Psalm 5:3, "O God, in the morning you hear my voice...."*

Tune: LAUDES DOMINI 6.6.6.6.6.6.
*Joseph Barnby, 1868*

# O Splendor of God's Glory Bright

*Ambrose of Milan (c. 340–c. 397)*
*Transl. composite* The New Century Hymnal, *1993*

1 O splen-dor of God's glo-ry bright, from light e - ter - nal bring-ing light;
2 O true Sun, fi - ery star, let fall per - pet-ual bril - liance on us all;
3 O fash-ion us to do your will, our en-vious thoughts and ac - tions still;
4 Make ho - ly this and ev-ery day: let mod-es - ty greet morn-ing's ray;

O light of light, light's liv - ing spring, O day of days, il - lu - min-ing.
The Ho - ly Spir - it's ra - diant beam up - on our earth - ly sens - es stream.
In ev - ery chal - lenge may we find the grace which guides both heart and mind.
And faith-ful love, the noon-day light; and hope, the sun - set calm and bright.

*St. Ambrose is noted for introducing congregational and antiphonal singing to the Western church. This hymn is an example of an early "protest song" written to preserve orthodox views of the divinity of Christ, which were threatened by the rise of Arianism in the fourth century.*

Tune: SPLENDOR PATERNAE L.M.
*Sarum plainsong, mode 1*
*Alternate tune:* PUER NOBIS NASCITUR

# Pero Queda Cristo
## (My Soul Overflows with Praise)

*Alfredo Colom M., 1954; alt.*
*English version by Carolyn Jennings, 1993*

1 Por la ma-ña-na di-ri-gi-mos la a-la-ban-za a Dios que ha
2 Cuan-do la no-che se a-pro-xi-ma, te-ne-bro-sa, en e-le-
1 At ear-ly dawn we sing a song of ad-o-ra-tion to God who
2 When night ap-proach-es and would cause us to be fear-ful, we lift our

si-do nues-tra ú-ni-ca es-pe-ran-za. Por la ma-ña-na le in-vo-
var-le u-na o-ra-ción el ser se go-za; Sien-te su paz i-na-go-
is our on-ly hope and our sal-va-tion. At ear-ly dawn we raise our
souls to God in prayer with spir-it cheer-ful. God's sooth-ing peace and com-fort

ca-mos con el al-ma, le su-pli-ca-mos que nos dé su dul-ce
ta-ble, dul-ce y gra-ta por-que te-mo-res y an-sie-dad, Je-sús nos
long-ing in-vo-ca-tion; for God's sweet calm we beg in fer-vent sup-pli-
fill our hearts with glad-ness, and Christ con-tin-ues to dis-pel our fear and

cal-ma. Dios nos es-cu-cha, pues nos a-ma tan-to, y nos a-
qui-ta. Y nues-tro cán-ti-co se e-le-va al cie-lo cuan-do a la
ca-tion. God's heart is full of love and mer-cy for us, from all our
sad-ness. Though shad-ows thick-en ev-ery-where a-round us, the sav-ing

*Born in Guatemala in 1904, Alfredo Colom M. was an evangelist and prolific writer and composer of hymns, although he did not have any formal musical training.*

Tune: POR LA MAÑANA 13.13.D.11.11.D.
*Alfredo Colom M., 1954*

li - via de cual-quier que - bran - to. Nos da su ma - no po - de - ro - sa y
tie - rra ba - ja os - cu - ro ve - lo. El sol se o - cul - ta, pe - ro que - da
bro-ken-ness God will re - store us. Our God is strong and will for-sake us
love of God will still sur - round us. The sun has gone but Christ is ev - er

fuer - te, pa - ra li - brar-nos de la mis - ma muer - te.
Cris - to, que nues-tros o - jos en el sue - ño han vis - to.
nev - er, from death it - self God sets us free for - ev - er.
near us, with - in our dreams a con-stant hope to cheer us.

3 Bri-lla su lum-bre bien-he-
cho-ra so-bre to-dos;
su ma-no po-ne so-bre los
que es-tán en-fer-mos.
Nos for-ta-le-ce, nos a-lien-ta
con el sue-ño;
es nues-tro Dios, el Re-den-tor
y nues-tro due-ño.
En la ma-ña-na al
des-per-tar sen-ti-mos
que Dios in-va-de el
ser y el pen-sa-mien-to;
Ve-mos a Cris-to el
Re-den-tor a-ma-do,
pa-ra sal-var-nos, en la
cruz cla-va-do.

3 The light of God shines over us
while we are sleep-ing;
our health and life and ver-y breath
are in God's keep-ing.
Through-out the night we trust in God
to stay be-side us,
the ver-y God who owns our be-ing
and re-deems us.
And when we wak-en
in the light of morn-ing,
the face of Je-sus,
still our thoughts a-dorn-ing,
Re-minds us that God came
and died to save us,
and through the cross
the joy of heav-en gave us.

89

# Awake, Awake to Love and Work

*Geoffrey A. Studdert-Kennedy, 1921; alt.*

1 A - wake, a - wake to love and work! The lark is in the sky;
2 Come, let your voice be one with theirs, shout with their shout of praise;
3 To give and give, and give a - gain, as God's own grace is free;

the fields are wet with dia - mond dew; The worlds a - wake to cry
See how the gi - ant sun soars up, God's gift for all your days!
To spend your-self nor count the cost; To serve most glo - rious - ly

their prais-es to the Fount of Life; Christ Je - sus pass-es by.
So let the love of Je - sus come and set your soul a - blaze,
the God who gave all worlds that are, and all that are to be.

*Geoffrey Studdert-Kennedy was known in the United States as an eloquent preacher. He was a famed chaplain (Woodbine Willie) in World War I and later chaplain to the King of England. This hymn is part of a longer poem, "At a Harvest Festival."*

Tune: MORNING SONG 8.6.8.6.8.6.
Kentucky Harmony, *1816*
Harm. C. Winfred Douglas, *1940*

# Rising in Darkness

## 90

*Attrib. to Gregory the Great (540–604)*
*Transl.* The New Century Hymnal, *1993*

1 Ris - ing in dark - ness, let us all keep watch - ing, let psalms pro -
2 As we might prais - es bring a ho - ly rul - er, so may we
3 Grant, O blessed God - head, this our prayer at dawn - ing, that we re -

vide our source of med - i - ta - tion; And sing with all our strength;
sing, your heaven - ly courts to en - ter, There with the saints to join,
flect the good - ness of your pres - ence; Your beau - ty shines, O Light,

hymns of ad - o - ra - tion to our Cre - a - tor bring.
now and ev - er af - ter, bless - ings on us con - fer.
O Sun, O Ra - diance, glo - ry re - ech - o - ing.

"Nocte surgentes" has been attributed to Gregory the Great, who
was the fourth of the traditional Latin "Doctors of the Church"
(including Ambrose, Augustine, and Jerome). It was written for
use at Matins—a service held in the hours before dawn.

Tune: CHRISTE SANCTORUM 11.11.12.6.
*La Feillée's* Méthode de plain-chant, *1782*

# 91

# Wake, My Soul

Friedrich R. L. von Canitz (1654–1699)
Transl. Madeleine Forell Marshall, 1993

*Heb. 12:28; Ps. 30:4–5, 11–12*

1 Wake, my soul, with all things liv - ing, thanks be giv - ing to the
2 All your hope - ful plans con - fess - ing, ask for bless - ing on that
3 Cry for help, when griefs as - sail you, good friends fail you, life is
4 Af - ter one last night of weep - ing, one last sleep - ing, you shall

Source of life and day. Sun - light comes and gone con -
good which you would do; But if you should need cor -
hope - less, death ap - pears. One whose child knew deep af -
wake to pure de - light. You at last shall know per -

fu - sion, night's il - lu - sion, like the star - light, fades a - way.
rec - tion, ask di - rec - tion, pray for pur - pose, clear and new.
flic - tion, cru - ci - fix - ion, ev - er waits to dry your tears.
fec - tion, pure af - fec - tion, bathed in God's own morn - ing light.

*Baron Friedrich R. L. von Canitz was famous in his lifetime as a successful diplomat—educated, refined, and gracious to all people. He allowed none of his hymns or poetry to be published during his lifetime.*

Tune: HAYDN 8.4.7.8.4.7.
*Franz Joseph Haydn, 1791*

# Day Is Done

*James Quinn, S. J., 1969; alt.*

1 Day is done, but love un-fail-ing dwells ev - er here;
2 Dusk de-scends, but light un-end-ing shines through our night;
3 Eyes will close, but you un-sleep-ing watch by our side;

Shad - ows fall, but hope, pre-vail-ing, calms ev - ery fear.
You are with us, ev - er lend-ing new strength to sight:
Death may come, in love's safe-keep-ing still we a - bide.

God, our Mak - er, none for-sak - ing, take our hearts, of Love's own mak-ing,
One in love, your truth con-fess - ing, one in hope of heav - en's bless-ing,
God of love, all e - vil quell-ing, sin for-giv - ing, fear dis-pel-ling,

Watch our sleep-ing, guard our wak-ing, be al - ways near.
May we see, in love's pos-sess-ing, love's end - less light!
Stay with us, our hearts in-dwell-ing, this e - ven - tide.

*Father James Quinn, S. J., has taught at several colleges in Scotland and is the author of articles and books, as well as hymns. He is active in ecumenical affairs and is one of the most distinguished hymnwriters of the Roman Catholic Church.*

Tune: AR HYD Y NOS 8.4.8.4.8.8.8.4.
*Traditional Welsh melody*
*For another harmonization, see 425*

# 93 Christ, Mighty Savior

*Mozarabic hymn, 10th century*
*Transl. Alan McDougall, 1916; rev. by Anne LeCroy, 1982*

1 Christ, might-y Sav-ior, Light of all cre-a-tion, you make the
2 Now comes the day's end as the sun is set-ting: mir-ror of
3 There-fore we come now eve-ning rites to of-fer, joy-ful-ly
4 Give heed, we pray you, to our sup-pli-ca-tion: that you may
5 Though bod-ies slum-ber, hearts shall keep their vig-il, for-ev-er

day-time ra-diant with the sun-light And to the night give
day-break, pledge of res-ur-rec-tion; While in the heav-ens
chant-ing ho-ly hymns to praise you, With all cre-a-tion
grant us par-don for of-fens-es, Strength for our weak hearts,
rest-ing in the peace of Je-sus, In light or dark-ness

glit-ter-ing a-dorn-ment, stars in the heav-ens.
choirs of stars ap-pear-ing hal-low the night-fall.
join-ing hearts and voic-es sing-ing your glo-ry.
rest for ach-ing bod-ies, sooth-ing the wea-ry.
wor-ship-ing our Sav-ior now and for-ev-er.

*"Christe lux mundi," a nine-stanza evening hymn of the Mozarabic rite, is the basis for the present hymn. "Mozarabic" refers to a body of rites and hymnody of the Spanish church before 1085.*

Tune: MIGHTY SAVIOR 11.11.11.5.
*David Hurd, 1984*

# Now All the Woods Are Sleeping

*Paul Gerhardt, 1647*
*Transl.* The Lutheran Book of Worship, *1978; alt.*

1 Now all the woods are sleep - ing, through fields the shad - ows creep - ing, and cit - ies pause to rest; Let us, as night is fall - ing, on God our Mak - er call - ing, sing praise to God who loves us best.

2 The ra - diant sun has van - ished, its gold - en rays are ban - ished from deep - ening skies of night; But Christ, the sun of glad - ness, dis - pel - ling all our sad - ness, shines in our hearts with warm - est light.

3 Now all the heaven-ly splen - dor breaks forth in star - light ten - der from myr - iad worlds un - known; And we, this mar - vel see - ing, for - get our self - ish be - ing and know a beau - ty not our own.

*Though beset with many professional difficulties and personal losses, the German hymnwriter Paul Gerhardt wrote more than one hundred hymns, including some of the finest and most beloved of Christian hymnody. This hymn was a favorite of the poet himself.*

Tune: NUN RUHEN ALLE WÄLDER 7.7.6.7.7.8.
(INNSBRUCK)
*Heinrich Isaac (1455–1517)*

# 95 The Day You Gave Us, God, Is Ended

*John Ellerton, 1870; alt.*

1 The day you gave us, God, is end-ed, the light now
2 We thank you that your Church, un-sleep-ing while earth rolls
3 As o'er each con-ti-nent and is-land the dawn leads
4 The sun that bids us rest is wak-ing our fam-i-ly
5 So be it, God. Your reign shall nev-er, like earth's proud

fades at your re-quest; To you our morn-ing hymns as-
on-ward in-to light, Through all the world its watch is
on an-oth-er day, The voice of prayer is nev-er
mem-bers far a-way, Who, while we sleep, are glad-ly
em-pires, fade and fall. Your reign en-dures, and grows for-

cend-ed, your praise shall sanc-ti-fy our rest.
keep-ing, and rests not now by day or night.
si-lent, nor dies the strain of praise a-way.
tak-ing their turn to wor-ship you and pray.
ev-er till all your crea-tures heed your call.

John Ellerton, a priest of the Church of England, wrote many
hymns and edited numerous hymnals. This text and music have
been together since they appeared in an important book edited
by Arthur Sullivan.

Tune: ST. CLEMENT 9.8.9.8.
*Clement E. Scholefield, 1874*

# Sun of My Soul, O Savior Dear

*John Keble, 1820; alt.*

*Luke 24:29; John 15:4–5*

1 Sun of my soul, O Sav - ior dear, it is not
2 A - bide with me from morn till eve, for with - out
3 Watch by the sick; en - rich the poor with bless - ings
4 Come near and bless us when we wake, as through the

night if you are near; O may no earth - born
you I can - not live; A - bide with me when
from your bound - less store; Be ev - ery mourn - er's
world our way we take, Till through your love which

cloud a - rise to hide you from your ser - vant's eyes.
night is nigh, for with - out you I dare not die.
sleep to - night, like in - fants' slum - bers, pure and light.
knows no end we gain at last the peace of heaven.

*John Keble, known for his volume of poems* The Christian
Year, *helped to initiate the Oxford Movement in 1833 with his
sermon on "National Apostasy." This movement sought to
reinstate the liturgical practices of the medieval church.*

Tune: HURSLEY L.M.
*Adapt. from* GROSSER GOTT, WIR LOBEN DICH
*Katholisches Gesangbuch, Vienna, c. 1774*

# Salup na ang Adlaw
## (Now the Sun Is Setting)

*Elena G. Maquiso, 1970; alt.*
*Transl. Fé Nebres, 1993*

1 Sa - lup na ang ad - law, ka - ngit - ngit ka - u - ban, ang lang - gam mi - ba - tog, i - lang hig - da - a - nan, ta - pos na ang bu - hat, ma - ka - pa - hu - lay, pa - sa - la - ma - tan Ka, a - mong A - ma - han.

2 Un - say bi - nu - ha - tan, sa ad - law'ng na - ta - pos, a - mo bang na - tu - man, I - mong ka - bu - but - on, kon wa man u - ga - ling, pag - pa - say - lo - on, ug sa bag - ong ad - law, pag - tul - tu - lan Mo.

1 Now the sun is set - ting, night on us de - scend - ing; Birds to trees a - light - ing, to their nests re - turn - ing. Day - time toil is o - ver, res - pite comes at last! We will praise and thank you, gra - cious, lov - ing God.

2 For this day that's end - ed, have we done what's pleas - ing? Did we faith - ful - ly o - bey your will, O God? . . . Grant us your for - give - ness when we've strayed a - way. Grant us for to - mor - row guid - ance for the day.

*Filipino hymnwriter Elena G. Maquiso has composed nearly 400 hymns and other sacred choral pieces, many of which have appeared in international publications. Her tune Moning bears the nickname of a classmate at the Divinity School, Silliman University.*

Tune: MONING 6.6.6.6.6.6.5.6.5.
*Elena G. Maquiso, 1970*

3 Kon du-nay na-sa-kit,
   gu-mi-kan ka-na-mo,
bi-san wa hi-baw-i
   un-sa ang hi-nung-dan,
I-tu-got-ka-na-mo,
   pag-pa-sig-u-li,
I-mong ka-bu-but-on
   ma-tu-man ga-yud.

4 Pa-sa-la-ma-tan, Ka,
   sa ad-law'ng na-ta-pos,
ma-nga ka-say-pa-nan,
   I-mong hi-ka-lim-tan,
Ka-li-naw ha-ta-gi
   sa pag-pa-hu-lay,
mag-ma-ta sa bun-tag
   sa ka-bag-o-han.

3 If to some a-round us
   pain we may have giv-en,
Caused un-know-ing-ly some
   soul a wound-ed heart,
Grant to us your mer-cy,
   bring us back a-gain.
May your love em-brace us,
   may your will be done.

4 Thank you, lov-ing God, for
   this day that has end-ed;
For our man-y fail-ures
   grant your grace and par-don.
On our sleep be-stow-ing
   peace and calm-ness, too.
Strength-ened for to-mor-row,
   Prais-ing each new day.

# Now the Day Is Over

98

*Sabine Baring-Gould, 1865; alt.*

*Matt. 11:28*

1 Now the day is o - ver, night is draw-ing nigh,
2 Je - sus, give the wear - y calm and sweet re - pose;
3 Grant to lit - tle chil - dren vi - sions of your care;
4 Com-fort ev - ery suf - ferer watch-ing late in pain;
5 When the morn-ing wak - ens, then may we a - rise

Shad - ows of the eve - ning steal a - cross the sky.
With your ten - der bless - ing may our eye - lids close.
Keep our trav - els safe by sea and land and air.
Those who plan some e - vil from their sin re - strain.
Pure and fresh and sin - less in your ho - ly eyes.

*Sabine Baring-Gould, author of a prodigious amount of literature in a wide variety of fields, was a priest of the Church of England. He wrote this hymn for the children of Horbury Bridge, Yorkshire, during his ministry there.*

Tune: MERRIAL 6.5.6.5.
*Joseph Barnby, 1868*

# 99                 Abide with Me

*Luke 24:29; 1 Cor. 15:55*                                *Henry F. Lyte, 1847; alt.*

1 A - bide with me; fast falls the e - ven - tide;
2 Swift to its close ebbs out life's lit - tle day;
3 I need your pres - ence ev - ery pass - ing hour;
4 I fear no foe, with you at hand to bless;
5 Hold now your cross be - fore my clos - ing eyes;

The shad - ows deep - en, Lord, with me a - bide;
Earth's joys grow dim, its glo - ries pass a - way;
I need your grace to foil the tempt-er's power.
Ills have no weight and tears no bit - ter - ness;
Shine through the gloom and point me to the skies;

When oth - er help - ers fail, and com - forts flee,
Change and de - cay in all a - round I see;
Give me your love my guide and stay to be.
Where is death's sting? where, grave, your vic - to - ry?
Heaven's morn - ing breaks, and earth's vain shad - ows flee;

Help of the help - less, O a - bide with me.
O Christ who chang - es not, a - bide with me.
Through cloud and sun - shine, O a - bide with me.
I tri - umph still if you a - bide with me.
In life, in death, O Christ, a - bide with me.

*Following the final sermon of his career, Henry F. Lyte handed a copy of this recently written hymn to a relative. He died two months later. The tune by W. H. Monk has contributed greatly to the popularity of the hymn.*

Tune: EVENTIDE 10.10.10.10.
*William H. Monk, 1861*

# All Praise Be Yours, My God, This Night

*St. 1–3, Thomas Ken, 1692; alt.*
*St. 4, Carl P. Daw, Jr., 1992*

1 All praise be yours, my God, this night, for all the bless-ings
2 For - give me, by Christ's vic - tory won, the ill that I this
3 O let me on your love re - pose, let wel - come sleep my
4 Praise God who gives all bless-ings birth; praise God all crea - tures

of the light; Keep me, kind Mak - er of all things,
day have done, That from the fear of sin set free,
eye - lids close, Sleep from whose balm new strength I take
on the earth; Praise God, who makes, sus - tains, sets free:

be - neath the shel - ter of your wings.
I, ere I sleep, at peace may be.
to serve my God when I a - wake.
one ho - ly God in per - sons three.

*Thomas Ken was a priest at Winchester Cathedral and College
and later ministered to the English royal family. Tallis' "Canon"
was one of the nine tunes composed for a book of metrical
psalms by Matthew Parker. The new fourth stanza was written
for The New Century Hymnal.*

Tune: TALLIS' CANON L.M.
*Thomas Tallis, c. 1567*

# 101
# Comfort, Comfort O My People

*Isa. 40:1–8*

*Johannes Olearius, 1671*
*Transl. Catherine Winkworth, 1863; alt.*

1 "Com - fort, com-fort O my peo - ple, tell of peace," thus says our God;
2 For the her - ald's voice is call - ing in the des - ert far and near,
3 Straight shall be what long was crook-ed, and the rough - er pla - ces plain!

Com-fort those whose hearts are shroud-ed, mourn-ing un - der sor-row's load.
Bid-ding us to make re - pen - tance since the realm of God is here.
Let your hearts be true and hum - ble, for Mes - si - ah's ho - ly reign.

Speak un - to Je - ru - sa - lem of the peace that waits for them;
Oh, that warn - ing cry o - bey! Now pre-pare for God a way;
For God's glo - ry ev - er-more shall be known o'er all the world;

Tell them that their sins I cov - er, and their war-fare now is o - ver.
Let the val - leys rise in meet-ing and the hills bow down in greet-ing.
And all flesh shall see the to - ken that God's word is nev - er bro - ken.

*Written for John the Baptist's Day, June 24, this hymn clearly*
*reflects the Isaiah text. Johannes Olearius, a Lutheran pastor,*
*held a faculty appointment at Wittenberg University as well as*
*church administration positions in his region.*

Tune: PSALM 42 8.7.8.7.7.7.8.8.
(FREU DICH SEHR)
Trente quatre Pseaumes, *Geneva, 1551*

# O How Shall I Receive You

*Paul Gerhardt, 1653*
*Transl. Catherine Winkworth, 1863, and others; alt.*

1 O how shall I re - ceive you, how meet you on your way,
2 Love caused your in - car - na - tion; love brought you un - to me;
3 You come, O Christ, with glad - ness, in mer - cy and good - will,

blessed hope of ev - ery peo - ple, my soul's de - light and stay?
your thirst for my sal - va - tion pro - cured my lib - er - ty.
to bring an end to sad - ness and bid our fears be still.

O Je - sus, Je - sus, give me now by your own pure light,
O love be - yond all tell - ing, that led you to em - brace
In pa - tient ex - pec - ta - tion we live for that great day

to know what-e'er is pleas - ing and wel - come in your sight.
in love, all love ex - cel - ling, our lost and fall - en race.
when a re - newed cre - a - tion your glo - ry shall dis - play.

*As a German Lutheran pastor serving during the Thirty Years'*
*War, Paul Gerhardt's trials were legion. In the midst of it all, he*
*composed more than a hundred hymns, among them some of the*
*finest and most beloved in Christian hymnody.*

Tune: ST. THEODULPH 7.6.7.6.D.
(VALET WILL ICH DIR GEBEN)
*Melchior Teschner, 1615*

# 103 Watcher, Tell Us of the Night

*Isa. 21:11–12*

*John Bowring, 1825; alt.*

1 Watch-er, tell us of the night, what its signs of prom-ise are.
2 Watch-er, tell us of the night, high-er yet that star as-cends.
3 Watch-er, tell us of the night, for the morn-ing seems to dawn.

Trav - eler, O a won-drous sight! See that glo-ry - beam-ing star!
Trav - eler, bless-ed - ness and light, peace and truth its course por - tends.
Trav - eler, shad-ows take their flight, doubt and ter-ror are with-drawn.

Watch-er, does its beau - teous ray news of joy or hope fore - tell?
Watch-er, will its beams a - lone gild the spot that gave them birth?
Watch-er, you may go your way; has-ten to your qui - et home.

Trav -eler, yes; it brings the day, prom - ised day of Is - ra - el!
Trav -eler, a - ges are its own; see, it bursts o'er all the earth!
Trav -eler, I re - joice to-day, for Em - man - u - el has come!

*This hymn, a dialogue between watcher and traveler, was
suggested by the dialogue in Isaiah 21:11–12. John Bowring was
a gifted linguist, worker for political and social reform, member
of Parliament, and governor of Hong Kong.*

Tune: ABERYSTWYTH 7.7.7.7.D.
*Joseph Parry, 1879*
*Alternate tune: ST. GEORGE'S WINDSOR*

# We Hail You God's Anointed

*James Montgomery, 1821; alt.*

*Ps. 72*

1 We hail you God's a - noint - ed, the long-a - wait - ed One!
2 You shall come down like show - ers up - on the fruit - ful earth;
3 The wise shall bow be - fore you and gold and in - cense bring;
4 O'er ev - ery foe vic - to - rious, you on your throne shall rest;

Hail in the time ap - point - ed, your reign on earth be - gun!
and joy and hope, like flow - ers, spring in your path to birth.
all na - tions shall a - dore you, and praise all peo-ples sing;
from age to age more glo - rious, all - bless-ing and all - blessed:

You come to break op - pres - sion, to set the cap-tive free;
Be - fore you on the moun - tains shall peace, the her - ald, go,
To you shall prayer un - ceas - ing and dai - ly vows be said,
The tide of time shall nev - er your cov - e - nant re - move;

to take a - way trans - gres - sion, and rule in eq - ui - ty.
and righ - teous-ness, in foun - tains, from hill to val - ley flow.
your realm is still in - creas - ing, with you, O Christ, as head.
your name shall stand for - ev - er, your change-less name of Love.

*Written as a Christmas hymn for the Moravian settlement in Yorkshire, England, this hymn has enjoyed widespread popularity from the beginning. It is characteristic of Montgomery's deep faith and passion for social justice.*

Tune: ELLACOMBE C.M.D.
Gesangbuch der herzoglichen Wirtembergischen katholischen Hofkapelle, *1784*

# Gentle Joseph, Joseph Dear

*Matt. 1:18–25*

*German carol, 15th century*
*Paraphr. by Carol Birkland, 1993*

*The German carol on which this is based appears in a mystery play, c. 1500. It is one of a group of related carols that also includes "In dulci jubilo"—"Good Christian friends, rejoice."*

Tune: JOSEPH LIEBER, JOSEPH MEIN 7.8.8.11.
*German carol, 15th century*
*Harm.* The New Century Hymnal, *1993*

# My Heart Sings Out with Joyful Praise

*Ruth Duck, 1985*

*Luke 1:46–55*

1 My heart sings out with joy-ful praise to God who rais-es me,
2 The arm of God is strong and just to scat-ter all the proud.
3 The prom-ise made in a-ges past at last has come to be,

Who came to me when I was low and changed my des-ti-ny.
The ty-rants tum-ble from their thrones and van-ish like a cloud.
for God has come in power to save, to set all peo-ple free.

The Ho-ly One, the Liv-ing God, is al-ways full of grace
The hun-gry all are sat-is-fied; the rich are sent a-way.
Re-mem-bering those who wait to see sal-va-tion's dawn-ing day,

To those who seek their Mak-er's will in ev-ery time and place.
The poor of earth who suf-fer long will wel-come God's new day.
Our Sav-ior comes to all who weep to wipe their tears a-way.

*The "Magnificat," a traditional text for evening prayer as well as Advent, is paraphrased here by Ruth Duck. She developed it to make the ancient rite of evening prayer available to her own worshipping communities.*

Tune: MARIAS LOVSÅNG C.M.D.
*Swedish folk melody*
*Alternate tunes: ELLACOMBE, TALLIS' THIRD*

# 107 Awake! Awake, and Greet the New Morn

*Isa. 12:6; 26:9; 35:6; Matt. 11:5*      *Marty Haugen, 1983; rev. 1993*

1 A - wake! a - wake, and greet the new morn, for
2 To us, to all in sor - row and fear, Em -
3 In deep - est night Christ's com - ing shall be, when
4 Re - joice, re - joice, take heart in the night, though

an - gels her - ald its dawn - ing, sing out your joy, for
man - u - el comes a - sing - ing, whose hum - ble song is
all the world is de - spair - ing, as morn - ing light so
cold the win - ter and cheer-less, the ris - ing sun shall

Je - sus is born, be - hold! the Child of our long - ing.
qui - et and near, yet fills the earth with its ring - ing.
qui - et and free, so warm and gen - tle and car - ing.
crown you with light, be strong and lov - ing and fear - less;

*Liturgical composer Marty Haugen wrote both words and music for this Advent hymn with the twofold aim of providing an easy congregational chorale and utilizing the images of the Isaiah passages.*

Tune: REJOICE, REJOICE 9.8.9.8.8.7.8.9.
*Marty Haugen, 1983*

# My Heart Sings Out with Joyful Praise

**106**

*Ruth Duck, 1985*

*Luke 1:46–55*

1 My heart sings out with joy - ful praise to God who rais - es me,
2 The arm of God is strong and just to scat - ter all the proud.
3 The prom - ise made in a - ges past at last has come to be,

Who came to me when I was low and changed my des - ti - ny.
The ty - rants tum - ble from their thrones and van - ish like a cloud.
for God has come in power to save, to set all peo - ple free.

The Ho - ly One, the Liv - ing God, is al - ways full of grace
The hun - gry all are sat - is - fied; the rich are sent a - way.
Re - mem-bering those who wait to see sal - va - tion's dawn-ing day,

To those who seek their Mak-er's will in ev - ery time and place.
The poor of earth who suf - fer long will wel-come God's new day.
Our Sav - ior comes to all who weep to wipe their tears a - way.

*The "Magnificat," a traditional text for evening prayer as well as Advent, is paraphrased here by Ruth Duck. She developed it to make the ancient rite of evening prayer available to her own worshipping communities.*

Tune: MARIAS LOVSÅNG C.M.D.
*Swedish folk melody*
*Alternate tunes: ELLACOMBE, TALLIS' THIRD*

# 107 Awake! Awake, and Greet the New Morn

*Isa. 12:6; 26:9; 35:6; Matt. 11:5*                                    *Marty Haugen, 1983; rev. 1993*

1 A - wake! a - wake, and greet the new morn, for
2 To us, to all in sor - row and fear, Em -
3 In deep - est night Christ's com - ing shall be, when
4 Re - joice, re - joice, take heart in the night, though

an - gels her - ald its dawn - ing, sing out your joy, for
man - u - el comes a - sing - ing, whose hum - ble song is
all the world is de - spair - ing, as morn - ing light so
cold the win - ter and cheer - less, the ris - ing sun shall

Je - sus is born, be - hold! the Child of our long - ing.
qui - et and near, yet fills the earth with its ring - ing.
qui - et and free, so warm and gen - tle and car - ing.
crown you with light, be strong and lov - ing and fear - less;

*Liturgical composer Marty Haugen wrote both words and music for this Advent hymn with the twofold aim of providing an easy congregational chorale and utilizing the images of the Isaiah passages.*

Tune: REJOICE, REJOICE 9.8.9.8.8.7.8.9.
*Marty Haugen, 1983*

Come as a ba - by weak and poor, to bring all hearts to -
Mu - sic to heal the bro - ken soul and hymns of lov - ing
One with-out voice breaks forth in song, a lame one leaps in
Love be our song and love our prayer, and love, our end - less

geth - er, to o - pen wide the heaven - ly door, and
kind - ness, the thun - der of the an - thems roll to
won - der, the weak are raised a - bove the strong, and
sto - ry, may God fill ev - ery day we share, and

lives now in-side us for ev - er.
shat - ter all hate and in - jus - tice.
weap-ons are bro-ken a - sun - der.
bring us at last in - to glo - ry.

# 108     Isaiah the Prophet Has Written of Old

Isa. 11:6–9; 55:10–13

*Joy F. Patterson, 1981; rev. 1993*

1 I - sa - iah the proph-et has
2 The moun-tains and hills shall break
3 Yet na - tions still prey on the
4 God, bring to fru - i - tion your

writ-ten of old how God's new cre - a - tion shall come. In - stead of the
forth in - to song, the peo - ples be led forth in peace; The earth shall be
meek of the world, and con - flict turns par-ent from child. Your peo - ple de -
will for the earth, that no one shall hurt or de - stroy, That wis - dom and

thorn tree, the fir tree shall grow; the wolf shall lie down with the
filled with the knowl-edge of God as the wa - ters cov - er the
spoil all the sweet-ness of earth; the brier and the thorn tree grow
jus - tice shall reign in the land and your peo - ple shall go forth in

*Joy Patterson, of Wausau, Wisconsin, served on the editorial
committee for The Presbyterian Hymnal, 1990. This text was one
of seven winning hymns published in New Hymns for Children
by Choristers Guild and The Hymn Society of America.*

Tune: JUDAS AND MARY Irr.
*Sydney Carter, 1964*

lamb, the lamb, the wolf shall lie down with the lamb.
sea, the sea, as the wa - ters cov - er the sea.
wild, grow wild, the brier and the thorn tree grow wild.
joy, in joy, your peo - ple shall go forth in joy.

# With Joy Draw Water

**109**

*Anne McKinstry, 1986, 1993*

*Isa. 11:1–10; 12:2–6*

1 With joy draw wa - ter from the spring; sal - va - tion's liv - ing well.
2 A shoot has sprung from Jes - se's tree; of God the cho - sen One.
3 With love the poor will be re - ceived; the proud will turn a - side;
4 The wolf shall lie down with the lamb; the calf and li - on play.
5 With joy draw wa - ter from the spring; sal - va - tion's liv - ing well.

The Ho - ly One is in your midst; glad prais - es sing and tell!
A branch of knowl-edge and of truth; a gift of love has come!
And faith - ful - ness will be a path, and righ-teous-ness the guide!
God's peace shall dwell with - in the land; a child shall show the way!
The Ho - ly One is in your midst; glad prais - es sing and tell!

*This text combines images from two Advent readings from the book of Isaiah, including the passage anticipating the reign of peace. The author, Anne McKinstry, has served as a writer-in-residence at Otis United Church of Christ in Massachusetts.*

Tune: ST. COLUMBA altered to 8.6.8.6.
*Irish traditional melody*
*Harm. Charles V. Stanford, 1906*

# 110       Now Bless the God of Israel

*Luke 1:68–79; Ps. 18:1–3; Isa. 9:2–7*       *Ruth Duck, 1985*

1 Now bless the God of Is - ra - el, who comes in love and power,
2 Re - mem-ber-ing the cov - e - nant, God res - cues us from fear,
3 In ten - der mer-cy, God will send the day - spring from on high,

who rais - es from the roy - al house de - liv - erance in this hour.
that we might serve in hol - i - ness and peace from year to year;
our ris - ing sun, the light of life for those who sit and sigh.

Through ho - ly proph-ets God has sworn to free us from a - larm,
And you, my child, shall go be - fore to preach, to proph-e - sy,
God comes to guide our way to peace, that death shall reign no more.

to save us from the heav-y hand of all who wish us harm.
that all may know the ten - der love, the grace of God most high.
Sing prais-es to the Ho - ly One! O wor - ship and a - dore!

*This text by United Church of Christ clergywoman Ruth Duck*
*is a paraphrase of the "Benedictus," which is often sung at*
*morning prayer. She came to appreciate daily prayer while*
*studying at the University of Notre Dame.*

Tune: FOREST GREEN C.M.D.
*Traditional English melody*
*Harm. Ralph Vaughan Williams, 1906*

# O Loving Founder of the Stars

*Latin, anon., 9th century; transl.* The New Century Hymnal, *1993*

Luke 2:1–7; John 1:1–5; Phil. 2:5–11

1 O lov - ing found - er of the stars, to all of faith light
2 Who griev - ing at the cry of pain— the an - guish of our
3 As Sav - ior from the heav - ens forth, when earth draws near its
4 O Christ, who braved earth's deep - est pain, all kneel - ing low your
5 Your judg - ment of this world draws near, O Ho - ly One, un -

with - out end, O Christ, re - deem - er of us all,
dy - ing race— Did death it - self for us de - stroy,
fi - nal hour, You from the vir - gin moth - er's womb
name a - dore; All heaven and earth your name con - fess
til that day pro - tect us all your faith - ful ones

to earn - est prayers your mer - cy lend.
and guilt as - sume through lov - ing grace:
ap - peared in love's re - deem - ing power.
and praise you, Sov - ereign, ev - er - more.
a - gainst the Faith - less One, we pray.

*The original Latin hymn, dating from the early Middle Ages, was sung at Vespers (sunset) during Advent. The tune referred to in old service books as the "Ambrosian Advent Hymn" is thought to be one of the earliest church tunes.*

Tune: CONDITOR ALME L.M.
*ancient Sarum plainsong, mode IV*

# 112 Keep Awake, Be Always Ready

*Isa. 2:1–5; 60:1–3; 64:1–9; Matt. 24:36–44;*
*Rom. 13:11–14; 1 Cor. 1:3–9; 1 Thess. 3:9–13*

*Arthur G. Clyde, 1993*

1 Keep a-wake, be al-ways rea - dy, God's time ap - proach-es
2 Rise and shine for One is com - ing whose love will quench all

sure and stea - dy, God's strength will keep your heart from blame.
na - ture's thirst - ing to be made whole for - ev - er more.

Clouds, the Spir - it's light con - ceal - ing, dis - perse, God's pur - est
On that day to end all weep - ing, death's swords trans - formed to

light re - veal - ing; cre - a - tion will its Sov-ereign name. Dry
tools of reap - ing, the God of might will mer - cy pour. In -

*This new text, written to reflect the readings for the first*
*Sunday in Advent, is set to a traditional tune of the season*
*by sixteenth-century Lutheran pastor Philipp Nicolai.*

Tune: WACHET AUF 8.9.8.8.9.8.6.6.4.8.8.
*Philipp Nicolai, 1599*
*Harm. J. S. Bach, 1731*

branch - es burst forth green, God's ad - vent signs are seen: Hal - le - lu - jah!
car - nate, God ap - pears em - brac - ing all our tears: Hal - le - lu - jah!

Christ's judg - ment won, God's will be done; God's new do - min - ion thus be - gun.
God's maj - es - ty e - ter - nal - ly re - vealed to set the cos - mos free.

## Little Bethlehem of Judah 113

*Calvin Seerveld, 1986; alt.*

*Mic. 5:2–4*

Unison

1 Lit - tle Beth - le - hem of Ju - dah, what good news you bear!
2 Though your peo - ple suf - fer trou - ble, wait - ing for the child,
3 Long - a - wait - ed comes the Shep-herd who will rule the earth;

Out of you will come the An - cient One as heir.
Soon all strife and ha - tred shall be rec - on - ciled.
God made low has come to serve in hu - man birth.

*Calvin Seerveld has held positions as professor of English
literature and philosophy and, since 1972, has been senior
member in the Institute for Christian Studies in Toronto. He
was on the committee appointed to revise the* Psalter Hymnal.

Tune: WESTRIDGE 8.5.8.3.
*Martin F. Shaw, 1929*

# 114 Return, My People

Joel 2:12–23; Isa. 11:1–12

James F. D. Martin, 1981; alt.

1 Return, my people, Israel, with penitential tear;
2 Fear not, beloved, hearken now: our God has done great things!
3 Then to the faithful of the earth the call of God rings clear:

just as the prophet did foretell the advent of Emmanuel,
Your vindication shall pour down like rain upon the barren ground,
"Return, my people, claim your worth, preparing for your Savior's birth;

God's reign on earth is near! God's reign on earth is near!
glad tidings to you bring, glad tidings to you bring.
my reign on earth is near. My reign on earth is near."

*This new Advent text by United Church of Christ minister James Martin is set to a tune by British composer Charles Hubert Hastings Parry, who is also known for his symphonies, organ works, and cantatas.*

Tune: REPTON 8.6.8.8.6.6.
C. Hubert H. Parry, 1888
Alternate tune: REST

# The Baptist Shouts on Jordan's Shore    115

*Charles Coffin, 1736*
*Transl. The New Century Hymnal, 1993*

*John 1:6–8, 19–28; Mark 1:1–8;*
*Luke 3:2–6, 15–18; Matt. 3:1–6, 11–12*

1 The Baptist shouts on Jordan's shore, the
2 The earth and sky and sea now feel that
3 Clean up your hearts, lay down the way, for
4 Through you, O Je - sus, you a - lone sal -

earth shakes with the might - y roar, A - wake, let laz - y
which their Au - thor will re - veal: The Child now leap - ing
God ap - proach-es day by day; Pre - pare for such a
va - tion, so - lace, strength are known; With - out your love we

sleep now flee: be - hold, the voice of proph - e - cy!
in the womb as God does hu - man form as - sume.
wor - thy heir, for such a guest your house pre - pare.
fade like grass, like wilt - ed flowers our lives will pass.

5 Your hands ex-tend, our pain em-brace,
   lift up the pros-trate, show your face;
Though we in part your beau-ty know,
   O blos-som forth, your splen-dor show.

6 O One who comes to set us free,
   O Child, to you our song will be,
With Fa-ther, Spir-it moth-er-ing,
   to you shall praise for-ev-er ring!

*Charles Coffin, distinguished scholar and Latin author,*
*was rector of the University of Paris for a time. The hymn,*
*appearing here in a new translation, is from a breviary ordered*
*by the archbishop of Paris to replace ancient Latin hymns with*
*newer ones.*

Tune: WINCHESTER NEW L.M.
Musikalisches Handbuch, *Hamburg, 1690*

# 116

# O Come, O Come, Emmanuel

*Isa. 11:1–12; Exod. 19–20:17*

*Psalteriolum Cantionum Catholicarum, 1710*
*Based on ancient antiphons from Advent Vespers*
*Transl. John Mason Neale, 1851, and others; alt.*
*St. 2, 7, transl. Henry Sloane Coffin, 1916; alt.*

Unison

1 O come, O come, Em - man - u - el, and
2 O come, O Wis - dom from on high, and
3 O come, O come, O A - do - nai, who
4 O come, O shoot of Jes - se, free your
5 O come, O Key of Da - vid, come, and

ran - som cap - tive Is - ra - el That mourns in lone - ly
or - der all things far and nigh; To us the path of
came to all on Si - nai high, And from its peak a
own from Sa - tan's tyr - an - ny, From depths of hell your
o - pen wide your heaven - ly home; Make safe the path to

ex - ile here, un - til the Child of God ap - pear.
knowl - edge show, and help us in that way to go.
sin - gle law pro - claimed in maj - es - ty and awe.
peo - ple save, and give them vic - tory o'er the grave.
end - less day, to hell's de - struc - tion close the way.

*In the medieval Western church, seven "Great O" antiphons,*
*the basis for this hymn, were sung consecutively on the*
*seven days before Christmas, ending with what appears*
*above as the first stanza.*

Tune: VENI EMMANUEL L.M. with refrain
*Melody from a 15th-century French "Processional"*
*Arr. Thomas Helmore, 1854*

Re-joice! Re-joice! Em-man - u-el shall come to you, O Is - ra-el!

6 O come, O Day-spring, come and cheer
  our spir-its by your ad-vent here;
Love stir with-in the womb of night,
and death's own shad-ows put to flight.
*(Refrain)*

7 O come, De-sire of Na-tions, bind
  all peo-ples in one heart and mind;
Make en-vy, strife, and quar-rels cease;
fill the whole world with heav-en's peace.
*(Refrain)*

# Lift Up Your Heads, O Mighty Gates  117

*Georg Weissel, 1641*
*Transl. Catherine Winkworth, 1865; alt.*

*Ps. 24:7–10*

1 Lift up your heads, O might-y gates; be-hold the glo - rious Rul - er waits!
2 Fling wide the por - tals of your heart; make it a tem - ple, set a - part
3 Re - deem - er, come! I o - pen wide my heart to you; here, Christ, a - bide!
4 So come, my Sov-ereign; en - ter in! Let new and no - bler life be - gin;

The Sov-ereign One is draw - ing near; the Sav - ior of the world is here.
From earth-ly use for heaven's em - ploy, a - dorned with prayer and love and joy.
Let me your in-ner pres - ence feel; your grace and love in me re - veal.
Your Ho - ly Spir-it guide us on, un - til the glo - rious crown be won.

*Georg Weissel, a Lutheran pastor, served a church in*
*Königsberg, East Prussia. He wrote some twenty hymns,*
*most of them for the great festivals of the church year.*
*This hymn was written for Advent.*

Tune: TRURO L.M.
*Thomas Williams'* Psalmodia Evangelica, *1789*

# 118 Of the Parent's Heart Begotten

*Marcus Aurelius Clemens Prudentius (348–413)*
*Transl.* The New Century Hymnal, *1993*

*Col. 1:15–17; John 1:1–5, 14*

1 Of the Par - ent's heart be - got - ten when the worlds were yet to be,
2 By this Word was all cre - a - ted, by this Word were all things done:
3 Bless - ed dawn - ing of sal - va - tion as the Word is breathed in grace
4 Now be - hold the One whom proph - ets have fore - told for a - ges long
5 Depths and heights break forth in sing - ing, an - gels, saints make mel - o - dy,

One there was with no be - gin - ning, One who is e - ter - nal - ly—
Land and air and deep-est o - cean, har - mo - ny of three in one,
In - to earth - ly flesh re - ceiv - ing— God in - car - nate tak - ing place;
On the faith-ful page of scrip - ture, seers and sag - es in their song;
All do - min - ions, ev - ery power sing, make new psalms of ec - sta - sy,

Source and End - ing of all things that have been,
And all grow - ing in the lu - mi - nance
Now the light of God re - vealed . . . . . . . .
Now the Prom - ised One shines forth! . . . . . . . . .
Let no heart re - frain from prais - ing God,

and all things that are to be, for - ev - er and for - ev - er.
shed forth from the moon and sun, for - ev - er and for - ev - er.
through the Child of hu - man face, for - ev - er and for - ev - er.
Let all earth its praise pro-long for - ev - er and for - ev - er.
cel - e - brate in har - mo - ny, for - ev - er and for - ev - er.

*"Corde natus ex parentis" is taken from twelve poems for the daily hours by Clemens Prudentius, who gave up a court office to enter a monastery, where he wrote a number of important and influential works.*

Tune: DIVINUM MYSTERIUM 8.7.8.7.8.7.7.
*Adapt. from a medieval plainsong in Petri's* Piae Cantiones, *1582 Harm. C. Winfred Douglas, 1940*

# My Soul Gives Glory to My God 119

*Miriam Therese Winter, 1987*

*Luke 1:46b–55; 1 Sam. 2:1–10*

1 My soul gives glo - ry to my God. My heart pours out its praise.
2 My God has done great things for me: yes, ho - ly is God's name.
3 From age to age, to all who fear, such mer - cy love im - parts,
4 Love casts the might-y from their thrones, pro-motes the in - se - cure,
5 Praise God, whose lov - ing cov - e - nant sup-ports those in dis - tress,

God lift - ed up my low - li - ness in man - y mar-vel-ous ways.
All peo - ple will de - clare me blessed, and bless - ings they shall claim.
dis - pens-ing jus-tice far and near, dis - miss - ing self - ish hearts.
leaves hun - gry spir-its sat - is - fied, the rich seem sud-den-ly poor.
re - mem-ber-ing past prom-is - es with pres - ent faith - ful - ness.

*This New Testament canticle, with its mosaic of liberation motifs that proclaim the justice of God, is known as the "Magnificat," the opening word of its Latin translation.*

Tune: MORNING SONG C.M.
*Melody from Kentucky Harmony, 1816 Harm. C. Winfred Douglas, 1940*

# 120 There's a Voice in the Wilderness

Isa. 40:3–11; Ps. 103:15–17

*J. Lewis Milligan, 1925; alt.*

1 There's a voice in the wil-der-ness cry-ing, a
2 O Zi-on, who of-fers good tid-ings, to the
3 But the word of our God is for-ev-er, our De-

call from the ways un-trod: Pre-pare in the des-ert a
height of the moun-tains dare! Lift your voice to the cit-ies of
fend-er's will is strong; God stands in the midst of

high-way, a high-way for our God! The
Ju-dah: "Be-hold your God!" de-clare. Like the
na-tions, to ren-der right the wrong. Then

*Before moving to Canada, J. Lewis Milligan was a successful British journalist and poet. This text was written in 1925 to celebrate the union of three churches into The United Church of Canada, a body he served as public relations director.*

Tune: ASCENSION Irr.
*H. Hugh Bancroft, 1938*

val - leys shall be ex - alt - ed, the loft - y hills brought
flowers of the field we per - ish, our hu - man works de -
God shall be as a shep-herd, the lambs gath-ered to God's

low: make straight all the crook - ed pla - ces
cay, the power and pomp of na - tions
breast; and pas - tures of peace shall greet them,

where Em - man - u - el may go!
shall pass like a dream a - way.
to give to the wea - ry rest.

# 121

# Toda la Tierra
## (All Earth Is Waiting)

*Isa. 40:3–5; Luke 3:4–6; Matt. 1:23*

*Alberto Taulé, 1972; alt.*
*Transl. Gertrude C. Suppe, 1987; alt.*

1 To - da la tie - rra es - pe - ra al Sal - va - dor y el sur - co a - bier - to, la
2 Di - ce el pro - fe - ta al pue - blo de Is - ra - el: "De ma - dre vir - gen ya
1 All earth is wait - ing to see the Prom - ised One, and o - pen fur - rows, the
2 Thus says the proph - et to those of Is - ra - el, "A vir - gin moth - er will

o - bra del Crea - dor; es el mun - do que lu - cha por la li - ber - tad,
vie - ne Em - ma - nuel," se - rá "Dios con no - so - tros," se - mi - lla se - rá,
sow - ing of our God. All the world, bound and strug - gling, seeks true lib - er - ty;
bear Em - man - u - el": One whose name is "God with us," our Sav - ior shall be,

re - cla - ma jus - ti - cia y bus - ca la ver - dad. (4 dar - nos li - ber - tad.)
con él la es - pe - ran - za al mun - do vol - ve - rá.
it cries out for jus - tice and search - es for the truth. (4 brings us lib - er - ty.)
through whom hope will blos - som once more with - in our hearts.

*Alberto Taulé, composer and author of this new Advent hymn, has served as a parish priest and music editor for the Roman Catholic Church in Spain. This hymn was his first to be published in the United States.*

Tune: TAULE 11.11.12.12.
*Alberto Taulé, 1972*
*Harm. Skinner Chávez-Melo, 1988*

3 Mon-tes y va-lles
   ha-brá que pre-pa-rar;
   nue-vos ca-mi-nos
   te-ne-mos que tra-zar.
   Dios es-tá ya muy cer-ca,
   ve-nid-lo a en-con-trar,
   y to-das las puer-tas
   a-brid de par en par.

4 En un pe-se-bre
   Je-sús a-pa-re-ció,
   pe-ro en el mun-do
   es-tá pre-sen-te hoy.
   Vi-ve en-tre la gen-te,
   con e-llas es-tá;
   y vuel-ve de nue-vo
   a dar-nos li-ber-tad.

3 Moun-tains and val-leys will
   have to be made plain;
   o-pen new high-ways,
   new high-ways for our God,
   Who is now com-ing closer,
   so come all and see,
   and o-pen the door-ways
   as wide as wide can be.

4 In low-ly sta-ble
   the Prom-ised One ap-peared,
   yet feel that pres-ence
   through-out the earth to-day,
   For Christ lives in all Chris-tians
   and is with us now;
   a-gain, on ar-riv-ing
   Christ brings us lib-er-ty.

# Come, O Long-Expected Jesus 122

*Charles Wesley, 1744; alt.*

1 Come, O long - ex - pect-ed Je - sus, born to set all peo-ple free;
2 Is - rael's strength and con - so - la - tion, hope to all the earth im - part;
3 Born all peo - ple to de - liv - er, born a child, you came to reign!
4 By your own e - ter - nal Spir - it, come to claim us as your own;

From our fears and sins re - lease us; grant us your true lib - er - ty.
Dear de - sire of ev - ery na - tion, en - ter ev - ery long-ing heart.
Born to rule on earth for - ev - er, come, be known to us a - gain.
By your all - suf - fi - cient mer - it, let us share your cross and crown.

*Charles Wesley, the brother of John, was one of the students known as "Methodists" at Oxford University. He wrote hymns for every occasion. This is from his small collection* Hymns for the Nativity.

Tune: STUTTGART 8.7.8.7.
*Melody attrib. to Christian F. Witt (1660–1716)*
*from* Psalmodia Sacra, *Gotha, 1715*
*Alternate tune: IN BABILONE*

# 123 Mary, Woman of the Promise

*Luke 1:39–55*

*Mary Frances Fleischaker, 1988*

1 Mar - y, wom - an of the prom - ise; ves - sel
2 Mar - y, song of ho - ly wis - dom sung be -
3 Mar - y, morn - ing star of jus - tice; mir - ror
4 Mar - y, mod - el of com - pas - sion; wound - ed
5 Mar - y, wom - an of the gos - pel; hum - ble

of your peo - ple's dreams: Through your o - pen,
fore the world be - gan: Faith - ful to the
of the Ra - diant Light: In the shad - ows
by your off - spring's pain: When our hearts are
home for trea - sured seed: Help us to be

will - ing spir - it wa - ters of God's good - ness streamed.
Word with - in you, as you bore God's won - drous plan.
of life's jour - ney, be a bea - con for our sight.
torn by sor - row, teach us how to love a - gain.
true dis - ci - ples, bear - ing fruit in word and deed.

*This text, selected as the winner in a regional Hymn Society competition seeking contemporary Marian hymns, portrays Mary's many roles in fulfilling God's promise. The author is an Adrian Dominican sister whose ministry has focused on worship and the arts.*

Tune: QUEM PASTORES 8.7.8.7.
*German carol, 14th century*
*Harm. Ralph Vaughan Williams, 1906*

# Away in a Manger

**124**

Anon., United States, 1885; st. 3, 1892; alt.

Luke 2:7

1 A - way in a man - ger, no crib for a bed, the
2 The cat - tle are low - ing, the poor ba - by wakes, but
3 Be near me, Lord Je - sus; I ask you to stay close

lit - tle Lord Je - sus laid down his sweet head. The
lit - tle Lord Je - sus, no cry - ing he makes. I
by me for - ev - er and love me, I pray. Bless

stars in the sky looked down where he lay, the
love you, Lord Je - sus; pro - tect me, I pray, and
all the dear chil - dren in your ten - der care, and

lit - tle Lord Je - sus, a - sleep on the hay.
stay by my side un - til night turns to day.
fit us for heav - en to live with you there.

*This anonymous United States carol is often misattributed to Luther. The poem first appeared in a Lutheran hymnal for schools and families. Though he never credited himself with it, the tune most likely was composed by Murray.*

Tune: **AWAY IN A MANGER** 11.11.11.11.
(MÜLLER)
*Attrib. to James R. Murray, 1887*

# 125     Angels We Have Heard on High

*Luke 2:15*

*Traditional French carol*
*Transl. st. 1–3, "Crown of Jesus Music II," 1862; alt.*
*St. 4, "Carols Old and Carols New," Boston, 1916; alt.*

1 An - gels we have heard on high, sweet - ly sing-ing o'er the plains,
2 Shep-herds, why this ju - bi - lee? Why your joy - ous strains pro - long?
3 Come to Beth-le - hem and see Christ whose birth the an - gels sing;
4 See the babe in man - ger laid whom the choirs of an - gels praise;

And the moun-tains in re - ply, ech - o back their joy - ous strains.
Say what may the tid - ings be, which in - spire your heaven-ly song.
Come a - dore on bend - ed knee, God, our world now en - ter - ing.
Mar - y, Jo - seph, lend your aid, while our hearts in love we raise.

**Refrain**

Glo - - - - - - - ri - a

in ex - cel - sis De - o, Glo - - - - -

*The earliest version of this anonymous French carol was first published in 1855. There have been numerous English translations since the 1860s, but the carol did not gain widespread ecumenical usage until the first half of the twentieth century.*

Tune: GLORIA 7.7.7.7. with refrain
(LES ANGES DANS NOS CAMPAGNES)
*French carol melody*

- - - ri - a in ex - cel - sis De - o.

## Angels, from the Realms of Glory                126

*James Montgomery, 1816; alt.*

Luke 2:8–20; Matt. 2:1–2, 9–11

1 An - gels, from the realms of glo - ry, wing your flight o'er all the earth;
2 Shep-herds, in the fields a - bid - ing, watch-ing o'er your flocks by night,
3 Sag - es, leave your con - tem-pla - tions, bright - er vi - sions beam a - far;
4 Saints, be - fore the al - tar bend-ing, watch-ing long in hope and fear,

As you sang cre - a - tion's sto - ry, now pro-claim Mes - si - ah's birth:
God with us is now re - sid - ing, yon - der shines the in - fant light:
Seek the great De - sire of Na - tions, guid - ed by Christ's na - tal star:
Sud-den-ly, your prayers at - tend-ing, Christ be - side you shall ap - pear.

*Refrain*

Come and wor-ship, come and wor-ship, wor-ship Christ, give thanks and sing.

*James Montgomery, English journalist, raised a strong voice
against injustice in his newspaper* Sheffield Iris, *in which this
hymn was first printed on December 24, 1816. The tune is named
for Regent Square Church in London, today a congregation of
the United Reformed Church in England and Wales.*

Tune: REGENT SQUARE 8.7.8.7.8.7.
*Henry T. Smart, 1867*

# 127

## Es ist ein' Ros entsprungen
### (Lo, How a Rose E'er Blooming)

*Isa. 11:1*

*German, 15th century; transl. Theodore Baker, 1894; alt.*

1 Es ist ein' Ros ent - sprun - gen aus ein - er Wur - zel zart,
1 Lo, how a Rose e'er bloom - ing from ten - der stem has sprung!
2 I - sa - iah had fore - told it, the Rose I have in mind,

wie uns die Al - ten sun - gen: von Jes - se kam die Art
Of Jes - se's lin - eage com - ing as saints of old have sung.
With Mar - y we be - hold it, the Vir - gin Moth - er kind.

und hat ein Blüm - lein bracht, mit - ten im kal - ten
It came a flow - er - et bright, a - mid the cold of
To show God's love a - right, she bore to us a

Win - ter wohl zu der hal - ben Nacht.
win - ter, when half spent was the night.
Sav - ior, when half spent was the night.

*Possibly dating from the fifteenth century, this anonymous hymn*
*was first published in a Catholic hymnal in Germany, where the*
*rose was held in special regard and was employed as a symbol*
*for Mary or for Christ.*

Tune: ES IST EIN' ROS 7.6.7.6.6.7.6.
Catholische Geistliche Kirchengesäng, Cologne, 1599
*Harm. Michael Praetorius, 1609*

# In the Bleak Midwinter

*Christina G. Rossetti, 1872; alt.*

1. In the bleak mid-win-ter, frost-y wind made moan,
2. Our God tran-scends all heav-en, earth, and its do-main;
3. An-gels and arch-an-gels may have gath-ered there,
4. What can I of-fer, poor as I am?

earth stood hard as i-ron, wa-ter like a stone;
heaven and earth shall flee a-way when Christ comes to reign;
cher-u-bim and ser-a-phim thronged the mid-night air;
If I were a shep-herd, I would bring a lamb.

Snow had fall-en, snow on snow, snow on snow,
In the bleak mid-win-ter a sta-ble place suf-ficed the
But his moth-er on-ly, in her maid-en bliss,
If I were a wise one, I would do my part; but

in the bleak mid-win-ter, long a-go.
sov-ereign God al-might-y, Je-sus Christ.
wor-shiped the be-lov-ed with a kiss.
what I can I of-fer: all my heart.

*Christina Rossetti has portrayed the Christmas story, not in
warm Bethlehem, but in the winter of her native England.
Rossetti was an accomplished writer of poetry and prose,
noted for her deep spirituality.*

Tune: CRANHAM Irr.
*Gustav Holst, 1906*

# 129 Good Christian Friends, Rejoice

German and Latin, 14th century
Transl. John Mason Neale, 1855; alt.

This carol is very old. Heinrich Suso, a German mystic who died in 1366, related a vision in which angels, singing this carol, drew him into a dance. The words were originally macaronic, combining Latin phrases with the vernacular.

Tune: IN DULCI JUBILO 6.6.7.7.7.8.5.5.
German melody, 14th century
Harm. adapt. from John Stainer, 1871
Descant, H. A. Chambers, 1931

last - ing hall.    Christ was born,    Christ was born to    save!

man-ger now.  Christ is born to - day,    Christ is born to - day!
ev - er-more.  Christ was born for    this,    Christ was born for    this!
last-ing hall.  Christ was born to    save,    Christ was born to    save!

# From Heaven unto Earth I Come

**130**

*Martin Luther, c. 1535*
*St. 1–2, transl. Catherine Winkworth, 1855; alt.*
*St. 3–5, transl. Lutheran Book of Worship, 1978; alt.*

*Luke 2:1–14*

1 "From heav-en un - to earth I come to bear good news to ev - ery-one!
2 "To you, this night, is born a child of Mar - y, cho-sen moth-er mild;
3 O dear-est Je - sus, ho - ly child, pre-pare a bed, soft, un - de - filed,
4 My heart for ver - y joy now leaps; my voice no long - er si - lence keeps;
5 "Glo - ry to God," the an-gels sing, "and peace on earth," let heav-en ring.

Glad tid-ings of great joy I bring where-of I now will glad-ly sing:
This lit - tle child, in Jo-seph's arms, with joy shall con-quer all earth's harms."
A ho - ly shrine, with-in my heart, that you and I need nev - er part.
I too must join the an - gel throng to sing this joy-ous cra - dle song.
With voic-es raised we greet the birth: a glad new year to all the earth.

*Martin Luther used a singing-game song as the model for the*
*first stanza of this hymn, then added fourteen more stanzas. The*
*hymn was written for his family's Christmas Eve celebration in*
*1534, and published the following year.*

Tune:  VOM HIMMEL HOCH L.M.
*Valentin Schumann's* Geistliche Lieder, *1539*
*Harm. Hans Leo Hassler in* Kirchengesäng,
Psalmen und Geistliche Lieder, *Nürnberg, 1608*

## 131 It Came upon the Midnight Clear

Edmund H. Sears, 1849; alt.

Luke 2:8–14

1 It came up-on the mid-night clear, that glo-rious song of old,
2 Still through the clo-ven skies they come, with peace-ful wings un-furled,
3 And you, be-neath life's crush-ing load, whose forms are bend-ing low,
4 For lo, the days are hasten-ing on, by proph-et bards fore-told,

from an-gels bend-ing near the earth to touch their harps of gold;
and still their heaven-ly mu-sic floats o'er all the wea-ry world;
who toil a-long the climb-ing way, with pain-ful steps and slow,
when with the ev-er-cir-cling years comes round the age of gold;

"Peace on the earth, good will to all, great news of joy we bring."
A-bove its sad and low-ly plains they bend on hover-ing wing,
Look now, for glad and gold-en hours come swift-ly on the wing;
When peace shall o-ver all the earth its an-cient splen-dors fling,

The world in sol-emn still-ness lay to hear the an-gels sing.
and ev-er o'er its Ba-bel sounds the bless-ed an-gels sing.
O rest be-side the wea-ry road, and hear the an-gels sing!
and all the world send back the song which now the an-gels sing.

*Edmund Sears, a Unitarian minister who served a number of congregations in the Boston area, wrote this Christmas hymn emphasizing the social implications of the Gospel for his congregation at Wayland, Massachusetts.*

Tune: CAROL C.M.D.
*Richard S. Willis, 1850*

# Joy to the World!

*Isaac Watts, 1719; alt.*

*Ps. 98:4–9; Luke 2:11–15*

1 Joy to the world! the Lord is come: let earth its
2 Joy to the earth! the Sav - ior reigns! Let all their
3 Christ rules the world with truth and grace, and makes the

prais - es bring; Let ev - ery heart pre - pare Christ room,
songs em - ploy; While fields and floods, rocks, hills, and plains
na - tions prove The glo - ries of God's righ - teous - ness

and heaven and na - ture sing, and heaven and na - ture
re - peat the sound-ing joy, re - peat the sound-ing
and won - ders of God's love, and won - ders of God's

and heaven and na - ture sing, and
re - peat the sound-ing joy, re -
and won - ders of God's love, and

sing, and heaven, and heaven and na - ture sing.
joy, re - peat, re - peat the sound-ing joy.
love, and won - ders, won - ders of God's love.

heaven and na - ture sing,
peat the sound-ing joy,
won - ders of God's love,

*Stanza 1 may be sung, "Joy to the world! the Sovereign comes: . . ."*

*Isaac Watts, an English Congregationalist, freely paraphrased
Old Testament psalms to glorify Christ and here develops a
hymn of advent and nativity from a psalm.*

Tune: ANTIOCH C.M.
*Lowell Mason, 1836*

# 133 O Little Town of Bethlehem

*Mic. 5:2; Luke 2:4–7*

*Phillips Brooks, 1868; alt.*

1 O lit - tle town of Beth - le - hem, how still we see you lie!
2 For Christ is born of Mar - y, and gath - ered all a - bove,
3 How si - lent - ly, how si - lent - ly, the won - drous gift is given!
4 O ho - ly Child of Beth - le - hem, de - scend to us, we pray;

A - bove your deep and dream-less sleep the si - lent stars go by;
While mor-tals sleep, the an - gels keep their watch of won-dering love.
So God im - parts to hu - man hearts the glo - rious love of heaven.
Cast out our sin and en - ter in; be born in us to - day.

Yet in your dark streets shines forth the ev - er - last - ing light,
O morn-ing stars, to - geth - er pro - claim the ho - ly birth!
No one dis - cerns God's com - ing, but in this world of sin,
We hear the Christ-mas an - gels the great glad tid - ings tell;

The hopes and fears of all the years are met in you to - night.
And prais - es sing, and voic - es ring with peace to all on earth.
Where yearn-ing souls long to be whole, the dear Christ en - ters in.
O come to us, a - bide with us, our Lord Em - man - u - el!

*Inspired by a visit to Bethlehem, Phillips Brooks, minister of
Holy Trinity Church, Philadelphia, wrote this hymn for the
Sunday School's Christmas service. The tune was hastily
sketched by the church organist in time for the service.*

Tune: ST. LOUIS 8.6.8.6.7.6.8.6.
*Lewis H. Redner, 1868*
*Alternate tune: FOREST GREEN*

# Silent Night, Holy Night

*Joseph Mohr, 1818*
*Transl. John F. Young, c. 1863; alt.*

*Luke 2:1–20*

1 Si - lent night, ho - ly night, all is calm, all is bright
2 Si - lent night, ho - ly night, shep-herds quake at the sight,
3 Si - lent night, ho - ly night, Child of God, love's pure light,

Round yon vir - gin moth-er and child. Ho - ly in - fant so ten - der and mild.
Glo - ries stream from heav-en a - far, heaven-ly hosts sing Al - le - lu - ia;
Ra - diant beams from your ho - ly face bring the dawn of re - deem - ing grace;

Sleep in heav - en - ly peace, sleep in heav - en - ly peace.
Christ the Sav - ior is born, Christ the Sav - ior is born.
Je - sus Christ at your birth, Je - sus Christ at your birth.

Stil-le Nacht, hei-li-ge Nacht!
Al-les schläft, ein-sam wacht
Nur das trau-te, hoch-hei-li-ge Paar
Hol-der Kna-be im lock-i-gen Haar,
Schlaf in himm-li-scher Ruh,
Schlaf in himm-li-scher Ruh!
*(Original German text by Joseph Mohr)*

Po-la'i e, po kama-ha'o,
Ma-lu-hia, Ma-lama-lama,
Ka ma-kua-hi-ne a-lo-ha, e,
Me ke kei-ki He-mo-lele e,
Moe me ka ma-lu-hia la-ni,
Moe me ka ma-lu-hia la-ni.
*(Hawaiian transl. Stephen Desha)*

¡No-che de paz; no-che de a-mor!
To-do duer-me en de-rre-dor.
En-tre los as-tros que es-par-cen su luz,
be-lla, a-nun-cian-do al ni-ñi-to Je-sús,
bri-lla la es-tre-lla de paz;
bri-lla la es-tre-lla de paz.
*(Spanish transl. Federico Fliedner; alt.)*

Csen-des éj, szent-sé-ges éj!
Min-de-nek nyug-ta mély;
Nincs fenn más, csak a szent szü-le pár,
Drá-ga kis-de-dük ál-ma-i-nál.
Szent fi-ú a-lud-jál,
Szent fi-ú a-lud-jál!
*(Hungarian transl. anon.)*

*This beloved carol was created when, the day before Christmas, the organ broke down in an Alpine village church. The priest, Joseph Mohr, gave a new poem to the organist, Franz Gruber, to be set to music. Gruber composed the music on the guitar, and it was sung with guitar on Christmas.*

Tune: STILLE NACHT Irr.
*Franz Gruber, 1818*

# 135

# Adeste Fideles
## (O Come, All You Faithful)

*Luke 2:11–15; John 1:14*

*Latin, 18th century; attrib. to John Francis Wade*
*Transl. Frederick Oakeley, 1841, and others; alt.*

1 A - des - te, fi - de - les, lae - ti tri - um - phan - tes; ve-
1 O come, all you faith - ful, joy - ful and tri - um - phant, O
2 God of true God . . . Light of true Light . . .
3 Sing, choirs of an - gels, sing in ex - ul - ta - tion,
4 A - men, Lord, we greet you, born this hap-py morn - ing;

ni - te, ve - ni - te in Beth - le - hem.
come now, O come now to Beth - le - hem.
born of the Vir - gin's womb in hu - man form;
sing, all you mes - sen - gers of heaven - ly love:
Je - sus to you shall all glo - ry be given;

Na - tum vi - de - te Re - gem an - ge - lo - rum.
Come and be - hold the rul - er of all an - gels:
Tru - ly our God, be - got - ten, not cre - at - ed:
"Glo - ry to God, all glo - ry in the high - est":
Word of our God . . . . now in flesh ap - pear - ing:

*Refrain*

Ve - ni - te a - do - re - mus, ve - ni - te a - do - re - mus,
O come in ad - o - ra - tion, O come in ad - o - ra - tion,

*The Latin text and tune of this familiar hymn are found*
*together in several eighteenth-century manuscripts signed*
*by John F. Wade. Wade lived among a group of English*
*Catholic refugees in northern France.*

Tune: ADESTE FIDELES Irr. with refrain
*English melody, 18th century*
*John F. Wade's Cantus Diversi, c. 1743*
*Harm. Collections of Motets or Antiphons, 1792*

ve - ni - te a - do - re - mus, Do - mi - num.
O come in ad - o - ra - tion: Christ is Lord!

# Jesus, Jesus, Oh, What a Wonderful Child 136

*African-American traditional; alt.*

*Luke 1:30–35; 2:8–14*

Je - sus, Je - sus, oh, what a won-der-ful child.

Je - sus, Je - sus, so ho - ly, meek, and mild; new

life, new hope the Child will bring. Lis - ten to the

an - gels sing, "Glo - ry, glo - ry, glo - ry," let the heav - ens ring!

*This gospel song praising the newborn Child might be effectively
used by repeating it several times. It could be sung softly as a
background for dance, story, or drama. Finger-snaps on the
off-beats might be used to fill the rests.*

Tune: WONDERFUL CHILD 11.10.8.7.11.
*African-American traditional
Arr. Jeffrey Radford, 1992*

# 137

# Hitsuji wa nemureri
## (Sheep Fast Asleep)

*Luke 2:8–14; Matt. 1:23; 2:1–2, 9–11*

*Genzō Miwa, 1907*
*Transl. John Moss, 1957; alt.*

1 Hi - tsu-ji wa ne - mu - re - ri, Ku - sa - no, to - ko ni,
2 Ma - hi-ru ni o - to-ra-nu Ku-shi - ki hi - ka - ri,
1 Sheep fast a-sleep, there on a hill, grass for a bed; all is still.
2 Star in the sky shin-ing; so bright! Si - lent and pure, won-drous light!

Sa - e-yu-ku fu - yu no yo, Shi - mo mo mi - e - tsu.
Mi - so-ra no ka - na-ta ni Te - ri-ka-ka-ya ku.
Cold win-ter night, the frost ap-pears; shep-herds keep watch by their fire.
What tid-ings brings it Is - ra - el? Can we new hope in it find?

Ha - ru-ka ni, hi - bi-ku wa Ka - ze - ka, mi - zu ka,
Su - ku-i wo mo - ta-ra-su Ka - mi no mi - ko no
Soft there a sound, far, far a-way; is it the stream? winds at play?
Good news it brings! "Fear not, I pray! Born is God's Child, born to-day!

I - na-to yo mi - tsu-ka-i U - ta-u mi - u - ta.
U - ma-re-shi yo - ro-ko-bi Tsu-gu-ru ho - shi ka.
Nay, friend, it is the heaven-ly choir, sing-ing through-out the spheres.
God's gift of love to all the earth, Je - sus, Em - man - u - el."

*Written by Genzō Miwa in 1907, the text of this popular*
*Japanese Christmas hymn was later revised and published in*
*Kyodan Sambika (1954) with the current tune. Translator John*
*Moss has served as a United Church of Christ missionary in*
*Niigata, Japan.*

Tune: KŌRIN 8.7.8.7.8.7.8.6.
*Chūgorō Torii, 1941*

# Jesus, Our Brother, Strong and Good

## 138

*French carol, 12th century*
*Transl. anon.*

*Luke 2:1–7; Matt. 1:23*

1 Je - sus, our broth - er, strong and good, was hum - bly
2 "I," said the don - key, shag - gy and brown, "I car - ried your
3 "I," said the cow, all white and red, "I gave you my
4 "I," said the sheep with curl - y horn, "I gave you my

born in a sta - ble rude, and the friend - ly beasts a -
moth - er up - hill and down, I car - ried your moth - er to
man - ger for your bed, I gave my hay to
wool for a blan - ket warm, you wore my coat on

round him stood, Je - sus our broth - er, strong and good.
Beth - le - hem town; I," said the don - key, shag - gy and brown.
pil - low your head; I," said the cow, all white and red.
Christ - mas morn; I," said the sheep with curl - y horn.

5  "I," said the dove, from the raf-ters high,
    "I cooed you to sleep that you should not cry,
   we cooed you to sleep, my love and I;
   I," said the dove, from the raf-ters high.

6  Thus all the beasts, by some good spell,
    in the sta-ble dark were glad to tell
   of the gifts they gave Em-man-u-el,
   the gifts they gave Em-man-u-el.

*Little is known of either the origins of this French text or its translation. The melody comes from a medieval French cathedral festival recognizing the role of the donkey in the flight into Egypt.*

Tune:  ORIENTIS PARTIBUS 7.7.7.7.
*French melody, early 13th century*
*Harm. Ralph Vaughan Williams, 1906*

# 139

# The First Nowell

*Luke 2:8–20; Matt. 2:1–12*

*Traditional English carol; alt.*

1 The first Now - ell, the an - gel did say,
2 They looked a - bove and saw a star
3 And by the light of that same star
4 This star shone bright in the north - west,
5 Then en - tered in those ma - gi three,

was to cer - tain poor shep - herds in fields as they lay;
shin - ing in the east, be - yond them far,
three sag - es came from coun - try far;
o'er Beth - le - hem it seemed to rest,
and bend - ing low up - on their knee,

In fields where they lay keep - ing their sheep,
And to the earth it gave great light,
To seek for a king was their in - tent,
And there it did both stop and stay,
They of - fered there, in great rev - erence,

on a cold win - ter's night that was so deep.
and so it con - tin - ued both day and night.
and to fol - low the star wher - ev - er it went.
right o - ver the place where Je - sus lay.
their gold and myrrh and frank - in - cense.

*Refrain*

*Refrain*

Now - ell, now - ell, now - ell, now -

ell, born in a man - ger, Em - man - u - el.

*Though perhaps of earlier origins, this anonymous English carol first appeared in print in the nineteenth century. "Nowell" stems from the Latin* novellae *(news) and is used as a joyous greeting to celebrate Jesus' birth.*

Tune: THE FIRST NOWELL  Irr. with refrain
*Traditional English melody*
*Harm.* Christmas Carols New and Old, *1871*
*Descant, Edward Shippen Barnes, 1937*

# 140 Break Forth, O Beauteous Heavenly Light

Luke 2:8–14

St. 1, Johann Rist, 1641
Transl. John Troutbeck, c. 1885; alt.
St. 2, Fred Pratt Green, 1986

1 Break forth, O beau-teous heaven - ly light, and ush - er in the
2 Come, dear - est child, in - to our hearts, and leave your crib be -

morn - ing; O shep - herds, shud - der not in fright, but
hind you! Let this be where the new life starts for

hear the an - gel's warn - ing. "This child, now weak in
all who seek and find you. To you the hon - or,

in - fan - cy, our con - fi - dence and joy shall be, the
thanks, and praise, for all your gifts this time of grace; come,

*This hymn combines the great talents of German artistry: seventeenth-century Rist, the prolific poet; Schop, brilliant instrumentalist of the same time; and Bach, who in the eighteenth century arranged both in a memorable setting for the "Christmas Oratorio."*

Tune: ERMUNTRE DICH 8.7.8.7.8.8.7.7.
*Johann Schop, 1641*
*Harm. J. S. Bach, 1734*

power of Sa - tan break - ing, our peace e - ter - nal mak - ing."
con - quer and de - liv - er this world, and us, for - ev - er.

## Carol Our Christmas

**141**

*Shirley Erena Murray, 1986*

1 Car - ol our Christ-mas, an up - side-down Christ-mas: snow is not
2 Sing of the gold and the green and the spar - kle, wa - ter and
3 Shep - herds and mus - ter - ers move o - ver hill - side, find - ing, not
4 Right - side - up Christ-mas be - longs to the u - ni - verse, made in the

fall - ing and trees are not bare. Car - ol the sum - mer, and
riv - er and lure of the beach. Sing in the hap - pi - ness
an - gels, but sheep to be shorn; Wise ones make jour - neys, what -
mo - ment a wom - an gives birth; Hope is the Je - sus gift,

wel - come the Christ Child, warm in our sun-shine and sweet-ness of air.
of o - pen spac - es, sing a na - tiv - i - ty sum - mer can reach!
ev - er the sea - son, search-ing for signs of the truth to be born.
love is the of - fering, ev - ery-where, an - y - where, here on the earth.

*Shirley Erena Murray, who lives in New Zealand, paints a picture of Christmas as it is experienced in the midst of summer in the southern hemisphere. Composer Colin Gibson has collaborated frequently with Murray. A "musterer" is a rancher.*

Tune: REVERSI 11.10.11.10.
*Colin Gibson, 1986*

# 142

# Manglakat na Kita sa Belen
### (Let Us Even Now Go to Bethlehem)

Luke 2:15; John 1:14–18

St. 1, Angel Sotto; st. 2–3, Lois Bello, 1981; rev. 1993

1 Mang - la - kat na ki - ta sa Be -
1 Let us e - ven now go to Beth - le - hem, go to
2 Let us e - ven now of - fer love and praise to our
3 Let us e - ven now sing with heart and soul: "Christ was

len sa Hu - di - ya. Kay ang Ha - ri
Beth - le - hem of Ju - de - a. Je - sus Christ,
God a - bove, to our God a - bove; who from heav - en's throne
born to save! Christ was born to save!" Let us sing our praise

sa ma - nga ha - ri sa Be - len na - ta - wo
who is our Sov - ereign, now in Beth - le - hem is
has sent a gift of love, Je - sus Christ, God's on - ly
that all the world may know, all the world may know God's

na, sa Be - len na - ta - wo na.
born! now in Beth - le - hem is born!
Child, Je - sus Christ, God's on - ly Child.
love, all the world may know God's love.

*This carol is part of a longer Christmas narrative originating in the*
*Philippines, in which singers and dancers parade from house to*
*house, often joined by neighbors and family members as they go.*

Tune: MANGLAKAT 10.10.11.7.7.
*Angel Sotto*
*Arr. Vérne de la Peña, 1994*

# On Christmas Night All Christians Sing

143

*Traditional English carol*

*Luke 2:8–14; John 1:1–5, 14; Acts 13:38–39*

1 On Christ-mas night all Chris - tians sing, to hear the news the an - gels bring; On Christ - mas night all Chris - tians sing, to hear the news the an - gels bring— News of great joy, news of great mirth, news of our gra-cious Rul-er's birth.

2 Then why should we on earth be sad, since our Re - deem - er made us glad; Then why should we on earth be sad, since our Re - deem - er made us glad, When from our sin Christ set us free, all for to gain our lib - er - ty.

3 From out of mys - tery came the Light, which made the an - gels sing this night; From out of mys - tery came the Light, which made the an - gels sing this night: "Glo - ry to God and peace to all, for - ev - er - more, Al - le - lu - ia!"

*The Puritan era in England sent the medieval carols underground. Many were not rediscovered until the early twentieth century when Ralph Vaughan Williams, Cecil Sharp, and others began collecting them. This tune is one found by Vaughan Williams in Sussex.*

Tune: SUSSEX CAROL 8.8.8.8.8.8.
*English traditional melody*
*Harm. Jonathan McNair, 1993*

# 144 Hark! The Herald Angels Sing

Luke 2:10–11, 25–32; 24:46–51;
1 Thess. 4:13–18; Isa. 60:19–20

Charles Wesley, 1739; alt.

1 Hark! the her - ald an - gels sing, "Glo - ry to the Christ-child bring;
2 Christ, by high - est heaven a - dored, Christ the ev - er - last - ing Lord!
3 Hail the Bear - er of God's peace! Hail the Sun of righ - teous-ness,

Peace on earth and mer - cy mild, God and sin - ner rec - on - ciled!"
Late in time the Sav - ior comes, off - spring of the Vir - gin's womb.
Light and life our Sav - ior brings, risen with ra - diant, heal-ing wings.

Joy - ful, all you saints a - rise, join the tri - umph of the skies;
Veiled in flesh, the God-head see; hail the in-car - nate De - i - ty,
Mild - ly lay - ing glo - ry by, born that we no more may die,

With the an - gel host pro - claim, "Christ is born in Beth - le - hem!"
Pleased on earth with us to dwell, Je - sus, our Em - man - u - el.
Born to raise us all from earth, born to give us sec - ond birth.

*This hymn by Charles Wesley, one of the founders of Methodism, is firmly wedded to Felix Mendelssohn's music. Composed for the four hundredth anniversary of the invention of printing, the music was adapted to this hymn fifteen years later.*

Tune: MENDELSSOHN 7.7.7.7.D. with refrain
*From Felix Mendelssohn's "Festgesang," 1840*
*Arr. William H. Cummings, 1855*

*Refrain*

Hark! the her-ald an-gels sing, "Glo-ry to the Christ-child bring!"

## Once in Royal David's City

145

Cecil F. Alexander, 1848; alt.

Luke 1:26–35; 2:1–7; 1 Thess. 4:13–18

1 Once in roy-al Da-vid's cit-y stood a low-ly cat-tle shed,
2 Je-sus came to earth from heav-en, who is God and Head of all,
3 And through all this won-drous child-hood Je-sus hon-ored and o-beyed,
4 Je-sus is our child-hood's pat-tern, dai-ly like us lived and grew,
5 We at last shall meet our Sav-ior, fount of God's re-deem-ing grace,

Where a moth-er laid her ba-by in a man-ger for a bed:
Shel-tered in a rus-tic sta-ble, cra-dled in a com-mon stall;
Loved and watched the ten-der moth-er whose strong arms a cra-dle made.
Je-sus, lit-tle, weak, and help-less, tears and smiles and com-fort knew.
For that Child so dear and gen-tle reigns with-in a glo-rious place;

Mar-y was that moth-er mild, Je-sus Christ her lit-tle child.
With the poor and meek and low-ly lived on earth our Sav-ior ho-ly.
So, like Je-sus, we should be serv-ing God o-be-dient-ly.
Je-sus felt the pain of sad-ness, and the joy-ous lift of glad-ness.
Lead-ing all God's chil-dren on to the heaven where saints have gone.

*Cecil Frances Alexander, wife of the bishop of Ireland, wrote a series of children's hymns commenting on the Apostles' Creed. This hymn, elaborating on the words "... born of the Virgin Mary," tells the whole life of Christ.*

Tune: IRBY 8.7.8.7.7.7.
*Henry J. Gauntlett, 1849*
*Harm. A. H. Mann, 1919*

# 146

# Nu Oli
## (Glad Tidings)

*Luke 2:10–11*

*Fanny Crosby, 1873; alt.*
*Transl. Laiana (Lorenzo Lyons, 1807–1886)*

1 Nu - o - li! nu - o - li! he nu ka - ma - ha'o!
1 Glad tid - ings! glad tid - ings! O won - der - ful love!
2 Nu - o - li! nu - o - li! ua pi - li ia nu
3 Nu - o - li! nu - o - li! hau - o - li ou - kou,

He nu no ke o - la mai lu - na mai no,
A mes - sage has come from the an - gels a - bove:
Ika po'e i - li - hu - ne, ka po - e lu'u - lu'u,
Ka po'e a - ka - hai, a ha'a - ha'a ka na - au;

No ka - na - ka nu - i, no ka - ma - li'i nei,
Good news of great joy comes to young and to old,
Ne'e mai a pau - le - le, ha - hai ia Ie - su,
Na Ie - su e ka - la a ho'o - ha - nau hou,

A oi ka na - ni i ke gu - la a'i - a'i.
For Je - sus brings mer - cy more pre - cious than gold.
A pau no ka hu - ne, a ma - ha ou - kou.
A ka'i mai nei a'e i ka na - ni ma - o.

In 1831 newly ordained Lorenzo Lyons and Betsy, his wife, sailed to Hawaii with the Sandwich Islands Mission. He served there over fifty years. Father Lyons (or "Laiana") translated a great number of hymns into Hawaiian. This one is very popular and is sung at Christmas.

Tune: NU OLI 11.11.11.11. with refrain
(GLAD TIDINGS)
*Robert Lowry, 1873*

# See the Little Baby

**147**

Luke 2:7–14; Matt. 2:1–2, 9–11

*Donald Swift, 1983; alt.*

Refrain

See the lit-tle ba-by born in a man-ger, on this Christ-mas morn-ing,

bright as the an-gels; See the lit-tle ba-by born in a man-ger,

*Last time, end*

sing No-el! Sing No-el! 1 There were shep-herds keep-ing their watch
2 "Come and see," said Mar-y and Jo-seph;

Sing No-el!

o - ver sheep as the an - gels sang. There were sa - ges
"Come and see what a won-der-ful child." Sheep and ox all

*to Refrain*

fol-low-ing the star. Sing No - el! Sing No - el!
gath-er-ing a - round. Sing No - el! Sing No - el!

This song was first performed in a choral arrangement by the
Spelman-Morehouse College Glee Clubs in 1985. Composer
Donald Swift is a graduate of Morehouse College, whose work
includes chamber pieces and choral collections such as "Three
Easter Spirituals."

Tune: LITTLE BABY Irr. with refrain
*Donald Swift, 1983*

# What Child Is This

William C. Dix, 1865; alt.

Luke 2:7–14, 25–32; Matt. 2:11; John 1:14;
John 19:16b–18, 34

1 What child is this, who, laid to rest, on Mar-y's lap is sleep-ing?
2 Why lies the Child in man-ger bare where ox and ass are feed-ing?
3 Bring gifts of in-cense, gold, and myrrh; come, join in ju-bi-la-tion;

Whom an-gels greet with an-thems sweet while shep-herds watch are keep-ing?
Give heed, draw near; for sin-ners here the si-lent Word is plead-ing.
The Ho-ly Child, though meek and mild, has come with God's sal-va-tion.

This, this, the an-gels sing, is Christ, God's ho-ly of-fer-ing;
Nails, spear shall pierce him through, the cross be borne for me, for you;
Raise, raise the song on high, the moth-er sings her lul-la-by;

Haste, haste your praise to bring the babe, the child of Mar-y!
Hail, hail the Word made flesh, the babe, the child of Mar-y!
Joy, joy, for Christ is born, the babe, the child of Mar-y!

William Chatterton Dix, manager of an English marine insurance company, wrote a number of fine hymns. This one is always sung to the tune Greensleeves, which first appeared in England in 1580 and is mentioned in one of Shakespeare's plays.

Tune: GREENSLEEVES 8.7.8.7.6.8.6.7. with refrain
English traditional melody, 16th century

# 149

# Pastores a Belén
## (As Shepherds Filled with Joy)

*Traditional Puerto Rican carol*
*Transl.* The New Century Hymnal, *1993*

1 Pas - to - res a Be - lén va - mos con a - le - grí - a,
2 Oh ni - ño ce - les - tial, ben - di - ce a los pas - to - res,

1 As shep-herds filled with joy, to Beth - le - hem we're go - ing,
2 O ho - ly, heaven-ly Child, the shep-herds seek your bless - ing,

que ha na - ci - do ya el hi - jo de Ma - rí - a.
que co - rren al por - tal can - tan - do tus lo - o - res.

for Mar - y's child is born this bless - ed Christ - mas morn - ing.
while sing - ing hap - py songs, our hope and joy con - fess - ing.

A - llí, a - llí, nos es - pe - ra Je - sús.
Co - rred, vo - lad, sus glo - rias a al - can - zar.

See there, see there, the ba - by Je - sus waits.
We run, we fly, to greet the glo - rious Child.

A - llí A - llí nos es - pe - ra Je - sús.
Co - rred, vo - lad, sus glo - rias a al - can - zar.

See there, see there, the ba - by Je - sus waits.
We run, we fly, to greet the glo - rious Child.

Lle - ve - mos pues tu - rro - nes y miel pa - ra o - fre - cer - le al ni - ño Ma - nuel.
O - fre - ce a mil a - mor y vir - tud, tra - ed, za - gal, al ni - ño Je - sús.
O let us bring our hon-ey so sweet, an of-fering for the Child to eat.
With thank-ful hearts we of - fer our best to Je - sus, at the man - ger we'll rest.

Lle - ve - mos pues tu - rro - nes y miel pa - ra o - fre - cer - le al
O - fre - ce a mil a - mor y vir - tud, tra - ed, za - gal, al
O let us bring our hon-ey so sweet, an of - fering for the
With thank - ful hearts we of - fer our best to Je - sus, at the

ni - ño Ma - nuel. Va - mos, va - mos, va-mos a ver, va-mos a ver al
ni - ño Je - sús. Va - mos, va - mos, va-mos a ver, va-mos a ver al
Child to eat. Hur - ry, hur - ry, hur-ry and see, hur-ry and see the
man - ger we'll rest. Hur - ry, hur - ry, hur-ry and see, hur-ry and see the

re - cién na - ci - do, va - mos a ver al ni - ño Ma - nuel.
re - cién na - ci - do, va - mos a ver al ni - ño Ma - nuel.
child born of Mar - y. Let's go and see Em - man - u - el.
child born of Mar - y. Let's go and see Em - man - u - el.

*This traditional carol from Puerto Rico invites the singer to*
*experience the wonder and joy of the shepherds as they came*
*to greet the Holy Child in the Bethlehem stable.*

Tune: PASTORES A BELEN Irr.
*Traditional Puerto Rican melody*
*Harm. Allena Luce, 1949*

# 150

# Sing a Different Song

*Isa. 9:2, 6–7; 42:10–11; Matt. 1:23*

*The Iona Community, 1987; alt.*

1 Sing a dif-ferent song now
2 Shout a dif-ferent shout now
3 Love a dif-ferent love now
4 Dance a dif-ferent dance now

Christ-mas is here, sing a song of peo-ple know-ing God's
Christ-mas is here, shout a shout of joy and gen - u - ine
Christ-mas is here, love with-out con-di - tion, love with - out
Christ-mas is here, dance a dance of war on suf - fering and

near: The Mes - si - ah is born in the
cheer: Fill the earth and the sky with the
fear: With the hum - ble and poor, with the
fear: Peace and jus - tice are one, in the

face of our scorn, sing a dif-ferent song to
news from on high, shout a dif-ferent shout that
shy and un - sure, love a dif-ferent love. Let
light of the sun. Dance a dif-ferent dance. God's

wel-come and warn.
all may come by.
Christ be the cure!
reign has be - gun!

This lively new carol from The Iona Community of Scotland
can be accompanied by drums and tambourines to enhance its
dance-like quality. The text invites enthusiastic participation in
celebrating the Christmas event.

Tune: DIFFERENT SONG 10.10.6.6.10.
John L. Bell, 1987

# 151 'Twas in the Moon of Wintertime

Matt. 1:23; Luke 2:11

Jean de Brébeuf, c. 1643
Transl. Jesse Edgar Middleton, 1926; alt.

1 'Twas in the moon of win-ter-time, when all the birds had fled, that
2 With-in a lodge of bro-ken bark the ten-der babe was found; a
3 The ear-liest moon of win-ter-time is not so round and fair as
4 O chil-dren of the for-est free, O seed of Man-i-tou, the

might-y Git-chi Man-i-tou sent an-gel choirs in-stead; Be-
rag-ged robe of rab-bit skin en-wrapped his beau-ty round; But
was the ring of glo-ry on the help-less in-fant there. The
ho-ly Child of earth and heaven is born to-day for you. Come

fore their light the stars grew dim, and won-dering hunt-ers heard the hymn:
as the hunt-er braves drew nigh, the an-gel song rang loud and high:
chiefs from far be-fore him knelt with gifts of fox and bea-ver pelt.
kneel be-fore the ra-diant Child, who brings you beau-ty, peace, so mild.

Jean de Brébeuf, a Jesuit priest, started a mission among native
Huron people in Canada in the early seventeenth century. Jesse
Middleton's translation moves beyond the original French poem
to include Huron folk symbols such as "rabbit skin" for
"swaddling clothes."

Tune: UNE JEUNE PUCELLE
8.6.8.6.8.8. with refrain
French folk melody, 16th century
Harm. Jonathan McNair, 1993

Je-sus Em-man-u-el, Je - sus is born, in ex-cel-sis glo - ri - a.

# Born in the Night, Mary's Child

**152**

*Geoffrey Ainger, 1964; alt.*

*Luke 2:1–7; Mark 10:18; John 1:1–5, 14;*
*John 19:16b–18*

1 Born in the night, Mar-y's Child, a long way from your home;
2 Clear shin-ing light, Mar-y's Child, your face lights up our way;
3 Truth of our life, Mar-y's Child, you tell us God is good;
4 Hope of the world, Mar-y's Child, you're com-ing soon to reign;

Com-ing in need, Mar-y's Child, born in a bor-rowed room.
Light of the world, Mar-y's Child, dawn on our shad-owed day.
Prove it is true, Mar-y's Child, go to your cross of wood.
Sov-ereign of earth, Mar-y's Child, walk in our streets a - gain.

*Methodist minister Geoffrey Ainger's song was part of a drama he
wrote for youth at his church in Loughton. Set in this section of
London, the play depicted Mary and Joe arriving on the subway,
with baby Jesus being born in a room above a filling station. The
carol made its way around the world, and on Christmas 1969,
Ainger recalls, it was being sung in India, Australia, in South
Pacific islands, and at Festival Hall in London.*

Tune:  MARY'S CHILD  7.6.7.6.
*Geoffrey Ainger, 1964*
*Harm. Richard D. Wetzel, 1972*

# 153 Who Would Think That What Was Needed

*Isa. 11:1–6; Matt. 2:1–11; Luke 2:8–14*

John Bell and Graham Maule, 1990; alt.

1 Who would think that what was need-ed to trans-form and save the earth
2 Shep-herds watch and sag - es won-der, mon-archs scorn and an - gels sing;
3 Cen - tu - ries of skill and sci-ence span the past from which we move,

might not be a plan or ar - my proud in pur-pose, proved in worth?
such a place as none would reck - on hosts a ho - ly, help-less thing;
yet ex - per-ience ques-tions wheth-er with such prog-ress we im-prove.

Who would think, de - spite de - ri - sion, that a child should lead the way?
Sta - bled beasts and pass-ing strang-ers watch a ba - by laid in hay:
In our search for sense and mean-ing, lest our hopes and hu-mor fray,

God sur - pris - es earth with heav-en, com-ing here on Christ-mas Day.
God sur - pris - es earth with heav-en, com-ing here on Christ-mas Day.
God sur - pris - es earth with heav-en, com-ing here on Christ-mas Day.

*This song was written by The Iona Community in Scotland,*
*which frequently develops hymn texts through a collaborative*
*process, often employing traditional tunes from the British Isles*
*such as "Scarlet Ribbons."*

Tune: SCARLET RIBBONS 8.7.8.7.D.
*English traditional melody*
*Arr. John Bell and others, 1990*

# Go Tell It on the Mountain

*African-American spiritual*
*Arr. John W. Work II, 1907*

*Luke 2:8–20; Isa. 18:3; 52:7*

**Refrain**

Go tell it on the moun - tain, o - ver the hill and ev - ery - where.

Go tell it on the moun - tain, that Je - sus Christ is born!

*Last time, end*

1 While shep-herds kept their watch-ing o'er si - lent flocks by night,
2 The shep-herds feared and trem-bled when lo! a - bove the earth
3 Down in a low - ly man - ger the hum - ble Christ was born,

Be - hold through-out the heav-ens there shone a ho - ly light.
Rang out the an - gel cho - rus that hailed our Sav - ior's birth.
And God sent us sal - va - tion that bless - ed Christ-mas morn.

*to Refrain*

*This is one of the few spirituals heard inside as well as outside African-American churches. It was adapted by John Wesley Work II, who is remembered as the director of the Jubilee Singers of Fisk University.*

Tune: African-American spiritual
*Adapt. Joyce Finch Johnson, 1992*

155

# Los magos que llegaron a Belén
## (The Magi Who to Bethlehem Did Go)

Matt. 2:1–12

*Manuel Fernández Juncas*
*English version, Carolyn Jennings, 1993*

**Introduction** *(one time only)*

Los ma-gos que lle-ga-ron a Be-lén a-nun-cia-ron la lle-ga-da del Me-
The ma-gi who to Beth-le-hem did go were the her-alds of the com-ing of Mes-

sí-as y no-so-tros, con a-le-grí-a, la a-nun-cia-mos hoy tam-bién.
si-ah; And with joy we al-so would has-ten to an-nounce the news to-day.

**Stanzas**

1 De tie-rra le-ja - na ve-ni-mos a ver-te,
2 Al re-cién na-ci - do que es Rey de los re-yes,
1 From a dis-tant land we come with hum-ble greet-ing,
2 To the new-born Child who has no earth-ly trea-sure

nos sir-ve de guí - a la es-tre-lla de O-rien-te.
o-ro le re-ga - lo pa-ra or-nar sus sie-nes.
where the east-ern star our car-a-van is lead-ing.
I have come with gold to bring de-light and plea-sure.

*This traditional Puerto Rican carol is frequently sung during one of the most cherished celebrations of the church year—the epiphany. The music is in the popular style of a "danza," a traditional dance form.*

Tune: LOS MAGOS 12.12. with refrain
*Traditional Puerto Rican carol*

Estribillo (Refrain)

(1–3) Oh bri - llan-te es-tre - lla que a-nun-cias la au-ro - ra    no nos
(4) Glo-ria en las al - tu - ras al Hi - jo de Dios,    Glo-ria en
(1–3) Ev - er - shin-ing star, God's bril - liant dawn re - veal - ing,    ev - er
(4) Glo - ry be to God, who sent the Child of Heav-en,    Glo - ry

fal - te nun - ca tu luz bien-he - cho-ra.
las al - tu - ras     (4) y en la tie-rra a-mor.
guide our way, God's pres-ence still as - sur-ing.
be to God, and     (4) peace to all on earth.

3. Co-mo es Dios el ni-ño
    le re-ga-lo in-cien-so,
  con a-ro-ma dul-ce
    que su-be has-ta el cie-lo.
   *Estribillo*

4. Al ni-ño del cie-lo
    que ba-jó a la tie-rra,
  le re-ga-lo mi-rra
    que ins-pi-ra tris-te-za.
   *Estribillo*

3. To the Child of God
    rich in-cense I am bring-ing,
  With a-ro-ma sweet
    that heav-en-ward is wing-ing.
   *Refrain*

4. To the Child who came
    to bring us heav-en's glad-ness,
  I have come with myrrh,
    a sign of com-ing sad-ness.
   *Refrain*

# 156

# Brightest and Best

Matt. 2:9–11; Luke 2:10–14

Reginald Heber, 1811; alt.

1 Bright-est and best of the stars of the morn - ing,
2 Cold on the cra - dle the dew - drops are shin - ing,
3 Shall we not of - fer our cost - ly de - vo - tion,
4 Vain - ly we of - fer each am - ple ob - la - tion,

dawn on our mid - night and lend us your aid.
God's ho - ly Child with the beasts of the stall;
fra - grance of E - dom and of - ferings di - vine,
vain - ly with gifts would we fa - vor se - cure;

Star of the East the ho - ri - zon a - dorn - ing,
An - gels a - dore while this ba - by lies sleep - ing,
Gems of the moun - tain and pearls of the o - cean,
Rich - er by far is the heart's ad - o - ra - tion;

guide where our in - fant Re - deem - er is laid.
Mak - er and Mon - arch and Sav - ior of all.
myrrh from the for - est or gold from the mine?
dear - er to God are the prayers of the poor.

*This is thought to be one of the earliest tunes to which "Brightest and Best" was sung in the United States. It appears to be named for William Walker, the compiler of* Southern Harmony, *a nineteenth-century collection of American tunes.*

Tune: WALKER 11.10.11.10
Southern Harmony, *1835*
*Harm. Jonathan McNair, 1994*
*Alternate setting: MORNING STAR*

# Brightest and Best

Reginald Heber, 1811; alt.

Matt. 2:9–11; Luke 2:10–14

1 Bright - est and best of the stars of the morn - ing,
2 Cold on the cra - dle the dew - drops are shin - ing,
3 Shall we not of - fer our cost - ly de - vo - tion,
4 Vain - ly we of - fer each am - ple ob - la - tion,

dawn on our mid - night and lend us your aid.
God's ho - ly Child with the beasts of the stall;
fra - grance of E - dom and of - ferings di - vine,
vain - ly with gifts would we fa - vor se - cure;

Star of the East the ho - ri - zon a - dorn - ing,
An - gels a - dore while this ba - by lies sleep - ing,
Gems of the moun - tain and pearls of the o - cean,
Rich - er by far is the heart's ad - o - ra - tion,

guide where our in - fant Re - deem - er is laid.
Mak - er and Mon - arch and Sav - ior of all.
myrrh from the for - est or gold from the mine?
dear - er to God are the prayers of the poor.

*An Anglican priest, Reginald Heber became bishop of Calcutta (including all of India), where he died of exhaustion at age forty-three. His Hymns (1827) was the first modern English hymnal arranged according to the church year.*

Tune: MORNING STAR 11.10.11.10.
*James P. Harding, 1892*
The New Psalms and Hymns, *Richmond, Va., 1901*
*Alternate setting: WALKER*

# 158 O Morning Star, How Clear and Bright

*Isa. 60:19–20; Rom. 15:7–13*

Philipp Nicolai, 1598
*Transl. Catherine Winkworth, 1863; alt.*

1 O Morn-ing Star, how clear and bright, your beam shines forth in
2 Come heaven-ly Bright-ness, Light di-vine, and deep with-in my

truth and light! My Sov-ereign meek and low-ly! O Root of Jes-se,
heart now shine, there make your-self an al-tar! Fill me with joy and

Prom-ised One, my God and Rul-er, you have won my heart to serve you
strength to be your mem-ber, joined e-ter-nal-ly in love that can-not

sole-ly! You are ho-ly, great and glo-rious, all-vic-to-rious,
fal-ter; Long-ing for you does pos-sess me; turn and bless me;

*This German chorale by Lutheran pastor Philipp Nicolai became so popular that its tune was chimed by church bells and its words engraved on pottery. It has been called "the queen of chorales."*

Tune: WIE SCHÖN LEUCHTET 8.8.7.8.8.7.4.8.4.8.
*Philipp Nicolai, 1598*
*Harm. J. S. Bach, c. 1731*

Rich in bless - ing, rule and might o'er all pos - sess - ing.
Here in sad - ness eye and heart long for your glad - ness.

## As with Gladness Those of Old 159

*William C. Dix, 1861; alt.*                                   *Matt. 2:1–12*

1 As with glad-ness those of old    did the guid-ing star be-hold;
2 As with joy-ful steps they sped   to that low-ly man-ger bed,
3 As they of-fered gifts most rare  at that man-ger plain and bare,
4 Ho-ly Je-sus, ev-ery day          keep us in the nar-row way;

As with joy they hailed its light,  lead-ing on-ward, beam-ing bright;
There to bend the knee be-fore      One whom heaven and earth a-dore;
So may we with ho-ly joy,           pure and free from sin's al-loy,
And when mor-tal things are past,   bring our ran-somed souls at last

So, true Morn-ing Star, may we      ev-er-more your splen-dor see.
So may we with will-ing feet        ev-er seek your mer-cy seat.
All our cost-liest trea-sures bring, Christ, to you from whom they spring.
Where they need no star to guide,   where no clouds your glo-ry hide.

*After reading the Epiphany gospel, William C. Dix penned this
hymn. Dix, the manager of a marine insurance company, was
also a gifted hymnwriter. Among his many fine contributions
is "What Child Is This."*

Tune: DIX 7.7.7.7.7.7.
*Conrad Kocher, 1838*
*Adapt. William H. Monk, 1861*

# 160

# Hark! the Herald Angels Sing
## (Jesus, the Light of the World)

John 8:12; 9:5

Charles Wesley, 1739; alt.; adapt. George D. Elderkin; alt.

1 Hark! the her-ald an-gels sing, Je-sus, the light of the world;
2 Joy-ful, all you saints a-rise, Je-sus, the light of the world;
3 Christ, by high-est heaven a-dored, Je-sus, the light of the world;
4 Hail the Bear-er of God's peace! Je-sus, the light of the world;

Glo-ry to the Christ-child bring, Je-sus, the light of the world.
Join the tri-umph of the skies, Je-sus, the light of the world.
Christ, the ev-er-last-ing Word, Je-sus, the light of the world.
Hail the Sun of righ-teous-ness! Je-sus, the light of the world.

*Refrain*

We will fol-low the light, beau-ti-ful light, come where the

dew-drops of mer-cy are bright, Shine all a-round us by

day and by night, Je-sus, the light of the world.

*The original version of Charles Wesley's hymn has received various alterations throughout the years. This adaptation by George Elderkin utilizes a repeated ascription, "Jesus, the light of the world," and a refrain to create a rousing carol of praise.*

Tune: ELDERKIN 7.7.7.7. with refrain
*George D. Elderkin*
*Arr. Jeffrey Radford, 1993*

# Amen, Amen

*African-American spiritual*

Mark 3:7–10; Luke 2:7, 46–47; Rom. 6:6–10

*Congregation/choir*

A - men, a - men, a - men, a - men,

*Solo*

1 O    see the lit-tle ba - by        ly - ing in a man-ger
2 See   Je - sus in the tem - ple      talk - ing to the el - ders;
3 See   Je - sus at the sea - shore    preach-ing to the peo-ple,
4 See   Je - sus on the cross . . . .  bear - ing all my sins . . . .
5 Yes,  Je - sus died to save us,      rose  on Eas-ter morn-ing,
6 We're sing-ing Al - le - lu - ia!    Je - sus is my Sav - ior,

*(Congregation/choir)*

a - men!    A - men,

on Christ - mas   morn - ing.     (2 See)
how they    all    mar - veled!   (3 See)
____  heal-ing all the sick  ones!  (4 See)
in  bit - ter   ag - o - ny!      (5 Yes,)
and lives   for - ev - er!        (6 We're)
who lives   for - ev - er!

a - men,           a - men, a - men, a - men!

*This is one of the many spirituals that found fame during the civil rights movement of the 1960s. Its pattern of call-and-response allowed the lead singer to create new verses while those gathered sang the response of "Amen."*

Tune: AMEN Irr.
*African-American spiritual*
*Arr. Nelsie T. Johnson, 1988*

# 162     In a Lowly Manger Born

*Matt. 8:20; John 19:5; Phil. 2:5–11; Heb. 5:1–11*

*Kō Yūki, 1923*
*Transl. Vern Rossman; alt.*

1 In a low-ly man-ger born, hum-ble life be-gun in scorn.
2 Vis-it-ing each out-cast soul, bring-ing peace to make them whole,
3 Came to earth for you and me, gave up life up-on the tree;

In a work-shop Je-sus grew, work-er's strug-gles knew.
Giv-ing self-less-ly in love, God's own love to prove.
There we saw God's love re-vealed, through that pain were healed.

Knew the suf-fering of the weak, knew the long-ing of the meek,
Sin-ners glad-ly heard Christ call, right-teous ones did hum-ble fall.
Lives a-gain in glo-ry bright, lives a-gain in power and might,

Knew the poor and suf-fering ones; this is God, the Hu-man One!
And in Christ new life be-gun, wor-shipped God, the Hu-man One!
Our sal-va-tion now has come, gift of God, the Hu-man One!

*In 1971 Kō Yūki was named pastor emeritus of a Tokyo church he had served for fifty years. He is known as a Christian educator, Pascal scholar, and prolific hymnwriter. Translator Vern Rossman was an American missionary to Japan.*

Tune: MABUNE 7.7.7.7.D.
*Seigi Abe, 1930*

# Many Are the Lightbeams

Cyprian of Carthage, "De unitate ecclesiae," 252 C.E.
Swedish paraphr. by Anders Frostenson (b. 1906)
Transl. David Lewis, 1983

John 8:12; 9:5; 15:1–5; 1 Cor. 12:4–27; Gal. 3:28

1 Man - y are the light-beams from the one light. Our one
2 Man - y are the branch-es of the one tree. Our one
3 Man - y are the gifts given, love is all one. Love's the
4 Man - y ways to serve God, the Spir-it is one; ser - vant
5 Man - y are the mem-bers, the bod-y is one; mem - bers

light is Je - sus. Man - y are the light-beams
tree is Je - sus. Man - y are the branch-es
gift of Je - sus. Man - y are the gifts given,
spir-it of Je - sus. Man - y ways to serve God, the
all of Je - sus. Man - y are the mem-bers, the

from the one light; we are one in Christ.
of the one tree; we are one in Christ.
love is all one; we are one in Christ.
Spir-it is one; we are one in Christ.
bod-y is one; we are one in Christ.

*The text upon which this hymn is based is by a bishop of the early church, Cyprian of Carthage. It was paraphrased from his 252 C.E. work, "De unitate ecclesiae" (Of church unity). He was martyred in Carthage c. 258.*

Tune: LIGHTBEAMS Irr.
*Olle Widestrand (b. 1906)*
*Arr. Darryl Nixon, 1987*

# 164

# Arise, Your Light Is Come

*Isa. 60:1; 61:1–2; Luke 4:14–21*

*Ruth Duck, 1973*

1 A - rise, your light is come! The Spir - it's call o - bey;
2 A - rise, your light is come! Fling wide the pris - on door;
3 A - rise, your light is come! All you in sor - row born,
4 A - rise, your light is come! The moun-tains burst in song!

Show forth the glo - ry of your God which shines on you to - day!
Pro - claim the cap-tive's lib - er - ty, good tid - ings to the poor.
Bind up the bro - ken - heart-ed ones and com - fort those who mourn.
Rise up like ea - gles on the wing; God's power will make us strong.

*This hymn was first published by the Ecumenical Women's
Center of Chicago in the 1974 collection of hymn adaptations,*
Because We Are One People. *Ruth Duck later included it in
her own collection,* Dancing in the Universe.

Tune: FESTAL SONG S.M.
*William Walter, 1872*

Words Copyright © 1992 by G.I.A. Publications, Inc.

# 165

# Love Came Down at Christmas

*Matt. 2:1–11; Luke 2:8–18*

*Christina G. Rossetti, 1885; alt.*

1 Love came down at Christ - mas, Love all love - ly, Love di - vine;
2 Wor - ship we the God - head, Love in - car - nate, Love di - vine;
3 Love shall be our to - ken; love be yours and love be mine;

*Christina Rossetti, author of the more familiar carol "In the
Bleak Midwinter," lived a very quiet life in England. This text
has been described by the noted editor Percy Dearmer as a
"gem, where so much is said in so little space."*

Tune: WHITNEY 6.7.6.7.
*Maurice C. Whitney, 1962*

Love was born at Christ - mas; star and an - gels gave the sign.
Wor - ship we our Je - sus, but where is God's sa - cred sign?
Love to God and neigh - bor, love for plea and gift and sign.

## Immortal Love, Forever Full 166

*John Greenleaf Whittier, 1867; alt.*  Phil. 2:9–11; Rom. 10:6–7; Mark 5:25–29

1 Im - mor - tal Love, for - ev - er full, for - ev - er flow - ing free,
2 Our out - ward lips con - fess the Name all oth - er names a - bove;
3 We may not climb the heaven - ly steeps to bring the Sov - ereign down;
4 But warm, sweet, ten - der, ev - en yet this One our help will be;

For - ev - er shared, for - ev - er whole, a nev - er - ebb - ing sea!
Love on - ly knows from where it came and com - pre - hends God's love.
In vain we search the low - est deeps for One no depths can drown.
For faith has still its Ol - i - vet, and love its Gal - i - lee.

5 The heal-ing of Christ's seam-less dress
  still soothes our beds of pain;
  We touch it in life's throng and press,
  and we are whole a-gain.

6 Through Christ our ear-liest prayers
  are said
  with words we scarce can frame;
  The last low whis-pers of our dead
  still ech-o with Christ's name.

*Though the American poet John Greenleaf Whittier did not write
hymnody as such, a number of hymns have been drawn from his
devotional poetry. This hymn was selected from* The Tent on the
Beach and Other Poems.

Tune: SERENITY C.M.
*Arr. from William V. Wallace, 1856*
*Alternate tune: BEATITUDO*

# 167 Mark How the Lamb of God's Self-Offering

Matt. 3:13–17; 4:1–2; Mark 1:9–13; Luke 3:21–22;
Acts 10:34–38; 2:38–42

Carl P. Daw, Jr., 1990

1 Mark how the Lamb of God's self - of - fering our hu - man
sin - ful-ness takes on In the birth - wa-ters of the Jor - dan
as Je - sus is bap-tized by John. Hear how the voice from heav-en
thun - ders, "Lo, this is my be - lov - ed Son." See how in

2 From this as - sur - ance of God's fa - vor Je - sus goes
to the wil - der - ness, There to en - dure a time of test - ing
that read-ied him to teach and bless. So we, by wa - ter and the
Spir - it bap-tized in - to Christ's min - is - try, Are of-ten

3 Grant us, O God, the strength and cour - age to live the
faith our lips de - clare; Bless us in our bap-tis-mal call - ing;
Christ's roy - al priest-hood help us share. Turn us from ev - ery false al -
le - giance, that we may trust in Christ a - lone: Raise up in

*Regarding this hymn for the first Sunday after the Epiphany,
hymnwriter Carl P. Daw, Jr., writes that "the Baptism of Christ
is one of the regular occasions for baptisms and for the making
and renewing of baptismal vows."*

Tune: RENDEZ À DIEU 9.8.9.8.D.
*Louis Bourgeois (c. 1510–c. 1561)*
Trente quatre Pseaumes, *Geneva, 1551*

dove-like form the Spir - it de - scends on God's A-noint-ed One.
led to paths of ser - vice through maz - es of ad-ver-si - ty.
us a cho-sen peo - ple trans-formed by love to be your own.

## O Radiant Christ, Incarnate Word
168

*Ruth Duck, 1989*  *Isa. 60:19–20; Matt. 3:13–17; Mark 1:9–11*

1 O ra - diant Christ, in - car - nate Word, e - ter - nal
2 Our bar - tered, bus - y lives burn dim, too tired to
3 Your glo - ry shone at Jor - dan's stream, the font where
4 O Light of Na - tions, fill the earth; our faith and

love re - vealed in time: Come, make your home with - in our
care, too numb to feel. Come, shine up - on our shad - owed
we were born a - new. At - tune your church to know you
hope and love re - new. Come, lead the peo - ples to your

hearts, that we may dwell in light sub - lime.
world: your ra - diance bathes with power to heal.
near; il - lu - mine all we say and do.
peace, as stars once led the way to you.

*Commissioned by the Lutheran School of Theology in Chicago, Ruth Duck's text provides a fitting center for Epiphany celebrations, with its sense of wonder at the incarnation and petition that through Christ's revelation our lives may be changed.*

Tune: DICKINSON COLLEGE L.M.
*Lee Hastings Bristol, Jr., 1962*
*Alternate tune: WAREHAM*

# 169 What Ruler Wades through Murky Streams

Matt. 3:13–17; Mark 1:9–11; Luke 3:21–22;
Col. 2:9–12

Thomas H. Troeger, 1984; rev. 1993

1 What rul - er wades through murk - y streams and bows be-neath the wave,
2 Christ gleams with wa - ter brown with clay from land the proph-ets trod.
3 Come bow be-neath the flow - ing wave. Christ stands here at your side

Ig - nor - ing how the world es - teems the pow - er - ful and brave?
A - bove while heav-en's clouds give way de - scends the dove of God.
and rais - es you as from the grave God raised the cru - ci - fied.

*Refrain*

Wa - ter, Riv - er, Spir - it, Grace, sweep o - ver me, sweep o - ver me!

*Thomas H. Troeger commented that this text "was inspired by seeing a picture of a muddy Jordan River and realizing the materiality of Christ's experience at baptism." The new musical setting was provided by David Hurd at the invitation of* The New Century Hymnal.

Tune: WATER OF BAPTISM C.M. with refrain
*David Hurd, 1994*

Re - carve the depths your fing-ers traced in sculpt - ing me.

# Your Ways Are Not Our Own

**170**

*Lavon Bayler, 1988, rev. 1993*

*Luke 6:17–38; Rom. 12:9–21*

1 Your ways are not our own, O gra-cious God most high,
2 Christ teach-es us to bless the ones who curse and harm,
3 Yet, we can-not ex - cuse a - buse in an - y form,
4 How shall we show your love, your par-don to be - lieve?
5 For - give-ness is our joy, re - ceiv-ing, giv-ing, too.

Yet we would fol - low in your paths and on your love re - ly.
To turn the oth - er cheek when struck, at - tack-ers to dis - arm.
For all are chil - dren of your care, and love must be our norm.
You bid us share as we are blessed and give as we re - ceive.
Keep us from judg-ments hard and cruel, that we may dwell with you.

*Lavon Bayler has served on the Illinois Conference staff of the United Church of Christ beginning in 1979. She maintains a faithful practice of writing worship materials as part of her daily spiritual discipline and has published several books of resources.*

Tune: SCHUMANN S.M.
Cantica Laudis,
*Lowell Mason and G. J. Webb, 1850*

# 171 Jesus Calls Us, o'er the Tumult

*Matt. 4:18–22; Mark 1:16–20; John 21:15*

*Cecil F. Alexander, 1852; alt.*

1 Je - sus calls us, o'er the tu - mult of our life's wild, rest-less sea; Day by day that voice still calls us, say - ing, "Chris - tian, fol - low

2 As of old, Saint An - drew heard it by the Gal - i - le - an lake, Turned from home and toil and kin - dred, leav - ing all for Je - sus'

3 Je - sus calls us from the wor - ship of the trea - sures we a - dore, From each i - dol that would keep us, say - ing, "Chris - tian, love me

4 In our joys and in our sor - rows, days of toil and hours of ease, Je - sus calls, in cares and plea - sures, "Chris-tian, love me more than

5 Je - sus calls us! By your mer - cies, Sav-ior, may we hear your call, Give our hearts to your o - be - dience, serve and love you best of

*David Hurd is an internationally recognized organist and composer who has served on the faculty of General Theological Seminary and Manhattan School of Music. This tune was composed especially for this text and should be performed simply, like a folk song.*

Tune: ST. ANDREW 8.7.8.7.7.
*David Hurd, 1980*
*Alternate setting: GALILEE*

*Last time only*

| | | |
|---|---|---|
| me," | say - ing, "Chris - | tian, fol - low me." |
| sake, | leav - ing all | for Je - sus' sake. |
| more," | say - ing, "Chris - | tian, love me more." |
| these, | Chris-tian, love | me more than these." |
| all, | serve and love | you best of all. |

*Last time only*

# Jesus Calls Us, o'er the Tumult

## 172

*Cecil F. Alexander, 1852; alt.*

*Matt. 4:18–22; Mark 1:16–20; John 21:15*

1 Je-sus calls us, o'er the tu-mult of our life's wild, rest-less sea;
2 As of old, Saint An-drew heard it by the Gal - i - le - an lake,
3 Je-sus calls us from the wor-ship of the trea - sures we a - dore,
4 In our joys and in our sor-rows, days of toil and hours of ease,
5 Je-sus calls us! By your mer-cies, Sav-ior, may we hear your call,

Day by day that voice still calls us, say - ing, "Chris-tian, fol - low me."
Turned from home and toil and kin-dred, leav - ing all for Je - sus' sake.
From each i - dol that would keep us, say - ing, "Chris-tian, love me more."
Je - sus calls, in cares and plea-sures, "Chris-tian, love me more than these."
Give our hearts to your o - be-dience, serve and love you best of all.

*Cecil Alexander, who in Ireland wrote sacred verse to teach
children the meaning of the catechism and liturgy, designated
this poem for St. Andrew's Day. Many years later Galilee was
composed for this text by an English organist, William Jude.*

Tune: GALILEE 8.7.8.7.
*William H. Jude, 1887
Alternate setting: ST. ANDREW*

# 173

## Tú has venido a la orilla
### (You Have Come down to the Lakeshore)

*Matt. 4:18–22; Mark 1:16–20; Luke 5:1–11*

*Cesáreo Gabaraín, 1979; alt.*
*Transl. Madeleine Forell Marshall, 1989; alt.*

1 Tú has ve-ni-do a la o-ri-lla, no has bus-
2 Tú sa-bes bien lo que ten-go: en mi

1 You have come down to the lake-shore seek-ing
2 You know full well my pos-ses-sions. Nei-ther

ca-do ni a sa-bios, ni a ri-cos, tan só-lo
bar-ca no hay o-ro ni es-pa-das; tan só-lo

nei-ther the wise nor the wealth-y, But on-ly
trea-sure nor weap-ons for con-quest, Just these my

*Estribillo (Refrain)*

quie-res que yo te si-ga. Je-
re-des y mi tra-ba-jo.

ask-ing for me to fol-low. O
fish-nets and will for work-ing.

sús, me has mi-ra-do a los o-jos;
Je-sus, you have looked in-to my eyes;

*One of the most popular hymns to emerge from the 1970s
revival of religious songs in Spain, this text has been translated
into nearly eighty languages. The Spanish composer-author was
a parish priest known for his work among youth.*

Tune: PESCADOR DE HOMBRES
8.10.10. with refrain
*Cesáreo Gabaraín, 1979*
*Harm. Skinner Chávez-Melo, 1987*

son - ri - en - do, has di - cho mi nom - bre;
kind - ly smil - ing, you've called out my name.

en la a - re - na he de - ja - do mi bar - ca;
On the sand I have a-ban-doned my small boat;

jun - to a ti bus-ca - ré o-tro mar.
now with you I will seek oth-er seas.

3. Tú ne-ce-si-tas mis ma-nos,
   mi can-san-cio que a o-tros des-can-se,
   a-mor que quie-ra se-guir a-man-do.
   *Estribillo*

4. Tú, Pes-ca-dor de o-tros ma-res,
   an-sia e-ter-na de al-mas que es-pe-ran.
   A-mi-go bue-no, que a-sí me lla-mas.
   *Estribillo*

3. You need my hands, my ex-haus-tion,
   work-ing love for the rest of the
   wea-ry—
   A love that's will-ing to go on lov-ing.
   *Refrain*

4. You who have fished oth-er wa-ters;
   you, the long-ing of souls that are
   yearn-ing:
   As lov-ing Friend, you have come
   to call me.
   *Refrain*

# 174 Hear the Voice of God, So Tender

Mark 2:21–22; Ps. 103

Lavon Bayler, 1987; rev. 1993

1 Hear the voice of God, so tender, gath-ering
2 God is heal-ing and for-giv-ing crea-tures
3 Lis-tening to the Spir-it's guid-ing, breath be-
4 Shed the old wine-skins of war-fare for the

us in righ-teous-ness, Giv-ing, as our sure de-fend-er,
who are sore dis-tressed, O-pening doors to hope-ful liv-ing,
yond the writ-ten code, We, in cov-e-nant a-bid-ing,
fresh new wines of peace, Know-ing God sus-tains our wel-fare

stead-fast love and faith-ful-ness. Bless God's ho-ly name to-geth-er,
as, by love, we're dai-ly blessed. Bless God's ho-ly name to-geth-er,
seek to write our let-ters bold. Bless God's ho-ly name to-geth-er,
with a love that will not cease. Bless God's ho-ly name to-geth-er,

as the Spir-it brings new life. Giv-ing, as our sure de-
as the Spir-it brings new life. O-pening doors to hope-ful
as the Spir-it brings new life. We, in cov-e-nant a-
as the Spir-it brings new life. Know-ing God sus-tains our

*This is one of the hundreds of hymn texts Lavon Bayler has provided in her books of liturgical resources related to the common lectionary. It appears in the volume for year B, aptly titled Whispers of God.*

Tune: RAQUEL 8.7.8.7.D.
*Skinner Chávez-Melo, 1985*
*Alternate tune: BEACH SPRING*

fend - er, stead-fast love and faith - ful - ness.
liv - ing, as, by love, we're dai - ly blessed.
bid - ing, seek to write our let - ters bold.
wel - fare with a love that will not cease.

## O Christ, the Healer, We Have Come
### 175

*Fred Pratt Green, 1967*

*Matt. 8:5–13; 15:21–28; Mark 5:25–34; Luke 7:1–10; 9:37–43a*

Unison

1 O Christ, the heal - er, we have come to
2 From ev - ery ail - ment flesh en - dures our
3 In con - flicts that de - stroy our health we
4 Grant that we all, made one in faith, in

pray for health, to plead for friends. How can we fail to be re-
bod - ies clam - or to be freed. Yet in our hearts we would con-
rec - og - nize the world's dis - ease; Our com - mon life de-clares our
your com-mu - ni - ty may find The whole-ness that, en - rich - ing

stored when reached by love that nev - er ends?
fess that whole-ness is our deep - est need.
ills. Is there no cure, O Christ, for these?
us, shall reach and pros - per hu - man - kind.

*Fred Pratt Green wrote this hymn in 1967 at the suggestion of the committee compiling* Hymns and Songs, *when they noted the need for a new healing text. Green immediately produced this prayer for wholeness of body, mind, and spirit.*

Tune: KENTRIDGE L.M.
*Richard Gieseke, 1988*
*Alternate tune: TALLIS' CANON*

# 176 "Silence! Frenzied, Unclean Spirit"

*Mark 1:21–28; Luke 4:33–37*

*Thomas H. Troeger, 1984; rev. 1993*

1 "Si - lence! Fren - zied, un-clean spir - it," cried God's heal - ing, Ho - ly One.
2 Christ, the de - mons still are thriv-ing in the grey cells of the mind:
3 Si - lence, Christ, the un-clean spir - it, in our mind and in our heart.

"Cease your rant - ing! Flesh can't bear it. Flee as night be - fore the sun."
Ty - rant voic - es, shrill and driv-ing, twist-ed thoughts that grip and bind,
Speak your word that when we hear it all our de - mons shall de - part.

At Christ's voice the de - mon trem - bled, from its vic - tim
Doubts that stir the heart to pan - ic, fears dis - tort - ing
Clear our thought and calm our feel - ing, still the frac - tured,

mad - ly rushed,    While the crowd that    was    as - sem - bled
rea - son's sight,   Guilt that makes our    lov - ing    fran - tic,
war - ring soul.     By    the    pow - er    of    your    heal - ing

stood    in    won - der,    stunned and    hushed.
dreams that    cloud    the    soul    with    fright.
make    us    faith - ful,                true,    and    whole.

Thomas H. Troeger has stated: "'Silence! Frenzied Unclean
Spirit' represented my personal desperation to come to terms
with the meaning of demons and the profound emotional
turmoil I encountered in many people when I was a pastor. I
wanted to draw on the strength of Christ's exorcism for facing
these painful situations."

Tune: AUTHORITY 8.7.8.7.D.
Carol Doran, 1984
Alternate tune: JEFFERSON

# 177 God of Change and Glory

1 Cor. 12:4–27

*Al Carmines, 1973*

1 God of change and glo - ry, God of time and space,
2 God of man - y col - ors, God of man - y signs,
3 Fresh-ness of the morn - ing, new - ness of each night,

when we fear the fu - ture, give to us your grace.
you have made us dif - ferent, bless - ing man - y kinds.
you are still cre - at - ing end - less love and light.

In the midst of chang-ing ways give us still the grace to praise.
As the old ways dis - ap-pear, let your love cast out our fear.
This we see, as shad-ows part, man - y gifts from one great heart.

*Refrain*

Man - y gifts, one Spir - it, one love known in man - y ways.

*Al Carmines, composer, playwright, performer, and teacher, has
served as minister for two United Church of Christ congregations
in New York City. This hymn, commissioned in 1973, was one
of the first modern texts to claim diversity as a gift from God.*

Tune: KATHERINE 6.5.6.5.7.7.
*Al Carmines, 1973*

# 178     We Have the Strength to Lift and Bear

Mark 2:1–12

Thomas H. Troeger, 1985; rev. 1993

1 We have the strength to lift and bear a friend's im - mo - bile weight,
2 It was this hope and trust that filled the four who walked the road
3 The awk-ward-ness of match-ing strides and one an - oth - er's pace
4 Christ, give your church that sin - gle hope by which those faith - ful four

The strength to watch and nurse and care through hours long and late,
And bore their friend whose limbs were stilled be - neath some hid - den load.
While hold - ing up the bed's two sides to keep their friend in place,
Could low - er down their friend by rope while oth - ers blocked the door.

Be - cause we trust in ways un-known the springs of health are stirred,
Each foot a stone, each leg a rod, for years he lay in bed,
The crowd - ed street, the roof of clay, the scribes who took of-fense—
Though we may lack your gift to heal, this task is sure - ly ours:

And thus the mind, the flesh and bone re - ceive Christ's heal-ing word.
in ter - ror of a judg - ing god and par - a - lyzed by dread.
Not all of these could turn a - way those stub - born lov - ing friends.
To bring to you the lost who feel their need of gra-cious powers.

*In writing this text based on the Mark narrative, Thomas H.
Troeger recalled his own observations of various people,
particularly nurses and spouses, who care for stroke victims.*

Tune: TALLIS' THIRD TUNE C.M.D.
*Thomas Tallis, c. 1557*

# We Yearn, O Christ, for Wholeness

**179**

*Dosia Carlson, 1986; rev. 1993*

1 We yearn, O Christ, for whole - ness and for your heal - ing touch;
2 We long to have com - pan - ions who trav - el by our side,
3 We need your liv - ing pres - ence, O Christ of Gal - i - lee,

too long have we felt help - less; our bur - dens seemed too much.
strong friends to call and an - swer with whom we are al - lied;
a pres - ence that re - vives us and sets our spir - its free.

For - get - ting all pre - tens - es we make our plead - ings heard,
As we lift up each oth - er when strug - gles lay us low,
No long - er are we fear - ful, your love per - vades each place.

in hope and ex - pec - ta - tion a - wait your gra - cious Word.
com - mu - ni - ty de - vel - ops; our faith and car - ing grow.
Em - pow - er us with cour - age to claim your heal - ing grace.

*Dosia Carlson is noted for her ministry at Beatitudes United*
*Church of Christ in Phoenix, Arizona, and for her hymnwriting.*
*This text was inspired by a sermon given by Harold Wilke*
*during the International Year of Persons with Disabilities (1983).*

Tune: PASSION CHORALE 7.6.7.6.D.
*Hans Leo Hassler, 1601*
*Harm. J. S. Bach, 1719*
*For another harmonization, see 202*

# 180 Blessed Are the Poor in Spirit

*Rusty Edwards, 1993*

Matt. 5:3–12; Luke 6:20–23; John 20:29; 2 Cor. 5:17–18

*Unison*

1 Blessed are the poor in spir-it: heav-en will some-day be theirs.
2 Blessed all who thirst or hun-ger: righ-teous-ly they will be fed.
3 Each seek-ing peace and jus-tice shall be known as God's own heir.

Blessed are the mourn-ing chil-dren: com-fort comes from One who cares.
Those who re-spond with mer-cy will see mer-cy up a-head.
Blessed, too, are those ill-treat-ed for what's good and right and fair.

Blessed the meek and pa-tient, hav-ing cour-age to hang on.
Blessed the clean in spir-it— beau-ti-ful, the pure in heart;
Blessed the New Cre-a-tion, joy be-yond what we con-ceive;

Soon all earth they will in-her-it; times of tri-als will be gone.
One day they will see their Mak-er, nev-er-more to live a-part.
Blessed all those who trust the prom-ise: with-out see-ing, they be-lieve!

*Howard M. Edwards III, who writes as Rusty Edwards, is an ordained Lutheran pastor from Illinois. The tune for this new Beatitudes paraphrase was composed especially to be interpreted by liturgical dancer Annika Gustafson.*

Tune: ANNIKA'S DANCE 7.7.7.7.6.7.8.7.
*Jane Marshall, 1993*

# You Are Salt for the Earth, O People

**181**

*Paraphr. by Marty Haugen, 1986; alt.*

*Matt. 5:13–15*

1 You are salt for the earth, O peo-ple: salt for the reign of God!
2 You are a light on the hill, O peo-ple: light for the Cit-y of God!
3 You are a seed of the Word, O peo-ple: bring forth the reign of God!
4 We are a blessed and a pil-grim peo-ple: bound for the reign of God!

Share the fla-vor of life, O peo-ple: life in the Cit-y of God!
Shine so ho-ly and bright, O peo-ple: shine for the Cit-y of God!
Seeds of mer-cy and seeds of jus-tice, grow in the Cit-y of God!
Love our jour-ney and love our home-land: love is the Cit-y of God!

*Refrain*

Bring forth the reign of mer-cy, bring forth the reign of peace;

Bring forth the reign of jus-tice, bring forth the Cit-y of God!

*During a residency at Holden Village, a retreat center in the state of Washington, Marty Haugen wrote this hymn to be used as a "processing song" for outdoor worship. The lectionary readings focusing on Jesus' teaching about the "reign of God" provided the basis for the text.*

Tune: BRING FORTH Irr. with refrain
*Marty Haugen, 1986*

# 182     We Have Come at Christ's Own Bidding

*Matt. 17:1–8; Mark 9:2–8; Luke 9:28–36*

*Carl P. Daw, Jr., 1988*

1 We have come at Christ's own bid-ding to this high and ho-ly place, Where we wait with hope and long-ing for some to-ken of God's grace. Here we pray for new as-sur-ance that our faith is not in vain, Search-ing like those first dis-ci-ples for a sign both clear and plain.

2 Light breaks through our clouds and shad-ows, splen-dor bathes the flesh-joined Word, Mo-ses and E-li-jah mar-vel as the heav-enly voice is heard. Eyes and hearts be-hold with won-der how the Law and Proph-ets meet: Christ with gar-ments drenched in bright-ness, stands trans-fig-ured and com-plete.

3 Strength-ened by this glimpse of glo-ry, fear-ful lest our faith de-cline, We, like Pe-ter, find it tempt-ing to re-main and build a shrine. But true wor-ship gives us cour-age to pro-claim what we pro-fess, That our dai-ly lives may prove us peo-ple of the God we bless.

*In his commentary on the text, hymnwriter Carl P. Daw, Jr.,*
*describes the "implicit comparison between the attitudes and*
*assumptions of the disciples on the Mount of the Transfiguration*
*and the expectations of present-day Christians as they gather*
*for worship."*

Tune: HYFRYDOL 8.7.8.7.D.
*Rowland H. Prichard, 1844*
*Arr. Ralph Vaughan Williams, 1906*

# Jesus, Take Us to the Mountain

183

*Jaroslav J. Vajda, 1991; alt.*

*Matt. 17:1–8; Mark 9:2–8; Luke 9:28–36;*
*John 19:30; Matt. 27:50–54; Mark 15:37–39*

Unison

1 Je - sus, take us to the moun-tain, where, with Pe - ter, James, and John,
2 What do you want us to see there, that your close com-pan - ions saw?
3 What do you want us to hear there, that your dear dis - ci - ples heard?
4 Take us to that oth - er moun-tain where we see you glo - ri - fied,
5 We who have be - held your glo - ry, ris - en and as - cend - ed Christ,

We are daz - zled by your glo - ry, light as blind-ing as the sun.
Your di - vin - i - ty re - vealed there fills us with the self - same awe.
Once a - gain the voice from heav - en says of the In - car - nate Word:
Where you shout-ed, "It is fin - ished!" where for all the world you died.
Can - not help but tell the sto - ry, all that you have sac - ri - ficed;

There pre - pare us for the night by the vi - sion of that sight.
Clothed in flesh like ours you go matched to meet our dead - liest foe.
"Lis - ten, lis - ten, ev - ery-one, this is my be - lov - ed One!"
Hear the stunned cen - tu - ri - on: "This was God's be - lov - ed One!"
Say with Pe - ter, James, and John: "You are God's be - lov - ed One!"

*Both text and tune were commissioned by St. Luke Lutheran*
*Church, Silver Spring, Maryland, to commemorate its fiftieth*
*anniversary. The hymnwriter, Jaroslav Vajda, tells of being*
*"as much at a loss for words contemplating the glory of the*
*transfigured Christ as were the disciples."*

Tune: SILVER SPRING 8.7.8.7.7.7.
*Carl F. Schalk, 1991*
*Alternate tune: IRBY*

# 184    O Wondrous Sight, O Vision Fair

*Luke 9:28–36; Matt. 17:1–5; Mark 9:2–7*

*Latin, "Sarum Breviary," 1495*
*Transl. John Mason Neale, 1851; alt.*

1 O won - drous sight, O vi - sion fair of glo - ry
2 From age to age the tale de - clare, how with the
3 The law and proph - ets there have place, two cho - sen
4 With shin - ing face and bright ar - ray, Christ deigns to
5 And faith - ful hearts are raised on high by this great

that the church shall share, Which Christ up - on the
three dis - ci - ples there, Where Mo - ses and E -
wit - ness - es of grace; The voice of God out
man - i - fest to - day What glo - ry shall be
vi - sion's mys - ter - y, For which in joy - ful

moun-tain shows, where bright - er than the sun, Christ glows!
li - jah meet, they with the Christ God's fu - ture greet.
from the cloud pro - claims the Hu - man One a - loud.
theirs be - yond, who live with - in God's lov - ing bond.
strains we raise the voice of prayer, the hymn of praise.

*This tune was composed in honor of the defeat of France at Agincourt by England under Henry V. The words, "Deo gracias . . . ," were added in honor of the English king's wish that the glory for the victory be given to God.*

Tune: DEO GRACIAS L.M.
*"The Agincourt Song," England, c. 1415*
*For other harmonizations, see 209, 259*

# Savior, When in Tears and Dust

**185**

*Robert Grant, 1815; alt.*

1 Sav - ior, when in tears and dust, low we bow to you in trust,
2 By your help-less in - fant years, by your life of want and tears,
3 By your hour of dire de - spair, by your ag - o - ny of prayer,
4 By your deep ex - pir - ing groan, by the sad se - pul-chral stone,

When re - pen - tant, to the skies scarce we lift our weep-ing eyes,
By your days of sore dis-tress in the sav - age wil - der - ness,
By the cross, the nail, the thorn, pierc-ing spear, and tor-turing scorn,
By the vault whose cold a - bode held in vain the ris - ing God:

Mind-ful how you suf - fered pain that God's love in us might reign—
By the dread mys - te - rious hour of the in-sult-ing tempt-er's power:
By the gloom that veiled the skies o'er the dread-ful sac - ri - fice:
O from earth to realms of light, Christ re - stored in power and might,

Help us claim what we would be, hear our sol - emn lit - a - ny.
Turn, O turn a fa - voring eye, hear our sol - emn lit - a - ny.
Lis - ten to our hum - ble cry, hear our sol - emn lit - a - ny.
Lis - ten, lis - ten to the cry of our sol - emn lit - a - ny.

*Robert Grant—English lawyer, member of Parliament, advocate general, humanitarian, and author of a number of significant hymns—was born in India. He returned near the end of his life to become governor of Bombay.*

Tune: SPANISH HYMN 7.7.7.7.D.
*Traditional melody*
*Arr. Benjamin Carr, 1824*

# Dust and Ashes Touch Our Face

186

Brian Wren, 1989

Gen. 3:17–19; Ps. 51:1–12

*Unison*

1 Dust and ash-es touch our face, mark our fail-ure and our
2 Dust and ash-es soil our hands— greed of mar-ket, pride of
3 Dust and ash-es choke our tongue in the waste-land of de-

fall-ing. Ho-ly Spir-it, come, walk with us to-mor-row,
na-tion. Ho-ly Spir-it, come, walk with us to-mor-row
pres-sion. Ho-ly Spir-it, come, walk with us to-mor-row

take us as dis-ci-ples, washed and wak-ened by your call-ing.
as we pray and strug-gle through the mesh-es of op-pres-sion.
through all gloom and griev-ing to the paths of res-ur-rec-tion.

*Refrain*

Take us by the hand and lead us, lead us through the des-ert sands,

*This hymn, exploring the different dimensions of repentance, was written for the choir of the United Church, Hyde Park, Chicago, with Ash Wednesday in mind. Brian Wren reminds us that the Holy Spirit is always with us, not only at Pentecost.*

Tune: DUST AND ASHES Irr. with refrain
Hal H. Hopson, 1989

bring us liv-ing wa-ter, Ho - ly Spir - it, come.

# Again We Keep This Solemn Fast

**187**

*"Ex more docti mystico"*
*Attrib. to Gregory the Great (c. 540–604)*
*Transl. Peter J. Scagnelli (b. 1949); alt.*

*Matt. 6:1–6, 16–21*

*To be sung freely*

1 A - gain we keep this sol - emn fast, a gift of faith from a - ges past, This
2 The law and proph-ets from of old in fig - ured ways this Lent fore-told, Which
3 More spar-ing, there-fore, let us make the words we speak, the food we take, Our
4 Let us a - void each harm-ful way that lures the care - less mind a - stray; By
5 We pray, O bless - ed Three-in - One, our God while end - less a - ges run, That

Lent which binds us lov - ing - ly to faith and hope and char - i - ty.
Christ, all a - ges' Sov-ereign Guide, in these last days has sanc - ti - fied.
sleep, our laugh-ter, ev - ery sense, learn peace through ho - ly pen - i - tence.
watch-ful prayer our spir - its free from schem - ing of the En - e - my.
this, our Lent of for - ty days, may bring us growth and give you praise.

*Ascribed by some to Gregory the Great, this Latin hymn, "Ex more docti mystico," has been found in several manuscripts, the earliest dating from the tenth century.*

Tune: ERHALT UNS, HERR L.M.
*Adapt. from "Jesu, dulce cordium" in Klug's Geistliche Lieder, 1543*
*Harm. The New Century Hymnal, 1993*

# 188

# Give Me a Clean Heart

*Margaret J. Douroux, 1970; alt.*

Ps. 51:1–12

Give me a clean heart so I may serve you.

God, fix my heart so that I may be used by you.

For I'm not wor - thy of all these bless - ings.

Give me a clean heart and I'll fol-low you.

*Margaret J. Douroux, the daughter of a Baptist minister, is known especially for this gospel song, which was recorded by singer James Cleveland. Among her other popular songs found in church hymnals is "God Is Not Dead."*

Tune: DOUROUX 10.12.10.10.
*Margaret J. Douroux, 1970*
*Arr. Albert Denis Tessier, 1987*

# Down at the Cross

*Elisha A. Hoffman (1839–1929); alt.*

*Gal. 2:20*

1 Down at the cross where my Sav - ior died, down where for cleans-ing from
2 I am so won - drous - ly saved from sin, Je - sus so sweet - ly a -
3 O pre - cious foun - tain that saves from sin, I am so glad I have
4 Come to this foun - tain so rich and sweet, cast your poor soul at the

sin I cried, there to my heart was the blood ap - plied—
bides with - in; there at the cross where Christ took me in—
en - tered in; there Je - sus saves me and keeps me clean—
Sav - ior's feet; plunge in to - day and be made com - plete—

*Refrain*

(1–4) Glo - ry to Christ's name. Glo - ry to Christ's name, glo - ry to Christ's

name; There to my heart was the blood ap-plied; glo - ry to Christ's name.

*While Elisha Hoffman pastored several congregations, he was associated with evangelical publishing houses as editor or compiler of fifty songbooks. Although never formally trained in music, he wrote texts and tunes for more than 200 hymns.*

Tune: DOWN AT THE CROSS
9.9.9.5. with refrain
*John H. Stockton (1813–1877)*

# 190

# Beneath the Cross of Jesus

*Isa. 32:2; Gal. 6:14*

*Elizabeth C. Clephane, 1872; alt.*

1 Be - neath the cross of Je - sus I glad - ly take my stand,
2 Up - on the cross of Je - sus with - in my mind I see
3 I take, O cross, your shad - ow for my a - bid - ing place;

the shad - ow of a might - y rock with - in a wea - ry land;
the ver - y dy - ing form of One who suf - fered there for me;
I ask no oth - er sun-shine than the sun - shine of Christ's face;

A home with-in the wil - der - ness, a rest up - on the way,
And from my griev-ing heart with tears two won - ders I con - fess—
Con - tent to let the world go by, to know no gain or loss,

from the burn-ing of the noon-tide heat, and the bur - den of the day.
the won-ders of Christ's glo - rious love and my un - wor-thi - ness.
my sin - ful self my on - ly shame, my glo - ry all the cross.

*Elizabeth Clephane was known during her short lifetime for her charitable work in her hometown of Melrose, Scotland. After her death, this hymn was compiled from several stanzas of a longer poem that had appeared in a popular Scottish religious magazine.*

Tune: ST. CHRISTOPHER 7.6.8.6.8.6.8.6.
*Frederick C. Maker, 1881*

# Before Your Cross, O Jesus

*Ferdinand Q. Blanchard, 1929; alt.*

*Mark 8:34; Gal. 6:14; Phil. 1:27; 3:7–10*

1 Be-fore your cross, O Je-sus,
   our lives are judged to-day;
   the mean-ing of our ea-ger strife
   is test-ed by your way.
   A-cross our rest-less liv--ing
   the light streams from your cross,
   and by its clear, re-veal-ing beams
   we mea-sure gain and loss.

2 The hopes that lead us on-ward,
   the fears that hold us back,
   our will to dare great things for God,
   the cour-age that we lack,
   The faith we keep in good--ness,
   our love, as low or pure,
   on all, the judg-ment of the cross
   falls stead-y, clear, and sure.

3 Yet hum-bly, in our striv-ing,
   we rise to face its test.
   We crave the power to do your will
   as once you did it best.
   On us let now the heal--ing
   of your great Spir-it fall,
   and make us brave and full of joy
   to an-swer to your call.

*Ferdinand Q. Blanchard, moderator of the General Council of Congregational Churches (1942–1944), was active in missions and was a leading advocate of educational opportunity for African-Americans. This hymn was written for Euclid Avenue Congregational Church in Cleveland, Ohio, which he served for forty years.*

Tune: ST. CHRISTOPHER 7.6.8.6.8.6.8.6.
*Frederick C. Maker, 1881*

# When Jesus Wept

*William Billings, 1770*

*John 11:35*

1 When Je - sus wept, the fall - ing tear in mer - cy
flowed be - yond all bound; When Je - sus groaned, a
trem - bling fear seized all the guilt - y world a - round.

*William Billings served as choir leader at Old South Church (Congregational) in Boston. A self-taught singing-school teacher and composer, he also worked as a tanner. "When Jesus Wept" is especially beautiful when sung as a canon, with groups entering as indicated by the numbers above.*

Tune: WHEN JESUS WEPT L.M.
*William Billings, 1770*
New England Psalm Singer

# In the Cross of Christ I Glory

*Gal. 6:14*

*John Bowring, 1825*

1 In the cross of Christ I glo - ry, tower - ing
2 When the woes of life o'er - take me, hopes de -
3 When the sun of bliss is beam - ing light and
4 Bane and bless - ing, pain and plea - sure, by the
5 In the cross of Christ I glo - ry, tower - ing

o'er the wrecks of time; All the light of
ceive, and fears an - noy, Nev - er shall the
love up - on my way, From the cross the
cross are sanc - ti - fied; Peace is there that
o'er the wrecks of time; All the light of

sa - cred sto - ry gath - ers 'round its head sub - lime.
cross for - sake me: Lo! it glows with peace and joy.
ra - diance stream - ing adds more lus - ter to the day.
knows no mea - sure, joys that through all time a - bide.
sa - cred sto - ry gath - ers 'round its head sub - lime.

*John Bowring's goal "to do something which may connect my work with the literature of the age" was attained with this enduring hymn. The gifted Bowring studied 200 languages and wrote extensively in many fields.*

Tune: RATHBUN 8.7.8.7.
*Ithamar Conkey, 1849*
*Alternate setting: TOMTER*

# In the Cross of Christ I Glory

*John Bowring, 1825*

*Gal. 6:14*

1 & 5 In the cross of Christ I glory, tower-ing o'er the
2 When the woes of life o'er-take me, hopes de-ceive, and
3 When the sun of bliss is beam-ing light and love up-
4 Bane and bless-ing, pain and plea-sure, by the cross are

wrecks of time; All the light of sa - cred
fears an - noy, Nev - er shall the cross for -
on my way, From the cross the ra - diance
sanc - ti - fied; Peace is there that knows no

sto - ry gath - ers 'round its head sub - lime.
sake me: Lo! it glows with peace and joy.
stream-ing adds more lus - ter to the day.
mea - sure, joys that through all time a - bide. *(repeat first stanza)*

*Composer Bruce Neswick wrote this tune to provide an
alternative to the traditional one. It is named for Episcopal priest
Patrick Tomter, in whose parish Neswick served as organist
during his undergraduate studies at Pacific Lutheran University.*

Tune: TOMTER 8.7.8.7.
*Bruce Neswick (b. 1956)*
*Alternate setting: RATHBUN*

# 195

# On a Hill Far Away
## (The Old Rugged Cross)

*Heb. 12:2; James 1:12*

*George Bennard, 1913; alt.*

1. On a hill far a-way stood an old rug-ged cross, the em-blem of suf-fering and shame; And I love that old cross where the dear-est and best for a world of lost sin-ners was slain.

2. Oh, that old rug-ged cross, so de-spised by the world, has a won-drous at-trac-tion for me; For the dear Lamb of God left the glo-ry of heaven to bear it to cold Cal-va-ry.

3. In that old rug-ged cross, which bore Love so di-vine, a won-drous beau-ty I see, For up-on that old cross Je-sus suf-fered and died to par-don and sanc-ti-fy me.

4. To the old rug-ged cross I will ev-er be true, its shame and re-proach glad-ly bear; When God calls me some-day to my home far a-way, there God's glo-ry for-ev-er I'll share.

*Refrain*

So I'll cher-ish the old rug-ged cross, cross, the old rug-ged cross, till my

*After serving as an officer in the Salvation Army, George Bennard was ordained by the Methodist Episcopal Church. In the midst of his travels through the Midwest conducting revival services, he was inspired to write this hymn.*

Tune: THE OLD RUGGED CROSS Irr.
*George Bennard, 1913*

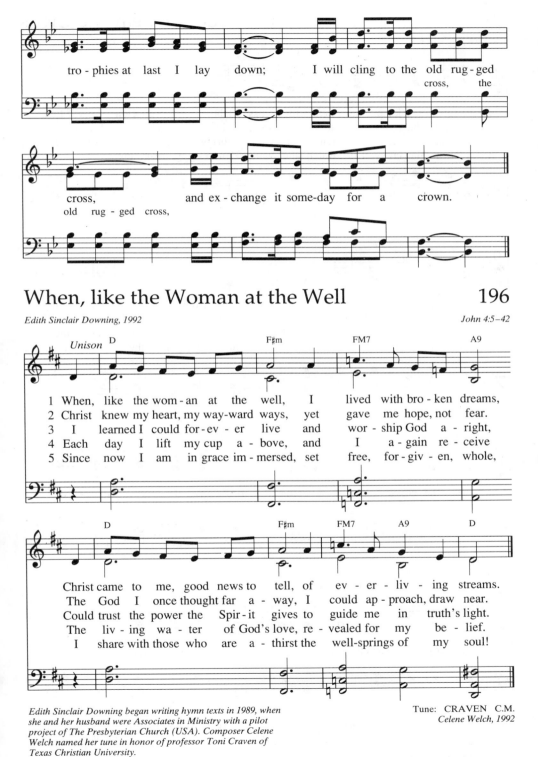

tro - phies at last I lay down; I will cling to the old rug-ged cross, the cross, and ex - change it some-day for a crown.
old rug - ged cross,

# When, like the Woman at the Well 196

*Edith Sinclair Downing, 1992*

*John 4:5–42*

Unison

1 When, like the wom - an at the well, I lived with bro - ken dreams,
2 Christ knew my heart, my way-ward ways, yet gave me hope, not fear.
3 I learned I could for - ev - er live and wor - ship God a - right,
4 Each day I lift my cup a - bove, and I a - gain re - ceive
5 Since now I am in grace im - mersed, set free, for - giv - en, whole,

Christ came to me, good news to tell, of ev - er - liv - ing streams.
The God I once thought far a - way, I could ap - proach, draw near.
Could trust the power the Spir - it gives to guide me in truth's light.
The liv - ing wa - ter of God's love, re - vealed for my be - lief.
I share with those who are a - thirst the well-springs of my soul!

*Edith Sinclair Downing began writing hymn texts in 1989, when
she and her husband were Associates in Ministry with a pilot
project of The Presbyterian Church (USA). Composer Celene
Welch named her tune in honor of professor Toni Craven of
Texas Christian University.*

Tune: CRAVEN C.M.
*Celene Welch, 1992*

# 197        Jesus, Keep Me near the Cross

*Gal. 6:14; Rev. 22:1–5*        *Fanny Crosby, 1869; alt.*

1 Je - sus, keep me near the cross; there a pre - cious foun - tain,
2 Near the cross, a trem - bling soul, love and mer - cy found me;
3 Near the cross! O Lamb of God, bring its scenes be - fore me;
4 Near the cross I'll watch and wait, hop - ing, trust - ing ev - er,

free to all, a heal - ing stream, flows from Cal - vary's moun - tain.
there the bright and morn - ing star sheds its beams a - round me.
help me live from day to day with its shad - ow o'er me.
till I reach the gold - en strand just be - yond the riv - er.

*Refrain*

In the cross, in the cross, be my glo - ry ev - er,

till my ran - somed soul shall find rest be - yond the riv - er.

"Aunt Fanny" Crosby was an inspiration to people around the world. Blind from infancy, she wrote about 8,000 gospel hymns using more than 200 pseudonyms. William H. Doane, an active layperson and philanthropist in Cincinnati and close personal friend, often collaborated with her.

Tune: NEAR THE CROSS 7.6.7.6. with refrain
William H. Doane, 1869

# Lift High the Cross

*George William Kitchin (1827–1912)*
*Rev. by Michael Robert Newbolt, 1916; alt.*

John 1:29–34; Rom. 5:6–11; 6:3–8; Rev. 7:9–17; 22:1–5

*Refrain, in unison*

Lift high the cross, the love of Christ pro - claim; Let

*Last time, end*

all a - dore and praise that sa - cred name.

*Stanzas, in harmony*

1 Come, Chris - tians, fol - low where our Sav - ior trod, the
2 Each new - born ser - vant of the Cru - ci - fied bears
3 O Christ, once lift - ed on the glo - rious tree, your
4 Set up your throne, that earth's de - spair may cease, be -
5 So shall our song of tri - umph ev - er be: praise

*to Refrain*

Lamb vic - to - rious, Christ the Child of God.
on the brow the seal of Christ who died.
death has brought us life e - ter - nal - ly.
neath the shad - ow of its heal - ing peace.
to the Cru - ci - fied for vic - to - ry.

*Since its first inclusion in a U.S. hymnal in the 1970s, this hymn has become enormously popular. G. W. Kitchin and M. R. Newbolt were Church of England ministers. Sydney Nicholson was organist of Westminster Abbey.*

Tune: CRUCIFER 10.10. with refrain
*Sydney Hugo Nicholson, 1916*

# Alas! and Did My Savior Bleed
## (At the Cross)

*Gal. 2:20; 6:14; Phil. 2:2–12; Heb. 12:1–3*

*Isaac Watts, 1707; alt.*
*Refrain by Ralph E. Hudson, 1885; alt.*

1 A - las! and did my Sav - ior bleed, and did my Sov-ereign die?
2 Was it for crimes that I have done, Christ groaned up - on the tree?
3 Well might the sun in shad-ows hide, and shut its glo - ries in,
4 But tears of grief can - not re - pay the debt of love I owe;

Would God de - vote that sa - cred head for sin - ners such as I?
A - maz - ing pit - y! Grace un-known! And love be - yond de - gree!
When Je - sus Christ my Sav - ior died for hu - man crea-tures' sin.
Here, Christ, I give my - self a - way as all that I can do!

*Refrain*

At the cross, at the cross where I first found the light, and the
bur-den of my heart rolled a - way,
rolled a-way,
It was there by faith all my

*After discharge from the Union army, Ralph Hudson taught music at Mt. Union College in Alliance, Ohio, where he founded a publishing company. He wrote the music for this Isaac Watts text and added a familiar camp-meeting chorus as a refrain.*

Tune: HUDSON C.M. with refrain
*Ralph E. Hudson, 1885*
*Alternate setting: MARTYRDOM*

fears took flight, and now I am hap-py all the day.

## Alas! and Did My Savior Bleed

**200**

*Isaac Watts, 1707; alt.*

*Gal. 2:20; 6:14; Phil. 2:2–12; Heb. 12:1–3*

1 A - las! and did my Sav - ior bleed, and did my Sov-ereign die?
2 Was it for crimes that I have done, Christ groaned up - on the tree?
3 Well might the sun in shad-ows hide, and shut its glo - ries in,
4 But tears of grief can - not re - pay the debt of love I owe;

Would God de - vote that sa - cred head for sin - ners such as I?
A - maz - ing pit - y! Grace un-known! And love be - yond de - gree!
When Je - sus Christ my Sav - ior died for hu - man crea - tures' sin.
Here, Christ, I give my-self a - way as all that I can do!

*This tune has also been called* Avon, Fenwick, Drumclog,
Inverness, *and* All Saints. *Although published by Hugh Wilson
(1827) and Robert Smith (1825), some claim it to be a Scottish
folk tune. In early America, the hymn appeared in shape note
books to at least five other tunes.*

Tune: MARTYRDOM C.M.
(AVON)
*Scottish folk tune*
*Alternate setting:* HUDSON

# 201

## An Outcast among Outcasts

Luke 17:11–19; Mark 15:32

Richard D. Leach, 1992

*Unison*

1 An out-cast a-mong out-casts, dis - missed with dou - ble scorn,
2 An out-cast a-mong out-casts, where three were cru - ci - fied,
3 For out-casts a-mong out-casts the bound-aries are re - drawn,

be - lit - tled by the la - bels: "un - clean" and "for-eign born"—
de - rid - ed by the oth - ers as they hung side by side—
by words, "Your faith has saved you," by cross and Eas-ter dawn.

came back with thanks for Je - sus, and then went on his way:
came back from death with pow - er, God had the fi - nal say:
The dis - tant longed-for cen - ters of pow - er, peace, and care,

An out-cast a-mong out - casts showed grate - ful faith that day.
An out-cast a-mong out - casts shows God to us to - day.
where life is free to flour - ish, are found now ev - ery - where.

*United Church of Christ minister Richard D. Leach has served churches in Connecticut since 1978, when he graduated from Princeton Theological Seminary. He began writing hymns in 1987 and had his first texts published in 1989.*

Tune: POST STREET 7.6.7.6.D.
*Dan Damon, 1994*

# O God, How We Have Wandered

Kevin Nichols, 1980; alt.

Luke 15:11–32; 2 Cor. 5:16–20

1 O God, how we have wan - dered and hid - den from your face;
2 And now at length dis - cern - ing the e - vil that we do,
3 O God of all the liv - ing, both ban - ished and re - stored,

In fool - ish - ness have squan - dered your leg - a - cy of grace.
By faith we are re - turn - ing with hope and trust in you.
Com - pas - sion - ate, for - giv - ing, our peace and hope as - sured.

But how, in ex - ile dwell - ing, we turn with fear and shame,
In haste you come to meet us, and home re - joic - ing bring,
Grant now that our trans - gress - ing, our faith - less - ness may cease.

As dis - tant but com - pell - ing, you call us each by name.
In glad - ness there to greet us with calf and robe and ring.
Stretch out your hand in bless - ing, in par - don, and in peace.

The tune for this contemporary text appears five times in J. S. Bach's *St. Matthew Passion, and first appeared as a hymn setting in the early 1800s. It has an ecumenical history reaching back many centuries. Originally it was a German love song.*

Tune: PASSION CHORALE 7.6.7.6.D.
(HERZLICH TUT MICH VERLANGEN)
*Melody by Hans Leo Hassler, 1601*
*Harm. J. S. Bach, 1729*
*For another harmonization, see 179*

## 203
### Ah, What Shame I Have to Bear

Luke 15:11–19

Sogo Matsumoto, 1895
Transl. Esther Hibbard, 1962

1 Ah, what shame I have to bear,
2 In this hut I sleep and wake,
3 Tat - tered sleeves are wet with dew

for I left my home To pur - sue an
tak - ing care of swine; No one has pit -
when I think of home. Wak - ing from my

emp - ty dream, spent my life in vain!
y on me: loud blows chil - ly wind.
fool - ish dreams, to my home I'll go.

*This Japanese text provides an opportunity to imagine and enter
into the experience of the prodigal child who longs for the
forgiveness of a parent. Translator Esther Hibbard was a United
Church of Christ missionary in Japan for many years.*

Tune: IMAYO 7.5.7.5.
*Japanese melody, 12th century*

## 204
### "Take Up Your Cross," the Savior Said

Mark 8:34

Charles W. Everest, 1883; alt.

1 "Take up your cross," the Sav - ior said, "if you would
2 Take up your cross; let not its weight fill your weak
3 Take up your cross, heed not the shame, and let your
4 Take up your cross and fol - low Christ, nor think till

my dis - ci - ple be; Take up your cross with
spir - it with a - larm; Christ's strength will bear your
fool - ish pride be still; For Christ did not re -
death to lay it down, For on - ly those who

will - ing heart and hum - bly fol - low af - ter me."
spir - it up and brace your heart, sup - port your arm.
fuse to die up - on a cross on Cal - vary's hill.
bear the cross may hope to wear the glo - rious crown.

*Charles Everest, after graduating from Trinity College, Hartford, was rector of a parish in Hamden, Connecticut, for thirty-one years. This sermon in verse is from his collection of hymns titled* Visions of Death and Other Poems.

Tune: DEUS TUORUM MILITUM L.M.
*Grenoble Antiphoner, 1753*

# Forty Days and Forty Nights

**205**

*George Hunt Smyttan, 1856; alt.*

*Matt. 4:1–11; Heb. 2:18*

1 For - ty days and for - ty nights you were fast - ing in the wild;
2 Shall we not your sor - row share and from world - ly joys ab - stain,
3 Then if Sa - tan on us press, flesh or spir - it to as - sail,
4 So shall we have peace di - vine: ho - lier glad - ness ours shall be;
5 Keep, O keep us, Sav - ior dear, ev - er con - stant by your side;

For - ty days and for - ty nights tempt - ed, and yet un - de - filed.
Fast - ing with un - ceas - ing prayer, strong with you to suf - fer pain?
Vic - tor in the wil - der - ness, grant that we not faint or fail!
'Round us, too, shall an - gels shine, such as served you faith - ful - ly.
That with you we may ap - pear at the e - ter - nal Eas - ter - tide.

*The son of a doctor in Bombay, George Hunt Smyttan became a priest in the Church of England. He published several collections of verse. This hymn was one of three Lenten hymns that appeared in* The Penny Post *(1856).*

Tune: HEINLEIN 7.7.7.7.
*Attrib. to Martin Herbst, 1676*

# A Woman Came Who Did Not Count the Cost

Mark 14:3–9

*Richard D. Leach, 1990*

*Unison*

1 A wom-an came who did not count the cost of do-ing what she
2 Some on-ly saw what she had spent— "Why such a waste with poor to
3 You give as she, sur-pris-ing-ly, you give with beau-ty as she

could, She broke an al - a - bas-ter flask, and sweet-ness
feed?" They served the poor well with their tongues! But she had
gave, You give as she, not hold-ing back, you make us

spilled on Je - sus' head.
done a love-ly deed. *Refrain* O God, you are the A-noint-ing
Christ - like with your love.

One who does not count your pas-sion's cost, And when we

United Church of Christ minister Richard D. Leach has stated
that much of his inspiration as a hymnwriter comes during his
sermon preparations. The theme of this text—God anointing us,
as the woman anointed Jesus with perfume—was first developed
in a sermon, and then given poetic form.

Tune: WEXFORD CAROL L.M.D.
*Irish folk melody*
*Arr. Arthur G. Clyde, 1994*

gath - er you will spill the sweet-ness of your grace on us.

## Just as I Am

**207**

*Charlotte Elliott, 1836; alt.*

*John 6:37; Eph. 2:14*

1 Just as I am, with-out one plea but that your
2 Just as I am, though tossed a-bout with man-y a
3 Just as I am, you will re-ceive, will wel-come,
4 Just as I am, your love un-known has bro-ken

blood was shed for me, And that you called in-
con-flict, many a doubt, Fight-ings and fears with-
par-don, cleanse, re-lieve; Be-cause your prom-ise
ev-ery bar-rier down; Now to be yours, and

vit-ing me, O Lamb of God, I come, I come!
in, with-out, O Lamb of God, I come, I come!
I be-lieve, O Lamb of God, I come, I come!
yours a-lone, O Lamb of God, I come, I come!

*This text appeared in Charlotte Elliott's Invalid's Hymn Book, published in England in 1836. Disabled at age thirty, she continued a career of writing and editing. This hymn has been translated into many languages.*

Tune: WOODWORTH L.M.
*William B. Bradbury, 1849*

# God Loved the World

John 3:16–17

Heiliges Lippen und Herzens Opfer, *Stettin, 1778*
*Transl. August Crull, 1845; alt.*

1 God loved the world, and loving gave
2 Christ Je - sus is the ground of faith,
3 If you are sick, if death is near,
4 Be of good cheer, for God in Christ

a won - drous gift, the lost to save,
who was made flesh and suf - fered death;
this truth your trou - bled heart can cheer;
for - gives the flock, by sin en - ticed,

That all who would in Christ be - lieve
All who con - fide in Christ a - lone
Christ Je - sus saves us all from death;
And jus - ti - fied by Je - sus' blood,

should ev - er - last - ing life re - ceive.
are built on this chief cor - ner - stone.
that is the firm - est ground of faith.
your bap - tism grants the high - est good.

*Edward Miller, a skilled flutist in G. F. Handel's orchestra,*
*adapted* Rockingham *from the tune* Tunbridge. *Miller named it*
*for the Marquis of Rockingham, a patron and friend, and prime*
*minister of Great Britain.*

Tune: ROCKINGHAM L.M.
*Anon.*
*Adapt. Edward Miller, 1790*

# O Love, How Vast, How Flowing Free

Latin, 15th century
*Transl.* The New Century Hymnal, *1994*

Matt. 4:1–11; Luke 4:1–13; Phil. 2:5–11;
John 17:1–26; 19:1–3, 16–18

1 O Love, how vast, how flow - ing free, O Love how
2 Not as an an - gel vis - it - ing, nor form ce -
3 For us bap - tized, and fast - ing long, for us was
4 For us was beat - en, whipped, and tried, and tak - en

filled with ec - sta - sy, That God a hu - man
les - tial or - bit - ing, But born in flesh God
tempt - ed by the wrong, For us the pangs of
to be cru - ci - fied, So Love all this for

form should take, and mor - tal be for mor-tals' sake.
chose to be, robed in our own hu - man - i - ty.
hun - ger knew; for us the Tempt - er o - ver - threw.
us en - dured, and dy - ing, life for us pro - cured.

5 A-ris-ing from the dead a-gain,
   our Sov-ereign goes on high to reign;
   And sends the Spir-it to a-bide
   for strength and sol-ace at our side.

6 Then for God's bound-less love
     sing praise
   through end-less a-ges, count-less days;
   By Love we have been rec-on-ciled:
   sal-va-tion gained through
     God's own Child.

*Recounting the life of Christ, this hymn comes from an*
*anonymous fifteenth-century Latin hymn of twenty-three*
*stanzas. It has been described as a precursor of Christmas*
*and Epiphany carols.*

Tune: DEO GRACIAS L.M.
*"The Agincourt Song," England, c. 1415*
*For another harmonization, see 184, 259*

# 210

# Said Judas to Mary

John 12:1–8

Sydney Carter, 1964; alt.

1 Said Ju-das to Mar-y, "Now what will you do with your oint-ment so rich and so rare?" "I'll pour it all o-ver the feet of the Christ, and I'll wipe it a-way with my

2 "O Mar-y, O Mar-y, O think of the poor. This oint-ment, it could have been sold; And think of the blan-kets and think of the bread you could buy with the sil-ver and

3 "To - mor-row, to-mor-row, I'll think of the poor; to - mor-row," she said, "not to - day; For dear-er than all of the poor in the world is my love who is go-ing a-

4 Said Je-sus to Mar-y, "Your love is so deep, to - day you may do as you will. To - mor-row, you say, I am go-ing a-way, but my bod-y I leave with you

*Sydney Carter has enjoyed a varied career as a schoolteacher, journalist, and songwriter, and was a leader of the folk-song renaissance in English church music in the early 1960s. This hymn imagines the dialogue between Mary of Bethany, Judas Iscariot, and Jesus.*

Tune: JUDAS AND MARY Irr.
*Sydney Carter, 1964*

hair," she said, "I'll wipe it a-way with my hair." (2 "O)
gold," he said, "you could buy with the sil - ver and gold." (3 "To-)
way," she said, "my love who is go - ing a - way." (4 Said)
still," he said, "my bo - dy I leave with you still." (5 "The)

(6 -way.")

5 "The poor of the world are my bod-y,"
   he said,
   "to the end of the world they shall be.
The bread and the blan-kets you give
   to the poor
you will know you have giv-en to me,"
   he said,
   "you'll know you have giv-en to me."

6 "My bod-y will hang on the cross
   of the world
   to-mor-row," he said, "not to-day.
And Mar-tha and Mar-y will find me
   a-gain
   and wash all my sor-row a-way,"
   he said,
   "and wash all my sor-row a-way."

# Lord Jesus, Who through Forty Days 211

*Claudia F. I. Hernaman, 1873; alt.*

*Mark 1:12–13; Luke 4:1–13*

1 Lord Je - sus, who through for - ty days for us did fast and pray,
2 As you with Sa - tan did con-tend, and did the vic-tory win,
3 And through these days of pen - i - tence, and through this Pas-sion - tide,
4 A - bide with us, till when this life of suf - fering shall be past,

Teach us with you to mourn our sins, and close by you to stay.
O give us strength to per - se - vere, in you to con-quer sin.
Yes, ev - er - more, in life and death, O Christ, with us a - bide.
An Eas - ter of un - end - ing joy we may at - tain at last.

*Unflagging in her zeal for religious education of children,*
*Claudia F. I. Hernaman wrote some 150 hymns. This one*
*appeared in her* Child's Book of Praise *(1873).*

Tune: ST. FLAVIAN C.M.
*Day's* The Whole Booke of Psalms, *1562*

# 212     O Jesus Christ, May Grateful Hymns

*Matt. 23:37–39; Luke 13:34–35*        *Bradford Gray Webster, 1954; alt.*

1 O Je-sus Christ, may grate-ful hymns be ris - ing, in ev-ery
2 Grant us new cour - age, nev - er proud, but hum - ble, strong in your
3 Show us your Spir - it, brood-ing o'er each cit - y, as you once

cit - y for your love and care; In - spire our wor - ship, grant the
strength to ven-ture and to dare; To lift the fall - en, guide the
wept a-bove Je - ru - sa - lem, Seek-ing to gath - er all in

glad sur - pris - ing that your blessed Spir - it rous - es ev - ery - where.
ones who stum - ble, seek out the lone - ly and God's mer - cy share.
love and pit - y, and heal - ing those who touch your gar - ment's hem.

*This text, written for a Convocation of Urban Life in America, was chosen by The Hymn Society for publication in* Five New Hymns on the City. *Bradford Webster, a Methodist minister, served churches in his native New York state for forty years.*

Tune: CHARTERHOUSE 11.10.11.10.
*David Evans, 1927*

# "Hosanna, Loud Hosanna"

*Jennette Threlfall, 1873; alt.*

Mark 11:8–10; Matt. 21:15

1 "Ho - san - na, loud ho - san - na," the lit - tle chil - dren sang;
2 From Ol - i - vet they fol - lowed a - mid a cheer - ing crowd,
3 "Ho - san - na in the high - est!" That an - cient song is ours.

through pil - lared court and tem - ple the love - ly an - them rang;
the vic - tor palm branch wav - ing, and chant - ing clear and loud.
We hail our great Re - deem - er and sing with all our powers:

To Je - sus, who had blessed them close fold - ed to his breast,
The one whom an - gels wor - ship rode on in low - ly state,
"Ho - san - na, Christ, we praise you with heart and life and voice.

the chil - dren sang their prais - es, the sim - plest and the best.
and glad to see the chil - dren, slowed down the don - key's gait.
Ho - san - na! In your pres - ence for - ev - er we'll re - joice!"

*Jennette Threlfall of England, who was disabled by two accidents,*
*wrote hymns that inspired hope and courage in others. This text was*
*published in her collection* Sunshine and Shadow.

Tune: ELLACOMBE C.M.D.
Gesangbuch der herzoglichen Wirtembergischen
katholischen Hofkapelle, *1784*

# 214

## Mantos y Ramos
### (Filled with Excitement)

Matt. 21:6–9; Luke 19:35–38; Mark 11:7; John 12:12–15

*Rubén Ruíz Avila, 1972; alt.*
*Transl. Gertrude C. Suppe, 1979, 1987; alt.*

1 Mantos y ramos esparciendo va
2 Como en la entrada a Jerusalén,
1 Filled with excitement, all the happy throng
2 As in that entrance to Jerusalem,

el pueblo alegre de Jerusalén.
todos cantamos a Jesús el rey,
spread cloaks and branches on the city streets.
hosannas we will sing to Jesus Christ,

Allá lo
al Cristo
There in the
To our Re-

lejos se vislumbra ya
vivo que nos llama hoy
distance they begin to see,
deemer who still calls today,

en un pollino al Salva-
para seguirle con a-
there on a donkey, comes the
asks us to follow with our

*Estribillo (Refrain)*

dor Jesús.
mor y fe.
Savior, Christ.
love and faith.

Mientras mil voces resuenan por doquier; ho-
From every corner a thousand voices sing

Mexican church musician Rubén Ruíz Avila composed
this hymn for the choir of the United Methodist Church in
Covington, Virginia. It was first published in Canciones de Fe y
Compromiso (1978) in the arrangement by Alvin Schutmaat.

Tune: HOSANNA 10.10.10.10. with refrain
*Rubén Ruíz Avila, 1972*
*Arr. Alvin Schutmaat, 1979*

san-na al que vie-ne en el nom - bre de Dios. Con un a-lien-to de
praise to the One who comes in the name of God. Our ac-cla-ma-tion breaks

gran ex-cla - ma-ción pro-rrum-pen con voz triun - fal:
forth in shouts of praise, our tri - um-phant song of joy:

"¡Ho - san - na! ¡Ho - san-na a Je - sús!"
"Ho - san - na, ho - san-na to Christ!

"¡Ho - san - na! ¡Ho - san-na a Je - sús!"
Ho - san - na, ho - san - na to Christ!"

**215**        # Ride On! Ride On in Majesty

*Luke 19:36–38; Zech. 9:9*        *Henry H. Milman, 1827; adapt. Lavon Bayler, 1993*

1 Ride on! Ride on in maj - es - ty!
2 Ride on! Ride on in maj - es - ty!
3 Ride on! Ride on in maj - es - ty!
4 Ride on! Ride on in maj - es - ty!

O Christ, with brave hu - mil - i - ty,
As crowds of peo - ple come to see
Ride on in hum - ble dig - ni - ty;
For you have set your peo - ple free

On low - ly colt, your road pur - sue,
And shout ho - san - nas, lift - ing high
Be - hold the ones you came to save
And we, re - mem - bering all your pain,

as palms and cloaks are spread for you.
their praise for one a - bout to die.
from sense - less life and end - less grave.
now meet a - gain to hail your reign.

Henry H. Milman, a priest of the Church of England,
served successively as professor of poetry at Oxford,
canon of Westminster, and dean of St. Paul's Cathedral,
London. He was also a successful playwright and historian.

Tune: ST. DROSTANE L.M.
*John B. Dykes, 1862*
*Alternate tune: WINCHESTER NEW*

# All Glory, Laud, and Honor

*Theodulph of Orléans, 9th century*
*Transl. John Mason Neale, 1854; alt.*

**216**

*Matt. 21:8–9*

1 All glo - ry, laud, and hon - or to you, O Christ, we sing,
2 O Prom-ised One of Is - rael, of Da - vid's roy - al line,
3 As you re-ceived their prais - es, re - ceive our prayers to - day,

to whom the lips of chil - dren made sweet ho - san - nas ring!
the one called "God's be - lov - ed," of flesh and yet di - vine,
whose jus - tice and whose mer - cy and sov-ereign-ty hold sway.

The peo - ple of the He - brews with palms a - dorned your way;
To you, be - fore your pas - sion, they sang their hymns of praise;
All glo - ry, laud, and hon - or to you, O Christ, we sing,

our praise and prayer and an - thems we of - fer you this day.
to you, now high ex - alt - ed, our mel - o - dy we raise.
to whom the lips of chil - dren made sweet ho - san - nas ring!

*Brought to France by Charlemagne, Theodulph became*
*bishop of Orléans but was later imprisoned by Charlemagne's*
*successor. According to legend, he was released when the*
*king, Louis the Pious, heard him sing this hymn from prison.*

Tune: ST. THEODULPH 7.6.7.6.D.
(VALET WILL ICH DIR GEBEN)
*Melchior Teschner, 1615*
*For another setting, see 217*

# 217 All Glory, Laud, and Honor

*Matt. 21:8–9*

*Theodulph of Orléans, 9th century*
*Transl. John Mason Neale, 1854; alt.*

1 All glo - ry, laud, and hon - or to you, O Christ, we
2 O Prom - ised One of Is - rael, of Da - vid's roy - al
3 As you re - ceived their prais - es, re - ceive our prayers to -

sing, to whom the lips of chil - dren made sweet ho -
line, the one called "God's be - lov - ed," of flesh, and
day, whose jus - tice and whose mer - cy, and sov - ereign -

san - nas ring! The peo - ple of the He - brews with
yet, di - vine, To you, be - fore your pas - sion, they
ty hold sway. All glo - ry, laud, and hon - or to

palms a - dorned your way; our praise and prayer and
sang their hymns of praise; to you, now high ex -
you, O Christ, we sing, to whom the lips of

*Vérne de la Peña is a Philippine composer and ethno-*
*musicologist whose studies have focused on the music of*
*indigenous peoples of Southeast Asia and the Pacific. His*
*tune,* Eulogia, *is reminiscent of that music through the use*
*of the "tritone" and ostinato accompaniment.*

Tune: EULOGIA 7.6.7.6.D.
*Vérne de la Peña, 1994*
*For another setting, see 216*

an - thems    we    of - fer you this    day.
alt - ed,    our    mel - o - dy we    raise.
chil - dren    made sweet ho - san - nas    ring!

## Ah, Holy Jesus

**218**

*Johann Heermann, 1630*
*Paraphr. by Robert Bridges, 1899; alt.*

*Isa. 53:3–5; John 1:11; 18:15–17*

1 Ah, ho - ly Je - sus, how have you of - fend - ed, that mor - tal
2 Who was the guilt - y? Who brought this up - on you? It is my
3 For me, kind Je - sus, was your in - car - na - tion, your mor - tal
4 There-fore, kind Je - sus, since I can-not pay you, I do a -

judg - ment has on you de - scend - ed? By foes de - rid - ed,
trea - son, Je - sus, that has slain you. And I, dear Je - sus,
sor - row, and your life's ob - la - tion, Your death of an - guish
dore you, and will ev - er pray you, Think on your pit - y

by your own re - ject - ed, O most af - flict - ed!
I it was de - nied you; I cru - ci - fied you.
and your bit - ter pas - sion, for my sal - va - tion.
and your love un - swerv - ing, not my de - serv - ing.

*Based on an eleventh-century Latin meditation by Jean de*
*Fécamp, this is one of many fine hymns by Johann Heermann.*
*Though poor, Heermann's parents prepared him for the*
*Lutheran pastorate. Much of his ministry took place during*
*the Thirty Years' War.*

Tune: HERZLIEBSTER JESU 11.11.11.5.
*Johann Crüger, 1640*

# 219 Journey to Gethsemane

John 18:1–20:18

*James Montgomery, 1820; alt.*

1 Jour - ney to Geth - se - ma - ne, go and feel the
2 Fol - low then to Pi - late's hall, view the Lord of
3 Cal - vary's mourn - ful moun - tain climb, see the Sav - ior
4 Ear - ly has - ten to the tomb, hear the cry of

tempt - er's power; Your Re - deem - er's con - flict see,
life ar - raigned; Crowned with thorns and mocked by all,
lift - ed high, Mark the mir - a - cle of time,
great sur - prise; Then the si - lence in the room,

watch the an - guish of this hour; Do not hide or
faith - ful - ly this pain sus - tained; Great - er still than
God's own Child is sac - ri - ficed; "It is fin - ished!"
Je - sus there no long - er lies: Christ is ris - en!

turn a - way: learn from Je - sus how to pray.
shame or loss, Je - sus now must face the cross.
Je - sus cries: learn from Je - sus how to die.
Re - al - ize that with Christ we, too, may rise.

*James Montgomery, born of Moravian missionary parents, edited a newspaper in England. Risking imprisonment, he published articles advocating human rights, including the abolition of slavery. He wrote more than 400 hymns.*

Tune: REDHEAD NO. 76  7.7.7.7.7.7.
*Richard Redhead, 1853*

# Sing, My Tongue

220

*Venantius Honorius Fortunatus (530–609)*
*Transl. The New Century Hymnal, 1995*

Unison

1 Sing, my tongue, the glo-rious bat-tle, right has tri-umphed
2 Since the first tree brought earth sor-row, griev - ing, God then
3 Thir - ty years of life com - plet-ed, now the hu - man
4 Of all trees is none so faith - ful, none of such no -

o - ver wrong; Now the cross stands as the to - ken
chose the way: Chose the tree to bear the Sav - ior,
form is spent; Born to fill this sa - cred mo - ment,
bil - i - ty As the cross, whose leaves, and blo - ssoms,

of the strug - gle, fierce and long; Christ the vic - tim
chose in man - ger poor to lay; Thus the plan of
fac - ing death with full in - tent, For the sac - ri -
and whose fruit shall match - less be— Sweet - est wood and

now is vic - tor, sing the no - ble tri - umph song.
our sal - va - tion: God for all our sin would pay.
fice of a - ges, to the cross the Lamb is sent.
nails of i - ron, sweet weight bear - ing grace - ful - ly.

*Taken from a long poem by Fortunatus, bishop of Poitiers,*
*France, this hymn tells a story beginning with the tree in the*
*Garden of Eden and ending with the cross. It was found in*
*most medieval breviaries and missals.*

Tune: FORTUNATUS NEW 8.7.8.7.8.7.
*Carl Schalk (b. 1929)*

# 221 The Royal Banners Forward Fly

*Venantius Honorius Fortunatus (530–609)*
*Transl.* The New Century Hymnal, *1994*

*Isa. 52:13; 53:4–5; John 19:17–18, 31–34*

1 The roy - al ban - ners for - ward fly, the cross, their
2 O sa - cred bod - y, wound - ed side by cru - el
3 The mys - tic proph - e - cy of old, which Da - vid
4 O won - drous tree by God or - dained, though now with

stan - dard, lights the sky; The mys - ter - y: as
spear is o - pened wide, That wa - ter stream - ing
faith - ful - ly fore - told: That God on earth should
roy - al pur - ple stained, Your bur - den once to

Life was slain, through death, e - ter - nal life to gain.
mixed with blood might cleanse us in the pre - cious flood.
sov - ereign be, ful - filled as God reigns from a tree.
all dis - played, the limbs on which our sin was weighed.

*This early hymn by Fortunatus was first sung as a processional on November 19, 569, and has been in general use at Passiontide at least since the tenth century. In more recent tradition it is sung on Good Friday.*

Tune: GONFALON ROYAL L.M.
*Percy C. Buck, 1918*
*Alternate tune:* ERHALT UNS, HERR

# My Song Is Love Unknown

**222**

Samuel Crossman, 1664; alt.

*2 Cor. 5:15–19; Heb. 5:7–10*

1 My song is love un-known, my Sav-ior's love to me,
2 God left the rich-est throne sal - va - tion to be - stow;
3 Some - times they threw down palms and sweet-est prais-es sang.
4 What has my Sov-ereign done? What makes this rage and spite?
5 I sing my plain be - lief, one song my heart out - pours:

Love to the love-less shown, that they might love-ly be.
But Christ as flesh and bone the world re-fused to know.
Ho - san - nas and glad psalms through streets and mar-kets rang.
Christ gave new strength to run, re - stored the gift of sight.
Nev - er was pain nor grief, nev - er was love like yours.

O who am I, that for my sake my God should take frail
But, O my Friend, my Friend in - deed, who at my need did
Then "Cru - ci - fy!" is all their breath, for blood and death they
Sweet in - ju - ries! Yet they at these them - selves dis - please, and
This is my Friend, in whose sweet praise I all my days could

flesh and die? My God should take frail flesh and die?
life ex - pend; who at my need did life ex - pend.
thirst and cry; for blood and death they thirst and cry.
'gainst Christ rise; them - selves dis - please, and 'gainst Christ rise.
glad - ly spend; I all my days could glad - ly spend.

*First published in 1664 by Samuel Crossman, one of the first
writers of English hymns, this hymn of praise for Christ's love
was not appreciated until 200 years later. The tune was named
for the parish in northeastern Wales where the composer served
as vicar.*

Tune: RHOSYMEDRE 6.6.6.6.8.8.8.
*John D. Edwards, c. 1840*

# 223 What Wondrous Love Is This

*John 19:17; Rev. 5:13*

*19th century, United States; alt.*
*First published in Mercer's Cluster, 1836*

1 What won-drous love is this, O my soul! O my soul! What
2 To God and to the Lamb I will sing, I will sing, to
3 And when from death I'm free, I'll sing on, I'll sing on, and

won-drous love is this, O my soul! What won-drous love is
God and to the Lamb, I will sing; To God and to the
when from death I'm free, I'll sing on! And when from death I'm

this! that Christ should come in bliss to bear the heav-y cross for my
Lamb who is the great I Am, while mil-lions join the theme, I will
free, I'll sing and joy-ful be, and through e-ter-ni-ty I'll sing

soul, for my soul, to bear the heav-y cross for my soul!
sing, I will sing; while mil-lions join the theme, I will sing.
on, I'll sing on, and through e-ter-ni-ty I'll sing on!

*This anonymous folk hymn, with its modal (dorian) tune, has appeared in many versions. William Walker, compiler of* Southern Harmony, *one of the most important nineteenth-century tune books in the United States, lived and died in Spartanburg, South Carolina.*

Tune: WONDROUS LOVE 12.9.12.12.9.
(CHRISTOPHER)
*Appendix to Wm. Walker's* Southern Harmony, *c. 1843*
Harm. The New Century Hymnal, *1993*

# When I Survey the Wondrous Cross

*Isaac Watts, 1707; alt.*

*Gal. 6:14; Phil. 3:7–8*

1 When I sur - vey the won - drous cross,
2 For - bid it, then, that I should boast,
3 From sa - cred head, from hands, and feet,
4 Were the whole realm of na - ture mine,

on which the Christ of glo - ry died,
save in the death of Christ, my God;
sor - row and love flow min - gled down!
that were a pres - ent far too small;

My rich - est gain I count but loss,
All the vain things that charm me most
Did e'er such love and sor - row meet,
Love so a - maz - ing, so di - vine,

and pour con - tempt on all my pride.
I sac - ri - fice them all to Christ's blood.
or thorns com - pose so rich a crown?
de - mands my soul, my life, my all.

*Originally titled "Crucifixion to the World by the Cross of Christ," this hymn has been acclaimed as one of the finest in the English language. Isaac Watts' hymnody grew out of his dissatisfaction with the restraints of the metrical psalters.*

Tune: HAMBURG L.M.
Lowell Mason, 1825

# 225 It Was a Sad and Solemn Night

*Mark 14:22–25; 1 Cor. 11:23–26*                                   *Isaac Watts, 1709; alt.*

1 It was a sad and sol-emn night, when powers of earth
2 Be-fore the mourn-ful scene be-gan, our Je-sus blessed
3 "This is my bod-y, broke for sin, re-ceive and eat
4 "Share this, my feast, till time shall end, in mem-ory of
5 O Christ your feast we cel-e-brate; we show your death,

and hell a-rose A-gainst the Child of
and broke the bread; What love through all these
the liv-ing food"; Then took the cup and
your dy-ing friend: Meet at my ta-ble
we sing your name, Till you re-turn, and

God's de-light, whom friends be-trayed to wick-ed foes.
ac-tions ran, what won-drous words of love were said!
blessed the wine, "This the new cov-enant in my blood."
and re-call the love which God has shown to all."
we shall eat the mar-riage sup-per of the Lamb.

*Isaac Watts, often considered the founder of English hymnody,
recalls very powerfully in this hymn the Maundy Thursday
events. The meal in the upper room is recounted, and the great
marriage feast of the Lamb is anticipated.*

Tune: BOURBON L.M.
*Melody attrib. to Freeman Lewis, 1825*
*Harm. Louise McAllister (1913–1960)*
Alternate tune: ERHALT UNS, HERR

# O Sacred Head, Now Wounded

**226**

*Medieval Latin, attrib. to Bernard of Clairvaux (1091–1153)*
*German paraphr. by Paul Gerhardt, 1656*
*Transl. James W. Alexander, 1830; alt.*

*Isa. 53; John 19:1–3*

1 O sa - cred Head, now wound - ed, with grief and shame weighed down,
2 What you, dear Sav - ior, suf - fered was all for sin - ners' gain;
3 What lan - guage shall I bor - row to thank you, dear - est friend;

Now scorn - ful - ly sur - round - ed with thorns, your on - ly crown,
Mine, mine was the trans - gres - sion, but yours the dead - ly pain.
For this your dy - ing sor - row, your pit - y with - out end?

How pale you are with an - guish, with sore a - buse and scorn!
Lo, here I fall, my Sav - ior, for I de - serve your place;
May I be yours for - ev - er; and though my days be few,

How does your vis - age lan - guish which once was bright as morn!
Look on me with your fa - vor, O grant to me your grace.
O Sav - ior, let me nev - er out - live my love for you!

*This hymn is drawn from an extended Latin poem in seven sections, each addressed to a member of Christ's body on the cross. It comes to us by way of a German translation by Lutheran pastor and hymnwriter Paul Gerhardt.*

Tune: PASSION CHORALE 7.6.7.6.D.
(HERZLICH TUT MICH VERLANGEN)
*Melody by Hans Leo Hassler, 1601*
*Harm. J. S. Bach, 1729*
*For another harmonization, see 179*

# 227 Christ at Table There with Friends

Matt. 26:39; Mark 14:36; Luke 22:42;
John 6:47–51; 1 Cor. 11:23–25

Anabel S. Miller, 1982; rev. 1994

1 Christ at ta - ble there with friends
2 In the gar - den Je - sus bows.
3 "Yet, your will, not mine, be done.
4 At our ta - ble Je - sus stands,

shar - ing bread and
Harsh the cry that
For this pur - pose
Word of God with

wine, and then
ris - es now:
I am come.
nail - scarred hands.

Speak - ing words of mys - ter - y:
"Fa - ther, some way let it be!
Thus to make all peo - ple new I
"Come, re - ceive the mys - ter - y.

"Thus re - mem - ber me,
Take this cup from me,
take this cup from you,
Take this cup from me,

I

thus re - mem - ber me."
take this cup from me!"
take this cup from you."
take this cup from me."

*Anabel Miller, born in China of American missionary parents, wrote this poem during Lent in 1982. Ten years later, she shared it with composer Emma Lou Diemer, who served as organist at her Presbyterian church in California. Diemer recognized its potential as a hymn text, and supplied the musical setting.*

Tune: MAUNDY THURSDAY 7.7.7.5.5.
Emma Lou Diemer, 1992

# Ruler of Life, We Crown You Now

**228**

*Jennie Evelyn Hussey, 1921; alt.*        *Matt. 26:36–39; Mark 14:32–36; 16:1–2; Luke 24:1–10; John 19:2; 20:11–13*

1 Rul-er of life, we crown you now   as   we your glo - ry   see;
2 Show us the tomb where you   were laid,   ten - der-ly mourned and   wept;
3 Let us, like Mar - y, through the gloom, come with a   gift   for   you;
4 May we be will - ing, Christ, to bear   dai - ly our cross   for   you,

Lest we for - get your thorn-crowned brow,   lead us   to Cal - va - ry.
An - gels in robes of   light   ar - rayed   guard-ed you while you   slept.
Show to us now the   emp - ty   tomb   lead-ing to life   a - new.
E - ven your cup of   grief   to   share;   your love will see   us   through.

*Refrain*

Lest we for-get Geth - sem - a - ne,   lest   we for-get your   ag - o - ny,

Lest we for-get love's vic - to - ry,   lead   us   to Cal - va - ry.

*A lifelong resident of New Hampshire, Jennie Evelyn Hussey began to write poems when she was eight and published her first hymns when she was twenty-four. Although her family had Congregational ties, Hussey was active in the Society of Friends.*

Tune: DUNCANNON C.M. with refrain
*William J. Kirkpatrick, 1921*

# 229

# Were You There?

John 19:16–18; 20:11–17

*African-American spiritual*

1 Were you there when they cru - ci - fied my Lord?
2 Were you there when they nailed him to the tree? Were you there?
3 Were you there when God wept at Mar - y's cry? Were you there?
4 Were you there when Christ rose up from the tomb?

Were you there when they cru - ci - fied my Lord?
Were you there when they nailed him to the tree? Were you there?
Were you there when God wept at Mar - y's cry? Were you there?
Were you there when Christ rose up from the tomb?

O    some-times it caus-es me to trem-ble, trem-ble, trem-ble.

Were you there when they cru - ci - fied my Lord?
Were you there when they nailed him to the tree? Were you there?
Were you there when God wept at Mar - y's cry? Were you there?
Were you there when Christ rose up from the tomb?

*While many spirituals begin solemnly but end on a high pitch of praise, this is one of the true "sorrow songs" that W. E. B. DuBois spoke about in his book* The Souls of Black Folk.

Tune: WERE YOU THERE  Irr.
*African-American spiritual*
*Arr. Joyce Finch Johnson, 1992*

# Come, You Faithful, Raise the Strain

*Attrib. to John of Damascus (c. 696–c. 754 C.E.)*
*Transl. John Mason Neale, 1872; alt.*

*Exod. 15; Luke 24*

1 Come, you faith - ful, raise the strain of tri - um - phant glad - ness;
2 Spring has dawned on earth to - day; Christ has burst from pris - on,
3 Now the joy - ous sea - son, bright with the day of splen - dor,
4 Nei - ther might the gates of death, nor the tomb's dim por - tal,

God has brought all Is - ra - el in - to joy from sad - ness;
And from three days' sleep in death as the sun has ris - en;
With the roy - al feast of feasts, comes its joys to ren - der;
Nor the watch - ers, nor the seal hold you as a mor - tal;

Loosed from Pha - raoh's bit - ter yoke Ja - cob's sons and daugh - ters;
All the win - ter of our sins, long and gray, is fly - ing
Comes to glad Je - ru - sa - lem who with true af - fec - tion
But to - day a - mid the twelve you still stand, be - stow - ing

Led them with un - moist-ened foot through the Red Sea wa - ters.
From the Light, to whom we give laud and praise un - dy - ing.
Wel-comes in un - wear - ied strains Je - sus' res - ur - rec - tion.
Peace and joy which ev - er - more pass - es hu - man know - ing.

*Little is known of St. John of Damascus, an early Greek*
*theologian, but his writings have survived. Among these are*
*poems that have been made into hymns and some that have*
*been integrated into Greek Orthodox liturgy.*

Tune: ST. KEVIN 7.6.7.6.D.
*Arthur S. Sullivan, 1872*

# 231

## Because You Live, O Christ

*Luke 24:1–10*

*Shirley Erena Murray, 1987*

1 Be - cause you live, O Christ, the gar - den of the
2 Be - cause you live, O Christ, the spir - it bird of
3 Be - cause you live, O Christ, the rain - bow of your

world has come to flow - er, the shad-ows of the tomb
hope is freed for fly - ing, our ca - ges of de - spair
peace will span cre - a - tion, the col - ors of your love

are flood - ed with your res - ur - rec - tion pow - er.
no long - er keep us closed and life - de - ny - ing.
will draw all hu - man - kind to ad - o - ra - tion.

The stone has rolled a - way and death can - not im - pris - on! O

*New Zealand hymnwriter Shirley Erena Murray expressed
her aims in writing this new text for the beloved Easter tune
Vruechten: "I wanted a fresh expression of community
joyfulness, with light, color, and the vision of the covenant
rainbow through the Resurrection."*

Tune: VRUECHTEN 6.7.6.7. with refrain
*Melody in David's Psalmen, 1685
J. Oudaen, Amsterdam*

sing this Eas-ter Day, for Je-sus Christ has ris - en, has

ris - en, has ris - en, has ris - en!

# This Joyful Eastertide 232

*George R. Woodward, 1894; alt.*

> *This text may be used with the above tune as a canticle for Easter.*

This joy-ful Eas-ter-tide, a-way with sin and sor---row!
My love, the Cru-ci-fied, has sprung to life this mor---row.
Had Christ, who once was slain,
   not burst from three days' pris-on,
    Our faith had been in vain.
But now has Christ a-ris-en, a-ris-en, a-ris-en;
   But now has Christ a-ris---en!

*George R. Woodward was a Cambridge Scholar and served*
*various parishes in England. He collaborated on the editing and*
*publishing of several collections of carols and hymns.*

Tune: VRUECHTEN 6.7.6.7.D.
*Melody in David's Psalmen, 1685*
*J. Oudaen, Amsterdam*

# 233       Christ the Lord Is Risen Today

Matt. 28:5–8; 1 Cor. 15:20–22; 54–57       *Charles Wesley, 1739; alt.*

1 Christ the Lord is risen to-day, Al - le - lu - ia!
2 Let the Vic-tor's peo-ple sing, Al - le - lu - ia!
3 Love's re-deem-ing work is done, Al - le - lu - ia!
4 Soar we now where Christ has led, Al - le - lu - ia!

Mor - tal tongues and an - gels say: Al - le - lu - ia!
Where, O death, is now your sting? Al - le - lu - ia!
Fought the fight, the bat - tle won, Al - le - lu - ia!
Fol - lowing our ex - alt - ed Head, Al - le - lu - ia!

Raise your joys and tri - umphs high, Al - le - lu - ia!
Dy - ing once, Christ lives to save, Al - le - lu - ia!
Death in vain for - bids Christ rise, Al - le - lu - ia!
Made like Christ, like Christ we rise, Al - le - lu - ia!

Sing, glad heavens, and earth re - ply: Al - le - lu - ia!
Where your vic - to - ry, O grave? Al - le - lu - ia!
God has o - pened par - a - dise, Al - le - lu - ia!
Ours the cross, the grave, the skies, Al - le - lu - ia!

*The unknown editor of Lyra Davidica wanted music with more movement and spirit than found in the grave, slow-paced psalm tunes, with one note to a syllable. Easter Hymn was among the first of a new popular style.*

Tune: EASTER HYMN 7.7.7.7. with alleluias
*Arr. from Lyra Davidica, London, 1708*

# I'll Shout the Name of Christ Who Lives

**234**

*Vivincio L. Vinluan, 1980; alt.*

*Rom. 6:5–11*

1 I'll shout the name of Christ who lives,
2 Dear broth - ers sing a - mong all here,
3 Once more we shout our joy and praise

who lives, who lives, that all might live;
and leap with joy, my sis - ters dear;
to One we love, whose throne is grace,

Christ broke death's power at Cal - va - ry,
A - lone at home we seek our peace,
Whose way is Life, whose Word ful - fills

and now I know from sin I'm free.
there Je - sus comes to bring re - lease.
as we in glad - ness do God's will.

This contemporary Filipino hymn incorporates a musical motive
from a traditional folk song, "Bahay Kubo." It was published in
the 1983 collection of Asian-American hymns, Hymns from the
Four Winds, *edited by I-to Loh.*

Tune: BAHAY KUBO L.M.
*Wesley Tactay Tabayoyong, 1981*
*Based on a Philippine folk song*

# 235

## ¡Cristo Vive!
### (Christ Is Living)

*1 Cor. 15:54–57; Luke 24:1–10; Col. 1:15–20; Rom. 5:12–21*

*Nicolás Martínez, 1960; alt.*
*English version, Carolyn Jennings, 1993*

*At a lively tempo*
*Unison*

1 ¡Cris-to vi - ve, fue-ra_el llan - to, los la - men - tos y_el pe - sar!
2 Que si Cris-to no vi - vie - ra va - na fue - ra nues-tra fe;
1 Christ is liv - ing, no more weep-ing, no more time for grief and pain!
2 If in truth Christ nev - er had lived faith would mere de - lu - sion give;

Ni la muer - te ni_el se - pul - cro lo_han po - di - do su - je - tar.
mas se cum - ple su pro - me - sa: 'Por - que vi - vo, vi - vi - réis.'
Nei-ther death nor tomb could hold Christ, who is liv - ing once a - gain.
But the prom - ise is ful - filled now: "Since I live, you too shall live."

No bus - quéis en - tre los muer - tos al que siem-pre_ha de vi - vir,
Si_en A - dán en - tró la muer - te, por Je - sús la vi - da_en - tró;
Do not look a - mong the dead for one who lives most cer - tain - ly;
If through Ad - am death came in, through Je - sus Christ came life in - stead;

*This resurrection hymn is the product of two Argentinean*
*talents. Author Nicolás Martínez was a Disciples of Christ*
*pastor, poet, and editor. Composer Pablo D. Sosa is known*
*as an international leader in liturgical music.*

Tune: CENTRAL 8.7.8.7.D.
*Pablo D. Sosa, 1960*

¡Cris - to vi - ve! es - tas nue - vas por do - quier de - jad o - ír.
No te - máis, el triun - fo es nues - tro: ¡Cris - to ya re - su - ci - tó!
Christ is liv - ing! Hear the good news that re - sounds so joy - ful - ly.
Have no fear! Ours is the tri - umph; Christ is ris - en from the dead.

3 Si es ver-dad que de la muer-te
   el pe-ca-do es a-gui-jón,
   no te-máis pues Je-su-cris-to
   nos da vi-da y sal-va-ción.
   Gra-cias de-mos a Dios siem-pre
   que nos da se-gu-ri-dad,
   que quien si-gue a Je-su-cris-to
   vi-ve por la e-ter-ni-dad.

3 E-ven if the sting of death is
   tru-ly found in hu-man sin,
   Be not fear-ful, for Christ Je-sus
   came our lib-er-ty to win.
   We give end-less thanks to God,
   who is our sure se-cu-ri-ty;
   Those who fol-low Christ the Sav-ior
   will have life e-ter-nal-ly.

## Halleluja 236

*Traditional*

Hal-le, hal-le, hal - le - lu - ja. Hal-le, hal-le, hal - le - lu - ja.

Hal-le, hal-le, hal - le - lu - ja. Hal-le - lu-ja, hal - le - lu - ja.

*This joyous response may be used following readings of scripture,
or as a processional or recessional, especially during Easter.*

Tune: HALLELUJA
*Caribbean melody*

# I Come to the Garden Alone
## (In the Garden)

*John 20:14–18*

*C. Austin Miles, 1912*

1 I come to the gar-den a-lone, while the dew is still on the
2 He speaks, and the sound of his voice is so sweet the birds hush their
3 I'd stay in the gar-den with him, though the night a-round me be

ros - es; And the voice I hear, fall-ing on my ear, the
sing - ing; And the mel - o - dy that he gave to me with-
fall - ing; But he bids me go; through the voice of woe his

*Refrain*

Son of God dis-clos - es.
in my heart is ring - ing. And he walks with me, and he
voice to me is call - ing.

talks with me, and he tells me I am his own, And the

joy we share as we tar - ry there, none oth-er has ev - er known.

*C. Austin Miles wrote this hymn and its music to tell the story of Mary Magdalene's encounter with Jesus at the tomb, when she recognizes him and calls him "Rabboni" ("Teacher").*

Tune: GARDEN 8.9.5.5.7. with refrain
C. Austin Miles, 1912

# Now the Green Blade Rises

John M. C. Crum, 1928; alt.

Matt. 27:57–28:7; Luke 23:50–24:12

1 Now the green blade ris - es from the bur - ied grain;
2 In the grave they laid their Love whom hate had slain,
3 Christ came forth at Eas - ter, like the ris - en grain,
4 When our hearts are win - try, griev - ing, or in pain,

Wheat that in dark earth for man - y days has lain;
Think - ing that their Love would nev - er wake a - gain,
Je - sus, who for three days in the grave had lain,
Christ's warm touch can call us back to life a - gain,

Love lives a - gain, that with the dead has been:
Laid in the earth like grain that sleeps un - seen:
Quick from the dead the ris - en One is seen:
Fields of our hearts that dead and bare have been:

*Refrain*

Love is come a - gain like wheat that ris - es green.

John M. C. Crum, an English priest who was canon of
Canterbury for fifteen years, wrote these words for this ancient
French Christmas carol tune when it was included in the Oxford
Book of Carols (1928).

Tune: NOËL NOUVELET 11.10.10.11.
*French noel, 15th century*
*Harm. Martin F. Shaw, 1928*

# Christ Rose Up from the Dead

*Matt. 28:2–6; John 19:16–18; 19:38–20:18*

*African-American traditional; alt.*

**Refrain**

Christ rose, Christ rose, Christ rose up from the dead, Christ rose,
a-rose a-rose, a-rose,

Christ rose, Christ rose from the dead, Christ rose Christ rose,
a-rose a-rose, a-rose,

*Last time, end*

Christ rose up from the dead, and God's grace will bear my spir-it home.

1 They cru-ci-fied my Sav-ior up-on a com-mon cross, they
2 And Jo-seph begged his bod-y, and laid it in the tomb, and
3 An an-gel came from heav-en and rolled a-way the stone, an
4 Oh, Mar-y, she came run-ning and found an emp-ty tomb, oh,

*This jubilee song, collected by K. D. Reddick and arranged by
Phil V. S. Lindsley, appeared around 1918 in shape note style in
a collection titled* The National Jubilee Melodies, *published by
the National Baptist Publishing Board.*

Tune: ASCENSIUS 7.6.7.6.7.6.9. with refrain
*African-American traditional*
*Arr. Phil V. S. Lindsley, 20th century*

cru - ci - fied my Sav - ior up - on a com - mon cross, They
Jo - seph begged his bod - y, and laid it in the tomb, And
an - gel came from heav - en and rolled a - way the stone, An
Mar - y, she came run - ning and found an emp - ty tomb, Oh,

cru - ci - fied my Sav - ior up - on a com - mon cross,
Jo - seph begged his bod - y, and laid it in the tomb,
an - gel came from heav - en and rolled a - way the stone,
Mar - y, she came run - ning and found an emp - ty tomb,

*to Refrain*

(1–4) and God's grace will bear my spir - it home.

# 240 Jesus Christ Is Risen Today

Matt. 28:1–10; Mark 16:1–8; Luke 24:1–10

St. 1 transl., Lyra Davidica, *London, 1708*
St. 2–5 transl., The New Century Hymnal, *1994*

1 Je - sus Christ is risen to - day, Al - le - lu - ia!
2 To the tomb the wom - en bring, Al - le - lu - ia!
3 There the an - gel clothed in white, Al - le - lu - ia!
4 "Has - ten now to Gal - i - lee," Al - le - lu - ia!
5 Christ ap - pears in full ar - ray, Al - le - lu - ia!

Our tri - um - phant ho - ly day, Al - le - lu - ia!
Spic - es rich, an of - fer - ing, Al - le - lu - ia!
Tells the news with great de - light, Al - le - lu - ia!
"Tell the oth - ers what you see!" Al - le - lu - ia!
Sing with joy this Pas - chal day, Al - le - lu - ia!

Who did once up - on the cross, Al - le - lu - ia!
Ask - ing where might Je - sus be, Al - le - lu - ia!
This the news the an - gel gives, Al - le - lu - ia!
With ex - cite - ment trem - bling, Al - le - lu - ia!
Christ now from the dead is raised, Al - le - lu - ia!

*In 1749, an English translation of this fourteenth-century Latin*
*hymn dropped all but the first stanza of the original. Most*
*hymnbooks have used that (1749) version. In this new*
*translation the original Latin verses of the medieval text are*
*restored, thus bringing to life the original Easter narrative.*

Tune: LLANFAIR 7.7.7.7. with alleluias
*Robert Williams, 1817*
Harm. *John Roberts (1822–1877)*

Unison

Suf - fer    to    re - deem our  loss,    Al  -  le - lu - ia!
Sav - ior   come  to    set  us    free,    Al  -  le - lu - ia!
That the    Sov - ereign glo - rious lives,  Al  -  le - lu - ia!
Off  they   run, good news to    bring,    Al  -  le - lu - ia!
Ho - ly    Trin - i - ty  be  praised,   Al  -  le - lu - ia!

# Joy Dawned Again on Easter Day                241

*Latin, c. 5th century*                                    *Luke 24:36–37*
*Transl. John Mason Neale, 1851; alt.*

1 Joy dawned a - gain    on  Eas - ter  Day, the  sun  shone
2 O  Je - sus, Sav - ior,  Gen - tle  One, come take  our
3 O  Sov - ereign One,  with  us   a - bide  in  this  our

out    with  bright  ar  -  ray;  For  when   the A - pos - tles
hearts  to   be    your  own,  That  we    may  give  you
joy - ful  Eas - ter - tide;  From  ev - ery  weap - on

hid  in   fear,  the  Ris - en  Christ  to  them  ap - peared.
all  our  days  the  will - ing  trib - ute  of  our  praise.
death can wield, your  own  re - deemed  for - ev - er  shield.

*This anonymous Latin hymn of uncertain date is one of the two
earliest hymns assigned to a special season. From that beginning
grew a full list of medieval Latin hymns assigned to specific times
and seasons.*

Tune:  PUER NOBIS NASCITUR  L.M.
*German carol, 15th century
Adapt. Michael Praetorius, 1609
Harm. George R. Woodward, 1910*

# 242

# The Strife Is O'er

*1 Cor. 15:53–57*

*Latin, c. 1695*
*Transl. Francis Pott, 1861; alt.*

**Refrain** (before st. 1 and after st. 4)

Al - le - lu - ia, al - le - lu - ia, al - le - lu - ia!

1. The strife is o'er, the bat - tle done, the vic - to -
2. The powers of death have done their worst, but Christ their
3. The three sad days are quick - ly sped, Christ ris - es
4. Christ, by your wounds on Cal - va - ry from death's dread

ry of life is won; The song of tri - umph
le - gions has dis - persed: Let shouts of ho - ly
glo - rious from the dead: All glo - ry to our
sting your ser - vants free, That we may live e -

has be - gun. Al - le - lu - ia!
joy out - burst. Al - le - lu - ia!
ris - en Head! Al - le - lu - ia!
ter - nal - ly. Al - le - lu - ia! *to Refrain*

*A seventeenth-century Jesuit collection published in Cologne,*
*Germany, is the earliest known source of this Latin hymn. The*
*hymn is firmly associated with this musical setting from a*
Magnificat *by the Italian composer Palestrina.*

Tune: VICTORY 8.8.8. with alleluias
*Giovanni Perluigi da Palestrina, 1591*
*Arr. William H. Monk, 1861*

# Alleluia! Alleluia! Hearts to Heaven 243

*Christopher Wordsworth, 1872; alt.*     *Matt. 28:5–8; Rom. 5:21; 6:4–11; 1 Cor. 15:20–22*

1 Al - le - lu - ia! Al - le - lu - ia! Hearts to heaven and voic - es raise;
2 Now the i - ron bars are bro - ken, Christ from death to life is born;
3 Christ is ris - en, we are ris - en; shed up - on us heaven-ly grace,
4 Al - le - lu - ia! Al - le - lu - ia! Glo - ry to the God of joy;

Sing to God a hymn of glad-ness, sing to God a hymn of praise.
Glo-rious life, and life im - mor - tal on this ho - ly Eas - ter morn;
Rain and dew, and gleams of glo - ry from the bright - ness of your face;
Al - le - lu - ia to the Sav - ior who came death's bonds to de - stroy;

Je - sus on the cross as Sav - ior for the world's sal - va - tion bled;
Christ has tri - umphed, and we con-quer by God's lib - er - at - ing deed;
That we, with our hearts in heav-en, here on earth may fruit-ful be,
Al - le - lu - ia to the Spir - it, Fount of love and sanc-ti - ty;

But the cru - ci - fied Re - deem - er now is ris - en from the dead!
Now the Christ with us a - bid - ing to e - ter - nal life shall lead.
And by an - gel hands be gath-ered, and be yours e - ter - nal - ly.
Al - le - lu - ia! Al - le - lu - ia! To the Tri - une Maj - es - ty.

*Christopher Wordsworth, gifted nephew of poet William Wordsworth, served the Church of England successively as canon at Westminster, parish priest in Berkshire, and, finally, bishop of Lincoln. This Easter hymn is one of his most enduring.*

Tune: WEISSE FLAGGEN 8.7.8.7.D.
*Tochter Sion, Cologne, 1741*
*Alternate tune: HYFRYDOL*

# 244

# O Sons and Daughters, Let Us Sing

Mark 16:1–7; John 20:19–29

*Attrib. to Jean Tisserand (d. 1494)*
*Transl. John Mason Neale, 1851; alt.*

Antiphon (may be sung at beginning and end)

Al - le - lu - ia! Al - le - lu - ia! Al - le - lu - ia! Al - le - lu - ia!

1 O sons and daugh - ters, let us sing the flower of heaven, a -
2 That Eas - ter morn at break of day, the faith - ful wom - en
3 An an - gel clad in white they see, who sat and spoke un -
4 When Thom - as first the tid - ings heard, he count - ed what they

live as spring, o'er death to - day rose
went their way to seek the tomb where
to the three, "Christ waits for you in
said ab - surd, but see - ing Christ his

tri - umph-ing, Al - le - lu - ia! Al - le - lu - ia!
Je - sus lay, Al - le - lu - ia! Al - le - lu - ia!
Gal - i - lee." Al - le - lu - ia! Al - le - lu - ia!
faith was stirred: Al - le - lu - ia! Al - le - lu - ia!

*Jean Tisserand, a Franciscan preaching friar, was well*
*known in Paris. He founded an order for women and*
*wrote a history commemorating some Franciscans*
*martyred in Morocco in 1220.*

Tune: O FILII ET FILIAE 8.8.8. with alleluias
Airs sur les hymnes sacrez, *Paris, 1623*

5  How blessed are they who have not seen
   and yet whose faith has con-stant been;
   for they e-ter--nal life shall win,
   Al-le-lu-ia! Al-le-lu-ia!

6  On this most ho-ly day of days,
   our hearts and voic-es, Christ, we raise
   to you in ju--bi-lee and praise.
   Al-le-lu-ia! Al-le-lu-ia! *(Antiphon)*

## The Day of Resurrection

**245**

*John of Damascus, 8th century*
*Transl. John Mason Neale, 1862; alt.*

*Mark 16:1–6*

1 The day of res-ur-rec-tion! Earth, tell it out a-broad;
2 Our hearts be pure from e-vil, that we may see a-right
3 Now let the heavens be joy-ful, let earth its song be-gin,

the Pass-o-ver of glad-ness, the Pass-o-ver of God.
the Christ who reigns e-ter-nal in res-ur-rec-tion light;
the whole world keep high tri-umph, and all that is there-in;

From death to life e-ter-nal, from earth un-to the sky,
We lis-ten for the teach-ings once heard so calm and plain,
Let all things seen and un-seen their notes of glad-ness blend,

our Christ has brought us o-ver with hymns of vic-to-ry.
for we, too, want to fol-low and raise the vic-tor strain.
for Christ a-gain has ris-en, our joy that has no end.

*A Greek canon—an extended poem of eight or nine odes, each*
*based on a scriptural canticle—was the source of this hymn.*
*John of Damascus gave up a high government position to enter a*
*monastery.*

Tune: LANCASHIRE 7.6.7.6.D.
*Henry T. Smart, 1836*

**246**

# Hoy celebramos con gozo al Dios
## (Come, Celebrate with Thanksgiving)

*Mortimer Arias; alt.*
*Transl. Roberto Escamilla and Elise S. Eslinger, 1981; alt.*

1 Hoy ce-le-bra-mos con go-zo al Dios to-do-po-de-
2 Hoy ce-le-bra-mos fes-ti-vos al Dios de li-be-ra-
1 Come, cel-e-brate with thanks-giv-ing, come and wor-ship God al-
2 Come, cel-e-brate in your feast-ing that the God of lib-er-

ro-so, al cre-a-dor de la tie-rra y da-
ción, que da vi-da y es-pe-ran-za y se
might-y, Who is cre-a-tor of all things, and the
a-tion Brings us to new life, new whole-ness, and for-

dor de to-do bien; al que vi-no has-ta no-
go-za en el per-dón. Con vo-ces y con pan-
giv-er of good gifts; Who came to be one a-
gives in joy and love. With voic-es and hap-py

so-tros y mu-rió en u-na cruz,
de-ros en-to-na-mos la can-ción,
mong us, e-ven dy-ing on a cross.
drum-ming let us sing the tri-umph song.

This hymn by Bolivian Methodists Mortimer Arias and Antonio Auza employs the Latin American "cueca" rhythm which juxtaposes contrasting meters. In Buenos Aires, Argentina, women whose husbands have 'disappeared' sometimes dance the "cueca" around a central square.

Tune: CHUQUISACA 8.8.8.7.D. with refrain
*Antonio Auza*
*Arr. Homero Perera*

que_ha ven-ci - do_a las ti - nie - blas y a la muer-te des - tru - yó.
ce - le-bran-do_al Dios vi - vien - te dan - za nues-tro co - ra - zón.
E - vil has been o - ver-come, and now death has been de - stroyed.
God is a - live and a - mong us, now our danc-ing hearts re - joice!

*Estribillo (Refrain)*

¡Cris-to vi - ve! Ce - le - bre - mos y es-pe - re - mos su gran
Cel - e - brate that Christ is liv - ing and then wait for God's great

don; San-to_Es-pí - ri - tu di - vi - no, ven a nues-tro co - ra-
gift: The di - vine and ho - ly Spir - it now may come in-to our

zón. nues - tro co - ra - zón.
hearts. come in - to our hearts.

3 Hoy a-cu-di-mos a-le-gres
  a_es-ta fies-ta del a-mor;
  res-pon-dien-do fer-vo-ro-sos
  a la san-ta_in-vi-ta-ción.
  En a-mor hoy ce-le-bra-mos
  es-ta san-ta co-mu-nión;
  es-tre-chán-do-nos las ma-nos
  so-mos pue-blo del Crea-dor.
  *(Estribillo)*

3 Come, cel-e-brate all to-geth-er
  in this feast of heaven-ly love.
  We come at God's in-vi-ta-tion
  on this hap-py, ho-ly day.
  Joy-ful-ly, let us now gath-er,
  cel-e-brat-ing u-ni-ty,
  Join-ing our hands in thanks-giv-ing
  as the fam-i-ly of God.
  *(Refrain)*

# 247 My Shepherd Is the Living God

*Ps. 23; John 10:11, 27–30*

*Composite from Thomas Sternhold, 1549, and Isaac Watts, 1719; alt.*

1 My shep-herd is the liv-ing God, I there-fore noth-ing need;
2 When I walk through the shades of death, your pres-ence is my stay;
3 The sure pro-vi-sions of my God at-tend me all my days;

In pas-tures fair, near pleas-ant streams you set-tle me to feed.
A word of your sup-port-ing breath drives all my fears a-way.
O may your house be my a-bode, and all my work be praise.

You bring my wan-dering spir-it back when I for-sake your ways,
Your hand, in sight of all my foes, does still my ta-ble spread;
There would I find a set-tled rest, while oth-ers come and go—

And lead me for your mer-cy's sake in paths of truth and grace.
My cup with bless-ings o-ver-flows, your oil a-noints my head.
No more a strang-er or a guest, but like a child at home.

*Isaac Watts, London's leading Congregational minister, wrote more than 600 hymns. His paraphrase of Psalm 23 has been altered here by combining a few phrases from Thomas Sternhold, a sixteenth-century English hymnwriter who also wrote metrical psalm texts.*

Tune: CONSOLATION C.M.D.
Southern Harmony, *1835*
Harm. Erik Routley, *1976*
Alternate tune: CRIMOND (Each stanza above becomes two stanzas.)

# Such Perfect Love My Shepherd Shows 248

*Henry W. Baker, 1868; alt.* *Ps. 23*

1 Such per-fect love my Shep-herd shows, whose good-ness fails me nev-er, Whose hand all things I need be-stows and watch-es me for-ev-er.

2 Where streams of liv-ing wa-ter flow, my lov-ing Shep-herd leads me, And where the ver-dant pas-tures grow with food from heav-en feeds me.

3 When vain and fool-ish oft I strayed, you, faith-ful Shep-herd, sought me, And on your shoul-der gent-ly laid, then home re-joic-ing brought me.

4 I do not fear death's shad-owed vale when you are here be-side me; Your rod and staff and strength pre-vail to com-fort and to guide me.

5 You spread a ta-ble in my sight,
your gifts of grace be-stow-ing;
And from your chal-ice I de-light
to taste your mer-cy flow-ing.

6 And so through all the length of days
your good-ness fails me nev-er;
Good Shep-herd, may I sing your praise
with-in your house for-ev-er.

*English clergyman Henry Baker greatly influenced hymnody in England and the United States through his leadership in preparing* Hymns Ancient and Modern *(1861). Baker's hymn is a recast of a George Herbert poem.*

Tune: DOMINUS REGIT ME 8.7.8.7.
*John B. Dykes, 1868*
*Alternate tune: ST. COLUMBA*

# 249 Peace I Leave with You, My Friends

John 14:18–29

Ray Repp, 1967

**Refrain**

Peace I leave with you, my friends, sha-lom, my peace, in all you do. Peace I leave with you, my friends. I give to you so you can give to oth-ers, too.

1 To share God's love is why I came, to show God's kind-ness with-out end.
2 Take my hand and be at peace; the spir-it of our love I send.
3 With this love now all will know that lone-li-ness is at an end.

Songwriter Ray Repp has composed and recorded numerous albums of liturgical songs since 1965, when he introduced guitar into worship with his "Mass for Young Americans."

Tune: PEACE, MY FRIENDS Irr. with refrain
Ray Repp, 1967
Arr. The New Century Hymnal, 1994

Go now, my friends, and do the same,
And with this love you will be free,
Re - joice, my friends, al - though I go,

un - til I come a - gain.
un - til I come a - gain.
for I will come a - gain.

## Listen to Your Savior Call

**250**

*William Cowper, 1768; alt.*

*John 21:15–16*

1  Lis - ten to your Sav - ior call, "Do you love me most of all?"
2  "I de - liv - ered you when bound, and, when bleed-ing, healed your wound.
3  "Mine is an un - chang-ing love, high - er than the heights a - bove,
4  O my Sav - ior, hear my need: though my love is faint in - deed,

Je - sus speaks, and speaks to you: "Love me as I first loved you."
Sought you wan - dering, set you right, for your path-way gave you light."
Deep - er than the depths be - neath, free and faith-ful, strong as death."
Still I love you and a - dore— oh, for grace to love you more!

*William Cowper was trained as a barrister. He suffered from severe depression, but during a time of wellness he wrote this hymn based on John 21:15—a dialogue between Jesus and the individual.*

Tune:  ORIENTIS PARTIBUS  7.7.7.7.
*French melody, early 13th century
Arr. Richard Redhead, 1853*

# 251  I Greet You, Sure Redeemer

*John 11:25–27*

Anon., *from* Strasbourg Psalter, *1545*
*Transl.* Elizabeth L. Smith, *1868; alt.*

1 I greet you, sure Re - deem - er, with my heart,
2 You are the source of mer - cy and of grace,
3 You are the life, by which a - lone we live,
4 You have the true and per - fect gen - tle - ness,
5 Our hope is all in you and you a - lone;

glad for the sav - ing love that you im - part,
reign - ing om - ni - po - tent in ev - ery place;
and all our sub - stance and our strength re - ceive.
no harsh - ness have you and no bit - ter - ness;
we trust the prom - ise that your word makes known.

Who pain did un - der - go for my poor sake;
So rule in us and our whole be - ing sway.
Sus - tain us by your faith and by your power,
Grant us the grace that flows in you so free
O dear Re - deem - er, make us calm and sure,

I pray you from our hearts all cares to take.
Shine on us with the light of your pure day.
and give us strength in ev - ery try - ing hour.
that we may dwell in per - fect u - ni - ty.
that in your strength we ev - er - more en - dure.

*This hymn first appeared in a sixteenth-century* Strasbourg
Psalter *edited by John Calvin. The original tune* Old 124th *and
text were both shortened to the present meter—the tune for an
early English psalter and the text for the 1920* Hymnal *of the
Reformed Church in the United States.*

Tune: TOULON 10.10.10.10.
*Adapt. from* OLD 124th
Trente quatre Pseaumes, *Geneva, 1551*

# Savior, like a Shepherd Lead Us

## 252

*Attrib. to Dorothy A. Thrupp (1779–1847)*
*From Hymns for the Young, 1836; alt.*
*St. 1 transl. to Hawaiian by Laiana (1807–1886)*

*John 10:1–29*

1 Sav-ior, like a shep-herd lead us, much we need your ten - der care;
1 Ie - su no ke Ka-hu - hi - pa, Ka - hu - hi - pa ma'i-ka'i e,
2 We are yours, in love be - friend us, be the guard-ian of our way;
3 Let us al - ways seek your fa - vor; let us al - ways do your will;

in your pleas - ant pas-tures feed us, for our use your folds pre - pare.
Ei - a ma - kou ka 'o - ha - na ke ho'o-lo - he a ha - hai:
keep your flock, from sin de - fend us, seek us when we go a - stray.
Je - sus Christ our on - ly Sav - ior, with your love our spir - its fill.

Bless-ed Je - sus, bless-ed Je - sus, you have bought us, yours we are;
E a - lo - ha, e a - lo - ha, a - la - ka'i a ha - nai mai,
Bless-ed Je - sus, bless-ed Je - sus, hear your chil - dren when we pray;
Bless-ed Je - sus, bless-ed Je - sus, you have loved us, love us still;

Bless-ed Je - sus, bless-ed Je - sus, you have bought us, yours we are.
E a - lo - ha, e a - lo - ha, a - la - ka'i a ha - nai mai.
Bless-ed Je - sus, bless-ed Je - sus, hear your chil - dren when we pray.
Bless-ed Je - sus, bless-ed Je - sus, you have loved us, love us still.

*The theme of Christ as shepherd is familiar and beloved to Christians. Emma Lyons Doyle, granddaughter of Laiana (translator Lorenzo Lyons), once said, "If you want to know the full beauty of this hymn, hear it sung in Hawaiian."*

Tune: BRADBURY 8.7.8.7.D.
William B. Bradbury, 1859

# 253

## A toi la gloire, ô Ressuscité!
### (Yours Is the Glory, Resurrected One!)

*Matt. 28:1–10; John 20:19–29; 1 Cor. 15:54–55*

Edmond L. Budry, 1904
*Transl.* The New Century Hymnal, 1993

1  A toi la gloi - re, ô Res - sus - ci - té! A toi la vic - toi - re,
1  Yours is the glo - ry, Res - ur - rect - ed One! End - less is the vic - tory
2  See, it is Je - sus, Je - sus has ap-peared; do not doubt at all for
3  Am I still fright-ened? One whom I a - dore, Je - sus, lives a - gain, gives

pour l'é - ter - ni - té! Bril-lant de lu - miè - re, l'ange est de - scen -
you o'er death have won. An - gels clothed in ra-diance rolled the stone a -
noth-ing you will fear. Let the church with glad-ness hymns of tri - umph
peace for - ev - er-more. Je - sus is my vic-tory, life and strength and

du, il rou - le la pier - re du tom-beau vain - cu.
way; con - quered is the grave in which your bod - y lay.
sing; tell it with-out ceas - ing: Death has lost its sting.
Head; Je - sus is my glo - ry, noth - ing shall I dread.

*Refrain*

A toi la gloi - re, ô Res - sus - ci - té!
Yours is the glo - ry, Res - ur - rect - ed One!

*Swiss pastor Edmond L. Budry may have drawn his inspiration for this hymn from a German Advent poem set to Handel's triumphant music. The tune* Judas Maccabeus *is adapted from a chorus in Handel's oratorio of the same name.*

Tune: JUDAS MACCABEUS
5.5.6.5.6.5.6.5. with refrain
G. F. Handel, 1751

A toi la vic - toi - re, pour l'é - ter - ni - té!
End - less is the vic - tory you o'er death have won.

# These Things Did Thomas Count

**254**

*Thomas H. Troeger, 1984*

*John 20:19–31*

1 These things did Thom - as count as real: the warmth of
2 The vi - sion of his skep - tic mind was keen e -
3 His rea - soned cer - tain - ties de - nied that one could
4 May we, O God, by grace be - lieve and thus the

blood, the chill of steel, The grain of wood, the heft of
nough to make him blind To an - y un - ex - pect - ed
live when one had died, Un - til his fin - gers read like
ris - en Christ re - ceive, Whose raw, im - print - ed palms reached

stone, the last frail twitch of flesh and bone.
act too large for his small world of fact.
Braille the mark - ings of the spear and nail.
out and beck - oned Thom - as from his doubt.

*The author cites his "reading of twentieth-century theology and
its coming to terms with the limits of the enlightenment and
rational cognition" as the foundational thought for this text.*

Tune: DISTRESS L.M.
The Sacred Harp, *1844*
Arr. *Jonathan McNair, 1993*

## 255

# Jesus, Sovereign, Savior

*Luke 24:13–48; John 20:19–23*

*Patrick M. Kirkland (1857–1943); alt.*

1 Je - sus, Sov - ereign, Sav - ior, once for sin - ners slain,
2 Faith-ful ones com - mun - ing towards the close of day,
3 In the up - per cham - ber, fol - low-ers, in fear,

cru - ci - fied in weak - ness, raised in power to reign,
des - o - late and wea - ry, met you on the way.
gath-ered sad and trou - bled, there you did ap - pear.

Dwell-ing now im - mor - tal, end-less in your days,
So, when sun is set - ting, come to us and show
Christ, be pres - ent with us, bid our sor - rows cease;

un - to you be glo - ry, hon - or, bless - ing, praise.
your truth, and with - in us make our hearts to glow.
breath - ing on us, Sav - ior, say, "I give you peace."

*Patrick M. Kirkland ministered to a Presbyterian church in Cheshire, England, for forty years. Named for a village near Bristol, King's Weston is one of several fine hymn tunes written by the English composer Ralph Vaughan Williams.*

Tune: KING'S WESTON 6.5.6.5.D.
*Ralph Vaughan Williams, 1925*

# We Live by Faith and Not by Sight

**256**

*Henry Alford, 1844; alt.*

*John 20:24–29*

Unison

1 We live by faith and not by sight;
2 We may not touch Christ's hands and side,
3 Help then, O Christ, our un - be - lief;
4 That, when our life of faith is done,

no gra - cious words we hear From Christ who spoke as
nor fol - low where Christ trod; But in con - fess - ing
and may our faith a - bound To call on you when
in realms of clear - er light We may be - hold you

none e'er spoke, who still we know is near.
we re - joice: our Sav - ior and our God!
you are near and seek where you are found:
as you are, with full and end - less sight.

*As dean of Canterbury, Henry Alford exemplified ecumenism by working closely with non-Anglican groups. He promoted New Testament scholarship with his famous commentary on the Greek New Testament, one of fifty books he published during his lifetime.*

Tune: DUNLAP'S CREEK C.M.
*Samuel McFarland, c. 1816*
*Harm. Richard Proulx, 1986*

# 257

# Alleluia! Gracious Jesus!

*Eph. 1:15–23; Heb. 9:11–14*

*William C. Dix, 1867; alt.*

1 Al - le - lu - ia! Gra - cious Je - sus! Yours the
2 Al - le - lu - ia! Not as or - phans are we
3 Al - le - lu - ia! Bread of an - gels, you on
4 Al - le - lu - ia! Christ e - ter - nal, noth - ing

scep - ter, yours the throne! Al - le - lu - ia! Yours the
left in sor - row now. Al - le - lu - ia! You are
earth our food, our stay. Al - le - lu - ia! Here the
can dis - rupt your reign; Al - le - lu - ia! Born of

tri - umph, yours the vic - to - ry a - lone!
near us; faith be - lieves, nor ques - tions how.
sin - ful flee to you from day to day.
Mar - y, heaven and earth are your do - main.

Hark! the songs of peace - ful Zi - on
Though the cloud from sight re - ceived you
In - ter - ces - sor, friend of sin - ners,
Hu - man life you ful - ly en - tered,

thun - der like a might - y flood; Je - sus, out of
when the for - ty days were o'er, shall our hearts for -
earth's Re - deem - er, plead for me, and the songs that
tend - ing those we count the least, serv - ing both as

ev - ery na - tion you've re - deemed us by your blood.
get your prom - ise, "I am with you ev - er - more."
sound in heav - en will re - peat your gra - cious plea.
Priest and Vic - tim in the eu - cha - ris - tic feast.

*William C. Dix, manager of a marine insurance company, was*
*also a gifted writer who made a significant contribution to*
*hymnody. This hymn was written to fill a need for communion*
*hymns in Church of England hymnals.*

Tune: HYFRYDOL 8.7.8.7.D.
*Rowland H. Prichard, 1844*
*Arr. Ralph Vaughan Williams, 1906*

# 258 Christ, Enthroned in Heavenly Splendor

John 6:51; Heb. 9:26; 1 Cor. 10:4

George Hugh Bourne, 1874; alt.

1 Christ, en-throned in heaven-ly splen-dor, first be-got-ten from the dead,
2 Here our hum-ble hom-age pay we, here in lov-ing rev-erence bow;
3 Pas-chal Lamb, your of-fering fin-ished once for all when you were slain,
4 Life-im-part-ing heaven-ly man-na, strick-en rock with stream-ing side,

You a-lone, our strong de-fend-er, now lift up your peo-ple's head.
Here for faith's dis-cern-ment pray we, lest we fail to know you now.
In its full-ness un-di-min-ished shall for-ev-er-more re-main,
Heaven and earth with loud ho-san-na wor-ship you, the Lamb who died,

Al-le-lu-ia! Al-le-lu-ia! Al-le-lu-ia!
Al-le-lu-ia! Al-le-lu-ia! Al-le-lu-ia!
Al-le-lu-ia! Al-le-lu-ia! Al-le-lu-ia!
Al-le-lu-ia! Al-le-lu-ia! Al-le-lu-ia!

Christ, our true and liv-ing Bread. Christ, our true and liv-ing Bread.
You are here, we ask not how. You are here, we ask not how.
Cleans-ing hearts from ev-ery stain. Cleans-ing hearts from ev-ery stain.
Risen, as-cend-ed, glo-ri-fied! Risen, as-cend-ed, glo-ri-fied!

*This post-communion hymn was one of seven by Anglican clergyman Bourne, who was headmaster at Chardstock College in England. It was first published in the United States in* The Hymnal *of the Evangelical and Reformed Church (1941).*

Tune: BRYN CALFARIA 8.7.8.7.4.7.
*William Owen,* Y Perl Cerddoral, 1852

# A Hymn of Glory Let Us Sing

## 259

*The Venerable Bede (673–735)*
*St. 1–2, transl. Elizabeth R. Charles, 1858; alt.*
*St. 3, transl. Benjamin Webb, 1854; alt.*

*Phil. 2:1–11; Eph. 1:15–23*

*Fanfare (introduction and coda, and interlude if desired)*

1 A hymn of glo - ry let us sing, new
2 You are a pres - ent joy, O Christ, tri -
3 O ris - en Christ, as - cend - ed now, to

hymns through-out the world shall ring; By a new way none
um - phant love once sac - ri - ficed, And great the light in
your blessed name all knees shall bow; You are, while end - less

ev - er trod Christ shares once more the throne of God.
you we see to guide us to e - ter - ni - ty.
a - ges run, in Tri - une God - head ev - er One.

*This Latin hymn by the Venerable Bede is possibly among the
first Christian hymns written in England. Bede's* Historia
Ecclesiastica *is an important source of early English history.*

Tune: DEO GRACIAS L.M.
*"The Agincourt Song," England, c. 1415*
*Arr. E. Power Biggs, 1947; adapt. Richard Proulx, 1985*
*For another harmonization, see 184, 209*

# 260 Hail the Day That Sees Christ Rise

*Acts 1:6–11; John 14:16*  
*Charles Wesley, 1739; alt.*

1 Hail the day that sees Christ rise, Al - le - lu - ia!
2 Christ, for you high tri - umph waits, Al - le - lu - ia!
3 See! The nail - marked hands a - bove; Al - le - lu - ia!
4 Christ for us still in - ter - cede, Al - le - lu - ia!

To a throne in par - a - dise; Al - le - lu - ia!
Lift your heads, e - ter - nal gates! Al - le - lu - ia!
Sing of God's re - deem - ing love; Al - le - lu - ia!
By your suf - fering for us plead; Al - le - lu - ia!

Christ, the Lamb for sin - ners given, Al - le - lu - ia!
You have con - quered death and sin; Al - le - lu - ia!
Hark! Christ's words our hearts as - sure: Al - le - lu - ia!
Make us wor - thy of the place, Al - le - lu - ia!

En - ters now the high - est heaven. Al - le - lu - ia!
You, our Sov - ereign, en - ter in! Al - le - lu - ia!
"I will send a Com - fort - er!" Al - le - lu - ia!
Which you of - fer us by grace. Al - le - lu - ia!

*Charles Wesley's original text was written for Ascension Day 1739 and had no alleluias; these were added in 1852 by G. E. White. Joseph Jones' tune bears the name of a twelfth-century bard and a town in Wales.*

Tune: GWALCHMAI 7.7.7.7. with alleluias  
*Joseph David Jones, 1868*  
Alternate tune: *LLANFAIR*

5  Now, though part-ed from our sight,
    Al-le-lu-ia!
  In the depths of star-ry night,
    Al-le-lu-ia!
  May our souls with you a-rise,
    Al-le-lu-ia!
  Seek-ing whole-ness at your side.
    Al-le-lu-ia!

6  There we will with you re-main,
    Al-le-lu-ia!
  Heirs in your e-ter-nal reign;
    Al-le-lu-ia!
  In the pres-ence of your face,
    Al-le-lu-ia!
  We will dwell in heav-en's grace.
    Al-le-lu-ia!

# Let Every Christian Pray        261

*Fred Pratt Green, 1970; rev. 1994*                    *Acts 2*

1 Let ev-ery Chris-tian pray, this day and ev-ery day,
2 The Spir-it brought to birth the church of Christ on earth
3 On-ly the Spir-it's power can fit us for this hour:

come, Ho-ly Spir-it, come! Was not the church we love
to seek and save the lost: God nev-er has with-drawn,
come, Ho-ly Spir-it, come! U-nite, in-struct, in-spire

com-mis-sioned from a-bove? Come, Ho-ly Spir-it, come!
since that tre-men-dous dawn, the gifts of Pen-te-cost.
and fill us with your fire: come, Ho-ly Spir-it, come!

*Noted contemporary British hymnwriter Fred Pratt Green retired from the parish ministry in 1969 and only then commenced his prolific output of hymn texts, which can be found in every major hymnal publication of the late twentieth century.*

Tune:  LAUDES DOMINI  6.6.6.6.6.6.
*Joseph Barnby, 1868*

# 262

# Hail, O Festal Day!

*Luke 24:1–12; Acts 1:6–11; 2:1–4; 3:12–21*

*Venantius Honorius Fortunatus (c. 530–609)*
*Stanzas 3, 5, 6 and Pentecost from York Processionals, 1530*
*Transl. The New Century Hymnal, 1995*

A poem of 110 lines by Fortunatus comparing the Resurrection to springtime and the renewal of nature is the basis for this ages-old hymn. It was adapted for major festivals, and new, anonymous verses and responses were added. This version takes centos found in the processionals used at York in 1530.

Tune: SALVE FESTA DIES  Irr. with refrain
*Ralph Vaughan Williams, 1906*

to Christ's re - turn: life's ver - y gift is re - newed.
gates o - pen wide, spil - ling forth in - crease of light.
tell of Christ's deeds, in ev - ery lan - guage on earth.
in, make us pure, that we your ves - sel may be.
life - giv - ing Light, re - new-ing life with your grace.

*(St. 2, 4, 6)*

2 *(Easter)* Now on the third day re - turned, a - rise now, O
2 *(Ascension)* The laws of hell now op - pressed, cre - a - tion re -
2 *(Pentecost)* Now to our lips the bright coal touch gen - tly, so
4 O Christ, Re - deem - er of all, our Sav - ior, the
6 Sov - ereign of all that is good, your sweet balm of

Christ, who was bur - ied; fill - ing your prom-ise of
sounds in thanks-giv - ing; field and sea, light and sky
we, too, are kin - dled— your love a - flame in our
Au - thor of good - ness, On - ly Be - got - ten of
peace pour up - on us; give us the wis-dom that

*to Refrain*

faith; nour - ish-ing Pow - er a - rise.
sing at the re - turn of their God.
hearts, lit from your own end - less love.
God, touch us with your heal - ing grace.
guides the u - ni - verse on its way.

# 263         O Spirit of the Living God

*Acts 2:1–4, 17–21*

*Henry Hallam Tweedy, 1933; alt.*

1 O  Spir - it  of  the  liv - ing  God, pure Light and  Fire  Di -
2 Blow, Wind of  God! With  wis - dom blow, dis - perse and  put  to
3 Teach  us  to  ut - ter  liv - ing  words of  truth which  all  may
4 So  shall  we  know the  power of  Christ, the  strength of  love  to

vine: burn bright - ly  in  your  church  once  more,  its  life  and
flight  the  mists of  er - ror,  clouds  of  doubt which hide  you
hear,  the  lan - guage  all  can  un - der - stand  when love speaks
save,  so  shall  we  rise  with  Christ  to  life  which soars  be -

faith  re - fine, Fill  it  with  love  and  joy  and  power, with
from  our  sight. Burn, Wing - ed  Fire!  In - spire  our  lips,  re -
loud  and  clear; Till  ev - ery  na - tion,  age,  and  race  shall
yond  the  grave; And  earth shall  win  true  ho - li - ness, which

righ - teous - ness  and  peace,  till  Christ  shall  dwell  in
new  in  us  your  call  to  preach  with  zeal  your
blend  their  creeds  in  one,  and  all  to - geth - er
makes  your  chil - dren  whole,  and  draws  us  on  by

hu - man hearts, and sin and sor - row cease.
great good news: God's love ex - tends to all.
use their gifts to see your will is done.
grace to reach cre - a - tion's glo - rious goal!

*Henry Hallam Tweedy served Congregational churches in New York and Connecticut from 1898 to 1909 before joining the faculty of Yale University Divinity School.*

Tune: ST. MATTHEW C.M.D.
William Croft, 1708

## Holy Spirit, Come, Confirm Us 264

*Brian Foley, 1971; alt.*

*John 14:25–27; 15:26–16:15*

1 Ho - ly Spir - it, come, con - firm us in the
2 Ho - ly Spir - it, come, con - sole us, come as
3 Ho - ly Spir - it, come, re - new us, come your -
4 Ho - ly Spir - it, come, ful - fill us, you the

truth that Christ makes known; We have faith and un - der -
ad - vo - cate to plead; Lov - ing Spir - it stand be -
self to make us live; Make us ho - ly through your
love of Three in One; Bring our lives to full com -

stand - ing through your help - ing gifts a - lone.
side us, grant in Christ the help we need.
pres - ence, ho - ly through the gifts you give.
ple - tion through your work in us be - gun.

*Author Brian Foley has served as a Roman Catholic priest in his native England since 1945. This text is a distillation of several scriptural passages, an example of his conviction that hymns should be based on theology, not mere sentiment.*

Tune: FOR THE BREAD 8.7.8.7.
V. Earle Copes, 1960

# 265          Come, O Spirit, with Your Sound

*Acts 2:1–24, 32–47; Joel 2:28*                              *John A. Dalles, 1983; rev. 1993*

1 Come, O Spir-it, with your sound like a wind, quick rush-ing;
2 Come, O Spir-it, with your flame, leap-ing tongues of fire; . . .
3 Come, O Spir-it, fill your church, mak-ing strong our mis-sion;

come from heav-en, stir our hearts, each dis-ci-ple touch-ing!
come, and with your glo-rious light all our thoughts in-spire! . . .
fill your daugh-ters and your sons with a might-y vi-sion,

Mold our ac-tions to your will, you our ser-vice giv-ing;
Rest up-on each ser-vant's head till each one is speak-ing
Till the great and glo-rious day when the whole cre-a-tion

move in our com-mu-ni-ty, trans-form now our liv-ing!
of our Christ, the Ho-ly One all the earth is seek-ing!
sings your praise as Sov-ereign One, giv-er of sal-va-tion!

*This hymn text was written for the Pentecost Worship*
*Celebration of Wabash Valley (Indiana) Presbytery in 1983 and*
*was first published in* The Presbyterian Hymnal *(1990). John A.*
*Dalles, a Presbyterian minister, is a graduate of Lancaster*
*Theological Seminary.*

Tune: BOUNDLESS MERCY 7.6.7.6.D.
Union Harmony, *1836*
Harm. Hilton Rufty, *1934*
Alternate tune: ST. KEVIN

# Filled with the Spirit's Power

*John R. Peacey, 1969; alt.*

*Acts 2:1–24, 32–47*

1 Filled with the Spir - it's power, all hearts as one,
2 Now with the mind of Christ set us on fire,
3 Wid - en our love, good Spir - it, to em - brace

the in - fant church con-fessed Christ's vic - to - ry won.
that u - ni - ty may be our great de - sire.
in your strong care all those of ev - ery race.

O Ho - ly Spir - it, in the church to - day
Give joy and peace; give faith to know your call,
Like wind and fire with life a - mong us move,

no less your un - i - fy - ing power dis - play.
and read - i - ness in each to work for all.
till we are known as Christ's, and Chris - tians prove.

*Following service during World War I with the British army in France, canon John Peacey was administrator and chaplain for colleges in England and India. He returned to England in 1945 and began writing hymns only after retiring in 1967.*

Tune: SHELDONIAN 10.10.10.10.
*Cyril V. Taylor, 1951*

# 267 Come, O Spirit, Dwell among Us

Acts 2:1–36; Exod. 13:18–22; Ps. 118:19–29

*Janie Alford, 1979; alt.*

1 Come, O Spir-it, dwell a-mong us, come with Pen-te-
2 We would raise our al-le-lu-ias for the grace of
3 Come, O Spir-it, dwell a-mong us; give us words of

cos-tal power; give the church a strong-er vi-sion,
for-mer years; for to-mor-row's un-known path-way,
fire and flame. Help our strug-gling voic-es praise you,

help us face each cru-cial hour. Built up-on a firm foun-da-tion,
hear, O God, our hum-ble prayers. In the church's pil-grim jour-ney
glo-ri-fy your ho-ly name. Good Cre-a-tor, Sav-ior, Spir-it,

Je-sus Christ, the Cor-ner-stone, still the church is
you have led us all the way, still in pres-ence
Three in One: what mys-ter-y! We would sing our

*Janie Alford is often described as "the Grandma Moses of hymnody." In her nineties, this retired medical secretary and Nashville, Tennessee, shop owner remained an active church worker and wrote many hymns. Nine of her texts were published in 1979.*

Tune: EBENEZER (TON-Y-BOTEL) 8.7.8.7.D.
*Thomas J. Williams, 1890*

called to mis - sion that God's love shall be made known.
move be - fore us, fire by night and cloud by day.
loud ho - san - nas now and through e - ter - ni - ty.

# Creator Spirit, Come, We Pray 268

*Latin, 9th century; attrib. to Rhabanus Maurus (d. 856)*
*Transl.* The New Century Hymnal, *1995*

1 Cre - a - tor Spir - it, come we pray, and vis - it
2 From God on high you are the gift: O Fount of
3 En - kin - dle us, set us a - glow, pour out your
4 De - fend us al - ways from the foe; on those who

ev - ery mind to - day; May hearts you made to be your
Life, your name we lift, O Par - a - clete, our Char - i -
love till hearts o'er - flow; To be made whole we sore - ly
fear, your peace be - stow; Pro - tect our jour - ney, be our

own be filled with heav - enly grace a - lone.
ty, O Fire, blessed Unc - tion flow - ing free.
long; O heal us, Spir - it ev - er strong.
guide, that we in safe - ty may a - bide.

*Although the author of this hymn is unknown, it is often attributed to Rhabanus Maurus, archbishop of Mainz. Manuscripts date from as early as the tenth century when it was used in the daily office during Pentecost.*

Tune: DICKINSON COLLEGE L.M.
*Lee Hastings Bristol, Jr., 1962*
Alternate tune: *PUER NOBIS NASCITUR*

269 Sweet Delight, Most Lovely

Paul Gerhardt, 1648
*Transl. Madeleine Forell Marshall, 1993*

Unison

1 Sweet de-light, most love-ly, shin-ing, faith-ful friend in love and grief,
2 Wise and care-ful, you have count-ed each e-lec-tron, all the sands.
3 When I fail you, please ex-hort me to re-turn to righ-teous ways.

Ho-ly Spir-it, all di-vin-ing, ev-er with us, our re-lief:
All-em-brac-ing, you have bound-ed space and time in your kind hands.
When I stag-ger, please sup-port me through the long and pain-ful days.

As the rain-fall comes, de-scend-ing, wash and bless us with your grace;
Source of life and ev-ery bless-ing, come in an-swer to our prayer—
Save me, hold me, ev-er stead-y, now in life as af-ter death:

All cre-a - tion com-pre-hend-ing, sanc-ti - fy our hu-man race.
As you came, our sin re-dress-ing, came to save us from de - spair.
Con-so-la - tion, ev-er read-y, ev-er-last-ing, vi-tal breath.

*This text is one of numerous new translations of German hymns*
*written for* The New Century Hymnal *by Madeleine Forell*
*Marshall. A comparative literary historian and professor,*
*Marshall specializes in devotional poetry and hymnody. She has*
*worked to support women who are victims of poverty and abuse,*
*and to facilitate intercultural communication.*

Tune: JOEL 8.7.8.7.D.
*Sally Ann Morris, 1991*
Alternate tune: NETTLETON

# Like the Murmur of the Dove's Song     270

Carl P. Daw, Jr., 1982                                    *Isa. 38:14; Rom. 8:26; 12:4–5; John 15:1–5*

1 Like the mur - mur of the dove's song, like the chal - lenge of her
2 To the mem - bers of Christ's bod - y, to the branch-es of the
3 With the heal - ing of di - vi - sion, with the cease-less voice of

flight,              like the vig - or        of the wind's rush,   like the
Vine,                to the church in         faith as - sem - bled,  to our
prayer,              with the power to         love and wit - ness,   with the

new flame's ea - ger might:       Come,   Ho - ly   Spir - it,   come.
midst as gift and sign:
peace be - yond com - pare:

*Carl P. Daw, Jr., wrote this text for* The Hymnal 1982
*(Episcopal), and expressly for the tune* Bridegroom. *Born and
educated in England, composer Peter Cutts has served as music
director for churches in Massachusetts and on the faculty of
Andover Newton Theological School.*

Tune:  BRIDEGROOM  8.7.8.7.6.
*Peter Cutts, 1969*

# 271 Wind Who Makes All Winds That Blow

*Acts 2:1–21*

*Thomas H. Troeger, 1983*

1 Wind who makes all winds that blow—
gusts that bend the sap-lings
2 Fire who fuels all fires that burn—
suns a-round which plan-ets
3 Ho - ly Spir - it, Wind and Flame,
move with-in our mor-tal

low, Gales that heave the sea in waves,
turn, Bea - cons mark-ing reefs and shoals,
frame. Make our hearts an al - tar pyre.

stir-rings in the mind's deep caves—
Aim your breath with
shin-ing truth to guide our souls—
Come to us as
Kin-dle them with your own fire.
Breathe and blow up -

Hymnwriter Thomas H. Troeger and composer Carol Doran
collaborated on this new hymn for a Pentecost celebration. The
tune is named for Father Sebastian Falcone, director of St.
Bernard's Institute of Rochester, New York, for whom the text
was written.

Tune: FALCONE 7.7.7.7.D.
*Carol Doran, 1985*
Alternate tune: ABERYSTWYTH

stead-y power on your church, this day, this hour.
once you came: burst in tongues of sa - cred flame!
on that blaze till our lives, our deeds and ways

Raise, re - new the life we've lost, Spir-it God of Pen - te - cost.
Light and Pow - er, Might and Strength, fill your church, its breadth and length.
Speak that tongue which ev - ery land by your grace shall un - der-stand.

# 272

# On Pentecost They Gathered

*Acts 2:1–24, 32–47*

*Jane Parker Huber, 1981; rev. 1993*

1 On Pen-te-cost they gath-ered quite ear-ly in the day,
2 The peo-ple all a-round them were star-tled and a-mazed
3 God pours the Ho-ly Spir-it on all who would be-lieve,
4 O Spir-it, sent from heav-en on that day long a-go,

a band of Christ's dis-ci-ples to wor-ship, sing, and pray.
to un-der-stand their lan-guage, as God in Christ they praised.
on wom-en, men, and chil-dren who would God's grace re-ceive.
re-kin-dle faith a-mong us in all life's ebb and flow.

A might-y wind came blow-ing, filled all the swirl-ing air,
What un-i-ver-sal mes-sage, what great good news was here?
That Spir-it knows no lim-it, be-stow-ing life and power.
O give us hearts to lis-ten and tongues a-flame with praise,

and tongues of fire a-glow-ing in-spired each per-son there.
That Christ, once dead, is ris-en to van-quish all our fear.
The church, formed and re-form-ing, re-sponds in ev-ery hour.
so folk of ev-ery na-tion glad songs of joy shall raise.

*Jane Parker Huber explained that she wrote this text in 1981
"to fill a gap in current hymnody," in that "many of the hymns
concerning the activity of the Holy Spirit do not mention
Pentecost."*

Tune: MUNICH 7.6.7.6.D.
Neuvermehrtes Gesangbuch, *Meiningen, 1693*
Harm. Felix Mendelssohn, 1847

# Praise with Joy the World's Creator

**273**

*The Iona Community, 1985; alt.*

1 Praise with joy the world's Cre - a - tor, God of jus - tice,
love, and peace, Source and end of hu - man knowl-edge,
grace be - stow - ing with - out cease. Cel - e - brate the
Ma - ker's glo - ry, power to res - cue and re - lease.

2 Praise to Christ who feeds the hun - gry, frees the cap - tive,
finds the lost, Heals the sick, up - sets re - li - gion,
fear - less both of fate and cost. Cel - e - brate Christ's
con - stant pres-ence— Friend and Strang-er, Guest and Host.

3 Praise the Spir - it sent a - mong us, lib - er - a - ting
truth from pride, Forg - ing bonds where race or gen - der,
age or na - tion dare di - vide. Cel - e - brate the
Spir - it's trea-sure— fool - ish - ness none dare de - ride.

4 Praise the Mak - er, Christ, and Spir - it, one God in Com-
mu - ni - ty, Call - ing Christ-ians to em - bod - y
one - ness and di - ver - si - ty. Thus the world shall
yet be - lieve when shown Christ's vi - brant un - i - ty.

*The Iona Community works and worships in a tenth-century abbey on the remote island of Iona, Scotland. Their output of hymns and songs includes this one written for the anniversary gathering of the World Student Christian Federation in Edinburgh in 1985.*

Tune: LAUDA ANIMA (PRAISE MY SOUL)
8.7.8.7.8.7.
*John Goss, 1869*

274 Womb of Life, and Source of Being

John 1:14; 20:19–23

*Ruth Duck, 1986, 1990*

1 Womb of life, and source of be - ing, home of ev -
2 Word in flesh, our broth - er Je - sus, born to bring
3 Brood - ing Spir - it, move a - mong us; be our part -
4 Moth - er, Broth - er, ho - ly Part - ner; Fa - ther, Spir -

- ery rest - less heart, in your arms the worlds a -
us sec - ond birth, you have come to stand be -
- ner, be our friend. When our mem - ory fails, re -
- it, On - ly Son: we would praise your name for -

wak - ened; you have loved us from the start.
side us, know - ing weak - ness, know - ing earth.
mind us whose we are, what we in - tend.
ev - er, one - in - three, and three - in - one.

*This hymn, which mixes old and new metaphors to express faith
and praise to God, known to us as Source, Word, and Spirit
(and many other names!), borrows a phrase from Charles
Wesley: "Born to give us second birth." According to Ruth
Duck, Trinitarian theology provides a model for the life of
community.*

Tune:  LADUE CHAPEL 8.7.8.7.D.
*Ronald Arnatt, 1968*
*Alternate tunes:  HYMN TO JOY; CENTRAL*

# Come Now, Almighty God

Anon., English, c. 1757; alt.

1 Come now, Al - might - y God, help us your
2 Come now, In - car - nate Word, by heaven and
3 Come, Ho - ly Com - fort - er, your sa - cred
4 To you, great One in Three, e - ter - nal

name to laud; our songs we raise:
earth a - dored; our prayer at - tend:
wit - ness bear in this glad hour.
prais - es be for ev - er - more.

Rul - er all glo - ri - ous, o'er all vic - to - ri - ous,
Come, and your peo - ple bless, and give your word suc - cess;
Your grace to us im - part, now rule in ev - ery heart,
Your sov - ereign maj - es - ty may we in glo - ry see,

come and reign o - ver us, An - cient of Days!
grant us your ho - li - ness, Sav - ior and Friend!
nev - er from us de - part, Spir - it of power!
and to e - ter - ni - ty love and a - dore.

*This anonymous English hymn to the Trinity was first published
in George Whitefield's Collection, 1757. This tune was composed
especially for this text by Giardini, who was a brilliant violinist.*

Tune: ITALIAN HYMN 6.6.4.6.6.6.4.
*Felice de Giardini, 1769*

# Holy God, We Praise Your Name

**276**

*Anon., German, c. 1774*

*Rev. 4:8–11*

*Transl. Clarence Alphonsus Walworth, 1853; alt.*

1 Ho - ly God, we praise your name; Sov - ereign God, we
2 Hark, the glad ce - les - tial hymn an - gel choirs a -
3 All a - pos - tles join the strain as your sa - cred
4 Ho - ly Fa - ther, Ho - ly Son, Ho - ly Spir - it,

bow be - fore you; All on earth your scep - ter claim,
round are rais - ing; Cher - u - bim and ser - a - phim,
name they hal - low; Proph - ets swell the glad re - frain,
Three we name you, While in es - sence tru - ly one,

all the heaven - ly hosts a - dore you. In - fi - nite your
in un - ceas - ing cho - rus prais - ing, Fill the heavens with
and the bless - ed mar - tyrs fol - low; And from morn to
un - di - vid - ed God we claim you; So we gath - er

vast do - main, ev - er - last - ing is your reign.
joys a - flame: ho - ly, ho - ly is your name.
set of sun, through the church the song goes on.
rev - erent - ly to a - dore the mys - ter - y.

*This German Catholic hymn, based on the* Te Deum Laudamus, *appeared with this tune in a hymnal published by command of Austrian empress Maria Theresa. In the nineteenth century it became popular in Protestant worship.*

Tune: GROSSER GOTT, WIR LOBEN DICH
7.8.7.8.7.7.
*Katholisches Gesangbuch, Vienna, c. 1774*
*Alt. Johann Gottfried Schicht, 1819*

# 277

# Holy, Holy, Holy

*Rev. 4:8–11; Isa. 6:1–8*

*Reginald Heber, 1826; alt.*

**Descant**

4 Ho - ly, ho - ly, ho - ly!

1 Ho - ly, ho - ly, ho - ly, God the Al - might - y!
2 Ho - ly, ho - ly, ho - ly! Saints a - dore you tru - ly,
3 Ho - ly, ho - ly, ho - ly! Though we know but dim - ly,
4 Ho - ly, ho - ly, ho - ly, God the Al - might - y!

Ho - ly, ho - ly, ho - ly!

Ear - ly in the morn - ing we praise your maj - es - ty.
Cast - ing down their gold - en crowns a - round the glass - y sea;
Though the eyes of hum - an - kind your glo - ry may not see,
All your works shall praise your name in earth and sky and sea.

Ho - ly, ho - ly, ho - ly!

Ho - ly, ho - ly ho - ly! Mer - ci - ful and might - y!
Cher - u - bim and ser - a - phim bow be - fore you on - ly,
You a - lone are ho - ly, you a - lone are wor - thy,
Ho - ly, ho - ly, ho - ly! Mer - ci - ful and might - y!

God in three per - sons, bless - ed Trin - i - ty.

God in three per - sons, bless - ed Trin - i - ty!
From the be - gin - ning, God e - ter - nal - ly.
Per - fect in power, in love and pur - i - ty.
God in three per - sons, bless - ed Trin - i - ty!

*This hymn by Reginald Heber was published in a book of hymns for Banbury Parish Church in England. Nicaea, one of nearly 300 tunes by John B. Dykes, was named for the famous council that defined the doctrine of the Trinity.*

Tune: NICAEA 11.12.12.10.
*John B. Dykes, 1861*
*Descant David McK.Williams, 1948*

# Creator God, Creating Still 278

*Jane Parker Huber, 1977; rev. 1993*                                        *Rom. 5:1–5*

1 Cre - a - tor God, cre - at - ing still, by will and word and deed,
2 Re - deem-er God, re - deem-ing still, with o - ver - flow-ing grace,
3 Sus - tain - er God, sus - tain - ing still, with strength for ev - ery day,
4 Great Tri - une God, for this new day we need your pres-ence still.

Cre - ate a new hu - man - i - ty to meet the pres - ent need.
Pour out your love on us, through us, make this a ho - ly place.
Em - power us now to do your will. Cor - rect us when we stray.
Cre - ate, re - deem, sus - tain us now to do your work and will.

*Jane Parker Huber's second hymn was written during a time of particular focus on language. By describing the Triune God in terms of function rather than in terms of persons, she hoped to avoid a tendency to think we know God by knowing formulas.*

Tune: ST. ANNE C.M.
*William Croft, 1708*

**279**

John 14:15–19, 25–27

# O God in Heaven

Elena G. Maquiso, 1961
Transl. D. T. Niles, 1964; alt.

1 O God in heav - en, grant to your chil - dren mer - cy and
2 Je - sus Re - deem - er, help us re - mem - ber your pain and
3 Spir - it un - end - ing, give us your bless - ing: strength for the

bless - ing, songs nev - er ceas - ing, Grace to in - vite us, peace to u -
pas - sion, your res - ur - rec - tion, Your call to fol - low, your love to -
wea - ry, help for the need - y, Hope for the scorn - ful, peace for the

nite us— O God in heav - en, auth - or of love.
mor - row— Je - sus Re - deem - er, sav - ior and friend.
mourn - ful— Spir - it un - end - ing, com-fort and guide.

This hymn, by Philippine composer and writer Elena G.
Maquiso, has appeared in a number of international hymn
collections. Professor Maquiso is known for her research on
indigenous hymnody of the Philippines, where she has served
on the faculty of Silliman University.

Tune: HALAD 5.5.5.5.
Elena G. Maquiso, 1961
Harm. Cantate Domino, 1980

**280**

Matt. 28:19; John 16:13

# O Trinity, Your Face We See

Douglas C. Eschbach, 1988; rev. 1994

1 O Trin - i - ty, your face we see through Christ in full hu -
2 O Ho - ly God, as three we bless the per - sons whom our
3 Through Christ you feed us as our host, you guide us by the
4 And yet, though in three ways you show your love, and grace on
5 For you are love with - in all three, and will be love e -

man - i - ty; For flesh has held di -
creeds con - fess; But each is nei - ther
Ho - ly Ghost. You fa - ther us in
us be - stow, our faith will e - ven
ter - nal - ly; May we in your love

vin - i - ty, that we might share your mys - ter - y.
more nor less, for all make up your ho - li - ness.
ways that boast of love for those who need you most.
strong - er grow when through each one all three we know.
ev - er be, most bless - ed Ho - ly Trin - i - ty.

*Douglas Eschbach was serving as minister at St. Paul Lutheran Church in Telford, Pennsylvania, and Arthur Clyde was director of music at Zwingli United Church of Christ in Souderton, Pennsylvania when they collaborated on this hymn.*

Tune: RELIANCE L.M.
*Arthur G. Clyde, 1988*
Alternate tune: WINCHESTER NEW

# Come, Holy Spirit, Heavenly Dove 281

*Isaac Watts, 1707; alt.* *John 1:32*

1 Come, Ho - ly Spir - it, heaven-ly Dove, with all your quick-ening powers;
2 In vain we tune our for - mal songs, in vain we strive to rise;
3 Come, Ho - ly Spir - it, heaven-ly Dove, with all your quick-ening powers;

Kin - dle a flame of sa - cred love in these cold hearts of ours.
Ho - san - nas lan - guish on our tongues, and our de - vo - tion dies.
Come, shed on us the Sav - ior's love, that it may kin - dle ours.

*This text from an early collection of Watts' Hymns and Spiritual Songs (1707) has seen many modifications through the years, including some made by John Wesley on theological grounds.*

Tune: ST. AGNES C.M.
*John B. Dykes, 1866*

282

# Every Time I Feel the Spirit

2 Sam. 22:9; Ps. 18:8

*African-American spiritual*

*Refrain*

Ev-ery time I feel the Spir-it mov-ing in my heart I will
pray. Yes, ev-ery time I feel the Spir-it mov-ing

*Last time, end*

in my heart I will pray.

1 Up-on the moun-tain my God
2 Oh, Jor-dan riv-er, chil-ly and

spoke, out of God's mouth came fire and smoke. Looked all a-
cold, it chills the bod-y, not the soul. There's on-ly

*to Refrain*

round me; looked so fine; I asked my God if all were mine.
one train on this track; it runs to heav-en, then right back.

*Among the thousands of spirituals that exist today are songs of
gladness and songs of sorrow. This well-known spiritual is a song
of joy, captured not only in the words, but in the lively rhythms.*

Tune: African-American spiritual
*Arr. Joyce Finch Johnson, 1992*

# Spirit of the Living God

**283**

Daniel Iverson, 1926

*Acts 11:15; 2 Cor. 3:1–6; Gal. 5:25*

Spir - it of the liv - ing God, fall a - fresh on me;

Spir - it of the liv - ing God, fall a - fresh on me.

Melt me, mold me, fill me, use me.

Spir - it of the liv - ing God, fall a - fresh on me.

*Presbyterian minister Daniel Iverson was inspired to write this chorus one evening while attending revival services led by the George T. Stephans Evangelistic Party in Orlando, Florida, in 1926. It became widely popular at similar meetings before it was published several years later.*

Tune: IVERSON 7.5.7.5.8.7.5.
*Daniel Iverson, 1926*

284       Joys Are Flowing like a River
(Blessed Quietness)

*Matt. 8:26; John 14:16; Ps. 46:4*       *Manie Payne Ferguson (b. 1850); alt.*

1 Joys are flow-ing like a riv - er, since the Com - fort - er has
2 Bring-ing life and health and glad-ness all a - round, this heaven-ly
3 Like the rain that falls from heav - en, like the sun - light from the
4 See, a fruit-ful field is grow-ing, bless-ed fruit of righ - teous -
5 What a won - der - ful sal - va - tion, when we al - ways see Christ's

come; Christ a - bides with us for - ev - er, makes the
Guest Ban-ished un - be - lief and sad - ness, changed our
sky, So the Spir - it too is giv - en, com - ing
ness; And the streams of life are flow - ing in the
face, What a per - fect hab - i - ta - tion, what a

*Refrain*

trust - ing heart a home.
wea - ri - ness to rest.
on us from on high.    Bless-ed qui - et-ness, ho - ly
lone - ly wil - der - ness.
qui - et rest - ing place.

qui - et-ness, what as - sur - ance in my soul. On the

storm-y sea, Je-sus speaks to me, and the bil-lows cease to roll.

*Manie Payne Ferguson, born in Ireland, was married to a Wesleyan evangelist who established several missions on England's west coast. Ferguson's hymns were published in* Echoes from Beulah.

Tune: BLESSED QUIETNESS 8.7.8.7. with refrain
*W. S. Marshall*
*Arr. J. Jefferson Cleveland*
*and Verolga Nix, 1981*

# O Holy Dove of God Descending 285

*Bryan Jeffery Leech, 1976*

1 O ho-ly Dove of God de-scend-ing, you are the love that knows no end-ing,
2 O ho-ly Wind of God now blow-ing, you are the seed that God is sow-ing,
3 O ho-ly Rain of God now fall-ing, you make the Word of God en-thrall-ing,
4 O ho-ly Flame of God now burn-ing, you are the power of Christ re-turn-ing,

All of our shat-tered dreams you're mend-ing: Spir-it, now live in me.
You are the life that starts us grow-ing: Spir-it, now live in me.
You are the in-ner voice now call-ing: Spir-it, now live in me.
You are the an-swer to our yearn-ing: Spir-it, now live in me.

*Bryan Jeffery Leech, educated in Britain and the United States, has served American churches since 1955. He has also written musical plays, assisted in preparing and editing hymnals, and co-edited* The Hymnal Companion *(1979).*

Tune: O HOLY DOVE 9.9.9.6.
*Bryan Jeffery Leech, 1976*

# 286

# Spirit, Spirit of Gentleness

James K. Manley, 1978; alt.

*Reduced-size notes may be played with organ pedals in lieu of or in combination with the other notes.*

This popular hymn by songwriter James K. Manley grew out
of a sabbatical leave at the School of Theology at Claremont,
California. It was first sung at Waiokeola Congregational
Church in Honolulu, after which Manley added the fourth
stanza at the suggestion of a church member.

Tune: SPIRIT Irr.
*James K. Manley, 1978*
*Arr.* The New Century Hymnal, *1993*

## 287          Come, Teach Us, Spirit of Our God

*Shirley Erena Murray, 1990*

*Unison*

1 Come, teach us, Spir - it of our God, the
2 Ex - cite our minds to fol - low you, to
3 En - gage our wits to dance with you, to
4 In - spire our spark to light from you to
5 De - light our hearts to wor - ship you, to

lan - guage of your way, the les - sons
trace new truths in store, new flight paths
leap from log - ic's base, to cap - ture
catch cre - a - tion's flair, new ar - tis -
learn com - pas - sion's code, to live in

that we need to live, the faith for ev - ery
for our spir - it space, new mar - vels to ex -
in - sight on the wing, to sense your cos - mic
try to cel - e - brate, new har - mo - nies to
con - text of your love, great teach - er who is

*For a hymn search sponsored by an educational institution, Shirley Erena Murray sought to utilize various images of creativity in learning. The tune was composed especially for this text.*

Tune: MURRAY C.M. extended
*Arthur G. Clyde, 1993*

day; the faith for ev - ery day.
plore: new mar - vels to ex - plore:
grace: to sense your cos - mic grace:
dare: new har - mo - nies to dare:
God! Great teach - er who is God!

# Let It Breathe on Me

**288**

*Magnolia Lewis-Butts, 1941; alt.*

*Job 33:4; Ezek. 37:1–14; John 20:19–23*

1 Let it breathe on me, let it breathe on me, let the breath of the
2 While I'm work - ing, God, in your vine - yard here, I can - not
3 When the path - way, God, I can - not see, when the way is

Spir - it breathe on me. Let it breathe on me, let it
serve with - out you near; O come, blessed Spir - it, so
hard, O breathe on me; Give me grace to know when

breathe on me, let the breath of God now breathe on me.
close to me that I may feel you breathe on me.
you are near, then, I pray, O Spir - it, breathe on me.

*Songwriter Magnolia Lewis-Butts helped form the National
Convention of Gospel Choirs and Choruses in 1932, which was
the model for all subsequent gospel music conventions.*

Tune: LET IT BREATHE  Irr.
*Magnolia Lewis-Butts, 1941*

# 289        Come Forth, O Love Divine

Acts 2:1–4

Bianco da Siena (d. 1434)
Transl. Richard F. Littledale, 1867; alt.

1 Come forth, O Love divine, seek now this soul of mine, and visit it with your own ardor glowing; O Comforter, draw near, within my heart appear, and kindle it, your holy flame bestowing.

2 O let it freely burn, till earthly passions turn to dust and ashes in its heat consuming; And let your glorious light shine ever on my sight, and clothe me round, the while my path illuming.

3 And so the yearning strong, with which the soul will long, shall far outpass the power of human telling; For none can guess its grace, till love create a place wherein the Holy Spirit makes a dwelling.

*Bianco da Siena lived in Venice, where he was a member of a religious order following the rule of St. Augustine. Ralph Vaughan Williams' tune composed for this hymn was named for his birthplace in England.*

Tune: DOWN AMPNEY 6.6.11.D.
*Ralph Vaughan Williams, 1906*

# Spirit of God, Descend upon My Heart

**290**

George Croly, 1854; alt.

Gal. 5:25; Matt. 22:37; John 1:32

1 Spir - it of God, de - scend up - on my heart;
2 I ask no dream, no proph - et ec - sta - sies,
3 Have you not bid us love you ev - ery way?
4 Teach me to feel that you are al - ways nigh;
5 Teach me to love you as your an - gels love,

wean it from earth, through all its puls - es move;
no sud - den rend - ing of the veil of clay,
All, all your own: soul, heart, and strength, and mind;
teach me the strug - gles of the soul to bear,
one ho - ly pas - sion fill - ing all my frame;

Stoop to my weak - ness, might - y as you are,
No an - gel vis - i - tant, no o - pening skies;
I see your cross— there teach my heart to stay:
To check the ris - ing doubt, the reb - el sigh;
The bap - tism of the heaven - de - scend - ed dove,

and make me love you as I ought to love.
but take the dim - ness of my soul a - way.
O let me seek you, and O let me find.
teach me the pa - tience of un - an - swered prayer.
my heart an al - tar, and your love the flame.

George Croly, ordained in the Church of Ireland, was well known in London literary circles and served a poor parish. This hymn is from a collection he compiled for that congregation. Hellespont was the original name for the tune Morecambe.

Tune: MORECAMBE 10.10.10.10.
Frederick C. Atkinson, 1870

# 291

# O God the Creator

Ps. 104:24–30; Acts 4:32–35

*Elizabeth Haile and Cecil Corbett, 1977; alt.*

1 O God, the Cre - a - tor, the Three - in -
2 For the earth is our moth - er where all things
3 We are one in the Spir - it, in the great mys-ter -
4 God, we ask you for lead - ers with your wis - dom

One, the Cre - a - tor of earth and moon and
grow, and her val - leys are green where the wa - ters
y, joined to - geth - er in beau-ty as we dwell in har-mo -
blessed, and we pray you will join us in our vi - sion

sun, You have loved and pro - tect-ed us since time first be -
flow, Gen - tle deer and the ea - gle and the might-y buf - fa -
ny, Bring-ing all of God's chil-dren in - to one com-mu - ni -
quest. God, we wel - come you in - to our hearts as our

Elizabeth Haile and Cecil Corbett are Native Americans who wrote
this text as the theme song of the 1977 Indian Youth Conference in
Tulsa, Oklahoma. It was published with Joy Patterson's tune in *The
Presbyterian Hymnal (1990)*. A "vision quest," referred to in stanza
four, is a Lakota Indian ritual of prayer and fasting carried out in
the form of a circle and a cross. Through this spiritual exercise, an
individual seeks wisdom and communion with "Wakan-Tanka"
(the Great Spirit), and may receive healing or new direction in life.

Tune: KASTAAK Irr.
*Joy F. Patterson, 1989*

*Refrain*

gun,
lo,
ty,
guest,

And we're broth-ers and sis-ters in God's love, in God's love, and we're broth-ers and sis-ters in God's love.

# Breathe on Me, Breath of God

292

*Edwin Hatch, 1886; alt.*

1 Breathe on me, Breath of God, fill me with life a - new
2 Breathe on me, Breath of God, un - til my heart is pure,
3 Breathe on me, Breath of God, stir in me one de - sire:
4 Breathe on me, Breath of God, so shall I nev - er die,

That I may love the way you love and do what you would do.
Un - til with you I will one will, to do and to en - dure.
That ev - ery earth - ly part of me may glow with ho - ly fire.
But live with you the per - fect life of your e - ter - ni - ty.

*Between parish assignments in London, Edwin Hatch taught classics at Trinity College, Quebec, and lectured at Oxford. This hymn appeared in a leaflet, "Between Doubt and Prayer" (1878). Other hymns were published posthumously in* Towards Fields of Light, *London (1890).*

Tune: TRENTHAM S.M.
*Robert Jackson, 1894*

# 293

## Sweet, Sweet Spirit

2 Cor. 3:17–5:5

*Doris Akers, 1962; alt.*

Slowly

1 There's a sweet, sweet Spir- it in this place, and I
2 There are bless- ings you can- not re - ceive till you

know that it's the Spir - it of the Lord; there are
know that Spir- it's full - ness and be - lieve; you're the

sweet ex - pres - sions on each face, and I
one to prof - it when you say, "I am

*to Refrain*

know they feel the pres - ence of the Lord.
going to stay with Je - sus all the way."

*This is one of the most popular gospel songs from the corpus of African-American songwriters who emerged during the golden age of gospel (1930–1969). Although this era was dominated by the Baptists, Doris Akers had Methodist roots.*

Tune: SWEET, SWEET SPIRIT
9.11.9.11. with refrain
*Doris Akers, 1962*

*Refrain*

Sweet Ho - ly Spir - it, sweet heav-en-ly Dove, stay right here

with us, fill-ing us with your love; And for these bless-ings we

lift our hearts in praise. With-out a doubt we'll know that we have

been re - vived when we shall leave this place.

# 294

# There's a Spirit in the Air

*John 6:24–35, 51–58; 1 Cor. 2:9–16; 1 John 4*

*Brian Wren, 1969; rev. 1987*

1 There's a spir - it in the air, tell - ing Chris-tians ev - ery-where:
2 Lose your shy - ness, find your tongue; tell the world what God has done:
3 When be - liev - ers break the bread, when a hun - gry child is fed:
4 Still the Spir - it gives us light, see - ing wrong and set - ting right:
5 When a strang-er's not a - lone, where the home-less find a home:

"Praise the love that Christ re-vealed, liv - ing, work - ing in our world."
God in Christ has come to stay. Live to - mor - row's life to - day.
Praise the love that Christ re-vealed, liv - ing, work - ing in our world.
God in Christ has come to stay. Live to - mor - row's life to - day.
Praise the love that Christ re-vealed, liv - ing, work - ing in our world.

6 May the Spir-it fill our praise,
    guide our thoughts and change our ways.
God in Christ has come to stay.
Live to-mor-row's life to-day.

7 There's a Spir-it in the air,
    call-ing peo-ple ev-ery-where:
Praise the love that Christ re-vealed,
liv-ing, work-ing in our world.

*Brian Wren celebrates the Spirit's work in the world in this text
written for Pentecost at Hockley, England. In it, Wren borrows
a poetic device from the Isaac Watts hymn "Give to Our God
Immortal Praise" with the alternating repetition of two choruses.*

Tune: ORIENTIS PARTIBUS 7.7.7.7.
*Medieval French melody
Harm. Richard Redhead, 1853*

# 295

# I Sing a Song of the Saints of God

*Lesbia Scott, 1929; alt.*

Unison

1 I sing a song of the saints of God, .... faith-ful their whole lives
2 They loved their God and they lived that love. It was lov - ing that made them
3 They lived not on - ly in a - ges past, there are hun-dreds of thou-sands

*This text was included in Lesbia Scott's Everyday Hymns for
Little Children with her original words, music, and illustrations.
A native of Britain, Scott was also the author of six published
plays and enjoyed painting until her death in 1986.*

Tune: GRAND ISLE Irr.
*John H. Hopkins, 1940*

through, who brave - ly la - bored, lived, and died for the God they
strong. They did what was right, for Je - sus' sake, lived just - ly their
still. The world is filled with liv - ing saints who choose to

loved and knew. And one was a doc - tor, and one was a queen, and an -
whole lives long. And one was a proph - et, and one was a priest, and an -
do God's will. You can meet them in school, on the road, or at sea, in a

oth - er a shep-herd in pas - tures green: they were saints of God, if you
oth - er was slain by a fierce wild beast: there is no earth-ly rea - son,
church, in a train, in a shop, or at tea: for the saints are folk like

know what I mean. God, help me to be one, too.
none in the least, why I should-n't be one, too.
you and like me, and I mean to be one, too.

# 296
# Behold the Host All Robed in Light

*Rev. 7:9–17*

*Hans A. Brorson, c. 1764*
*Transl. Carl Doving, 1909; alt.*

1 Be - hold the host all robed in light, ar - rayed like snow - clad
2 Their work was hard, their jour - ney long, but by God's grace their

moun - tains bright, With palms they stand— who is this band who
faith was strong, These saints made pure, their trials en-dured, for -

gath - er in God's sight? These are the faith-ful ones, the same who
ev - er to God be - long. How of-ten in their earth-ly day they

through the time of tri - al came, Who Christ has raised that
si - lent-ly did weep and pray, But con - flicts past, brought

*Danish Lutheran pastor and hymnwriter Hans A. Brorson*
*was bishop of Ribe for many years, a position in which he was*
*greatly loved and respected. The Norwegian folk melody from*
*Heddal was harmonized by Norwegian composer Edvard Grieg.*

Tune: DEN STORE HVIDE FLOK 8.8.4.4.6. Triple
*Norwegian folk tune*
*Arr. Edvard Grieg (1843–1907)*

they might praise un - end - ing - ly God's name;
home at last, God wiped their tears a - way;

And now their jour - ney fin - ished they with
No hun - ger now, nor thirst they know; op -

joy - ful voic - es join to pray, glad songs they sing. Their
pres - sion can - not cause them woe. The Shep - herd feeds and

thanks they bring to God both night and day.
gent - ly leads where liv - ing wa - ters flow.

# 297

# Give Thanks for Life

*1 Thess. 5:18; Rom. 16:1–16; Eph. 1:15–16*

*Shirley Erena Murray, 1986*

1 Give thanks for life, the mea - sure of our days,
2 Give thanks for those who made their life a light
3 And for our own, our liv - ing and our dead,
4 Give thanks for hope, that like the wheat, the grain

mor - tal, we pass through beau - ty that de - cays,
caught from the Christ-flame, burst - ing through the night,
thanks for the love by which our life is fed,
that lies in dark - ness does its life re - tain

Yet sing to God our hope, our love, our praise,
Who touched the truth, who burned for what was right,
A love not changed by time or death or dread,
In res - ur - rec - tion to grow green a - gain,

*Shirley Erena Murray wrote this text "as a celebration for someone who has lived a full life." The tune by Nancy M. René was originally composed as a setting for her own version of "For All the Saints," and was dedicated to her mother and grandmother.*

Tune: ROBINSON 10.10.10. with alleluias
*Nancy M. René, 1994*

# O Savior, for the Saints

### 298

*Richard Mant, 1837; alt.*

*Rom. 14:7–9*

1 O Sav-ior, for the saints who strove in you to live,
2 O Sav-ior, for the saints who strove in you to die,
3 They all in life and death, with you, O Christ, in view,
4 For this, your name we bless and hum-bly pray a - new

Who fol-lowed you with-out com-plaint, our grate-ful hymn re-ceive.
Who loved and served with-out re-straint, ac - cept our thank-ful cry.
Learned from the Ho - ly Spir-it's breath to suf - fer and to do.
That we, like them, in ho - li - ness may live and die in you.

*This was one of several original hymns appended to Richard Mant's book of translations of Latin hymns from the Roman Breviary. A priest of the Church of England, Mant was for many years a bishop in Ireland.*

Tune: FESTAL SONG S.M.
*William Walter, 1872*

# 299 For All the Saints

*Heb. 12:1*

*William W. How, 1864; alt.*

1 For all the saints who from their la - bors rest, who to the world their stead-fast faith con - fessed, your name, O Je - sus, be for - ev - er blessed.

2 You were their rock, their ref - uge, and their might: you, Christ, the hope that put their fears to flight; 'mid gloom and doubt, you were their one true light.

3 Still may your peo - ple, faith - ful, true, and bold, live as the saints who no - bly fought of old, and share with them a glo - rious crown of gold. Al - le - lu - ia! Al - le - lu - ia!

4 Ringed by this cloud of wit - ness - es di - vine, we fee - bly strug - gle, they in glo - ry shine; yet in your love our faith - ful lives en - twine.

5 And when the strife is fierce, the war - fare long, steals on the ear the dis - tant tri - umph song, then hearts are brave a - gain, and faith grows strong.

*This traditional All Saints Day hymn originally consisted of eleven stanzas written for the* Sarum Hymnal *(1869) and set to a tune by that name,* Sarum. *It has grown in popularity since it was later paired with the enduring* Sine Nomine *in* The English Hymnal *(1906).*

Tune: SINE NOMINE 10.10.10.4.
*Ralph Vaughan Williams, 1906*

# Jesus Shall Reign

**300**

*Isaac Watts, 1719; alt.*

*Ps. 72; Rev. 1:4b–8*

1 Je - sus shall reign wher - e'er the sun
2 Through Christ shall end - less prayer be made,
3 Peo - ple and realms of ev - ery tongue
4 Bless - ings a - bound where - e'er Christ reigns:
5 Let ev - ery crea - ture rise and bring

does its suc - ces - sive jour - neys run;
borne by the Spir - it's cease - less aid;
dwell on God's love with sweet - est song,
the pris - oners leap to lose their chains,
trib - utes of praise for all to sing;

God's realm shall stretch from shore to shore
Like sweet per - fume new hymns shall rise
And in - fant voic - es shall pro - claim
The wea - ry find e - ter - nal rest,
An - gels de - scend with songs a - gain,

till moons shall wax and wane no more.
with ev - ery morn - ing sac - ri - fice.
their ear - liest prayers in Je - sus' name.
and all who suf - fer want are blessed.
and earth re - peat the loud a - men.

*The second half of a longer paraphrase of Psalm 72, this hymn
was included in Isaac Watts' Psalms of David, a collection of
psalm-based poems with New Testament orientation. John Hatton
once lived on Duke Street in St. Helen's, Lancaster, England.*

Tune: DUKE STREET L.M.
*Attrib. to John Hatton, c. 1793*

# 301      Crown with Your Richest Crowns

*John 19:16–18, 31–34; Rev. 7:9–10*

*Matthew Bridges, 1851, and Godfrey Thring, 1874*
*Adapt. Thomas H. Troeger, 1993*

1 Crown with your rich-est crowns the Lamb up - on the throne;
2 Crown Christ whose love has flowed down hands and feet and side.
3 Crown Christ the truth, the life who tri - umphed o'er the grave
4 Crown Christ who rules in peace, whose power a scep - tre sways
5 Crown Christ who holds the years, em - brac - ing space and time,

Hark! how the heaven-ly an - them drowns all mu - sic but its own.
Look past the peak of Cal - vary's road to Christ the glo - ri - fied.
And rose vic - to - rious in the strife, this fal - len world to save.
From pole to pole, that wars may cease, and all be prayer and praise:
Cre - a - tor of the roll - ing spheres, in - ef - fa - bly sub - lime:

A - wake, my soul, and sing of Christ who died for you, And
The sun that lights the sky is pale be - fore that sight. At
Christ's glo - ries now we sing, Christ's name we mag - ni - fy, Who
Christ's reign shall have no end, for 'round those wound-ed feet a
All hail, Re - deem - er, hail! For you have died for me; Your

*This hymn has evolved as a composite of the original text by Matthew Bridges and Godfrey Thring's version written twenty-three years later. Diademata was composed for Bridges' text and is titled for the Greek word meaning "crowns."*

Tune: DIADEMATA S.M.D.
*George J. Elvey, 1868*

to your ris - en Sav - ior bring your thanks for life made new.
prayer we glimpse then turn the eye from mys - ter - ies so bright.
died e - ter - nal life to bring, and lives that death may die.
fra - grant gar - den shall ex - tend for - ev - er green and sweet.
praise shall nev - er, nev - er fail through-out e - ter - ni - ty.

## Eternal Christ, You Rule                                   302

*Dan Damon, 1990*                                     *Eph. 1:15–23; 5:1–2*

Unison

1 E - ter - nal Christ, you rule keep - ing com - pa - ny with pain;
2 E - ter - nal Christ, you rule speak - ing par - don from the cross;
3 E - ter - nal Christ, you rule tak - ing chil - dren by the hand;
4 E - ter - nal Christ, you rule fast - ing for - ty days a - lone;
5 E - ter - nal Christ, you rule keep - ing com - pa - ny with pain;

en - dur - ing rid - i - cule, re - ject - ed, still you reign.
for - giv - ing pound-ed nails; death did its worst and lost.
the proud re - turn to school; the meek re - ceive the land.
the tempt - er played the fool, ex - pect - ing bread from stone.
with love and truth as tools, come build in us your reign.

*Hymnwriter Daniel Charles Damon credits a sermon given by
United Church of Christ minister Ansley Coe Throckmorton at
Pacific School of Religion in Berkeley, California, as his
inspiration for this text. To the question, "How does Christ
rule?" Throckmorton replied, "By keeping company with pain."*

Tune: THROCKMORTON 6.7.6.6.
*Dan Damon, 1990*

303 Rejoice, Give Thanks and Sing

Phil. 4:4; Rev. 3:7; 19:6–7

Charles Wesley, 1746; alt.

1 Re - joice, give thanks and sing; your Sov-ereign God a - dore!
2 Our Sav - ior Je - sus reigns, the God of truth and love;
3 Christ Je - sus can - not fail to rule both earth and heaven;
4 Re - joice in glo - rious hope, for Christ the Judge shall come,

For Christ has robbed death's sting and tri - umphs ev - er - more. Lift
The Lamb who purged our stains is crowned with power a - bove. Lift
The keys of death and hell are to the Sav - ior given. Lift
And take the faith - ful up to their e - ter - nal home. We

up your heart, lift up your voice! Re - joice, a - gain I say, re - joice.
up your heart, lift up your voice! Re - joice, a - gain I say, re - joice.
up your heart, lift up your voice! Re - joice, a - gain I say, re - joice.
soon shall hear a heaven-ly voice a - bove the trum-pet's sound, "Re - joice!"

*This Ascension text, one of the festival hymns by Charles Wesley,*
*was published originally in John Wesley's* Moral and Sacred Poems
*(1744). Somewhat altered, it appeared in this familiar version in*
*Charles' 1746 collection,* Hymns for Our Lord's Resurrection.

Tune: DARWALL'S 148th 6.6.6.6.8.8.
*John Darwall, 1770*

# All Hail the Power of Jesus' Name

**304**

*St. 1–3, Edward Perronet, 1779, 1780; alt.*
*St. 4, John Rippon, 1787; alt.*

*Rev. 19; 5:9; Phil. 2:9–11*

1 All hail the power of Je - sus' name! Let an - gels pros - trate fall;
2 A - dorn, O mar - tyred saints of old, the cor - o - na - tion hall;
3 All heirs of Is - rael's chos - en race, now ran-somed from the fall,
4 Be - fore the cross, with heav-en's throng, we on our knees shall fall;

Bring forth the roy - al di - a - dem, and crown Christ ser - vant of all.
Ex - tol the wound-ed One fore - told, and crown Christ bear - er of all.
Pro - claim the won - ders of God's grace, and crown Christ heal - er of all.
We'll join the ev - er - last-ing song, and crown Christ sav - ior of all.

At - tend the Sav - ior's sov -ereign claim, and crown Christ ser - vant of all.
Ex - tol the wound-ed One fore - told, and crown Christ bear - er of all.
Pro - claim the won - ders of God's grace, and crown Christ heal - er of all.
We'll join the ev - er - last-ing song, and crown Christ sav - ior of all.

*Edward Perronet, long a worker for English Methodism, later became a Congregational minister near Canterbury. John Rippon, an English Baptist minister, wrote more than 1,000 hymns. The tune is by Oliver Holden, an early American carpenter, legislator, musician, and hymnal editor.*

Tune: CORONATION C.M.
*Oliver Holden, 1793*

# 305 You Servants of God, Your Sovereign Proclaim

*Rev. 4:9–11; 5:11–14*

*Charles Wesley, 1744; alt.*

1 You servants of God, your Sovereign proclaim,
2 God rules from on high, almighty to save,
3 Salvation to God who sits on the throne!
4 Then let us adore and render God's right,

and publish abroad that wonderful name:
and still God is nigh, whose presence we have.
Let all cry aloud for what God has done.
all glory and power, all wisdom and might,

The name, all victorious, of Jesus extol,
The great congregation God's triumphs shall praise,
The praises of Jesus the angels proclaim,
All honor and blessing with angels above,

who, sovereign and glorious, now rules over all.
ascribing salvation to Jesus always.
still veiling their faces, they worship the Lamb.
and thanks never ceasing and infinite love.

*Written at a time of anti-Methodist sentiment, this hymn was
included in Charles Wesley's* Hymns for Times of Trouble and
Persecution. *The tune is attributed to William Croft, composer at
England's Chapel Royal and organist at Westminster Abbey.*

Tune: HANOVER 10.10.11.11.
*Attrib. to William Croft, 1708*

# The Church of Christ, in Every Age

**306**

*Fred Pratt Green, 1969*

1 The church of Christ, in ev - ery age be -
set by change, but Spir - it led, Must
claim and test its her - i - tage and
keep on ris - ing from the dead.

2 A - cross the world, a - cross the street, the
vic - tims of in - jus - tice cry For
shel - ter and for bread to eat, and
nev - er live be - fore they die.

3 Then let the ser - vant church a - rise, a
car - ing church that longs to be A
part - ner in Christ's sac - ri - fice, and
clothed in Christ's hu - man - i - ty.

*Poet Fred Pratt Green has been a chaplain, parish minister, administrator, and playwright. Since retiring from parish responsibilities in 1969, he has been an active hymnwriter and makes his home in Norwich, England.*

Tune: WAREHAM L.M.
*William Knapp, 1738*

# 307 Glorious Things of You Are Spoken

Ps. 87:3; Isa. 33:20–21; 60:18; 26:4; Exod. 13:22

John Newton, 1779; alt.

1 Glo - rious things of you are spo - ken, Zi - on, cit - y of our God;
2 See! the streams of liv-ing wa - ters, spring - ing from e - ter - nal Love,
3 'Round each hab - i - ta-tion hov-ering, see the cloud and fire ap - pear
4 Sav - ior, if of Zi-on's cit - y we through grace a part may claim,

One whose word can - not be bro - ken formed you for a blessed a - bode.
Well sup - ply your sons and daugh-ters, and all fear of want re - move.
For a glo - ry and a cov - er-ing, show - ing that their God is near!
Let the world de - ride or pit - y, we will glo - ry in your name.

On the Rock of A - ges found - ed, what can shake your sure re - pose?
Who can faint, while such a riv - er ev - er will their thirst as-suage:
Thus de - riv - ing from their ban - ner light by night and shade by day,
Fad - ing is all world-ly plea - sure, all earth's boast - ed pomp and show;

With sal - va-tion's walls sur-round-ed, you may smile at all your foes.
Grace which, like our God, the Giv - er, nev - er fails from age to age?
Safe they feed up - on the man - na which God gives them when they pray.
Sol - id joys and last - ing trea - sures, none but Zi - on's chil - dren know.

Filled with Old Testament scriptural allusions, this was one of few
hymns of praise included among the many subjective, sometimes
brooding, hymns in Newton and Cowper's Olney Hymns. It has
enjoyed great popularity in many English-speaking countries.

Tune: AUSTRIAN HYMN 8.7.8.7.D.
Franz Joseph Haydn, 1797
Alternate tune: ABBOT'S LEIGH

# At the Font We Start Our Journey

*Jeffery Rowthorn, 1992*

*Col. 3:15; Acts 10:36–43*

1 At the font we start our jour-ney, in the Eas - ter
2 At the pul - pit we are fash-ioned by the Eas - ter
3 At the al - tar we are nour-ished with the Eas - ter
4 At the door we are com - mis-sioned, now the Eas - ter

faith bap - tized; doubts and fears no long - er blind us,
tale re - told in - to wit - nes - ses and proph - ets,
gift of bread; in our break - ing it to piec - es
vic - tory's won, to re - store a world di - vid - ed

by the light of Christ sur - prised. Al - le - lu - ia,
by the power of Christ made bold. Al - le - lu - ia,
see the love of Christ out - spread. Al - le - lu - ia,
to the peace of Christ as one. Al - le - lu - ia,

al - le - lu - ia! Hope held out and re - al - ized.
al - le - lu - ia! Faith pro - claimed, yet still un - told.
al - le - lu - ia! Life em - braced, yet free - ly shed.
al - le - lu - ia! Eas - ter's work must still be done.

*This text was written for a parish in the Episcopal Diocese of Connecticut, where the author served as bishop suffragan. Born and educated in Britain, Rowthorn has held positions at Union Theological Seminary and Yale University Divinity School, and more recently was appointed bishop in charge of the Convocation of American Churches in Europe.*

Tune: WESTMINSTER ABBEY 8.7.8.7.8.7.
*Henry Purcell, c. 1680*
*Arr. Ernest Hawkins, 1842*

# 309 We Are Your People

Brian Wren, 1973; rev. 1993

*Unison*

1 We are your peo - ple: Spir - it of grace,
2 Joined in com - mu - ni - ty, trea - sured and fed,
3 Rich in di - ver - si - ty, help us to live
4 Glad of tra - di - tion, help us to see

you dare to make us Christ to our neigh - bors
may we dis - cov - er gifts in each oth - er,
clos - er than neigh-bors, o - pen to strang - ers,
in all life's chang-ing, where Christ is lead - ing,

1 & 6 — *Last time, end* — 2–5

of ev - ery cul - ture and place.
will - ing to lead and be led.
a - ble to clash and for - give.
where our best ef - forts should be.

5  Give, as we ven-ture
   jus-tice and care
      (peace-ful, in-sist-ing,
      risk-ing, re-sist-ing),
   wis-dom to know when and where.

6  Spir-it, u-nite us,
   make us, by grace,
      will-ing and read-y,
      Christ's liv-ing bod-y,
   lov-ing the whole hu-man race.

*Originally written in 1973 for the hymnal of the United
Reformed Church in England and Wales,* New Church Praise,
*this text was revised by Brian Wren in 1993. The tune is named
for the composer's father-in-law, who served as chair of the
Congregational Union of England and Wales.*

Tune: WHITFIELD Irr.
*John Wilson, 1975*

# It's the Old Ship of Zion

*African-American spiritual*

Refrain

It's the old ship of Zi - on, it's the old ship of Zi - on,

It's the old ship of Zi - on, get on board, get on board. *Last time, end*

*Leader* 1 It has land-ed man-y a thou-sand, it has land-ed man-y a thou-sand,
2 There's no dan-ger in the wa - ter, there's no dan-ger in the wa - ter, *All*

*to Refrain*

It has land-ed man-y a thou-sand, get on board, get on board.
There's no dan-ger in the wa - ter, get on board, get on board.

3 It was good for my dear moth-er, . . . Get on board.
4 It was good for my dear fa-ther, . . . Get on board.
5 It will take us home to Glo-ry, . . . Get on board.

*The image of the ship is like the image of the train in many other spirituals, where the same train that carried relatives of the enslaved to freedom would return tomorrow. In each instance, everyone is encouraged to "get on board."*

Tune: OLD SHIP OF ZION  8.8.8.6. with refrain
*African-American spiritual*

# 311          Renew Your Church

*Matt. 5:13–16; Luke 11:1–4; Mark 12:28–34*        *Kenneth L. Cober, 1960; alt.*

1 Re - new your church, its min - is - tries re - store: both to serve
2 Teach us your word, re - veal its truth di - vine; on our path
3 Teach us to pray, for you are ev - er near; your still voice
4 Teach us to love, with strength of heart and mind, each and all—

and a - dore. Make us a - gain as salt through-out the land,
let it shine. Tell of your works, your might - y acts of grace;
let us hear. Our souls are rest - less till they rest in you;
hu - man-kind! Break down old walls of prej - u - dice and hate;

and as light from a stand. 'Mid som - ber shad - ows
from each page show your face. As you have sent your
this is life, full and true. Be - fore your pres - ence
leave us not to our fate. As you have loved and

of the night, where greed and ha - tred spread their blight, O
Christ to save, in love to tri - umph o'er the grave, O
keep us still that we may find for us your will And
given your life to end hos - til - i - ty and strife, Your

*Kenneth L. Cober grew up in Puerto Rico, the son of missionary parents. Cober has served churches in many states and has written several books about church education.*

Tune: ALL IS WELL 10.6.10.6.8.8.8.8.6.
*Traditional English melody*

send us forth  with  power en-dued.  Help us, God,  be  re-newed.
let  our hearts  with  love be stirred.  Help us, God,  know your word.
seek your guid - ance  ev - ery day.  Teach us, God,  how  to  pray.
grace we must  be  mind-ful of:  Teach us, God,  how  to  love.

## We Love Your Realm, O God  312

*Timothy Dwight, 1801*
*Adapt. Lavon Bayler, 1992*

*Ps. 26:8*

1 We  love  your realm, O  God,  all  plac - es  where you  reign.
2 We  love  your church, O  God,  for  Christ has  giv - en  life
3 We  rec - og - nize, with  pain,  that  we  have not  a - chieved
4 Yet  Christ, our  friend  and  guide,  con - tin - ues  to  for - give,

We  rec - og - nize, with  hope and joy,  the  world as  your do - main.
To  form com-mu - ni - ties  of  love that  seek to  heal our  strife.
The  faith-ful-ness  of  our  re - solve when  we  at  first be - lieved.
De - liv - ering us  from  our  mis-takes, in - vit - ing  us  to  live.

5  Be-yond our bro-ken-ness,
   we seek to know your ways
Of deep com-mu-nion, sol-emn vows,
   and hymns of love and praise.

6  We know your truth will last.
   We trust your reign is sure.
E-quip us for those dai-ly tasks
   that help your world en-dure.

*This poem by Lavon Bayler, a United Church of Christ minister,*
*was inspired by and modeled after the oldest commonly used*
*American hymn, "I Love Thy Kingdom" by Timothy Dwight.*

Tune:  ST. THOMAS  S.M.
*Williams'* New Universal Psalmodist, *1770*

# 313

# Like a Tree beside the Waters

*Jer. 17:7–8*

*James F. D. Martin, 1992*

1 Like a tree be-side the wa-ters, nur-tured by your lov - ing care,
2 Like a tree be-side the riv - er, draw-ing life from ho - ly streams,
3 We, be - side the liv-ing wa-ters, drink from your e - ter - nal life.

We, O God, your sons and daugh-ters, your en - dur-ing wit - ness bear.
Fill us with your love for - ev - er; re - cre - ate our hopes and dreams.
Give to all, your sons and daugh-ters, faith that ris - es o - ver strife.

In each pass - ing gen - er - a - tion may your voice of love be heard.
Through the storms of life sus - tain us by the wis-dom of your grace.
O Liv - ing God, most glo-rious, strength-en us for life to - day.

Bless, we pray, this con - gre - ga - tion with your ho - ly, liv - ing Word.
May the chang-ing of the sea - sons find us in your warm em - brace.
By the hope of time-less prom-ise guide your church up - on the Way.

*James Martin wrote this text at the invitation of Campbellsport (Wisconsin) United Church of Christ for the celebration of its 125th anniversary year in 1993. Ordained to the United Church of Christ in 1980, Martin has served as pastor to churches in Wisconsin.*

Tune: SILVER CREEK 8.7.8.7.D.
*Roy Hopp, 1989*
*Alternate tune: HYFRYDOL*

# Community of Christ

*Shirley Erena Murray, 1985*

1 Com - mu - ni - ty of Christ, who make the Cross your own,
2 Com - mu - ni - ty of Christ, look past the church's door
3 Com - mu - ni - ty of Christ, through whom the word must sound—
4 When men-ace melts a - way, so shall God's will be done,

live out your creed and risk your life for God a - lone:
and see the ref - u - gee, the hun - gry, and the poor.
cry out for jus - tice and for peace the whole world 'round:
the cli - mate of the world be peace and Christ its Sun;

The God who wears your face, to whom all worlds be - long,
Take hands with the op - pressed, the job - less in your street,
Dis - arm the powers that war and all that can de - stroy,
Our cur - ren - cy be love and kind - li - ness our law,

whose chil - dren are of ev - ery race and ev - ery song.
take towel and wa - ter, that you wash your neigh-bor's feet.
turn bombs to bread, and tears of an - guish in - to joy.
our food and faith be shared as one for ev - er - more.

*Shirley Erena Murray has grown up within the Ecumenical
Movement and addresses related themes such as Christian unity
and social justice in her hymnody. This text was first sung at the
General Assembly of the Presbyterian Church of New Zealand.*

Tune: LEONI 6.6.8.4.D.
*Traditional Hebrew melody
Adapt. Meyer Lyon, 1770*

# 315

# O Word of God Incarnate

*Ps. 119:105*

*William W. How, 1867; alt.*

1 O Word of God in-car-nate, O Wis-dom from on high,
2 O God, we hold this trea-sure from you, its source di-vine,
3 O make your church, dear Sav-ior, a lamp of pur-est gold,

O Truth un-changed, un-chang-ing, O Light of cloud-ed sky:
a light that to all a-ges through-out the earth will shine;
to bear be-fore all peo-ple your true light as of old!

We praise you for the ra-diance that from the hal-lowed page,
It is the chart and com-pass that all life's voy-age through,
O teach your wan-dering pil-grims by this their path to trace,

a lan-tern to our foot-steps, shines on from age to age.
'mid mists and rocks and tem-pest, still guides, O God, to you.
till, doubt and striv-ing end-ed, they meet you face to face.

*William W. How, author and hymnwriter, is remembered
especially for his work among the poor of London's East End.
Felix Mendelssohn harmonized this German hymn tune, which
appeared with a different text for his oratorio* Elijah.

Tune: MUNICH 7.6.7.6.D.
Neuvermehrtes Gesangbuch, *Meiningen, 1693*
*Harm. Felix Mendelssohn, 1847*

# We Limit Not the Truth of God

316

*George Rawson, 1853; alt.*

1 We lim-it not the truth of God to our poor reach of mind,
2 Who dares to bind to one's own sense the or-a-cles of heaven,
3 E-ter-nal God, In-car-nate Word, Spir-it of flame and dove:

to no-tions of our day and place, crude, par-tial, and con-fined;
for all the na-tions, tongues, and climes and all the a-ges given?
en-large, ex-pand all liv-ing souls to com-pre-hend your love;

No, let a new and bet-ter hope with-in our hearts be stirred:
That u-ni-verse, how much un-known! that o-cean un-ex-plored!
And help us all to seek your will with wis-er powers con-ferred:

O God, grant yet more light and truth to break forth from your Word.

*George Rawson based this text on the parting words of Pastor*
*John Robinson to the Pilgrim founders in 1620.*

Tune: OLD 22nd C.M.D.
Anglo-Genevan Psalter, *1556*
Alternate tunes: *FOREST GREEN; ELLACOMBE*

# 317

## Mikotoba o kudasai
### (Make a Gift of Your Holy Word)

*Deut. 32:1–2; Amos 8:11; Matt. 8:8*

*Yasushige Imakoma, 1965; transl. Paul R. Gregory, 1994*

1 Mi - ko - to - ba　o　ku - da - sai,　fu - ri　so - so - gu　A - me　no　yo - o　ni,　me - gu - mi　no　Shu　yo.　U - e　to　Ka - wa - ki　ni,　ku - ru - shi - mi　u - me - ki,　ya - mi - ji　sa - ma - yo - o

1 Make a　gift　of　your　ho - ly　Word,　let　it　pour　on　my　head and　heart like　your　rain,　sov-ereign and　lov - ing　God.　Let　it　fill　my　life　each　day,　touch my　hun - ger　and　my　thirst,　The deep suf - fering　that　I　know

2 Let　your Word come　in - to　our　lives,　as　your winds blow　o'er　all　the　earth,　we　pray.　God　of　sal - va - tion,　come,　That we　shall　be　ful - ly　free　from the　sins that　keep　us　bound,　made pure　by　your　Spir - it's　gift

3 Grant all　peo - ple　your　ho - ly　Word.　Quench the　thirst - y　earth　as　the　first　morn-ing　dew,　O　gra - cious God　of　life.　Let　it　teach love's heal - ing　way,　in　our　war - torn　suf - fering　world.　Let　it　bind　us　one　to　one

*Selected by the Hymnal Committee of the United Church of
Christ in Japan from many original submissions, this hymn
was first published in Sambike (Hymns of Praise), 1967. The
winning tune provided by Shōzō Koyama was the composer's
first encounter with a text in colloquial Japanese verse and
moved him deeply.*

Tune: MIKOTOBA 8.11.6.7.7.7.7.
*Shōzō Koyama, 1965*

| | | | | | | | |
|---|---|---|---|---|---|---|---|
| I | no | chi | no | ta | me | ni. | |
| on | life's | lone | ly, | wan | dering | way. | |
| of | re | sound | ing | vic | to | ry. | |
| toward | a | just | and | peace | ful | day. | |

## Almighty God, Your Word Is Cast

318

*John Cawood, 1815; alt.*

*Matt. 13:1–9, 18–23*

1 Al - might-y God, your Word is cast like seed in - to the ground;
2 Let not the sly sa - tan-ic foe this ho - ly seed re - move,
3 Let not the world's de - ceit-ful cares the ris - ing plant de - stroy,
4 So when the pre - cious seed is sown, your quick-ening grace be - stow,

Now let the dew of heaven de - scend and righ - teous fruits a - bound.
But give it root in ev - ery heart to bring forth fruits of love.
But let it yield a hun - dred-fold the fruits of peace and joy.
That all whose souls the truth re - ceive its sav - ing power may know.

*The parable of the sower from Matthew's Gospel was the basis for this hymn. Growing up on a small farm, John Cawood, a priest of the Church of England, surely had a special understanding of this parable.*

Tune: ST. FLAVIAN C.M.
*Day,* The Whole Booke of Psalms, *1562*

# 319

# Sing Them Over Again to Me
### (Wonderful Words of Life)

*Philip P. Bliss, 1874; alt.*

1 Sing them o - ver a - gain to me, won-der-ful words of life;
2 Christ, the bless-ed one, gives to all won-der-ful words of life;
3 Sweet - ly ech - o the gos - pel call, won-der-ful words of life;

let me more of their beau - ty see, won-der-ful words of life;
sin - ner, wake to the lov - ing call, won-der-ful words of life;
of - fer par-don and peace to all, won-der-ful words of life;

Words of life and beau - ty teach me faith and du - ty.
All so free - ly giv - en, our sure hope of heav - en.
Je - sus, on - ly Sav - ior, keep me with you for - ev - er.

**Refrain**

Beau-ti - ful words, won-der-ful words, won-der-ful words of life.

Beau-ti - ful words, won-der-ful words, won-der-ful words of life.

*Philip Bliss wrote this text and tune for the first issue of* Words of Life *(1874). A few years later it was sung as a duet during an evangelistic campaign and became popular immediately.*

Tune: WORDS OF LIFE C.M. with refrain
*Philip P. Bliss, 1874*

# Deep in the Shadows of the Past

**320**

*Brian Wren, 1973; rev. 1993*

1 Deep in the shad-ows of the past, far out from set-tled lands,
2 While oth-ers bowed to change-less gods, they met a mys-ter-y:
3 From A-bra-ham to Naz-a-reth the prom-ise changed and grew,
4 For all the writ-ings that sur-vived, for lead-ers, long a-go,

some no-mads trav-eled with their God a-cross the des-ert sands.
a hid-den, un-com-plet-ed Name— "I AM WHAT I WILL BE";
while some, re-mem-ber-ing the past, re-cord-ed what they knew,
who sift-ed, cop-ied, and pre-served the Bi-ble that we know,

The dawn-ing hope of hu-man-kind by them was sensed and shown:
And by their tents, a-round their fires, in sto-ry, song, and law,
and some, in let-ters and la-ments, in proph-e-cy and praise,
Give thanks and find its sto-ry yet our prom-ise, strength, and call:

a prom-ise call-ing them a-head, a fu-ture yet un-known.
they praised, re-mem-bered, hand-ed on, a past that prom-ised more.
re-cov-ered, kin-dled, and ex-pressed new hope for chang-ing days.
the work-ing-mod-el of our faith, a-live with hope for all.

*Brian Wren has commented: "The hymn tries to tell the story
of the Bible in a manner acceptable to different beliefs about
its inspiration." Wren credits James Barr's* The Bible in the
Modern World *for the idea of the Bible as a "working-model"
of our faith.*

Tune: SHEPHERDS' PIPES C.M.D.
*Annabeth McClelland Gay, 1952*

# 321

# Break Now the Bread of Life

*Matt. 14:13–21; Mark 6:30–44*

*Mary A. Lathbury, 1877; alt.*

1 Break now the bread of life, Sav-ior, to me, as you once
2 Bless now the truth, dear Christ, to me, to me, as you once

broke the loaves be-side the sea; Be-yond the sa-cred page
blessed the bread by Gal-i-lee; Then shall all bond-age cease,

I seek you, Lord; my spir-it yearns for you, O Liv-ing Word.
all shack-les fall, and I shall find my peace, my all in all.

*Mary Lathbury, "poet laureate of Chautauqua," wrote her prayer hymn to enrich the lives of those gathered for summer study at the lakeside conferences near Jamestown, New York. The tune was written for it by the chorus director of Chautauqua that same season.*

Tune: BREAD OF LIFE 6.4.6.4.D.
William F. Sherwin, 1877

# 322

# Take Me to the Water

*Acts 8:36–39; 10:47–48*

*African-American spiritual*

1 Take me to the wa - ter, take me to the wa -
2 None but the righ - teous, none but the righ -
3 I love Je - sus, I love Je -
4 Je - sus is my Sav - ior, Je - sus is my Sav -

ter, take me to the wa - ter to be bap - tized.
teous, none but the righ - teous . . . shall see God.
sus, I love Je - sus, . . . yes, I do.
ior, Je - sus is my Sav - ior for - ev - er more.

*During the antebellum era the enslaved either worshipped secretly in the woods or in small one-room churches built on the plantations. This spiritual reminds us that in either case baptisms were done down at the riverside.*

Tune: African-American spiritual
*Arr. Jeffrey Radford, 1993*

## Little Children, Welcome                                      323

*Fred Pratt Green, 1973*

*1 Lit - tle chil - dren, wel - come! Earth is yours to live in;
2 Lit - tle chil - dren, wel - come! Je - sus cares a - bout you;
3 Lit - tle chil - dren, wel - come! We, the church of Je - sus,
4 Lit - tle chil - dren, wel - come! God will make you hap - py,

arms of love pro - tect you, lit - tle chil - dren, wel - come!
Je - sus now en - folds you, lit - tle chil - dren, wel - come!
we will help your grow - ing, lit - tle chil - dren, wel - come!
Je - sus save and keep you, lit - tle chil - dren, wel - come!

*Other words may be substituted as appropriate; for example, "Sisters, brothers, welcome!" "Little sister, welcome!" or "Little brother, welcome!"

*Fred Pratt Green is a noted British hymnwriter who was awarded an honorary doctorate from Emory University in Atlanta, Georgia, where his papers will be held. The uncomplicated tune by contemporary composer Roy Hopp makes this an easy hymn for people of all ages.*

Tune: SAIPAN 6.6.6.6.
*Roy Hopp, 1988*

# 324     Baptized into Your Name Most Holy

*Matt. 28:19; Rom. 6:1–3, 10–11*

*Johann J. Rambach, 1734*
*Transl. Catherine Winkworth (1829–1878); alt.*

1 Bap-tized in - to your name most ho - ly, O Fa - ther, Son,
2 My lov - ing Fa - ther, here you take me hence-forth to be
3 O faith-ful God, you nev - er fail me; your cov-enant sure -
4 All that I am and love most dear - ly, re - ceive it all,

and Ho - ly Ghost, I claim a place, though weak and low - ly,
your child and heir; My faith-ful Sav - ior, here you make me
ly will a - bide. Let not e - ter - nal death as - sail me
O God, from me. Oh, let me make my vows sin-cere - ly,

A - mong your seed, your cho - sen host. Bu - ried with
The fruit of all your sor - rows share; O Ho - ly
should I trans - gress it on my side! Have mer - cy
and help me your own child to be! Let noth - ing

Christ and dead to sin, I have your Spir - it now with - in.
Ghost, you com-fort me though threat-ening clouds a - round I see.
when I come de - filed; for - give, lift up, re - store your child.
that I am or own serve an - y will but yours a - lone.

*Although this hymn originated in eighteenth-century Germany, it could be found two centuries later in the United States in hymnals of the Evangelical and German Congregational churches. Johann Jakob Rambach was a popular preacher and professor of theology.*

Tune: O DASS ICH TAUSEND ZUNGEN HÄTTE
9.8.9.8.8.8.
*Johann B. König, Harmonischer Liederschatz, 1738*

# Child of Blessing, Child of Promise

**325**

*Ronald S. Cole-Turner, 1981*

1 Child of bless-ing, child of prom-ise, bap-tized with the Spir-it's sign;
2 Child of love, our love's ex-pres-sion, love's cre-a-tion, loved in-deed!
3 Child of joy, our dear-est trea-sure, God's you are, from God you came.
4 Child of God your lov-ing Par-ent, learn to know whose child you are.

With this wa-ter God has sealed you un-to love and grace di-vine.
Fresh from God, re-fresh our spir-its, in-to joy and laugh-ter lead.
Back to God we hum-bly give you; live as one who bears Christ's name.
Grow to laugh and sing and wor-ship, trust and love God more than all.

*Ronald Cole-Turner, a teacher of theology, is an ordained minister of the United Church of Christ. He is an award-winning author on the interface of science and religion.*

Tune: STUTTGART 8.7.8.7.
*Attrib. to Christian F. Witt (1660–1716), in Psalmodia Sacra, Gotha, 1715*

# Crashing Waters at Creation

**326**

*Sylvia G. Dunstan, 1991*

*Gen. 1:1–5; Exod. 14:21–22; Mark 1:9–11; John 4:13–14*

1 Crash-ing wa-ters at cre-a-tion
   or-dered by the Spir-it's breath,
   First to wit-ness day's be-gin-ning
   from the bright-ness of night's death.

2 Part-ing wa-ter stood and trem-bled
   as the cap-tives passed on through,
   Wash-ing off the chains of bond-age—
   chan-nel to a life made new.

3 Cleans-ing wa-ter once at Jor-dan
   closed a-round the One fore-told,
   O-pened to re-veal the glo-ry
   ev-er new and ev-er old.

4 Liv-ing wa-ter, nev-er end-ing,
   quench the thirst and flood the soul.
   Well-spring, Source of life e-ter-nal,
   drench our dry-ness, make us whole.

*Hymnwriter Sylvia Dunstan wrote this text to accompany a prayer for blessing the water in the United Church of Canada baptismal rites. She has credited the work of Miriam Therese Winter as her inspiration for some of the imagery in the last stanza.*

Tune: STUTTGART 8.7.8.7.
*Attrib. to Christian F. Witt (1660–1716), in Psalmodia Sacra, Gotha, 1715*

# 327

# Jesus Loves Me

St. 1, Anna B. Warner, 1860
St. 2–3, David Rutherford McGuire, 1971

1 Jesus loves me! This I know, for the Bible tells me so.
2 Jesus loves me! This I know, as he loved so long a-go,
3 Jesus loves me! Still to-day, walk-ing with me on my way,

Lit-tle ones to him be-long; they are weak, but he is strong.
Tak-ing chil-dren on his knee, say-ing, "Let them come to me."
Want-ing as a friend to give light and love to all who live.

*Refrain*

Yes, Jesus loves me! Yes, Jesus loves me!

Yes, Jesus loves me! The Bible tells me so.

1  Deer He-soos zis guh see-reh,
    eem soorp keer-kus ice guh-seh,
Inch koo-tov ink un-toon-etz
    po-ker dug-hak, yev orh-netz.

    Vo, guh see-reh ziss!
    Vo, guh see-reh ziss!
    Vo, guh see-reh ziss!
    Soorp Kirk-uh ice guh-seh.
*(Armenian transliteration Vartan Hartunian)*

1  Lo'u A-lii ua faa-fe-tai
    I lou sa-ga a-lo-fa-mai,
Ua i-lo-a-ti-no ai
    I lou tau-si pe-a mai.

    O lou a-lo-fa!
    O lou a-lo-fa!
    O lou a-lo-fa!
    E si-li la-va lea.
*(Samoan transl. anon.)*

*Anna B. Warner collaborated with her sister, Susan, on several
novels. In one,* Say and Seal, *this hymn was sung to comfort a
sick child. Two new stanzas have been provided by Canadian
David R. McGuire, an Anglican priest.*

Tune: JESUS LOVES ME  7.7.7.7. with refrain
William B. Bradbury, 1862

1   Cris-to me a-ma, bien lo sé,
      Su pa-la-bra me ha-ce ver
    Que los ni-ños son de A-quél,
    Quien es nues-tro A-mi-go fiel.

      Cris-to me a-ma,
      Cris-to me a-ma,
      Cris-to me a-ma,
      La Bib-lia di-ce a-sí.
*(Spanish transl.* Himnario Metodista, *1968)*


1   Saq wa-re o a-i-su,
      Saq wa tsu-yo ke-re ba,
    Wa-re yo-wa-ku-to-mo,
    O-so-re wa a-ra-ji.

      Wa-ga Shu ye-su,
      Wa-ga Shu ye-su,
      Wa-ga Shu ye-su,
      Wa-re o a-i-su.
*(Japanese phonetic transcription*
  *Mas Kawashima, 1988)*


1   Je-sus liebt mich ganz ge-wiss,
      Denn die Bi-bel sagt mir dies,
    Al-le Kind-er schwach und klein,
    Lad't Er herz-lich zu sich ein.

      Ja, Je-sus liebt mich,
      Ja, Je-sus liebt mich,
      Ja, Je-sus liebt mich,
      Die Bi-bel sagt mir dies.
*(German transl.* Psalter und Harfe, *1876)*


1   Ye-su sa-rang Ha-si-man
      Geo-ruk-ha-sin ma-ril-sei
    Wo-o-ri-drn Ya-ka-na
    Ye-su gwon-sei man-to-da.

      Nal sa-rang ha-sim
      Nal sa-rang ha-sim
      Nal sa-rang ha-sim
      Seong gyon-gei sse-oit-ne.
*(Korean transl. anon. in*
Hymnal: A Worship Book, *1992)*


1   Je-sus Christ wa-śte-ma-da,
      Wo-wa-pi Wa-kan he-ye:
    Mi-ye on te hi qon he,
    Wan-na he wa-na-ka-ja.

      Han Je-sus wa-śte;
      Han Je-sus wa-śte;
      Han Je-sus wa-śte;
      Wa-śte ma-da-ka ye.
*(Lakota transl.* Dakota Odowan, *1842)*


1   He a-lo-ha ko Ie-su
      I ke kei-ki li'i-li'i no,
    No-na no ka po'e li'i-li'i,
    No-na wau ka po-ki'i nei.

      Kei-ki a-lo-ha!
      Kei-ki a-lo-ha!
      Kei-ki a-lo-ha!
      Ke a-lo-ha! o Ie-su!
*(Hawaiian transl.* Laiana, *19th century)*


1   En-gem sze-ret Jé-zu-som,
      Bib-li-ám-ból jól tu-dom.
    Mind ö-vé a kis gyer-mek,
    E-rőt ád a gyön-gék-nek!

      Úgy van ő sze-ret,
      Ő sze-ret na-gyon;
      Úgy van ő sze-ret,
      Í-gé-jé-ből tudom.
*(Hungarian transl. János Victor)*


1   Me-nya be Ye-su lɔa mí.
      E-fe nya gblɔ ne-ne-ma.
    E-lɔa ɖe-vi-wo ka-tã
    'La-be e-fe dɔ-me nyo.

      Ẽ, Ye-su lɔa mí,
      Ẽ, Ye-su lɔa mí,
      Ẽ, Ye-su lɔa mí,
      'La-be e-fe dɔ-me nyo.
*(Ghanaian transl. anon.)*

# 328 Wonder of Wonders, Here Revealed

*Jane Parker Huber, 1980*

1 Won - der of won - ders, here re - vealed;
2 Here in this sac - ra - ment we see
3 This child of God, though young or old,
4 Now we our vow of faith re - new,

God's cov - e - nant with us is sealed.
God's grace un - bound, for all, for me!
we wel - come now in - to Christ's fold,
stretch wide our sights to glob - al view,

And long be - fore we know or pray,
May we re - spond with joy - ful praise
To know with us God's lov - ing care;
And claim with Chris - tians far and near

God's love en - folds us ev - ery day.
in lov - ing ser - vice all our days.
here all our joys and sor - rows share.
a larg - er fam - i - ly held dear.

*Jane Parker Huber has noted two important ideas she addressed in this text: "The fact that God loves each of us before we know how to love in return, and . . . in baptism we become part of a worldwide family."*

Tune: PENTECOST L.M.
*William Boyd, 1864*

# Jesus, the Joy of Loving Hearts

**329**

*Attrib. to Bernard of Clairvaux, c. 1150*
*Transl. Ray Palmer, 1858; alt.*

*John 6:52–58; Heb. 13:8*

1 Je - sus, the joy of lov - ing hearts, fount of our lives, and
2 Your truth un - changed has ev - er stood; you plead with all to
3 We taste of you, the liv - ing bread, and long to feast up -
4 For you our rest - less spir - its yearn, wher-e'er our chang - ing
5 O Je - sus, ev - er with us stay! Make all our mo - ments

light of all: From ev - ery bliss that earth im - parts
call on you; To those still seek - ing, you are good;
on you still; We drink of you, the foun - tain - head;
lot is cast; Glad, when your smile on us you turn,
calm and bright! Oh, chase the cloud of sin a - way!

we turn, un - filled, to hear your call.
to those who find you, life is new.
our thirst - y souls from you we fill.
blessed, when by faith we hold you fast.
Shed o'er the world your ho - ly light.

*Bernard, founder of the monastery at Clairvaux, was respected*
*by popes and royalty alike. From the forty-two-verse Latin*
*poem, American Congregational minister Ray Palmer freely*
*translated selected verses to create this version.*

Tune: HESPERUS L.M.
(QUEBEC)
*Henry W. Baker, 1854*

# 330

# Let Us Break Bread Together

*Acts 2:42*

*African-American spiritual*

1 Let us break bread to-geth-er on our knees;
*2 Let us drink wine to-geth-er on our knees;
3 Let us praise God to-geth-er on our knees;

let us break bread to-geth-er on our knees.
let us drink wine to-geth-er on our knees.
let us praise God to-geth-er on our knees.

*Refrain*

When I fall on my knees, with my face to the ris-ing sun,

* "Share the cup" *may be substituted for "drink wine."*

*The earliest version of this spiritual probably began with the current stanza three, and was a song some of the enslaved in Virginia used when gathering for secret meetings. The communion stanzas were added some time after the Civil War.*

Tune: LET US BREAK BREAD
10.10. with refrain
*Harm. David Hurd, 1983*

# Come, My Way, My Truth, My Life 331

*George Herbert, 1633; alt.* *John 8:12; 14:1–7; 15:11*

Unison

1 Come, my Way, my Truth, my Life: such a way as gives us
2 Come, my Light, my Feast, my Strength: such a light as shows a
3 Come, my Joy, my Love, my Heart: such a joy as none can

breath; Such a truth as ends all strife;
feast; Such a feast as mends in length;
move; Such a love as none can part;

such a life as con - - - quers death.
such a strength as makes a guest.
such a heart as joys in love.

*Shortly before his death, the poet George Herbert entrusted his manuscript of* The Temple *(including this hymn) to a friend for publication. The musical setting by English composer Ralph Vaughan Williams is from* Five Mystical Songs from George Herbert.

Tune: THE CALL 7.7.7.7.
*Ralph Vaughan Williams, 1911*

# 332 As We Gather at Your Table

*Matt. 22:1–10; Luke 14:16–24*                    *Carl P. Daw, Jr., 1989*

1 As we gath-er    at your ta - ble, as we lis-ten to your word,
2 Turn our wor-ship in-to    wit - ness in the sac-ra-ment of    life;
3 Gra-cious Spir-it, help us    sum-mon oth-er guests to share that feast

help us know, O  God, your pres-ence; let  our hearts and minds be stirred.
send us forth to  love and  serve you, bring-ing peace where there is  strife.
where tri-um-phant Love will wel-come those who had  been  last and least.

Nour-ish  us  with sa-cred sto - ry till we claim it  as  our own;
Give us, Christ, your great com-pas - sion to for-give as  you for-gave;
There no  more will en-vy bind  us  nor will pride our  peace de-stroy,

teach us through this ho - ly  ban-quet how to  make Love's vic-tory known.
may we  still  be-hold your  im - age in the world you  died  to  save.
as  we  join  with saints and  an - gels to re-peat  the  sound-ing joy.

*In this hymn, commissioned by an Episcopal parish in Virginia for the celebration of its tricentennial, Carl P. Daw, Jr., utilized a familiar phrase from Isaac Watts' "Joy to the World," which was the motto for the celebration: "Repeat the sounding joy."*

Tune: BEACH SPRING  8.7.8.7.D.
The Sacred Harp, *1844*
Harm. The New Century Hymnal, *1992*

# O Bread of Life

*Timothy Tingfang Lew, 1934*
*Transl. Greer Anne Wenh-In Ng, 1986*

*John 6:35*

1 O Bread of life, for all things break - ing,
2 We come this day in hum - ble wor - ship - ing;
3 Stand in our midst, eyes and hearts o - pen - ing;

the bit - ter cup on Cal - vary drain - ing;
our land is scarred, earth's peo - ple suf - fering;
your mys - tic self to us re - veal - ing;

Re - deemed by grace, we join in feast - ing,
O sa - cred face, blood and tears min - gling,
U - nite us in life ev - er - last - ing,

at your com - mand the past re - mem - bering.
all hu - man pain you are still bear - ing.
Im - man - u - el, bless - ing un - end - ing.

*One of fifty indigenous hymns to be included in the Protestant Chinese publication Hymns of Universal Praise, this text employs some Buddhist terms and images with which many Chinese people can identify. The tune can be translated as "God's, or holy, grace."*

Tune: SHENG EN 9.9.9.9.
*Yin-Lan Su, 1936*
*Arr. Darryl Nixon, 1986*

# 334 Graced with Garments of Great Gladness

*Isa. 61:10; John 6:35–58*

*Johann Franck, c. 1649*
*Transl. Catherine Winkworth, 1863; alt.*

1 Graced with gar-ments of great glad - ness, I shall leave the depths of
2 Bright - ness, that my life so bright - ens, Light, that all my soul en-
3 Je - sus, Bread of Life, I pray you, let me glad-ly here o-

sad - ness, En - ter in - to glo-ry's splen - dor, there with
light - ens, Joy, that joins my heart in know - ing, Fount, that
bey you, To your ta - ble here in - vit - ed be your

joy my prais-es ren - der To the One whose grace un-bound - ed
is all be - ing flow - ing, At your name I cry, "My Mak - er!"
love by love re - quit - ed. From this ban - quet let me mea - sure,

has this won-drous ban-quet found - ed. Sing my soul, your sto - ry
Let me be a fit par - tak - er Of this bless - ed food from
oh, how vast, how deep its trea - sure. Through the mer - cies that you

*One of Germany's leading hymnwriters, Johann Franck was*
*also a secular poet of some renown. Born at the beginning of*
*the Thirty Years' War, Franck became a lawyer and served as*
*a councillor, a mayor, and finally a provincial representative.*

Tune: SCHMÜCKE DICH L.M.D.
*Johann Crüger, 1649*
*Harm.* The English Hymnal, *1906*

tell - ing: Christ e - ter - nal in me dwell - ing.
heav - en, for our good through Je - sus giv - en.
give me as your own in heaven re - ceive me.

## Come, Gather in This Special Place

**335**

*Phil Porter, 1991*

1 & 4 Come, gath - er in this spe - cial place; the ta - ble here is
2 The grapes have yield - ed es - sence pure, a drink to quench the
3 The bread is fresh - ly baked to - day, a fra - grant feast of

long and wide; For all who heed com - mu - nion's call, there's
grav - est thirst; The cup is passed from hand to hand, and
grain sup - plied; And e - ven crumbs that dust our palms will

room for thou - sands side by side.
each will sense de - spair re - versed.
leave souls ful - ly sat - is - fied.

*Elaine Kirkland and Phil Porter, both United Church of Christ
artists, have been composing songs, hymns, and chants together
since 1989. This is the first communion hymn they created, which
appeared in their collection* Fire Will Shine.

Tune: GATHER L.M.
*Elaine Kirkland, 1991*

336 Here, O My Lord, I See You Face to Face

*Horatius Bonar, 1855; alt.*

1 Here, O my Lord, I see you face to face;
here would I touch and han - dle things un - seen;
Here grasp with firm - er hand the e - ter - nal grace,
And all my wea - ri - ness up - on you lean.

2 Here would I feed up - on the bread of God,
here share the cup, the gra - cious gift of heaven;
Here would I lay a - side each earth - ly load,
here taste a - fresh the calm of sin for - given.

3 This is the hour of ban - quet and of song;
this is the heaven - ly ta - ble spread a - new;
Here let me feast, and, feast - ing, still pro - long
the brief, bright hour to - geth - er here with you.

4 Too soon we rise; the sym - bols dis - ap - pear;
the meal, but not your love, is past and gone.
This joy - ful feast con - firms that you are here,
now and for - ev - er, as our shield and sun.

5 We have no help but yours, nor do we need
an - oth - er strength than yours to lean up - on.
It is e - nough, O Lord, e - nough in - deed;
our faith is in your might, your might a - lone.

*Horatius Bonar, a founder of the Free Church of Scotland and author of 600 hymns, wrote this hymn at his brother's request. It was first printed in a leaflet for the author's church, St. Andrew's Free Church in Greenock, Scotland.*

Tune: MORECAMBE 10.10.10.10.
*Frederick C. Atkinson, 1870*
*Alternate tune: LANGRAN*

# Draw Us in the Spirit's Tether

337

*Percy Dearmer, 1925; alt.*

*Matt. 18:20*

Unison

1 Draw us in the Spir-it's teth - er, for when hum - bly
2 As dis - ci - ples used to gath - er in the name of
3 All our meals and all our liv - ing make as sac - ra -

in your name, two or three are met to - geth - er,
Christ to sup, then with thanks to God the Giv - er,
ments of you, that by car - ing, help-ing, giv - ing,

you are in the midst of them; Al - le - lu - ia!
break the bread and bless the cup, Al - le - lu - ia!
we may be dis - ci - ples true. Al - le - lu - ia!

Al - le - lu - ia! Touch we now your gar - ment's hem.
Al - le - lu - ia! So now bind our friend - ship up.
Al - le - lu - ia! We may serve with faith a - new.

*British hymnal editor Percy Dearmer originally wrote these stanzas under a pseudonym as part of a postcommunion hymn by George H. Bourne. The tune was adapted from an anthem by Harold Friedell and is named for Union Theological Seminary in New York.*

Tune: UNION SEMINARY 8.7.8.7.4.4.7.
*Harold Friedell, 1957*
*Adapt. Jet Turner, 1967*

# 338

# Una Espiga
## (Sheaves of Summer)

*Cesáreo Gabaraín, 1973; alt.*
*Transl. George Lockwood, 1989*

1 U - na es - pi - ga do - ra - do por el sol, el ra -
2 Com - par - ti - mos la mis - ma co - mu - nión, so - mos
1 Sheaves of sum - mer turned gold - en by the sun, grapes in
2 We are shar - ing the same com - mu - nion meal; we are

ci - mo que cor - ta el vi - ña - dor, Com - par -
tri - go del mis - mo sem - bra - dor, Un mo -
bunch - es cut down when ripe and red, Are con -
wheat by the same great Sow - er sown; Like a

ti - mos a - ho - ra en pan y vi - no de a - mor: que son
li - no, la vi - da, nos tri - tu - ra con do - lor, Dios nos
vert - ed in - to the bread and wine of God's love in the
mill - stone life grinds us down with sor - row and pain, but God

cuer - po y san - gre del Se - ñor.
ha - ce pue - blo nue - vo en el a - mor.
bod - y and blood of our dear Lord.
makes us new peo - ple bound by love.

3 Co-mo gra-nos que han
   he-cho el mis-mo pan,
  co-mo no-tas que te-jen un can-tar,
  Co-mo go-tas de a-gua que se
   fun-den en el mar,
  los cris-tia-nos un cuer-po
   for-ma-rán.

3 Like the grains which be-come
   one same whole loaf,
  like the notes that are wo-ven in-to song,
  Like the drop-lets of wa-ter
   that are blend-ed in the sea,
  we, as Chris-tians, one bod-y
   shall be-come.

4 A la me-sa de Dios se
   sen-ta-rán,
  co-mo i-gle-sia su pan
   com-par-ti-rán,
  U-na mis-ma es-pe-ran-za
   ca-mi-nan-do can-ta-rán,
  en la vi-da her-ma-na-dos
   se a-ma-rán.

4 At God's ta-ble to-geth-er
   we shall sit.
  As God's chil-dren, Christ's
   bod-y we will share.
  One same hope we will sing
   to-geth-er as we walk a-long.
  Broth-ers, sis-ters, in life,
   in love, we'll be.

*Author and composer of a number of Spanish hymns that have gained
widespread popularity in the late twentieth century, Cesáreo Gabaraín
was a parish priest who received postgraduate degrees in theology,
journalism, and musicology from the University of Madrid.*

Tune: UNA ESPIGA Irr.
*Cesáreo Gabaraín, 1973*
*Harm. Skinner Chávez-Melo, 1987*

# 339

# Adoro te devote
## (Truth Whom We Adore)

Thomas Aquinas *c. 1260*
*Transl.* The New Century Hymnal, *1995*

*Gently flowing*
Unison

1 A - do - ro te de - vo - te, la - tens De - i - tas,
1 Truth whom we a - dore though hid - den you may be,
2 Of your death, O Sav - ior, this me - mo - ri - al:
3 Je - sus, now but dim - ly we be - hold your grace;

quae sub his fi - gu - ris ve - re la - ti - tas:
Un - der - neath these forms lies your re - al - i - ty;
Through this bread you of - fer true life, rich and full.
We a - wait the day when you re - veal your face;

Ti - bi se cor me - um to - tum sub - ji - cit,
To know you com - plete - ly my heart seeks in vain;
Clean me spot - less, Je - sus, by your blood a - lone,
Then un - veiled to us your splen - dor we may see—

qui - a te con - tem - plans to - tum de - fi - cit.
Thus, my Sov - ereign, I give all un - to your reign.
That for all the world's sin can one drop a - tone.
Blessed, to view your glo - ry in hu - mil - i - ty.

*J. M. Neale, previous translator of this hymn, commented that Aquinas, ". . . as if afraid to employ any pomp of words on approaching so tremendous a Mystery, has used the very simplest expressions throughout." The words have been linked to the above tune since the seventeenth century.*

Tune: ADORO TE DEVOTE 11.11.11.11.
*Plainsong melody from* Processionalle, *Paris, 1697*
*Harm.* The New Century Hymnal, *1994*

# Somos pueblo que camina

### 340

(We Are People on a Journey)

*"Misa Popular Nicaragüense," 20th century; alt.*
*English version, Carolyn Jennings, 1993*

*John 6:32–35*

1  So-mos pue-blo que ca - mi - na    por la sen - da del do - lor.
2  Los hu - mil-des y los po - bres    in - vi - ta - dos son de Dios.
1  We are peo-ple on a  jour - ney;    pain is with us  all  the way.
2  God has sent the in - vi - ta - tion    to the hum-ble and the poor.

**Estribillo (Refrain)**

A - cu - da-mos ju - bi - lo - sos    a la  san - ta co - mu - nión.
Joyful - ly  we come to - geth - er    at the  ho - ly feast of  God.

3  Es-te pan que Dios nos brin-da
   a-li-men-ta nues-tra u-nión. *(Estribillo)*

3  This is bread that God pro-vides us,
   nour-ish-ing our u-ni-ty. *(Refrain)*

4  Cris-to a-quí se ha-ce pre-sen-te;
   al reu-nir-nos es su a-mor. *(Estribillo)*

4  Christ is ev-er pres-ent with us
   to u-nite us all in love. *(Refrain)*

5  Los se-dien-tos de jus-ti-cia
   bus-can su li-be-ra-ción. *(Estribillo)*

5  All who tru-ly thirst for jus-tice
   seek their lib-er-a-tion here. *(Refrain)*

*The "Misa Popular Nicaragüense," in which this hymn*
*appeared, was composed for the Eucharist liturgy by members*
*of the "comunidades de base"—a group of laypersons who*
*organized to deal with issues in the Latin American church and*
*community.*

Tune: SOMOS PUEBLO  8.7. with refrain (8.7.)
   *"Misa Popular Nicaragüense," 20th century*

# 341

# Great Spirit God

*Jer. 10:12–13; Matt. 6:25–33*

*Dakota hymn, Joseph R. Renville, 1842*
*Transl. Sidney H. Byrd, 1993*
*For another translation, see 3*

*Optional hand-drum rhythm:*

1 Great Spir-it God, the things which are yours are nu-mer-ous and great. The heavens a-bove you set in their place, and earth re-ceived its form by your hands. The o-cean depths re-spond to your will, for you can do all things.

2 Your will, mys-ter-i-ous and so strong, brings growth to all the earth. Food for our souls and cloth-ing to wear, are like your cup that bless-es and fills. Pro-vide for us each day of our lives suf-fi-cient for our needs.

3 You gave your law to Ad-am and Eve, fore-bears of hu-man-kind. That law I dis-o-beyed with my sin, and now I suf-fer pain and dis-grace. Je-sus, ex-press your mer-cy to me, and pay for all my sins.

4 That day you came to dwell on the earth, bring-ing us all great joy! The na-tions scat-tered o-ver the world, to them you gave the light of all life. O Je-sus, O Com-pas-sion-ate One, we of-fer praise to you.

*Recollecting the accounts told by his grandfather and others, Sidney Byrd stated: "This hymn was sung by thirty-eight Dakota Indian prisoners of war as they went to the gallows at Mankato, Minnesota, on December 26, 1862, in the largest mass execution in American history."*

*Tune: LACQUIPARLE 9.6.9.9.9.6.*
*Native American melody (Dakota)*
*Adapt. Joseph R. Renville, 1842*
*Harm. J. R. Murray, 1877*

5  Your sac-ra-ment en-trust-ed to us,
    Je-sus, now share with me.
   Your bread of life and drink
      for our souls,
   which you have of-fered,
      pur-i-fy now.
   Sanc-ti-fy minds and bod-ies to you;
      re-store us by your love.

6  "Take now my flesh as food
      for your soul,"
   these are your words, O Christ.
   "Take my shed blood and drink
      from my cup,
   that it may serve to strength-en
      your faith."
   En-trance in-to your door I de-sire;
   Je-sus, now hear my plea.

7  Your plan for our sal-va-tion, O God,
      grant to my sin-ful soul.
   Be-yond the heavens is your great a-bode;
      all good-ness is se-cure in your hands.
   This life di-vine which you gave to me
      is one that has no end.

# Be Known to Us in Breaking Bread 342

*James Montgomery, 1825; alt.*                                    *Luke 24:30–31, 35*

1 Be known to us in break-ing bread, but do not then de-part;
2 Here share with us in love di-vine, your bod-y and your blood;

O Sav-ior, stay with us and spread your ta-ble in our heart.
That liv-ing bread, that heaven-ly wine, be our im-mor-tal food.

*This hymn is sometimes found as the second and third stanzas*
*of an American hymn, "Shepherd of Souls, Refresh and Bless."*
*Montgomery—Moravian poet, journalist, humanitarian, and author*
*of more than 400 hymns—titled this hymn "The Family Table."*

Tune: ST. FLAVIAN C.M.
*Day, The Whole Booke of Psalms, 1562*

# 343 Jesus Took the Bread

Matt. 26:26–28; Luke 9:16; 22:19; 24:30

Ruth Duck, 1982

1 Je - sus took the bread, dai - ly gift of God,
2 Je - sus blessed the bread, thanked the God of grace,
3 Je - sus broke the bread; then he poured the wine.
4 Je - sus gives the bread at our ta - ble still,

formed of wheat and sweat and toil, sun, rain, and sod.
thanked the One who made all worlds, all time, all space.
Bro - ken bod - y, life poured out, God gives as sign.
gives the cup to those who seek God's lov - ing will.

In our hands we take gifts of bread and wine,
Bless - ing, hon - or, praise, all to God be - long.
Weak, a - fraid, and lost: that is when we're healed.
Let us go in peace; let us free - ly give,

gath - ered from the fields of earth, signs of love di - vine.
Let us lift our hearts to God in a thank - ful song.
In our hu - man bro - ken - ness: there God is re - vealed.
shar - ing love with all the world dai - ly as we live.

Ruth Duck wrote this hymn emphasizing the actions of
communion—taking, blessing, breaking, and giving the
bread—following a summer study of liturgy at the University
of Notre Dame. It was first used at New Hope United Church
of Christ in Milwaukee.

Tune: NEW HOPE 10.11.10.12.
Ruth Duck, 1982
Arr. Randall Sensmeier, 1982

# The Time Was Early Evening

**344**

*The Iona Community, 1988*

Mark 14:12–25

1 The time was ear-ly eve - ning, the place a room up - stairs;
2 The com - pa - ny of Je - sus had met to share a meal;
3 "The bread and bod - y bro - ken, the wine and blood out - poured,
4 Christ Je - sus, now a - mong us, con - firm our faith's in - tent,

The guests were the dis - ci - ples, few in num-ber and few in prayers.
The One who made them wel-come had much more to re - veal.
The cross and kitch - en ta - ble are one by my sign and word."
As, with your words and ac - tions, we u - nite in this sac - ra - ment.

*Refrain*

Oh, the food comes from the bak - er; the drink comes from the vine;

The words come from the Sav - ior, "I will meet you in bread and wine."

In the Iona Community collection Enemy of Apathy, this piece
is titled "The Song of the Supper" and is accompanied by an
instruction that it is an "effective song for a house communion,
or when the sacrament is celebrated in the usual eating place."

Tune: AFTON WATER Irr. with refrain
*Traditional Scottish melody*
Harm. The New Century Hymnal, *1994*

# 345      Let All Mortal Flesh Keep Silence

*Isa. 6:1–3; 1 Tim. 6:13–15*

*From the Liturgy of St. James, 4th century*
*Transl. Gerard Moultrie, 1864; alt.*

1 Let all mor-tal flesh keep si - lence, and with fear and
2 Mon-arch great, yet born of Mar - y, as of old on
3 Rank on rank the host of heav - en spreads its van-guard
4 At Christ's feet the six - winged ser - aphs, cher - u - bim with

trem - bling stand; Pon-der noth-ing earth - ly - mind - ed,
earth Christ stood, Lord of all, in hu - man ves - ture—
on the way, As the Light of light de - scend - ing
sleep - less eye, Veil their fac - es to the Pres - ence,

for with bless - ing in the hand, Christ our God to
in the bod - y and the blood— Christ will give to
from the realms of end - less day, That the powers of
as with cease-less voice they cry, Al - le - lu - ia,

*This Greek hymn comes from the Liturgy of St. James of Jerusalem. It has been paraphrased by Gerard Moultrie, a priest of the Church of England. The French folk melody first appeared with these words in* The English Hymnal *(1906).*

Tune: PICARDY 8.7.8.7.8.7.
*French carol melody, 17th century*
*Harm. Ralph Vaughan Williams, 1906*

earth de - scend - ing, our full hom-age to de - mand.
all the faith - ful bread of life for heaven-ly food.
hell may van - ish as the shad-ows clear a - way.
al - le - lu - ia, al - le - lu - ia, God most high!

## Bread of the World, in Mercy Broken 346

*Reginald Heber, 1827; alt.*                                      John 6:35–58

1 Bread of the world, in mer - cy bro - ken, Wine of the soul in
2 Look on the heart by sor - row bro - ken, look on the tears by

mer - cy shed, By whom the words of life were spo - ken,
sin - ners shed, And be your feast to us the to - ken

and in whose death our sins are dead,
that by your grace our lives are fed.

*Author of a number of familiar hymns, Reginald Heber published
the first modern English hymnal arranged according to the church
year. The musical setting for this hymn was written by Episcopal
priest and hymnal editor John Sebastian Bach Hodges.*

Tune: EUCHARISTIC HYMN  9.8.9.8.
*J. S. B. Hodges, 1868*
*Alternate tune:  RENDEZ À DIEU*
*(sung in one stanza)*

# 347 Let Us Talents and Tongues Employ

*Luke 10:1–9*  
*Fred Kaan, 1975; alt.*

1 Let us tal-ents and tongues em-ploy, reach-ing out with a shout of joy:
2 Christ is a-ble to make us one, at his ta-ble he set the tone,
3 Je-sus calls us in, sends us out bear-ing fruit in a world of doubt,

bread is bro-ken, the wine is poured, Christ is spo-ken and seen and heard.
teach-ing peo-ple to live to bless, love in word and in deed ex-press.
gives us love to tell, bread to share: God (Im-man-u-el) ev-ery-where!

*Refrain (first time p, second time f)*

Je-sus lives a-gain, earth can breathe a-gain, pass the Word a-round: loaves a-bound!

*This hymn came into being when composer Doreen Potter asked poet Fred Kaan to write a text for her adaptation of a Jamaican folk melody. It was first used at the World Council of Churches Assembly in Nairobi (1975), and in Vancouver (1983).*

Tune: LINSTEAD L.M. with refrain  
*Jamaican folk song*  
*Adapt. Doreen Potter, 1975*

# Jesus Is Here Right Now

348

Leon C. Roberts, 1986; alt.

Je - sus is here right now. Je - sus is
here. With this bread and wine true peace you'll
find; Christ Je - sus is here right now. (right now).

*Somewhat detached throughout*

*to beginning* | *Last time, end*

*Composer Leon C. Roberts is perhaps best known for his "Mass of St. Augustine" and other liturgical compositions that appear in* Lead Me, Guide Me: The African-American Catholic Hymnal. *His work is greatly influenced by priest and composer Clarence Joseph Rivers.*

Tune: JESUS IS HERE  6.4.5.4.6.
*Leon C. Roberts, 1986*

# 349

# I Come with Joy

Brian Wren, 1968; rev. 1982, 1994

*Unison*

1 I come with joy, a child of God, for - giv - en, loved, and
2 I come with Chris - tians far and near to find, as all are
3 As Christ breaks bread, and bids us share, each proud di - vi - sion
4 And thus we meet, and bet - ter know the Pres - ence, ev - er
5 To - geth - er met, to - geth - er bound, in friend - ship we will

free, The life of Je - sus to re - call, in
fed, The new com - mu - ni - ty of love in
ends. The love that made us, makes us one, and
near, And join our hearts and sing with joy that
stay, And go with joy to love the world and

love laid down for me, in love laid down for me.
Christ's com - mu - nion bread, in Christ's com - mu - nion bread.
strang - ers now are friends, and strang - ers now are friends.
Christ is ris - en here, that Christ is ris - en here.
live the way we pray, and live the way we pray.

*One of Brian Wren's most widely published texts, this hymn was
originally written to "sum up a series of sermons on the meaning
of communion. It tries to use simple words to suggest important
theological themes."*

Tune: DOVE OF PEACE 8.6.8.6.6.
Southern Harmony, *1835*
Arr. Austin Lovelace, 1977

# Now in the Days of Youth

Walter J. Mathams, 1913; alt.
Adapt. Sylvia G. Dunstan, 1992

*Eccles. 12:1; 1 Cor. 16:13; Deut. 30:19–20*

1 Now in the days of youth when life is filled with choice, when
2 Teach us to use our lives with pur-pose and with power for
3 Teach us to love in truth, to give and to re - ceive with
4 Teach-er, Cre-a - tor, God, en - fold us in your arms; be

hope and doubt touch ev - ery hour, when all thoughts find a voice,
vi - sions of a bet - ter world and for de - ci - sion's hour;
joy - ful and with o - pen hearts, with all that we be - lieve;
with us as we try our wings, and keep us safe from harm.

We turn, O God, to you for guid-ance and for grace. In
To choose the way of life, re - ject the way of death, un -
To seek an-oth-er's good, to hon - or what is right, to
All good and per - fect gifts come to us from your hand. O

all our days, in all our ways, help us to seek your face.
til the ra-diant force of God fills mind and strength and breath.
let our will and our de - sire be held in ho - ly light.
help us use them care-ful - ly and live by love's com - mand.

*When the Rev. Walter J. Mathams of London wrote this hymn for use at Christian Endeavor and Sunday School conventions, he did not realize it would receive wide circulation. It was introduced in the United States in 1913 in* Worship and Song.

Tune: DIADEMATA S.M.D.
George J. Elvey, 1868

**351**

# I Was There to Hear Your Borning Cry

*John Ylvisaker, 1985; alt*

**Unison**

1. I was there to hear your born - ing cry, I'll be there when you are old. I re - joiced the day you were bap - tized, to see your life un - fold. I was there when you were but a child, with a

2. When you found the won - der of the Word, I was there to cheer you on; You were raised to praise the liv - ing God, to whom you now be - long. Should you find some-one to share your time and you

3. In the mid - dle a - ges of your life, not too old, no long - er young, I'll be there to guide you through the night, com-plete what I've be - gun. When the eve - ning gent-ly clos - es in and you

4. I was there to hear your born - ing cry, I'll be there when you are old. I re - joiced the day you were bap - tized, to see your life un - fold. *St. 4, end*

*John Ylvisaker is the composer of a number of collections of music in the "contemporary" or "folk" idiom, as well as soundtracks for various media productions. This is perhaps his best-known song.*

Tune: BORNING CRY 9.7.9.6.D.
*John Ylvisaker, 1985*

Am   D   G   G/B   C

faith    to   suit   you   well;   I'll be   there   in case   you
join    your hearts   as   one,   I'll be   there   to make   your
shut    your wea - ry   eyes,   I'll be   there   as   I   have

G   A7   D   *to beginning*

wan - der   off   and   find   where   de - mons   dwell.
vers - es   rhyme   from   dusk   till   ris - ing   sun.
al - ways   been   with   just   one   more   sur - prise.

# My God, Accept My Heart This Day   352

*Matthew Bridges, 1848; alt.*                                    *Gal. 4:5; Eph. 1:5*

1 My   God, ac - cept   my   heart this   day,   and   make   it   al - ways   yours,
2 Be - fore the cross   of   One who   died,   I   bow   in   deep re - gret.
3 A - noint me with   your   love and   grace, a -   dopt   me   for your   own,
4 Let   ev - ery thought and   work and   word   be   given, O   God, to   you.

That   I   from you   no   more may stray   as   long   as   life   en - dures.
Let   ev - ery   sin   be   cru - ci - fied,   and   ev - ery   wrong off - set.
That   I   in heaven may   find   my place   and   wor - ship   at   your   throne.
In   life and death, may   I   be stirred your   pur - pose   to   pur - sue.

*Influenced by the Oxford Movement, Matthew Bridges left the*
*Church of England and became a Roman Catholic in 1848, the*
*year this confirmation hymn was published. He wrote numerous*
*other prose and poetry works.*

Tune:  ST. STEPHEN  C.M.
*William Jones, 1789*

# 353      Great Work Has God Begun in You

*Phil. 1:6; Col. 2:6; Eph. 5:1*

*Carol Birkland, 1995*

1 Great work has God be - gun in you, so let the Spir - it
2 In love, God calls you to this day, and gives you strength, these
3 A - round God's ta - ble cel - e - brate the end of bond - age,
4 Great work has God be - gun in you; take on God's love in

fol - low through; The mark of Christ up - on your brow, bap -
vows to say; Take up the faith that you were shown, and
sin, and hate: A feast of love and vic - to - ry, the
all you do, And may that love in you in - crease— now,

tis - mal touch re - mem - ber now.
grow, as - sured you are God's own.
gift of Christ who sets us free.
with God's bless - ing, go in peace.

*Carol Birkland has served as director of Christian education in Lutheran and United Church of Christ congregations, and has written and edited curriculum. William Rowan's tune first appeared in* Together Met, Together Bound, *a collection of his hymn settings.*

Tune: VERBUM DEI L.M.
*William P. Rowan, 1993*
*Alternate tune: PUER NOBIS NASCITUR*

# God, When I Came into This Life

**354**

*Fred Kaan, 1979*

*Isa. 43:1*

1 God, when I came in-to this life, you
2 You give me free-dom to be-lieve; to-
3 With-in the cir-cle of the faith, as
4 In all the ten-sions of my life, be-
5 So help me in my un-be-lief and

called me by my name; To-day I come, com-
day I make my choice, And to the wor-ship
mem-ber of your cast, I take my place with
tween my faith and doubt, Let your great Spir-it
let my life be true: Feet firm-ly plant-ed

mit my-self, re-spond-ing to your claim.
of the church I add my learn-ing voice.
all the saints of fu-ture, pres-ent, past.
give me hope, sus-tain me, lead me out.
on the earth, my sights set high on you.

*The musical setting for this text by contemporary poet Fred Kaan is an Appalachian folk tune of possible British origin. Annabel Morris Buchanan, an organist, music teacher, and scholar of American hymnody, collected and arranged this and other tunes in* Folk Hymns of America, *1938.*

Tune: LAND OF REST C.M.
The Christian Harp, *1832*
*Harm. Annabel Morris Buchanan, 1938*

# 355 God the Spirit, Guide and Guardian

*Gen. 2:7; John 10:11–16*

*Carl P. Daw, Jr., 1987*

1 God the Spir - it, guide and guard - ian, wind - sped
2 Christ our Sav - ior, sov - ereign, shep - herd, Word made
3 Great Cre - a - tor, life - be - stow - er, truth be -
4 Tri - une God, mys - te - rious be - ing, un - di -

flame and hov - ering dove, Breath of life and voice of
flesh, love cru - ci - fied, Teach - er, heal - er, suf - fering
yond all thought's re - call, Fount of wis - dom, womb of
vid - ed and di - verse, Deep - er than our minds can

proph - ets, sign of bless - ing, power of love: Give to
ser - vant, friend of sin - ners, foe of pride: In your
mer - cy, giv - ing and for - giv - ing all: As you
fath - om, great - er than our creeds re - hearse: Help us

those who lead your peo - ple fresh a - noint - ing
tend - ing may all pas - tors* learn and live a
know our strength and weak - ness, so may those the
in our var - ied call - ings your full im - age

*Where appropriate, "ministers" may be substituted for "pastors."*

Words Copyright © 1989 by Hope Publishing Company
Harmonization Copyright ©, Oxford University Press. From *The English Hymnal 1906.*

| | | |
|---|---|---|
| of your grace; | Send them forth | as bold a- |
| shep - herd's care; | Grant them cour - age | and com- |
| church ex - alts | O - ver - see | its life stead- |
| to pro - claim, | That our min - is - tries | u- |

| | | |
|---|---|---|
| pos - tles to your church | in ev - ery | place. |
| pas - sion shown through word | and deed and | prayer. |
| fast - ly yet not | o - ver - look its | faults. |
| nit - ing may give | glo - ry to your | name. |

*A gift from Carl P. Daw, Jr., to Episcopal colleague Jeffery*
*Rowthorn for his consecration as bishop suffragan of the*
*Diocese of Connecticut, this text calls on the Triune God*
*to aid and bless the person being ordained in his or her ministry.*

Tune: HYFRYDOL 8.7.8.7.D.
*Rowland H. Prichard, 1844*
*Arr. Ralph Vaughan Williams, 1906*
*Alternate tune: JEFFERSON*

# 356 God, Who Summons through All Ages

*Eph. 4:11–12*

*Edith Sinclair Downing, 1992*

1 God, who sum-mons through all a - ges men and wom - en to or - dain,
2 Called to keep your house-hold's mys-teries, guar-dian, coun - sel-or, and friend,
3 God, E - ter - nal Word With - in Us, help us lis - ten so that we

now a - noint your cho - sen ser-vant, join *her** to the a-pos - tles' train.
blessed with gifts u - nique and pre-cious, may *she* these with your grace blend.
hear your call to be Christ's bod - y, claim our gifts, serve faith - ful - ly.

*Or *him, he,* as appropriate.

*Edith Sinclair Downing wrote this text "to affirm persons called to the pastoral ministry, particularly women, and to encourage believers to claim their gifts for mutual ministry." The tune by David Hurd was first published in a collection of the composer's works in 1983, and later appeared in several hymnals.*

Tune: JULION 8.7.8.7.8.7.
*David Hurd, 1974*
Alternate tune: *REGENT SQUARE*

Give *her* pa-tience, cour-age, wis-dom, as *she* serves your tri-une name. *St. 1, 2, to 𝄋*
As *she* an-swers Christ's com-mis-sion, keep *her* stead-fast to life's end.
May we each in word and ac-tion join in mu-tual min-is-try! *St. 3, to Coda*

Coda

# You Are Called to Tell the Story    357

*Ruth Duck, 1991*                                              *Eph. 3:14–21*

1 You are called to tell the sto-ry,
   pass-ing words of life a-long,
 Then to blend your voice with oth-ers
   as you sing the sa-cred song.
 Christ be known in all our sing-ing,
   fill-ing all with songs of love.

2 You are called to teach the rhy-thm
   of the dance that nev-er ends,
 Then to move with-in the cir-cle,
   hand in hand with strang-ers, friends.
 Christ be known in all our danc-ing,
   touch-ing all with hands of love.

3 You are called to set the ta-ble,
   bless-ing bread as Je-sus blessed,
 Then to come with thirst and hun-ger,
   need-ing care like all the rest.
 Christ be known in all our shar-ing,
   feed-ing all with signs of love.

4 May the One whose love is broad-er
   than the mea-sure of all space
 Give us words to sing the sto-ry,
   move a-mong us in this place.
 Christ be known in all our liv-ing,
   fill-ing all with gifts of love.

*In this text, hymnwriter Ruth Duck sought to "set ordained
ministry in the larger context of the ministry of the whole people
of God." It was written for the ordination of her longtime friend,
Elizabeth Caldwell.*

Tune: JULION 8.7.8.7.8.7.
*David Hurd, 1974*
Alternate tune: REGENT SQUARE

# 358

# God of the Prophets

*2 Kings 2:9; Exod. 28:1–3; 1 Sam. 16:1, 13; Rom. 1:1–6*

Denis Wortman, 1884; alt.

1 God of the proph - ets, bless the proph-ets' heirs,
2 A - noint them proph - ets! Make their ears at - tend
3 A - noint them priests! Strong in - ter - ces - sors they
4 Make them a - pos - tles! Her - alds of your cross,

E - li - jah's man - tle o'er E - li - sha cast.
to your di - vin - est speech; their hearts a - wake
for par - don, and for char - i - ty and peace!
forth may they go to tell all realms your grace.

Each age for its own sol - emn tasks pre - pares:
To hu - man need; their lips make el - o - quent
O might with them the world, though gone a - stray,
In - spired of you, may they count all but loss,

make each one no - bler, strong-er than the last.
for righ-teous - ness that shall all e - vil break.
pass in - to Christ's pure life of sac - ri - fice.
and stand at last with joy be - fore your face.

*Denis Wortman wrote "God of the Prophets" for the centenary of
the New Brunswick Theological Seminary (Reformed) in New
Jersey. A pastor of the Reformed Church in America, Wortman
became president of its General Synod in 1901.*

Tune: TOULON 10.10.10.10.
*Adapt. from OLD 124TH,*
Trente quatre Pseaumes, *Geneva, 1551*

# O God, Who Teaches Us to Live

**359**

*Tom Hunter, 1992*

1 O God, who teach - es us to live and
2 For love that wel - comes chil - dren in and
3 For wis - dom, skills, and con - fi - dence where
4 For words and num - bers, hopes and dreams that
5 For all who fol - low teach - ing's call with

guides us on our way, For all the teach - ers
holds them when they stray, For knowl - edge hearts and
won - der leads to faith, For those who ask and
grow from day to day, For in - spi - ra - tion's
cour - age and with grace To build a fu - ture

in our midst, we give you thanks and praise.
souls re - ceive, we give you thanks and praise.
those who hear, we give you thanks and praise.
mes - sen - gers, we give you thanks and praise.
for us all, we give you thanks and praise.

*United Church of Christ minister Tom Hunter describes himself as a "minstrel" for schools and churches across the United States. This hymn was written "to celebrate and thank teachers in both Sunday and weekday schools because their work shapes the future for us all."*

Tune: ST. ANNE C.M.
*William Croft, 1708*

# 360

# Thuma Mina
## (Send Me, Lord)

*Isa. 6:8*

*South African traditional song*

Transcribed from recordings of South African worship, this
prayer-song has gained international popularity since its use
at the seventh assembly of the World Council of Churches at
Canberra, Australia, 1991, and subsequent publication.

Tune: THUMA MINA  Irr.
*South African traditional song*

# Your Love, O God, Has Called Us Here

**361**

*Russell Schulz-Widmar, 1982*

*Heb. 13:1; 1 Pet. 1:22*

1 Your love, O God, has called us here, for all love
2 O gra-cious God, you con - se - crate all that is
3 O God of love, in - spire our life, re - veal your

finds its source in you, The per - fect love that casts out
love - ly, good, and true. Bless those who in your pres - ence
will in all we do; Join ev - ery hus - band, ev - ery

fear, the love that Christ makes ev - er new.
wait, and ev - ery day their love re - new.
wife in mu - tual love and love for you.

*Russell Schulz-Widmar of Austin, Texas, has been a lecturer, music director, and professor of church music. He has served as president of The Hymn Society and co-editor of* A New Hymnal for Colleges and Schools, *1992.*

Tune: GERMANY (GARDINER) L.M.
*William Gardiner's* Sacred Melodies, *1815*

# 362

# When Love Is Found

Matt. 19:6; Mark 10:8

Brian Wren, 1978; rev. 1992

*Unison*

1 When love is found and hope comes home, sing and be
2 When love has flowered in trust and care, build both each
3 When love is tried as loved-ones change, hold still to
4 When love is torn, and trust be - trayed, pray strength to
5 Praise God for love, praise God for life, in age or

glad that two are one. When love ex - plodes and fills the
day, that love may dare to reach be - yond home's warmth and
hope, though all seems strange, till ease re - turns and love grows
love till tor - ments fade, till lov - ers keep no score of
youth, in calm or strife. Lift up your hearts! Let love be

sky, praise God, and share our Mak - er's joy.
light, to serve and strive for truth and right.
wise through lis - tening ears and o - pened eyes.
wrong, but hear through pain love's Eas - ter song.
fed through death and life in bro - ken bread.

*Brian Wren has noted one important hope for all committed
Christian relationships, "that love may reach out beyond the nuclear
family, rather than the more cozy and familiar theme of inviting
others into 'home's warmth and light.'"*

Tune: O WALY WALY L.M.
*English folk melody
Arr. Jonathan McNair, 1993*

# O God of Love
### 363

*William Vaughan Jenkins (1868–1920); alt.*

*Gen. 2:24; Matt. 19:5; Mark 10:7–9*

1 O God of love, to you we bow
  and pray for these be-fore you now,
That close-ly knit in ho-ly vow
  they may in you be-come as one.

2 What-ev-er comes to be their share
  of quick-ening joy or bur-dening care,
In power to do and grace to bear,
  may they in you re-main as one.

3 E-ter-nal Love, with them a-bide;
  through change and chance, O be their guide,
Let noth-ing in this life di-vide
  those whom you now have joined as one.

*William Vaughan Jenkins, by profession a chartered accountant in England, was active in mission work of Baptist and Congregational churches and was involved in the Adult School Movement. This hymn, written for his wedding in 1900, was published in 1909.*

Tune: O WALY WALY L.M.
*English folk melody*
*Arr. Jonathan McNair, 1993*

# God, Today Bless This New Marriage
### 364

*Marie J. Post, 1974; alt.*

1 God, to-day bless this new mar-riage, guide this un-ion in your way.
2 Fill their lives with love and ser-vice where their dai-ly path may be.
3 May the home they are pre-par-ing be a place of faith and prayer,

With the bless-ing of your Spir-it, may they live from day to day.
Grant them hum-ble hearts when pros-pered, pa-tience in ad-ver-si-ty.
fruit-ful for this life and your do-min-ion which they glad-ly share.

*Marie Post wrote poetry for the* Grand Rapids Press *in Michigan for thirty years, and published a collection of her work titled* I Had Never Visited an Artist Before *(1977). Her text was inspired by a traditional wedding prayer of the Christian Reformed Church.*

Tune: SERVANT SONG 8.7.8.7.
*Richard Gillard, 1977*
*Arr. Betty Carr Pulkingham, 1977; adapt.*

# 365 How Blessed Are They Who Trust in Christ

John 3:13–16; Jude 1:20–21

*Fred Pratt Green, 1972*

1 How blessed are they who trust in Christ when we and
2 In rip-ened age, their har-vest reaped, or gone from
3 In Christ, who tast-ed death for us, we rise a-

those we love must part; We yield them up, for
us in youth or prime, In Christ they have e-
bove our nat-ural grief, and wit-ness to a

go they must, but do not lose them from our heart.
ter-nal life, re-leased from all the bonds of time.
strick-en world the strength and splen-dor of be-lief.

*This text was one of four chosen from 457 entries for publication by The Hymn Society of America in 1980. Works of this eminent British writer have been published in* The New Yorker *and in anthologies.*

Tune: MARYTON L.M.
*H. Percy Smith, 1874*

# God of Our Life

*Hugh T. Kerr, 1916; alt.*

1 God of our life, through all the cir-cling years, we trust in you.
2 God of the past, our times are in your hand; with us a-bide.
3 God of the com-ing years, through paths un-known we fol-low you;

In all the past, through all our hopes and fears, your care shines through.
Lead us by faith to hope's true prom-ised land; be now our guide.
When we are strong, O leave us not a-lone, our ref-uge true.

With each new day, when morn-ing lifts the veil,
Bless us in times of dark-ness and of light,
Be now for us in life our dai-ly bread,

We own your mer-cies, God, which nev-er fail.
Then faith's fair vi-sion chang-es in-to sight.
Our heart's true home when all our years have sped.

*Hugh Kerr was educated in Canada and the United States and was a pioneer in religious broadcasting. He wrote this hymn for the fiftieth anniversary of Shadyside Presbyterian Church in Pittsburgh, where he had a long tenure as pastor.*

Tune: SANDON 10.4.10.4.10.10.
*Charles Henry Purday, 1860*
*For another harmonization, see 466*

# 367

# Christ the Victorious

*Gen. 1:26–27; 3:19*

*Carl P. Daw, Jr., 1982*

1 Christ the Vic - to - ri - ous, give to your ser - vants
2 On - ly Im - mor - tal One, might - y Cre - a - tor!
3 God - spo - ken proph - e - cy, word at cre - a - tion:
4 Christ the Vic - to - ri - ous, give to your ser - vants

rest with your saints in the re - gions of light.
We are your crea - tures and chil - dren of earth.
"You came from dust and to dust shall re - turn."
rest with your saints in the re - gions of light.

Grief and pain end - ed, and sigh - ing no long - er,
From earth you formed us, both glo - rious and mor - tal,
Yet at the grave shall we raise up our glad song,
Grief and pain end - ed, and sigh - ing no long - er,

there may they find ev - er - last - ing life.
and to the earth shall we all re - turn.
"Al - le - lu - ia, al - le - lu - ia!"
there may they find ev - er - last - ing life.

*Carl P. Daw, Jr.'s paraphrase of the "Kontakion for the Departed" from the Eastern Orthodox memorial service was written specifically for this tune to preserve some of the flavor of the original text for congregations unable to sing the traditional Kiev melody.*

Tune: RUSSIAN HYMN 11.10.11.9.
*Alexis F. Lvov, 1833*

# Sheltered by God's Loving Spirit

**368**

*Deborah Patterson, 1993*

*1 Cor. 13:4–13; Rom. 5:8*

1 Shel-tered by God's lov - ing Spir - it, gath-ered here we share our grief:
2 Giv - en breath by God's own pur-pose, back to God our breath does go.

Seek-ing so - lace, seek - ing cour-age— know-ing God does bring re - lief.
Life e - ter - nal in our pres - ent here we on - ly part - ly know.

We are free to name our sor-rows, speak our an - ger, weep our loss,
But for-give-ness, love, and cour-age show us God's a - maz - ing grace,

For our God did suf - fer al - so when Christ died up - on a cross.
Strength-en us to face the jour-ney till we know God face to face.

*Reflecting on the love she had experienced while going through deep pain, Deborah Patterson wrote this text for the funeral of a parishioner at St. John's United Church of Christ in Smithton, Illinois, while serving as minister.*

Tune: BEECHER 8.7.8.7.D.
*John Zundel, 1855*

# 369     Keep Your Lamps Trimmed and Burning

*Matt. 25:1–13; Gal. 6:9*                                                  *African-American spiritual*

1 Keep your lamps trimmed and burn-ing, keep your lamps trimmed and burn-ing, keep your lamps trimmed and burn-ing, for this work's al-most done.

2 It's our faith makes us hap-py, it's our faith makes us hap-py, it's our faith makes us hap-py, for this work's al-most done.

3 We are climb-ing Ja-cobs's lad-der, we are climb-ing Ja-cob's lad-der, we are climb-ing Ja-cob's lad-der, for this work's al-most done.

4 Ev-ery round goes high-er, high-er, ev-ery round goes high-er, high-er ev-ery round goes high-er, high-er, for this work's al-most done.

*Last time, end*

**Refrain**

Sis-ters, don't grow wear-y, broth-ers, don't grow wear-y, chil-dren, don't grow wear-y, for this work's al-most done.

*By tradition, a leader may call out substitute words for the refrain,*
*such as "Christians don't grow weary, Christians don't grow weary, . . ."*
*etc., or "people," "preacher," or any others that may be appropriate.*

*This spiritual is possibly one of the code songs in which to keep*
*one's lamp "trimmed and burning" could have meant keeping a*
*lookout for a conductor of the underground railroad, such as*
*Harriet Tubman. It is often sung at church dedication services.*

Tune: KEEP YOUR LAMPS 7.7.7.6.6.6.6.6
*African-American spiritual*
*Harm. The New Century Hymnal, 1994*

# What Gift Can We Bring?

Jane Marshall, 1980

*1 Sam. 9:7; 1 Cor. 3:8–9; 1 John 4:13–16*

*Unison*

1 What gift can we bring, what pres - ent, what to - ken?
2 Give thanks for the past, for those who had vi - sion,
3 Give thanks for to - mor - row, full of sur - pris - es,
4 This gift we now bring, this pres - ent, this to - ken,

What words can con - vey it, the joy of this day?
who plant - ed and wa - tered so dreams could come true.
for know - ing what - ev - er to - mor - row may bring,
these words can con - vey it, the joy of this day!

When grate - ful we come, re - mem - bering, re - joic - ing,
Give thanks for the now, for stud - y, for wor - ship,
The Word is our prom - ise al - ways, for - ev - er;
When grate - ful we come, re - mem - bering, re - joic - ing,

what song can we of - fer in hon - or and praise?
for mis - sion that bids us turn prayer in - to deed.
we rest in God's keep - ing and live in God's love.
this song we now of - fer in hon - or and praise!

Jane Marshall received the first "Woman of Achievement"
award at Perkins School of Theology, Southern Methodist
University, where she teaches. She wrote this hymn for the
twenty-fifth anniversary of her home church, Northaven United
Methodist Church in Dallas.

Tune: ANNIVERSARY SONG 11.11.11.11.
*Jane Marshall, 1980*

# 371

# God, Creation's Great Designer

Gen. 1:1–2:7; 1 Pet. 2:4–9

*Jane Parker Huber, 1984*

1 God, cre - a - tion's great de - sign - er, ar - chi - tect, and ar - ti - san,
2 Hear our thanks for those who found-ed in this place a church for praise.
3 Sing we, too, of church-es stand-ing not a - lone in wood and stone,
4 Shape us as your con - gre - ga - tions, called to - geth - er, sent a - far,

dream-er, build - er, and re - fin - er— how we mar - vel at your plan.
Firm in Christ their faith was ground-ed as they lived their earth - ly days.
but in hu - man lives com-mand-ing con - fi - dence in you a - lone.
so as peo - ple or as na - tions we can serve you where we are.

You have formed us to re - flect you, filled us with your Spir-it's breath,
Build-ers, they, in brick and stone-work, walls sup-port - ing roof and floors,
For high arch - es, ris - ing, yearn-ing, soar-ing towers that fill with song,
O ac - cept the praise we bring you, bless the work of hu-man hands.

freed us to ac - cept, re - ject you, and in Christ, de - feat-ed death.
prais-ing you in all their own work— sol - id stee - ple,
win-dows o - pened for our learn-ing— God, we praise you all day long.
Hear the hymns our voic - es sing you, ech - o - ing through years and lands.

*Jane Parker Huber wrote this text specifically for the dedication of an Indiana church's rebuilding program to be sung with this twentieth-century tune, New Reformation. "It celebrates the skill and labor of human workers as well as of our creating God."*

Tune: NEW REFORMATION 8.7.8.7.D.
*J. T. Morrow, 1950*
*Alternate tunes: WEISSE FLAGGEN,*
*HOLY MANNA*

# God, You Have Set Us

**372**

*Jane Parker Huber, 1984; rev. 1993*

*1 Cor. 4:1; 1 Pet. 4:10–11*

1 God, you have set us in this time and place,
2 We ded - i - cate this work of hu - man hand;
3 Let doors and hearts pro-vide a wel - come here.
4 Call youth and age in - to these halls for praise.
5 So may the world be-come our neigh-bor - hood,

Called us as stew - ards of your love and grace.
Built for your glo - ry, may it firm - ly stand.
Let walls and voic - es ring with songs of cheer.
Then send us out for ser - vice all our days,
Each wish - ing each the right, the true, the good,

O keep us faith - ful, set our souls a - fire,
Let truth be preached and jus - tice right - ly done.
Let win - dows speak of beau - ty and of light.
Your word of peace and chal-lenge here made real
Word, font, and ta - ble call - ing us to be

And by your Spir - it all our work in - spire.
In Christ our Sav - ior make us tru - ly one.
Let smile and ges - ture show your love a - right.
Spurs us to act with en - er - gy and zeal.
Bound up in Christ, in Christ set bold - ly free.

*Commissioned to write a hymn for the dedication of a remodeled sanctuary and the twenty-fifth anniversary of the Church of Saint Andrew in Roswell, Georgia, Jane Parker Huber provided a text that could be used by others for related occasions.*

Tune: NATIONAL HYMN 10.10.10.10.
*George William Warren, 1892*

# 373

# They Did Not Build in Vain

Acts 2:1–4, 43–47; 1 Cor. 3:11; Eph. 2:19–22; Heb. 12:1–2

*Alan Luff, 1989; alt.*

1 They did not build in vain who found-ed here a church
2 Those who have loved this place, a cloud of wit-nes-ses,
3 In ev-ery place our world is storm and tem-pest tossed,
4 Make this the meet-ing place where doubt finds grounds of faith,

as wit-ness to God's love a-mid a world of pain;
sur-round and urge us on as we now run our race;
the flames of fear and hate are e-vil's flags un-furled;
where hurt finds heal-ing love, our pen-i-tence your grace;

They built up-on the rock that is the ris-en Christ,
Though the ho-ri-zon's bend con-ceals the way a-head,
Yet still the Spir-it's power in wind and fire of love
Where God in Trin-i-ty is bridge from death to life,

the one foun-da-tion laid, that stands each earth-ly shock.
the foot-prints on the road show Christ waits at the end.
pours gifts up-on the church for ser-vice in this hour.
from sin to ho-li-ness, time to e-ter-ni-ty.

*Alan Luff, a graduate of the Royal College of Music, has served the Anglican Church as parish priest, precentor of Westminster Abbey, and canon of Birmingham Cathedral. He is also known as the author of* Welsh Hymns and Their Tunes *(1990).*

Tune: LEONI 6.6.8.4.D.
*Traditional Yigdal melody*
*Adapt. Meyer Lyon, 1770*

# O God of All Your People Past

**374**

*Thomas H. Gill, 1868; alt.*

*Ps. 90:1*

1 O God of all your peo-ple past, your grace is our sal - va - tion;
2 Their joy in you, the joy we bring, rings thrill-ing in its blend - ing;
3 O saints to come, take up the strain, and bless the Bound-less Giv - er.

your arms of love, their home se-cure, re - main our hab - i - ta - tion.
the Spir - it who in them did sing to us new song is lend - ing.
Un - bro-ken be the gold-en chain! Let not di - vi-sions sev - er.

We bring to you the praise they brought, we seek you as the
That song in them, in us, is one; we raise it high, we
But safe in that dear dwell-ing place, and rich with that e -

saints have sought in ev - ery gen - er - a - tion.
send it on, the mus - ic nev - er end - ing.
ter - nal grace, sing on, sing on for - ev - er.

*Barred from studies at Oxford University because of his Unitarian heritage, Thomas Gill pursued his own study of history and theology. He wrote several volumes of poetry and historical writings. Later in life, Gill associated with the evangelical branch of the Anglican church.*

Tune: NUN FREUT EUCH 8.7.8.7.8.8.7.
*Melody by Martin Luther*
*Klug's* Geistliche Lieder, *1535*

# 375     Christ Jesus, Please Be by Our Side

*Rev. 4:8*

*Attrib. to Wilhelm August II, 17th century*
*Cantionale Sacrum, Gotha, 1651*
*Transl. Madeleine Forell Marshall, 1992*

1 Christ Je - sus, please be by our side, your
2 Pre - pare our hearts to sing your praise, in -
3 So shall we join that faith - ful crowd, who,
4 Now hon - or God who shaped this earth; praise

Ho - ly Spir - it send as guide: With gra - cious help, your
struct our lips, re - fine each phrase, Em - power our mind, our
"Ho - ly, ho - ly," cry a - loud: E - ter - nal joy, most
Je - sus Christ of mor - tal birth; A - dore the Ho - ly

peo - ple may keep to the true and righ - teous way.
faith in - flame, that hu - man - kind may bless your name.
ho - ly light, the face of God is their de - light.
Spir - it: three in One, the bless - ed Trin - i - ty.

*Wilhelm August II was severely wounded twice during the Thirty Years' War, the second time left for dead, but he recovered to devote himself to the rebuilding of his country and to poetry and music. His authorship of this hymn is uncertain.*

Tune: HERR JESU CHRIST,
DICH ZU UNS WEND L.M.
*Pensum Sacrum, Görlitz, 1648*
*Arr. J. S. Bach, c. 1708*

# God, We Thank You for Our People

**376**

*Ruth Duck, 1986*

1 God, we thank you for our peo-ple, roots dug deep with-in the soil,
2 Thank you, God, for gen-tle plea-sure: les-sons learned and se-crets told,
3 Still we must con-fess be-fore you, some-times, Sav - ior, we have failed;
4 By your Spir-it of cre-a-tion keep us bold for risk-ing still,

har - dy spir-its, rich in lov-ing, strong for strug-gle, bold for toil.
hopes and mem-ories saved as trea-sure, passed to young ones by the old,
though we wor-ship and a-dore you, some-times love has not pre-vailed.
ea - ger in an-ti-ci-pa-tion, ev-er strong to do your will.

Faith-ful Rock of gen-er-a-tions, you whom par-ents' par-ents praised:
Pranks and glo-ries, songs and sto-ries, food by lov-ing hands pre-pared.
Tem-pers rac-ing, dev-il chas-ing, hearts es-tranged by ice or flame
Bind us close to one an-oth-er, shar-ing life and death and birth,

Here in hope as we re-mem-ber may our song to you be raised.
God, we bless you for your pres-ence in our tears and laugh-ter shared.
You trans-form by ways for-giv-ing. Grace a-maz-ing! Grace, your name!
Wel-com-ing as sis-ter, broth-er, all your chil-dren on the earth.

*Ruth Duck created this text at the request of Harold (Hal)
McSwain, Jr., for a family reunion. She found her inspiration
in the stories of Harold, Sr., and in her own family heritage.
The hymn speaks to any community that has shared life together
for a long time.*

Tune: HOLY MANNA 8.7.8.7.D.
*William Moore, 1825*

# 377

# Forward through the Ages

*Heb. 11; 1 Cor. 12*

*Frederick Lucian Hosmer, 1908; alt.*

1 For-ward through the a - ges, in un-bro-ken line,
2 Wide grows God's do - min - ion, reign of love and peace;
3 Not a - lone we con - quer, not a - lone we fall;

move the faith-ful spir - its at the call di - vine;
for it we must la - bor, till all striv-ings cease.
in each loss or tri - umph, lose or tri-umph all.

Gifts in dif-fering mea - sure, hearts of one ac - cord,
Proph-ets have pro - claimed it, teach-ers tes - ti - fied,
Bound by God's far pur - pose in one liv-ing whole,

man - i - fold in ser - vice, one the sure re - ward.
po - ets sung its glo - ry, mar - tyrs for it died.
move we on to - geth - er to the shin - ing goal.

*Frederick Hosmer, educated at Harvard and ordained to the
Unitarian ministry, served Congregational and Unitarian
churches throughout the country. He was known for his concern
for social issues, his service book for Sunday schools, and his
lectures on hymnology.*

Tune: ST. GERTRUDE 6.5.6.5.D. with refrain
*Arthur S. Sullivan, 1871*

**Refrain**

For-ward through the a - ges, in un-bro-ken line,

Move the faith-ful spir - its at the call di - vine.

# Jerusalem, My Happy Home   378

*F. B. P., c. 16th century; alt.*                              *Ps. 144:9–10; 1 Cor. 13:12; Luke 1:46–55*

1 Je - ru - sa - lem,     my hap-py home, when will  you wel - come me?
2 There saints are crowned with glo - ry great; they see  God face  to  face;
3 There Da - vid stands  with harp in hand  as  mas - ter of  the  choir;
4 There Mar - y sings  Mag - ni - fi - cat  with tune  both strong and  sweet;

When shall my  sor - rows have  an end?  Your joys, when  shall I  see?
They tri - umph still,  they will  re - joice,  de - light - ing  in God's grace.
Ten thou-sand times would they  be blessed that might such  mu - sic  hear.
And choirs of  saints in  har - mo - ny  re - sound through ev - ery  street.

5 There Mag-da-len no more la-ments
   but joins the ris-ing sound;
   What tongue can tell or heart con-ceive
   the joys that there are found!

6 Je - ru - sa - lem, Je - ru - sa - lem,
   God grant that I may see
   your end-less joy, and of the same
   par-tak-er ev-er be!

*The earliest known version of this hymn (1585) is forty-four
stanzas long. A later and shorter version, found in the British
Museum, credits "F. B. P.," about whom nothing is known. The
American tune was often sung with the words "O Land of rest,
for thee I sigh."*

Tune:  LAND OF REST  C.M.
The Christian Harp, *1832*
*Adapt. and harm. Annabel Morris Buchanan, 1938*

# 379 Come, We Who Love God's Name

*Ps. 48:1–2; Heb. 12:22–24; Rev. 4:2–11*　　　　　　　　　　　　　　　　　*Isaac Watts, 1707; alt.*

1 Come, we who love God's name, and let our joys be known;
2 Let those re - fuse to sing who nev - er knew our God;
3 God's grace on earth is found, the seeds of glo - ry sown;
4 The hill of Zi - on yields a thou - sand sa - cred sweets
5 Then let our songs a - bound, and ev - ery tear be dry;

To - geth - er God's great love pro - claim, and thus sur-round the throne.
But we our thanks and praise will bring for love so deep and broad.
Ce - les - tial fruits on earth - ly ground from faith and hope have grown.
Be - fore we reach the heaven-ly fields, or walk the gold - en streets.
We're trav-eling through Em - man - uel's ground, to great-er worlds on high.

*A story concerning this hymn holds that the pastor of a New England church once asked the choir to lead the singing of the second stanza on a Sunday when it threatened to "refuse to sing" because of a disagreement in the congregation. Needless to say, the choir acquiesced.*

Tune: ST. THOMAS S.M.
*Williams'* New Universal Psalmodist, *1770*
*Alternate setting:* MARCHING TO ZION

# 380 O Saints in Splendor Sing

*Rev. 7*　　　　　　　　　　　　　　　　　　　　　　*Sylvia G. Dunstan, 1991*

1 O saints in splen-dor sing
 the praise of God Most High.
 Through trib-u-la-tion you have come,
 through blood been sanc-ti-fied.

2 Robed in bap-tis-mal grace
 a-mid the world's de-spair,
 Pro-claim the glo-ry of our God
 whose love has con-quered fear.

3 Those saints who went be-fore
 pre-pared for us the way;
 The church ex-pec-tant, yet to come,
 re-lies on us to-day.

4 O wor-thy is the Lamb!
 the Lamb that once was slain!
 Of hon-or, bless-ing, thanks, and praise,
 lift up the glad re-frain!

*Sylvia Dunstan wrote this hymn based on the Revelation 7 text to accompany a sermon preached for a small struggling congregation. It was intended to encourage them to identify with the saints and to persevere as a community of faith.*

Tune: ST. THOMAS S.M. (see above)

# Faith of the Martyrs

*Frederick W. Faber, 1849; alt.*

1 Faith of the mar - tyrs, liv - ing still in spite of dun - geon, fire, and sword; O how our hearts beat high with joy, when we re - call their faith's re - ward:

2 Mar - tyrs con - fined in pris - ons bleak were still in heart and con - science free; and no less blessed will be our fate if we, like them, live faith - ful - ly:

3 Faith of the mar - tyrs! We will love both friend and foe in peace or strife; and sow the seeds of hope and faith by strength-ening word and fear - less life:

4 Faith of the mar - tyrs! Faith and prayer shall long out - live sin's ty - ran - ny; and through the truth that comes from God all hu - man - kind shall then be free:

**Refrain**

Faith of the mar - tyrs, liv - ing faith! We would be true in life and death.

The Greek term martures *is translated in the New Testament as "witness" and forms the basis for the English word "martyr." The hymn was written as a call for the return of the Church of England to the Roman Catholic church, and "our fathers . . ." in the original text referred to those faithful to Rome who had suffered martyrdom.*

Tune: ST. CATHERINE L.M. with refrain
*Henri F. Hemy, 1864*
*Adapt. James G. Walton, 1874*

# 382    Come, We Who Love God's Name

*Ps. 48:1–2; Heb. 12:22–24; Rev. 4:2–11*

*Isaac Watts, 1707; alt.*
*Refrain by Robert Lowry, 1867; alt.*

1 Come, we who love God's name, and let our joys be known; To-
2 Let those re - fuse to sing who nev - er knew our God; But
3 God's grace on earth is found, the seeds of glo - ry sown; Ce-
4 The hill of Zi - on yields a thou-sand sa - cred sweets Be-
5 Then let our songs a - bound, and ev - ery tear be dry; We're

geth - er God's great love pro - claim, to - geth - er God's great love pro-
we our thanks and praise will bring, but we our thanks and praise will
les - tial fruits on earth - ly ground, ce - les - tial fruits on earth - ly
fore we reach the heaven-ly fields, be - fore we reach the heaven-ly
trav - eling through Em - man - uel's ground, we're trav - eling through Em - man - uel's

claim, and thus sur - round the throne, and thus sur-round the throne.
bring for love so deep and broad, for love so deep and broad.
ground from faith and hope have grown, from faith and hope have grown.
fields, or walk the gold - en streets, or walk the gold - en streets.
ground to great - er worlds on high, to great-er worlds on high.

And thus sur-round the throne, and thus sur - round the throne.

*Isaac Watts' joyous hymn was a favorite of the early American singing schools and was set to a variety of fuguing tunes. This gospel tune by Baptist preacher Robert Lowry incorporates a camp-meeting style refrain and is a favorite of many Christians.*

Tune: MARCHING TO ZION S.M. with refrain
*Robert Lowry, 1867*
*Alternate setting: ST. THOMAS*

*Refrain*

We're march - ing to Zi - on, beau-ti-ful, beau-ti-ful Zi - on; We're

We're march-ing on to Zi - on,

march-ing on-ward to Zi - on, the beau - ti-ful cit-y of God.

Zi - on, Zi - on, the

# Come, Let Us Join with Faithful Souls

**383**

*William G. Tarrant, 1892; alt.*

*Rev. 5:11–14*

1 Come, let us join with faith-ful souls our song of faith to raise;
2 Faith - ful are all who love the truth and per - fect truth pro - claim,
3 And faith-ful are the gen - tle hearts to whom the power is given
4 O God of hosts, our faith re-new, and grant us, in your grace,

One fam - i - ly in heart are we, and one the God we praise.
Who stead-fast stand at God's right hand and glo-ri - fy God's name.
Of ev - ery hearth to make a home, of ev-ery home a heaven.
To join the songs sung by the saints in ev-ery time and place.

*A leader of the Unitarian Church in England, William Tarrant*
*edited a Unitarian weekly and for thirty-seven years ministered*
*to the Unitarian Christian Church in London. This hymn was*
*one of many he wrote for use by that congregation.*

Tune: AZMON C.M.
*Carl G. Gläser, 1828*
*Arr. Lowell Mason, in* Modern Psalmody, *1839*

# 384 For the Faithful Who Have Answered

Heb. 11:4–12:2

*Sylvia G. Dunstan, 1986; alt.*

1 For the faith-ful who have an-swered when they heard your call to serve,
2 Man-y minds have glimpsed the prom-ise; man-y hearts have yearned to see;
3 For this cloud of faith-ful wit-ness, for the com-mon life we share,

for the man-y ways you led them, test-ing will and stretch-ing nerve,
man-y souls have heard you call-ing us to great-er lib-er-ty.
for the work of peace and jus-tice, for the gos-pel that we bear,

For their work and for their wit-ness as they strove a-gainst the odds,
Some have fall-en in the strug-gle; oth-ers still are press-ing on.
For the vi-sion that our home-land is your love— deep, high, and broad—

for their cour-age and o-be-dience, we give thanks and praise, O God.
You are not a-shamed to own us; we give thanks and praise, O God.
for the dif-ferent roads we trav-el, we give thanks and praise, O God.

*In commissioning a hymn for the fiftieth anniversary of women's ordination in 1986, the United Church of Canada specified that it should concentrate on all people's faithful response to God's call. Sylvia Dunstan selected Hebrews 11 and 12 as her primary reference.*

Tune: OMNI DIE 8.7.8.7.D.
*German melody, 1625*
Trier Gesangbuch, *1695*

# O What Their Joy and Their Glory Must Be 385

*Peter Abelard (1079–1142)*
*Transl. composite John M. Neale, 1841, and S. W. Duffield, 1886; alt.*

*Rev. 7:9–17; 21:1–6*

1 O what their joy and their glo - ry must be,
2 The true Je - ru - sa - lem ho - ly is there,
3 Long - ing for home now let ev - ery heart raise
4 There in a Sab - bath of un - end - ing light,

as end - less Sab - baths the bless - ed ones see;
whose peace-ful du - ties give joy free from care;
prayers of de - vo - tion and an - thems of praise;
joy - ful - ly keep - ing that ho - ly day bright,

Crowns for the val - iant, for wea - ry ones rest;
Where dis - ap - point - ment no heart can as - sail,
From streams of sor - row we lift up our eyes,
We join in chant - ing the song with - out cease

God shall be all, and in all ev - er blessed.
where each prayer whis - pered is heard with - out fail.
to the blessed cit - y, our home and our prize.
with all the saints in that sweet realm of peace.

*Peter Abelard, a brilliant and daring thinker, was a founder of the University of Paris. His questioning and reasoning approach to Scripture made enemies. This was one of ninety-three hymns to the Spirit (Hymnus Paraclitensis) he wrote for the Convent of Heloisa.*

Tune: O QUANTA QUALIA 10.10.10.10.
*La Feillée's* Nouvelle Méthode de Plain Chant, *1808*

# 386 The Church's One Foundation

*Eph. 2:13–22; 4:4–6; 1 Cor. 3:11*                                        *Samuel J. Stone, 1866; alt.*

1 The church's one foun - da - tion is Je - sus Christ our Lord;
2 E - lect from ev - ery na - tion, yet one o'er all the earth,
3 'Mid toil and trib - u - la - tion, and tu - mult of our war,
4 Yet we on earth have un - ion with God, the Three - in - One,

we are Christ's new cre - a - tion by wa - ter and the word;
one char - ter of sal - va - tion, one God, one faith, one birth,
we wait the con - sum - ma - tion of peace for - ev - er - more;
and mys - tic sweet com - mu - nion with those whose rest is won.

From heaven Christ came and sought us in love to set us free;
One name to - geth - er bless - ing, one ho - ly food we share,
Till with the vi - sion glo - rious, our long - ing eyes are blessed,
O hap - py ones and ho - ly! God, give us grace that we,

with pre - cious blood Christ bought us for all e - ter - ni - ty.
to one hope we are press - ing, at one in work and prayer.
and the great church vic - to - rious shall be the church at rest.
like them, the meek and low - ly, may live e - ter - nal - ly.

*Like the writings of Ambrose many centuries earlier, this hymn was born out of a doctrinal dispute. The young priest Samuel J. Stone composed twelve hymns on the articles of the Apostles' Creed in support of those reacting against nontraditional views of biblical scholarship. This hymn is based on article nine, "the holy Catholic Church."*

Tune: AURELIA 7.6.7.6.D.
Samuel S. Wesley, 1864

# O Christ, the Great Foundation

## 387

*Timothy Tingfang Lew, 1933; alt.*
*Transl. Frank W. Price, 1953; alt.*

*Acts 2:17–21; Eph. 4:4–6; Col. 1:18–20*

1 O Christ, the great foun-da-tion
   on which your peo-ple stand
to preach your true sal-va-tion
   in ev-ery age and land:
Pour out your Ho-ly Spir-it
   to make us strong and pure,
to keep the faith un-bro-ken
   as long as worlds en-dure.

2 Bap-tized in one con-fes-sion,
   one church in all the earth,
we bear Christ's own im-pres-sion,
   the sign of sec-ond birth:
One ho-ly peo-ple gath-ered
   in love be-yond our own,
by grace we were in-vit-ed,
   by grace we make you known.

3 Where ty-rants' hold is tight-ened,
   where strong de-vour the weak,
where in-no-cents are fright-ened,
   the righ-teous fear to speak,
There let your church a-wak-ing
   at-tack the powers of sin
and, all their ram-parts break-ing,
   with you the vic-tory win.

4 This is the mo-ment glo-rious
   when Christ who once was dead
shall lead the church vic-to-rious,
   their cham-pion and their head.
The Sov-ereign of cre-a-tion
   a new do-min-ion brings,
the fi-nal con-sum-ma-tion,
   the glo-ry of all things.

*Timothy Tingfang Lew was born in China and was educated*
*both there and in the United States. He served as representative*
*to the World Council of Churches from 1927 to 1939 and*
*chaired the commission that prepared the Chinese Union*
*hymnbook in 1936.*

Tune: AURELIA 7.6.7.6.D.
*Samuel S. Wesley, 1864*

# Help Us Accept Each Other

## 388

*Fred Kaan, 1974; alt.*

*John 15:12; 17:20–23; Eph. 4:1–6, 11–16*

1 Help us ac-cept each oth-er
   as Christ ac-cept-ed us;
teach us as sis-ter, broth-er,
   each per-son to em-brace.
Be pres-ent, God, a-mong us,
   and bring us to be-lieve
we are our-selves ac-cept-ed
   and meant to love and live.

2 Teach us, O God, your les-sons,
   as in our dai-ly life
we strug-gle to be hu-man
   and search for hope and faith.
Teach us to care for peo-ple,
   for all, not just for some,
to love them as we find them,
   or as they may be-come.

3 Let your ac-cep-tance change us,
   so that we may be moved
in liv-ing sit-u-a-tions
   to do the truth in love;
To prac-tice your ac-cep-tance,
   un-til we know by heart
the ta-ble of for-give-ness
   and laugh-ter's heal-ing art.

4 God, for to-day's en-coun-ters
   with all who are in need,
who hun-ger for ac-cep-tance,
   for righ-teous-ness and bread,
Bring us new eyes for see-ing,
   new hands for hold-ing on;
re-new us with your Spir-it;
   God! Free us, make us one!

*Dutch theologian Fred Kaan was ordained in the United*
*Reformed Church in England and Wales and has served as an*
*international church administrator. Author of more than 200*
*hymns, Kaan frequently has addressed contemporary issues in*
*his texts.*

Tune: AURELIA 7.6.7.6.D.
*Samuel S. Wesley, 1864*

# 389

# Un mandamiento nuevo

Matt. 22:34–40; Mark 12:28–34;
John 13:34–35; 14:6; 15:9–12; 1 John 4:7–21

William Loperena, 1965; rev. 1993
English version, Carolyn Jennings, 1993

Estribillo (Refrain)

Un man - da-mien-to nue - vo Je-sús nos dio
Je - sus a new com - mand-ment has giv - en us:

que nos a - me - mos siem - pre co-mo nos a - ma
that we should love each oth - er just as our God loves

1. Dios. / us.
2. to Stanzas Dios. / us. — Last time, end

Estrofas (Stanzas)

1 La se - ñal de cris-tian - dad
2 Quien al pró - ji - mo no a - ma,
1 The clear sign of all true Chris - tians
2 Those who do not love their neigh - bors

*Originally written for a Maundy Thursday service, this hymn has
received widespread use throughout Puerto Rico, where William
Loperena is a Dominican priest working on the development of
ecumenical liturgies.*

Tune: LOPERENA 8.8. with refrain (10.7.6.)
William Loperena, 1965
Arr. Luis Olivieri and Roberto Milano, 1993

es    a  -  mar  -  se en her-man - dad.
mien-te    si a    Dios  di - ce    que a - ma.    *(Estribillo)*
is  the    way    they  love each  oth - er.
do  not    tru -  ly  love their    Sav - ior.    *(to Refrain)*

3  Cris-to, Luz, Ver-dad y Vi-da
   al per-dón y a-mor in-vi-ta.

4  Per-do-ne-mos los a-gra-vios
   co-mo Dios ha or-de-na-do.
   *(Estribillo)*

5  De Je-sús her-ma-nos so-mos
   si de ve-ras per-do-na-mos.

6  En la vi-da y en la muer-te
   Dios nos a-ma pa-ra siem-pre.
   *(Estribillo)*

7  Don-de hay ca-ri-dad y a-mor.
   siem-pre es-tá pre-sen-te Dios.

8  Co-mul-gue-mos con fre-cuen-cia
   pa-ra a-mar-nos a con-cien-cia.
   *(Estribillo)*

9  Glo-ria a Dios el Cre-a-dor
   y a Cris-to el Sal-va-dor.

10  Y al Es-pí-ri-tu di-vi-no
    en Tri-ni-dad han vi-vi-do.
    *(Estribillo)*

3  Christ, the Light, the Truth, and true Life,
   bids us share our love and par-don.

4  Let us all for-give each oth-er
   as by God we are com-mand-ed.
   *(Refrain)*

5  We are tru-ly friends of Je-sus
   if we free-ly give our par-don.

6  In our liv-ing and our dy-ing,
   God is ev-er there to love us.
   *(Refrain)*

7  In true char-i-ty and lov-ing,
   God is pres-ent here a-mong us.

8  Let us come to Je-sus' ta-ble
   with our love for one an-oth-er.
   *(Refrain)*

9  Glo-ry be to the Cre-a-tor;
   glo-ry be to Christ, our Sav-ior;

10  Glo-ry be to God, the Spir-it,
    Ho-ly Trin-i-ty for-ev-er.
    *(Refrain)*

# 390

## Eternal Christ, Who, Kneeling

*John 17:20–23*

*William W. Reid, Jr., 1976; alt.*

1 E - ter - nal Christ, who, kneel - ing when earth - ly tasks were done,
2 But we have of - ten slight - ed the ties de - signed to hold
3 Ac - cept our deep con - tri - tion for all our sun - dering ways

turned un - to God ap - peal - ing, "That they may all be one,"
your fol - low - ers u - nit - ed with - in one com - mon fold.
which still dis - rupt your mis - sion, which mock our words of praise.

We thank you for your vi - sion of u - ni - ty un - torn,
On his - tory's tat - tered pa - ges we see, O Christ, with shame,
Christ, may your Spir - it guide us that we may find, be - yond

of faith with - out di - vi - sion with which your church was born.
the strife which through the a - ges has marred your church's name.
the things which still di - vide us, love's all - em - bra - cing bond.

*William Watkins Reid, Jr., is a pastor, author, hymnwriter, and*
*past member of the executive committee of The Hymn Society.*
*He takes an active part in politics at all levels, and his hymns are*
*often written as responses to current events.*

Tune: NYLAND 7.6.7.6.D.
*Finnish hymn melody*
*Harm. David Evans, 1927*

# In the Midst of New Dimensions

391

*Julian Rush, 1985; alt.*

*Gen. 9:12–16; Exod. 13:21–22; Num. 14:14*

1 In the midst of new di-men-sions, in the face of chang-ing ways,
2 Through the flood of starv-ing peo-ple, war-ring fac-tions and de-spair,
3 As we stand a world di-vid-ed by our own self-seek-ing schemes,
4 We are man and we are wom-an, all per-sua-sions, old and young,
5 Should the threats of dire pre-dic-tions cause us to with-draw in pain,

Who will lead the pil-grim peo-ples wan-dering in their sep-arate ways?
Who will lift the ol-ive branch-es? Who will light the flame of care?
Grant that we, your glob-al vil-lage, might en-vi-sion wid-er dreams.
Each a gift in your cre-a-tion, each a love song to be sung.
May your blaz-ing phoe-nix spir-it res-ur-rect the church a-gain.

*Refrain*

God of rain-bow, fier-y pil-lar, lead-ing where the ea-gles soar, We your

peo-ple, ours the jour-ney now and ev-er, now and ev-er, now and ev-er-more.

*Julian Rush, an ordained minister in the United Methodist Church, has spent more than a decade as director of the Colorado AIDS Project. He wrote this hymn on the theme of "diversity" for a meeting of the Rocky Mountain Conference (United Methodist).*

Tune: NEW DIMENSIONS 8.7.8.7. with refrain
*Julian Rush, 1985*
Arr. The New Century Hymnal, *1994*

# 392

# En santa hermandad
## (United by God's Love)

*Eph. 3:14–21; Col. 1:11–12*

*William Loperena*
*Transcribed by Luis Olivieri*
*English version, Carolyn Jennings, 1994*

1 En san-ta her-man-dad va-mos a can-
2 Al Cre-a-dor can-te - mos que nos dio su
1 U - nit-ed by God's love, let us sing to -
2 Sing praise to our Cre-a - tor, God of grace and

tar. (Al)
geth - er. (Sing)

*Estribillo (Refrain)*

gra - cia.
mer - cy,

Tú e-res Cris-to_el
You are the one Re -

Re - den - tor; llé-na-nos de_a-mor.
deem-er Christ, fill our hearts with love;

Tú e-res nues-tro
You are the Sav-ior,

*Last time, end*

Sal - va - dor y Li-ber-ta - dor.
Je - sus Christ, Lib-er-a - tor God. *(to stanzas 3, 4)*

*Many of the hymns of William Loperena employ folk music and rhythms, such as the popular "guaracha" used here.*

Tune: EN SANTA HERMANDAD Irr.
*William Loperena*
*Transcribed by Luis Olivieri*
*Arr. Roberto Milano, 1989*

3 A Cris-to en-sal-ce-mos
   por su san-ta a-lian-za.
4 Al Fiel Con-so-la-dor
   de-mos a-la-ban-za.
   *(Estribillo)*

3 Sing praise to Christ the Sav-ior,
   Bring-er of sal-va-tion.
4 And praise the Ho-ly Spir-it,
   Com-fort-er most ho-ly.
   *(Refrain)*

# Blessed Be the Tie That Binds 393

*John Fawcett, 1782; alt.*                                    *Gal. 3:28; 6:2; Col. 3:13–15*

1 Blessed be the tie that binds our hearts in Chris - tian love;
2 Be - fore our God we come and pour our ar - dent prayers;
3 We share each oth - er's woes, each oth - er's bur - dens bear,
4 When we are called to part it gives us in - ward pain,

The shar - ing of a com - mon life is like to that a - bove.
Our fears, our hopes, our aims are one, our com - forts and our cares.
And of - ten for each oth - er flows a sym - pa - thiz - ing tear.
But we shall still be joined in heart, and hope to meet a - gain.

*An English Baptist minister, John Fawcett published a number of poetic works. His entire ministry was spent at a church near Hebden Bridge, Yorkshire, where he wrote most of his hymns to follow his sermons.*

Tune: DENNIS S.M.
*Melody by Johann G. Nägeli (c. 1768–1836)*
*Adapt. Lowell Mason, 1845*

## 394 In Christ There Is No East or West

*1 Cor. 12:13; Gal. 3:28; Eph. 2:14–22*

*John Oxenham, 1908; alt.*
*St. 3, Laurence Hull Stookey, 1987*

1 In Christ there is no East or West, in Christ no South or North;
2 In Christ shall true hearts ev-ery-where their high com-mu-nion find;
3 In Christ is nei-ther Jew nor Greek, and nei-ther slave nor free;
4 In Christ now meet both East and West, in Christ meet South and North;

But one com-mu-ni-ty of love through-out the whole wide earth.
God's ser-vice is the gold-en cord close-bind-ing hu-man-kind.
For men and wom-en live in God, and all are kin to me.
One joy-ous, true com-mu-ni-ty through-out the whole wide earth.

*Singer and composer Harry T. Burleigh studied at the National Conservatory of Music from 1892 to 1896. He is recognized as the first African-American composer to employ spirituals in concert arrangements. This tune is named after the rector of St. George's Episcopal Church in New York City, where Burleigh served as baritone soloist for more than fifty years.*

Tune: McKEE C.M.
*African-American melody*
*Arr. Harry T. Burleigh, 1939*
Alternate setting: ST. PETER

## 395 In Christ There Is No East or West

*1 Cor. 12:13; Gal. 3:28; Eph. 2:14–22*

*John Oxenham, 1908; alt.*
*St. 3, Laurence Hull Stookey, 1987*

1 In Christ there is no East or West, in Christ no South or North;
2 In Christ shall true hearts ev-ery-where their high com-mu-nion find;
3 In Christ is nei-ther Jew nor Greek, and nei-ther slave nor free;
4 In Christ now meet both East and West, in Christ meet South and North;

*At the beginning of the twentieth century, many hymns were written to promote the oneness of humanity. English Congregationalist John Oxenham's text is a lasting example. His great concern for those in military service led to the publication of a World War I hymnbook that exceeded eight million in circulation.*

Tune: ST. PETER C.M.
*Alexander R. Reinagle, 1836*
Alternate setting: McKEE

But      one com-mu - ni - ty    of  love through-out the whole wide    earth.
God's    ser-vice  is  the    gold-en cord close - bind-ing hu - man -  kind.
For      men and wom-en   live in God, and    all  are kin  to     me.
One      joy-ous, true com - mu - ni - ty  through-out the whole wide    earth.

## Where Charity and Love Prevail 396

*Latin hymn, "Ubi caritas et amor," 9th century*          John 13:34–35; 15:9–12; 2 Cor. 5:17–20; 1 John 4:7–21
*Paraphr. by Omer Westendorf, 1961; alt.*

**With freedom**

1 Where char - i - ty and love pre - vail, there God is  ev - er found; Brought
2 With grate-ful joy and ho - ly fear  true char - i - ty we learn;  Let
3 For - give we now each oth-er's faults as   we our faults con-fess;  And
4 Let  strife a - mong us be un-known, let  all con - ten - tion cease;  Be

here  to-geth - er  by Christ's love,    by  love  are   we thus bound.
us   with heart and mind and  strength   now  love Christ in  re - turn.
let  us  love each oth - er  well    in  Chris-tian  ho - li - ness.
Christ the glo - ry  that we   seek,    be  ours Christ's ho - ly  peace.

*Believed to date from the time of Charlemagne (768–814), this hymn was, before Vatican II (1962–1965), the last and indispensable song during the Maundy Thursday foot-washing service. Benedictine priest Paul Benoit composed many organ works.*

Tune: CHRISTIAN LOVE C.M.
*Paul Benoit, 1961*
*Alternate tune: ST. FLAVIAN*

# 397 Thank Our God for Sisters, Brothers

*Roger Powell, 1948; alt.*

1 Thank our God for sis - ters, broth-ers, one by grace, in har - mo - ny,
2 Praise to God for con - gre - ga - tions, keep-ing faith with Christ as guide;
3 Ho - ly is your name for - ev - er! Heal di - vi - sions that re - main;

Join - ing heart to heart with oth - ers, mak - ing strong com - mu - ni - ty.
Man - y tongues of man - y na - tions, song and ser - vice u - ni - fied.
Bless the church's new en - deav-ors; make our wit - ness one a - gain.

With the cross of Christ our stan-dard, let us sing as with one voice,
Sweet the psalm and sweet the car - ol, when our song is raised as one.
One in Christ and in Christ's gos - pel, make us one we now im - plore.

Glo - ry, glo - ry, yours the prom-ise: we who are the church re - joice.
Glo - ry, glo - ry, yours the pow - er, as in heaven your will be done.
Glo - ry, glo - ry, yours the glo - ry, then and now and ev - er - more.

*This hymn was written for a Union Thanksgiving service in 1948 by the Rev. Roger Powell of Camillus, New York. It served as a rallying song for the first meeting of the National Council of Churches in 1952.*

Tune: PLEADING SAVIOR 8.7.8.7.D.
*Melody from* The Christian Lyre, *1831*

# Shadow and Substance

**398**

*Dan Damon, 1989*

*Gen. 1:26–27*

1 Shad - ow and sub - stance, won - der and mys - ter - y,
2 We are your im - age, formed in com - mu - ni - ty;
3 Nam - ing the name - less Spir - it of u - ni - ty,

spell-bind-ing spin -ner of at - oms and earth; Soul of the cos-mos,
sis - ters and broth-ers of Ad - am and Eve. You gave us col - or,
scan-ning the heav-ens for signs of your care; God of the a - ges,

per - son and en-er-gy, source of our be - ing: we sing of your worth.
cus-tom and his-to-ry; teach us to hon - or what oth - ers re - ceive.
give us hu - mil-i - ty; guide us to mys - ti - cal un - ion in prayer.

*This hymn by writer and composer Dan Damon exemplifies one of the goals he has articulated about his work: "To keep things simple and singable while at the same time exploring the edges of our spoken and sung faith."*

Tune: TWILIGHT 5.6.10.D.
*Dan Damon, 1989*

# 399 When Minds and Bodies Meet as One

*Gal. 3:28; Eph. 4:1–16*

*Brian Wren, 1980; rev. 1993*

1 When minds and bod - ies meet as one and
2 When lead - ers meet with an - gry sound, yet
3 When team - work serves a com - mon aim, and
4 When peo - ple feel the lash - ing claws of
5 In Christ we come to break and bless the

find their true af - fin - i - ty, we join the dance in
bri - dle their hos - til - i - ty, to bar - gain for a
play - ers move in sym - pa - thy, the flow - ing rhy - thm
greed and in - hu - man - i - ty, yet strug - gle in a
bread of new so - ci - e - ty, cre - a - ted for to -

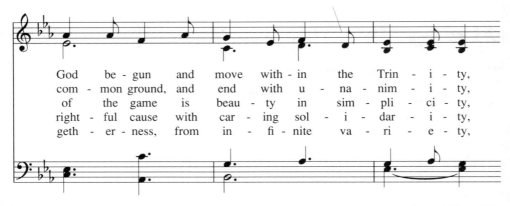

God be - gun and move with - in the Trin - i - ty,
com - mon ground, and end with u - na - nim - i - ty,
of the game is beau - ty in sim - pli - ci - ty,
right - ful cause with car - ing sol - i - dar - i - ty,
geth - er - ness, from in - fi - nite va - ri - e - ty,

*British poet Brian Wren and composer Peter Cutts were both encouraged in their work by the renowned hymnologist Erik Routley. They later collaborated in the 1983 collection* Faith Looking Forward, *in which this hymn was first published.*

Tune: TRINITY CAROL  L.M.D.
*Peter Cutts, 1980*

# 400      Christ Is Made the Sure Foundation

*Eph. 2:20–22; 1 Pet. 2:4–7*

*Latin, 6th–8th century*
*Transl. John Mason Neale, 1851; alt.*
*St. 3 adapt. Thomas H. Troeger, 1992*

1 Christ is made the sure foun - da - tion, Christ the head and cor - ner-stone,
2 To this tem - ple, where we call you, come, O God of Hosts, to - day!
3 Here re - new your ser - vants' vis - ion, that by faith they may at - tain

chos - en of our God and pre - cious, bind - ing all the Church in one;
With your con-stant, lov - ing kind-ness hear your peo - ple as they pray.
peace and hope, re - newed com-pas - sion, strength to com-fort those in pain,

Ho - ly Zi - on's help for-ev - er, and our con - fi - dence a - lone.
Give your full - est ben - e - dic - tion: grace to fol - low Christ the Way.
Tears and grief trans-formed to glad-ness in your ev - er - last - ing reign.

*The hymn has its origins in an early Latin poem,* Urbs beata
Jerusalem, *based on passages from Ephesians, 1 Peter, and
Revelation. "Holy Zion" refers to the church transcendent, built
of "living stones"—the saints of God.*

Tune: REGENT SQUARE 8.7.8.7.8.7.
*Henry T. Smart, 1867*
*Alternate tune:  WESTMINSTER ABBEY*

# O God in Whom All Life Begins

**401**

*Carl P. Daw, Jr., 1992*

1 O God in whom all life be-gins, who births the seed to fruit,
2 U - nite in mu - tual min - is - try our minds and hands and hearts
3 Through tears and laugh-ter, grief and joy, en - large our trust and care;

be - stow your bless-ing on our lives; here let your love find root.
that we may have the grace to seek the power your peace im - parts.
so bind us in com - mu - ni - ty that we may risk and dare.

Bring forth in us the Spir - it's gifts of pa - tience, joy, and peace;
So let our var - ied gifts com-bine to glo - ri - fy your Name
Be with us when we gath - er here to wor-ship, sing, and pray,

de - liv - er us from numb - ing fear, and grant our faith in - crease.
that in all things by word and deed we may your love pro - claim.
then send us forth in power and faith to live the words we say.

*Carl P. Daw, Jr., is an Episcopal priest who began hymnwriting while serving on the text committee for* The Hymnal 1982. *He has held academic positions at the College of William and Mary and the University of Connecticut, where he was also vicar-chaplain.*

Tune: NOEL C.M.D.
*Traditional English melody*
*Arr. Arthur S. Sullivan, 1874*

# 402

# De colores
## (Sing of Colors)

*Mexican folk song*
*Transl.* The New Century Hymnal, *1995*

1 De colores, de colores se vis-ten los
1 Sing of col-ors, sing of col-ors that o-ver the
2 Sing, re-joic-ing! Ev-ery crea-ture that breathes raise a

cam-pos en la pri-ma-ve-ra. De co-
hills in pro-fu-sion are spring-ing; Sing of
song to the God of cre-a-tion. Sing, re-

lo-res, de co-lo-res son los pa-ja-ri-tos que vie-nen de a-
col-ors of the birds that fly out-side my win-dow their can-ti-cles
joic-ing! Sing to God who so ear-nest-ly cares, who has of-fered sal-

fue-ra. De co-lo-res, de co-
sing-ing; Sing of col-ors, in the
va-tion. Sing the good news! Sing the

*This Mexican folk song is known by many Mexican-American churchgoers, and has also been popular among the United Farm Workers.*

Tune:  DE COLORES
*Mexican folk song*
*Arr. Alfredo Morales, F.S.C.*

# 403 My Hope Is Built on Nothing Less

*Matt. 7:24–27; 1 Cor. 3:11; Heb. 6:19; Rev. 11:15*

*Edward Mote, c. 1834; alt.*

1 My hope is built on noth-ing less than Je - sus' love and
2 When shad-ows veil my Sav-ior's face, I rest up - on un -
3 Christ's oath and cov - e - nant and blood sup - port me in the
4 When Christ shall come with trum-pet sound, oh, may I then in

righ - teous-ness; I dare not trust this earth - ly frame, but
chang-ing grace; In ev - er - y high and storm - y gale, my
ris - ing flood; When all a - round my soul gives way, Christ
Love be found, Dressed in God's righ - teous - ness a - lone, fault -

**Refrain**

whol-ly lean on Je - sus' name.
an - chor holds with - in the veil.    On Christ, the sol - id Rock, I stand;
then is all my hope and stay.
less to stand be - fore the throne.

all oth - er ground is sink-ing sand, all oth - er ground is sink-ing sand.

*William Bradbury met great success by composing hymn tunes and religious songs in a lively, popular style. He also helped establish music programs in New York public schools, served a church, and co-founded a piano company.*

Tune: SOLID ROCK L.M. with refrain
*William B. Bradbury, 1863*

# Give Up Your Anxious Pains

*Paul Gerhardt, 1656*
*Transl. Madeleine Forell Marshall, 1994*

1 Give up your anx - ious pains, con - fu - sion, and re - morse,
2 All things con - form to please the faith - ful when they pray,
3 "Don't let us be dis - mayed by griev - ous so - cial wrong;

To God, who set and still main - tains cre - a - tion's com - plex course.
So fall up - on your trust - ing knees and all to - geth - er say:
Re - spon - sive, ac - tive, un - a - fraid, may we be brave and strong.

God leads what may ap - pear cha - o - tic, ran - dom, wild: So
"O faith - ful God of grace who rules the rag - ing storm, En -
Ex - tend your lov - ing care through all our live - long days; And

God has planned and will make clear a path for you, dear child.
light - en our poor mor - tal race; your prom - ised works per - form."
when we die, bring us to where bright an - gels sing your praise."

*Each word of Martin Luther's German translation of Psalm 37:5 provided a beginning word for Paul Gerhardt's twelve-stanza hymn of comfort. While traveling to America, John Wesley heard Moravians sing this hymn; he later translated it into English.*

Tune:  ICH HALTE TREULICH STILL  S.M.D.
J. S. Bach, 1736

# 405 There Are Some Things I May Not Know
## (Yes, God Is Real)

*Kenneth Morris, 1942; alt.*

**Unison**

1 There are some things | I may not know, | there are some
2 Some folks may doubt, | some folks may scorn, | all can de -
3 I can - not tell | just how you felt | when Je - sus

plac - es I can't go, | But I am sure | of this one
sert and leave me a - lone, | But as for me | I'll take God's
took your sins a - way, | But since that day, | yes, since that

thing, | that God is real | for I can feel | God deep with - in.
part, | for God is real | and I can feel | God in my heart.
hour, | God has been real | for I can feel | God's ho - ly power.

**Refrain**

Yes, God is real, | real in my soul; | yes, God is real | for God has

This gospel song by Kenneth Morris is considered his most
successful composition. It has become a standard in many
African-American churches, and has been translated into
twenty-four languages. Morris is also known for his musical
arrangements, which number more than 3,000.

Tune: YES, GOD IS REAL 8.8.8.12. with refrain
*Kenneth Morris, 1942*

washed and made me whole; God's love for me is like pure gold, yes, God is real for I can feel God in my soul.

# Not with Naked Eye, Not with Human Sense    406

*Dan Damon, 1989*

John 1:18; 20:26–29

1 Not with na-ked eye, not with hu-man sense:
2 Not a gold-en king, not a might-y queen:
3 Chil-dren learn of God sit-ting in the grass,
4 Thom-as saw the Christ break-ing earth's rou-tine;
5 Not with craft-ed scope, not with crys-tal lens:

Through the eye of faith ob-serve om - ni - po - tence.
God's in earth and heaven and all that lies be - tween.
Touch-ing, tast-ing, smil-ing, hear-ing Je - sus pass.
Blessed are those who trust the Ho-ly One un - seen.
Vi - sion of the Christ be-gins where see - ing ends.

*Dan Damon commented about this hymn: "People who do not see with their physical eyes learn to rely on other senses. Sometimes faith is one of them." The tune is named for Valerie Stiteler, a United Church of Christ minister.*

Tune: STITELER 5.5.5.6.
*Dan Damon, 1989*

# 407        How Firm a Foundation

*Isa. 43:2–5; 2 Tim. 2:19; Heb. 13:5*        *"K" in John Rippon's Selection of Hymns, 1787; alt.*

1 How firm a foun - da - tion for you has been laid,
2 "Fear not, I am with you, oh, be not dis - mayed,
3 "When through the deep wa - ters I call you to go,
4 "When through fi - ery tri - als your path - way shall lie,
5 "The soul that on Je - sus has leaned for re - pose,

by God in the Word, in the sac - ri - fice paid!
for I am your God, I will still give you aid;
the riv - ers of woe shall not o - ver you flow;
my grace all - suf - fi - cient shall be your sup - ply;
I will not, I will not de - sert to its foes;

What more can God say than to you has been said,
I'll strength - en you, help you, and cause you to stand
For I will be with you, your trou - bles to bless,
the flame shall not hurt you; for I have de - signed
That soul, though all hell should en - deav - or to shake,

to you, who for ref - uge to Je - sus have fled?
up - held by my gra - cious, om - ni - po - tent hand."
de - liv - er - ing you from your deep - est dis - tress."
your soul to make pure just as gold is re - fined."
I'll nev - er, no nev - er, no nev - er for - sake!"

*In 1787, John Rippon, English Baptist clergyman, identified the author of this hymn as "K"; no one has yet verified a complete name. The pentatonic melody has been known by several names since it first appeared in Funk's Genuine Church Music (1832).*

Tune: FOUNDATION 11.11.11.11.
*Early United States melody from Funk's Genuine Church Music, 1832*
*Alternate tune: ADESTE FIDELES*

# All My Hope on God Is Founded

*Joachim Neander, c. 1680*  
*Paraphr. by Robert Bridges, 1899; alt.*

Ps. 62:5–8; 1 Tim. 6:17

1 All my hope on God is found-ed: who else can my hope re-new?  
2 Well does the al-might-y Giv-er boun-teous gifts on us be-stow!  
3 In glad hymns to God e-ter-nal sac-ri-fice of praise be done,

Still through change and chance God guides me, on-ly good and on-ly true.  
With de-light our souls are nour-ished; plea-sure leads us where we go.  
high a-bove all prais-es prais-ing for the love in Christ made known.

God un-known, grace a-lone, calls my heart to be God's own.  
At God's hand does love stand; joy a-waits each new com-mand.  
Hear Christ's call, one and all; those who fol-low shall not fall.

*British composer Herbert Howells studied with Charles V. Stanford at the Royal College of Music in London and later taught there. The tune was composed for an English school and was named for Howells' son who died in childhood.*

Tune: MICHAEL 8.7.8.7.3.3.7.  
*Herbert Howells, 1930, 1977*

# I Heard My Mother Say

*African-American traditional*

1 I heard my moth-er say, I heard my moth-er say,
2 At mid-night was my cry, at mid-night was my cry,
3 Oh, when I come to die, oh, when I come to die,
4 In the morn-ing when I rise, in the morn-ing when I rise,

I heard my moth-er say, "Give me Je - sus."
at mid-night was my cry, "Give me Je - sus."
oh, when I come to die, give me Je - sus.
in the morn-ing when I rise, give me Je - sus.

*Refrain*

Give me Je - sus, give me Je - sus, you may

have all this world, give me Je - sus.

*This spiritual is better known as "Give Me Jesus." The musical arrangement was created for* The New Century Hymnal *by Joyce Finch Johnson, organist and professor of music at Spelman College, Atlanta, Georgia.*

Tune:  GIVE ME JESUS  6.6.10. with refrain
*African-American traditional*
*Harm. Joyce Finch Johnson, 1992*

# If You But Trust in God to Guide You

*Georg Neumark, 1641*
*Transl. Catherine Winkworth, 1863; alt.*

*Ps. 55:22*

1 If you but trust in God to guide you, with hope-ful heart through
2 On - ly be still, and wait God's plea - sure in cheer-ful hope, with
3 Sing, pray, and keep God's ways un - swerv-ing; of - fer your ser - vice

all your ways, you will find strength, with God be - side you,
heart con - tent, trust-ing that grace which knows no mea-sure
faith - ful - ly, and trust God's word, though un - de - serv-ing,

to bear the worst of e - vil days; For those who trust God's
will by un - bound - ed Love be sent; Nor doubt our in - most
there find the truth to set you free; God will not fail to

change-less love build on the rock that will not move.
wants are clear to One who holds us al - ways near.
guide and bless those who em - brace God's faith - ful - ness.

*The comforting words of Psalm 55:22 inspired this beautiful*
*hymn by Georg Neumark, who wrote both words and music.*
*Neumark was a German poet who suffered much during the*
*Thirty Years' War.*

Tune: NEUMARK 9.8.9.8.8.8.
*Georg Neumark, 1657*

# 411 Praise the Source of Faith and Learning

*Prov. 2:6*

*Thomas H. Troeger, 1987, 1989*

1 Praise the Source of faith and learn - ing that has sparked and stoked the mind
2 God of wis - dom, we ac - knowl-edge that our sci - ence and our art
3 May our faith re - deem the blun - der of be - liev - ing that our thought
4 As two cur - rents in a riv - er fight each oth - er's un - der-tow

with a pas - sion for dis - cern - ing how the world has been de-signed.
and the breadth of hu - man knowl-edge on - ly par - tial truth im - part.
has dis-placed the grounds for won - der which the an - cient proph-ets taught.
till con-verg - ing they de - liv - er one co - her - ent stead - y flow,

Let the sense of won-der flow - ing from the won - ders we sur - vey
Far be-yond our cal - cu - la - tion lies a depth we can - not sound
May our learn-ing curb the er - ror which un - think - ing faith can breed
Blend, O God, our faith and learn-ing till they carve a sin - gle course,

*Thomas Troeger's text was commissioned by Duke University to honor Waldo Beach, a retired professor of ethics who has written about the theology conveyed by hymns. Composer William Albright has served as professor of music at the University of Michigan.*

Tune: PROCESSION 8.7.8.7.D.
*William Albright, 1992*
*Alternate tune: HYFRYDOL*

keep our faith for - ev - er grow-ing and re - new our need to pray:
where your pur-pose for cre - a - tion and the pulse of life are found.
lest we jus - ti - fy some ter - ror with an an - ti - quat - ed creed.
till they join as one, re - turn - ing praise and thanks to you, their Source.

## God Moves in a Mysterious Way  412

*William Cowper, 1774; alt.*  Ps. 77:19; Rom. 11:33–36

1 God moves in a mys - te - rious way great won - ders to per - form;
2 Deep in un - fath - om - a - ble mines of nev - er - fail - ing skill
3 O fear - ful saints, fresh cour-age take, the clouds you so much dread
4 Judge not God's way through hu - man sense, but trust un - fail-ing grace:

God plants firm foot - steps in the sea and rides up - on the storm.
God floods the earth with bright de - signs, guards with a sov-ereign will.
Are big with mer - cy and shall break in bless - ings on your head.
Be - hind a frown-ing prov - i - dence there shines a smil-ing face.

5  God's pur-pos-es will rip-en fast,
   un-fold-ing ev-ery hour;
   The bud may have a bit-ter taste,
   but sweet will be the flower.

6  Our un-be-lief is sure to err
   and scan God's work in vain;
   God is God's own in-ter-pret-er,
   whose truth shall be made plain.

*This hymn by the English poet William Cowper seems to have been written a few months after his suicide attempt. It was first published in John Newton's* Twenty-six Letters on Religious Subjects.

Tune: DUNDEE C.M.
The 150 Psalms of David, *Edinburgh, 1615*

# By Gracious Powers

*Dietrich Bonhoeffer, 1944*
*Transl. Fred Pratt Green, 1972; alt.*

Unison

1 By gra-cious powers so won-der-ful-ly shel-tered,
2 Yet is this heart by its old foe tor-ment-ed,
3 And when this cup you give is filled to brim-ming
4 Yet when a-gain in this same world you give us

and con-fi-dent-ly wait-ing, come what may,
still e-vil days bring bur-dens hard to bear;
with bit-ter sor-row, hard to un-der-stand,
the joy we had, the bright-ness of your sun,

We know that God is with us night and morn-ing,
O give our fright-ened souls the sure sal-va-tion
We take it thank-ful-ly and with-out trem-bling,
We shall re-mem-ber all the days we lived through,

and nev-er fails to greet us each new day.
for which, O God, you taught us to pre-pare.
out of so good and so be-loved a hand.
and our whole life shall then be yours a-lone.

*Dietrich Bonhoeffer, theologian, professor, and leader of the German Opposition, composed the poem on which this hymn is based, "New Year 1945," while imprisoned by the Gestapo in Berlin. Four months later, Bonhoeffer was executed by special order of Himmler.*

Tune: BONHOEFFER 11.10.11.10.
*Herbert G. Hobbs, 1976*
*Harm. Jan Helmut Wubbena, 1976*

# Incarnate God, Immortal Love

*Alfred Tennyson, 1850; alt.*

*2 Cor. 5:7*

1 In - car - nate God, im - mor - tal Love, whom we, that
2 You will not leave us in the dust; you gave us
3 In you meet hu - man and di - vine, the high - est,
4 Our lit - tle sys - tems have their day; they have their

have not seen your face, by faith, and faith a -
life, we know not why. We trust we were not
ho - liest un - ion known. We false - ly call our
day and cease to be; They are but fleet - ing

lone, em - brace, be - liev - ing where we can - not prove:
made to die, for you have made us, you are just.
powers our own un - til our wills with yours com - bine.
cer - tain - ty, and you, O Christ, are more than they.

5  We have but faith; we can-not know,
   for knowl-edge is of things proved true;
   And yet we trust it comes from you,
   a sign of prom-ise; let it grow.

6  Let knowl-edge grow from more to more,
   but more of rev-erence in us dwell;
   That mind and soul, ac-cord-ing well,
   may make one music as be-fore.

*The English poet laureate Alfred Tennyson included an eleven-stanza prologue to his* In Memoriam *(1850), written in memory of a friend, Arthur Hallam. Some stanzas of the prologue have been selected to form this hymn.*

Tune: ROCKINGHAM L.M.
*Anon.*
*Adapt. Edward Miller, 1790*

# 415 God's Actions, Always Good and Just

*Samuel Rodigast, 1675; transl. Madeleine Forell Marshall, 1992*

1 God's ac-tions, al-ways good and just, pro-ceed from God's per-fec-tion; So we our world's af-fairs en-trust to god-ly just pro-tec-tion. When all I see is mis-e-ry, when rank op-pres-sion pains me, God's right-eous-ness sus-tains me.

2 My gra-cious guide in righ-teous ways, God sets my course of ac-tion; And I may trace life's seem-ing maze as-sured of sat-is-fac-tion. For, just and fair, God shall re-pair all e-vil and dis-tor-tion, and can-cel each mis-for-tune.

3 The lamp of truth, my God dis-pels the shad-ows that a-larm me. A liv-ing shield, my God re-pels the death-beams that would harm me. The truth will win, the light break in, a-chiev-ing rev-e-la-tion, com-plet-ing my sal-va-tion.

4 God's ways are ev-er lov-ing-kind, what-ev-er our de-lu-sion, And if I taste the bit-ter wine, the cup of my con-fu-sion, Take heart, my soul, for you shall know, sweet com-fort fol-lows sad-ness. The pain shall end in glad-ness.

*When Severus Gastorius suffered a serious illness in 1675, his friend Samuel Rodigast wrote this hymn to comfort him. Gastorius was a German Lutheran music director at Jena. Rodigast was a scholar and educator in Berlin.*

Tune: WAS GOTT TUT 8.7.8.7.8.7.7.
*Severus Gastorius, c. 1675*

# I Will Trust in the Lord

*African-American traditional*

*Ps. 37:3*

1 I will trust in the Lord, I will trust in the
2 I'm gon-na treat ev-ery-bod-y right, I'm gon-na treat ev-ery-bod-y

Lord, I will trust in the Lord, till I die.
right, I'm gon-na treat ev-ery-bod-y right, till I die.

I will trust in the Lord, I will trust in the
I'm gon-na treat ev-ery-bod-y right, I'm gon-na treat ev-ery-bod-y

Lord, I will trust in the Lord, till I die.
right, I'm gon-na treat ev-ery-bod-y right, till I die.

*One use of this traditional song has been in African-American churches, where someone giving a testimony would raise a verse or two, and be joined by the congregation in singing. Then the person would build a testimony upon the hymn's thematic language.*

Tune:  TRUST IN THE LORD  Irr.
*African-American traditional*
*Arr. Jeffrey Radford, 1993*

# 417          This Is a Day of New Beginnings

2 Cor. 5:16–17

*Brian Wren, 1978; rev. 1983*

1 This is a day of new be - gin - nings, time to re -
2 For by the life and death of Je - sus, God's might - y
3 Then let us, with the Spir - it's dar - ing, step from the
4 Christ is a - live, and goes be - fore us to show and
\* In faith we'll gath - er 'round the ta - ble to taste and

mem - ber and move on, time to be - lieve what love is
Spir - it, now as then, can make for us a world of
past and leave be - hind our dis - ap - point - ment, guilt, and
share what love can do. This is a day of new be -
share what love can do. This is a day of new be -

*1–3*

bring - ing, lay - ing to rest the pain that's gone.
dif - ference, as faith and hope are born a - gain.
griev - ing, seek - ing new paths, and sure to find.
gin - nings— our God is mak - ing all things new.
gin - nings— our God is mak - ing all things new.

*4*

\*Alternate fourth stanza for Holy Communion

*Brian Wren wrote this hymn in 1978 for a New Year's Day service in Oxford, England. The music is by the editor of two hymnals of the United Methodist Church and was composed for the original Wren text.*

Tune: BEGINNINGS 9.8.9.8.
*Carlton R. Young, 1987*

# My Faith, It Is an Oaken Staff

*Thomas T. Lynch, 1855; alt.*

1 My faith, it is an oak-en staff, the trav-eler's well-loved aid;
2 My guide is Je-sus Christ whose steps, when trav-el-ers have trod,
3 My faith, it is an oak-en staff, O let me on it lean.

My faith, it is a song of trust, sus-tains me un-dis-mayed.
Wheth-er be-neath was flint-y rock or yield-ing grass-y sod,
My faith pro-vides the ground of hope, sup-ports a pur-pose keen.

I'll trav-el on and still be stirred by si-lent thought or so-cial
They car-ried on, their joy un-spent; through pain and trial they on-ward
Your Spir-it, God, up-on me send, that I may be what you in-

word; By all my per-ils un-de-terred, a pil-grim un-a-fraid.
went, Un-stayed by plea-sure, still they bent their zeal-ous course to God.
tend. With pa-tient cour-age, we'll con-tend as ra-diant saints se-rene.

*A gifted Congregational minister in London, Thomas Toke Lynch was the subject of controversy within the churches upon the publication of his hymn collection,* The Rivulet, *which received poor reviews. This hymn was labeled Lynch's "best" when it appeared in* Congregational Praise *(1951).*

Tune: THE STAFF OF FAITH  8.6.8.6.8.8.8.6.
*Swiss folk melody*
Fellowship Hymn Book, *1910*

# 419

# Nun danket alle Gott
## (Now Thank We All Our God)

*Sir. 50:20–24; 39:35; Ps. 67*

*Martin Rinkart, 1647; transl. Catherine Winkworth, 1858; alt.*

1 Nun dank - et al - le Gott, mit Herz - en, Mund und Händ - en,
1 Now thank we all our God with heart and hands and voic - es,
2 O may this boun-teous God through all our life be near us,
3 All praise and thanks to God our Mak - er now be giv - en,

der gro - sse Ding - e tut an uns und al - len End - en;
Who won - drous things has done, in whom this world re - joic - es,
With ev - er joy - ful hearts and bless - ed peace to cheer us,
To Christ, and Spir - it, too, our help in high - est heav - en,

der uns von Mut - ter - leib und Kind - es - bein - en an
Who, from our par - ents' arms, has blessed us on our way
And keep us still in grace, and guide us when per - plexed,
The one e - ter - nal God, whom earth and heaven a - dore,

un - zäh - lig viel zu gut bis hier - her hat ge - tan.
With count-less gifts of love, and still is ours to - day.
And free us from all ills in this world and the next.
For thus it was, is now, and shall be ev - er - more.

*For much of his life, German Lutheran pastor and musician Martin Rinkart ministered to the walled city of Eisleben amidst the horrors of the Thirty Years' War. This hymn has become one of the most widely used hymns of the church.*

Tune: NUN DANKET  6.7.6.7.6.6.6.6.
*Johann Crüger, 1647*
*Harm. Felix Mendelssohn, 1840*

# We Praise You, O God

*Julia C. Cory, 1902; alt.*

1 We praise you, O God, our Re - deem - er, Cre - a - tor;
2 We wor - ship you, God of our moth - ers and fa - thers;
3 With voic - es u - nit - ed our prais - es we of - fer,

in grate - ful de - vo - tion our trib - ute we bring.
through life's storm and tem - pest our guide you have been.
and glad - ly our song of thanks - giv - ing we raise.

We lay it be - fore you, we kneel and a - dore you;
When per - ils o'er - take us, you nev - er will for - sake us,
Our sins now con - fess - ing, we pray for your bless - ing;

we bless your ho - ly name, glad prais - es we sing.
and with your help, O God, in life's strug - gles we win.
to you, our great Re - deem - er, for - ev - er be praise!

*Julia Bulkley Cady Cory wrote this hymn for Thanksgiving in 1902 at the invitation of the organist of New York's Brick Presbyterian Church who felt that the familiar words to Kremser contained too much militaristic imagery.*

Tune: KREMSER 12.11.12.11.
*Valerius,* Nederlandtsch Gedenkclanck, *1626*

# 421

# We Gather Together

*Netherlands folk hymn, 16th century*
*Transl. Theodore Baker, 1894*
*Adapt. Lavon Bayler, 1992*

1 We gath-er to-geth-er
  to ask for God's bless-ing,
    to live in com-mu-ni-ty,
    seek-ing God's will.
  We come now, as sis-ters
  and broth-ers, con-fess-ing
    the sins that di-vide
    and the wrong in us still.

2 Be-side us, for-giv-ing,
  en-a-bling, sus-tain-ing,
    you call us, O Sav-ior,
    to life that is new.
  You draw us a-way
  from self-cen-tered com-plain-ing.
    You lead us and guide us
    in ways that are true.

3 All praise to the Spir-it,
  pro-vid-er, de-fend-er.
    You of-fer us free-dom,
    to fol-low or stray,
  Em-pow-er-ing all by
  the hope you en-gen-der.
    Grant wis-dom and cour-age
    to fol-low your way.

*The original text of this hymn was one of thanksgiving for The*
*Netherlands' independence from Spanish domination in the*
*sixteenth century. It has been reinterpreted for contemporary*
*congregations by United Church of Christ minister and writer*
*Lavon Bayler.*

Tune:  KREMSER  12.11.12.11.
*16th-century Dutch melody*
*Arr. Edward Kremser, 1877*

# 422

# Come, O Thankful People, Come

*Exod. 23:16*

*St. 1, Henry Alford, 1844; alt.*
*St. 2, Anna Laetitia Aiken Barbauld, 1772; alt.*
*St. 3, composite of Alford and Barbauld; alt.*

*This hymn represents the joining of two Thanksgiving hymns by*
*nineteenth-century poet Henry Alford and eighteenth-century*
*poet Anna Laetitia Aiken Barbauld. The creator of this*
*combined form, which appeared early in the twentieth century,*
*is not known.*

Tune:  ST. GEORGE'S WINDSOR  7.7.7.7.D.
*George J. Elvey, 1858*
*Descant:  H. A. Chambers, 1931*

# 423

# Great Is Your Faithfulness

*Lam. 3:22–23*

*Thomas O. Chisholm, 1923; alt.*

1 Great is your faith - ful - ness, O God, Cre - a - tor,*
2 Sum - mer and win - ter, and spring-time and har - vest,
3 Par - don for sin and a peace so en - dur - ing,

with you no shad - ow of turn - ing we see.
sun, moon, and stars in their cours - es a - bove,
your own dear pres - ence to cheer and to guide.

You do not change, your com - pas - sions they fail not;
Join with all na - ture in man - i - fold wit - ness
Strength for to - day and bright hope for to - mor - row,

all of your good - ness for - ev - er will be.
to your great faith - ful - ness, mer - cy, and love.
bless - ings all mine with ten thou - sand be - side.

*originally "my Father"

*This hymn was one of a number sent by poet Thomas O. Chisholm to composer William M. Runyan for musical settings. It became a favorite of Will Houghton, president of Moody Bible Institute, whose enthusiasm helped establish its popularity.*

Tune: FAITHFULNESS 11.10.11.10. with refrain
*William M. Runyan, 1923*

*Refrain*

Great is your faith-ful-ness! Great is your faith-ful-ness! Morn-ing by

morn-ing new mer-cies I see; All I have need-ed your

hand has pro-vid-ed, Great is your faith-ful-ness, God, un-to me!

# 424

# Praise Our God Above

*Matt. 6:25–33; Deut. 8:1–3, 6–10*

*Tzu-chen Chao, 1931*
*Transl. Frank W. Price, 1953; alt.*

Unison

1 Praise our God a-bove, Source of bound-less love: spring wind,
2 God's care like a cloak wraps us hum-ble folk, makes all

sum-mer rain, then the har-vest grain; Pearl-y
green things grow, rip-ens what we sow. Through God

rice and corn, fra-grant au-tumn morn.
we are strong; sing our har-vest song.

Though our work is hard, God gives us re-ward.
Sing praise, field and flower, praise God's might-y power.

*Frank Price, a Presbyterian missionary to China, titled this hymn*
*"Harvest Song" in* Chinese Christian Hymns—*a collection of*
*English hymn translations. The tune is a Confucian chant*
*proclaiming peace, harmonized by W. H. Wong for the 1977*
*edition of* Hymns of Universal Praise.

Tune: HSUAN P'ING 5.5.5.5.D.
*Confucian Dacheng chant*
*Arr. W. H. Wong, 1973*

# For the Fruit of All Creation

*Fred Pratt Green, 1970*

1 For the fruit of all cre-a-tion, thanks be to God.
2 In the just re-ward of la-bor, God's will is done.
3 For the har-vests of the Spir-it, thanks be to God.

For God's gifts to ev-ery na-tion, thanks be to God.
In the help we give our neigh-bor, God's will is done.
For the good we all in-her-it, thanks be to God.

For the plow-ing, sow-ing, reap-ing, si-lent growth while we are sleep-ing,
In our world-wide task of car-ing for the hun-gry and de-spair-ing,
For the won-ders that as-tound us, for the truths that still con-found us,

Fu-ture needs in earth's safe-keep-ing, thanks be to God.
In the har-vests we are shar-ing, God's will is done.
Most of all that love has found us, thanks be to God.

*This text was written in response to a request for a new harvest hymn for an existing tune. After its publication in England in 1970, it became popular in many countries and can be found set to various tunes.*

Tune: AR HYD Y NOS 8.4.8.4.8.8.8.4.
*Welsh traditional melody*
Musical Relicks of the Welsh Bards, *Dublin, 1784*
*Harm. L. O. Emerson, 1906*
*For another harmonization, see 82*

# 426
# O God, Whose Steadfast Love

*Gen. 18:9–15; 1 Sam. 1:1–20; Luke 1:26–56; 2:1–7*

*James L. Haddix, 1986; rev. 1994*

1 O God, whose stead-fast love true moth-er-hood has blessed;
2 Your prom-is-es, O God, so sure through-out the years,
3 In your great love, O God, full par-ent-hood is known:
4 May your house-hold of faith one fam-i-ly be - come,

who shields the in - fant small up - on its moth-er's breast:
have lived in moth-ers' hearts, have bloomed from moth-ers' tears.
a fa - ther mourns his child, a moth-er's strength is shown.
that love may be in - creased and none may be a - lone;

Em - brace us, too, O God, our God, and hold us in your
So Sar - ah laughed, and Han - nah wept, and sing-ing Mar - y
Let par - ents' faith - ful lives un - bind your love that through them
That moth-er's love and fa - ther's care and chil-dren's joy we

lov - ing arms, and hold us in your lov - ing arms.
se - crets kept, and sing - ing Mar - y se - crets kept.
we might find Christ's deep - er love for hu - man - kind.
all may share, and chil - dren's joy we all may share.

*United Church of Christ minister James Haddix wrote this text for the "Festival of the Christian Home." It was dedicated and sung to his mother, Margaret Ann Lewis Haddix, at a reception in Missouri recognizing her thirty-year career as a first-grade teacher.*

Tune: RHOSYMEDRE 6.6.6.6.8.8.8.
*John D. Edwards, c. 1840*

# God Made from One Blood

**427**

*Thomas H. Troeger, 1988*

1 God made from one blood all the fam-ilies of earth,
2 We turn to you, God, with our thanks and our tears
3 Through fam-ilies we've tast-ed the val-ue of trust
4 Help fam-ilies in all of their var-i-ous forms

the cir-cles of nur-ture that raise us from birth,
for all of the fam-ilies we've known through the years,
and felt what it means to be lov-ing and just,
to face with in-teg-ri-ty strug-gles and storms;

Com-pan-ions who join us to work through each stage
The in-ti-mate net-works on whom we de-pend
Yet fam-ilies have al-so be-trayed their best goals,
Grant peace to our homes that will nur-ture the bud

of child-hood and youth and a-dult-hood and age.
of par-ents and part-ners and chil-dren and friends.
mis-treat-ing their mem-bers and bruis-ing their souls.
of peace for the fam-ilies you made from one blood.

*This text was commissioned by Yale University Press for A New
Hymnal for Colleges and Schools (1992) to provide a hymn that
recognizes the many different kinds of families that are
represented when a campus congregation gathers to worship.*

Tune: ST. DENIO 11.11.11.11.
*Adapt. from a Welsh ballad in John Roberts'*
Caniadaeth y Cysegr, *1839*

# 428

# Malipayong Adlaw'ng Natawhan
## (What a Glad Day)

Grace R. Tabada
*Transl. Fé Nebres, 1993*

Ma-li-pa-yong ad-law'ng na-taw-han ka-ni-mo a-mong ig-
What a glad day, to-day's your birth-day, our lov-ing greet-ings we

so-on, Ma-li-pa-yong ad-law'ng na-taw-han, pa-na-
say! What a glad day, to-day's your birth-day, may God's

la-ngi-nan ka sa Dios. Ma-ga-du-yog ka-
bless-ings up-on you stay! We your friends join with

mi sa i-mo nga pag-sa-u-log. Ma-li-
you in cel-e-brat-ing this day! What a

It is the custom of some churches in the Visayas provinces in
the Philippines to serenade individuals at early dawn on their
birthday. This song by Grace Tabada is a new addition to the
serenaders' repertoire.

Tune: TABADA 9.8.9.8.6.8.9.8.8.
Grace R. Tabada
Arr. Vérne de la Peña, 1994

pa - yong ad - law'ng na - taw - han, pa - na -
glad day, to - day's your birth - day, may God's

la - ngi-nan ka sa Dios. Pa - na - la - ngi-nan ka sa Dios.
bless - ings up-on you stay! May God's bless - ings up-on you stay!

# 429

# God, Bless Our Homes

*Frank von Christierson, 1957*

1 God, bless our homes with peace and love and laugh - ter,
2 May ev - ery heart re - ceive God's lov - ing spir - it
3 For - give the hurts our self - ish - ness in - flict - ed
4 O God, in grat - i - tude for homes and loved ones,

with un - der - stand-ing and with loy - al - ty.
and know the truth that makes life tru - ly free;
on those we love and those who love us best.
we o - pen now our hearts to hu - man - kind.

May we to - geth - er fol - low Christ our Sav - ior
Then, in that spir - it may we live u - nit - ed,
Christ, heal the scars, and draw us all to - geth - er
Grant us your spir - it— love for all our neigh - bors—

*Frank von Christierson was born in Finland and came to the United States as a child. After completing degrees at Stanford University and San Francisco Theological Seminary, he ministered to and founded several Presbyterian congregations in California.*

Tune: CHARTERHOUSE 11.10.11.10.
*David Evans, 1927*

Music Copyright ©, Oxford University Press. From the *REVISED CHURCH HYMNARY*, 1927.

and know the bless-ing of com - mu - ni - ty.
and find in God our deep se - cu - ri - ty.
in God whose will is peace and joy and rest.
so in your peace may we our con - cord find.

# Praise to God, Your Praises Bring    430

*William C. Gannett, 1872; alt.*

1 Praise to God, your prais-es bring; hearts bow down and voic - es sing
2 Praise God for the bud-ding green, A - pril's res - ur - rec - tion scene;
3 Praise God for the sum-mer rain, feed - ing, day and night, the grain;
4 Praise God for the gar - den root, mead-ow grass, and or - chard fruit:

Prais - es to the glo - rious One, all God's year of won - der done.
Praise God for the shin - ing hours, star-ring all the land with flowers.
Praise God for the ti - ny seed, hold-ing all the world shall need.
Praise for hills and val - leys broad, each the ta - ble of our God.

5  Praise God for the win-ter's rest,
    snow that falls on na-ture's breast;
   Praise for hap-py dreams of birth,
    brood-ing in the qui-et earth.

6  For God's year of won-der done,
    praise to the all-glo-rious One!
   Hearts bow down and voic-es raise
    songs of thanks for all God's days.

*Most of William C. Gannett's hymns were written for special occasions, including this one for a harvest festival in St. Paul, Minnesota. Gannett and Frederick L. Hosmer, both Unitarian ministers, edited* The Thought of God in Hymns and Poems.

Tune: SAVANNAH 7.7.7.7.
The Foundery Collection, *1742*

# 431 Now Greet the Swiftly Changing Year

*Luke 2:8–14*

*17th-century Slovak*
*Transl. Jaroslav J. Vajda, 1969; alt.*

1. Now greet the swift - ly chang - ing year with
2. Christ's love a - bun - dant far ex - ceeds the
3. With such a God to lead our way in
4. "All glo - ry be to God on high and

joy and pen - i - tence sin - cere; re - joice, re - joice, with
vol - ume of a whole year's needs; re - joice, re - joice, with
haz - ard and pros - per - i - ty, what need we fear in
peace on earth," the an - gels cry; re - joice, re - joice, with

thanks em - brace an - oth - er year of grace.
thanks em - brace an - oth - er year of grace.
earth or space in this new year of grace?
thanks em - brace an - oth - er year of grace.

*This seventeenth-century New Year's hymn was included in the*
*Tranoscius, a collection published by the Czech Lutheran pastor*
*Juraj Tranovský (1591–1637). Translator Jaroslav Vajda is also*
*known for his original hymn texts.*

Tune: SIXTH NIGHT 8.8.8.6.
*Alfred V. Fedak, 1984*

# 'Tis Winter Now; the Fallen Snow

**432**

*Samuel Longfellow, 1864; alt.*

Unison

1 'Tis win-ter now; the fal-len snow has left the
2 And yet God's love is not with-drawn; new life with-
3 And though a-broad the sharp winds blow, and skies are
4 O God! who gives the win-ter's cold, as well as

heavens all cold-ly clear; Through leaf-less boughs the sharp winds
in the keen air breathes; God's beau-ty paints the crim-son
chill, and frosts are keen, Home clos-er draws its cir-cle
sum - mer's joy-ous rays, Us warm-ly in your love en-

blow, and all the earth lies dead and drear.
dawn, and clothes the boughs with glit-tering wreaths.
now, and warm-er glows the light with-in.
fold, and keep us through life's win-try days.

*Samuel Longfellow served as a Unitarian minister in Fall River, Massachusetts, Brooklyn, New York, and finally, Germantown, Pennsylvania. Among his published works was a biography of his brother, Henry Wadsworth Longfellow. With Samuel Johnson he published* Hymns of the Spirit.

Tune: DANBY L.M.
*Traditional English melody*
*Arr. Ralph Vaughan Williams, 1925*
*Alternate tune: O WALY WALY*

# 433

# In the Bulb There Is a Flower

*Natalie Sleeth, 1985*

*Unison*

1 In the bulb there is a flow - er; in the seed, an ap-ple tree;
2 There's a song in ev-ery si - lence, seek-ing word and mel-o - dy;
3 In our end is our be - gin - ning; in our time, in - fin - i - ty;

in co-coons, a hid-den prom-ise: but-ter-flies will soon be free!
there's a dawn for ev-ery dark-ness, bring-ing hope to you and me.
in our doubt there is be-liev-ing; in our life, e - ter-ni - ty.

In the cold and snow of win-ter there's a spring that waits to be,
From the past will come the fu - ture; what it holds, a mys-ter - y,
In our death, a res - ur - rec - tion; at the last, a vic-to - ry,

un-re-vealed un-til its sea - son, some-thing God a-lone can see.
un-re-vealed un-til its sea - son, some-thing God a-lone can see.
un-re-vealed un-til its sea - son, some-thing God a-lone can see.

*Natalie Sleeth composed her "Hymn of Promise" first*
*as a choral anthem and then adapted it to this version for*
*congregational singing. It was dedicated to her husband,*
*Ronald Sleeth, who died shortly after she completed it.*

Tune: PROMISE 8.7.8.7.D.
*Natalie Sleeth, 1985*

# All Beautiful the March of Days

**434**

*Frances W. Wile, 1910; alt.*

1 All beau-ti-ful the march of days, as sea-sons come and go;
2 O'er bril-liant fields of spar-kling snow the ra-diant morns un-fold;
3 O you from whose un-fath-omed law the year in beau-ty flows,

the hand that shaped the rose has formed the crys-tal of the snow,
The sol-emn splen-dors of the night burn bright-ly through the cold.
your-self the splen-did vi-sion seen in crys-tal and in rose,

Has sent the sil-ver frost of heaven, the flow-ing wa-ters sealed,
Life mounts in ev-ery puls-ing vein, love deep-ens 'round the hearth,
The pass-ing days with grace de-clare, and pass-ing nights pro-claim,

And laid a si-lent love-li-ness on hill and wood and field.
And clear-er sounds the an-gel hymn, "Good will to all on earth."
In ev-er-chang-ing words of light, the won-der of your name.

*Frances Wile wrote this hymn extolling the beauty of winter
at the suggestion of her pastor, William Gannett, and Frederick
Hosmer, both of whom were hymnwriters.*

Tune: FOREST GREEN C.M.D.
*Traditional English melody
Harm. Ralph Vaughan Williams, 1906*

Harmonization Copyright ©, Oxford University Press. From *The English Hymnal 1906.*

# 435 Each Winter as the Year Grows Older

*William Gay, 1969; alt.*

1 Each win-ter as the year grows old-er, we all grow old-er too. The chill sets in a lit-tle cold-er; the ver-i-ties I knew seem shak-en and un-true.

2 When race and class cry out for trea-son, when si-rens call for war, They o-ver-shout the voice of rea-son, and scream till we ig-nore all we held dear be-fore.

3 But I be-lieve be-yond be-liev-ing, that life can spring from death; That growth can flow-er from our griev-ing; that we can catch our breath and turn trans-fixed by faith.

4 So e-ven as the sun is turn-ing to jour-ney to the north, The liv-ing flame, in se-cret burn-ing, can kin-dle on the earth, and bring God's love to birth.

5 O Child of ec-sta-sy and sor-rows, O Child of peace and pain, Bright-en to-day's world by to-mor-row's, re-new our lives a-gain; Christ Je-sus, come and reign!

*This hymn is a collaboration between United Church of Christ minister William Gay and composer-organist Annabeth McClelland Gay. It is one of several Christmas carols the couple wrote to send to their friends during the Vietnam War era of the 1960s.*

Tune: CAROL OF HOPE 9.6.9.6.6.
*Annabeth McClelland Gay, 1969*

# God of Grace and God of Glory

**436**

*Harry Emerson Fosdick, 1930; alt.*

1 God of grace and God of glory, on your people
2 From the e - vils that sur - round us and as - sail the
3 Cure your chil - dren's war - ring mad - ness; bend our pride to
4 Set our feet on loft - y plac - es; gird our lives that
5 Save us from weak res - ig - na - tion to the e - vils

pour your power; crown your an - cient church - 's sto - ry;
Sav - ior's ways, from the fears that long have bound us—
your con - trol. Shame our reck - less, self - ish glad - ness,
they may be ar - mored with all Christ - like grac - es,
we de - plore; let the search for your sal - va - tion

bring its bud to glo - rious flower. Grant us wis - dom, grant us cour - age,
free our hearts for faith and praise. Grant us wis - dom, grant us cour - age,
rich in things and poor in soul. Grant us wis - dom, grant us cour - age,
in the fight to set us free. Grant us wis - dom, grant us cour - age,
be our glo - ry ev - er - more. Grant us wis - dom, grant us cour - age,

for the fac - ing of this hour, for the fac - ing of this hour.
for the liv - ing of these days, for the liv - ing of these days.
make our bro - ken spir - its whole, make our bro - ken spir - its whole.
in the quest for lib - er - ty, in the quest for lib - er - ty.
serv - ing you whom we a - dore, serv - ing you whom we a - dore.

*Harry Emerson Fosdick, a prophetic preacher and writer, taught at Union Theological Seminary from 1915 to 1946. This hymn was written for the opening service and dedication of Riverside Church, New York City, which he served for twenty years.*

Tune: CWM RHONDDA 8.7.8.7.8.7.7.
*John Hughes, c. 1907*

437

# We Shall Not Give Up the Fight

*South African freedom song*

*Descant, st. 4 only*

we have on-ly start-ed, we

1 & 4 We shall not give up the fight, we have on-ly start-ed, we have on-ly

have on-ly start-ed, we have on-ly start - ed.

start-ed, we have on-ly start - ed. We shall not give up the fight, we

we have on-ly start-ed, we have on-ly start-ed, on-ly start-ed.

*Last time, end*

have on-ly start-ed, we have on-ly start-ed, we have on-ly start-ed.

*This protest song of South Africa came to Europe via Tanzania.*
*It reflects the determined faith and unity of those who fought*
*against apartheid, and offers hope and strength to all Christians*
*struggling against the evils of injustice.*

Tune: ONLY STARTED Irr.
*South African freedom song*

# 438

# When Peace, Like a River
## (It Is Well with My Soul)

*Ps. 146; Col. 1:19–23; 2:13–14; 3 John 1:2*

*Horatio G. Spafford, 1873; alt.*

1 When peace, like a riv - er, up - holds me each day, when
2 Though e - vil should tempt me, though tri - als should come, let
3 My sin— oh, the bliss of this glo - ri - ous thought— my
4 O God, speed the day that is filled with your light, when

sor - rows like sea bil - lows roll, What - ev - er my lot, you have
this blessed as - sur - ance con - trol, That Christ has re - gard - ed my
sin— not in part, but the whole— Is nailed to the cross and I
clouds are rolled back as a scroll; The trum - pet shall sound and the

*Refrain*

taught me to say, "It is well, it is well with my soul."
help - less es - tate, and has paid life and blood for my soul:
bear it no more. Praise the Lord! Praise the Lord, O my soul!
Lord shall ap - pear, "e - ven so"— it is well with my soul.

It is

well with my soul, it is well, it is well with my soul.
It is well with my soul.

*This hymn was written out of grief over the loss of the author's four daughters in the sinking of the SS Ville du Havre. After leaving his Chicago law practice, Horatio G. Spafford and his wife settled in Jerusalem.*

Tune: VILLE DU HAVRE 11.8.11.9. with refrain
*Philip P. Bliss, 1876*

# A Mighty Fortress Is Our God

**439**

*Martin Luther, c. 1529*

*Ps. 46*

*Transl. Frederick H. Hedge, 1853; adapt. Ruth Duck, 1981*

1 A might-y for-tress is our God, a bul-wark nev-er fail-ing,
2 Did we in our own strength con-fide, our striv-ing would be los-ing,
3 And though this world with dev-ils filled should threat-en to un-do us,
4 That word be-yond all earth-ly powers for-ev-er is a-bid-ing;

Our pres-ent help a-mid the flood of mor-tal ills pre-vail-ing.
But there is one who takes our side, the One of God's own choos-ing.
We will not fear for God has willed the truth to tri-umph through us.
The Spir-it and the gifts are ours, for Christ is with us sid-ing.

For still our an-cient foe does seek to work us woe with craft and pow-er
You ask who that may be? Christ Je-sus sets us free! With might-y power to
The powers of e-vil grim, we trem-ble not for them; their rage we can en-
Let goods and kin-dred go, this mor-tal life al-so; the bod-y they may

great, and armed with cru-el hate, on earth with-out an e-qual.
save, vic-to-rious o'er the grave, Christ will pre-vail tri-um-phant.
dure, for lo, their doom is sure: one lit-tle word shall fell them.
kill; God's truth shall tri-umph still; God's reign en-dures for-ev-er.

*There is speculation that this psalm paraphrase was written in 1527 when Martin Luther's friend was burned at the stake, or in 1529, when Lutheran German princes protested the revocation of their liberties. It has been translated into more than fifty languages.*

Tune: EIN' FESTE BURG (isometric) 8.7.8.7.6.6.6.6.7.
*Martin Luther, c. 1529*
*Harm. The New Hymnal for American Youth, 1930; alt.*
*For another version, see 440*

# 440

# A Mighty Fortress Is Our God

*Ps. 46*

*Martin Luther, c. 1529*
*Transl. Madeleine Forell Marshall, 1993*

1 A might-y for-tress is our God, our strong and sure pro-tec - tion;
2 These hu-man hands, for all their skill, can-not shape our sal-va - tion.
3 When e - vil pow-ers rage and swear and threat-en mass de-struc - tion,
4 God's ev - er - last - ing Word a - bides, our strong and sure sal-va - tion.

Our God, who loves us, has re - solved to free us from sub-jec - tion.
We need a cham-pion, one who will a - chieve our lib - er - a - tion.
When we are tempt-ed to de - spair, to yield to their se - duc - tion—
The Spir - it here and now pro - vides rich gifts and con - so - la - tion.

With bold Sa - tan - ic pride and ha - tred well sup - plied,
Who is there, good and brave, with strength and will to save
Then may we stand as - sured by God's most ho - ly Word,
Let wealth and fam - ily go, this bod - y be brought low.

the dead - ly force of sin has sworn to do us in.
our weak and fear - ful race? Who will our cause em - brace?
the e - vil one shall fail, God's righ - teous-ness pre - vail:
What - ev - er loss we bear God will at last re - pair.

*Reformation-era psalm and hymn tunes usually did not have regular rhythms, but combined duple and triple groupings. This version of the tune is much as Martin Luther wrote it. Later generations "squared up" the rhythm, as in the previous setting.*

Tune: EIN' FESTE BURG
(rhythmic) 8.7.8.7.6.6.6.6.7.
*Martin Luther, c. 1529*
*For another version, see 439*

Mere hu - man strength will per - ish.
God's on - ly Child, Christ Je - sus!
Then why should we be fear - ful?
God's realm is ours for - ev - er.

## Jesus, Savior, Pilot Me 441

*Edward Hopper, 1871; alt.*

*Mark 4:35–41*

1 Je - sus, Sav - ior, pi - lot me o - ver life's tem-pes-tuous sea;
2 As a moth - er stills her child, you can hush the o - cean wild;
3 When at last I near the shore, and the fear - ful break-ers roar,

Un - known waves be - fore me roll, hid - ing rock and treach-erous shoal;
Bois-terous waves o - bey your will when you say to them, "Be still."
Keep-ing me from peace-ful rest, then, while lean-ing on your breast,

Chart and com - pass ev - er be; Je - sus, Sav - ior, pi - lot me.
Won-drous Sov - ereign of the sea, Je - sus, Sav - ior, pi - lot me.
May I hear your words so true, "Fear not, I will pi - lot you."

*Inspired by the many sailors in his congregation in New York
City, Edward Hopper wrote these lines. They were first sung for
an anniversary service of the American Seamen's Friend Society
at Broadway Tabernacle (Congregational).*

Tune: PILOT 7.7.7.7.7.7.
*John E. Gould, 1871*

# 442

# I'm Pressing on the Upward Way
## (Higher Ground)

*Johnson Oatman, Jr., 1892; alt.*

1 I'm press-ing on the up-ward way, new heights I'm gain-ing ev-ery
2 My heart has no de-sire to stay where doubts a-rise and fears dis-
3 I want to live be-yond the world, though Sa-tan's darts at me are
4 I want to scale the ut-most height, and catch a gleam of glo-ry

day; Still pray-ing as I'm on-ward bound, "O plant me,
may; Though some may dwell where these a-bound, my prayer, my
hurled; For faith has caught a joy-ful sound, the song of
bright; But still I'll pray till heaven I've found, "God, lead me

*Refrain*

God, on high-er ground."
aim is high-er ground.
saints on high-er ground. O lift me up, and I shall be by faith in heaven e-ter-nal-ly,
on to high-er ground."

A high-er plane than I have found, O plant me, God, on high-er ground.

*Johnson Oatman, Jr., wrote hymns while in the insurance business in Mount Holly, New Jersey. Words for more than 5,000 gospel songs are credited to him. Iowa-born Charles Gabriel taught singing schools and compiled many collections of gospel and Sunday School songs.*

Tune: HIGHER GROUND L.M. with refrain
*Charles H. Gabriel, 1898*

# How Like a Gentle Spirit

443

*C. Eric Lincoln, 1987; alt.*

*1 John 4:16*

*May be sung in unison*

1 How like a gen - tle spir - it deep with - in
2 Let God be God wher - ev - er life may be;
3 God like a moth - er ea - gle hov - ers near
4 When in our vain pre - ten - sions we con - spire
5 Through all our fret - ful claims of sex and race

God reins our fer - vent pas - sions day by day,
let ev - ery tongue bear wit - ness to the call;
on might - y wings of pow - er man - i - fest;
to shape God's im - age as we see our own,
the un - i - ver - sal love of God shines through,

and gives us strength to chal - lenge and to win
all hu - man - kind is one by God's de - cree;
God like a gen - tle shep - herd stills our fear,
hark to the voice a - bove our base de - sire;
for God is love tran - scend - ing style and place

de - spite the per - ils of our cho - sen way.
let God be God, let God be God for all.
and com - forts us a - gainst a peace - ful breast.
God is the sculp - tor, we the fash - ioned stone.
and all the i - dle op - tions we pur - sue.

*The author of this hymn has been a professor at several universities and seminaries and has received thirteen honorary degrees. C. Eric Lincoln is also known for his scholarly books on the African-American church and for his poems and novels.*

Tune: SURSUM CORDA 10.10.10.10.
*Alfred M. Smith, 1941*

# 444 We Are Often Tossed and Driven
## (We'll Understand It Better By and By)

*Charles Albert Tindley, c. 1906; alt.*

1 We are of-ten tossed and driven on the rest-less sea of time,
2 We are of-ten des-ti-tute of the things that life de-mands,
3 Tri-als harsh on ev-ery hand, and we can-not un-der-stand
4 Temp-ta-tions, hid-den snares of-ten take us un-a-wares,

Som-ber skies and howl-ing tem-pests oft suc-ceed a bright sun-shine;
Want of food and want of shel-ter, thirst-y hills and bar-ren lands;
All the ways that God would lead us to that bless-ed prom-ised land;
And our hearts are made to bleed for man-y a thought-less word or deed,

In that land of per-fect day, when the mists have rolled a-way,
In our God our trust's as-sured, and ac-cord-ing to the Word,
We are guid-ed by God's eye, and we'll fol-low till we die,
And we won-der, why the test, when we try to do our best,

*to Refrain*

We will un-der-stand it bet-ter by and by.
We will un-der-stand it bet-ter by and by.
For we'll un-der-stand it bet-ter by and by.
But we'll un-der-stand it bet-ter by and by.

*Refrain*

By and by, when the morn-ing comes, when the saints of

God are gath - ered home, We'll tell the sto - ry

how we've o - ver-come: for we'll un - der-stand it bet-ter by and by. (by and by.)

*This is probably Charles A. Tindley's most celebrated gospel hymn of the early twentieth century. Far from being a song that merely looks heavenward, Tindley's song identifies poverty as a social problem.*

Tune: BY AND BY Irr. with refrain
*Charles Albert Tindley, c. 1906*
*Transcribed by F. A. Clark, 1906*

# 445 Lift Your Heads, O Martyrs, Weeping

*Deut. 31:6; Ps. 36:7; Matt. 8:23–26*

*Károly Jeszensky, 1890; based on a hymn by*
*Pauli Joachim (1636–1708); transl. William Tóth, 1938*
*Adapt. Theodore S. Horvath, 1994*

1 Lift your heads, O mar-tyrs, weep - ing, God our Mak - er
2 Though the storms may rage and roil . . . . o'er the vast and
3 Though the hills and vales be riv - en, once con-ceived by
4 Though in chains you now are griev - ing, though a tor - tured

still does reign! You are dai - ly in God's keep - ing,
fear - ful sea, Though you cry from wretch-ed toil, . . . .
God's own hand, Though the signs of earth and heav - en
slave you die, Mar - tyrs, if you die be - liev - ing,

God is with you in your pain. Rise and be of val - iant heart,
"O my Sav - ior, res - cue me!" Though it seems that God does sleep,
sig - nal doom in ev - ery land, Yet, O mar - tyrs, have no fear;
heav-en's path shall o - pen lie. Up - ward gaze and trust a - new,

and with cour-age bear your part; Soon a - gain God's
hope and trust in God still keep; Calm your hearts though
ev - er is your help - er near; God has sought you,
God has not for - sak - en you; You are God's own

*In the Counter-Reformation of the 1670s, Hungarian Reformed ministers were imprisoned, and forty-two who would not recant their faith were sold as galley slaves. This hymn of faith reflects the strain and rhythm of their oars. It eventually became an anthem of liberation for Hungarian Protestants.*

Tune: MAGYAR 8.7.8.7.7.7.8.8.
*"Hymn of the Hungarian Galley Slaves," 1674*
*Adapt. and harm. G. J. Neumann, 1938*

arms will fold     you     to God's lov - ing heart and hold     you.
they be quak - ing,     God is faith - ful, none for - sak - ing.
God has found     you;     God's pro - tec - tive wings sur - round     you.
peo - ple, sure - ly     God will fold God's own se - cure - ly.

# Jesus, Still Lead On                    446

*Nicolaus Ludwig von Zinzendorf, 1721; transl. Jane Borthwick, 1846; alt.*

1 Je - sus, still     lead     on,     till     our     rest     be     won;
2 If     the     way     be     drear,     if     the     woe     be     near,
3 When we     seek     re - lief     from     a     long - felt     grief,
4 Je - sus, still     lead     on,     till     our     rest     be     won;

And     al - though the     way be cheer - less, we will fol - low, calm and fear - less;
Let     not faith - less     fears o'er - take us,     let not faith and     hope for - sake us;
When temp - ta - tions     come al - lur - ing, make us pa - tient and en - dur - ing;
Heaven - ly Lead - er     still di - rect us,     still sup - port, con - sole, pro - tect us,

Guide us     by     your     hand     to     the prom - ised     land.
For through man - y a     woe     to     our home     we     go.
Show us     that     bright     shore     where we weep     no     more.
Guide us     by     your     hand     to     the prom - ised     land.

*Selections from two German hymns written by Count Nicolaus von Zinzendorf in 1721 were combined by Christian Gregor in 1778 to create this hymn. Zinzendorf, who gave the Moravian Brethren asylum on his estate, later became a Moravian pastor.*

Tune: SEELENBRÄUTIGAM 5.5.8.8.5.5.
*Adam Drese* in
Geistreiches Gesangbuch, *Darmstadt, 1698*

# 447

# Beams of Heaven as I Go

*Charles Albert Tindley, c. 1906; alt.*

1 Beams of heav-en, as I go, through this wil-der-ness of woe,
2 Of-ten-times my sky is clear, joy a-bounds with-out a tear,
3 Bur-dens now may crush me down, dis-ap-point-ments all a-round,

guide my heart in peace-ful ways, turn my mid-nights in-to days;
though a day so bright be-gun, clouds may hide to-mor-row's sun.
trou-bles speak in mourn-ful sigh, sor-row through a tear-stained eye;

When in life's shad-ows I would grope, faith al-ways finds a star of hope,
There'll be a day that's al-ways bright, a day that nev-er yields to night,
There is a world where plea-sure reigns, no mourn-ing soul shall roam its plains,

And soon from all life's grief and dan-ger, I shall be free some day.
And in its light the streets of glo-ry I shall be-hold some day.
And to that land of peace and glo-ry I want to go some day.

*Refrain*

I do not know how long 'twill be, nor what the fu-ture holds for me,

But this I know, if Je-sus leads me, I shall get home some day.

Composer Charles A. Tindley, a prolific writer of gospel hymns, was a highly respected African-American Methodist minister in Philadelphia. It is Rev. Tindley whom Thomas Dorsey, perhaps the most famous gospel songwriter, credited as his influential predecessor.

Tune: SOME DAY 7.7.7.7.8.8.9.6. with refrain
Charles Albert Tindley, c. 1906
Transcribed by F. A. Clark, 1906

## Take My Life, God, Let It Be

448

*Frances R. Havergal, 1874; alt.*

*Rom. 12:1*

1 Take my life, God, let it be con-se-crat-ed faith-ful-ly.
2 Take my spir-it, let it move at the im-pulse of your love.
3 Take my will; your will be done! Make your will and mine be one.
4 Take my love and help it grow; let my lov-ing ov-er-flow.

Take my mo-ments and my days, let them flow in cease-less praise.
Take my in-tel-lect and use all its pow-ers as you choose.
Take my heart, and by your grace make of it your dwell-ing place.
Take me now, and help me be part of Christ's com-mu-ni-ty.

Frances R. Havergal wrote her hymn following a visit to Areley House in Worcestershire, England. Among the ten persons at the house were "some unconverted . . . some converted but not rejoicing." Before she left, "everyone had got a blessing."

Tune: VIENNA 7.7.7.7.
Justin H. Knecht, 1797
Alternate tune: HENDON

449

# Softly and Tenderly

Will L. Thompson, 1880; alt.

1 Soft - ly and ten - der - ly Je - sus is call - ing, call - ing for
2 Why should we tar - ry when Je - sus is plead-ing, plead-ing for
3 Time is now fleet-ing, the mo-ments are pass - ing, pass - ing from
4 O for the won - der - ful love Je - sus prom-ised, prom-ised for

you and for me; See at the por - tals Christ wait - ing and
you and for me? Why should we lin - ger and heed not God's
you and from me; Shad - ows are gath - er - ing, death-beds are
you and for me; Though we have sinned Je - sus of - fers us

*Refrain*

watch-ing, watch-ing for you and for me. Come home, come
mer - cies, mer - cies for you and for me? Come home,
com - ing, com - ing for you and for me.
par - don, par - don for you and for me.

home, All who are wea-ry, come home;
come home,

Will Thompson established publishing firms in Chicago and East
Liverpool, Ohio, the community to which he left a legacy of song.
Dwight L. Moody once remarked that he would rather have
written "Softly and Tenderly" than anything he had ever done.

Tune: SOFTLY AND TENDERLY
11.7.11.7. with refrain
Will L. Thompson, 1880

Ear-nest-ly, ten-der-ly Je-sus is call-ing— call-ing, "O sin-ner, come home!"

# O for a Closer Bond with God          450

*William Cowper, 1769; alt.*                    *Ps. 119:105; Isa. 30:18–22*

1 O   for   a   clos - er   bond   with   God,
2 Where is   the   bless - ed - ness   we   knew
3 Re - turn,   O   ho - ly   Dove,   re - turn,
4 The   dear - est   i - dols   we   have   known,
5 So   shall   our   bond   be   close   with   God,

a   calm   and   heav - enly   frame,   A   light   to   shine   up -
when first   our   hearts   were   stirred?   Where is   the   soul - re -
sweet mes - sen - ger   of   peace!   For - give   our   sins   and
as   we   our   ways   pur - sue;   Help   us   to   tear   them
calm   and   se - rene   our   frame;   So   pur - er   light   shall

on   the   road   that   leads   us   to   the   Lamb!
fresh - ing   view   of   Je - sus   Christ,   the   Word?
help   us   learn   in   Christ   to   find   re - lease.
from   your   throne,   and   wor - ship   on - ly   you.
mark   the   road   that   leads   us   to   the   Lamb!

*This hymn was written during the illness of William Cowper's*
*dear friend, Mary Unwin. Cowper wrote poetry and, together*
*with John Newton, published* Olney Hymns. *John B. Dykes,*
*organist and Church of England priest, wrote many hymn tunes.*

Tune: BEATITUDO C.M.
*John B. Dykes, 1875*

# 451          Be Now My Vision

*Ancient Irish text, c. 8th century; transl. Mary E. Byrne, 1905*
*Versified by Eleanor H. Hull, 1912; adapt.*

1 Be now my vi - sion, O God of my heart;
2 Be now my wis - dom, and be my true word;
3 Rich - es I need not, nor life's emp - ty praise,
4 Sov - ereign of heav - en, my vic - to - ry won,

noth - ing sur - pass - es the love you im - part—
ev - er with - in me, my soul is as - sured;
you, my in - her - i - tance, now and al - ways;
may I reach heaven's joys, O bright heav - en's Sun!

You my best thought, by day or by night,
Moth - er and Fa - ther, you are both to me,
You and you on - ly are first in my heart,
Heart of my own heart, what - ev - er be - fall,

wak - ing or sleep - ing, your pres - ence my light.
now and for - ev - er your child I will be.
great God, my trea - sure, may we nev - er part.
still be my vi - sion, O Rul - er of all.

*Dating from the eighth century or earlier, this Irish hymn was*
*translated into prose by Mary Byrne. It was then versified by Eleanor*
*Hull, author of several books on Irish literature and history. David*
*Evans arranged the Irish melody for this text in 1927.*

Tune: SLANE 10.10.9.10.
*Traditional Irish melody*
*Harm. David Evans, 1927*

# Savior, Who Dying Gave

**452**

*Sylvanus Dryden Phelps, 1862*
*Adapt. Thomas H. Troeger, 1992*

*Rom. 5:6–11; Gal. 5:22–24*

1 Sav - ior, who dy - ing gave your love to me,
2 Give me a faith - ful heart guid - ed by you,
3 All that I am and have is yours a - lone,

that all God made me for might come to be—
that ev - ery day may bring your love to view
my love for you the fruit your love has sown.

I make this sol - emn vow: my heart will al - ways bow
through some small kind - ness done, some work of love be - gun,
Not doubt, nor fear, nor wrong, nor death can still this song:

when I re - mem - ber how you died for me.
some thread of jus - tice spun, some life made new.
my gifts of love be - long to you a - lone.

*Both author and composer of this hymn were ministers. Sylvanus*
*Phelps' text first appeared in a denominational journal and was*
*later altered to be used in the collection* Pure Gold *by Robert*
*Lowry, music editor for Biglow Publishing Company.*

Tune: SOMETHING FOR JESUS 6.4.6.4.6.6.6.4.
*Robert Lowry, 1872*

# 453 When the Morning Stars Together

*Ps. 150; Job 38:7; 2 Chron. 5:13–14*        *Albert F. Bayly, 1969; alt.*

1 When the morn-ing stars to - geth-er their Cre-a - tor's glo - ry sang,
2 When in syn - a - gogue and tem-ple voic - es raised the psalm-ists' songs,
3 Voice and in - stru-ment in un - ion through the a - ges spoke your praise;
4 God, we bring our gift of mu - sic; touch our lips and fire our heart,

And the an - gel host all shout-ed till with joy the heav-ens rang,
Of - fer - ing the ad - o - ra - tion which a - lone to you be - longs,
Plain-song, tune - ful hymns, and an - thems told your faith-ful, gra-cious ways.
Teach our minds and train our sens - es, fit us for this sa - cred art.

Then your wis - dom and your great-ness their ex - ul - tant mu - sic told,
When the sing - ers, trum-pets, cym-bals all com - bined, your praise to share,
Choir and or - ches - tra and or - gan each a sa - cred of - fering brought,
Then with skills and con - se - cra - tion we would serve you, God, and give

All the beau - ty and the splen-dor which your might-y works un - fold.
Then the peo - ple saw your glo - ry fill the sa - cred house of prayer.
While, in - spired by your own Spir - it, po - et and com-pos - er wrought.
All our powers to glo - ri - fy you, and in serv-ing ful - ly live.

*Albert Bayly, a British shipbuilder and, later, minister of the United Reformed Church, was an outstanding twentieth-century hymnwriter. He also produced books of verse, missionary pageants, and librettos for some of W. L. Lloyd Webber's cantatas.*

Tune: OFFERING 8.7.8.7.D.
*Jean Slates Hawk, 1991*
*Alternate tune: WEISSE FLAGGEN*

# Lord, I Want To Be a Christian

**454**

*African-American spiritual*

Deut. 6:5–6; 10:12–16

1 Lord, I want to be a Chris-tian in my heart, in my heart;
2 Lord, I want to be more lov - ing in my heart, in my heart,
3 Lord, I want to be more ho - ly in my heart, in my heart;
4 Lord, I want to be like Je - sus in my heart, in my heart;

Lord, I want to be a Chris-tian in my heart.
Lord, I want to be more lov - ing in my heart.
Lord, I want to be more ho - ly in my heart.
Lord, I want to be like Je - sus in my heart.

*Refrain*

In my heart, in my heart,
In my heart, in my heart,

Lord, I want to be a Chris-tian in my heart.
Lord, I want to be more lov - ing in my heart.
Lord, I want to be more ho - ly in my heart.
Lord, I want to be like Je - sus in my heart.

*Many of the enslaved of antebellum America did not want to become Christians because they did not want to adopt the religion of their captors. But this spiritual attests that the Christian faith was an internal strength and aim for many.*

Tune: I WANT TO BE A CHRISTIAN
8.6.8.3. with refrain
*African-American spiritual*
*Arr. Joyce Finch Johnson, 1992*

# 455

# I Am Yours, O Lord

*Ps. 119:94*

*Fanny Crosby, 1874; alt.*

1 I am yours, O Lord, I have heard your voice, and it
2 O the pure de - light of a sin - gle hour that be -
3 Con - se - crate me now to your ho - ly work by the
4 There are depths of love that I can - not know till I

told your love to me; But I long to rise in the
fore your throne I spend, When I kneel in prayer, and with
power of grace di - vine; Let my soul look up with a
cross the nar - row sea; There are heights of joy that I

*Refrain*

arms of faith, drawn to you e - ter - nal - ly.
you, my God, I com - mune as friend with friend!
stead - fast hope; let your will be done, not mine.
may not reach till I rest e - ter - nal - ly.

Draw me

near - er, near-er, bless-ed Lord, to the cross where you have died;
near - er, near - er

*Fanny Crosby, blind from infancy, wrote more than 8,500 gospel hymns. On a speaking tour, she composed this hymn while she was a guest in the Cincinnati home of William Doane, a wealthy manufacturer, amateur musician, and gospel songwriter.*

Tune: I AM YOURS 10.7.10.7. with refrain
*William H. Doane, 1874*

Draw me near-er, near-er, near-er, bless-ed Lord, to your pre-cious, bleed-ing side.

# More Love to You, O Christ 456

*Elizabeth P. Prentiss, c. 1856; alt.*

1 More love to you, O Christ, more love to you! Hear now the
2 Once earth-ly joy I craved, sought peace and rest; Now you a -
3 Then shall my lat - est breath whis - per your praise; This be the

prayer I make faith to re - new.
lone I seek, give what is best: In all I say and do,
part - ing cry my heart shall raise:

*Refrain*

more love, O Christ, to you, more love to you, more love to you!

*Elizabeth Prentiss, a teacher and author of numerous books,*
*wrote this hymn at a time of grief and physical illness. It was*
*published some fifteen years later, together with William H.*
*Doane's tune.*

Tune: MORE LOVE TO YOU 6.4.6.4.6.6.4.4.
*William H. Doane, 1870*

## 457          Jesus, I Live to You

*Rom. 14:8; Phil. 1:21*

*Henry Harbaugh, c. 1850; alt.*

1 Je - sus, I live to you, the love - li - est and best;
2 Je - sus, I die to you, when - ev - er death shall come;
3 Wheth - er to live or die, I know not which is best;
4 Liv - ing or dy - ing, Lord, I ask to be your own;

My life will be your life in me, in your blessed love I rest.
Un - ceas - ing - ly, you'll live in me in my e - ter - nal home.
To live will be your bliss in me, to die is end - less rest.
My life will be your life in me, and heaven on earth be known.

*This is the most famous of all hymns from the German Reformed tradition of the United Church of Christ. Henry Harbaugh, a noted educator and clergyman, was associated with institutions that became Franklin and Marshall College, Lancaster Theological Seminary, and The Mercersberg Academy.*

Tune: LAKE ENON S.M.
*Isaac B. Woodbury, 1856*

## 458          I've Got a Feeling

*African-American traditional; alt.*

*In a relaxed, "swing" style*

Leader (Unison)

1 I've got a feel - ing, ev - ery -

Leader (Unison)

2      Je - sus al - read - y told me, ev - ery -
3 The Spir - it has con - firmed it, ev - ery -

*All (Harmony; see st. 2–3)*

thing is gon-na be all right. O . . . . I've got a

*All (Harmony)*

thing is gon-na be all right. O . . . . Je - sus al - read-y
thing is gon-na be all right. O the Spir - it has con -

feel - ing, ev-ery-thing is gon-na be all right. O . . . .
told me, ev-ery-thing is gon-na be all right. O . . . .
firmed it, ev-ery-thing is gon-na be all right. O the

I've got a feel - ing, ev-ery-thing is gon-na be all right,
Je - sus al - read-y told me, ev-ery-thing is gon-na be all right,
Spir - it has con - firmed it, ev-ery-thing is gon-na be all right,

(1–3) be all right, be all right, be all right.

This traditional song is often sung in churches that have a
devotional service prior to the worship service. A worshiper
might raise this song to encourage another whose testimony
indicated he or she is going through difficult times.

Tune: I'VE GOT A FEELING Irr.
*African-American traditional*
*Arr. Jeffrey Radford, 1993*

# 459     Come, O Fount of Every Blessing

*Ps. 36:7–9*

*Robert Robinson, 1758; alt.*

1 Come, O Fount of ev-ery bless-ing, tune my heart to sing your grace;
2 Here I pause in my so-journ-ing, giv-ing thanks for hav-ing come,
3 O to grace how great a debt-or dai-ly I am drawn a-new!

streams of mer-cy, nev-er ceas-ing, call for songs of end-less praise.
come to trust, at ev-ery turn-ing, God will guide me safe-ly home.
Let that grace now, like a fet-ter, bind my wan-dering heart to you.

Teach me some me-lo-dious son-net, sung by flam-ing tongues a-bove.
Je-sus sought me when a strang-er, wan-dering from the fold of God,
Prone to wan-der, I can feel it, wan-der from the love I've known:

Praise the mount; I'm fixed up-on it, mount of God's un-fail-ing love.
Came to res-cue me from dan-ger, bless-ed bod-y, pre-cious blood.
Here's my heart, O take and seal it, seal it for your ver-y own.

*Converted to Methodism at age twenty, Robert Robinson soon became a Calvinistic Methodist preacher and later gained great popularity. The melody, associated with this text since 1813, is an American folk tune.*

Tune: NETTLETON 8.7.8.7.D.
*John Wyeth's* Repository of Sacred Music, *1813*

# Be Not Dismayed
## (God Will Take Care of You)

**460**

*Civilla D. Martin, 1904; alt.*

*Ps. 91*

1 Be not dis-mayed what-e'er be - tide, God will take care of you;
2 Through days of toil when heart grows frail, God will take care of you;
3 All you may need God will pro - vide, God will take care of you;
4 No mat - ter what may be the test, God will take care of you;

Be - neath God's wings of love a - bide, God will take care of you.
When dan - gers fierce your path as - sail, God will take care of you.
Noth - ing you ask will be de - nied, God will take care of you.
Lean, wea - ry one, up - on God's breast, God will take care of you.

*Refrain*

God will take care of you, through ev - ery day, o'er all the way;

God will take care of you, God will take care of you.

take care of you

*This early hymn by Civilla Martin was written in 1904 and set to music by her husband, a Baptist minister, as a contribution to a songbook he was compiling for a school. This is one of several such collaborations.*

Tune: MARTIN C.M. with refrain
W. Stillman Martin, 1905

# 461 Let Us Hope when Hope Seems Hopeless

*Ps. 126:5–6; Rom. 4:18; 1 Cor. 13*                    *David Beebe, 1989*

1 Let us hope when hope seems hope - less, when the
2 Faith and hope in love's com - pas - sion will sur -
3 Like a child out - grow - ing child - hood, set - ting

dreams we dreamed have died. When the morn - ing
vive though knowl - edge cease, though the tongues of
child - hood things a - way, we will learn to

breaks in bright - ness, hun - ger shall be sat - is - fied.
joy fall si - lent, dull the words of proph - e - cies.
live in free - dom, in the life of God's new day.

*Emma Lou Diemer, organist since the age of thirteen, studied composition at Yale University and Eastman School of Music, and has published orchestra, chamber, choral, and organ works. David Beebe wrote this text while teaching a course on creative writing. A minister of the United Church of Christ, Beebe has served on the staff of the denomination's Stewardship Council.*

Tune: LET US HOPE 8.7.8.7.D.
*Emma Lou Diemer, 1994*
*Alternate tune: HYFRYDOL*

One who sows the fields with weep - ing shall re - trace the
Faith shall see and trust its ob - ject; hope shall set its
Now we see as in a mir - ror. Then we shall see

sor - row - ing way and re - joice in har - vest
an - chor sure; love shall bloom in Love e -
face to face, un - der - stand how love's com -

boun - ty at the break - ing of the day.
ter - nal. Faith and hope and love en - dure.
pas - sion blos - soms through a - maz - ing Grace.

# 462 Creating God, Your Fingers Trace

Ps. 148

*Jeffery Rowthorn, 1979*

1 Cre - at - ing God, your fin - gers trace the bold de - signs of
2 Sus - tain - ing God, your hands up - hold earth's mys - teries known or
3 Re - deem - ing God, your arms em - brace all now de - spised for
4 In - dwell - ing God, your gos - pel claims one fam - ily with a

far - thest space; . . . . . Let sun and moon and stars and light
yet un - told; . . . . . . Let wa - ter's frag - ile blend with air,
creed or race; . . . . . . Let peace, de - scend - ing like a dove,
bil - lion names; . . . . . Let ev - ery life be touched by grace

and what lies hid - den praise . . . . your might.
en - a - bling life, pro - claim . . . . your care.
make known on earth your heal - ing love.
un - til we praise you face . . . . to face.

*Jeffery Rowthorn's paraphrase of Psalm 148 was one of two winning texts in the 1979 Hymn Society competition seeking "New Psalms for Today." It is set to the first published tune by composer Eugene Hancock and appears in* The Presbyterian Hymnal, *1990.*

Tune: HANCOCK L.M.
*Eugene W. Hancock, 1989*
*Alternate tunes: DEO GRACIAS,
DICKINSON COLLEGE*

# I Look to You in Every Need

*Samuel Longfellow, 1864; alt.*

1 I look to you in ev - ery need, and nev - er look in vain; I
2 Dis - cour-aged in the work of life, dis - heart-ened by its load, Shamed
3 Se - rene and calm, you cir - cle me, my rest - less-ness to still; A -
4 En - fold - ed deep in your dear love, held in your law, I stand; Your

feel your strong and ten - der love, and all is well a - gain: The
by its fail - ures or its fears, I sink be - side the road; But
round me flows your quick-ening life, to nerve my fal-tering will: Your
hand in all things I be - hold, and all things in your hand; You

thought of you is might-ier far than sin and pain and sor - row are.
let me on - ly think of you and all my strength re - turns a - new.
pres - ence fills my sol - i - tude; your prov - i - dence turns all to good.
lead me in sur - pris - ing ways, and turn my mourn-ing in - to praise.

*Samuel Longfellow—poet, hymnwriter, and Unitarian
minister—was the brother of Henry Wadsworth Longfellow.
The German organist Reimann was a contemporary of J. S.
Bach and traveled to Leipzig to hear Bach perform.*

Tune: O JESU 8.6.8.6.8.8.
*Reimann's* Sammlung Alter und Neuer
Melodien, *1747*

# 464 The Weaver's Shuttle Swiftly Flies

*Job 7:6*

*James Gertmenian, 1990*

1 The weav-er's shut-tle swift-ly flies a-cross the tap-es-
2 The Weav-er's shut-tle swift-ly flies a-cross the earth-ly
3 Who knows the pat-terns of our lives be-fore our days are
4 When will we find the true de-sign in-tend-ed for our
5 O gen-tle Weav-er, lov-ing God, we are your works of

try; then pat-terns, tex-tures, var-ied hues e-merge for
loom. Our sto-ries all too quick-ly pass from cra-dle
spun? Who knows the rea-son why, and how, be-fore it's
days? In heaven to come, when life is done and noth-ing's
art, and so we see e-ter-ni-ty with-in each

all to see. And so our lives are wo-ven fine as
to the tomb. Day fol-lows day and year on year; they
all be-gun? The One whose hand weaves all with love and
left but praise? Or shall we see in glimps-es now the
hu-man heart. In all we think and do and say, in

*Developing an image from Job 7:6, United Church of Christ
minister James Gertmenian reminds us of the swift passage of
our days and invites us to seek glimpses of God, the Eternal
Weaver, in them.*

Tune: ST. MATTHEW C.M.D.
William Croft, 1708

in | that | weav - er's | hand, | a | fair | de - sign | and
fade | as | in | a | dream. And | none | can | hold | the
mys - ter - y | and | care; | The | One | whose thread | and
pat - tern | God | re - veals, | and | here | em - brace | this
all | we | hope | and | fear, | give | us | the | eyes | to

rich - er | still | than | we | can | un - der - stand.
shut - tle | still | or | stop | the | flow - ing | stream.
warp | and | weft | are | flesh | and | earth | and | air!
earth - ly | race | that | wounds | us | and | that | heals?
rec - og - nize | the | heav - en | al - ways | here.

465

# Teach Me, O Lord, Your Holy Way

*William Matson, 1866; alt.*

1 Teach me, O Lord, your ho - ly way,
2 Help me, O Sav - ior, here to trace
3 Guard me, O Christ, that I may ne'er
4 Bless me in ev - ery task I face,

and give me an o - be - dient mind,
the sa - cred foot - steps you have trod;
for - sake the right, or do the wrong;
be - gun, con - tin - ued, done for you;

That in your ser - vice I may find
and ful - ly trust - ing in my God,
A - gainst temp - ta - tion make me strong,
Ful - fill your will in all I do,

my heart's de - light from day to day.
to grow in good - ness, truth, and grace.
and keep me in your shel - tering care.
and grant me your a - bun - dant grace.

*William Matson, English poet and Congregational minister,*
*wrote a poem of 321 four-line stanzas titled "The Inner Life"*
*(1866). This hymn of obedience to Christ has been drawn from*
*that extended poem.*

Tune: ROCKINGHAM L.M.
*Anon.*
*Adapt. Edward Miller, 1790*

# Unto the Hills We Lift Our Longing Eyes

**466**

*John Campbell, Duke of Argyll, 1877; alt.*

*Ps. 121*

1 Un - to the hills we lift our long - ing eyes with yearn-ing sighs.
2 God will not let our ser - vant feet be moved; safe we will be.
3 God is our keep - er, change-less through the years, a shel - ter strong.
4 From ev - ery e - vil, God will keep our lives, from ev - ery sin.

Who will pro - vide the help we sore - ly need? Who hears our cries?
God will sup - ply, for all our nights and days, se - cu - ri - ty.
God is our shade, pro - tect - ing ev - ery hand, through a - ges long.
God will pre - serve and guard our go - ing out, our com - ing in.

From our Cre - a - tor comes our cer - tain aid.
God does not sleep when we are tak - ing rest.
Sun will not strike or harm through-out the day,
Ev - er a - round, with - in, we will a - dore

Our help is from our God, who all things made.
God's cov - e - nant en - dures through ev - ery test.
Nor moon by night, those liv - ing by God's way.
our God who holds and guides for - ev - er - more.

John Campbell's paraphrase of Psalm 121 was a favorite with
Canadian soldiers during World War II. Campbell, a member of
Parliament, was married to Queen Victoria's daughter, Princess
Louise. For six years he was governor-general of Canada.

Tune: SANDON 10.4.10.4.10.10.
*Charles Henry Purday, 1860*
*For another harmonization, see 366*

# 467      Mothering God, You Gave Me Birth

*Gen. 1:1–5; Matt. 26:26–29;*                                            *Jean Janzen, 1991*
*Mark 14:22–25; Luke 22:15–20*                            *Based on the writings of Julian of Norwich*

1 Moth - er - ing God, you gave me birth in the bright
2 Moth - er - ing Christ, you took my form, of - fer - ing
3 Moth - er - ing Spir - it, nur - turing One, in arms of

morn - ing of this world. Cre - a - tor,
me your food of light, Grain . . . of
pa - tience hold me close, So that in

Source of ev - ery breath, you are my rain, my wind, my
life, and grape of love, your ver - y bod - y for my
faith I root and grow un - til I flower, un - til I

*In the late fourteenth century in Norwich, England, a*
*well-educated Christian woman, Julian of Norwich, devoted her*
*life to God through the study and contemplation of scripture.*
*This hymn by Jean Janzen is based on some of the ideas from*
*Julian's important theological treatise,* Showings.

Tune: ANDREW 8.8.8.8.8.
*Jonathan McNair, 1994*

1–2   3

sun;    you are my   rain,   my wind, my   sun.
peace;  your ver - y  bod - y for my  peace.
know;   un - til I   flower,  un - til   I   know.

1–2   3

# The Care the Eagle Gives Her Young 468

*R. Deane Postlethwaite, 1980*       *Deut. 32:11–12a; Exod. 19:4*

1 The  care  the  ea - gle  gives  her  young, safe  in  her
2 As  when  the  time  to  ven - ture  comes, she  stirs  them
3 And  if  we  flut - ter  help - less - ly,  as  fledg - ling

loft - y  nest,  Is  like  the  ten - der
out  to  flight,  So  we  are  pressed  to
ea - gles  fall,  Be - neath  us  lift  God's

love  of  God  for  us  made  man - i - fest.
bold - ly  try,  to  strive  for  dar - ing  height.
might - y  wings  to  bear  us,  one  and  all.

*This text was originally titled "For a Recognition of God's Feminine Attributes." The author explains: "I find a deep meaning and power in the image of a God who, like a mother eagle, pushes me from her nest, but who catches me, bears me up, when I fall."*

Tune: CRIMOND C.M.
*Jesse Seymour Irvine, 1872*
*Harm. T. C. L. Pritchard, 1929*

# 469

# O Grant Us Light

Ps. 43:3

Lawrence Tuttiett, 1864; alt.

1 O grant us light, that we may know wis-dom that you a -
lone can give, That truth may guide us as we go,
and vir - tue bless the lives we live.

2 O grant us light that we may find where er - ror lurks in
hu - man lore, And turn to you our seek - ing minds,
and love your ho - ly Word the more.

3 O grant us light, that we may learn how dead is life from
you a - part, How sure is joy for all who turn
to you an un - di - vid - ed heart.

4 O grant us light, when soon or late, all earth-ly scenes shall
pass a - way, In you to find the o - pen gate,
to death - less home and end - less day.

*Ordained a priest of the Church of England, Lawrence Tuttiett
served a parish at Warwickshire. His last two appointments were
in Scotland. Henry W. Baker, an important English hymnal
editor, wrote this tune while an undergraduate at Oxford.*

Tune: HESPERUS L.M.
(QUEBEC)
*Henry W. Baker, 1854*

# Golden Breaks the Dawn

**470**

*Tzu-chen Chao (b. 1888)*
*Paraphr. by Frank W. Price (b. 1895); alt.*

*Ps. 50:1–2; Matt. 6:11–12*

1 Gold-en breaks the dawn, comes the east-ern sun
2 Give me dai - ly bread, while I do my part;

o - ver lake and lawn, new day has be - gun.
bright skies o - ver - head, glad - ness in my heart.

Birds a - bove me fly, flow-ers bloom be - low;
Sim-ple wants pro - vide, e - vil let me shun;

through the earth and sky God's great mer-cies flow.
Je - sus at my side, till the day is done.

*Tzu-chen Chao was a prominent Chinese Christian leader,*
*theologian, and dean of the School of Religion of Yenching*
*University. He was elected one of the first vice presidents of the*
*World Council of Churches at its inaugural meeting in 1948.*

Tune: LE P'ING 10.10.10.10.
*Chinese folk tune; adapt. Te-ngai Hu*
*Harm. Bliss Wiant, 1936*

# 471

# What a Covenant

*Deut. 33:27*

*Elisha A. Hoffman, 1887; alt.*

1 What a *cov - e - nant, what a joy di - vine, lean - ing on the ev - er -
2 Oh, how sweet to walk in this pil-grim way, lean - ing on the ev - er -
3 What have I to dread, what have I to fear, lean - ing on the ev - er -

last - ing arms. What a bless - ed - ness, what a peace is mine, lean - ing
last - ing arms. Oh, how bright the path grows from day to day, lean - ing
last - ing arms? I have bless - ed peace with my Sav - ior near, lean - ing

*Refrain*

on the ev - er - last-ing arms.
on the ev - er - last-ing arms. Lean - ing, lean - ing, safe and se-cure from
on the ev - er - last-ing arms.

all a-larms; lean - ing, lean - ing, lean-ing on the ev - er - last-ing arms.

*Or, "fellowship"

*In a letter to two grieving friends, A. J. Showalter quoted*
*Deuteronomy 33:27, ". . . underneath are the everlasting arms."*
*Showalter then wrote this music and the refrain and sent them to*
*E. A. Hoffman to provide the stanzas.*

Tune: LEANING 5.5.9.D. with refrain
*Anthony J. Showalter, 1887*

# Precious Lord, Take My Hand

**472**

*Thomas A. Dorsey, 1932; alt.*

1 Pre - cious Lord, take my hand, lead me on, let me stand,
2 When my way grows drear, pre-cious Lord, lin - ger near,
3 When the shad - ows ap - pear and the night draws near,

I am tired, I am weak, I am worn;
when my life is al - most gone,
and the day is past and gone,

Through the storm, through the night, lead me on to the light:
Hear me cry, hear my call, hold my hand, lest I fall:
At the riv - er I stand, guide my feet, hold my hand:

*Refrain*

Take my hand, pre - cious Lord, lead me home.

*Thomas A. Dorsey was known as "Georgia Tom" when he
played piano for blues singer Ma Rainey. He started writing
gospel songs after what he called "a definite spiritual change."
This inspirational song, composed following the deaths of his
wife, Nettie, and a newborn child, derives from the tune Maitland.*

Tune:  PRECIOUS LORD  Irr. with refrain
*Thomas A. Dorsey, 1932*

# 473

## Blessed Assurance

Acts 17:30–31; Rev. 7:9–14

Fanny Crosby, 1873; alt.

1 Bless-ed as - sur - ance, Je - sus is mine! O what a
·2 Per - fect sub - mis - sion, per - fect de - light! Vi - sions of
3 Per - fect sub - mis - sion, all is at rest, I in my

fore - taste of glo - ry di - vine! Heir of sal - va - tion, pur - chase of
rap - ture now burst on my sight; An - gels de - scend-ing, bring from a -
Sav - ior am hap - py and blessed; Watch-ing and wait - ing, look-ing a -

God, born of the Spir - it, washed in Christ's blood.
bove ech - oes of mer - cy, whis - pers of love.
bove, filled with God's good - ness, lost in Christ's love.

*Refrain*

This is my sto - ry, this is my song, prais-ing my Sav - ior all the day long;

*After hearing Phoebe Knapp play this tune on the piano, Fanny Crosby composed the poem on the spot. In her almost 95 years, Crosby wrote more than 8,500 gospel hymns and songs.*

Tune: ASSURANCE Irr.
Phoebe P. Knapp, 1873

This is my sto - ry, this is my song, prais-ing my Sav-ior all the day long.

# I'm So Glad, Jesus Lifted Me  474

*African-American spiritual*

1 I'm so glad, Je-sus lift-ed me, I'm so glad,
2 Sa - tan had me bound, Je-sus lift-ed me, Sa - tan had me bound,
3 When I was in trou-ble, Je-sus lift-ed me, when I was in trou-ble,

Je - sus lift - ed me, I'm so glad,
Je - sus lift - ed me, Sa - tan had me bound,
Je - sus lift - ed me, when I was in trou - ble,

Je-sus lift-ed me, sing-ing glo-ry, hal-le-lu-jah, Je-sus lift-ed me.

*Just as the spirituals were adapted to be sung in a folk-song style during the 1960s music festivals and civil rights marches, so have they been adapted in a gospel style. This is a spiritual that especially lends itself to gospel rendering.*

Tune: I'M SO GLAD Irr.
*African-American spiritual*

# 475 God's Eye Is on the Sparrow

*Matt. 10:26–30; Luke 12:4–7*

*Civilla D. Martin, c. 1905; alt.*

*Civilla Martin, a native of Nova Scotia, assisted her husband in his evangelistic campaigns. Charles Gabriel was editor for Rodeheaver Publishing Company, Chicago, and one of the most popular gospel songwriters of the early 1900s.*

Tune: SPARROW Irr.
*Charles H. Gabriel, 1905*

know God watch-es me; God's eye is on the spar-row, and I
know God watch-es me; God's eye is on the spar-row, and I
know God watch-es me; God's eye is on the spar-row, and I

*Refrain, in harmony*

know God watch-es me.
know God watch-es me. I sing be-cause I'm
know God watch-es me.

hap-py, I sing be-cause I'm free, God's
I'm hap-py, I'm free,

eye is on the spar-row, and I know God watch-es me.

# 476

## My Life Flows on in Endless Song
### (How Can I Keep from Singing)

*Ps. 46:1–7; 1 Cor. 3:21–23; 2 Cor. 5:17*

*Anon. in* Bright Jewels for the Sunday School,
*ed. Robert Lowry, 1869; alt.*
*St. 3, Doris Plenn, c. 1957*

1 My life flows on in end - less song; a - bove earth's lam - en -
2 What though my joys and com - forts die? My Sav - ior still is
3 When ty - rants trem - ble, sick with fear, and hear their death knells
4 I lift my eyes; the cloud grows thin; I see the blue a -

ta - tion, I hear the sweet, though far - off hymn that
liv - ing. What though the shad - ows gath - er 'round? A
ring - ing; When friends re - joice both far and near, how
bove it; And day by day this path - way smooths, since

hails a new cre - a - tion. Through all the tu - mult
new song Christ is giv - ing. No storm can shake my
can I keep from sing - ing? In pris - on cell and
first I learned to love it. The peace of Christ makes

and the strife, I hear the mu - sic ring - ing; It
in - most calm, while to that Rock I'm cling - ing; Since
dun - geon vile our thoughts to them are wing - ing; When
fresh my heart, a foun - tain ev - er spring - ing; All

*In various nineteenth-century hymnals this hymn was attributed to different poets, including Anna Warner. The earliest published source credits Robert Lowry as the composer, although Silas Vail later claimed the music. The third stanza was written by Doris Plenn in the 1950s when her friends were imprisoned during the McCarthy era.*

Tune: ENDLESS SONG 8.7.8.7.D.
*Attrib. to Robert Lowry in* Bright Jewels
for the Sunday School, *New York, 1869*

finds an ech-o in my soul— how can I keep from sing-ing?
Love com-mands both heaven and earth, how can I keep from sing-ing?
friends by shame are un - de - filed, how can I keep from sing-ing?
things are mine since I am Christ's— how can I keep from sing-ing?

# Though Falsely Some Revile or Hate Me 477

*1 Kings 17:1–16; Matt. 28:20*

Chi-pi Ni, 1929
Transl. Frank W. Price; alt.

1 Though false - ly some re - vile or hate me, friends for-sake me, too,
2 My path may be hedged up with briars, fierce foes my life sur - round;
3 Though parched my pas - ture - land be - come and fears of fam-ine haunt,
4 The brook of Cher-ith may dry up, the rav - ens hun-gry cry,
5 In ev - ery cir-cum - stance of life God's pow - er will pre - vail;

I will re - mem-ber Christ's own word: "I'll al - ways be with you."
God's mer - cy is for - ev - er sure, it makes God's love a - bound.
My Shep-herd leads me all the way; I shall not suf - fer want.
The Shep-herd will God's ser - vants feed, their ev - ery need sup - ply.
The jar of meal and cruse of oil will nev - er, nev-er fail.

*With echoes of the psalms and a direct reference to 1 Kings 17,*
*this moving hymn from the East Asia Christian Council hymnal*
*blends imagery from both the Hebrew Scriptures and the New*
*Testament, assuring us of God's eternal presence and provision.*

Tune: THE BROOK CHERITH C.M.
*Maryette H. Lum, 1936*

# 478

## I've Got Peace Like a River

*Isa. 66:12; 1 Pet. 1:8–9; 1 John 4:7–12*

*African-American spiritual*

1 I've got peace like a riv-er, I've got peace like a
2 I've got joy like a foun-tain, I've got joy like a
3 I've got love like an o-cean, I've got love like an
4 I've got faith like an an-chor, I've got faith like an

riv-er, I've got peace like a riv-er, in my
foun-tain, I've got joy like a foun-tain, in my
o-cean, I've got love like an o-cean, in my
an-chor, I've got faith like an an-chor, in my

soul.    I've got riv-er in my soul.
soul.    I've got foun-tain in my soul.
soul.    I've got o-cean in my soul.
soul.    I've got an-chor in my soul.

*Congregations or individuals may wish to add additional verses of their own making.*

*Most of the spirituals that drew from biblical stories and images used the Hebrew scriptures, rather than the New Testament, as their inspiration. The imagery of "peace like a river" derives from the book of Isaiah.*

Tune: PEACE LIKE A RIVER   7.7.10.D.
*African-American spiritual*

# God Is My Shepherd

**479**

Scottish Psalter, *1650*
Adapt. Lavon Bayler, *1992*

*Ps. 23*

1 God is my shep-herd, I'll not want, I feed in pas-tures green.
2 Re - stored to life each morn-ing new, I rise up from the dust
3 When I must pass through shad-owed vale, where loss and death a - wait,
4 No en - e - my can o - ver-come, no power on earth de - feat
5 Good-ness and mer - cy all my days will sure - ly fol-low me;

God grants me rest and bids me drink from wa - ters calm and clean.
to fol - low God whose pres - ence gives me con - fi - dence and trust.
I will not fear for God is there, my shep-herd strong and great,
the ones a - noint-ed by God's grace and fed with man - na sweet.
and where God reigns in heaven and earth, my dwell-ing place will be.

Through dai - ly tasks, I'm blessed and led by One I have not seen.
I praise the name of God to - day; in God I put my trust.
Whose rod and staff will com - fort me and all my fears a - bate.
My cup is filled and o - ver-flows as I my Sav - ior greet.
My shep-herd bless - es, cares, and leads through all e - ter - ni - ty.

The Scottish Psalter *of 1650, developed over a span of 100 years,*
*is still in use today. Its metrical version of Psalm 23 is the most*
*popular entry in this classic work of Protestantism.*

Tune: BROTHER JAMES' AIR 8.6.8.6.8.6.
*James Leith Macbeth Bain, c. 1840–1925*
*Arr. Gordon Jacob, 1934*

# 480

# Jesus, Priceless Treasure

*John 15:15; 1 Pet. 1:19*

*Johann Franck, 1653*
*Trans. Catherine Winkworth, 1863; alt.*

1 Je-sus, price-less trea - sure, source of pur-est plea - sure,
2 Let your arms en - fold me: those who try to wound me
3 Ban-ish thoughts of sad - ness, for the source of glad - ness,

friend most sure and true: Long my heart was burn - ing,
can - not reach me here. Though the earth be shak - ing,
Je - sus, en - ters in; Though the clouds may gath - er,

faint - ing much and yearn - ing, thirst-ing af - ter you.
ev - ery heart be quak - ing, Je - sus calms my fear.
those who love the Sav - ior still have peace with - in.

Yours I am, O spot - less Lamb, so will I let
Fires may flash and thun - der crash; yet, though sin and
Though I bear much sor - row here, still in you lies

*A contemporary of German pietist Paul Gerhardt, Johann Franck was a lawyer and a poet. Modeled on a love song by Heinrich Albert, "Flora, meine Freude," this hymn has had many translations, including one in Russian attributed to Peter the Great in 1724.*

Tune: JESU, MEINE FREUDE 6.6.5.6.6.5.7.8.6.
*Johann Crüger, 1653*
*Arr. J. S. Bach (1685–1750)*

noth - ing hide you, seek no joy be - side you.
hell as - sail me, Je - sus will not fail me.
pur - est plea - sure, Je - sus price - less trea - sure!

# As Pants the Hart for Cooling Streams 481

A New Version of the Psalms of David,
*ed. Nahum Tate and Nicholas Brady, 1696; alt.*

*Ps. 42*

1 As pants the hart for cool - ing streams when
2 Why rest - less, why cast down, my soul? Trust
3 God of my strength, how long shall I, like
4 Why rest - less, why cast down, my soul? Hope

heat - ed in the chase, So longs my soul, O
God, who will em - ploy All grace for you, and
one for - got - ten, mourn, For - lorn, for - sak - en,
still, and you shall sing The praise of One who

God, for you, and your re - fresh - ing grace.
change your sighs to thank - ful hymns of joy.
and ex - posed to my op - pres - sor's scorn?
is your God, your health's e - ter - nal spring.

*Both Nahum Tate and Nicholas Brady were Irish. Brady, a priest, held various posts, including that of royal chaplain. Tate made his living writing for the state. This is one of the most enduring paraphrases from their* A New Version of the Psalms of David. *(A "hart" is a deer.)*

Tune: MARTYRDOM C.M.
(AVON)
*Hugh Wilson, 1825*

# 482       I Will Lift the Cloud of Night

*Charles P. Jones, 1916; alt.*

1. I will lift the cloud of night be - fore you, what is
2. With an ev - er - last - ing love I'll love you, though with
3. Al - though Sa - tan in a rage would tear you, and with
4. I will lift the cloud of night be - fore you, I will

wrong I'll make it right be - fore you, all your bat - tles I will
tri - als I will test and prove you, still there's noth - ing that can
ev - ery win - ning art would snare you, yet from youth to your old
make the crook-ed straight be - fore you, I will spread my wings pro -

fight be - fore you, and the high place I'll bring down.
hurt or move you; and the high place I'll bring down.
age I'll bear you and the high place I'll bring down.
tect - ing o'er you; and the high place I'll bring down.

*Refrain*

When you walk and lose the way I'll lead you; on the

*African-American hymnwriter Charles P. Jones was the founder and first bishop of the Church of Christ (Holiness) U.S.A. He composed more than 1,000 gospel hymns, texts and music, which appeared in numerous hymnbooks Jones published beginning in 1899.*

Tune: JONES 10.10.10.7. with refrain
*Charles P. Jones, 1916*

pro-duce of the land I'll feed you; And a home with-in my heart I'll

deed you; and the high place I'll bring down.

## Out of the Depths I Call 483

A New Version of the Psalms of David,
*ed. Nahum Tate and Nicholas Brady, 1696; alt.*

*Ps. 130*

1 Out of the depths I call, to God I send my cry: Oh,
2 For you my soul still waits with pa-tience un - de - terred; My
3 My faint-ing spir - it longs for your en - liv-ening ray, More
4 Let Is - rael trust in God, whose mer-cy bound-less grows, The

hear my sup-pli - ca - ting voice and gra-cious-ly re - ply.
hopes are on your prom - ise built, your nev - er - fail - ing word.
ea - ger than the morn - ing watch to greet the dawn-ing day.
plen-teous source and spring from whom re - demp-tion ev - er flows.

*In seventeenth-century England, the "old" Sternhold and*
*Hopkins psalter was being displaced by the "new" Tate and*
*Brady version, while in America, the* Bay Psalm Book *was*
*gaining great popularity. All this preceded the outpouring of*
*psalm hymns by the prolific Congregationalist Isaac Watts.*

Tune: ST. BRIDE S.M.
*Samuel Howard, 1762*

# 484

# O Come to Me, You Weary

*Matt. 11:28–30; John 6:35–40; 11:25–26*

*William C. Dix, 1867; alt.*

1 "O come to me, you wea - ry, and I will give you rest."
2 "O come to me, you wan - derers, and I will give you light."
3 "O come to me, you faint - ing, and I will give you life!"
4 "All you who come and seek me will nev - er be cast out."

The bless - ed voice of Je - sus, which comes to hearts op - pressed!
The lov - ing voice of Je - sus, which comes to cheer the night!
The cheer-ing voice of Je - sus, which stills our in - ner strife!
The wel - come voice of Je - sus, which drives a - way our doubt!

It tells of ben - e - dic - tion, of par - don, grace, and peace,
Our hearts were filled with sad - ness, and we had lost our way;
The e - vil one sur - rounds us and would our faith sub - due,
And though we are un - wor - thy of love so free and true,

of joy that has no end - ing, of love which does not cease.
but morn - ing brings us glad - ness and songs for each new day.
but you are strong with - in us, our cour - age brave and true.
we hear your call to sin - ners; in trust we come to you.

*William C. Dix, manager of a marine insurance company, wrote this hymn after many weeks of illness. Shortly thereafter, he began to recover. William Lloyd, a Welsh farmer and cattle drover, had a good voice and conducted singing classes.*

Tune: MEIRIONYDD 7.6.7.6.D.
*Welsh hymn tune*
*Attrib. to William Lloyd, 1840*

# O Love That Will Not Let Me Go

*George Matheson, 1882; alt.*

*Rom. 8:38–39; John 8:12*

1 O Love that will not let me go,
2 O Light that fol - lows all my way,
3 O Joy that seeks me through my pain,
4 O Cross that rais - es up my head,

I rest my wea - ry soul in you;
to you I yield my flick - ering flame;
to you I can - not close my heart;
from you I dare not seek to flee;

I give you back the life I owe, that
Re - new my spir - it's fee - ble ray, that
I trace the rain - bow through the rain, and
Life's glo - ries with - er and are dead, but

in your o - cean depths its flow may swell with ar - dor true.
from your bril - liant sun - lit day it may new bright - ness claim.
know the prom - ise is not vain that you will ne'er de - part.
from the ground there blos - soms red, life that shall end - less be.

*Although he was nearly blind, George Matheson studied for the Church of Scotland ministry, assisted by his sisters, who learned Latin, Greek, and Hebrew to help him. Matheson wrote this hymn in five minutes on June 6, 1882, at his parsonage.*

Tune: ST. MARGARET 8.8.8.8.6.
*Albert L. Peace, 1885*

# 486

# I Must Tell Jesus

Heb. 2:18

*Elisha A. Hoffman, 1894; alt.*

1 I must tell Je - sus all of my tri - als, I can - not
2 I must tell Je - sus all of my trou - bles, Je - sus my
3 Tempt-ed and tried, I need a great Sav - ior, One who can
4 Oh, how the world to e - vil al - lures me! Oh, how my

bear these bur - dens a - lone; In my dis - tress my Je - sus will
kind, com - pas - sion-ate Friend; If I but ask, my Sav - ior will
help my bur - dens to bear; I must tell Je - sus, I must tell
heart is tempt-ed to sin! I must tell Je - sus, my Friend who

help me, who ev - er loves and cares for God's own.
an - swer, all of my trou - bles quick-ly will end.
Je - sus, who all my cares and sor - rows will share.
helps me o - ver the world the vic - tory to win.

*Refrain*

I must tell Je - sus! I must tell Je - sus! I can - not

*An Evangelical minister, Elisha Hoffman also served the Evangelical Publications House in Cleveland, Ohio, for eleven years. This hymn was inspired by a parishioner in Lebanon, Pennsylvania. Orwigsburg (Pennsylvania) was the place of Hoffman's birth.*

Tune: ORWIGSBURG 10.9.10.9. with refrain
*Elisha A. Hoffman, 1894*

bear my bur-dens a - lone; I must tell Je - sus! I must tell

Je - sus! Je - sus can help me, Je - sus a - lone.

## Surely No One Can Be Safer

487

*Lina Sandell, 1855*
*Transl. The New Century Hymnal, 1994*

Rom. 8:38–39

1 Sure - ly no one can be saf - er than God's chil - dren, held in fa - vor,
2 With the flock God is a - bid-ing, heav-en's plen - ty all pro - vid-ing,
3 None shall ev - er meet re - jec-tion, be de - nied God's own pro - tec-tion;
4 Wheth-er tak - ing, wheth-er giv-ing, God a - lone re - mains for - giv-ing,

Not the stars so bright-ly burn-ing, not the birds to nests re - turn-ing.
Rich in mer - cy, nev - er spar-ing, like a fa - ther, gent - ly car - ing.
Has there been a friend who bet - ter knows our hopes, our fears that fet - ter?
And with one true pur - pose ho - ly to pre - serve our wel - fare sole - ly.

*Lina Sandell endured many hardships in her early years,*
*including illness, the death of a child, and the drowning of her*
*father, who was a Swedish Lutheran pastor. She maintained a*
*deep piety and strong commitment to mission, and wrote more*
*than 650 hymns and poems.*

Tune:  TRYGGARE KAN INGEN VARA  L.M.
*Swedish folk melody*
*Harm.* Song Book for Sunday School, *1871*

# 488

# Be Still, My Soul

*Ps. 37:7; Ps. 46:10; 1 Tim. 4:10*

*Katharina von Schlegel, 1752*
*Transl. Jane Laurie Borthwick, 1855; alt.*

1 Be still, my soul: for God is on your side; bear pa-tient-
2 Be still, my soul: for God will un-der-take to guide in
3 Be still, my soul: the hour will soon be here when we shall

ly the cross of grief or pain; Leave to your God to
fu-ture days as in the past. Your hope, your con-fi-
be with God whom we a-dore, with dis-ap-point-ment

or-der and pro-vide; in ev-ery change God
dence let noth-ing shake; all now mys-te-rious
gone, no grief nor fear, sor-row re-placed with

faith-ful will re-main. Be still, my soul: your best e-ter-nal
shall be clear at last. Be still, my soul: the waves and winds still
joy for-ev-er-more. Be still, my soul: when change and tears are

*Little is known about Katharina von Schlegel, the author of twenty-six hymns, except that she seems to have been a member of the duke's court at Cöthen, Germany. The tune is adapted from an orchestral work by Finland's great composer Jean Sibelius.*

Tune: FINLANDIA 10.10.10.10.10.10.
*Jean Sibelius, 1899*
*Arr. The Hymnal, 1933*

friend     through thorn - y    ways   leads   to   a   joy - ful   end.
know       how   Je - sus'   pow - er   ruled them long   a - go.
past,       all   safe and   bless - ed   we   shall meet   at   last.

# I Heard the Voice of Jesus Say      489

*Horatius Bonar, 1846; alt.*      *Matt. 11:28–30; John 4:7–15; 8:12*

1 I   heard the voice of   Je-sus say, "Come   un-to me   and   rest;
2 I   came to Je - sus   as I was,   so   wea-ry, worn, and   sad,
3 I   heard the voice of   Je-sus say, "Be - hold, I free - ly   give
4 I   came to Je - sus,   and I drank of   that life-giv - ing   stream;

Lay   down, O   wea - ry   one, lay down your head up - on   my   breast."
And   there I   found   a   rest-ing place, where Je - sus made me   glad!
The   liv - ing   wa - ter;   thirst-y one, draw near, and drink, and   live."
My   thirst was quenched, my   soul re-vived, and   now I   am   re - deemed.

5   I heard the voice of Je-sus say,
    "I am this lost world's Light,
    Look un-to me; your morn shall rise,
    and all your day be bright."

6   I looked to Je-sus, and I found
    my guid-ing Star, my Sun;
    And in that light of life I'll go
    till trav-eling days are done.

*Horatius Bonar was one of the founders of the Free Church of Scotland. A man of wide scholarship and great devotion to his ministry, he wrote nearly one book a year, as well as some 600 hymns.*

*Tune: EVAN C.M.*
*William H. Havergal, 1847*
*Arr. Lowell Mason, 1850*
*Alternate tune: KINGSFOLD*
*(Pair stanzas 1–2, 3–4, 5–6)*

# 490

# I Want Jesus to Go with Me

*African-American spiritual; alt.*

*Unison*

1 I want Je - sus to go with me;
2 In my tri - als, O com - fort me;
3 When I'm in trou - ble, O stay with me;

I want Je - sus to go with me;
In my tri - als, O com - fort me;
When I'm in trou - ble, O stay with me;

All a - long my pil - grim jour - ney,
When my heart is al - most break - ing,
When my head is bowed in sor - row,

O I want Je - sus to go with me.
O I want Je - sus to com - fort me.
O I want Je - sus to stay with me.

*Most spirituals were congregational songs, but such "sorrow songs" as this convey the image of a lone person singing prayerfully to God. The solemnity of this particular spiritual reminds us of the oppression and tragedy with which slavery afflicted so many lives.*

Tune: African-American spiritual 8.8.8.9.
*Harm. J. Jefferson Cleveland and Verolga Nix, 1981*

# Awake, My Soul, Stretch Every Nerve

**491**

*Philip Doddridge (1702–1751); alt.*

*2 Tim. 4:7–8; Phil. 3:12–14*

1 A - wake, my soul, stretch ev - ery nerve, and
2 A cloud of wit - ness - es a - round holds
3 For God's all - an - i - mat - ing voice still
4 O Sav - ior, shown the way by you, I

press with vig - or on; A heaven - ly race de - mands your zeal,
you in full sur - vey; For - get the steps al - read - y trod,
calls us to the race; And God's own hand still gives the prize
have my race be - gun; And, crowned with vic - tory, at your feet

and an im - mor - tal crown, and an im - mor - tal crown.
and on - ward urge your way, and on - ward urge your way.
with nev - er - end - ing grace, with nev - er - end - ing grace.
I'll lay my hon - ors down, I'll lay my hon - ors down.

*This hymn is one of more than 400 written by a Congregational minister, Philip Doddridge, but none of them were published in his lifetime. Pressing on in the heavenly race is a theme found in several New Testament passages.*

Tune: CHRISTMAS C.M.
*G. F. Handel, 1728*

# 492

# I Would Be True

*Phil. 4:8–9*

*St. 1, 2, Howard Arnold Walter, 1917*
*St. 3, anon.; alt.*

1 I would be true, for there are those who trust me;    I would be
2 I would be friend of all, the foe, the friend-less;    I would be
3 I would be prayer-ful through each bus-y mo-ment;    I would be

pure, for there are those who care;    I would be strong, for
giv-ing, and for-get the gift;    I would be hum-ble,
con-stant-ly in touch with God;    I would be tuned to

there is much to suf-fer;    I would be brave, for
for I know my weak-ness;    I would look up, and
sense God's slight-est whis-per;    I would have faith to

there is much to dare,    I would be brave, for there is much to dare.
laugh, and love, and live,    I would look up, and laugh, and love, and live.
keep the path Christ trod,    I would have faith to keep the path Christ trod.

*The first two stanzas of this hymn are from "My Creed," a poem that Howard Walter sent to his mother from Japan, where he taught English before becoming a Congregational minister. Walter died at the age of thirty-five while working for the Y.M.C.A. in India.*

Tune: PEEK 11.10.11.10.10.
*Joseph Y. Peek, 1911*

# O Jesus, I Have Promised

**493**

*John E. Bode, 1868; alt.*

*Luke 9:57; John 14:1–4*

1 O Je - sus, I have prom - ised to serve you to the end;
2 O let me hear you speak - ing in ac - cents clear and still,
3 O Je - sus, you have prom - ised to all who fol - low you

re - main for - ev - er near me, my Sav - ior and my Friend:
a - bove the storms of pas - sion, the mur - murs of self - will!
that where you are in glo - ry your ser - vant shall be, too;

I shall not fear life's strug - gles if you are by my side,
O speak to re - as - sure me, to has - ten or con - trol!
And, Je - sus, I have prom - ised to serve you to the end;

nor wan - der from the path - way if you will be my guide.
O speak, and make me lis - ten, O guar - dian of my soul!
O give me grace to fol - low my Sav - ior and my Friend!

*John Ernest Bode wrote these words when his daughter and two sons were confirmed. Although the Oxford scholar and rector wrote books of hymns, this is the only one to achieve lasting fame.*

Tune: ANGEL'S STORY 7.6.7.6.D.
A. H. Mann, 1883
Alternate tune: MUNICH

# 494          We Who Would Valiant Be

*John Bunyan, 1684; alt.*

1 We who would valiant be: let us not waver,
2 Those who may us sur-round with dis-mal sto-ries,
3 Since, Sav-ior, you de-fend us with your Spir-it,

but in true con-stan-cy fol-low the Sav-ior.
on-ly them-selves con-found; our strength the more is.
we know we at the end shall life in-her-it.

There's no dis-cour-age-ment shall make us once re-lent
No foes shall give us fright, ours is the one true Light;
Cruel ru-mors, flee a-way! We'll fear not what they say;

our first a-vowed in-tent to live as pil-grims.
we will make good our right to live as pil-grims.
we'll la-bor night and day to live as pil-grims.

The English author John Bunyan became an influential
Congregational and Baptist preacher, for which he was
imprisoned for many years. Part One of his Pilgrim's Progress
was written in prison. Lines from Pilgrim's Progress, Part Two,
have been recast as this hymn.

Tune: ST. DUNSTAN'S 6.5.6.5.6.6.6.5.
C. Winfred Douglas, 1917

# Called as Partners in Christ's Service

### 495

*Jane Parker Huber, 1981*

*John 15:12–17; Gal. 6:2; Eph. 2:14–22*

1 Called as part-ners in Christ's ser-vice, called to min - is - tries of grace,
2 Christ's ex - am - ple, Christ's in - spir-ing, Christ's clear call to work and worth,
3 Thus new pat-terns for Christ's mis-sion, in a small or glob-al sense,
4 So God grant us for to - mor-row ways to or - der hu - man life

We re-spond with deep com - mit-ment fresh new lines of faith to trace.
Let us fol - low, nev - er fal-tering, rec - on - cil - ing folk on earth.
Help us bear each oth - er's bur-dens, break-ing down each wall or fence.
That sur-round each per - son's sor-row with a calm that con - quers strife.

May we learn the art of shar-ing, side by side and friend with friend,
Men and wom-en, rich - er, poor-er, all God's peo - ple, young and old,
Words of com-fort, words of vi - sion, words of chal-lenge, said with care,
Make us part-ners in our liv - ing, our com - pas - sion to in - crease,

E - qual part - ners in our car-ing to ful - fill God's cho - sen end.
Blend-ing hu - man skills to - geth-er gra-cious gifts from God un - fold.
Bring new power and strength for ac-tion, make us col-leagues, free and fair.
Mes - sen - gers of faith, thus giv-ing hope and con - fi - dence and peace.

*One of Jane Parker Huber's most widely sung texts, this hymn was originally written for a women's breakfast at the 1981 Presbyterian General Assembly meeting to celebrate the partnership of women and men in service of the church.*

Tune: BEECHER 8.7.8.7.D.
*John Zundel, 1855*
*For another key, see 43, 368*

# 496

## Ekolu Mea Nui
### (Three Greatest Things)

*1 Cor. 13:13*

*Robert Nawahine (1868–1951)*

1 E - ko-lu me-a nu-i ma ka ho - nu - a,
2 E na ma - ku-a, na ke - i - ki,

ho - nu - a,

O ka ma-na-'o i - 'o, ka ma-na-'o la - na,
Na ma-mo a Iu - da me E - pe-lai - ma,

e - pe-lai - ma,

a me ke-a - lo - ha. Ke-a - lo - ha kai oi a - 'e,
E pa'a ka ma-na - 'o i ka po-no i oi a - e.

Po-mai-ka'i na mea a - pau, po-mai-ka'i na mea a - pau.
Po-mai-ka'i na mea a - pau, po-mai-ka'i na mea a - pau.

*This translation is not intended to be sung.*

1 Three important things in the world, faith, hope, and aloha, aloha is the best, and everything is blessed, and everything is blessed.

2 O parents, children, descendants of Judah and Ephraim, think always that righteousness is best, and everything is blessed, and everything is blessed.

*Composed by Robert Nawahine, the "Three Greatest Things" are from 1 Corinthians 13, which ends "And now faith, hope, and love abide, these three; and the greatest of these is love." Nawahine was a leader among the churches of Maui.*

Tune: NAWAHINE Irr.
*Robert Nawahine (1868–1951)*
*Arr. Martha Hohu, 1971*

# Guide My Feet

*African-American traditional; alt.*

*Heb. 12:1–15*

1 Guide my feet while I run this race, guide my feet
2 Hold my hand while I run this race, hold my hand
3 I'm your child while I run this race, I'm your child
4 Stand by me while I run this race, stand by me

Yes, my God.

while I run this race, guide my feet while I run this race,
while I run this race, hold my hand while I run this race,
while I run this race, I'm your child while I run this race,
while I run this race, stand by me while I run this race,

Yes, my God.

For I don't want to run this race in vain.

*This stanza may be added following stanza 1:*
Wheel with me while I run this race . . .

*The words and music of some African-American spirituals have been widely adapted during the twentieth century, especially in the civil rights movement of the 1960s. The alternate words were suggested by a fifth-grade church school class to include those who must "run this race" in a wheelchair.*

Tune:  GUIDE MY FEET  8.8.8.10.
*African-American traditional*
*Arr. Joyce Finch Johnson, 1992*

# 498

## Jesu, Jesu, Fill Us with Your Love

*John 13:1–20; Gal. 5:13–14*

*Tom Colvin, 1969; rev. 1994*

Refrain
Unison

Je - su, Je - su, fill us with your love, show
us how to serve the neigh-bors we have from you. *Last time, end*

1 Knelt at the feet of his friends, si - lent - ly wash - ing their
2 Neigh-bors are rich and poor, var - ied in col - or and
3 These are the ones we should serve, these are the ones we should
4 Lov - ing puts us on our knees, show - ing our faith by our
5 Kneel at the feet of our friends, si - lent - ly wash - ing their

feet, Je - su, you act - ed as ser - vant to them.
race, neigh-bors are near and far a - way.
love; all these are neigh-bors to us and you.
deeds, serv - ing the neigh-bors we have from you.
feet, this is the way we should live with you.

*This African folk melody was presented to the Church at Cshereponi, Northern Ghana, by Ghanaian musicologist, A. A. Mensah, when United Church of Christ missionaries, Al and Sue Krass were serving there. Like Tom Colvin, a Scottish missionary in neighboring Tamale, Al Krass was encouraging the making of hymns to indigenous melodies. Tom Colvin wrote these words to this adapted form of the melody in dedication to the Church at Chereponi.*

Tune: CHEREPONI Irr. with refrain
*Ghanaian folk song; adapt. Tom Colvin, 1969*
*Arr. Jane Marshall, 1982*

# Pues si vivimos
## (In All Our Living)

*St. 1, Mexican folk hymn; transl. anon.*
*St. 2, Elise S. Eslinger, 1983*

1 Pues si vi-vi-mos, pa-ra Dios vi-vi-mos
1 In all our liv-ing, we be-long to God;
2 God sent Christ Je-sus to be our sha-lom,

y si mo-ri-mos, pa-ra Dios mo-ri-mos.
and in our dy-ing, we are still with God;
to show us mer-cy and heal-ing love;

Se-a que vi-va-mos o que mu-ra-mos,
So, wheth-er liv-ing, or wheth-er dy-ing,
So in our liv-ing, and in our dy-ing,

so-mos del buen Dios, so-mos del buen Dios.
we be-long to God; we be-long to God.
Christ is our sha-lom; Christ is our sha-lom.

*This anonymous Mexican folk hymn was transcribed by hymnologist Gertrude Suppe after she first heard it sung by two church women visiting California from Mexico. It was published in* Celebremos II *(1983).*

Tune: PUES SI VIVIMOS Irr.
*Anon.; arr. B. C. M., 1988*

# 500     We Are Climbing Jacob's Ladder

*Gen. 28:10–17*

*African-American spiritual*

1 We are climb-ing Ja-cob's lad-der, we are climb-ing Ja-cob's lad-der,
2 Ev-er-y round goes high-er, high-er, ev-er-y round goes high-er, high-er,
3 Rise, shine, give God glo-ry, rise, shine, give God glo-ry,

we are climb-ing Ja-cob's lad-der, bear-ers of the cross.
ev-er-y round goes high-er, high-er, bear-ers of the cross.
rise, shine, give God glo-ry, bear-ers of the cross.

*Like many spirituals, this one uses a story from the Hebrew scriptures as its starting point and the element of the ladder as a creative device to draw us into the narrative. In like manner, the following twentieth-century adaption of the song by Carole Etzler employs the story of Sarah, the matriarch of the Hebrew people, and extends the direction of the pilgrimage from the upward climb of the ladder to the outward embrace of a circle.*

Tune: JACOB'S LADDER   8.8.8.5.
*African-American spiritual*

# 501     We Are Dancing Sarah's Circle

*Gen. 17:15–19; 18:9–15*

*Carole A. Etzler, 1975*

1 We are danc-ing Sar-ah's cir-cle, . . . sis-ters, broth-ers, all.
2 Here we seek and find our sto-ry, . . . sis-ters, broth-ers, all.
3 We will all do our own nam-ing, . . . sis-ters, broth-ers, all.
4 Ev-ery round a gen-er-a-tion, . . . sis-ters, broth-ers, all.
5 On and on the cir-cle's mov-ing, . . . sis-ters, broth-ers, all.

Tune: JACOB'S LADDER   8.8.8.5.
*African-American spiritual*

# Dear God, Embracing Humankind

**502**

*John Greenleaf Whittier, 1872; alt.*

*Mark 1:16–20; Matt. 14:22–23; 1 Kings 19:11–12*

1 Dear God, em-brac-ing hu-man-kind, for - give our fool-ish
2 In sim - ple trust like theirs who heard, be - side the Syr - ian
3 O sab - bath rest by Gal - i - lee! O calm of hills a -
4 Drop your still dews of qui - et - ness, till all our striv-ings
5 Breathe through the puls - es of de - sire your cool-ness and your

ways; Re - clothe us in our right - ful mind, in
sea, The gra - cious call - ing of your word, let
bove! There Je - sus met you prayer - ful - ly: the
cease; Take from our souls the strain and stress, and
balm; Let sense be numb, let flesh re - tire; speak

pur - er lives your ser - vice find, in deep - er rev-erence, praise.
us, like them, by spir - it stirred, rise up and fol-lowers be.
si - lence of e - ter - ni - ty, in - ter - pret - ed by love.
let our or - dered lives con - fess the beau - ty of your peace.
through the earth-quake, wind, and fire, O still, small voice of calm.

*In his poem "The Brewing of Soma," New England poet John Greenleaf Whittier compares frenzied ecstasies of a sect of Hindu priests to the noisy Christian revivals he found so offensive. This hymn of quiet worship is from the final stanzas.*

*Tune: REST 8.6.8.8.6.*
*Frederick C. Maker, 1887*
*Alternate tune: REPTON*
*(repeating last phrase)*

# 503       O Savior, Let Me Walk with You

*Washington Gladden, 1879; alt.*

1. O Sav-ior, let me walk with you in earth-ly
2. Help me the slow of heart to move by some clear
3. Teach me your pa-tience; let me be in clos-er,
4. In hope that sends a shin-ing ray far down the

paths of ser-vice true; Tell me your se-cret,
win-ning word of love. Teach me the way-ward
dear-er com-pa-ny, In work that keeps faith
fu-ture's broad-ening way, In peace that on-ly

help me bear the strain of toil, the fret of care.
feet to stay, and guide them in the home-ward way.
sweet and strong, in trust that tri-umphs o-ver wrong.
you can give, with you, O Sav-ior, let me live.

*Washington Gladden was a Congregational minister,
distinguished preacher and lecturer, and author of over thirty
works. Gladden wrote extensively on civic and social affairs of
his day. This hymn was penned in 1879 and published in his
periodical,* The Sunday Afternoon.

Tune: MARYTON L.M.
*H. Percy Smith, 1874*

# You Walk along Our Shoreline

*Sylvia G. Dunstan, 1984; alt.*                                    *Mark 1:16–20; John 17:20–26*

1 You walk a - long  our  shore - line  where  land meets un - known sea.
2 You call  us, Christ, to  gath - er  the  peo - ple  of  the  earth.
3 We  cast our net,  O  Je - sus; we  seek your prom - ised reign;

We  hear your voice of  pow - er, "Now come and fol - low  me. And
We  can - not fish for  on - ly  those lives we think  have  worth. We
We  work for  love and  jus - tice; we  learn to hope through pain. You

if  you still will  fol - low through storm  and wave and  shoal,
spread your net of  gos - pel a - cross  the  wa - ter's  face,
call  on  us  to  gath - er God's daugh - ters and God's sons,

Then  I  will make you  fish - ers, but  of  the  hu - man soul."
Our  boat a  com - mon shel - ter for  all found by  your grace.
To  let your judg - ment heal  us  so  that all  may  be  one.

*Hymnwriter Sylvia Dunstan credited an article by Michael Steinhauser in the March 1984 issue of* Practice of Ministry in Canada *entitled "Fishing: A Metaphor for Ministry" as the inspiration for her text. Dunstan was an ordained minister of the United Church of Canada.*

Tune:  SALLEY GARDENS  7.6.7.6.D.
*Traditional Irish melody*
*Harm. The New Century Hymnal, 1994*

# 505

# Sweet Hour of Prayer

*William Walford, 1845; alt.*

1 Sweet hour of prayer! Sweet hour of prayer! that calls me from a world of care,
2 Sweet hour of prayer! Sweet hour of prayer! the joys I feel, the bliss I share
3 Sweet hour of prayer! Sweet hour of prayer! whose wings shall my pe - ti - tion bear

and bids me at my Ma-ker's throne let all my needs and wants be known.
of those whose anx-ious spir-its burn with strong de-sires for your re-turn!
to One whose truth and faith-ful - ness en-gage the wait-ing soul to bless.

In sea - sons of dis-tress and grief, my soul has of - ten found re - lief,
With them I has-ten to the place where I would know my Sav-ior's face,
And since I'm bid to seek God's face, be - lieve God's word, and trust God's grace,

and oft es-caped the tempt-er's snare by your re - turn, sweet hour of prayer!
And glad - ly take my sta - tion there, and wait for you, sweet hour of prayer!
I'll cast a - way my ev - ery care, and wait for you, sweet hour of prayer!

*Although credited to a different poet when first published in 1845, researchers believe this hymn was written by William Walford. William Bradbury, a highly trained musician, sang under Lowell Mason in Boston and also wrote "Jesus Loves Me."*

Tune: SWEET HOUR L.M.D.
*William B. Bradbury, 1861*

# What a Friend We Have in Jesus

## 506

*Joseph Scriven, 1855; alt.*

*Phil. 4:6–7*

1 What a friend we have in Je - sus, all our sins and griefs to bear!
2 Have we tri - als and temp-ta - tions? Is there trou-ble an - y - where?
3 Are we weak and heav - y lad - en, bur-dened with a load of care?

What a priv-i-lege to car - ry ev - ery-thing to God in prayer!
We should nev - er be dis - cour - aged; take it to our God in prayer!
Pre - cious Sav-ior, still our ref - uge, take it to our God in prayer!

Oh, what peace we of - ten for - feit, oh, what need-less pain we bear,
Can we find a friend so faith - ful, who will all our sor-rows share?
Do your friends de-spise, for - sake you? Take it to our God in prayer!

All be-cause we do not car - ry ev - ery-thing to God in prayer.
Je - sus knows our ev - ery weak - ness; take it to our God in prayer!
Je - sus' arms will take and shield you; you will find a sol-ace there.

*No stranger to sorrow himself, Joseph Scriven wrote this hymn
to comfort his mother in Ireland. Scriven, who moved to Canada
as a young man, attempted to follow literally the teachings of the
Sermon on the Mount.*

Tune: ERIE 8.7.8.7.D.
*Charles C. Converse, 1868*

# 507

## Jesus—The Very Thought to Me

Phil. 2:1–11; 1 Pet. 1:1–9

Latin, possibly 12th century
Transl. Edward B. Caswall, 1849; alt.

1 Je-sus— the ver - y thought to me with sweet-ness fills my breast;
2 No voice can sing, no heart can frame, nor can the mem-ory find
3 O hope of ev - ery con - trite heart, O joy of all the meek,
4 But what to those who find? Ah this, no tongue nor pen can show
5 Je - sus, our joy, our great - est bliss, and you our prize will be;

But sweet-er far your face to see, and in your pres - ence rest.
A sweet-er sound than your blessed name, Sav - ior of hu - man-kind.
How kind you are to those a - part, how good to those who seek!
Your love, O Je - sus, what it is none but your loved ones know.
Our glo - ry here and now is this, and through e - ter - ni - ty.

"Jesus dulcis memoria" was an anonymous medieval poem originally
forty-two stanzas long. Several hymns have been derived from it,
including this one set to John B. Dykes' tune named for a young
Roman girl, Christian by birth, who was martyred in 304 C.E.

Tune: ST. AGNES C.M.
John B. Dykes, 1866

# 508

## Prayer Is the Soul's Sincere Desire

Luke 11:1; Rom. 8:26–28

James Montgomery, 1818; alt.

1 Prayer is the soul's sin-cere de-sire,
   ut-tered or un-ex-pressed;
   The mo-tion of a hid-den fire
   that trem-bles in the breast.

2 Prayer is the sim-plest form of speech
   that in-fant lips can try;
   Prayer, the sub-lim-est strains that reach
   the Maj-es-ty so nigh.

3 Prayer is the con-trite sin-ner's voice,
   turn-ing from thought-less ways,
   While an-gels in their songs re-joice
   and cry, "Be-hold, one prays!"

4 No prayers do hu-mans make a-lone;
   the Ho-ly Spir-it pleads,
   And Je-sus on the e-ter-nal throne
   for sin-ners in-ter-cedes.

5 O Christ, by whom we come to God,
   the Life, the Truth, the Way,
   The path of prayer you too have trod:
   Christ, teach us how to pray.

This hymn by Moravian journalist and hymnwriter James
Montgomery was written for Edward Bickersteth's Treatise
on Prayer to answer the question, "What is prayer?" The hymn
closes with the disciples' request of Jesus, "Teach us to pray."

Tune: ST. AGNES C.M.
John B. Dykes, 1866

# How Deep the Silence of the Soul

*Sylvia G. Dunstan, 1989*

1 How deep the si - lence of the soul that lives with - in your grace.
2 Like un - seen chimes on mov-ing air, like warm and morn-ing sun,

How full the grat - i - tude of heart in your a - bid - ing place.
Like glad-dening, green - ing, grow-ing things, like trees with blooms be - gun.

What rich se - ren - i - ty is found, what cour - age and re - lease
Such is your pres - ence in our lives, you touch with-out a trace,

when wis - dom teach - es us to seek the gen - tle path to peace.
un - til we turn and find our-selves held fast in your em - brace.

This hymn by Sylvia Dunstan, entitled "Morning Meditation,"
recounts the Canadian writer's experience one February when
she left cold, snowy Toronto to visit her mother in California.
There she enjoyed meditating in the garden that was abloom
with camellias.

Tune: TALLIS' THIRD TUNE C.M.D.
*Thomas Tallis, c. 1557*
*For another key, see 178*

## 510     Grant Us Wisdom to Perceive You

*Rae Whitney, 1991; rev. 1994*

1 Grant us wis - dom to per - ceive you, hearts a -
2 Grant us faith - ful - ness in pray - ing, strength to
3 Grant us dil - i - gence in do - ing, pa - tience
4 Grant us cour - age to pro - claim you; Sav - ior

wak - ened to re - ceive you, minds a - lert to
keep our souls from stray - ing, sense to cease from
when your truth pur - su - ing, ea - ger to re -
of our lives we name you! May our ac - tions

thoughts that grieve you, God of mer - cy, hear us.
dis - o - bey - ing, God of mer - cy, hear us.
ceive re - new - ing, God of mer - cy, hear us.
nev - er shame you; God of mer - cy, hear us.

*This text was inspired by a prayer of St. Benedict, the founder
of the Benedictine monastic order, c. 529 C.E. Rae Whitney
grew up in England, but settled in Nebraska with her American
husband in 1960. She is the author of some 300 hymns.*

Tune: QUEM PASTORES 8.8.8.6.
*German carol, 14th century
Harm. Ralph Vaughan Williams, 1906*

## 511     I Love My God, Who Heard My Cry

*Ps. 116:1–2*

*Isaac Watts, 1719; alt.*

1 I love my God, who heard my cry and pit - ied
2 I love my God, who heard my cry and chased my

ev - ery groan. Long as I live and trou-bles
grief a - way. O let my heart no more de -

rise, I'll has-ten to God's throne.
spair while I have breath to pray.

*This African-American spiritual has become a popular setting for
Isaac Watts' text. The harmonization by Richard Smallwood is an
example of the contemporary gospel sound that he helped to pioneer
with his singing group, "The Richard Smallwood Singers."*

Tune: SMALLWOOD C.M.
*African-American spiritual*
*Arr. Richard Smallwood, 1975*

# Sovereign and Transforming Grace     512

*Frederick H. Hedge, 1829; alt.*

1 Sov-ereign and trans-form-ing Grace, we in-voke your quick-ening power;
2 Ho - ly and cre - a - tive Light, we in-voke your kin - dling ray;
3 To the anx-ious soul im - part hope, all oth - er hopes a - bove;
4 Work in all; in all re - new, day by day, the life di - vine;

Reign the spir - it of this place, bless the pur-pose of this hour.
Dawn up - on our spir - it's night, as the dark-ness turns to day.
Stir the dull and hard-ened heart with a long-ing and a love.
All our wills to you sub - due, all our hearts to you in - cline.

*Frederick Henry Hedge, a professor and Unitarian minister, was
perhaps best known for his translations of German hymns. He was
also a hymnwriter, and contributed this text to* Hymns for the
Church of Christ, *a Unitarian hymnal, which he co-edited in 1853.*

Tune: MANTON 7.7.7.7.
*Jane Marshall, 1992*
*Alternate tune: MERCY*

# 513

# O Source of All That Is

Johann Heermann, 1630
Transl. Madeleine Forell Marshall, 1993

1 O Source of all that is, most good-ly Fount of fa - vor,
2 Help me to Christ-like speech, my care-less tongue re - strain - ing.
3 Let me en - joy, with friends, a life of mu - tual car - ing,
4 Re - mind me, as I die, of Je - sus' cru - ci - fix - ion.

Al - low me health and strength, and bless my dai - ly la - bor.
Pre - vent the i - dle vow and si - lence dull com - plain - ing.
Com - mu - ni - ty in Christ, each oth - er's bur - dens bear - ing.
Be - stow on me, that hour, your fi - nal ben - e - dic - tion.

Grant that I may com - plete the good works you as - signed,
But should in - jus - tice rage, the strong op - press the weak,
If I find wealth or fame, if I live man - y years,
Then wel - come my glad soul in - to that glo - rious place,

My con-science clear and sweet, my words both true and kind.
My el - o - quence en - gage, and teach me how to speak.
Save me from sin and shame, and calm my mor - tal fears.
Where I shall, pure and whole, a - dore you face to face.

*Amid the fighting of the Thirty Years' War, Lutheran pastor Johann Heermann wrote this hymn of faith. The chorale tune is one of several sometimes referred to as O Gott, du frommer Gott through association with this text.*

Tune: O GOTT, DU FROMMER GOTT
(DARMSTADT) 6.7.6.7.6.6.6.6.
Neuvermehrtes Gesangbuch, *Meiningen*, 1693

# Over My Head

*African-American traditional*

1 O-ver my head    I hear mu-sic in the air.
2 O-ver my head    I hear sing-ing in the air.
3 O-ver my head    I see trou-ble in the air.
4 O-ver my head    I see Je-sus in the air.

O-ver my head    I hear mu-sic in the air.
O-ver my head    I hear sing-ing in the air.
O-ver my head    I see trou-ble in the air.
O-ver my head    I see Je-sus in the air.

O-ver my head    I hear mu-sic in the air,
O-ver my head    I hear sing-ing in the air,
O-ver my head    I see trou-ble in the air,
O-ver my head    I see Je-sus in the air,

there must be a God some-where.

*This African-American spiritual was widely sung during the 1960s folk-song movement. It was also a freedom song for the civil rights struggle and sometimes included the stanza: "Over my head I see freedom in the air."*

Tune: African-American traditional
*Arr. J. Jefferson Cleveland and Verolga Nix, 1981*

# 515

# O God, My God

Ps. 22:1–2

*The Iona Community, 1988; alt.*

*Refrain*
*Not too fast*

O God, my God, O gra - cious God, why do you seem so

*Last time, end*

far from me, O God, my God, O gra - cious God?

O gra - cious God, O gra - cious God?

O gra - cious God, O gra - cious God?

1 Night and morn - ing I make my prayer: Peace for
2 Pain and suf - fering un - bound and blind Plague the
3 Why, oh, why do the wick - ed thrive, Poor folk
4 Turn a - gain as you hear my plea; Tend the

this place and help for there; Wait - ing and won - dering,
prog - ress of hu - man - kind, Al - ways de - mand - ing,
per - ish, the rich sur - vive; Beg - ging the ques - tion,
tor - ment in all I see: Lov - ing and heal - ing,

*In the Iona Community collection* Enemy of Apathy, *this hymn
is described as a "protest song or a complaint." It exhibits the
kind of "stark honesty before God" characteristic of many of the
psalms.*

Tune: O GOD MY GOD 8.8.5.5.3.3. with refrain
*John Bell, 1988*
*The Iona Community*

*to Refrain*

wait-ing and won-dering, does God care? Does God care?
al-ways de-mand-ing, does God mind? Does God mind?
beg-ging the ques-tion, is God a - live? Is God a - live?
lov-ing and heal-ing, set me free. Set me free.

# O Grant Us, God, a Little Space

**516**

*John Ellerton, 1870; alt.*

1 O grant us, God, a lit - tle space from dai - ly tasks set free.
2 A - round us rolls the cease-less tide of busi-ness, toil, and care,
3 Yet this is not the on - ly place your pres-ence may be found;
4 Yours are the work-place, home, and mart, the wealth of sea and land;
5 Work shall be prayer, if all be wrought as you would have it done;

We meet with-in this ho - ly place and find se - cu - ri - ty.
And scarce-ly can we turn a - side for one brief hour of prayer.
On dai - ly work you shed your grace, and bless-ings all a - round.
The worlds of sci - ence and of art are fash-ioned by your hand.
And prayer, by you in - spired and taught, shall then with work be one.

*John Ellerton's hymn, written for a noonday service in a city church, is one of the earliest to speak of science and art as part of God's creation. Thomas Este was a famous English printer and music publisher.*

Tune: WINCHESTER OLD C.M.
*Este's* Whole Book of Psalmes, *1592*

# 517

# I Need You Every Hour

*Annie S. Hawks, 1872; alt.*
*Refrain added by Robert Lowry, 1872; alt.*

1 I need you ev-ery hour, O God of grace;
the peace your voice af-fords, I now em - brace.

2 I need you ev-ery hour, in faith or fear;
temp - ta - tions lose their power when you are near.

3 I need you ev-ery hour, in joy or pain;
come quick - ly and a - bide or life is vain.

4 I need you ev-ery hour; teach me your will,
and your rich prom-is - es in me ful - fill.

*Refrain*

I need you, how I need you! Ev - ery hour I need you;
O bless me now, my Sav - ior; I come to you.

First sung at a convention of the National Baptist Sunday School
Association, this hymn was used by Dwight Moody and Ira
Sankey in both England and the United States. Annie S. Hawks,
a Baptist, was the author of some 400 hymns.

Tune: NEED 6.4.6.4. with refrain
Robert Lowry, 1872

# Father Almighty, Bless Us

## 518

L. J. W., in The Sunny Side, 1875; alt.

Ps. 23

1 Fa - ther al - might - y, bless us with your bless - ing;
2 Christ of com - pas - sion, car - ry all who seek you
3 Moth - er of mer - cy, from your watch and keep - ing

an - swer in love your chil - dren's sup - pli - ca - tion;
to pas - tures green be - side the peace-ful wa - ters;
no space can part, nor hour of time re - move us;

Hear now our prayer, the spo - ken and un -
Most ten - der guide, in ways of cheer - ful
Give us your good, and save us from our

spo - ken; hear us, E - ter - nal God.
du - ty lead us, good Shep - herd.
e - vil, In - fi - nite Spir - it.

Credited to the Rev. L. J. W.—possibly the Rev. Loammi J.
Ware—this hymn appeared in The Sunny Side, a Unitarian
collection. Berlin physician Friedrich F. Flemming wrote the
music as a male chorus setting of an ode by Horace.

Tune: INTEGER VITAE 11.11.11.5.
Friedrich F. Flemming (1778–1813)

# 519 Not My Brother, nor My Sister

## (Standing in the Need of Prayer)

*African-American spiritual; alt.*

**Leader**

1 Not my broth-er, nor my sis-ter, but it's me, O God,
2 Not the preach-er, nor the dea-con, but it's me, O God,
3 Not my fa-ther, nor my moth-er, but it's me, O God,
4 Not the strang-er, nor my neigh-bor, but it's me, O God,

**All** ... **Leader**

stand-ing in the need of prayer; Not my broth-er, nor my sis-ter, but it's
stand-ing in the need of prayer; Not the preach-er, nor the dea-con, but it's
stand-ing in the need of prayer; Not my fa-ther, nor my moth-er, but it's
stand-ing in the need of prayer; Not the strang-er, nor my neigh-bor, but it's

**All** ... **Refrain**

me, O God, stand-ing in the need of prayer.
me, O God, stand-ing in the need of prayer.
me, O God, stand-ing in the need of prayer.
me, O God, stand-ing in the need of prayer.

It's

me, it's me, O God, stand-ing in the need of prayer;

it's me,

*James Weldon Johnson included this African-American spiritual in his historic collection of 1925,* The Book of American Negro Spirituals. *It was popularized by Mahalia Jackson, who specialized in such spirituals when she began her public singing career.*

Tune: NEED OF PRAYER 13.7.13.7. with refrain
*African-American spiritual*

It's me, it's me, O God, stand-ing in the need of prayer.

it's me,

# Eternal Spirit of the Living Christ

520

*Frank von Christierson, 1974; rev. 1979*

*Rom. 8:26–27*

*Unison*

1 E - ter-nal Spir-it of the liv-ing Christ, I know not how to
2 Come, pray in me the prayer I need this day; help me to see your
3 Come with the vi-sion and the strength I need to serve my God, and

ask or what to say; I on-ly know my need, as deep as
pur-pose and your will, Where I have failed, what I have done a -
all hu-man-i-ty; Ful - fill-ment of my life in love out-

life, and on - ly you can teach me how to pray.
miss; held in for-giv-ing love, let me be still.
poured— my life in you, O Christ, your love in me.

*Frank von Christierson's text was published by The Hymn Society in the 1974 collection* New Hymns, Songs, and Prayers for Church and Home. *Alfred Smith, an Episcopal minister who first studied music as an adult, composed* Sursum Corda *for a hymn, "Lift up your hearts. . . ."*

Tune: SURSUM CORDA 10.10.10.10.
*Alfred M. Smith, 1941*

Words Copyright © 1974 by The Hymn Society

# 521

# In Solitude

*Rom. 8:26–27; Eph. 5:18–20*

*Ruth Duck, 1983*

1 In sol - i - tude, in sol - i - tude, I come to God in prayer.
2 When-e'er the world is troub-ling me, and stress is all a - round,
3 In sea - sons of per - plex - i - ty, in times of deep de - spair,
4 And when my heart is bur - dened down with cares for those I love,
5 With psalms and hymns and songs of praise be - fore my God I'll come,

In si - lence and sim - plic - i - ty, my spir - it blos-soms there.
I seek the pres - ence of my God, and heal - ing light is found.
I light a can - dle in the night and turn to God in prayer.
too deep for words, with groans and sighs, de - scends the ho - ly dove.
till death it - self is past and gone, and I ar - rive at home.

*Ruth Duck has commented that "these words were inspired by a pentatonic melody which came to me as I taught myself to play the mandolin." They are an expression of her "deep-rooted southern spirituality."*

Tune: LAND OF REST C.M.
*Traditional United States melody*
*Harm. Annabel Morris Buchanan, 1938*

Words Copyright © 1985 by G.I.A. Publications, Inc.

# 522

# I Love to Tell the Story

*Katherine Hankey, 1866; alt.*

1 I love to tell the sto - ry of un - seen things a - bove.
2 I love to tell the sto - ry; more won - der - ful it seems
3 I love to tell the sto - ry; it's pleas - ant to re - peat
4 I love to tell the sto - ry, for those who know it best

*Born in Clapham, England, Katherine Hankey belonged to the Clapham Sect of Evangelicals and established a Bible class for girls in London's West End. This hymn is drawn from her extended poem on the life of Jesus, which also contains "Tell me the old, old story."*

Tune: HANKEY 7.6.7.6.D. with refrain
*William G. Fischer, 1869*

Of Je - sus' ra - diant glo - ry, of Je - sus' end - less love.
than all the gold - en vi - sions of all our gold - en dreams.
what seems, each time I tell it, more won - der - ful - ly sweet.
seem hun - ger - ing and thirst - ing to hear it, like the rest.

I love to tell the sto - ry, be - cause I know it's true;
I love to tell the sto - ry, I tell it now to you
I love to tell the sto - ry, for some have nev - er heard
And when I sing in glo - ry, I know the new, new song

it sat - is - fies my long - ings as noth - ing else can do.
be - cause I want to share it, be - cause I know it's true.
the mes - sage of sal - va - tion from God's own ho - ly Word.
will be the old, old sto - ry that I have loved so long.

*Refrain*

I love to tell the sto - ry; and when I am in glo - ry

I'll tell the old, old sto - ry of Je - sus' end - less love.

# 523 Someone Asked the Question
## (Why We Sing)

*Matt. 10:26–31; Luke 12:4–7*

*Kirk Franklin, 1993*

1. Some-one asked the ques-tion, "Why do we sing? When we
   Some-one may be won-dering when we sing our song, at
2. When the song is o - ver, we've all said "A - men," in your
   if some-bod - y asks you, "Was it just a show," lift your
3. When we cross that riv - er to stu - dy war no more, we will

lift our hands to Je - sus what do we real - ly mean?"
times we may be cry-ing and noth-ing's real - ly wrong.
heart just keep on sing-ing and the song will nev - er end. And
hands and be a wit-ness and tell the whole world, "No!"
sing our song to Je - sus, the One whom we a - dore! *(to Refrain)*

*St. 3, 2nd ending only*

**Refrain**

I sing be-cause I'm hap-py! I sing be-cause I'm free!

*Kirk Franklin began to compose and arrange gospel music at the age of eleven, when he was appointed Minister of Music at Mt. Rose Baptist Church in Ft. Worth, Texas. The recording of "Why We Sing" by Kirk Franklin and the Family became immediately popular.*

Tune: WHY WE SING Irr.
*Kirk Franklin, 1993*

God's eye is on the spar-row— That's the rea-son why I sing.

*(Harmony)*

Glo-ry hal - le - lu - jah! You're the rea-son why I sing.

Glo-ry hal - le-lu - jah! I give the prais-es to you.

Glo-ry hal - le-lu - jah! You're the rea-son why I sing.

# 524

# This Little Light/This Joy I Have

Matt. 5:14-16

*African-American spiritual*

1 This lit-tle light of mine,     I'm gon-na let it shine. . . . . .
1 This . . . joy I have,     the world did-n't give to me. . . . . .

I am gon - na let    it,     let it shine,
oh, the world did    not     give to me,

This lit - tle light of mine,     I'm gon-na let it shine.
This joy . . . . I have,     the world did-n't give to me.

This lit - tle light of mine,     I'm gon-na let it shine,
This . . . joy I have,     the world did-n't give to me.

Hal - le-lu - jah,
Hal - le-lu, the

let it shine, . . . let it shine, . . . let it shine, (oh let it shine.)
No, the world did-n't give it, the world can't take it a - way.

*The texts of these two spirituals may be used interchangeably
with the tune This Joy. For an alternate version, this melody may
be sung with the accompaniment of "Glory, Glory Hallelujah."
A more traditional setting of "This Little Light" is provided with
the tune Lattimer.*

Tune: THIS JOY Irr.
*African-American spiritual
Arr. Jeffrey Radford, 1993
See also LATTIMER*

"This Little Light" continued:
2  Ev-ery-where I go . . .
3  All--through the night . . .

"This Joy I Have" continued:
2  This love I have . . .
3  This hope I have . . .
4  This faith I have . . .
5  This peace I have . . .

# This Little Light of Mine
*African-American spiritual*

**525**

*Matt. 5:14–16*

1 This lit-tle light of mine, I'm gon-na let it shine,

this lit-tle light of mine, I'm gon-na let it shine,

This lit-tle light of mine, I'm gon-na let it shine, let it

shine, let it shine, let it shine. (let it shine.)

2  Ev-ery-where I go, I'm gon-na let it shine . . .
3  All--through the night, I'm gon-na let it shine . . .

*This was the favorite song of civil rights activist Fannie Lou
Hamer, who could sing as well as she could give powerful
speeches. During that era this spiritual was sometimes modified
and sung as "This little light of freedom."*

Tune: LATTIMER Irr.
*African-American spiritual*
*Adapt. William Farley Smith, 1987*

# 526

## Siyahamb' ekukhanyen' kwenkhos'
### (We Are Marching in the Light of God)

*Ps. 89:15*

*South African freedom song; transl. Freedom Is Coming, 1984*

Lyrics under the music:

Si - ya - hamb' e - ku - kha - nyen' kwen-khos', si - ya-hamb' e - ku - kha - nyen' kwen-khos'. Si - ya - hamb' e - ku - kha - nyen' kwen - khos', kha - nyen' kwen - khos', Si - ya - ham - ba, ham - ba, si - ya - march-ing, Oo, ham - ba, ham - ba, si - ya - hamb' e - ku - kha - nyen' kwen-khos'.

We are march - ing in the light of God, we are march-ing in the light of God. We are march-ing in the light of God, the light of God. We are march-ing, march-ing, we are march-ing, march-ing, Oo, we are march-ing in the light of God.

*1 D* ... *2 D* ... *Last time, end*

This South African song and fourteen others were first recorded
and published in 1980 by the Church of Sweden Mission and the
singing group "Fjedur" after a visit they made to South Africa.
The subsequent 1984 collection *Freedom Is Coming* brought the
songs to a worldwide audience.

Tune: SIYAHAMBA Irr.
*South African song*

# We Offer Christ

**527**

*Brian Wren, 1986*

1 We of-fer Christ to all the world a-round us, born in-to faith,
2 We of-fer Christ from all our best tra-di-tions, by grace a-lone,
3 We of-fer Christ the bar-ri-er-be-strid-er, whose full-ness far
4 We of-fer Christ and, God-be-loved, our Sav-ior now of-fers us,

re-leased from pride and shame; Em-braced by love, we show how
a-mazed and strange-ly warmed, Cre-a-ted e-qual, stirred by
ex-ceeds our lo-cal view, Whose Spir-it, breath-ing deep in
born of the Spir-it's kiss, to love cre-a-tion and cre-

love has found us; at peace with God, we speak our Sav-ior's name.
free-dom-vi-sions, self-crit-i-cal, pre-pared to be re-formed.
ev-ery cul-ture, brings Christ to us, the same, yet strange-ly new.
a-tion's Lov-er, with skill, com-pas-sion, jus-tice, care and peace.

*"We Offer Christ" was commissioned by St. Paul's United Methodist Church, Orangeburg, South Carolina, for its 150th anniversary. The opening phrase derives from John Wesley's advice to Thomas Coke as he departed for America: "Offer them Christ."*

Tune: CHARTERHOUSE 11.10.11.10.
*David Evans, 1927*

# 528

# Sois la Semilla
## (You Are the Seed)

Matt. 13:24–30, 33, 36–43; 5:13–16; 28:18–20

*Cesáreo Gabaraín, 1979; alt.*
*Transl. Raquel Gutiérrez-Achon and Skinner Chávez-Melo, 1987; alt.*

mor, men - sa - je - ras de la vi - da,
ción. Id lle - van - do mi pre - sen - cia;
all, mes - sen - gers of my for - giv - ing peace,
rose; "Lo, I'll be with you for - ev - er,

de la paz y el per - dón.
e - ter - nal love.

con u - ste - des es - toy.
till the end of the world."

2 Sois u-na lla-ma
   que ha de_en-cen-der
      res-plan-do-res de fe y ca-ri-dad.
     Sois los pas-to-res que han de lle-var
     al mun-do por sen-das de paz.
     Sois los a-mi-gos que qui-se_es-co-ger,
      sois pa-la-bra que_in-ten-to_es-par-cir.
     Sois rei-no nue-vo
     que_em-pie-za_a_en-gen-drar
      jus-ti-cia, a-mor y ver-dad.
   *Estribillo*

3 Sois fue-go y sa-bia
   que vi-ne_a tra-er,
     sois la o-la que_a-gi-ta la mar.
     La le-va-du-ra pe-que-ña de_a-yer
      fer-men-ta la ma-sa del pan.
     U-na ciu-dad no se pue-de_es-con-der,
      ni los mon-tes se han de_o-cul-tar,
     en es-tas o-bras que bus-can el bien,
     el mun-do a Dios ha de ver.
   *Estribillo*

2 You are the flame that will bright-en
     the way,
     send-ing spar-kles of hope, faith,
     and love;
  you are the shep-herds
  to lead the whole world
     through val-leys and pas-tures of peace.
  You are the friends that I chose for my-self,
     the word that I want to pro-claim.
  You are the cit-y that's built on a rock
     where jus-tice and truth al-ways reign.
   *Refrain*

3 You are the life that will nur-ture the plant;
     you're the waves in a tur-bu-lent sea;
  yes-ter-day's yeast is be-gin-ning to rise,
     a new loaf of bread it will yield.
  There is no place for a cit-y to hide,
     nor a moun-tain can cov-er its might;
  may your good deeds
  show a world in de-spair
     a path that will lead all to God.
   *Refrain*

*This hymn by Spanish theologian Cesáreo Gabaraín first appeared in the collection* Dios con nosotros, *published in Madrid. The tune, which can be translated in English as "Go and Teach," was arranged by Mexican organist and choral director Skinner Chávez-Melo.*

Tune: ID Y ENSEÑAD 10.9.10.8.D. with refrain
*Cesáreo Gabaraín, 1979*
*Harm. Skinner Chávez-Melo, 1987*

# 529       Now Let Us All, in Hymns of Praise

*Fred Pratt Green, 1982*

1 Now let us all, in hymns of praise, bear wit-ness with one voice
2 What chang-es, chal-leng - es, and tests the church of Christ sur - vives!
3 Of all our la - bors, who can say what har - vest there shall be,

to God's re-deem-ing work in Christ, and bid the world re - joice.
How rich the rec - ords left to us of ded - i - cat - ed lives!
when time, that lim - its and dis-torts, be - comes e - ter - ni - ty?

To - day we call to mind the things that time can-not e - rode:
Still must the church pro - claim to all that now, and ev - er - more,
Then shall our hymns, re - hearsed be - low, be per - fect praise a - bove,

what God, Cre - a - tor of the world, is do - ing for our good.
the house of God is o - pen house, and Christ the O - pen Door.
as, face to face, we ful - ly know what this means: God is love!

*This setting of Fred Pratt Green's 1982 text appears in the composer's collection of thirty-five hymns, The Roy Hopp Hymnary (1990). Hopp holds master's degrees in both choral conducting and composition, and has served as a director of music in Michigan.*

Tune: OPEN DOOR C.M.D.
*Roy Hopp, 1990*
*Alternate tune: ELLACOMBE*

# God Our Author and Creator

## 530

*Carl P. Daw, Jr., 1985*

*Gen. 1:1–2:3; Acts 17:22–31; Rom. 12:2; John 3:16–17*

*Unison*

1 God our Au - thor and Cre - a - tor, in whose life we find our own,
2 Like those first a - pos - tles, Sav - ior, give us strength to love and serve:
3 Keep us faith - ful, Ho - ly Spir - it, help us bear the mes - sage true,

make our dai - ly wit - ness great - er, by our lives make your love known.
when our faint - ing spir - its wa - ver, fire our hearts and steel our nerve.
that at last all lands may hear it: "God is love; Christ died for you."

Help us show how love em - brac - es those whom fear and greed down - trod;
Teach us wis - dom and com - pas - sion: bid our rest - less thoughts be still;
Join our lives in might - y cho - rus till we come from ev - ery place,

in all yearn - ing hearts and fac - es let us see a child of God.
by your guid - ance help us fash - ion lives con - formed un - to your will.
with all those who went be - fore us, to the full - ness of God's grace.

*In 1985, a hymn competition was held to commemorate the centennial of the Women's Missionary Union of the Southern Baptist Convention. This winning text by Carl P. Daw, Jr., fulfilled the guideline that the hymn address mission in the context of daily life.*

Tune: JEFFERSON 8.7.8.7.D.
Southern Harmony, *1835*
Harm. John Ferguson, 1973

# 531 God, Speak to Me, That I May Speak

*Frances Ridley Havergal, 1872; alt.*

1 God, speak to me, that I may speak in
2 O lead me, God, that I may lead some
3 O fill me with your full - ness, God, your
4 O use me, God, use ev - en me just

liv - ing ech - oes of your tone; as you have sought, so
wan - der - ers a - long life's way; O feed me so that
ov - er - flow - ing love to know; In glow - ing word and
as you will, and when, and where, un - til your bless - ed

let me seek your err - ing chil - dren lost and lone.
I may feed your hun - gry ones with - out de - lay.
kin - dling thought, your love to tell, your praise to show.
face I see, your rest, your joy, your glo - ry share.

*Daughter of the English hymnwriter William H. Havergal,*
*Frances Ridley Havergal was a gifted poet and student of several*
*languages, including Hebrew and Greek. She also composed*
*several hymn tunes. Canonbury was adapted from one of Robert*
*Schumann's piano pieces.*

Tune: CANONBURY L.M.
*Arr. from Robert Schumann, 1872*

# Come, Labor On

# 532

*Jane Laurie Borthwick, 1859, rev. 1863; alt.*

*Matt. 9:37–38; 20:1–7*

1 Come, la-bor on. Who dares stay i-dle on the har-vest plain
2 Come, la-bor on. Claim the high call-ing an-gels can-not share;
3 Come, la-bor on. A-way with gloom-y doubts and faith-less fear!
4 Come, la-bor on. No time for rest, till glows the west-ern sky,

while all a-round us waves the gold-en grain? And to each ser-vant
to young and old the gos-pel glad-ness bear. Re-deem the time; its
No one so weak but may do ser-vice here; Though fee-ble a-gents,
till the long shad-ows o'er the path-way lie, And a glad sound comes

does the Sav-ior say, "Go work to-day."
hours too swift-ly fly. The night draws nigh.
may we all ful-fill God's righ-teous will.
with the set-ting sun, "Well done, well done!"

*Jane Laurie Borthwick, along with her sister, Sarah, was a member of the Scottish Free Church and translated many German hymns. English-born Thomas Tertius Noble was organist-choirmaster at St. Thomas' Church, New York City, for thirty-five years.*

Tune: ORA LABORA 4.10.10.10.4.
*Thomas Tertius Noble, 1918*

# 533

# Children of God

*Eph. 4:31–5:2*

*John Greenleaf Whittier, 1848; alt.*

1 Chil - dren of God, lift hearts to one an - oth - er;
2 For God whom Je - sus loved has tru - ly spo - ken:
3 Fol - low with rev - erent steps the great ex - am - ple
4 Then shall all shack - les fall; the storm - y clan - gor

where pit - y dwells, the peace of God is there;
the ho - lier wor - ship which Christ deigns to bless
of Christ whose ho - ly work was do - ing good;
of wild war mu - sic o'er the earth shall cease;

To wor - ship right - ly is to love each oth - er,
Re - stores the lost, and binds the spir - it bro - ken,
So shall the wide earth seem a ho - ly tem - ple,
Love shall tread out the bale - ful fire of an - ger,

each smile a hymn, each kind - ly deed a prayer.
and feeds the wid - ow and the par - ent - less.
each lov - ing life a psalm of grat - i - tude.
and in its ash - es plant the tree of peace.

*Of Puritan ancestry and Quaker parentage, the American poet and journalist John Greenleaf Whittier was a strong supporter of the abolition of slavery. This hymn is comprised of the final stanzas of "Worship," a poem expressing his views on the life of faith.*

Tune: WELWYN 11.10.11.10.
*Alfred Scott-Gatty, 1900*

# O God of Strength

534

*Shepherd Knapp, 1907; alt.*

1  O God of strength, whose
    pur-pose, nev-er swerv-ing,
shall make com-plete the
    work Christ has be-gun,
Grant us to join and__
    work with all dis-ci-ples,
filled with your strength
    to see your will is done.

2  O Word Made Flesh, whose
    work God's work con-tin-ued,
one with the Spir-it's thought
    and deed and word,
Now make us one,
    com--pan-ions in your ser-vice,
your liv-ing bod-y
    by the Spir-it stirred.

3  O Power of Peace,
    who brings to us good tid-ings,
teach us to speak your word
    of hope and cheer:
Rest for the soul, and__ strength
    for all our striv-ing,
light for the path of life,
    your truth brought near.

4  O God, whose grace
    has called us to your ser-vice,
how good your thoughts toward us,
    how great their sum!
We work with you, we__ go
    where you will lead us,
un-til in all the earth
    your reign shall come.

*This hymn was written for a meeting of the Men's Association of the Brick Presbyterian Church, New York, while Shepherd Knapp was assistant minister there. It later became very popular among the students at Eden Seminary, St. Louis.*

Tune:  WELWYN  11.10.11.10.
*Alfred Scott-Gatty, 1900*

# O Holy God, Whose Gracious Power

535

*Jane Parker Huber, 1978*

*Matt. 28:19–20; Acts 1:8*

1  O ho-ly God, whose
    gra-cious power re-deems us,
Make us by faith, true
    stew-ards of your grace.
Help us to hear and__ heed
    Christ's great com-mis-sion,
Shar-ing good news in this
    our time and place.

2  Go we to all the world
    as Christ com-mand-ed
To be your wit-ness-es
    both far and near,
To feed the flock and to
    nour-ish flesh and spir-it,
Sens-ing in sac-ra-ment,
    Christ's pres-ence here.

3  Spir-it di-vine, we need
    your lov-ing fa-vor,
For we con-fess we
    can-not stand a-lone.
May we re-ceive and__ give
    with e-qual plea-sure,
Thus build-ing strong
    your church in flesh, not stone.

4  So may we face the fu-ture
    with-out swerv-ing,
Al-ways em-powered to
    wit-ness to your grace,
In thank-ful-ness for__
    gifts re-ceived and giv-en,
And for those mo-ments
    when we glimpse your face.

*Jane Parker Huber has commented: "This hymn was written early in my time of experimenting with new words for familiar tunes." Huber wanted to provide an alternative for the original Whittier text.*

Tune:  WELWYN  11.10.11.10.
*Alfred Scott-Gatty, 1900*

# 536 Savior, an Offering Costly and Sweet

*John 12:1–3; Eph. 5:1–2*                                             *Edwin Parker, 1888; alt.*

1 Sav - ior, an of - fer - ing cost - ly and sweet
2 Dai - ly our lives would show weak - ness made strong,
3 Some word of hope for hearts bur - dened with fears,
4 Thus, ev - er serv - ing you, till e - ven - tide

Mar - y of Beth - an - y laid at your feet;
toil - some and gloom - y ways bright - ened with song,
some balm of peace for eyes swol - len with tears,
clos - es the day of life, may we a - bide;

May our love's in - cense rise sweet - er than sac - ri - fice,
Some deeds of kind - ness done, some souls by pa - tience won,
Some dews of mer - cy shed, some way - ward foot - steps led,
And when earth's la - bors cease, bid us de - part in peace,

Sav - ior to you, dear Sav - ior to you.
Sav - ior to you, dear Sav - ior to you.
Sav - ior to you, dear Sav - ior to you.
Sav - ior to you, dear Sav - ior to you.

*Edwin P. Parker served as the minister of the Second Church of Christ (South Congregational Church) in Hartford, Connecticut, for fifty years. Parker was also a choir director, composer, and arranger. He wrote this hymn to summarize a sermon.*

Tune: LOVE'S OFFERING 6.4.6.4.6.6.4.5.
*Edwin Parker, 1888*

# Christian, Rise and Act Your Creed

*Francis Albert Rollo Russell, 1893; alt.*

1 Chris - tian, rise and act your creed; let your
2 Hearts a - round you sink with care; you can
3 Of - fer oth - ers hope and joy, and God's
4 Come then, law di - vine, and reign: faith that

prayer be in your deed; Seek the right, per - form the
help their load to bear; You can bring in - spir - ing
wor - ship your em - ploy; Giv - ing thanks in hum - ble
doubt as - sails in vain, Per - fect love be - reft of

true, raise your work and life a - new.
light, strength - en them to do the right.
zeal, learn - ing all God's will to feel.
fear, born in heaven and ra - diant here.

*Francis Albert Rollo Russell was a writer on scientific subjects and a Fellow of the Royal Meteorological Society. This hymn was first published in the* Pilgrim Hymnal *(1904). The tune originated with a text used for the Feast of the Holy Innocents.*

Tune: INNOCENTS 7.7.7.7.
The Parish Choir, *1850*

# 538     Standing at the Future's Threshold

Matt. 25:31–40

*Paul R. Gregory, 1985; rev. 1994*

1 Stand-ing at the fu-ture's thresh-old, grate-ful for God's guid-ing hand,
2 Midst the teem-ing cit-ies' mil-lions, wit-ness to God's bound-less love,
3 O-pen-heart-ed in ex-chang-es with the faith-ful not our own,
4 Build-ing jus-tice as the bul-wark of the peace that God would give,
5 Je-sus Christ, e-ter-nal Sav-ior, Source of life and truth and grace,

Ask-ing no pro-tect-ed strong-hold, called to be a pil-grim band,
Reach-ing for each sys-tem's lost ones, seek-ing jus-tice with each move;
Trust-ing God's way with these strang-ers not to leave the truth un-known,
Mak-ing sac-ri-fice the hall-mark of the life we're called to live:
We would ask no spe-cial fa-vor, with the low-liest seek our place,

Seek-ing ev-er for new vi-sion of the gos-pel for our day,
Grant us cour-age, strength, and pa-tience to con-tend with vi-cious power,
Join-ing them in shared en-deav-or where we have Christ's clear com-mand,
Grant us, God, to bear our wit-ness to this peace in Christ, and move
Know the in-as-much of serv-ing, have your cross as our com-mand:

*Paul Gregory served as East and Southeast Asia secretary of
the United Church Board for World Ministries from 1957 to
1986. This hymn was written for the conclusion of the 175th
anniversary of that board, and looked to the mission challenges
of the future. "Inasmuch" in stanza five is a reference to the
command Jesus gives in Matthew 25:40.*

Tune: LUX EOI 8.7.8.7.D.
*Arthur S. Sullivan (1842–1900)*

We move for-ward in God's mis - sion with our faith to show the way.
Lead us for-ward in the faith that gives us hope in test - ing's hour.
We have faith that calls us ev - er toward this good earth's prom-ised land.
For-ward with our faith's own ac - cess to the life of hope and love.
Lead us in this faith un - swerv-ing for - ward as your pil - grim band.

# Won't You Let Me Be Your Servant? 539

*Richard Gillard, 1977; alt.*

*Rom. 12:9–18; Col. 1:24–29*

1 & 6 Won't you let me be your ser - vant, let me be as Christ to you?
2 We are pil - grims on a jour-ney, we are trav - elers on the road;
3 I will hold the Christ-light for you in the shad - ow of your fear;
4 I will weep when you are weep-ing; when you laugh, I'll laugh with you.
5 When we sing to God in heav - en we shall find such har - mo - ny,

Pray that I may have the grace to let you be my ser-vant, too.
We are here to help each oth - er go the mile and bear the load.
I will hold my hand out to you, speak the peace you long to hear.
I will share your joy and sor-row till we've seen this jour-ney through.
Born of all we've known to - geth-er of Christ's love and ag - o - ny.

*(repeat stanza 1)*

*Richard Gillard was born in England and later made his home in New Zealand. Largely self-taught, Gillard has described his musical style as "folk." This is the best known of his many songs in the United States.*

Tune: SERVANT SONG 8.7.8.7.
*Richard Gillard, 1977*
*Arr. Betty Carr Pulkingham, 1977; adapt.*

# 540 We Plant a Grain of Mustard Seed

Matt. 13:31–32; Mark 4:30–32; Luke 13:18–19;
John 13:34–35; 15:12–17

*Mary Bryan Matney, 1990*

1 We plant a grain of mus-tard seed, and in our faith we find
2 Our ac-tions, more than words, de-fine how love's ex-am-ple feeds
3 When stooped to lend a help-ing hand, we find a touch that heals,
4 Make love our pur-pose, love our aim, for love en-dures all things,

the proof of God is love, in-deed, which blos-soms from its kind;
a great-er love, for love di-vine bursts forth from small-est seeds;
for love in-vest-ed will ex-pand to bear the fruit love yields;
and choos-ing love our lives will claim the peace for-give-ness brings;

the proof of God is love, in-deed, which blos-soms from its kind.
a great-er love, for love di-vine bursts forth from small-est seeds.
for love in-vest-ed will ex-pand to bear the fruit love yields.
and choos-ing love our lives will claim the peace for-give-ness brings.

5  So may our new be-gin-nings prove,
   like liv-ing bread and wine,
  that through our com-mon hu-man love
   we taste what is di-vine;
  that through our com-mon hu-man love
   we taste what is di-vine.

6  Our lives will be ful-filled and blessed
   if through the seeds we've sown
  and by the love that we pro-fess
   the love of Christ is known;
  and by the love that we pro-fess
   the love of Christ is known.

*Mary Bryan Matney and Sally Ann Morris wrote this hymn in
1990 for the marriage of friends. In 1992, it won first prize
in its category in a hymnwriting competition sponsored by
the Charlotte, North Carolina, chapter of the American Guild
of Organists.*

Tune: NEW BEGINNINGS 8.6.8.6.8.6.
*Sally Ann Morris, 1990*

# They Asked, "Who's My Neighbor?"

*Jan Wesson, 1981; alt.*                                    *Luke 10:29–37*

1 They asked, "Who's my neigh - bor and whom should I love; for
2 There once was a trav - el - er set on by thieves who
3 A cer - tain Sa - mar - i - tan then came a - long to
4 I know who's my neigh - bor and whom I should love, for

whom should I do a good deed?" Then Je - sus re - lat - ed a
beat him and left him to die; A priest and a Le - vite each
bind up his wounds and give aid; He took him to stay at an
whom I should do a good deed; For Je - sus made clear in the

sto - ry and said, "It's an - y - one who has a
saw him in pain; but they turned a - way and walked
inn un - til well, and for all the ser - vice he
sto - ry he told, it's an - y - one who has a

need, yes, an - y - one who has a need."
by, yes, they turned a - way and walked by.
paid, yes, for all the ser - vice he paid.
need, yes, an - y - one who has a need.

*Ruth Janelle (Jan) Wesson wrote this hymn for the dedication of her church in Nashville, Tennessee, and was encouraged to submit it to a Hymn Society competition. It was published at the society's national conference in 1982.*

Tune: NEIGHBOR 11.8.11.8.8.
*Jan Wesson, 1981*

# 542

# Born of God, Eternal Savior

1 Pet. 4:8–11; John 17:11; Matt. 6:10

*Somerset T. C. Lowry, 1893; alt.*

1 Born of God, E - ter - nal Sav - ior, source of life, of truth and grace,
2 Christ, as you have lived for oth - ers, so may we for oth - ers live;
3 Come, O Christ, and reign a - mong us, grant - ing love and joy and peace;
4 See the Christ-like host ad - vanc - ing, high and low - ly, great and small,

Hu - man One, whose birth in - car - nate hal - lows all our hu - man race,
Free - ly have your gifts been grant - ed, free - ly may your ser - vants give.
Hush the storm of strife and pas - sion, bid its cru - el dis-cords cease.
Linked in bonds of com - mon ser - vice, an - swer-ing the Sav-ior's call.

Come a - gain, in all your glo - ry; come to us, in - spire and lead;
All the wealth that we may gath - er is for use in caus - es just.
By your pa - tient years of toil - ing, by your si - lent hours of pain,
Je - sus Christ, we hear your plead-ing that your peo - ple should be one.

Fill us with your lov - ing-kind-ness; heal our wrongs, and help our need.
We are stew-ards of the boun - ty loaned to us in sol - emn trust.
Quench our fe - vered thirst for plea-sure, shame our self - ish greed for gain.
Grant, O grant our hope's fru - i - tion: here on earth, your will be done.

*Born in Dublin, Ireland, Somerset T. C. Lowry was a priest of
the Church of England and author of several prose and poetic
works. This hymn, originally titled "For Unity," was written
while he served in North Holmwood, Surrey.*

Tune: WEISSE FLAGGEN 8.7.8.7.D.
Tochter Sion, *Cologne, 1741*
*Alternate tune: BEECHER*

# Where Cross the Crowded Ways of Life 543

*Frank Mason North, 1903; alt.*                                     Luke 19:41; Matt. 10:42; Rev. 22:20

1 Where cross the crowd - ed ways of life, where sound the
2 In haunts of wretch - ed - ness and need, on shad-owed
3 From ten - der child - hood's help - less - ness, from hu - man
4 The cup of wa - ter given for you still holds the

cries of clan and race, A - bove the noise of self - ish
thresh-olds framed with fears, From paths where hide the lures of
griefs and bur - dened toil, From fam - ished souls, from sor - rows'
fresh - ness of your grace; Yet long these mul - ti - tudes to

strife, O Christ, we hear your voice of grace.
greed, we catch the vi - sion of your tears.
stress, we know your heart does not re - coil.
view the deep com - pas - sion of your face.

5  O Sav-ior, from
      the moun-tain-side,
   Make haste to heal
      these hearts of pain;
   A-mong these rest-less
      throngs a-bide,
      O tread the cit-y's streets a-gain:

6  Till all shall learn
      com-pas-sion's might,
   And fol-low where
      your feet have trod,
   Till glo-rious from
      your realm of light,
   Shall come the cit-y of our God.

*This hymn was written for the 1905 Methodist Hymnal by Frank
Mason North, a Methodist minister who was deeply committed to
the role of the church in urban life. North later served as president
of the Federal Council of Churches of Christ in America.*

Tune:  GERMANY (GARDINER) L.M.
*William Gardiner's* Sacred Melodies, *1815*

# 544 Si Fui Motivo de Dolor, Oh Dios
### (If I Have Been the Source of Pain, O God)

*Spanish text, Sara M. de Hall; based on a text by C. M. Battersby*
*English transl., Janet W. May, 1992*

3 Si por la vi-da qui-se an-dar en paz,
   tran-qui-lo, li-bre y sin lu-char por ti
   cuan-do an-he-la-bas ver-me en la lid,
   ¡per-dón, oh Dios!

4 Es-cu-cha oh Dios, mi hu-mil-de
   con-fe-sión
   y lí-bra-me de ten-ta-ción su-til;
   pre-ser-va siem-pre mi al-ma en
   tu re-dil.
   A-mén, A-mén.

3 If I've in-sist-ed on a peace-ful life,
   Far from the strug-gles that the
   gos-pel brings,
   When you pre-fer to guide me to the strife,
   For-give me, God.

4 Re-ceive, O God, this ar-dent word of prayer,
   And free me from temp-ta-tion's
   sub-tle snare,
   With ten-der pa-tience, lead me to your care.
   A-men, A-men.

*The gospel hymn "If I Have Wounded Any Soul Today"*
*was translated into Spanish and set to a new tune. This new*
*setting and its English re-translation provide a strikingly fresh*
*understanding of the poetic intent. Pablo Sosa is an international*
*composer and leader in church music.*

Tune: CAMACUA 10.10.10.4.
*Pablo D. Sosa (b. 1933)*

# There Was Jesus by the Water

545

*Versified by Gracia Grindal, 1983; alt.*

*Matt. 9:18–25; Mark 5:21–42; Luke 8:40–56*

Unison

1 There was Je - sus by the wa - ter speak-ing to the press-ing
2 As the Sav - ior healed an - oth - er, news was brought that she was
3 Je - sus went back with the rul - er where they heard the mourn-ers
4 Je - sus touched the lit - tle daugh-ter, say - ing, "Lit - tle girl, a -

crowd, when, be - hold, there came a rul - er from the syn - a - gogue, who
dead. "Do not trou - ble Je - sus fur-ther." Je - sus heard the news and
weep. Je - sus said un - to the wail-ers, "Why this tu - mult— she's a -
rise!" And she rose to see her fa-ther's and her moth-er's stunned sur -

bowed, say - ing, "Come and heal my daugh - ter, lay your
said, "I will come and see your daugh - ter, I will
sleep. I will go un - to his daugh - ter, and will
prise. They then held their lit - tle daugh - ter and they

heal - ing hands up - on her, heal her, please, that she may live."
lay my hands up - on her, do not fear, she yet may live."
lay my hands up - on her, do not laugh, on - ly be - lieve."
laid their hands up - on her, trust-ing how he made her live.

*Hymnwriter Gracia Grindal is also a teacher, poet, and published hymnologist. Her text first appeared with Rusty Edwards' tune in* Songs of Rejoicing *(1989). Talitha Cumi is an Aramaic command that means "little girl, arise."*

Tune: TALITHA CUMI 8.7.8.7.8.8.7.
*Rusty Edwards, 1983*

# 546

# Jesus, Lover of My Soul

*Charles Wesley, 1740; alt.*

1 Je - sus, lov - er of my soul, let me to your bos - om fly,
2 Oth - er ref - uge have I none; in your hands, my des - ti - ny;
3 Plen-teous grace in you is found, grace to cov - er all my sin;

While the near - er wa - ters roll, while the tem - pest still is high;
Leave, O leave me not a - lone, still sup-port and com - fort me.
Let the heal - ing streams a-bound, make and keep me pure with - in.

Hide me, O my Sav - ior, hide, till the storm of life is past;
All my trust on you is stayed, all my help from you I bring;
Fount of life, your love im - part, fill my cup a - bun - dant - ly;

Safe in - to the ha - ven guide, O re-ceive my soul at last!
Cov - er my de - fense-less head with the shad - ow of your wing.
Spring up now with - in my heart, rise to all e - ter - ni - ty.

*Charles Wesley wrote this hymn soon after his 1738 conversion and titled it "In Temptation." Once considered so intimate that it was omitted from many eighteenth-century hymnals, it is presently found in many languages in collections around the world.*

Tune: MARTYN 7.7.7.7.D.
*Simeon B. Marsh, 1834*
*Alternate tune: ABERYSTWYTH*

# Amazing Grace, How Sweet the Sound

**547**

*St. 1–4, John Newton, 1779; alt.*
*St. 5, A Collection of Sacred Ballads, 1790*

1 A - maz - ing grace, how sweet the sound, that
2 'Twas grace that taught my heart to fear, and
3 Through man - y dan - gers, toils, and snares, I
4 My God has prom - ised good to me, whose
5 When we've been there ten thou - sand years, bright

saved a wretch like me! I once was lost, but
grace my fears re - lieved; How pre - cious did that
have al - read - y come; 'Tis grace has brought me
word my hope se - cures; God will my shield and
shin - ing as the sun, We've no less days to

now am found, was blind but now I see.
grace ap - pear the hour I first be - lieved!
safe thus far, and grace will lead me home.
por - tion be as long as life en - dures.
sing God's praise than when we'd first be - gun.

*John Newton's autobiographical hymn reflects his conversion
from his earlier existence as a slave trader. While serving as
curate in the English village of Olney, Newton met William
Cowper, and together they published* Olney Hymns, *which
included this hymn.*

Tune: AMAZING GRACE C.M.
(NEW BRITAIN)
Columbia Harmony, *Cincinnati, 1829*
*Arr. Edwin O. Excell, 1900*

## 548

# Onuniyan tehanl waun
### (Amazing Grace, How Sweet the Sound)

*St. 1–4, John Newton, 1779; alt.; st. 5, A Collection of Sacred Ballads, 1790*
*Lakota transl. Stephen W. Holmes, 1987*

1 O-nu-ni-yan te-hanl wa-un,
   Ma-shi-cha tke wa-ni,
   Wo-wash-te kin i-ye-wa-ye,
   wi-cho-ni wan-bla-ke.

2 Wo-wash-te he chan-te ma-hel,
   wash-ag-ma-ya-yin kte,
   Wo-wi cha-ke kin un le-hanl,
   o-a-pe kin wan-na.

3 O-ta kig-le te-ke wan el,
   eg-na i-ma-cha-ge,
   Wo-wash-te kin hel ma-wa-ni,
   Wash-te o-ma-ju-la.

4 O-to-ka-he-ya chi-ya-tan,
   o-hin-ni-yan ya-un,
   Wa-kan-tan-ka wo-wi-tan kin,
   yu-ha ma-wa-ni kte.

5 Wa-kan-tan-ka ya-tan un-we,
   Wa-kan-tan-ka ya-tan,
   Wa-kan-tan-ka ya-tan un-we,
   wa-kan-tan-ka a-men.

*United Church of Christ minister Stephen Holmes developed this translation in collaboration with Lakota members of a church he served in South Dakota. "Amazing Grace" has long been a favorite hymn among the Lakota people, but it does not appear in* Dakota Odowan, *the hymnbook published by the Dakota Mission.*

Tune: AMAZING GRACE C.M.
(NEW BRITAIN)
*Columbia Harmony, Cincinnati, 1829*
*Arr. Edwin O. Excell, 1900*

## 549

# Bless God, O My Soul

*Ps. 103*

*Russell E. Sonafrank II, 1987; rev. 1993*

(1–4) Bless God, O my soul! All with-in me bless God's name!
(5) Bless God, hosts of heaven, ev-ery-one who does God's will!

*Last time, end*
*Cue notes, last time only*

Bless God, who was, and is, and shall ev-er be the same!
God's do-min-ion nev-er ends! Bless . . . God, O my soul!

1 When we suf - fer, God sends heal - ing; when we sin, our
2 With com - pas - sion God works jus - tice when op - pres - sion
3 God will not be al - ways chid - ing, nor for - ev - er
4 As a par - ent's love is end - less, so God's mer - cy
5 God re - moves all our trans - gres - sions far as east is

God for - gives; From the grave our God re - deems us,
shac - kles truth; Like the phoen - ix, God re - stores us
an - gry be; God will deal with us in mer - cy,
fol - lows us; For the One who framed our be - ing
from the west; For the grace of God is great as

*to Response*

and by grace, we rise to live!
to the vig - or of our youth.
not ac - cord - ing to our sin.
well re - calls that we are dust!
heaven stands high a - bove the earth!

*This paraphrase of Psalm 103 by Russell E. Sonafrank II and Stephen J. Morris was awarded first place among fifty-nine unsolicited new hymns submitted to The Hymn Society in 1988. It was subsequently published in that organization's journal, The Hymn.*

Tune: SPRING WOODS 8.7.8.7. with response
*Stephen J. Morris, 1987*

# 550 O God, as with a Potter's Hand

*Gen. 2:4b–8; 1 Cor. 15:21–22; 2 Cor. 4:7–12*

*Herman G. Stuempfle, Jr., 1991; rev. 1994*

1 O God, as with a pot-ter's hand, when earth was morn - ing
2 Can clay de - fy the pot - ter's touch, a - lone its form de -
3 But once you shaped from hu - man clay a life whose truth and
4 O God, you hold our earth - en lives with - in your shap - ing

bright, you shaped from clay a hu - man form that
fine, or spoil with wild, re - bel - lious will the
grace re - vealed an im - age pure and whole that
hand and turn our form - ing clay to show the

gave your eye de - light; You breathed in love your
art - ist's true de - sign? Yet we, in whom your
sin could not de - face. And when we seized your
im - age you have planned. For - give the sin that

*Composer Sally Ann Morris has frequently collaborated with hymnwriter Herman Stuempfle, Jr., who dedicated this text to his son, David, a potter. Morris named the tune Winston-Salem for her hometown in North Carolina.*

Tune: WINSTON-SALEM C.M.D.
*Sally Ann Morris, 1993*

Spir - it's breath: a liv - ing crea - ture stirred and
hand has formed an im - age good and fair, dis -
choic - est work and broke its frag - ile clay, your
mars your work and strives a - gainst your will. Con -

stood with - in the gar - den green, a - wake to hear your Word.
fig - ure what you meant to be a work be - yond com - pare.
hands re-stored the shat - tered shards on earth's first Eas - ter day.
form our lives to Je - sus Christ with wis - dom, love, and skill.

# 551      Pass Me Not, O Gentle Savior

*Luke 18:35–43*            *Fanny Crosby (1820–1915); alt.*

1 Pass me not, O gen-tle Sav - ior, hear my hum-ble cry;
2 Let me at your throne of mer - cy find a sweet re - lief;
3 Trust-ing on - ly in your mer - it, would I seek your face;
4 Be the Spring of all my com - fort, more than life to me;

While on oth-ers you are call - ing, do not pass me by.
Kneel-ing there in deep con-tri - tion, help my un - be - lief.
Heal my wound-ed, bro-ken spir - it, save me by your grace.
Not just here on earth be - side me, but e - ter - nal - ly.

*Refrain*

Sav - ior, Sav - ior, hear my hum - ble cry;

While on oth - ers you are call - ing, do not pass me by.

*Fanny Crosby was already a successful writer when she became associated with gospel hymnists Sankey, Sweney, Root, and others. She directed her talent to gospel songs in her early forties, and collaborated with William Doane on many hymns.*

Tune: PASS ME NOT 8.5.8.5. with refrain
*William H. Doane (1832–1915)*

# From the Crush of Wealth and Power

**552**

Kendyl L. R. Gibbons, 1992

*Luke 10:34; James 5:14–16*

1 From the crush of wealth and pow-er some-thing bro-ken in us
2 E-ven now our hearts are wa-ry of the friend we need so
3 When our love for one an-oth-er makes our bur-dens light to
4 Ev-ery time our spir-its lan-guish, ter-ri-fied to draw too

all waits the Spir-it's si-lent hour .... plead-ing
much. When I see the pain you car-ry, shall I,
bear, find the sis-ter and the broth-er, hun-gry
near, may we know each oth-er's an-guish and, with

with a poi-gnant call, bind all my wounds a-gain.
with a gen-tle touch, bind all your wounds a-gain?
for the feast we share; bind all their wounds a-gain.
love that casts out fear, bind all our wounds a-gain.

*This text was commissioned by the Unitarian Universalist*
*Association for the 1993 hymnal* Singing the Living Tradition. *It*
*was written for Peter Cutts' tune* Bridegroom *by Kendyl Gibbons,*
*a Unitarian Universalist minister serving churches in Illinois.*

Tune: BRIDEGROOM 8.7.8.7.6.
*Peter Cutts, 1969*

# 553

# There Is a Balm in Gilead

*Jer. 8:18–22; 46:11; Acts 10:34–43*

*African-American spiritual; alt.*

Refrain

There is a balm in Gil-e-ad, to make the wound-ed whole,

*Last time, end*

there is a balm in Gil-e-ad, to heal the sin-sick soul.

1 Some - times I feel dis - cour-aged, and think my work's in vain,
2 Don't ev - er feel dis - cour-aged, for Je - sus is your friend,
3 If you can - not preach like Pe - ter, if you can - not pray like Paul,

*to Refrain*

But then the Ho - ly Spir - it re - vives my soul a - gain.
who, if you ask for knowl-edge, will nev - er fail to lend.
you can tell the love of Je - sus, who died to save us all.

*This is one of the most moving of the African-American
spirituals because it illustrates the way in which the enslaved tried
to encourage those who were feeling especially weighed down by
the burden of their captivity.*

Tune: BALM IN GILEAD Irr. with refrain
*African-American spiritual*

# Out of the Depths, O God, We Call

**554**

*Ruth Duck, 1988*

*Ps. 130:1–8*

1 Out of the depths, O God, we call to you.
2 Out of the depths of fear, O God, we speak.
3 God of the lov - ing heart, we praise your name.

*Wounds of the past re - main, af - fect - ing all we do.
Break - ing the si - lenc - es, the sear - ing truth we seek.
Dance through our lives and loves; a - noint with Spir - it flame.

Fac - ing our lives, we need your love so much.
Safe a - mong friends, our grief and rage we share.
Your light il - lu - mines each fa - mil - iar face.

Here in this com-mu - ni-ty, heal us by your touch.
Here in this com-mu - ni-ty, hold us in your care.
Here in this com-mu - ni-ty, meet us with your grace.

*Ruth Duck has provided the following words that may be
substituted for those who are seriously ill:*
Free us from fear of death, our faith and hope re-new. . . .
*or, for those who have been abused:*
Wounds of a-buse re-main, af-fect-ing all we do. . . .

Tune: FENNVILLE 10.12.10.12.
*Robert J. Batastini, 1994*

# 555

# Here, Savior, in this Quiet Place

*James 5:13–16; Mark 9:14–29*                                    *Fred Pratt Green, 1974; alt.*

1 Here, Sav-ior, in this qui-et place, where an-y-one may kneel, I al-so come to ask for grace, be-liev-ing you can heal.

2 If pain of bod-y, stress of mind, de-stroys my in-ward peace, In prayer for oth-ers may I find the se-cret of re-lease.

3 If self up-on its sick-ness feeds and turns my life to gall, Let me not brood up-on my needs, but sim-ply tell you all.

4 You nev-er said, "You ask too much," to an-y trou-bled soul. I long to feel your heal-ing touch— will you not make me whole?

5 But if the thing I most de-sire
   is not your way for me,
   May faith, when test-ed in the fire,
   prove its in-teg-ri-ty.

6 Of all my prayers, may this be chief:
   till faith is ful-ly grown,
   Christ, dis-be-lieve my un-be-lief,
   and claim me as your own.

*Peter Cutts, Director of Music and Associate Dean of Chapel
at Andover Newton Theological School, was commissioned to
provide a musical setting for this text especially for* The New
Century Hymnal. *Cutts' work appears in numerous hymnals
in the United States and his native Great Britain.*

Tune: CHATHAM C.M.
*Peter Cutts, 1994*

# God, Who Stretched the Spangled Heavens 556

*Catherine Cameron, 1967*

*Gen. 5:1–2; Isa. 42:5–9*

1 God, who stretched the span-gled heav - ens in-fi - nite in time and place,
2 We have ven - tured worlds un - dreamed of since the child-hood of our race;
3 As each far hor - i - zon beck - ons, may it chal-lenge us a - new,

Flung the suns in burn-ing ra - diance through the si - lent fields of space;
Known the ec - sta - sy of wing-ing through un - trav-eled realms of space;
Chil - dren of cre - a - tive pur - pose, serv - ing oth - ers, hon-oring you.

We, your chil - dren, in your like-ness, share in - ven-tive powers with you;
Probed the se - crets of the at - om, yield-ing un - i - mag - ined power,
May our dreams prove rich with prom-ise, each en-deav-or, well be - gun;

Great Cre - a - tor, still cre - a - ting, show us what we yet may do.
Fac - ing us with life's de - struc - tion or our most tri - um-phant hour.
Great Cre - a - tor, give us guid - ance till our goals and yours are one.

*Catherine Cameron, a professor of social psychology in
California, wrote this text in 1967 with Haydn's Austrian
Hymn in mind. This tune, Holy Manna, appeared in The
Columbian Harmony (1825), and was attributed to the compiler
of that volume, William Moore.*

Tune: HOLY MANNA 8.7.8.7.D.
*William Moore, 1825*

# 557

# Pray for the Wilderness

*Dan Damon, 1989; rev. 1994*

1 Pray for the wil - der - ness, van - ish - ing fast,
2 Learn from the el - e - phant, ea - gle, and whale,
3 Work for the jus - tice cre - at - ed things need,
4 Trust that God's Christ o - ver - came nails and wood,
5 Pray for the at - mos-phere, pray for the sea,

pray for the rain for - est, o - pen and vast;
learn from the drag - on - fly, spi - der, and snail;
work for the health of each plant and its seed;
trust that earth's peo - ple will turn to the good;
learn from the riv - er, the rock, and the tree;

Pray for the wa - ter - falls, pray for the trees,
Learn from the peo - ple in neigh - bor - ing lands,
Work for the crea - tures a - buse has be - trayed,
Trust that cre - a - tion for - ev - er will grow,
Work till sha - lom in full har - mo - ny rings.

pray for the plan - et brought down by de - grees.
learn from the chil - dren who play in their sands.
work for the gar - den God's wis - dom once made.
trust that God's good - ness to us o - ver - flows.
Trust the con - nec - tion of all liv - ing things.

*Hymnwriter Dan Damon tried for several months to write a*
*hymn for the earth. A movie about the vanishing rain forest*
*finally provided the inspiration he needed, along with his*
*seven-year-old daughter, Heather, who suggested including*
*"waterfalls."*

Tune: WILDERNESS 10.10.10.10.
*Lee Yu San, 1967*

# O How Glorious, Full of Wonder

**558**

*Curtis Beach, 1958, rev. 1980; alt.*

*Ps. 8*

1 O how glo-rious, full of won-der is your name o'er all the earth,
2 When we see your lights of heav-en, moon and stars, your power dis-played,
3 You have set us in com-mu-nion with the won-ders of your hand,
4 O how won-drous, O how glo-rious is your name in ev-ery land,

God, who wrought cre-a-tion's splen-dor, bring-ing suns and stars to birth!
Who are we that you should love us, crea-tures that your hand has made?
Made us fly with ea-gle pin-ion, pil-grims o-ver sea and land.
God, whose pur-pose shines be-fore us toward the goal that you have planned!

Rapt in rev-erence we a-dore you, mar-veling at your mys-tic ways.
Born of earth, yet full of yearn-ing, mix-ture strange of good and ill,
Soar-ing spire and ru-ined cit-y, these our hopes and fail-ures show.
Yours the will our hearts are seek-ing, con-scious of our hu-man need.

Hum-bly now we bow be-fore you, lift-ing up our hearts in praise.
From your ways so of-ten turn-ing, yet your love does seek us still.
Teach us more of hu-man pit-y, that we in your im-age grow.
Spir-it in our spir-it speak-ing, make us yours, O God, in-deed.

United Church of Christ minister Curtis Beach submitted this
hymn to the editorial committee of the Pilgrim Hymnal (1958). It
was one of two psalm paraphrases by Beach to be accepted. The
hymn was also included in The Hymnal of the United Church
of Christ (1974).

Tune: IN BABILONE 8.7.8.7.D.
*Traditional Dutch melody*
*Arr. Julius Röntgen, c. 1906*
*Alternate tune: HYMN TO JOY*

# 559

# Thank You, God

*Brian Wren, 1973*

1 Thank you, God, for wa - ter, soil, and air, large gifts sup-port - ing
2 Thank you, God, for min - er - als and ores, the ba - sis of all
3 Thank you, God, for price-less en - er - gy, stored in each at - om,
4 Thank you, God, for weav-ing na - ture's life in - to a seam-less
5 Thank you, God, for mak - ing plan - et earth a home for us and

ev - ery-thing that lives. For - give our spoil - ing and a - buse of
build-ing, wealth, and speed. For - give our reck - less plun-der - ing and
gath-ered from the sun. For - give our greed and care-less - ness of
robe, a frag - ile whole. For - give our haste that tam-pers un - a -
a - ges yet un - born. Help us to share, con - sid - er, save, and

them. Help us re - new the face of the earth.
waste. Help us re - new the face of the earth.
power. Help us re - new the face of the earth.
ware. Help us re - new the face of the earth.
store. Come and re - new the face of the earth.

*John Weaver composed the tune* Amstein *for Brian Wren's text for*
*The Presbyterian Hymnal (1990). It is named for Charles A.*
*Amstein, associate pastor of Madison Avenue Presbyterian Church*
*in New York, where Weaver was named music director in 1970.*

Tune: AMSTEIN 9.10.10.9.
*John Weaver, 1988*

# By Whatever Name We Call You

**560**

*Dosia Carlson, 1990*

*1 Pet. 4:10; Job 11:7–9*

*Unison*

1 By what-ev-er name we call you Fash-ion-er of spheres,
2 In what-ev-er way we wor-ship, Mys-ter-y di-vine,
3 In what-ev-er gifts we of-fer, All-in-clu-sive One,

you are grand-er, so much wis - er than our minds per - ceive.
you are on - ly dim-ly known through ri-tu - al and creed.
you ac-cept your own cre - a - tion, frag-ments we re - turn.

La - bels lim-it un-der - stand-ing, God, you have no peers.
Though we try to cap-ture you in sym-bol or in sign,
Not as own-ers but as stew-ards is our giv-ing done.

So, we ques-tion— chang-ing, grow - ing— want-ing to be - lieve.
on - ly as we let you be can long-ing hearts be freed.
In true won-der we re - ceive the love we can-not earn.

*Dosia Carlson credits "sermons preached by Culver Nelson when he was senior pastor at Church of the Beatitudes, United Church of Christ, in Phoenix, Arizona," as her inspiration for this text. Peter Niedmann, a composer and church music director, provided this musical setting especially for* The New Century Hymnal.

Tune: OGONTZ 8.5.8.5.D.
*Peter Niedmann, 1994*

# 561 When in Our Music God Is Glorified

*2 Chron. 5:11–14*

*Fred Pratt Green, 1972*

1 When in our mu - sic God is glo - ri - fied, and ad - o -
2 How of - ten, mak - ing mu - sic, we have found a new di -
3 So has the church, in lit - ur - gy and song, in faith and
4 Let ev - ery in - stru-ment be tuned for praise! Let all re -

ra - tion leaves no room for pride, It is as though the whole cre -
men - sion in the world of sound, As wor-ship moved us to a
love, through cen - tu - ries of wrong, Borne wit - ness to the truth in
joice who have a voice to raise! And may God give us faith to

*1–3*
a - tion cried: Al - le - lu - ia!
more pro-found Al - le - lu - ia!
ev - ery tongue: Al - le - lu - ia!
sing al - ways:

*4*
Al - le - lu - ia!

*Fred Pratt Green wrote this text at the request of British editor
and composer John Wilson, who asked for a "festival" hymn
to be set with* Engelberg. *Charles Villiers Stanford originally
composed the tune for the text "For All the Saints" in* Hymns
Ancient and Modern *of 1904.*

Tune: ENGELBERG 10.10.10.4.
*Charles V. Stanford, 1904*

# Take My Gifts

*Shirley Erena Murray, 1991*

1 Take my gifts and let me love you, God who first of all loved me,
2 Take the fruit that I have gath - ered from the tree your Spir-it sowed,
3 Take what-ev - er I can of - fer— gifts that I have yet to find,

gave me light and food and shel - ter, gave me life and set me free,
har - vest of your own com-pas - sion, juice that makes the wine of God,
skills that I am slow to sharp - en, tal - ents of the hand and mind,

now be - cause your love has touched me, I have love to give a - way,
spiced with hu - mor, laced with laugh - ter— fla-vor of the Je - sus life,
things made beau - ti - ful for oth - ers in the place where I must be:

now the bread of love is ris - ing, loaves of love to mul - ti - ply!
tang of risk and new ad - ven-ture, taste and zest be - yond be - lief.
take my gifts and let me love you, God who first of all loved me.

*Shirley Erena Murray recounted that Colin Gibson composed
this tune for her stewardship text "almost instantaneously."
Gibson has served as professor at the University of Otago, as
well as organist and choir director in Dunedin, New Zealand.*

Tune: TALAVERA TERRACE 8.7.8.7.D.
*Colin Gibson, 1991*
*Alternate tune: HOLY MANNA*

# 563

# We Cannot Own the Sunlit Sky

*John 10:10*

*Ruth Duck, 1984; rev. 1989*

1 We can-not own the sun-lit sky, the moon, the wild - flowers
2 When bod-ies shiv - er in the night and, wea - ry, wait for
3 God calls hu-man - i - ty to join as part - ners in cre -

grow - ing, for we are part of all that is with -
morn - ing, when chil - dren have no bread but tears, and
a - ting a fu - ture free from want or fear, life's

in life's riv - er flow - ing. With o - pen hands re -
war - horns sound their warn - ing, God calls hu - man - i -
good - ness cel - e - brat - ing. That new world beck - ons

ceive and share the gifts of God's cre - a - tion, that
ty to wake, to join in com - mon la - bor, that
from a - far, in - vites our shared en - deav - or, that

*Ruth Duck wrote this text while she was serving as a corporate member of the United Church Board for World Ministries. In it, she wanted to "emphasize humanity's shared partnership with God in caring for one another and the whole creation."*

Tune: ENDLESS SONG 8.7.8.7.D.
*Attrib. to Robert Lowry in* Bright Jewels
for the Sunday School, *New York, 1869*

all may have a-bun-dant life in ev-ery earth-ly na-tion.
all may have a-bun-dant life in one-ness with their neigh-bor.
all may have a-bun-dant life and peace en-dure for-ev-er.

# We Are Not Our Own

## 564

*Brian Wren, 1987*

*Unison*

1 We are not our own. Earth forms us, hu-man leaves on na-ture's grow-ing
2 We are not a-lone. Earth names us: past and pres-ent, peo-ples near and
3 Through a hu-man life God finds us; dy-ing, liv-ing, love is ful-ly
4 There-fore let us make thanks-giv-ing, and with jus-tice, will-ing and a-

vine, Fruit of man-y gen-er-a-tions, seeds of life di-vine.
far, fam-i-ly and friends and strang-ers show us who we are.
known, and in bread and wine re-minds us: we are not our own.
ware, give to earth, and all things liv-ing, lit-ur-gies of care.

5 And if love's en-coun-ters lead us
    on a way un-cer-tain and un-known,
    All the saints with prayer sur-round us:
    we are not a-lone.

6 Let us be a house of wel-come,
    liv-ing stone up-hold-ing liv-ing stone,
    Glad-ly show-ing all our neigh-bors
    we are not our own!

*This hymn was commissioned for the tenth anniversary of the Liturgical Studies Program of Drew University, New Jersey, in 1987. Brian Wren's melody came to him early on in the writing process and was helpful in the creation of the final hymn text.*

Tune: YARNTON 8.9.8.5.
*Brian Wren, 1987*
*Arr. Fred Graham, 1987*

# 565 God, Whose Giving Knows No Ending

*Robert L. Edwards, 1961; alt.*

1 God, whose giv-ing knows no end-ing, from your rich and
2 Skills and time are ours for serv-ing, that your will on
3 Trea-sure, too, you have en-trust-ed, gain through powers your
4 Lend your joy to all our giv-ing, let it light our

end-less store, Na-ture's won-der, Je-sus' wis-dom, cost-ly cross, grave's
earth be done: All at peace in health and free-dom, rac-es joined, the
grace con-ferred; Ours to use for home and kin-dred, and to spread the
pil-grim way; From the night of anx-ious keep-ing, loose us in-to

shat-tered door: Gift-ed by you, we turn to you
Church made one. Now di-rect our dai-ly la-bor,
gos-pel Word. O-pen wide our hands in shar-ing
gen-erous day. Then when years on earth are o-ver,

of-fering up our-selves in praise; Thank-ful song shall
lest we strive for self a-lone; born with tal-ents,
as we heed Christ's age-less call, Heal-ing, teach-ing,
and we've lived our hu-man span, God, ful-fill be-

*Robert L. Edwards, an ordained United Church of Christ minister, has served several churches in Connecticut. He wrote this text for a competition of The Hymn Society, and it was subsequently published in* Ten New Stewardship Hymns *in 1961.*

Tune: AUSTRIAN HYMN 8.7.8.7.D.
*Franz Joseph Haydn, 1797*
*Alternate tune: HYFRYDOL*

rise for - ev - er, gra - cious do - nor of our days.
make us ser - vants fit to an - swer at your throne.
and re - claim - ing, hon - oring you by lov - ing all.
yond our dream - ing, all our stew - ard - ship be - gan.

# Heaven and Earth, and Sea and Air 566

*Joachim Neander, 1680*  
*Transl. Madeleine Forell Marshall, 1993*

Ps. 57:7–11; 108:1–5

1 Heaven and earth, and sea and air all their Mak-er's praise de - clare.
2 See, at dawn, the ris - ing sun, show the won - ders God has done!
3 Look a - round this earth - ly ball, God has rich - ly dressed it all,
4 Wa - ters surge and wind-storms blow, thun-der, light-ning, hail, and snow:
5 All these things with cu - rious force, find them drawn to praise their source:

Wake, my soul, a - wake and sing, with cre - a - tion prais - es bring!
Moon and stars with sil - very light praise God through the si - lent night.
Ur - ban lights and can - yons deep, for - ests, fields, with cows and sheep.
Through their fren - zy, e - ven these, God would praise and God would please.
Wake, my soul, a - wake and sing, to your Mak - er prais - es bring.

*Words and music of this hymn come to us from two German Pietists: Joachim Neander, writer of both hymns and tunes, and Johann Freylinghausen, known especially as editor and compiler of the most important Pietist hymnbook.*

Tune: GOTT SEI DANK 7.7.7.7.  
*Freylinghausen's* Geistreiches Gesangbuch  
Halle, 1704

# 567 Stars and Planets Flung in Orbit

Ps. 148

Herman G. Stuempfle, Jr., 1989

1 Stars and plan - ets flung in or - bit, gal - ax - ies that
2 Skies a - dorned with sun - set splen - dor, si - lent peaks in
3 Life in won - drous, wild pro - fu - sion, seed and fruit, each
4 Hu - man - kind, earth's deep - est mys - tery, born of dust but

swirl through space, Pow - ers hid with - in the at - om,
calm re - pose, Gold - en fields a - wait - ing har - vest,
flower and tree, Beast and fish and swarm - ing in - sect,
touched by grace, Torn a - part by tongue and col - or,

cells that form an in - fant's face: These, O God, in
foam - ing surf and fra - grant rose: Earth, its boun - ty
soar - ing bird, re - joic - ing, free: These, your crea - tures,
yet a sin - gle, striv - ing race: We, in whom you

si - lence praise you; by your wis - dom they are made.
clothed with beau - ty, ech - oes all cre - a - tion's praise.
join in cho - rus, prais - ing you in word - less song.
trace your im - age, add our words to na - ture's song.

*Herman G. Stuempfle, Jr., began his ministry as a parish pastor.*
*His long association with Lutheran Theological Seminary in*
*Gettysburg began in 1962 when he joined the faculty as professor*
*of preaching, and continued until 1989 when he retired as*
*president emeritus.*

Tune: LAUDA ANIMA 8.7.8.7.8.7.
John Goss, 1869

5 Gra-cious God, we bring be-fore you
   gifts of hu-man life a-lone,
   Truth that throbs through song and sto-ry,
   vi-sions caught in paint and stone:
   These, O God, we glad-ly of-fer,
   gifts to praise the Giv-er's name.

6 Christ, the Word be-fore cre-a-tion
   as cre-a-tion's fin-al goal,
   Once you came for earth's re-demp-tion;
   by your Spir-it make earth whole.
   Then, O God, the new cre-a-tion
   will your praise for-ev-er sing.

# God Marked a Line and Told the Sea    568

*Thomas H. Troeger, 1986*                    *Job 38:1–11; Gen. 2:15–17; 3:1–7*

1 God marked a line and told the sea its
2 God set one lim-it in the glade where
3 The line, the lim-it, and the law are
4 But, dis-con-tent with fi-nite powers, we
5 We are not free when we're con-fined to

surg-ing tides and waves were free To trav-el up the
tempt-ing, fruit-ed branch-es swayed. And that first lim-it
pat-terns meant to help us draw A bound be-tween what
reach to take what is not ours And then de-fend our
ev-ery wish that sweeps the mind. But free when free-ly

slop-ing strand but not to o-ver - take the land.
stands be-hind the lim-its that the law de-fined.
life re-quires and all the things our heart de-sires.
claim by force and swerve from life's in - tend-ed course.
we ac-cept the sa-cred bounds that must be kept.

*Thomas Troeger has provided the following commentary on this text: "It was written as a polemical poem to counter spurious ideas of freedom as undisciplined license, and to affirm how the profoundest liberty involves a sense of boundaries and structure."*

Tune: KEDRON L.M.
*Attrib. to Elkanah Kelsay Dare in*
*Amos Pilsbury's* United States Harmony, *1799*

# 569 Touch the Earth Lightly

*Shirley Erena Murray, 1992*

Unison
Brightly

1 Touch the earth light - ly, use the earth gent - ly,
*2 We who en - dan - ger, who cre - ate hun - ger,
3 Let there be green - ing, birth from the burn - ing,
4 God of all liv - ing, God of all lov - ing,

*The second verse only may be sung in A minor, omitting
the sharps except where indicated in parentheses.

nour-ish the life of the world in our care:
a - gents of death for all crea - tures that live,
wa - ter that bless - es, and air that is sweet,
God of the seed - ling, the snow, and the sun,

Gift of great won - der, ours to sur - ren - der,
We who would fos - ter clouds of dis - as - ter—
Health in God's gar - den, hope in God's chil - dren,
Teach us, de - flect us, Christ re - con - nect us,

trust for the chil - dren to - mor - row will bear.
God of our plan - et, fore - stall and for - give!
re - gen - er - a - tion that peace will com - plete.
us - ing us gent - ly, and mak - ing us one.

Shirley Erena Murray's notes on this hymn state that the title line
is borrowed from an Australian Aboriginal saying. The "clouds
of disaster" mentioned in stanza 2 refer to nuclear testing by
France, which New Zealand has protested at the United Nations
many times.

Tune: TENDERNESS 5.5.10.D.
*Colin Gibson, 1992*

# We Shall Overcome

*United States traditional*

570

*John 8:31–32; Rom. 12:21; 2 Cor. 13:11*

1 We shall o - ver - come, we shall o - ver -
2 We'll go hand in hand, we'll go hand in
3 We are not a - fraid, we are not a -
4 Our God will see us through, our God will see us

come, we shall o - ver - come some day;
hand, we'll go hand in hand some day;
fraid, we are not a - fraid to - day;
through, our God will see us through some day;

(1–6) Oh, deep in my heart, I do be - lieve,

we shall o - ver - come some day.
we'll go hand in hand some day.
we are not a - fraid to - day.
our God will see us through some day.

5 The truth shall make us free . . . some day.
6 We shall live in peace . . . some day.

*This anthem of the 1960s civil rights movement was frequently sung at mass meetings and marches. Several sources have been cited as its origins, including the spiritual "No more auction block for me" based on the tune known as Sicilian Mariners; an old Baptist hymn "I'll Be All Right"; and part of the text from C. A. Tindley's gospel hymn "I'll Overcome Someday."*

Tune: WE SHALL OVERCOME Irr.
*United States traditional*
*Harm. J. Jefferson Cleveland, 1981*

# 571     O God of Love, O God of Peace

Isa. 2:2–4

Henry W. Baker, 1861; alt.

1 O God of love, O God of peace, make wars through-out the world to cease; The wrath of hu - man wrong re - strain:
2 Re - mem-ber, God, your works of old, the won - ders that our peo - ple told; Heal ev - ery mal - ice, harm, and pain:
3 Whom shall we trust, O God, but you? For you are con - stant, strong, and true. None ev - er called on you in vain:

Give peace, O God, give peace a - gain!

*Both words and music of this hymn were composed by Henry W. Baker. A priest of the Church of England, Baker was the first committee chair for* Hymns Ancient and Modern, *which sold sixty million copies in fifty years.*

Tune: HESPERUS L.M.
(QUEBEC)
Henry W. Baker, 1854

# When Israel Was in Egypt's Land

**572**

*African-American spiritual; alt.*

*Exod. 3:7–12; 7:16; 8:1, 20; 9:1, 13; 10:3*

1 When Is-rael was in E-gypt's land, Let my peo-ple go,
2 "Thus spoke our God," bold Mo-ses said, "Let my peo-ple go;
3 No more in bond-age shall they toil, Let my peo-ple go,
4 Oh, let us all from bond-age flee, Let my peo-ple go,

Op-pressed so hard they could not stand, Let my peo-ple go.
If not I'll smite your first-born dead, Let my peo-ple go."
Nor spill their blood on E-gypt's soil, Let my peo-ple go.
And let us all in Christ be free, Let my peo-ple go.

*Refrain*

Go down, Mo-ses, way down in E-gypt's land,

Tell old Pha-raoh to let my peo-ple go.

*According to historian Jon Michael Spencer, this is the most famous of the spirituals to speak subtly of the desire the enslaved had for freedom, believing that God would set them free just as God had set the Hebrew people free from captivity in Egypt.*

Tune: GO DOWN, MOSES 8.5.8.5. with refrain
*African-American spiritual*

# 573

# Lead On Eternal Sovereign

*Ernest W. Shurtleff, 1887; alt.*

1 Lead on e-ter-nal Sov-ereign, we fol-low in your way;
loud rings your cry for jus-tice, your call for peace this day:
Through prayer-ful prep-a-ra-tion, your grace will make us strong,
to car-ry on the strug-gle to tri-umph o-ver wrong.

2 Lead on e-ter-nal Sov-ereign, we fol-low not with fear,
for in each hu-man con-flict your words of strength we hear:
That when we serve with glad-ness, you will not let us fall,
our trust is in your prom-ise that love will con-quer all.

3 Lead on e-ter-nal Sov-ereign, till sin's fierce war shall cease,
and all your saints to-geth-er will sing a hymn of peace;
Then all in your do-min-ion will live with hearts set free,
to love and serve each oth-er for all e-ter-ni-ty.

*At Andover Seminary, fellow students asked Ernest W. Shurtleff to write a hymn for their graduation. This is the result. Shurtleff became a Congregational minister and in his last years established churches in Europe and did relief work during World War I.*

Tune: LANCASHIRE 7.6.7.6.D.
*Henry T. Smart, 1836*

# In Egypt under Pharaoh
**574**

*Dosia Carlson, 1989*                    *Exod. 1:1–14; 7:8–11:10; 14:21–31*

1. In E-gypt un-der Pha-raoh the Is-rael-ites were bound,
   from plagues and trib-u-la-tions no re-spite could be found.
   Praise God who in sur-pris-ing ways gave pas-sage through the waves.
   Our Lib-er-a-tor res-cues, our Lib-er-a-tor saves.

2. From Af-ri-ca to gang-planks, a-cross a friend-less sea,
   black cap-tives harsh-ly treat-ed all strug-gled to be free.
   Praise God who strength-ened ad-vo-cates with power that does and dares.
   Our Lib-er-a-tor res-cues, our Lib-er-a-tor cares.

3. Wher-ev-er hurt-ing hu-mans un-just-ly live in pain,
   the hun-gry, home-less, hope-less, cry out for growth and gain.
   Praise God whose great re-deem-ing love each ser-vant free-ly gives.
   Our Lib-er-a-tor res-cues, our Lib-er-a-tor lives!

*Dosia Carlson wrote this text in 1989 for the United Church of Christ celebration of the 150th anniversary of the Amistad event.*

Tune: LANCASHIRE  7.6.7.6.D.
*Henry T. Smart, 1836*

# O for a World
**575**

*Miriam Therese Winter, 1987*              *Acts 4:32–35; 1 Cor. 1:26–31; 1 Pet. 3:8–12*

1 O for a world where ev-ery-one re-spects each oth-er's ways,
2 O for a world where goods are shared and mis-er-y re-lieved,
3 We wel-come one world fam-i-ly and strug-gle with each choice
4 The poor are rich, the weak are strong, the fool-ish ones are wise.
5 O for a world pre-par-ing for God's glo-rious reign of peace,

Where love is lived and all is done with jus-tice and with praise.
Where truth is spo-ken, chil-dren spared, e - qual-i-ty a - chieved.
That o-pens us to u-ni-ty and gives our vi-sion voice.
Tell all who mourn: out-casts be-long, who per-ish-es will rise.
Where time and tears will be no more, and all but love will cease.

*Inspired by Charles Wesley's phrase "O for a thousand tongues" and the familiar tune Azmon, Miriam Therese Winter wrote this hymn envisioning a new world order for the Presbyterian Women's Triennial Conference in 1982. It was later recrafted and recorded by the Medical Mission Sisters.*

Tune: AZMON C.M.
*Carl G. Gläser, 1828*
*Adapt. Lowell Mason in* Modern Psalmody, *1839*

# 576 For the Healing of the Nations

Fred Kaan, 1965

1 For the heal - ing of the na - tions, God, we pray with one ac - cord; for a just and e - qual shar - ing of the things that earth af - fords; to a life of love in ac - tion help us rise and pledge our word.

2 Lead us for - ward in - to free-dom; from de - spair your world re - lease, that, re - deemed from war and ha - tred, all may come and go in peace. Show us how through care and good - ness fear will die and hope in - crease.

3 All that kills a - bun - dant liv - ing, let it from the earth be banned; pride of sta - tus, race, or school - ing, dog - mas that ob - scure your plan. In our com - mon quest for jus - tice may we hal - low life's brief span.

4 You, Cre - a - tor God, have writ - ten your great name on hu - man - kind; for our grow - ing in your like - ness bring the life of Christ to mind, that by our re - sponse and ser - vice earth its des - ti - ny may find.

Fred Kaan's most widely published text was first sung at
Pilgrim Church in Plymouth, England, at a service of worship
marking Human Rights Day in 1965. It has been used for many
subsequent occasions, including the twenty-fifth anniversary of
the United Nations.

Tune: WESTMINSTER ABBEY 8.7.8.7.8.7.
Henry Purcell, c. 1680
Arr. Ernest Hawkins, 1842

# God the Omnipotent!

577

*St. 1–2, Henry F. Chorley, 1842; alt.*
*St. 3–4, John Ellerton, 1870; alt.*

1 God the Om - ni - po - tent! bold - ly or - dain - ing
2 God the All - mer - ci - ful! earth has for - sak - en
3 God the All - righ - teous One! earth has de - fied you,
4 God the All - prov - i - dent! by your great chas - tening

thun - der and light - ning your strength to dis - play,
all you make ho - ly, and slight - ed your way;
yet to e - ter - ni - ty stands what you say;
earth shall see free - dom and truth hold - ing sway;

Bring forth com - pas - sion where vi - o - lence is reign - ing;
Bid not your wrath in its ter - rors a - wak - en:
False - hood and wrong shall not tar - ry be - side you:
Through the thick cha - os your reign is still has - tening:

give to us peace in our time, we pray.
give to us peace in our time, we pray.
give to us peace in our time, we pray.
you will give peace in your time, we pray.

*Two English hymns, one by Henry F. Chorley, a friend of*
*Charles Dickens, and another by Church of England priest John*
*Ellerton, are combined in this text. The tune was originally*
*written for the Russian national anthem.*

Tune: RUSSIAN HYMN 11.10.11.9.
*Alexis F. Lvov, 1833*

# 578

# Profetiza, Pueblo mío
## (You Shall Prophesy, All My People)

*Acts 2:17–21; Rev. 10:11*

*Rosa Martha Zárate Macías, 1989; rev. 1994*
*Transl. The New Century Hymnal, 1994*

**Estribillo (Refrain)**
Unison

Pro - fe - ti - za, Pue-blo mí - o, pro-fe - ti-za u-na vez más.
You shall proph-e-sy, all my peo - ple, you shall proph-e-sy once more,

Que tu voz sea el e - co del cla-mor de los Pue-blos en o - pre - sión.
That your voice may ech - o all the cries of the peo-ple who are op - pressed.

Pro - fe - ti - za, Pue-blo mí - o, pro-fe - ti-za u-na vez más,
You shall proph - e-sy, my peo - ple, you shall proph-e-sy once more,

a-nun-cián - do-le a los po - bres u-na nue-va so-cie - dad.
to the poor an-nounce the com - ing of a new so-ci-e - ty.

*to Stanzas*

*Last time, end*

*Rosa Martha Zárate Macías wrote this hymn for her Mexican*
*People and other Pueblos deprived of their homeland, whom the*
*Great Spirit calls to be prophets, men and women of courage,*
*responsible for constructing the new society based in justice and love.*

Tune: PROPHESY Irr. with refrain
*Rosa Martha Zárate Macías, 1989*
*Harm. Raquel Gutiérrez-Achon, 1993*

1 Pro - fe - ta te con - sa - gro,  no ha-ya du-da y te - mor
2 A - nún - cia-le a los Pue - blos  que se re - no - va - rá
1 "I con - se-crate you proph-ets!"  Ban - ish all doubt and fear;
2 An-nounce to all the peo - ples  the cov - e - nant re - newed:

*to Refrain*

en tu an-dar por la his - to - ria;  sé fiel a tu mi - sión.
el pac - to en la jus - ti - cia;  la paz flo - re - ce - rá.
be faith - ful to your mis - sion,  lead-ing through his - to - ry.
the prom-ise of God's jus - tice,  blos-som - ing forth in peace.

3 De-nun-cia a quie-nes cau-san
   el llan-to y la o-pre-sión
   la ver-dad sea tu es-cu-do
   sé luz de un nue-vo sol.
   *Estribillo*

4 Es-ta sea tu es-pe-ran-za,
   es-te sea tu lu-char,
   cons-tru-ir en la jus-ti-cia
   la nue-va so-cie-dad.
   *Estribillo*

3 De-nounce those who are caus-ing,
   all those op-pressed to cry,
   Truth will be your pro-tec-tion,
   the light of a new sun.
   *Refrain*

4 Let this hope be your mis-sion,
   let hope be-come your fight,
   To build a so-cial or-der
   with jus-tice at its base.
   *Refrain*

# 579

# Great God of Earth and Heaven

*Shirley Erena Murray, 1986*

*Unison*

1 Great God of earth and heav - en whose Spir - it is our breath,
2 While ref - u - gees go home - less and die be - fore they live,
3 Where hun - ger kills your peo - ple, in - jus - tice cries a - loud,

at Christ-mas-time born hu - man, at Eas - ter shared our death:
while chil - dren have no fu - ture— our ap - a - thy for - give!
while weap - ons grow more le - thal and on - ly power stands proud—

All - gen - er - ous, all - lov - ing, in whom all beau - ty thrives—
Where hope fades to de - pres - sion, de - spair e - rodes the soul,
God of our flesh and fi - ber, whose mer - cy does not cease,

for - give your sons and daugh - ters the com - fort of our lives!
re - store in us a pas - sion to make the bro - ken whole.
im - plant your mind with - in us, cre - ate a world for peace!

*This text by New Zealand writer Shirley Erena Murray was
first used for a Refugee Sunday at the inner-city parish of St.
Andrew's-on-the-Terrace, Wellington. It was intended as "a
protest against apathy and 'the comfortable pew.'"*

Tune: KING'S LYNN 7.6.7.6.D.
*Traditional English melody
Arr. Ralph Vaughan Williams, 1906*

# O Kou Aloha No

580

(The Queen's Prayer)

*Queen Liliuokalani, 1893*

1 O   kou a-lo-ha   no        A   i - a   i   ka   La - ni,
2 Kou no-ho mi-hi     a  -  na A   pa - 'a-ha-o     la,
3 Mai   na-na 'i - no - 'i   no Na   he-wa o ka - na  -  ka,
4 No - lai - la e   ka   Ha  -  ku Ma - la - lo okou e - he - u

A     o kou oi - a - i' - o,   He   he - mo-le - le   ho'i.
O     o - e   ku - 'u     la  - ma kou     na - ni,   ko - 'u   ko'o.
A - ka,  e   hu - i - ka  - la,  a     ma - 'e - ma - 'e   no.
Ko   ma-kou ma-lu - hi  - a,   a   mau loa a - ku   no.

*This translation is not intended to be sung.*

Your love is in heaven and your truth so perfect. I live in sorrow imprisoned; you are my light, your glory my support. Behold not with malevolence the sins of humankind, but forgive and cleanse. And so, O Lord, beneath your wings be our peace forever more.

*In June 1893, after having been deposed from her throne in Hawaii, the imprisoned Queen Liliuokalani wrote a hymn to tell of her love of God, so great that she asked that even the sins of those who imprisoned her be forgiven.*

Tune:   LILIUOKALANI   6.7.7.6.
*Queen Liliuokalani (1838–1917)*
*Arr. Emerson C. Smith, 1954*

# 581

## Lead Us from Death to Life

2 John 1:3; Isa. 2:2–4

*Refrain, Satish Kumar*
*Stanzas, Marty Haugen, 1985*

*Last time, end*

**Dm7 · G · Em7 · Am**

1 Still all the an-gry cries, still all the an-gry guns, still now your
2 So man-y lone-ly hearts, so man-y bro-ken lives, long-ing for
3 Let jus-tice ev-er roll, let mer-cy fill the earth, let us be-

**Dm7 · G7 · C · Am · Dm7**

peo-ple die, earth's sons and daugh-ters. Let jus-tice roll, let
love to break in-to their an-guish. Come, teach us love,
gin to grow in-to your peo-ple. We can be love,

**E7 · Am · F · D7/F♯ · C/G · G7 · C to Refrain**

mer-cy pour down, come and teach us your way of com-pas-sion.
come, teach us peace, come and teach us your way of com-pas-sion.
we can bring peace, we can still be your way of com-pas-sion.

*The text for the refrain of this hymn is known as the "World Peace Prayer." It is a paraphrase of a verse from the* Upanishads, *the most ancient scriptures of Hinduism. Since its introduction at a service in Westminster Abbey on Hiroshima Day, 1981, the prayer has been translated into numerous languages and circulated around the world. The musical setting and additional stanzas were composed by Marty Haugen, composer-in-residence at Mayflower United Church of Christ, Minneapolis, Minnesota.*

Tune: WORLD PEACE PRAYER
12.11.9.10. with refrain
*Marty Haugen, 1985*

# 582  O God of Earth and Altar

St. 1–2, Gilbert K. Chesterton, 1906; alt.
St. 2, alt. Jane Parker Huber, 1985
St. 3, Jane Parker Huber, 1985

1 O God of earth and al - tar, bow down and hear our cry;
2 From all that ter - ror teach - es, from lies of pen and voice,
3 A - wak - en us to ac - tion and forge us in - to one,

Our earth-ly rul - ers fal - ter, our peo - ple drift and die;
From all the eas - y speech - es that make our hearts re - joice,
de - fy - ing sect and fac - tion; O God, your will be done!

The walls of gold en - tomb us, the swords of scorn di - vide;
From val - ue's pro - fan - a - tion, from hon - or sac - ri - ficed,
Op - pres-sive sys-tems snare us; our ap - a - thies in - crease.

Take not your thun - der from us, but take a - way our pride.
From sleep and from dam - na - tion, de - liv - er us, O Christ!
Great God, in mer - cy spare us for jus - tice and for peace!

*G. K. Chesterton of England was a prolific journalist, lecturer, and author of some one hundred literary works. This hymn has been updated by Jane Parker Huber to "incorporate contemporary concerns for the church's mission."*

Tune: LLANGLOFFAN 7.6.7.6.D.
*Traditional Welsh melody*
Harm. The English Hymnal, 1906

# Like a Mother Who Has Borne Us

**583**

*Daniel Bechtel, 1986*

*Hos. 11:1–9; 2 Tim. 1:8–10*

*1* Like a moth - er who has borne us, held us
*2* Like a fa - ther who has taught us, grasped our
*3* Though as chil - dren we have wan - dered, placed our
*4* When we of - fer food and com - fort, grasp our

close in her de - light, Fed us free - ly from her
hand and been our guide, Lift - ed us and healed our
trust in power and might, Left be - hind our broth - ers,
neigh - bor's hand in love, Tread the path of peace and

bod - y, God has called us in - to life.
sor - rows, God has walked with us in life.
sis - ters, God still calls us in - to life.
jus - tice, God still walks with us in life.

*This hymn was inspired by Hosea's depiction of the parental aspects of God's relationship with Israel. It was first sung at a chapel service at Dickinson College, where Daniel Bechtel, an ordained minister in the United Church of Christ, began his tenure as professor of religion in 1964.*

Tune: AUSTIN 8.7.8.7.
*William P. Rowan, 1992*
*Alternate tune: STUTTGART*

# 584
# I Am the Light of the World

John 8:12

*Jim Strathdee, 1969; rev. 1981*
*In response to a Christmas poem by Howard Thurman*

"I am the light of the world!

You peo-ple come and fol-low me!" If you fol-low and love you'll

learn the mys-ter-y of what you were meant to do and be.

1 When the song of the an-gels is stilled, when the
2 ⁷ To find the lost and lone-ly one, ⁷ to
3 ⁷ To free the pris-oner from all chains, ⁷ to
4 To bring hope to ev-ery task you do, ⁷ to

This text is based on a Christmas poem by Howard Thurman,
a prolific twentieth-century writer, theologian, and teacher.
The song grew out of Jim Strathdee's music ministry at an
intercultural, bilingual congregation in Los Angeles.

Tune: LIGHT OF THE WORLD Irr.
*Jim Strathdee, 1969*

star       in    the    sky        is         gone,                                        When the
heal       the    bro - ken   soul   with    love,                              ⅞    To
make      the    pow - er - ful        care,                                    To    re -
dance     at     a      ba  -    by's   new     birth,                          ⅞    To

sag  -  es    and    the    shep - herds  have    found    their  way  home,              the
feed    the   hun - gry    chil -  dren   with   warmth    and   good food,                To
build          the   na  -  tions   with    strength   of   good will,                      to
make          mu - sic    in . . . .   an     old    per - son's heart,                     and

work         of      Christ-mas   is    be  -  gun:
feel     the earth   be - low,   the   sky    a - bove!
see     all   God's    chil - dren  ev - ery - where!
sing         to    the   col - ors   of    the    earth!

*Return to 𝄋*

585 · O God, We Bear the Imprint of Your Face

*Shirley Erena Murray, 1981; rev. 1994*

Unison

1 O God, we bear the im-print of your face: the col-ors of our
2 Where we are torn and pulled a-part by hate be-cause our race, our
3 O God, we share the im-age of the One whose flesh and blood are

skin are your de-sign, and what we have of beau-ty in our race as
skin is not the same, while we are judged un-e-qual by the state and
ours, what-ev-er skin; in Christ's hu-man-i-ty we find our own, and

man or wom-an, you a-lone de-fine, who stretched a liv-ing fab-ric
vic-tims made be-cause we own our name, hu-man-i-ty re-duced to
in your fam-i-ly our prop-er kin: Je-sus our broth-er we still

on our frame and gave to each a lan-guage and a name.
lit-tle worth, dis-hon-ored is your liv-ing face on earth.
cru-ci-fy; love is the lan-guage we must learn, or die.

*Composer Bruce Neswick provided this setting at the request*
*of The New Century Hymnal. Neswick, Organist-Choirmaster*
*of Christ Church Episcopal Cathedral, Lexington, Kentucky,*
*is a graduate of the Institute of Sacred Music of Yale*
*University Divinity School.*

Tune: ROSEBERRY 10.10.10.10.10.10.
*Bruce Neswick, 1994*

# Come to Tend God's Garden

## 586

John A. Dalles, 1992

Luke 13:6–9; Gal. 5:22–26

1 Come to tend God's gar - den, seeds of hope to sow, plant-ing fields of
2 As we tend God's gar - den, from its fur-rows rise stems of fresh be -
3 May God's gar - den flour - ish, may our toil suc - ceed, may God bless our

*Whenever this repeated figure appears in the bass,
the organist should tie the eighth notes in the bass part.

jus - tice, watch-ing mer - cy grow! In an ar - id waste - land,
gin - nings, stretch-ing toward the skies! Gra-cious-ness, our mead - ow,
ac - tions, ev - ery word and deed! Serv-ing Christ each sea - son,

spread a ver - dant heath! In a land of tu-mult, cul - ti - vate God's peace!
joy - ful - ness, our root, u - ni-ty, our fo-liage, right-eous-ness, our fruit!
with God's di - a - gram, chart-ed by the Spir-it, for the task at hand!

John Dalles is the author of more than 200 hymn texts. This one
was written for the 275th anniversary of the Synod of the Trinity
(Pennsylvania), where Dalles has served as a pastor at Fox
Chapel Presbyterian Church, Pittsburgh.

Tune: KING'S WESTON 6.5.6.5.D.
Ralph Vaughan Williams, 1925
For another setting see 255

# 587  Through All the World, a Hungry Christ

Mark 1:40–42; Luke 4:16–20; 16:19–22

*Shirley Erena Murray, 1992; alt.*

1 Through all the world, a hun-gry Christ  must
2 Be - yond the church, a lep - er Christ  takes
3 In tor - ture cell, a pris-oner Christ  for
4 We do not know you, beg-gar Christ,  we

scav - enge far for dai - ly bread,  Must beg the
each un - touch-a - ble by hand,  Gives hope to
jus - tice and for truth must cry  To free the
do not rec - og - nize your sores,  We do not

rich for crumb and crust—  we are the
those who have no trust,  whose stig - ma
in - no - cent op - pressed  while we at
see, for we are blind:  for - give us,

*The small notes in the right hand of the accompaniment may be
played on the keyboard by an assistant or by a solo instrument.
*Play this note for st. 2, 3, 4 only.*

rich, the dai - ly fed.
is our so - cial brand.
lib - er - ty pass by.
touch us, make us yours.

Shirley Erena Murray's text addresses "the Christ presence in
the victims of the world, including the differently abled and
AIDS sufferers." Calvin Hampton's innovative tune is named
for Vernon De Tar, organist and retired faculty member of The
Juilliard School of Music. Hampton served as music director at
Calvary/St. George's Episcopal Parish in New York City.

Tune: DE TAR L.M.
Calvin Hampton, 1973
Alternate tune: GERMANY

# Let Justice Flow like Streams

## 588

Jane Parker Huber, 1984

Amos 5:14–15, 24; 7:7–8

1 Let  jus - tice  flow  like  streams  of  spark-ling  wa - ter,  pure,
2 Let  right-teous - ness  roll  on  as  oth - ers'  cares  we  heed,
3 So  may God's plumb line,  straight, de - fine  our  mea - sure  true,

En - a - bling growth, re - fresh-ing life, a - bun - dant, cleans-ing, sure.
An  ev - er - flow - ing  stream of faith trans - lat - ed  in - to  deed.
And  jus-tice, right, and  peace per-vade this  world our  whole life  through.

This is one of two hymns Jane Parker Huber wrote for special
events emphasizing economic justice for women at the time of
the reunification of two Presbyterian denominations in 1983. The
text's brevity underscores the urgency of Amos' pronouncements
against injustice.

Tune: ST. THOMAS S.M.
Aaron Williams' New Universal Psalmodist, 1770

# 589

# Let There Be Light, O God of Hosts

*William M. Vories, 1908; alt.*

1 Let there be light, O God of hosts!
2 With-in our pas - sioned hearts in - still
3 Give us the peace of sens - es clear
4 Let woe and waste of war - fare cease,

Let there be wis - dom on the earth!
the calm that ends all strain and strife;
to know our neigh - bors' good our own;
that use - ful la - bor yet may build

Let broad hu - man - i - ty have birth!
Make us your min - is - ters of life;
To hope and suf - fer not a - lone,
Its homes with love and laugh - ter filled!

Let there be deeds, in - stead of boasts!
purge us from lusts that curse and kill!
bond - ed in love that con - quers fear!
God, give your way - ward chil - dren peace!

*William Vories, founder of the vast, interdenominational Omi Mission in Japan, wrote this hymn as a response to the rising threat of German militarism in 1908. It exemplifies the vision of world peace and unity Vories strove to promote through his lifelong missionary work.*

Tune: PENTECOST L.M.
*William Boyd, 1864*

# Spirit of Jesus, If I Love My Neighbor

**590**

*Brian Wren, 1973; rev. 1994*

*Rom. 13:8–14*

1 Spir - it of Je - sus, if I love my neigh - bor,
2 And if, when I have an - swered need with kind - ness,
3 If I am hug - ging safe - ty or pos - ses - sions,

out of my knowl - edge, lei - sure, power or wealth,
my neigh - bor ris - es, wak-ened from de - spair,
un - curl my spir - it, as your love pre - vails,

o - pen my mind to un - der-stand the an - ger of
o - pen my heart to hear the cry for jus - tice that
to join my neigh - bors, work for lib - er - a - tion, and

help - less-ness that hates my power to help.
strug-gles for the chang - es that I fear.
find . . . my free - dom at the mark of nails.

*Brian Wren gave this poem the subtitle "Pilgrimage of
Confession" when it was first written, referring in part to the
walk made by nine white South Africans in 1972 to draw
other whites' attention to the injustice of migrant labor laws.*

Tune: BENJAMIN 11.10.11.10.
*Jonathan McNair, 1994*

# 591

## This Is My Song

Ps. 82:8

*Lloyd Stone, 1934*

1 This is my song, O God of all the na - tions, a song of
2 My coun - try's skies are blu - er than the o - cean, and sun-light

peace for lands a - far and mine. This is my home, the
beams on clo - ver - leaf and pine; But oth - er lands have

coun - try where my heart is; here are my hopes, my
sun - light, too, and clo - ver, and skies are ev - ery -

dreams, my ho - ly shrine; But oth - er hearts in oth - er lands are
where as blue as mine. O hear my song, O God of all the

beat - ing with hopes and dreams as true and high as mine.
na - tions, a song of peace for their land and for mine.

*These stanzas, published during the period between the two world wars, express a hope for lasting peace among all nations, races, and cultures. Finlandia is derived from a "tone poem" of the same name by Finnish composer Jean Sibelius.*

Tune: FINLANDIA 10.10.10.10.10.10.
*Jean Sibelius, 1899*
*Arr. for The Hymnal, 1933*

# God of the Ages, Who with Sure Command  592

*Daniel Crane Roberts, 1876; alt.*

1 God of the a - ges, who with sure com-mand
2 Your pur-pose, just, en - vi-sions mor-tals free;
3 From war's a - larms, from dead-ly pes - ti - lence,
4 Re - fresh your peo - ple on life's toil-some way;

brought forth in beau - ty all the star - ry band
God, set our path toward hu - man lib - er - ty.
with stead - fast care be ev - er our de - fense;
lead us from night to nev - er - end - ing day;

of shin - ing worlds in splen-dor through the skies,
Still be our rul - er, guard-ian, guide, and stay—
Your love and faith with - in our hearts in - crease;
With truth and love guide us through er - ror's maze,

our grate - ful songs be - fore your throne a - rise.
your Word our law, your paths our cho - sen way.
with boun-teous good - ness nour - ish us in peace.
and we shall give you glo - ry, laud, and praise.

Episcopal priest Daniel Crane Roberts wrote this hymn for
a July 4, 1876, centennial celebration at Brandon, Vermont.
George W. Warren, composer of the tune, was organist at St.
Thomas' Church in New York City for thirty years.

Tune: NATIONAL HYMN 10.10.10.10.
*George William Warren, 1892*

# 593

# Lift Every Voice and Sing

*James Weldon Johnson, 1921; alt.*

1 Lift ev-ery voice and sing, till earth and heav-en ring, ring with the
2 Ston-y the road we trod, bit-ter the chas-tening rod, felt in the
3 God of our wea-ry years, God of our si-lent tears, God who has

har-mo-nies of lib-er-ty; Let our re-joic-ing
days when hope un-born had died; Yet with a stead-y
brought us thus far on the way; God, who by your

rise, high as the lis-tening skies, let it re-sound loud as the
beat, have not our wea-ry feet, come to the place for which our
might, led us in-to the light, keep us for-ev-er in the

roll - ing sea. Sing a song full of the
peo - ple sighed? We have come o-ver a
path, we pray. Lest our feet stray from the

*Poet James Weldon Johnson was the first African-American to pass the bar examination in the state of Florida, and served as U.S. consul in Venezuela and Nicaragua. He collaborated with his composer brother, John Rosamond Johnson, to write Broadway operettas and edit song collections. John appeared in vaudeville, directed London musicals, and headed the Music School Settlement in New York.*

Tune: LIFT EVERY VOICE Irr.
*J. Rosamond Johnson, 1921*

faith that the harsh past has taught us, Sing a song full of the
way that with tears has been wa - tered, We have come, tread - ing our
plac - es, our God, where we met you, Lest our hearts, drunk with the

hope that the pres - ent has brought us; Fac - ing the
path through the blood of the slaugh - tered, Out from the
wine of the world, for - get you; Shad - owed be -

ris - ing sun of our new day be - gun, let us march
gloom - y past, till now we stand at last where the white
neath your hand, may we for - ev - er stand, true to our

on till vic - to - ry is won.
gleam of our bright star is cast.
God, true to our na - tive land.

# 594      How Beautiful, Our Spacious Skies

*Miriam Therese Winter, 1993; Adapted from*
*"America the Beautiful" by Katharine Lee Bates, 1893*

1 How beau-ti-ful, our spa-cious skies, our am-ber waves of grain;
2 In-dig-e-nous and im-mi-grant, our daugh-ters and our sons:
3 How beau-ti-ful, sin-cere la-ment, the wis-dom born of tears,
4 How beau-ti-ful, two con-ti-nents, and is-lands in the sea

our pur-ple moun-tains as they rise a-bove the fruit-ful plain.
O may we nev-er rest con-tent till all are tru-ly one.
the cour-age called for to re-pent the blood-shed through the years.
that dream of peace, non-vi-o-lence, all peo-ple liv-ing free.

A-mer-i-ca! A-mer-i-ca! God's gra-cious gifts a-bound,
A-mer-i-ca! A-mer-i-ca! God grant that we may be
A-mer-i-ca! A-mer-i-ca! God grant that we may be
A-mer-i-cas! A-mer-i-cas! God grant that we may be

and more and more we're grate-ful for life's boun-ty all a-round.
a sis-ter-hood and broth-er-hood from sea to shin-ing sea.
a na-tion blessed with none op-pressed, true land of lib-er-ty.
a hem-i-sphere where peo-ple here all live in har-mo-ny.

*On her first trip west in the summer of 1893 the distinguished*
*New England educator Katharine Lee Bates was inspired to*
*write "O Beautiful for Spacious Skies." One hundred years later*
*Miriam Therese Winter wrote new stanzas to clearly include all*
*of the Americas.*

Tune: MATERNA C.M.D.
*Samuel A. Ward, 1882*

# Some Glad Morning

**595**

(I'll Fly Away)

*Albert E. Brumley, 1932*

*Ps. 55:6*

1 Some glad morn-ing when this life is o'er, I'll fly a-way;
2 When the shad-ows of this life have gone, fly a-way, fly a-way;
3 Just a few more wea-ry days and then,

to a home on God's ce-les-tial shore, I'll fly a-way.
Like a bird from pris-on bars has flown, fly a-way, fly a-way.
To a land where joys shall nev-er end,

*Refrain*

I'll fly a-way, O glo-ry, I'll fly a-way;
fly a-way, fly a-way, in the morn-ing;

When I die, hal-le-lu-jah, by and by, I'll fly a-way.
fly a-way, fly a-way.

*This is a favorite song of the golden age of gospel music, in which heaven is vividly described and highly desired. Albert E. Brumley's musical style grew out of his Ozark mountain roots. He wrote this song while working in a cotton field.*

Tune: I'LL FLY AWAY 9.4.9.4. with refrain
*Albert E. Brumley, 1932*

# 596

# Rock of Ages, Cleft for Me

*Isa. 26:4; John 19:34*

*Augustus M. Toplady, 1776; alt.*

1 Rock of a - ges, cleft for me, let me hide; my shel - ter be!
2 Not the la - bors of my hands can ful - fill your law's de - mands;
3 Noth - ing in my hand I bring, sim - ply to your cross I cling;
4 While I draw this fleet-ing breath, when my eyes shall close in death,

Let the wat - er and the blood, from your wound - ed side which flowed,
Could my zeal no re - spite know, could my tears for - ev - er flow,
Na - ked, come to you for dress; help-less, look to you for grace;
When I soar to worlds un - known, meet you at your judg-ment throne,

Be of sin the dou - ble cure, cleanse me from its guilt and power.
All for sin could not a - tone; you must save, and you a - lone.
Stained, I to the foun-tain fly; wash me, Sav - ior, or I die!
Rock of a - ges, cleft for me, let me hide; my shel - ter be!

Augustus Toplady first published this poem as part of an
extensive article in which he likened the English national debt to
the burden of sin. The present form is a hybrid of the original
and revisions in 1815 by Thomas Cotterill.

Tune: TOPLADY 7.7.7.7.7.7.
*Thomas Hastings, 1830*
*Alternate tune: REDHEAD NO. 76*

# Shall We Gather at the River

597

*Robert Lowry, 1864; alt.*

*Rev. 22:1–5*

1 Shall we gath-er at the riv - er, where bright an-gel feet have trod,
2 On the mar-gin of the riv - er, wash-ing up its sil - ver spray,
3 As we reach the shin-ing riv - er, lay we ev-ery bur-den down;
4 Soon we'll reach the shin-ing riv - er, soon our pil-grim-age will cease;

with its crys-tal tide for-ev - er flow-ing by the throne of God?
we will walk and wor-ship ev - er, all the hap-py gold-en day.
grace our spir-its will de-liv - er, and pro-vide a robe and crown.
soon our hap-py hearts will quiv - er with the mel-o-dy of peace.

*Refrain*

Yes, we'll gath-er at the riv - er, the beau-ti-ful, the beau-ti-ful riv - er,

Gath-er with the saints at the riv - er that flows by the throne of God.

*Written during a time when an epidemic was claiming many lives in New York, Robert Lowry's hymn raised the question "Shall we meet again?" Lowry was pastor at Hanson Place Baptist Church in Brooklyn from 1861 to 1869, and collaborated on numerous hymn collections with William H. Doane.*

Tune: HANSON PLACE 8.7.8.7. with refrain
*Robert Lowry, 1864*

598

# On River Jordan's Banks I Stand

*Samuel Stennett, 1787; alt.*

1 On River Jordan's banks I stand, and cast a wish-ful eye
2 There gen-erous fruits that nev-er fail on trees im-mor-tal grow.
3 All o'er those wide ex-tend-ed plains shines one e-ter-nal day.
4 When shall I reach that hap-py place, and be for-ev-er blessed?
5 Filled with de-light, my rap-tured soul can here no long-er stay.

Up-on the fair and hap-py land where my pos-ses-sions lie.
There rocks and hills and brooks and vales with milk and hon-ey flow.
There God, the Sun, for-ev-er reigns, and scat-ters night a-way.
When shall I see my Mak-er's face, when in God's bo-som rest?
Though Jor-dan's waves a-round me roll, fear-less I'll sail a-way.

**Refrain**

I am bound for the prom-ised land, I am bound for the prom-ised land.

Oh, who will come and go with me? I am bound for the prom-ised land.

*Born into an English family that had been active for generations in Seventh Day Baptist churches, Samuel Stennett became an outstanding Baptist preacher. He was a personal friend of King George III. The hymn originally had no refrain.*

Tune: PROMISED LAND C.M. with refrain
Southern Harmony, *1835; alt.*
*Arr. Rigdon M. McIntosh, 1875*

# Steal Away

*African-American spiritual; alt.*

Matt. 24:27; 27:52–53; 1 Cor. 15:51–52; 1 Thess. 4:13–18

*Slowly, with feeling*

Refrain

Steal a - way, steal a - way, steal a - way to Je - sus!

Last time, end

Steal a - way, steal a - way home, I don't have long to stay here!

1 I hear God call - ing, God calls me by the thun - der; the
2 Green trees are bend - ing, poor sin - ner stands a - trem - bling; the
3 I hear God call - ing, God calls me by the light - ning; the
4 Tomb - stones are burst - ing, poor sin - ner stands a - trem - bling; the

to Refrain

trum - pet sounds with - in my soul, I don't have long to stay here.
trum - pet sounds with - in my soul, I don't have long to stay here.
trum - pet sounds with - in my soul, I don't have long to stay here.
trum - pet sounds with - in my soul, I don't have long to stay here.

*This is an example of the spiritual with coded meaning that Frederick Douglass spoke of in his narrative of 1855, My Bondage and My Freedom. To "steal away home" could have meant to run away to freedom.*

Tune: STEAL AWAY 5.7.8.7. with refrain
*African-American spiritual*

# 600 — How Lovely Is Your Dwelling

Ps. 84

*Jean Janzen, 1991*

1 How love - ly is your dwell-ing, O God, my hope and strength.
2 How blessed are those whose trav - els are strength-ened by your hand,
3 Look on me, God of good-ness, you are my sun and shield.

My spir - it longs for shel - ter, my flesh cries out for
who pass through shad-owed val - leys and find re - fresh - ing
One day with - in your house-hold is what I most de -

home, where ev - en swal-lows nest - ing be - side your al - tar
springs. Your rains fall soft as kind - ness on all your faith-ful
sire. O guide me in your mer - cy a - long my lone - ly

rest - ing are ev - er prais - ing you.
pil - grims un - til they come to you.
path - way; O bring me safe - ly home.

*Jean Wiebe Janzen is a published poet who also teaches poetry writing at Fresno Pacific College and Eastern Mennonite College. She began writing hymns at the invitation of the Mennonite Church for their* Hymnal: A Worship Book *(1992) where this text appears with the setting by Heinrich Schütz.*

Tune: ES IST EIN' ROS'
altered to 7.6.7.6.7.7.6.
Catholische Geistliche Kirchengesäng, *Cologne, 1599*

# How Lovely Is Your Dwelling

**601**

*Jean Janzen, 1991*

*Ps. 84*

1 How love-ly is your dwell-ing, O God, my hope and strength.
2 How blessed are those whose trav-els are strength-ened by your hand,
3 Look on me, God of good-ness, you are my sun and shield.

My spir-it longs for shel-ter, my flesh cries out for home,
who pass through shad-owed val-leys and find re-fresh-ing springs.
One day with-in your house-hold is what I most de-sire.

where ev-en swal-lows nest-ing be-side your al-tar rest-ing
Your rains fall soft as kind-ness on all your faith-ful pil-grims
O guide me in your mer-cy a-long my lone-ly path-way;

are ev-er prais - ing you.
un-til they come to you.
O bring me safe - ly home.

*Some performing editions show G natural in soprano.

Tune: PSALM 84   7.6.7.6.7.7.6.
*Heinrich Schütz, Psalter, 1628*

## 602

# Savior God Above

*Ps. 108:5–6; Rom. 13:9–12; Rev. 1:4–6*

*Duke Ellington, 1943; alt.*

**Refrain**

Sav-ior God a-bove,    God al-might-y, God of    love,

please look down and   see my peo - ple   through.

*Last time, end*

1  I be-lieve that   God put   sun and moon up in   the   sky.
2  Heav-en is   a    good-ness time, a   bright-er light on   high.
3  I be-lieve God   is   now, was then, and al-ways will   be.

*This song is part of the jazz suite Black, Brown and Beige by African-American jazz classicist Duke Ellington. The suite had its premiere in Carnegie Hall in 1943 as a musical portrait of African-American social history.*

Tune: COME SUNDAY  Irr. with refrain
*Duke Ellington, 1943*

to Refrain

I don't mind the gray skies, 'cause they're just clouds pass-ing by.
Love your neigh-bor as your - self, and have a bright-er by and by.
With God's bless-ing we can make it through e - ter - ni - ty.

to Refrain

## Giver of Life, Where'er They Be

**603**

*Frederick Lucian Hosmer, 1888; alt.*

1 Giv - er of life, wher - e'er they be, safe in your own e -
2 All souls you call, both here and there, do rest with - in your
3 Your word is true, your ways are just; a - bove the chant - ed
4 Hap - py are they in God who rest, no more by fear and

ter - ni - ty, now live your chil - dren glo - rious - ly.
shel - ter - ing care; one prov - i - dence a - like they share:
"Dust to dust" shall rise our song of grate - ful trust:
doubt op - pressed; liv - ing or dy - ing they are blessed:

Al - le - lu - ia! Al - le - lu - ia! Al - le - lu - ia!

*Frederick Hosmer wrote this hymn for Easter services at the Church of Unity in Cleveland, Ohio, where he served as minister for many years. Hosmer wrote more than fifty hymns.*

Tune: GELOBT SEI GOTT  8.8.8. with alleluias
*Melchior Vulpius, 1609*

# 604 Hush, Hush, Somebody's Calling My Name

*African-American spiritual*

*Slowly, with feeling*

1 Hush, Hush, Some-bod-y's call-ing my
2 Sounds like Je - sus. Some-bod-y's call-ing my
3 I'm so glad. Trou - ble won't last al -

name. Hush, Hush,
name. Sounds like Je - sus.
ways. I'm so glad.

Hal - le-lu - jah

Some-bod - y's call-ing my name. Oh, Hush,
Some-bod - y's call-ing my name. Oh, Sounds like
Trou - ble won't last al - ways. Oh, I'm so

Hush, Some-bod - y's call-ing my name. O my God,
Je - sus. Some-bod - y's call-ing my name. O my God,
glad. Trou - ble won't last al - ways. O my God,

O my God, what shall I do? What shall I do?
O my God, what shall I do? What shall I do?
O my God, what shall I do? What shall I do?

*This spiritual is an example of the call to personhood that Jesus was able to evoke within the hearts of the enslaved. It suggests that the inward "call" also anticipated physical freedom. Jeffrey Radford has served as Director of Music at Trinity United Church of Christ, Chicago.*

Tune: African-American spiritual
Arr. Jeffrey Radford, 1993

# As Moses Raised the Serpent Up 605

*Versification* The New Century Hymnal, *1993*

John 3:14–17

1 As Mo - ses raised the ser - pent up, God's
2 For God so loved the world that God, all
3 That Child was sent in - to the world not

Child is lift - ed high; And all who in that
hu - man life to free, Gave to the world God's
to con - demn but save; Now through Christ's name all

Child be - lieve shall nev - er, nev - er die.
Child that all might live e - ter - nal - ly.
are re - deemed— what won - drous love God gave.

*This hymn is a paraphrase of the gospel for Holy Cross Day, traditionally a time for reflection on faith and the meaning of the cross. In this reading, the image of Christ on the cross as the way to eternal life is related to the story of redemption of God's rebellious people in the wilderness.*

Tune: MORNING SONG C.M.
*Melody from* Sixteen Tune Settings, *1812*
*Harm. C. Winfred Douglas, 1940*

## 606        Nearer, My God, to You

*Gen. 28:10–22; Matt. 16:24*

*Sarah Flower Adams, 1841*
*Adapt. Thomas H. Troeger*

1 Near - er, my God, to you, near - er to you. I'll bear the
2 When I am wan - der - ing as Ja - cob did, and in the
3 Let Ja - cob's lad - der fill the sky a - bove, and an - gels
4 Then, wak - ing from the night to morn - ing air by Beth - el's

cross as Christ calls me to do and pray each day a - new:
deep - est night the path is hid, my dreams will bring me, too,
car - ry down the faith and love to keep this goal in view:
stone, I'll know you heard my prayer, and how my yearn - ing grew:

1–4 Near - er my God, to you, near - er my God, to you, near - er to you.

*Sarah Flower Adams, daughter of a well-known English editor,*
*was a successful actress in London. During her short life she*
*wrote prose and poetry for religious publications, a five-act*
*drama, and a children's catechism.*

Tune: BETHANY 6.4.6.4.6.6.6.4.
*Lowell Mason, 1856*

## 607        We Would Be Building

*Matt. 7:24–27; Luke 6:47–49; 1 Esd. 5:56–7:15*

*Purd E. Deitz, 1935; alt.*

1 We would be build - ing; tem - ples still un - done o'er crum - bling
2 Teach us to build; up - on the sol - id rock we set the
3 O keep us build - ing, Sav - ior; may our hands ne'er fal - ter

walls    their    cross-es    scarce-ly    lift,    wait-ing    till    love    can
dream    that    hard-ens    in-to    deed,    ribbed with fine    steel,    both
when    the    dream is    in    our    hearts,    when to    our    ears    there

raise    the    bro-ken    stone,    and hearts cre-a-tive
time    and change    to    mock,    the un-fail-ing    pur-pose
come    di-vine    com-mands    and    all    the    pride    of

bridge the    hu-man    rift.    We    would be    build-ing,
of    our    no-blest    creed.    Teach us    to    build;    O
sin-ful    will    de-parts.    We    build with    you;    O

Ar-chi-tect Di-vine,    re-veal the    shape of    life    in    your de-sign.
Mak-er, lend us    sight    to see the    tow-ers gleam-ing    in    the light.
grant en-dur-ing    worth    un-til your prom-ised realm shall come on earth.

*Purd Deitz, pastor of Trinity Evangelical and Reformed Church
in Philadelphia, wrote this hymn to express the youth conference
theme, "Christian Youth Building a New World." Set to one of
his favorite tunes,* Finlandia, *it became popular around the
world.*

Tune:  FINLANDIA  10.10.10.10.10.10.
*Jean Sibelius, 1899*
*Arr. for* The Hymnal, *1933*

# 608 Christ Will Come Again

*Matt. 13:24–30; John 14:3*                                                                                     *Brian Wren, 1987*

*Unison*

1 Christ will come a - gain, God's jus - tice to com - plete, to
2 Christ will come a - gain and life shall be com - plete. The
3 Christ will come a - gain, and joy shall be com - plete as

reap the fields of time and sift the weeds from wheat: then
wa - ters from the throne shall wash the na - tions' feet: then
flames of light-ning love be - deck the judg - ment seat: then

let us pas-sion-ate-ly care for peace and jus - tice here on earth,
let us pas-sion-ate-ly care for health and whole-ness here on earth,
let us pas-sion-ate-ly share the whole great gos - pel here on earth,

and e - vil's rage re - strain with love, till Christ shall come a - gain.
and ease our neigh-bor's pain with love, till Christ shall come a - gain.
un - til all things at - tain their end, when Christ shall come a - gain.

*This hymn was written during a Seventh Day Adventist
Musicians Convention in 1987. Brian Wren wanted to honor his
hosts with "a hymn on the Second Advent which, whether
understood literally or symbolically, would connect ultimate
hope with present action."*

Tune: IDA 5.6.6.6.8.8.8.8.6.
*Joan Collier Fogg, 1987*

# Now Is the Time Approaching

**609**

*Jane Laurie Borthwick, 1859; alt.*

*Jer. 33:14–16; Isa. 11:6–9; 61:11*

1 Now is the time ap - proach - ing, by proph-ets long fore - told,
2 Let all that now di - vides us re - move and pass a - way,
3 O long - ex - pect - ed dawn - ing, come with your cheer-ing ray!

when all shall dwell to - geth - er, se - cure and man - i - fold.
like mists of ear - ly morn - ing be - fore the blaze of day.
Yet shall the prom-ise beck - on and lead us not a - stray.

Let war be learned no long - er, let strife and tu - mult cease,
Let all that now u - nites us more sweet and last - ing prove,
O sweet an - tic - i - pa - tion! It cheers the watch-ers on

all earth a bless - ed gar - den that God shall tend in peace.
a clos - er bond of un - ion, in bless - ed lands of love.
to pray, and hope, and la - bor till Christ's new realm is come.

*Jane Laurie Borthwick's text titled "Anticipation of Heaven" was published in her* Thoughts for Thoughtful Hours *(1859). George J. Webb, American organist and music publisher, originally wrote this music for a secular song, "'Tis dawn, the lark is singing."*

Tune: WEBB 7.6.7.6.D.
*George J. Webb, 1837*

# 610

# My Eyes Have Seen the Glory

Acts 7:55–59; 2 Cor. 5:1–10

*Julia Ward Howe, 1861; alt.*

1 My eyes have seen the glo - ry of the com - ing of the Lord,
2 God has been there in the watch-fires of a hun - dred cir - cling camps,
3 God has sound-ed forth the trum - pet that shall nev - er call re - treat;
4 In the beau - ty of the lil - ies Christ was born a-cross the sea,

who is tram-pling out the vin - tage where the grapes of wrath are stored,
where they built a sa - cred al - tar in the eve - ning dews and damps;
and is sift - ing out the hearts of all be - fore the judg - ment seat;
with a glo - ry in whose bo - som that trans-fig - ures you and me;

And has loosed the fate - ful light-ning of a ter - ri - ble swift sword;
I can read the righ - teous sen - tence by the dim and flar - ing lamps;
O be swift, my soul, to an - swer and be ju - bi-lant, my feet!
As Christ died to make us ho - ly, let us die to make all free;

*Refrain*

God's truth is march-ing on.
God's day is march-ing on.
Our God is march-ing on.
While God is march-ing on.

Glo - ry, glo - ry, hal - le - lu - jah!

*Julia Ward Howe, an early leader in the movement for women's suffrage and an abolitionist, wrote this text specifically for a familiar camp-meeting tune one night after reviewing Union troops near Washington, D.C. It was published on the front page of the* Atlantic Monthly, *which added the title "Battle Hymn of the Republic."*

Tune: BATTLE HYMN OF THE REPUBLIC  Irr.
*United States camp-meeting tune, 19th century*

Glo - ry, glo - ry, hal - le - lu - jah! Glo - ry, glo - ry, hal - le -
lu - jah! God's truth is march - ing on.

# O Day of God, Draw Near

**611**

*R. B. Y. Scott, 1937; alt.*

*Ps. 105:7; 2 Pet. 3:8–15*

1 O Day of God, draw near in beau - ty and in power,
2 Bring to our trou - bled minds, un - cer - tain and a - fraid,
3 Bring jus - tice to our land, that all may dwell se - cure,
4 Bring to our world of strife your sov-ereign word of peace,
5 O Day of God, draw near as at cre - a - tion's birth;

Come with your time-less judg-ment now to match our pres - ent hour.
The qui - et of a stead-fast faith, calm of a call o - beyed.
And fine - ly build for days to come foun - da - tions that en - dure.
That war may haunt the earth no more and des - o - la - tion cease.
Let there be light a - gain, and let your reign be - gin on earth.

*R. B. Y. Scott was a theologian, Old Testament scholar, and
social reformer who taught at McGill University, Montreal, and
at Princeton University. A minister in the United Church of
Canada, he wrote this text in 1937 for the Fellowship for a
Christian Social Order.*

Tune: ST. MICHAEL S.M.
Trente quatre Pseaumes, *Geneva, 1551*
*Adapt. William Crotch, 1836*

# 612

## Strengthen All the Weary Hands

*Isa. 35*

*Martie McMane, 1991; rev. 1993*

1 Strength-en all the wea - ry hands, stead - y all the
2 Wa - ters flow in the wil - der - ness, streams break forth a -
3 Then the ran - somed shall re - turn, they shall come to
4 Let the wil - der - ness be glad, and the des - ert

trem - bling knees, and say to all faint hearts:
mid ar - id des - erts, burn - ing sands turn to pools.
Zi - on with sing - ing. Joy shall crown their heads.
burst in - to blos - som, dance and sing for joy!

"Cour - age, cour - age, do not be a - fraid.
Be strong, fear not, for your God is near.
Sor - row, sigh - ing, all shall flee a - way.
Hal - le - lu - jah! Hal - le - lu - jah!

(1-4) Look, your God is com - ing. God comes, comes to save you.

*Martie McMane, an ordained United Church of Christ minister, wrote many songs for worship as a pastor-evangelist in local church and national settings. This one first appeared in* Worship Comes Alive, *a resource developed for a denominational program, "The Evangelism Institutes."*

Tune: SONG OF REJOICING  Irr.
*Martie McMane, 1991*
*Harm. Don Brandon, 1991*

## O Holy City, Seen of John — 613

Walter Russell Bowie, 1910; alt.

Rev. 21:1–22:5; Heb. 11:16

1 O ho - ly cit - y, seen of John, where Christ, the Lamb, does reign,
2 O shame to us who rest con-tent while lust and greed for gain
3 Give us, O God, the strength to build the cit - y that has stayed
4 Al - read - y in the mind of God that cit - y is pre - pared:

with-in whose four - square walls shall come no night, nor need, nor pain,
in street and shop and ten - e - ment wring gold from hu - man pain,
too long a dream, whose laws are love, whose ways are your own ways,
oh, how its splen - dor chal - leng - es the souls that great - ly dare,

And where the tears are wiped from eyes that shall not weep a - gain.
And bit - ter lips in deep de - spair cry, "Christ has died in vain!"
And where the sun that blaz - es is your grace for all our days.
Yes, bids us seize the whole of life and build its glo - ry there.

Walter Russell Bowie, Episcopal priest and seminary professor, was a member of the committee that prepared the Revised Standard Version of the Bible. This hymn expresses a hope for a realm of God beginning here and now.

Tune: MORNING SONG 8.6.8.6.8.6.
Melody from Sixteen Tune Settings, 1812
Harm. C. Winfred Douglas, 1940

# 614

## Camina, Pueblo de Dios
### (Go Forth, O People of God)

*Rom. 7:5–8:4; 2 Cor. 5:14–19; Rev. 21:1–7*

*Cesáreo Gabaraín, 1979*
*Transl. George Lockwood, 1987; alt.*

Unison

Estribillo (Refrain)

Ca - mi - na, pue-blo de Dios, ca - mi - na, pue-blo de Dios.
Go forth, O peo-ple of God; go forth, O peo-ple of God!

Nue-va ley, nue-va a - lian - za en la nue-va cre-a - ción.
A new law, and a new prom-ise, all cre - a - tion is re - born.

*Last time, end*

Ca - mi - na, pue-blo de Dios, ca - mi - na, pue-blo de Dios.
Go forth, O peo-ple of God; go forth, O peo-ple of God!

1 Mi - ra a-lláen el Cal - va - rio en la ro-ca hay u - na cruz;
2 Cris - to to-maen su cuer-po el pe - ca - do, la es-cla - vi - tud.
1 Look on Cal - va - ry's sum-mit; on the rock there tow - ers a cross;
2 Christ's own bod - y is bur-dened by our sin, en - slave-ment, and pain.

*Cesáreo Gabaraín was a Roman Catholic priest who was very active as a congregational composer and head of a liturgical music association. He also served as the Spanish chaplain to Pope Paul VI, and was given the title "emeritus" shortly before his death in 1991.*

Tune: NUEVA CREACION 7.8.8.7.D. with refrain
*Cesáreo Gabaraín, 1979*
*Harm. Juan Luis García, 1987*

muer - te que en-gen-dra la vi - da, nue-vos se - res, nue - va luz.
Al des-tru - ir - los, nos tra - e u - na nue-va ple - ni - tud.
death that gives birth to new liv - ing, a new peo-ple, a new light.
Crush-ing all e - vil, Christ brings us life's a - bun-dance, life's new joy.

Cris - to nos ha sal - va - do con su muer-te y re - su-rrec-ción.
Po - ne en paz a los pue-blos, a las co - sas y al Cre - a - dor.
Christ has brought us sal - va - tion, dy-ing there and ris - ing a - gain.
Christ brings rec - on-cil - ia - tion to all things and peo-ple with God.

to Refrain
(Estribillo)

To-das las co - sas re - na - cen en la nue-va cre - a - ción.
To-do re - na - ce a la vi - da en la nue-va cre - a - ción.
Ev - ery-thing comes to new birth-ing, all cre - a - tion is re - born.
Na-ture bursts in - to new flow-ering, all cre - a - tion is re - born.

3  Cie-lo y tie-rra se a-bra-zan,
    nues-tra al-ma ha-lla el per-dón.
   Vuel-ven a a-brir-se los cie-los
    pa-ra el mun-do pe-ca-dor.
   Is-ra-el pe-re-gri-no,
    vi-ve y can-ta tu re-den-ción.
   Hay nue-vos mun-dos a-bier-tos
    en la nue-va cre-a-ción.
   *Estribillo*

3  Heav-en and earth are em-brac-ing,
    and our souls find par-don at last.
   Now heav-en's gates are re-o-pened
    to the sin-ner, to us all.
   This is Is-ra-el's jour-ney;
    now we live, sal-va-tion's our song;
   Christ's re-sur-rec-tion has freed us.
    There are new worlds to ex-plore.
   *Refrain*

# 615 Enter in the Realm of God

*Mark 4:26–32; 10:13–16; 1 John 4:7–12*

*Lavon Bayler, 1994*

**Unison**

1 En - ter in the realm of God.
2 In com - mu - ni - ties that serve,
3 God has loved, and so we love,
4 Come a - gain, O Christ, to rule

It has come, and yet will be.
and a - mong the saints who care,
and we give that all may share
in that realm that has no end.

It is known, and yet un - known.
There is jus - tice for the poor,
In the heal - ing God sup - plies,
May your chil - dren ev - ery - where

Christ re - vealed its mys - ter - y.
and new free - dom from de - spair.
in good news that we de - clare.
hear your greet - ing: "Wel - come, friend!"

*Hymnwriter Lavon Bayler referred to Jesus' teachings about the realm of God in the Gospel of Mark when asked to provide a text on this theme. Contemporary Philippine composer Vérne de la Peña provided the arrangement of the traditional Visayan folk melody.*

Tune: DANDANSOY 7.7.7.7.
*Visayan folk melody, Philippines*
*Arr. Vérne de la Peña, 1994*

# I Want to Be Ready

*African-American spiritual*

Rev. 21:1–4, 10–27; John 11:1–44; Acts 2:14, 36–41

*Refrain*

I want to be read - y, I want to be read - y,

*Last time, end*

I want to be read-y to walk in Je-ru-sa-lem just like John.

*Leader* ... *All*

1 Oh, John, oh, John, what do you say?
2 When Mar - tha spoke the Sav - ior's name,
3 When Pe - ter was preach-ing at Pen - te - cost, walk in Je-ru-sa-lem just like John.
4 When Mar-y asked Je - sus to "come and see,"
5 John said the cit - y was just four-square,

*All* ... *to Refrain*

That I'll be there at the com-ing day,
She knew she'd nev - er be the same,
He was en - dowed with the Ho - ly Ghost, walk in Je-ru-sa-lem just like John.
Her faith gave Laz - a - rus vic - to - ry,
And he de - clared he'd meet me there,

*Leader*

*This African-American spiritual is one of a small number based
not on the Hebrew Scriptures but the New Testament, specifically
the book of Revelation. Stanzas two and four are additions to the
traditional text and include some of the female followers of Jesus.*

Tune:  I WANT TO BE READY  Irr.
*African-American spiritual*
Arr. J. Jefferson Cleveland and Verolga Nix, 1981

## 617     Unite and Join Your Cheerful Songs

*Rev. 5:9–14*

Hymns and Spiritual Songs,
*ed. James O'Kelly, 1816; alt.*

1 U - nite and join your cheer - ful songs, with
2 This is the way the church should strive, in
3 Wor - thy the Lamb, the an - gels say, to
4 As - sist us, all a - bove the sky, on

an - gels 'round the throne; Ten thou - sand thou - sand
har - mo - ny be - low; As mem - bers of one
be ex - alt - ed thus; A - men, a - men the
earth, and on the seas; U - nite and raise God's

are their tongues, yet all their joys are one.
bod - y live, one Sov - ereign shall you know.
saints re - ply, the Lamb was slain for us.
hon - ors high, in hymns of end - less praise.

*This hymn appears in* Hymns and Spiritual Songs, *a collection of hymn texts (without tunes), published in 1816 in Raleigh, North Carolina. It may have been written by the book's editor, James O'Kelly, an itinerant preacher who broke away from the Methodist Church because of its hierarchical government. O'Kelly founded the Christian Church in the southern United States in 1794. In 1931, the Christian Church merged with the Congregational Church to form a predecessor denomination of the United Church of Christ. The themes of unity and freedom appear throughout O'Kelly's collection of hymns.*

Tune: AMAZING GRACE (NEW BRITAIN) C.M.
*from* Columbia Harmony, Cincinnati, 1829
*Arr. Edwin O. Excell, 1900*
*Alternate tune:* LAND OF REST

# PSALMS AND CANTICLES

# PSALMS AND CANTICLES

The psalms and canticles of Judeo-Christian worship heritage link Christians of today with their earliest roots. The Israelites sang psalms in worship and for other religious occasions. Early Christians continued the practice, and in one form or another the saying or singing of psalms has been a thread through centuries of Christian worship. During a long period of Reformed history, psalms were sung in meter, for example, the *Bay Psalm Book*. In early times, however, they were sung antiphonally, leader and congregation alternating verses, or with the congregation singing a response. Although exact performance practices and tunes are not known, it is clear that corporate participation in the singing of the psalms was the common practice.

Psalms were originally intended for singing, and this century has seen a revival in this ancient custom. This section of *The New Century Hymnal* presents the Psalms in their biblical form, with verses arranged in balance for antiphonal use. They are pointed to be sung to simple tunes, or tones. The format also allows for their use as readings for private or corporate meditation. The same is true for the canticles, Bible texts that were traditionally sung, but taken from sources other than the Book of Psalms.

The translation used for this adaptation is the New Revised Standard Version of the Bible, 1990. In addition to adjustments in the verses for musical flow, the text has been rendered using the same language standards found throughout the hymnal. The selection of psalms and verses is based on the *Revised Common Lectionary*, 1992, and psalms have been added for use in morning and evening prayer. When the lectionary designates varied selections of verses on different days, directions are given following the psalm. At the end of this section are several psalms set in Anglican-style chant, and two hymns, "Phos Hilaron" and "O Wisdom," for use in evening prayer.

## USING THE PSALMS AND CANTICLES IN WORSHIP

The psalms and canticles in this section of the book may be used in a variety of ways:

They may be read by an individual for private devotions.

They may be sung responsively:

    a solo voice (*cantor*) alternating with congregation;

    choir alternating with congregation;

    one part of the congregation alternating with another part of the congregation.

They may be sung through entirely by congregation, without alternating.

They may be read responsively (when reading, the points ['] are ignored):

    leader alternating with congregation;

    two sides of congregation alternating;

    alternating by half couplet or whole couplet.

## SINGING THE PSALMS AND CANTICLES
## USING A PSALM TONE AND POINTS

The psalms and canticles have been arranged into couplets, each with an A phrase and a B phrase (indented), to match the melody of a *tone*. The point (') in the text is positioned to indicate exactly where the melody note changes. If the choice is to have a cantor alternate with congregation, the cantor sings the first couplet as follows:

Protect        me,  O  God,      for in you       I   take refuge.

The congregation then answers with the indented couplet, repeating the same melody (tone) "by ear," and observing the point as the place to change the note.

I say to God, "You are my God; I have no good a - part from you."

This alternating continues for the desired number of verses.

## USING THE RESPONSE (𝑅.)

The symbol 𝑅 indicates the singing, by all, of the response. If the psalm or canticle is read responsively, instead of being sung, the response may be spoken or sung by all at the designated places.

## ONE WAY TO USE A PSALM OR CANTICLE IN WORSHIP

1. The response is played through once.
2. The response is sung by all.
3. The tone is played.
4. The first couplet is sung by the cantor or choir, accompanied by the tone.
5. The second couplet is sung by the congregation, accompanied by the tone.
6. Continue alternating couplets. Where indicated, the response is played and sung (with no musical introduction).
7. The singing of the psalm or canticle continues as before.
8. The response is sung by all at the end (with no introduction).

## ADDITIONAL HELPS

1. The points are always placed so that an accented syllable will fall on the last note of musical phrase A or B in the tone. If there are extra syllables, they are also sung on the last note.

2. The psalms and canticle texts are to be sung in a natural speech rhythm, at a comfortable pace, and with minimal (if any) pause for punctuation.

3. Several tones have been provided here. These, plus additional tones, will be found in the accompanist edition in various transpositions.

4. This form of psalm singing can be learned with little difficulty, and the same tone may be used for any psalm.

5. Double tones are designed to carry the text of two couplets. The above guidelines for singing will apply, except that two couplets will be matched with phrases A, B, C, and D of the tone. Thus, alternating may be accomplished by having the cantor sing the first *two* couplets, with the congregation responding with the next *two* couplets. Or the congregation, by itself, may sing the entire selection to the double tone, and with the designated response.

# Psalm tones

Interlude
between verses

## 11 (Double tone)

# Psalm 1

*Antiphon: Judy Hunnicutt, 1994*

My de - light is in the law of God.

℟

¹Happy are those who do not follow
the advice óf the wicked,
or take the path that sinners tread,
or sit in the séat of scoffers;

²but their delight is in the láw of God,
and on God's law they meditate dáy
and night.

³They are like trees planted by stréams
of water,
which yield their fruit ín its season,

and their leaves dó not wither.
In all that they dó they prosper.

⁴The wicked áre not so,
but are like chaff that the wind
dríves away.

⁵Therefore the wicked will not stand ín
the judgment,
nor sinners in the congregation óf
the righteous;

⁶for God watches over the way óf the
righteous,
but the way of the wickéd will
perish. ℟

# Psalm 2

*Antiphon: Carolyn Jennings, 1994*

Hap - py are all who take ref - uge in God.

℟

¹Why do the natíons conspire,
and the peoples plót in vain?

²The rulers of the earth set themselves,
and the leaders take counsél together,

against God and those God has
anointed, saying,

³"Let us burst their bonds asunder,
and cast their cords from us."

⁴The one who sits in the heavens
laughs;
God has them in derision. ℟

⁵Then God will speak to them in
wrath,
and terrify them in fury, saying,

⁶"I have set my ruler on Zion,
my holy hill."

⁷I will tell of the decree of God:
God said to me, "You are my child;
today I have begotten you.

⁸"Ask of me, and I will make the
nations your heritage,

and the ends of the earth your
possession. ℟

⁹"You shall break them with a rod of
iron,
and dash them in pieces like a
potter's vessel."

¹⁰Now therefore, O rulers, be wise;
be warned, O leaders of the earth.

¹¹Serve God with fear, with trembling
¹²kiss God's feet,
or God will be angry, and you will
perish in the way;

for God's wrath is quickly kindled.
Happy are all who take refuge in
God. ℟

*(May be sung with double tone.)*

# Psalm 4

℟esponse

*Antiphon: Peter Niedmann, 1994*

Let the light of your face shine on us, O God.

℟

¹Answer me when I call,
O God of my right!

You gave me room when I was in
distress.
Be gracious to me, and hear my
prayer.

²How long, you people, shall my
honor suffer shame?

How long will you love vain
words, and seek after lies?

³But know that God has set apart the
faithful for God;
God hears when I call. ℟

⁴When you are disturbed, do not sin;
ponder it on your beds, and be
silent.

⁵Offer right sacrifices, and put your
trust in God.

⁶There are many who say, "O that
we might see some good!

Let the light of your face shine on us,
O God!"

⁷You have put gladness in my heart
more than when their grain and
wine abound.

⁸I will both lie down and sleep in
peace;
for you alone, O God, make me lie
down in safety. ℛ

*(May be sung with double tone.)*

# Psalm 5

Response — Antiphon: Martie McMane, 1994

Lead me, O God, in your righ-teous - ness.

ℛ

¹Give ear to my words, O God;
give heed to my sighing.

²Listen to the sound of my cry,
my Sovereign and my God, for to
you I pray.

³O God, in the morning you hear
my voice;
in the morning I plead my case to
you, and watch.

⁴For you are not a God who delights
in wickedness;
evil will not sojourn with you. ℛ

⁵The boastful will not stand before
your eyes;
you hate all evildoers.

⁶You destroy those who speak lies;
God abhors the bloodthirsty and
deceitful.

⁷But I, through the abundance of your
steadfast love, will enter your house,
I will bow down toward your holy
temple in awe of you.

⁸Lead me, O God, in your
righteousness because of my enemies;
make your way straight before me.
ℛ

*(May be sung with double tone.)*

# Psalm 8

How ma - jes - tic is your name in all the earth.

Antiphon: Lee Dengler, 1994

𝓡

[1]O God, our Sovereign, how majestic
is your name in áll the earth!
    You have set your glory abóve the
    heavens.

[2]Out of the mouths of babes and
infants you have founded a bulwark
because óf your foes,
    to silence the enemy and t́he
    avenger.

[3]When I look at your heavens, the
work óf your fingers,
    the moon and the stars that you
    háve established;

[4]what are human beings that you are
mindf́ul of them,
    mortals t́hat you care for them? 𝓡

[5]Yet you have made them a little
loẃer than God,
    and crowned them with gloŕy and
    honor.

[6]You have given them dominion over
the works óf your hands;
    you have put all things und́er their
    feet,

[7]all sheep and oxen, and also the beasts
óf the field,
    [8]the birds of the air, and the fish of
    the sea, whatever passes along the
    paths óf the seas.

[9]O Gód, our Sovereign,
    how majestic is your name in áll
    the earth! 𝓡

*(May be sung with double tone.)*

# Psalm 9

Antiphon: *Elaine Kirkland, 1994*

ℛesponse

You, O God, have not for-sak-en those who seek you.

ℛ

⁹God is a stronghold for the oppressed,
  a stronghold in times of trouble.

¹⁰And those who know your name put
  their trust in you,
    for you, O God, have not forsaken
    those who seek you.

¹¹Sing praises to God, who dwells in
Zion.
    Declare God's deeds among the
    peoples.

¹²For God who avenges blood is
  mindful of them;
    God does not forget the cry of the
    afflicted. ℛ

¹³Be gracious to me, O God.
    See what I suffer from those who
    hate me;

you are the one who lifts me up from
the gates of death,
  ¹⁴so that I may recount all your
    praises, and, in the gates of
    daughter Zion, rejoice in your
    deliverance.

¹⁵The nations have sunk in the pit that
  they have made;
    in the net that they hid has their
    own foot been caught.

¹⁶God has made God known,
    God has executed judgment; the
    wicked are snared in the work of
    their own hands. ℛ

¹⁷The wicked shall depart to Sheol,
    all the nations that forget God.

¹⁸For the needy shall not always be
  forgotten,
    nor the hope of the poor perish
    forever.

¹⁹Rise up, O God! Do not let mortals
  prevail;
    let the nations be judged before
    you.

²⁰Put them in fear, O God;
    let the nations know that they are
    only human. ℛ

*(May be sung with double tone.)*

# Psalm 13

Antiphon: David Hurd, 1994

*Response*

Con - sid - er    and    an - swer me, O    God,    my    God!

*R*

¹How long, O God? Will you forget
me forever?

> How long will you hide your face
> from me?

²How long must I bear pain in my
soul, and have sorrow in my heart
all day long?

> How long shall my enemy be
> exalted over me?

³Consider and answer me, O God, my
God!

> Give light to my eyes, or I will
> sleep the sleep of death,

⁴and my enemy will say, "I have
prevailed";

> my foes will rejoice because I am
> shaken.

⁵But I trusted in your steadfast love;

> my heart shall rejoice in your
> salvation.

⁶I will sing to God,

> because God has dealt bountifully
> with me. *R*

# Psalm 14

Antiphon: Hyeon Jeong, 1994

*Response*

O    that    de - liv - er-ance would    come    from    from    Zi - on.

from

*R*

¹Fools say in their hearts, "There is no
God."

> They are corrupt, they do
> abominable deeds; there is no one
> who does good.

²God looks down from heaven on
humankind

> to see if there are any who are wise,
> who seek after God.

[3]They have all gone astray, they are all
alike perverse;
> there is no one who does good, no,
> not one.

[4]Have they no knowledge, all the
evildoers who eat up my people as
they eat bread,
> and do not call úpon God? ℟

[5]There they shall be in great terror,
for God is with the company óf the
righteous.

[6]You would confound the plans óf the
poor,
> but God is their refuge.

[7]O that deliveránce for Israel
would cóme from Zion!

When God restores the fortunes
óf God's people,
> Jacob will rejoice; Israel will be
> glad. ℟

*(May be sung with double tone.)*

<br>

# Psalm 15

℟espone

Antiphon: *Emma Lou Diemer, 1994*

Who may dwell on the ho-ly hill of God?

℟

[1]O God, who may abide in your tent?
Who may dwell on your holy hill?

[2]Those who walk blamelessly,
and do what is right,

who speak the truth from their heart,
[3]and do not slander with their
tongue,

who do no evil to their friends,
nor take up a reproach against
their neighbors; ℟

[4]in whose eyes the wicked áre despised,
but who honor those who fear God;

who stand by their oath
even to their hurt;

[5]who do not lend money at interest,
and do not take a bribe against the
innocent.

Those who do these things
shall never be moved. ℟

*(May be sung with double tone.)*

# Psalm 16

*Antiphon: Carolyn Jennings, 1994*

Response

In your right hand are plea-sures for - ev - er-more.

𝓡

¹Protect me, O God,
  for in you I take refuge.

²I say to God, "You are my God;
  I have no good apart from you."

³As for the holy ones in the land,
  they are the noble, in whom is all
  my delight.

⁴Those who choose another god
  multiply their sorrows; 𝓡

their drink offerings of blood I will
not pour out
  or take their names upon my lips.

⁵God is my chosen portion and my
cup;
  you hold my lot.

⁶The boundary lines have fallen for me
in pleasant places;
  I have a goodly heritage.

⁷I bless God who gives me counsel;
  in the night also my heart instructs
me. 𝓡

⁸I keep God always before me;
  because God is at my right hand,
  I shall not be moved.

⁹Therefore my heart is glad, and my
soul rejoices;
  my body also rests secure.

¹⁰For you do not give me up to Sheol,
  or let your faithful one see the Pit.

¹¹You show me the path of life. In
  your presence there is fullness of joy;
  in your right hand are pleasures
  forevermore. 𝓡

*(May be sung with double tone.)*

# Psalm 17

*Antiphon: Jane Marshall, 1994*

Won - drous - ly show your stead - fast love, O God.

ℛ

¹Hear a just cause, O God; attend to
my cry;
> give ear to my prayer from lips
> free of deceit.

²From you let my vindication come;
> let your eyes see the right.

³If you try my heart, if you visit me
by night, if you test me, you will
find no wickedness in me;
> my mouth does not transgress.

⁴As for what others do,
> by the word of your lips I have
> avoided the ways of the violent.

ℛ

⁵My steps have held fast to your paths;
> my feet have not slipped.

⁶I call upon you, for you will answer
me, O God;
> incline your ear to me, hear my
> words.

⁷Wondrously show your steadfast love,
> O savior of those who seek refuge
> from their adversaries at your
> mighty hand.

⁸Guard me as the apple of the eye; hide
me in the shadow of your wings,
> ⁹from the wicked who despoil me,
> my deadly enemies who surround
> me.

¹⁵As for me, I shall behold your face in
righteousness;
> when I awake I shall be satisfied,
> beholding your likeness. ℛ

*Proper 13 [18] A vs. 1–7, 15; Proper 27 [32] C vs. 1–9.*

# Psalm 19

Response       Antiphon: *Jean Slates Hawk, 1994*

O God, you are my rock and my re-deem - er.

R

¹The heavens are telling the glory of God;
    and the firmament proclaims God's handiwork.

²Day to day pours forth speech,
    and night to night declares knowledge.

³There is no speech, nor are there words;
    their voice is not heard;

⁴yet their voice goes out through all the earth,
    and their words to the end of the world.

In the heavens God has set a tent for the sun,
    ⁵which comes out like a beloved from a wedding canopy, and like an athlete runs its course with joy.

⁶Its rising is from the end of the heavens,
    and its circuit to the end of them, and nothing is hid from its heat. R

⁷The law of God is perfect, reviving the soul;
    the decrees of God are sure, making wise the simple;

⁸the precepts of God are right, rejoicing the heart;

the commandment of God is clear, enlightening the eyes;

⁹the fear of God is pure, enduring forever;
    the ordinances of God are true and righteous altogether.

¹⁰More to be desired are they than gold, even much fine gold;
    sweeter also than honey, and drippings of the honeycomb.

¹¹Moreover by them is your servant warned;
    in keeping them there is great reward.

¹²But who can detect their errors?
    Clear me from hidden faults.

¹³Keep back your servant also from the insolent;
    do not let them have dominion over me.

Then I shall be blameless,
    and innocent of great transgression.

¹⁴Let the words of my mouth and the meditation of my heart be acceptable to you,
    O God, my rock and my redeemer.
R

*Proper 21 [26] B vs. 7–14.*

# Psalm 20

An-swer us, O God, when we call.

R

¹May God answer you in the day of trouble!
>The name of the God of Jacob protect you!

²May God send you help from the sanctuary,
>and give you support from Zion.

³May God remember all your offerings,
>and regard with favor your burnt sacrifices.

⁴May God grant you your heart's desire,
>and fulfill all your plans. R

⁵May we shout for joy over your victory, and in the name of our God set up our banners.
>May God fulfill all your petitions.

⁶Now I know that God will help God's anointed,
>and will answer them from God's holy heaven with mighty victories by God's strong hand.

⁷Some take pride in chariots, and some in horses,
>but our pride is in the name of the Sovereign our God.

⁸They will collapse and fall, but we shall rise and stand upright.
>⁹Give victory to the ruler, O God; answer us when we call. R

*(May be sung with double tone.)*

# Psalm 22

Response

Antiphon: *Marty Haugen, 1994*

O God, do not be far a-way; O God, do not be far a-way.

℟

¹My God, my God, why have you forsaken me?
Why are you so far from helping me, from the words of my groaning?

²O my God, I cry by day, but you do not answer;
and by night, but find no rest.

³Yet you are holy, enthroned on the praises of Israel.
⁴In you our ancestors trusted; they trusted, and you delivered them.

⁵To you they cried, and were saved;
in you they trusted, and were not put to shame. ℟

⁶But I am a worm, and not human;
scorned by others, and despised by the people.

⁷All who see me mock at me;
they make mouths at me, they shake their heads;

⁸"Commit your cause to God;
let God deliver — let God rescue the one in whom God delights!" ℟

⁹Yet it was you who took me from the womb;
you kept me safe on my mother's breast.

¹⁰On you I was cast from my birth,
and since my mother bore me you have been my God.

¹¹Do not be far from me,
for trouble is near and there is no one to help.

¹²Many bulls encircle me, strong bulls of Bashan surround me;
¹³they open wide their mouths at me, like a ravening and roaring lion.

¹⁴I am poured out like water, and all my bones are out of joint;
my heart is like wax; it is melted within my breast;

¹⁵my mouth is dried up like a potsherd, and my tongue sticks to my jaws;
you lay me in the dust of death. ℟

¹⁹O God, do not be far away!
O my help, come quickly to my aid!

²⁰Deliver my soul from the sword,
my life from the power of the dog!

²¹Save me from the mouth of the lion!
From the horns of the wild oxen you have rescued me.

²²I will tell of your name to my brothers and sisters;

in the midst of the congregation
I will praise you: ℛ

²³You who fear God, praise God!
All you offspring of Jacob, glorify
God;

stand in awe of God,
all you offspring of Israel!

²⁴For God did not despise or abhor
the affliction of the afflicted;
God did not hide God's face from
me, but heard when I cried to God.
ℛ

²⁵From you comes my praise in the
great congregation;
my vows I will pay before those
who fear God.

²⁶The poor shall eat and be satisfied;
those who seek God shall praise
God. May your hearts live forever!

²⁷All the ends of the earth shall
remember and turn to God;
and all the families of the nations
shall worship before God.

²⁸For dominion belongs to God,
and God rules over the nations. ℛ

²⁹To God, indeed, shall all who sleep in
the earth bow down;
before God shall bow all who go
down to the dust, and I shall live
for God.

³⁰Posterity will serve God;
future generations will be told
about God,

³¹and proclaim God's deliverance to a
people yet unborn,
saying that God has done it. ℛ

*Good Friday ABC, the entire Psalm; Lent 2 B vs. 23–31;*
*Easter 5 B vs. 25–31; Proper 23 [28] B vs. 1–15; Proper 7*
*[12] C vs. 19–28.*

# Psalm 23

ℛesponse

*Antiphon: Carolyn Jennings, 1994*

God re - stores my soul and leads me in right paths.

ℛ
¹God is my shepherd, I shall not want.
²God makes me lie down in green
pastures, and leads me beside still
waters;

³God restores my soul,
and leads me in right paths for the
sake of God's name.

⁴Even though I walk through the
darkest valley, I fear no evil;
for you are with me; your rod and
your staff — they comfort me.

⁵You prepare a table before me in the
presence of my enemies;
you anoint my head with oil; my
cup overflows.

⁶Surely goodness and mercy shall
follow me all the days óf my life,
 and I shall dwell in the house of
 God my whole life long. *R*

# Psalm 24

Response            Antiphon: Peter Niedmann, 1994

Vs. 1–6   Who shall as - cend the hill of God?
Vs. 7–10   God is the Rul - er of glo - ry.

*R*

¹The earth is God's and all that is in it,
 the world, and those who live in it;

²for God has founded it ón the seas,
 and established it ón the rivers.

³Who shall ascend the hill of God?
 And who shall stand in God's
 holy place?

⁴Those who have clean hands ánd
pure hearts,
 who do not lift up their souls to
 what is false, and do not swear
 deceitfully.

⁵They will receive blessing from God,
 and vindication from the God of
 their salvation.

⁶Such is the company of those who
seek God,

who seek the face of the God of
Jacob. *R*

⁷Lift up your heads, O gates! and be
lifted up, O áncient doors!
 that the Ruler of glory máy
 come in.

⁸Who is the Ruler of glory?
 God, strong and mighty, God,
 mighty in battle.

⁹Lift up your heads, O gates! and be
lifted up, O áncient doors!
 that the Ruler of glory máy
 come in.

¹⁰Who is this Ruler of glory?
 The Sovereign of hosts — God is
 the Ruler of glory. *R*

*Presentation ABC vs. 7–10 (Alt.).*

# Psalm 25

Antiphon: *Judy Hunnicutt, 1994*

Your mer-cy and love have been from of old.

℟

¹To you, O God,
I lift up my soul.

²O my God, in you I trust; do not let
me be put to shame;
do not let my enemies exult over
me.

³Do not let those who wait for you be
put to shame;
let them be ashamed who are
wantonly treacherous.

⁴Make me to know your ways, O God;
teach me your paths. ℟

⁵Lead me in your truth, and teach me,
for you are the God of my salvation;
for you I wait all day long.

⁶Be mindful of your mercy, O God,
and of your steadfast love,
for they have been from of old.

⁷Do not remember the sins of my
youth
or my transgressions;

according to your steadfast love
remember me,
for your goodness' sake, O God! ℟

⁸Good and upright is God;
therefore God instructs sinners in
the way.

⁹God leads the humble in what is
right,
and teaches the humble God's way.

¹⁰All the paths of God are steadfast love
and faithfulness,
for those who keep God's covenant
and God's decrees. ℟

*Proper 21 [26] A vs. 1–9.*

# Psalm 26

Response

Antiphon: *Elaine Kirkland, 1994*

Your stead - fast love is be - fore my eyes.

℟

¹Vindicate me, O God, for I have
  walked in mý integrity,
    and I have trusted in God withóut
    wavering.

²Prove me, O God, and try me;
  test my heart and mind.

³For your steadfast love is befóre my
eyes,
  and I walk in faithfulnéss to you.

⁴I do not sit with the worthless,
  nor do I consórt with hypocrites;  ℟

⁵I hate the companý of evildoers,
  and will not sit with the wicked.

⁶I wash my hands in innocence,
  and go around your altar, O God,

⁷singing aloud a song óf thanksgiving,
  and telling all your wóndrous deeds.

⁸O God, I love the house in which you
  dwell,
    and the place where your glorý
    abides.  ℟

⁹Do not sweep me awáy with sinners,
  nor my life with the bloodthirsty,

¹⁰those in whose hands are evíl devices,
  and whose right hands are fúll of
  bribes.

¹¹But as for me, I walk in mý integrity;
  redeem me, and be gracíous to me.

¹²My foot stands on lével ground;
  in the great congregation I will
    bless God.  ℟

*Proper 17 [22] A vs. 1–8. (May be sung with double tone.)*

# Psalm 27

Response

Antiphon: Lee Dengler, 1994

Do not for - sake me, O God of my sal - va - tion.

*R*

¹God is my light and my salvation;
whom shall I fear?

God is the stronghold of my life; of
whom shall I be afraid?

²When evildoers assail me to devour
my flesh —

my adversaries and foes — they
shall stumble and fall.

³Though an army encamp against me,
my heart shall not fear.

Though war rise up against me, yet
I will be confident.

⁴One thing I asked of God, that will
I seek after:

to live in the house of God all the
days of my life, *R*

to behold the beauty of God, and to
inquire in God's temple.

⁵For God will hide me in God's
shelter in the day of trouble;

God will conceal me under the cover
of God's tent;

God will set me high on a rock.

⁶Now my head is lifted up above my
enemies all around me,

and I will offer in God's tent
sacrifices with shouts of joy;

I will sing and make melody to God.

⁷Hear, O God, when I cry aloud, be
gracious to me and answer me! *R*

⁸"Come," my heart says, "seek God's
face!"

Your face, O God, do I seek.

⁹Do not hide your face from me.

Do not turn your servant away in
anger, you who have been my help.

Do not cast me off, do not forsake
me,

O God of my salvation!

¹⁰If my father and mother forsake me,
God will take me up. *R*

¹¹Teach me your way, O God,

and lead me on a level path because
of my enemies.

¹²Do not give me up to the will of my
adversaries, for false witnesses have
risen against me,

and they are breathing out violence.

¹³I believe that I shall see the goodness
of God

in the land of the living.

¹⁴Wait for God, be strong;

let your heart take courage, wait for
God! *R*

*Epiphany 3 [3] A vs. 1, 4–9.*

*(May be sung with double tone.)*

# Psalm 29

*Antiphon: David Hurd, 1994*

The voice of God is full of maj - es - ty.

**R**

¹Ascribe to God, O heavenly beings,
 ascribe to God glory and strength.

²Ascribe to God the glory of God's
 name;
  worship God in holy splendor.

³The voice of God is over the waters;
 the God of glory thunders, God,
 over mighty waters.

⁴The voice of God is powerful;
 the voice of God is full of majesty.
**R**

⁵The voice of God breaks the cedars;
 God breaks the cedars of Lebanon.

⁶God makes Lebanon skip like a calf,
 and Sirion like a young wild ox.

⁷The voice of God flashes forth
 in flames of fire.

⁸The voice of God shakes the
 wilderness;
  God shakes the wilderness of
  Kadesh. **R**

⁹The voice of God causes the oaks to
 whirl, and strips the forest bare;
  and in God's temple all say,
  "Glory!"

¹⁰God sits enthroned over the flood;
 God sits enthroned as ruler forever.

¹¹May God give strength to the people!
 May God bless the people with
 peace! **R**

# Psalm 30

Antiphon: *Martie McMane, 1994*

God, you a-lone are ho-ly, you turn our sor-row to joy.

℟

¹I will extol you, O God, for you
have drawn me up,
   and did not let my foes rejoice
   over me.

²O God my God, I cried to you for
help,
   and you have healed me.

³O God, you brought up my soul from
Sheol,
   restored me to life from among
   those gone down to the Pit.

⁴Sing praises to God, O you God's
faithful ones,
   and give thanks to God's holy
   name. ℟

⁵For God's anger is but for a moment;
God's favor is for a lifetime.
   Weeping may linger for the night,
   but joy comes with the morning.

⁶As for me, I said in my prosperity,
   "I shall never be moved."

⁷By your favor, O God, you had
established me as a strong mountain;
   you hid your face; I was dismayed.

⁸To you, O God, I cried,
   and to you I made supplication: ℟

⁹"What profit is there in my death, if I
go down to the Pit?
   Will the dust praise you? Will it
   tell of your faithfulness?

¹⁰"Hear, O God, and be gracious to me!
   O God, be my helper!"

¹¹You have turned my mourning into
dancing;
   you have taken off my sackcloth
   and clothed me with joy,

¹²so that my soul may praise you and
not be silent.
   O God, my God, I will give thanks
   to you forever. ℟

*(May be sung with double tone.)*

# Psalm 31a

Antiphon: *Robert Train Adams, 1994*

Response

You are in - deed my rock and my fort - ress.

℟

¹In you, O God, I seek refuge; do not
let me ever be put to shame;
    in your righteousness deliver me.

²Incline your ear to me; rescue me
speedily.
    Be a rock of refuge for me, a strong
    fortress to save me.

³You are indeed my rock and my
fortress;
    for your name's sake lead me and
    guide me,

⁴take me out of the net that is hidden
for me,
    for you are my refuge.

⁵Into your hand I commit my spirit;
    you have redeemed me, O God,
    O faithful God.

¹⁵My times are in your hand;
    deliver me from the hand of my
    enemies and persecutors.

¹⁶Let your face shine upon your
servant;
    save me in your steadfast love. ℟

¹⁹O how abundant is your goodness that
you have laid up for those who fear
you,

and accomplished for those who
take refuge in you, in the sight of
everyone!

²⁰In the shelter of your presence you
hide them from human plots;
    you hold them safe under your
    shelter from contentious tongues.

²¹Blessed be God, who has wondrously
shown steadfast love to me
    when I was beset as a city under
    siege.

²²I had said in my alarm, "I am driven
far from your sight."
    But you heard my supplications
    when I cried out to you for help.

²³Love God, all you God's saints.
    God preserves the faithful, but
    abundantly repays the one who acts
    haughtily.

²⁴Be strong, and let your heart take
courage,
    all you who wait for God. ℟

*Holy Saturday ABC vs. 1–4, 15–16; Easter 5 A vs. 1–5,*
*15–16; Proper 4 [9] A vs. 1–5, 19–24.*

# Psalm 31b

Response

Antiphon: *Robert Train Adams, 1994*

Let your face shine up-on your ser - vant.

*(Selection for Palm/Passion Sunday)*

℟

⁹Be gracious to me, O God, for I am ín
distress;
> my eye wastes away from grief, my
> soul and bódy also.

¹⁰For my life is spent with sorrow, and
my ýears with sighing;
> my strength fails because of my
> misery, and my bones wáste away.

¹¹I am the scorn of all my adversaries, a
horror to my neighbors, an object of
dread to mý acquaintances;
> those who see me in the street flee
> from me.

¹²I have passed out of mind like one
who is dead;
> I have become like a bróken vessel.

℟

¹³For I hear the whispering of many —
terror áll around! —
> as they scheme together against me,
> as they plot to táke my life.

¹⁴But I trust in ýou, O God;
> I say, "You áre my God."

¹⁵My times are ín your hand;
> deliver me from the hand of my
> enemíes and persecutors.

¹⁶Let your face shine upón your
servant;
> save me in your steadfast love. ℟

*(May be sung with double tone.)*

# Psalm 32

R

¹Happy are those whose transgression
is forgiven,
>whose śin is covered.

²Happy are those to whom God
imputes no iniquity,
>and in whose spirit there is no
>deceit.

³While I kept silence, my body
wasted away
>through my groaning all day long.

⁴For day and night your hand was
heavy upon me;
>my strength was dried up as by the
>heat of summer. R

⁵Then I acknowledged my śin to you,
>and I did not hide my iniquity;

I said, "I will confess my
transgressions to God,"
>and you forgave the guilt of my
>sin.

⁶Therefore let all who are faithful offer
prayer to you;

at a time of distress, the rush of
mighty waters shall not reach them.

⁷You are a hiding place for me; you
preserve me from trouble;
>you surround me with glad cries of
>deliverance. R

⁸I will instruct you and teach you the
way you should go;
>I will counsel you with my eye
>upon you.

⁹Do not be like a horse or a mule,
without understanding,
>whose temper must be curbed with
>bit and bridle, else it will not stay
>near you.

¹⁰Many are the torments of the wicked,
>but steadfast love surrounds those
>who trust in God.

¹¹Be glad in God and rejoice, O
righteous,
>and shout for joy, all you upright
>in heart. R

*Proper 26 [31] C vs. 1–7. (If all verses are used, may be
sung with double tone.)*

# Psalm 33

Response

*Antiphon: Robert Fryson, 1994*

The earth is full of the stead-fast love of God.

ℛ

¹Rejoice in God, O you righteous.
  Praise befits the upright.

²Praise God with the lyre;
  make melody to God with the harp
  of ten strings.

³Sing to God a new song;
  play skillfully on the strings, with
  loud shouts.

⁴For the word of God is upright,
  and all God's work is done in
  faithfulness. ℛ

⁵God loves righteousness and justice;
  the earth is full of the steadfast love
  of God.

⁶By the word of God the heavens
  were made,
  and all their host by the breath of
  God's mouth.

⁷God gathered the waters of the sea as
  in a bottle;
  God put the deeps in storehouses.

⁸Let all the earth fear God;
  let all the inhabitants of the world
  stand in awe of God. ℛ

⁹For God spoke, and it came to be;
  God commanded, and it stood firm.

¹⁰God brings the counsel of the nations
  to nothing;

God frustrates the plans of the
  peoples.

¹¹The counsel of God stands forever,
  the thoughts of God's heart to all
  generations.

¹²Happy is the nation whose God is the
  Sovereign,
  the people whom God has chosen
  as God's own heritage.

¹³God looks out from heaven;
  God sees all humankind.

¹⁴From where God sits enthroned, God
  watches all the inhabitants of the
  earth —
  ¹⁵God who fashions the hearts of
  them all, and observes all their
  deeds.

¹⁶A ruler is not saved by a great army;
  a warrior is not delivered by great
  strength.

¹⁷The war horse is a vain hope for
  victory,
  and by its great might it cannot
  save. ℛ

¹⁸Truly the eye of God is on those who
  fear God,
  on those who hope in God's
  steadfast love,

℟ *The earth is full of the steadfast love of God.*

¹⁹to deliver their soul from death,
  and to keep them alive in famine.

²⁰Our soul waits for God,
  who is our help and shield.

²¹Our heart is glad in God,

because we trust in God's holy
  name.

²²Let your steadfast love, O God,
  be upon us,
    even as we hope in you. ℟

*Proper 5 [10] A vs. 1–12; Proper 14 [19] C vs. 12–22.*

# Psalm 34

℟

¹I will bless God at all times;
  God's praise shall continually be in
  my mouth.

²My soul makes its boast in God;
  let the humble hear and be glad.

³O magnify God with me,
  and let us exalt God's name
  together.

⁴I sought God, and God answered me,
  and delivered me from all my fears.
℟

⁵Look to God, and be radiant;
  so your faces shall never be
  ashamed.

⁶This poor soul cried, and was heard by
  God,
    and was saved from every trouble.

⁷The angel of God encamps around
  those who fear God;
    God's angel delivers them.

⁸O taste and see that God is good;
   happy are those who take refúge in
   God. ℛ

⁹O fear God, all you holy ónes of God,
   for those who fear God háve no
   want.

¹⁰The young lions suffer ẃant and
   hunger,
      but those who seek God lack ńo
      good thing.

¹¹Come, O children, listén to me;
   I will teach you the fear of God.

¹²Which of you desires life, and covets
   many days to énjoy good?
      ¹³Keep your tongue from evil, and
      your lips from speaking deceit. ℛ

¹⁴Depart from evil, ánd do good;
   seek peace, ánd pursue it.

¹⁵The eyes of God are ón the righteous,
   God's ears are open to their cry.

¹⁶The face of God is against évildoers,
   to cut off the remembrance of them
   from the earth.

¹⁷When the righteous cry for help, God
   hears,
      and rescues them from áll their
      troubles. ℛ

¹⁸God is near to the brokenhearted,
   and saves the crushed in spirit.

¹⁹Many are the afflictions óf the
   righteous,
      but God rescues them from them
      all.

²⁰God keeps áll their bones;
   not one of them ẃill be broken.

²¹Evil brings death to the wicked,
   and those who hate the righteous
   will be condemned.

²²God redeems the life of those who
   serve God;
      none of those who take refuge in
      God will be condemned.

*All Saints A vs. 1–10, 22; Proper 14 [19] B vs. 1–8;*
*Proper 15 [20] B vs. 9–14; Proper 16 [21] B vs. 15–22;*
*Proper 25 [30] B vs. 1–8, (19–22).*

# Psalm 36

*Antiphon: Jean Slates Hawk, 1994*

ℛesponse

How pre - cious is your stead - fast love, O God.

ℛ

⁵Your steadfast love, O God, extends
to the heavens,
   your faithfulness to the clouds.

⁶Your righteousness is like the mighty
mountains, your judgments are like
the great deep;

you save humans and animals alike,
O God.

⁷How precious is your steadfast love,
O God!
All people may take refuge in the
shadow óf your wings.

⁸They feast on the abundance óf your
house,
and you give them drink from the
river of ýour delights. ℟

⁹For with you is the fountain of life;
in your light wé see light.

¹⁰O continue your steadfast love to
those who know you,
and your salvation to the upright
of heart!

¹¹Do not let the foot of the arrogant
tread on me,
or the hand of the wicked drive me
away. ℟

*Monday in Holy Week ABC vs. 5–11; Epiphany 2 [2] C vs. 5–10.*

# Psalm 37

℟esponse                                          Antiphon: *Vérne de la Peña, 1994*

God will give you the de-sires of your heart.

℟

¹Do not fret because of the wicked; do
not be envióus of wrongdoers,
²for they will soon fade like the
grass, and wither like the green
herb.

³Trust in God, ánd do good;
so you will live in the land, and
enjoy security.

⁴Take delíght in God,
who will give you the desires óf
your heart.

⁵Commit your wáy to God;
trust in God, and God will act. ℟

⁶God will make your vindication shine
like the light,
and the justice of your cause like
the day at noon.

⁷Be still before God, ánd wait
patiently;
do not fret over those who prosper
in their way, over those who carry
out evíl devices.

⁸Refrain from anger, and forsake wrath.
Do not fret — it leads onlý to evil.

⁹For the wicked shall be cut off,
but those who wait for God shall
inherit the land. ℟

¹⁰Yet a little while, and the wicked will
be no more;

though you look diligently for their
place, they will not be there.

¹¹But the meek shall inherit the land,
and delight themselves in abundant
prosperity.

³⁹The salvation of the righteous is from
God,

who is their refuge in the time of
trouble.

⁴⁰God helps them and rescues them;
God rescues them from the wicked,
and saves them, because they take
refuge in God. *R*

*Epiphany 7 [7] C all verses; Proper 22 [27] C vs. 1–9.*

*(May be sung with double tone.)*

# Psalm 40

*Antiphon: Marty Haugen, 1994*

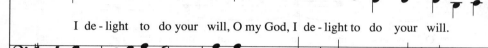

I de-light to do your will, O my God, I de-light to do your will.

*R*

¹I waited patiently for God,
who inclined to me and heard my
cry.

²God drew me up from the desolate pit,
out of the miry bog;

God set my feet upon a rock,
making my steps secure.

³God put a new song in my mouth, a
song of praise to our God.

Many will see and fear, and put
their trust in God.

⁴Happy are those who make God their
trust,

who do not turn to the proud, to
those who go astray after false
gods. *R*

⁵You have multiplied, O God my God,
your wondrous deeds and your
thoughts toward us;

none can compare with you.

Were I to proclaim and tell of them,
they would be more than can be
counted.

⁶Sacrifice and offering you do not
desire, but you have given me an
open ear.

Burnt offering and sin offering you
have not required.

⁷Then I said, "Here I am;
in the scroll of the book it is
written of me. *R*

*R  I delight to do your will, O my God, I delight to do your will.*

8"I delight to do your will, O my God;
your law is within my heart."

9I have told the glad news of
deliverance in the great congregation;
see, I have not restrained my lips,
as you know, O God.

10I have not hidden your saving help
within my heart,
I have spoken of your faithfulness
and your salvation;

I have not concealed your steadfast
love and your faithfulness,
I have not concealed them from the
great congregation.

11Do not, O God, withhold your mercy
from me;
let your steadfast love and your
faithfulness keep me safe forever. *R*

*Epiphany 2 [2] A vs. 1–11; Annunciation ABC vs. 5–10
(Alt.).*

# Psalm 41

*Response*                                    *Antiphon:  Peter Niedmann, 1994*

O set me in your pres - ence for - ev - er.

*R*

1Happy are those who consider the
poor;
God delivers them in the day of
trouble.

2God protects them and keeps them
alive; they are called happy in the
land.
You do not give them up to the
will of their enemies.

3God sustains them on their sickbed;
in their illness you heal all their
infirmities.

4As for me, I said, "O God, be
gracious to me;
heal me, for I have sinned against
you." *R*

5My enemies wonder in malice when I
will die,
and when my name will perish.

6And when they come to see me, they
utter empty words, while their hearts
gather mischief;
when they go out, they tell it
abroad.

7All who hate me whisper together
about me; they imagine the worst for
me.
8They think that a deadly thing has
fastened on me, that I will not rise
again from where I lie.

9Even my friend in whom I trusted,
who ate of my bread,
has exalted at my misfortune. *R*

¹⁰But you, O God, be gracious to me,
    and raise me up, that I may repay
    them.

¹¹By this I know that you are pleased
with me;
    because my enemy has not
    triumphed over me.

¹²But you have upheld me because of
my integrity,
    and set me in your presence forever.

¹³Blessed be the Sovereign, the God of
Israel,
    from everlasting to everlasting.
    Amen and Amen. ℛ

*(May be sung with double tone.)*

## Psalm 42, 43

Antiphon:  *Carolyn Jennings, 1994*

Response — Unison

My soul thirsts for God, for the liv - ing God.
(Alt. for Ps. 43) Why have you cast me off, O God?

ℛ

¹As a deer longs for flowing streams,
    so my soul longs for you, O God.

²My soul thirsts for God, for the
living God.
    When shall I come and behold the
    face of God?

³My tears have been my food day and
night,
    while people say to me continually,
    "Where is your God?"

⁴These things I remember,
    as I pour out my soul:

how I went with the throng, and led
them in procession to the house of
God,
    with glad shouts and songs of
    thanksgiving, a multitude keeping
    festival. ℛ

⁵Why are you cast down, O my soul,
    and why are you disquieted within
me?
    Hope in God; for I shall again
    praise God, my help ⁶and my God.

My soul is cast down within me;
    therefore I remember you from the
    land of Jordan and of Hermon, from
    Mount Mizar.

⁷Deep calls to deep at the thunder of
your cataracts;
    all your waves and your billows
    have gone over me.

⁸By day God commands God's steadfast
love,
    and at night God's song is with me,
    a prayer to the God of my life. ℛ

℟ *My soul thirsts for God, for the living God.*

⁹I say to God, my rock, "Why have
you forgotten me?
  Why must I walk about mournfully
  because the enemy oppresses me?"

¹⁰As with a deadly wound in my body,
my adversaries taunt me,

while they say to me continually,
  "Where is your God?"

¹¹Why are you cast down, O my soul?
  Why are you disquieted within me?

Hope in God; for I shall again praise
the one,
  who is my help and my God. ℟

(Psalm 43)

℟ *Why have you cast me off, O God?*

℟

¹Vindicate me, O God, and defend my
cause against an ungodly people;
  from those who are deceitful and
  unjust deliver me!

²For you are the God in whom I take
refuge;
  why have you cast me off?

Why must I walk about mournfully
because of the oppression of the
enemy?

³O send out your light and your truth;
let them lead me;

let them bring me to your holy hill
  and to your dwelling.

⁴Then I will go to the altar of God, to
God my exceeding joy;
  and I will praise you with the harp,
  O God, my God.

⁵Why are you cast down, O my soul,
  and why are you disquieted within
  me?

Hope in God; for I shall again praise
the one,
  who is my help and my God. ℟

Psalms 42 and 43 Easter Vigil ABC and Proper 7 [12] C;
Psalm 43 Proper 26 [31] A.

# Psalm 45

℟esponse

Antiphon: Judy Hunnicutt, 1994

Your throne, O God, en - dures for-ev - er and ev - er.

℟

¹My heart overflows with a goodly
theme; I address my verses to the
king;
  my tongue is like the pen of a ready
  scribe.

²You are the most handsome of men;
grace is poured upon your lips;
  therefore God has blessed you
  forever.

³Gird your sword on your thigh, O
mighty one,
> in your glory and majesty.

⁴In your majesty ride on victoriously
for the cause of truth and to defend the
right;
> let your right hand teach you dread
> deeds. ℟

⁵Your arrows are sharp in the heart of
the king's enemies;
> the peoples fall únder you.

⁶Your throne, O God, endures forever
and ever.
> Your royal scepter is a scepter of
> equity;

⁷you love righteousness ánd hate
wickedness.
> Therefore God, your God, has
> anointed you with the oil of
> gladness beyond your companions;

⁸your robes are all fragrant with myrrh
and alóes and cassia.
> From ivory palaces stringed
> instruments make you glad; ℟

⁹daughters of kings are among those
who serve you,
> at your right hand stands the queen
> in gold of Ophir.

¹⁰Hear, O daughter, consider and incline
your ear;

forget your people and your parents'
house,

¹¹and the king will desire your beauty.
> Since he is your lord, bow to him;

¹²the people of Tyre will seek your
favor with gifts,
> the richest of the people ¹³with all
> kinds of wealth. ℟

The princess is clothed in her chamber
with gold-woven robes;
> ¹⁴in many-colored robes she is led
> to the king;

behind her the virgins, her
companions, follow.
> ¹⁵With joy and gladness they are led
> along as they enter the palace óf the
> king.

¹⁶In the place of ancestors you, O king,
shall have descendants;
> you will make them nobles in áll
> the earth.

¹⁷I will cause your name to be
celebrated in all generations;
> therefore the peoples will praise
> you forever and ever. ℟

*Annunciation ABC (Alt.) all verses; Proper 9 [14] A vs.*
*10–17; Proper 17 [22] B vs. 1–2, 6–9. (If all verses are*
*used, may be sung with double tone.)*

# Psalm 46

Response        Antiphon: Lee Dengler, 1994

The God of hosts is with us, there-fore we will not fear.

℞

¹God is our refuge and strength,
    a very present help in trouble.

²Therefore we will not fear, though the
    earth should change,
      though the mountains shake in the
      heart of the sea;

³though its waters roar and foam,
      though the mountains tremble with
      its tumult.

⁴There is a river whose streams make
    glad the city of God,
      the holy habitation of the Most
      High. ℞

⁵God is in the midst of the city; it
    shall not be moved;
      God will help it when the morning
      dawns.

⁶The nations are in an uproar, the
    empires totter;
      God's voice resounds and the earth
      melts.

⁷The God of hosts is with us;
      the God of Jacob is our refuge.

⁸Come, behold the works of God;
      see what desolations God has
      brought on the earth. ℞

⁹God makes wars cease to the end of
    the earth;
      God breaks the bow, and shatters
      the spear; God burns the shields
      with fire.

¹⁰"Be still, and know that I am God!
    I am exalted among the nations, I
    am exalted in the earth."

¹¹The God of hosts is with us;
      the God of Jacob is our refuge. ℞

# Psalm 47

Antiphon: Elaine Kirkland, 1994

Response

Sing prais-es to God, sing prais - es to our Rul - er.

𝑅

¹Clap your hands, áll you peoples;
shout to God with loud songs of
joy.

²For God, the Most High, is awesome,
a great ruler over áll the earth.

³God subdued peoples under us, and
nations under our feet.
⁴God chose our heritage for us, the
pride of Jacob whom God loves.

⁵God has gone up with a shout,
God has gone up with the sound óf
a trumpet. 𝑅

⁶Sing praises to God, sing praises;
sing praises to our Ruler, sing
praises.

⁷For God is the ruler of áll the earth;
sing praises with a psalm.

⁸God is ruler over the nations;
God sits on God's holy throne.

⁹The nobles of the peoples gather
as the people of the God of Sarah
and Abraham.

For the shields of the earth belong to
God;
God is highly exalted. 𝑅

# Psalm 48

Response

*Antiphon: Martie McMane, 1994*

We pon-der your stead-fast love, O God.

𝓡
¹Great is God and greatly to be praised
in the city óf our God.

God's holy mountain, ²beautiful in
élevation,
is the joy of áll the earth,

Mount Zion, in the far north,
the city of the great Ruler.
³Within its citadels God is a
sure defense. 𝓡

⁴Then the rulers assembled,
they came ón together.
⁵As soon as they saw it, they
were astounded; they were in
panic, they took to flight;

⁶trembling took hold of them there,
pains as of a woman in labor,
⁷as when an east wind
shatters the ships of
Tarshish.

⁸As we have heard, so have we
seen in the city of the God of hosts,
in the city of our God, which
God establishes forever.

⁹We ponder your steadfast love, O
God,
in the midst óf your temple. 𝓡

¹⁰Your name, O God, like your praise,
reaches to the ends óf the earth.
Your right hand is filled with
victory.

¹¹Let Mount Zión be glad,
let the towns of Judah rejoice
because óf your judgments.

¹²Walk about Zion, go all around
it, count its towers,
¹³consider well its ramparts;
go through its citadels,

that you may tell the next
generation¹⁴that this is God,
our God forever and ever.
God will be our guide forever. 𝓡

# Psalm 49

Antiphon:   *David Hurd, 1994*

The med - i - ta - tion  of  my heart shall  be  my  un - der - stand - ing.

℟

¹Hear this, all you peoples; give ear,
  all inhabitants of the world,
    ²both low and high, rich and
    poor together.

³My mouth shall speak wisdom;
  the meditation of my heart
  shall be understanding.

⁴I will incline my ear to a proverb;
  I will solve my riddle to the
  music of the harp. ℟

⁵Why should I fear in times of trouble,
  when the iniquity of my persecutors
  surrounds me,

⁶those who trust in their wealth
  and boast of the abundance of
  their riches?

⁷Truly, no ransom avails for one's life,
  there is no price one can give
  to God for it.

⁸For the ransom of life is costly,
  and can never suffice
    ⁹that one should live on forever
    and never see the grave. ℟

¹⁰When we look at the wise, they die;
  the foolish and stupid perish
  together and leave their wealth to
  others.

¹¹Their graves are their homes forever,
  their dwelling places to all
  generations, though they named
  lands their own.

¹²Mortals cannot abide in their pomp;
  they are like the animals that
  perish. ℟

# Psalm 50

Response

Antiphon: Hyeon Jeong, 1994

Our God comes and does not keep si - lence.

R

¹The mighty one, God the Sovereign,
speaks and summons the earth:
   from the rising of the sun to
   its setting.

²Out of Zion, the perfection of beauty,
God shines forth.
   ³Our God comes and does not
   keep silence,

before God is a devouring fire,
   and a mighty tempest all around. R

⁴God calls to the heavens above
and to the earth,
   that God may judge God's
   people:

⁵"Gather to me my faithful ones,
   who made a covenant with me
   by sacrifice!"

⁶The heavens declare God's
righteousness,
   for God indeed is judge. R

⁷"Hear, O my people, and I will speak,
   O Israel, I will testify against
   you for I am God, your God.

⁸"Not for your sacrifices do I
rebuke you;
   your burnt offerings
   are continually before me. R

⁹"I will not accept a bull from your
house, or goats from your folds.

¹⁰For every animal of the forest is
   mine, the cattle on a thousand hills.

¹¹"I know all the birds of the air,
   and all that moves in the field
   is mine.

¹²"If I were hungry,
   I would not tell you,
   for the world and all that is
   in it is mine. R

¹³"Do I eat the flesh of bulls,
   or drink the blood of goats?

¹⁴"Offer to God a sacrifice of
thanksgiving,
   and pay your vows to
   the Most High.

¹⁵"Call on me in the day of trouble;
   I will deliver you,
   and you shall glorify me." R

²²"Mark this, then, you who forget
God,
   or I will tear you apart, and there
   will be no one to deliver.

²³"Those who bring thanksgiving
as their sacrifice honor me;
   to those who go the right way I
   will show the salvation of God." R

*Proper 5 [10] A vs. 7–15; Epiphany Last and Trans-
figuration B vs. 1–6; Proper 14 [19] C vs. 1–8, 22–23.*

# Psalm 51

Response

*Antiphon: Emma Lou Diemer, 1994*

Cre - ate in me a clean heart, O God.

℟

¹Have mercy on me, O God,
according to your steadfast love;
according to your abundant mercy
blot out my transgressions.

²Wash me thoroughly from my
iniquity, and cleanse me from my sin.
³For I know my transgressions,
and my sin is ever before me.

⁴Against you, you alone, have I
sinned, and done what is evil
in your sight,
so that you are justified in your
sentence and blameless when you
pass judgment.

⁵Indeed, I was born guilty,
a sinner when my mother
conceived me. ℟

⁶You desire truth in the inward being;
therefore teach me wisdom in
my secret heart.

⁷Purge me with hyssop,
and I shall be clean;
wash me, and I shall be
purer than snow.

⁸Let me hear joy and gladness;
let the bones that you have
crushed rejoice.

⁹Hide your face from my sins,
and blot out all my iniquities. ℟

¹⁰Create in me a clean heart, O God,
and put a new and right spirit
within me.

¹¹Do not cast me away from
your presence,
and do not take your
holy spirit from me.

¹²Restore to me the joy of your
salvation,
and sustain in me a willing spirit.

¹³Then I will teach transgressors
your ways,
and sinners will return to you. ℟

¹⁴Deliver me from bloodshed, O God,
O God of my salvation,
and my tongue will sing aloud
of your deliverance.

*R̰ Create in me a clean heart, O God*

¹⁵O God, opén my lips,
and my mouth will declare
your praise.

¹⁶For you have no delight in sacrifice;
if I were to give a burnt offering,
you would not be pleased.

¹⁷The sacrifice acceptable to God
is a troubled spirit;
a broken and contrite heart, O God,
you will not despise. *R̰*

*Ash Wednesday ABC vs. 1–17; Lent 5 B vs. 1–12 (Alt.);*
*Proper 13 [18] B vs. 1–12; Proper 19 [24] C vs. 1–10.*
*(If all verses are used, may be sung with double tone.)*

## Psalm 52

*R̰esponse*     *Antiphon: Jane Marshall, 1994*
*Unison*

Trust in the stead-fast love of God for - ev - er and ev - er.

*R̰*

¹Why do you boast, O mighty one,
of mischief done against the godly?

All day long ²you are plotting
destruction.
Your tongue is like a sharp razor,
you worker of treachery.

³You love evil more than good, and
lying more than speaking the truth.
⁴You love all words that devour,
O deceitful tongue.

⁵But God will break you down forever;
God will snatch and tear you from
your tent and uproot you from the
land of the living. *R̰*

⁶The righteous will see, and fear,
and will laugh at the evildoer, saying,
⁷"See the one who would not take
refuge in God, but trusted in
abundant riches, and sought refuge
in wealth!"

⁸But I am like a green olive tree
in the house of God.
I trust in the steadfast love of God
forever and ever.

⁹I will thank you forever,
because of what you have done.
In the presence of the faithful I will
proclaim your name,
for your name is good. *R̰*

# Psalm 54

*Antiphon: Robert Fryson, 1994*

God is the up - hold - er of my life.

℟

¹Save me, O God, by your name,
  and vindicate me by your might.

²Hear my prayer, O God;
  give ear to the words óf my
    mouth.

³For the insolent have risen
against me,
  the ruthless seek my life;
  they do not set God before them.

⁴But surely, God is my helper;
  God is the upholder óf my life. ℟

⁵God will repay my enemies
for their evil.
  In your faithfulness,
  put an end to them.

⁶With a freewill offering I will
sacrifice to you;
  I will give thanks to your name,
  O God, for it is good.

⁷For God has delivered me from
évery trouble,
  and my eye has looked in triumph
  ón my enemies. ℟

# Psalm 62

*Antiphon: Jean Slates Hawk, 1994*

Trust God at all times, O peo - ple.

℟

⁵For God alone my soul waits in
silence,
  for my hope is from God.

⁶God alone is my rock
 and my salvation, my fortress;

I shall not be shaken.

⁷On God rests my deliverance
ánd my honor;
  my mighty rock, my refuge is
  in God.

659

⁸Trust in God at all times, O people;
  pour out your heart before God
  who is a refuge for us.  ℟

⁹Those of low estate are but a breath,
  those of high estate are á delusion;
    in the balances they go up; they
    are together lighter than a breath.

¹⁰Put no confidence in extortion,
  and set no vain hopes on robbery;

if riches increase, do not set
  your heart on them.

¹¹Once God has spoken;
  twice have I heard this:

that power belongs to God,
  ¹²and steadfast love belongs to you,
  O God.

For you repay to all
  according to their work.  ℟

# Psalm 63

℟esponse

Antiphon:  *Vérne de la Peña, 1994*

I  will  bless  God  as  long  as  I  live.

℟

¹O God, you áre my God.
  I seek you, my soul thirsts for you;

my flesh faints for you,
  as in a dry and weary land where
  there is no water.

²So I have looked upon you in the
  sanctuary,
    beholding your power and glory.

³Because your steadfast love is better
  than life,
    my lips will praise you.

⁴So I will bless you as long ás I live;
  I will lift up my hands and call ón
  your name.  ℟

⁵My soul is satisfied as with á rich
  feast,
    and my mouth praises you with
    joyful lips

⁶when I think of you ón my bed,
  and meditate on you in the watches
  óf the night;

⁷for you have been my help,
  and in the shadow of your wings I
  sing for joy.

⁸My soul clings to you;
  your mighty hand upholds me.  ℟

# Psalm 65

*Antiphon: Marty Haugen, 1994*

God is the hope of all the ends of the earth.

𝓡

¹Praise is due to you, O God, in Zion;
  and to you shall vows
  be performed,

²O you who answer prayer!
  To you all flesh shall come.

³When deeds of iniquity overwhelm us,
  you forgive our transgressions.

⁴Happy are those whom you choose
and bring near to live in your courts.
  We shall be satisfied with the
  goodness of your house, your
  holy temple. 𝓡

⁵By awesome deeds you answer us
with deliverance,
  O God of our salvation;

you are the hope of all
the ends of the earth
  and of the farthest seas.

⁶By your strength you established the
mountains;
  you are girded with might.

⁷You silence the roaring of the seas,
the roaring of their waves,
  the tumult of the peoples. 𝓡

⁸Those who live at earth's farthest
bounds are awed by your signs;

you make the gateways of the
morning and the evening
shout for joy.

⁹You visit the earth and water it,
  you greatly enrich it;
    the river of God is full of water;

you provide the people with grain,
  for so you have prepared it.

¹⁰You water its furrows abundantly,
  and settle its ridges; 𝓡

you soften the earth with showers,
  and you bless its growth.

¹¹You crown the year with
  your bounty;
    your wagon tracks overflow
    with richness.

¹²The pastures of the wilderness
  overflow,
    the hills gird themselves with joy,

¹³the meadows clothe themselves with
flocks, the valleys deck themselves
with grain,
  they shout and sing together
  for joy. 𝓡

*Proper 10 [15] A vs. (1–8), 9–13.*

# Psalm 66

Antiphon: *Carolyn Jennings, 1994*

Let the sound of God's praise be heard.

𝓡
¹Make a joyful noise to God, áll
the earth;
²sing the glory of God's name;
give to God gloríous praise.

³Say to God, "How awesome áre
your deeds!
Because of your great power,
your enemies ćringe before you.

⁴"All the earth worships you;
they sing praises to you,
sing praises ío your name."

⁵Come and see what Gód has done:
God is awesome in deeds
ámong mortals. 𝓡

⁶God turned the sea ínto dry land;
they passed through the rivér
on foot.

There we rejoiced in God, ⁷who
rules by God's míght forever,
whose eyes keep watch on the
nations — let the rebellious
not exált themselves.

⁸Bless our God, O peoples, let the
sound of God's práise be heard,
⁹who has kept us among the
living, and has not lét our feet slip.

¹⁰For you, O Gód, have tested us;
you have tried us as silvér is tried.
𝓡
¹¹You brought us into the net;
you laid burdens ón our backs;
¹²you let people ride ovér our heads;

we went through fire
ánd through water;
yet you have brought us out to
a śpacious place.

¹³I will come into your house
wíth burnt offerings;
I will pay you my vows ¹⁴that my
lips uttered and my mouth promised
when I wás in trouble.

¹⁵I will offer to you burnt offerings of
fatlings, with the smoke of the
sacrifíce of rams;
I will make an offering
of búlls and goats. 𝓡

[16]Come and hear, all you who fear God,
   and I will tell what God
has done for me.
   [17]I cried aloud to God,
      and extolled God with my tongue.

[18]If I had cherished iniquity in my heart,
   God would not have listened.

[19]But truly God has listened;

God has given heed to the words
   of my prayer.

[20]Blessed be God, because God
   has not rejected my prayer
      or removed God's steadfast
love from me. ℟

*Easter 6 A vs. 8–20; Proper 9 [14] C vs. 1–9; Proper 23 [28] C vs. 1–12. (If all verses are used, may be sung with double tone.)*

# Psalm 67

℟
[1]May God be gracious to us and
bless us
   and make God's face to shine
   upon us,

[2]that your way may be known
upon earth,
   your saving power
   among all nations.

[3]Let the peoples praise you, O God;
   let all the peoples praise you.

[4]Let the nations be glad and
sing for joy,

for you judge the peoples with
equity and guide the nations
upon earth. ℟

[5]Let the peoples praise you, O God;
   let all the peoples praise you.

[6]The earth has yielded its increase;
   God, our God, has blessed us.

[7]May God continue to bless us;
   let all the ends of the earth
   revere God. ℟

# Psalm 68

Antiphon: *Judy Hunnicutt, 1994*

Sing, sing to God, sing prais-es to God's ho - ly name.

ℛ

¹Let God rise up, let God's enemies
be scattered;
    let those who hate God
    flee before God.

²As smoke is driven away,
so drive them away;
    as wax melts before the fire,
    let the wicked perish before God.

³But let the righteous be joyful;
    let them exult before God;
    let them be jubilant with joy. ℛ

⁴Sing to God, sing praises
to God's name;
    lift up a song to the one who rides
    upon the clouds;

be exultant before God
    whose name is the Sovereign.

⁵Father-Mother of orphans and
protector of widows
    is God in God's holy habitation.

⁶God gives the desolate a home to
live in; God leads out the prisoners
to prosperity,
    but the rebellious live in
    a desolate land. ℛ

⁷O God, when you went out before
your people,

when you marched through the
wilderness, ⁸the earth quaked,

the heavens poured down rain at the
presence of God, the God of Sinai,
    at the presence of God,
    the God of Israel.

⁹Rain in abundance, O God, you
showered abroad;
    you restored your heritage
    when it languished;

¹⁰your flock found a dwelling in it;
    in your goodness, O God, you
    provided for the needy. ℛ

³²Sing to God, O nations of the earth;
    sing praises to God,

³³O rider in the heavens,
the ancient heavens;
    listen, God sends out a voice,
    a mighty voice.

³⁴Ascribe power to God, whose
majesty is over Israel;
    and whose power is in the skies.

³⁵Awesome is God in God's sanctuary;
    the God of Israel gives power
    and strength to God's people.
    Blessed be God! ℛ

# Psalm 69

Antiphon: *Lee Dengler, 1994*

An - swer me, O God, for your stead-fast love is good.

℟

⁷It is for your sake that I have
borne reproach,
that shame has covered my face.

⁸I have become a stranger to my
kindred,
an alien to my mother's children.

⁹It is zeal for your house that has
consumed me;
the insults of those who insult you have
fallen on me. ℟

¹⁰When I humbled my soul with
fasting, they insulted me for doing so.
¹¹When I made sackcloth my
clothing, I became a
byword to them.

¹²I am the subject of gossip for those
who sit in the gate,
and the drunkards make songs
about me.

¹³But as for me, my prayer is to
you, O God.

At an acceptable time, O God,
in the abundance of your
steadfast love, answer me.

With your faithful help ¹⁴rescue me
from sinking in the mire;
let me be delivered from my
enemies and from the deep waters.
℟

¹⁵Do not let the flood sweep over me,
or the deep swallow me up,
or the Pit close its mouth over me.

¹⁶Answer me, O God, for your
steadfast love is good;
according to your abundant mercy,
turn to me.

¹⁷Do not hide your face from your
servant, for I am in distress–
make haste to answer me.

¹⁸Draw near to me, redeem me,
set me free because of my enemies.
℟

# Psalm 70

Response          *Antiphon: Elaine Kirkland, 1994*

Has - ten to help me, O God.

℟

¹Be pleased, O God, to deliver me.
  O God, make haste to help me!

²Let those be put to shame and
confusion who seek my life.
  Let those be turned back and
  brought to dishonor who
  desire to hurt me.

³Let those who say, "Aha, Aha!"
  turn back because of their shame.

⁴Let all who seek you rejoice and
  be glad in you.
    Let those who love your
    salvation say evermore,
    "God is great!"

⁵But I am poor and needy;
  hasten to me, O God!
    You are my help and my
    deliverer; O God, do not delay! ℟

# Psalm 71

Response          *Antiphon: David Hurd, 1994*

Unison

You, O God, are my hope, my trust, O God from my youth.

℟

¹In you, O God, I take refuge;
  let me never be put to shame.

²In your righteousness deliver me
and rescue me;
  incline your ear to me and save me.

³Be to me a rock of refuge,
a strong fortress, to save me,

for you are my rock and my
fortress.

⁴Rescue me, O my God, from the
hand of the wicked,
  from the grasp of the unjust
  and cruel.

⁵For you, O God, are my hope,
my trust, O God, from my youth.
  ⁶Upon you I have leaned from
  my birth;

it was you who took me from my
mother's womb.
  My praise is continually of you. ℛ

⁷I have been like a portent to many,
  but you are my strong refuge.

⁸My mouth is filled with your praise,
  and with your glory all day long.

⁹Do not cast me off in the
time of old age;
  do not forsake me when my
  strength is spent.

¹⁰For my enemies speak
concerning me,

and those who watch for my
life consult together.

¹¹They say, "Pursue and seize that
person whom God has forsaken,
  for there is no one to deliver." ℛ

¹²O God, do not be far from me;
  O my God, make haste to help me!

¹³Let my accusers be put to shame
and consumed;
  let those who seek to hurt me be
  covered with scorn and disgrace.

¹⁴But I will hope continually,
  and will praise you yet more
  and more. ℛ

*Tuesday in Holy Week ABC vs. 1–14; Epiphany 4 [4] C;*
*Proper 16 [21] C vs. 1–6.*

# Psalm 72

*Antiphon: Hyeon Jeong, 1994*

Give the rul-er your jus-tice, O God.

ℛ

¹Give the ruler your justice, O God,
  and your righteousness
  to a ruler's heir.

²May the ruler judge your people
with righteousness,
  and your poor with justice.

³May the mountains yield prosperity
for the people,
  and the hills, in righteousness. ℛ

⁴May the ruler defend the cause of the
poor of the people,
  give deliverance to the needy,
  and crush the oppressor.

⁵May the ruler live while
the sun endures,
  and as long as the moon,
  throughout all generations.

⁶May the ruler be like rain
  that falls on the mown grass,
    like showers that water the earth.

⁷In the ruler's days may
  righteousness flourish
    and peace abound, until the
    moon is no more. ℟

¹⁰May the monarchs of Tarshish and of
  the isles render the ruler tribute,
    may the monarchs of Sheba
    and Seba bring gifts.

¹¹May all monarchs fall down
  before the ruler,
    all nations give the ruler service.

¹²For the ruler delivers the needy
  when they call,
    the poor and those who have
    no helper.

¹³The ruler has pity on the weak
  and the needy,
    and saves the lives of the needy.

¹⁴From oppression and violence
  the ruler redeems their life;
    and precious is their blood in
    the ruler's sight. ℟

¹⁸Blessed be the Sovereign,
  the God of Israel,
    who alone does wondrous things.

¹⁹Blessed be God's glorious name
  forever;
    may the whole earth be filled
    with God's glory.

Amen and Amen.
  Amen and Amen. ℟

*Epiphany ABC, end with vs. 14; Advent 2 A, omit vs.
10–14.*

# Psalm 77

℟esponse                                          Antiphon: *Emma Lou Diemer, 1994*

I will call to mind the deeds of God.

℟
¹I cry aloud to God,
    aloud to God, that God may
    hear me.

²In the day of my trouble I seek God;
    in the night my hand is stretched
    out without wearying;
    my soul is not comforted.

¹¹I will call to mind the deeds of God;
    I will remember your
    wonders of old.

¹²I will meditate on all your work;
    I will muse on your mighty deeds.
℟

¹³Your way, O God, is holy.
    What god is so great as our God?

<sup>14</sup>You are the God who works wonders;
  you have displayed your might
  among the peoples.

<sup>15</sup>With your strong arm you
  redeemed your people,
    you redeemed the descendants
    of Jacob and Joseph.

<sup>16</sup>When the waters saw you, O God,
  when the waters saw you,
  they were afraid;
    the very deep trembled. ℛ

<sup>17</sup>The clouds poured out water;

the skies thundered; your arrows
  flashed on every side.

<sup>18</sup>The crash of your thunder was
  in the whirlwind;
    your lightnings lit up the world;
    the earth trembled and shook.

<sup>19</sup>Your way was through the sea,
  your path, through the mighty waters;
    yet your footprints were unseen.

<sup>20</sup>You led your people like a flock
  by the hand of Moses and Aaron. ℛ

# Psalm 78

Antiphon: Robert Fryson, 1994

ℛesponse

For - get not the works of God.

ℛ

<sup>1</sup>Give ear, O my people,
  to my teaching;
    incline your ears to the words
    of my mouth.

<sup>2</sup>I will open my mouth in a parable;
  I will utter dark sayings
  from of old,

<sup>3</sup>things that we have heard and known,
  that our ancestors have told us.

<sup>4</sup>We will not hide them
  from their children;
    we will tell to the coming
    generation the glorious deeds
    of God,

we will tell of God's might,
  and the wonders that God has done.
ℛ

<sup>5</sup>God established a decree in Jacob,
  and appointed a law in Israel,
    which God commanded our
    ancestors to teach to their children;

<sup>6</sup>that the next generation might
  know them, the children yet unborn,
    that they might rise up and tell
    them to their children,

<sup>7</sup>so that they should set their
  hope in God,
    and not forget God's works,
    but keep God's commandments. ℛ

℟ *Forget not the works of God.*

¹²In the sight of their ancestors
God worked marvels in the land
of Egypt, in the fields of Zoan.
¹³God divided the sea and let them
pass through it, and made the
waters stand like a heap.

¹⁴In the daytime God led them
with a cloud,
and all night long with
a fiery light.

¹⁵God split rocks open
in the wilderness,
and gave them drink abundantly
as from the deep.

¹⁶God made streams come out of
the rock,
and caused waters to flow
down like rivers. ℟

²³Yet God commanded the skies above,
and opened the doors of heaven;

²⁴God rained down on them manna
to eat,
and gave them the grain of heaven.

²⁵Mortals ate of the bread of angels;
God sent them food in abundance.
℟

²⁶God caused the east wind to blow
in the heavens,
and by God's power led out
the south wind;

²⁷God rained flesh upon them like dust,
winged birds like the sand
of the seas;

²⁸God let them fall within their camp, and
all around their dwellings.

²⁹And they ate and were well filled,
for God gave them
what they craved. ℟

³²In spite of all this they still sinned;
they did not believe
in God's wonders.

³³So God made their days vanish
like a breath,
and their years in terror. ℟

³⁴When God killed them,
they sought for God;
they repented and sought God
earnestly.

³⁵They remembered that God
was their rock,
the Most High God their redeemer.

³⁶But they flattered God
with their mouths;
they lied to God with their tongues.

³⁷Their heart was not steadfast
toward God;
they were not true
to God's covenant.

³⁸Yet God, being compassionate,
forgave their iniquity,
and did not destroy them;
often God was restrained in anger,
and did not stir up all God's wrath.
℟

*Proper 21 [26] A vs. 1–4, 12–16; Proper 27 [32] A vs. 1–7;*
*Proper 13 [18] B vs. 23–29; Holy Cross ABC vs. 1–2,*
*34–38 (Alt.).*

*(Verses 32 and 33 have been added here to the lectionary*
*verses.)*

# Psalm 79

*Antiphon: Jane Marshall, 1994*

How long, O God? Will you be an-gry for-ev-er?

℟

¹O God, the nations have come
into your inheritance;
   they have defiled your holy temple;
   they have laid Jerusalem in ruins.

²They have given the bodies
of your servants to the birds
of the air for food,
   the flesh of your faithful
   to the wild animals of the earth.

³They have poured out their blood like
water all around Jerusalem,
   and there was no one to bury them.

⁴We have become a taunt
to our neighbors,
   mocked and derided by those
   around us.

⁵How long, O God? Will you
be angry forever?

Will your jealous wrath burn
like fire? ℟

⁶Pour out your anger on the nations
that do not know you,
   and on the nations that do not
   call on your name.

⁷For they have devoured Jacob
and laid waste his habitation.

⁸Do not remember against us the
iniquities of our ancestors;
   let your compassion come speedily
   to meet us, for we are brought
   very low.

⁹Help us, O God of our salvation,
for the glory of your name;
   deliver us, and forgive our sins,
   for your name's sake. ℟

# Psalm 80

Antiphon: *Vérne de la Peña, 1994*

Stir up your might and come to save us.

℟

¹Give ear, O Shepherd of Israel,
  you who lead Joseph líke a flock!
    You who are enthroned upón
    the cherubim,

shine forth ²before Ephraim
and Benjamin ánd Manasseh.
  Stir up your might, and cóme
  to save us!

³Restore ús, O God;
  let your face shine, that
  we máy be saved.

⁴O Sovereign God of hosts, how long
will you be angry with your
péople's prayers?
    ⁵You have fed them with the
    bread of tears, and given them tears
    to drink ín full measure.

⁶You make us the scorn
óf our neighbors;
    our enemies laugh
    amóng themselves.

⁷Restore us, O Gód of hosts;
  let your face shine,
  that we máy be saved. ℟

⁸You brought a vine óut of Egypt;
  you drove out the natións
  and planted it.

⁹You cléared the ground for it;
  it took deep root and fílled the land.

¹⁰The mountains were covered
  wíth its shade,
    the mighty cedars wíth its branches;

¹¹it sent out its branches ío the sea,
  and its shoots ío the River.

¹²Why then have you broken dówn
  its walls,
    so that all who pass along the
    way pluck its fruit?

¹³The boar from the forest raváges it,
  and all that move in the field
  féed upon it. ℟

¹⁴Turn again, O God of hosts; look
  down from heaven, and see;
    have regard for this vine,
    ¹⁵the stock that your
    strong hand planted.

¹⁶They have burned it with fire,
  they have cút it down;
    may they perish at the rebuke
    óf your countenance.

¹⁷But let your hand be upon the
  one at your right hand,
    the one whom you made strong
    for yourself.

672

¹⁸Then we will never turn back
from you;
give us life, and we will
call on your name.

let your face shine,
that we may be saved. ℛ

*Advent 4 A and 1 B vs. 1–7, 17–19; Proper 22 [27] A vs.
7–15; Advent 4 C vs. 1–7 (Alt.); Proper 15 [20] C vs. 1–2,
8–19.*

¹⁹Restore us, O Sovereign
God of hosts;

# Psalm 81

ℛesponse

Antiphon: *Jean Slates Hawk, 1994*

Shout for joy . . . . . to the God of Ja - cob.

ℛ

¹Sing aloud to God our strength;
shout for joy to the God of Jacob.

²Raise a song, sound the tambourine,
the sweet lyre with the harp.

³Blow the trumpet at the new moon,
at the full moon, on our festal day.

⁴For it is a statute for Israel,
an ordinance of the God of Jacob. ℛ

⁵God made it a decree in Joseph, when
he went out over the land of Egypt.
I hear a voice I had not known:

⁶"I relieved your shoulder
of the burden;
your hands were freed
from the basket.

⁷"In distress you called,
and I rescued you;
I answered you in the secret place
of thunder; I tested you at the
waters of Meribah.

⁸"Hear, O my people, while I
admonish you;
O Israel, if you would but
listen to me! ℛ

⁹"There shall be no strange god
among you;
you shall not bow down to a
foreign god.

¹⁰"I am the Sovereign your God,
who brought you up out of the
land of Egypt.
Open your mouth wide and I
will fill it.

¹¹"But my people did not listen to
my voice;
Israel would not submit to me.

¹²"So I gave them over to their
stubborn hearts,
to follow their own counsels. ℛ

¹³"O that my people would
listen to me,
that Israel would walk in my ways!

14"Then I would quickly subdue
their enemies,
and turn my hand against their foes.

15"Those who hate God would
cringe before God,
and their doom would last forever.

16"I would feed you with the finest
of the wheat,
and with honey from the rock
I would satisfy you." R

*Epiphany 9 [9] B, Proper 4 [9] B vs. 1–10; Proper 17 [22]*
*C vs. 10–16. (If all verses are used, may be sung with*
*double tone.)*

# Psalm 82

Response

Antiphon: Marty Haugen, 1994

Rise up, O God, judge the earth; for all na-tions be-long to you.

R

1In the divine council God has
taken God's place;
God holds judgment in the
midst of the gods:

2"How long will you judge unjustly
and show partiality to the wicked?

3"Give justice to the weak
and the orphan;
maintain the right of the
lowly and the destitute.

4"Rescue the weak and the needy;
deliver them from the hand of
the wicked." R

5They have neither knowledge
nor understanding, they walk
around in shadows;

all the foundations of the
earth are shaken.

6I say, "You are gods,
children of the Most High,
all of you;

7"nevertheless, you shall die
like mortals,
and fall like any noble."

8Rise up, O God, judge the earth;
for all the nations belong to you! R

*(May be sung with double tone.)*

674

# Psalm 84

Response — Antiphon: Peter Niedmann, 1994

Unison

Hap-py are those who live in your house, ev - er sing-ing your praise.

R

¹How lovely is your dwelling place,
  O God of hosts!

²My soul longs, indeed it faints
for the courts of God;
    my heart and my flesh sing
    for joy to the living God.

³Even the sparrow finds a home,
    and the swallow a nest for herself,

where she may lay her young,
at your altars,
    O God of hosts, my Ruler
    and my God. R

⁴Happy are those who live
in your house,
    ever singing your praise.

⁵Happy are those whose strength
is in you,
    in whose heart are the
    highways to Zion.

⁶As they go through the valley of Baca
they make it a place of springs;
    the early rain also covers it
    with pools.

⁷They go from strength to strength;
    the God of gods will be seen
    in Zion. R

⁸O Sovereign God of hosts, hear
my prayer;
    give ear, O God of Jacob!

⁹Behold our shield, O God;
    look on the face of your anointed.

¹⁰For a day in your courts is better than
a thousand elsewhere.
    I would rather be a doorkeeper
    in the house of my God than live
    in the tents of wickedness.

¹¹For the Sovereign God is a sun
and shield;
    God bestows favor and honor.

No good thing does God withhold
    from those who walk uprightly.

¹²O God of hosts,
    happy is everyone who trusts
    in you. R

*Proper 25 [30] C vs. 1–7.*

# Psalm 85

*Antiphon: Carolyn Jennings, 1994*

Show us your stead-fast love, O God, and grant us your sal - va - tion.

ℛ
¹O God, you were favorable
to your land;
  you restored the fortunes of Jacob.

²You forgave the iniquity
of your people;
  you pardoned áll their sin.

³You withdrew áll your wrath;
  you turned from ýour hot anger.

⁴Restore us again, O God of óur
salvation,
  and put away your indignation
  toward us. ℛ

⁵Will you be angry with ús forever?
  Will you prolong your anger
  to all génerations?

⁶Will you not revive ús again,
  so that your people máy
  rejoice in you?

⁷Show us your steadfast love, O God,
  and grant us ýour salvation. ℛ

⁸Let me hear what God the
Sovereign will speak,
  for God will speak peace
  to the people;

God will speak to the faithful,
  to those who turn to God in
  their hearts.

⁹Surely God's salvation is at hand for
those who fear God,
  that God's glory may dwell in
  our land. ℛ

¹⁰Steadfast love and faithfulness
will meet;
  righteousness and peace will
  kiss each other.

¹¹Faithfulness will spring up
from the ground,
  and righteousness will look
  down from the sky.

¹²God will give what is good,
  and our land will yield its increase.

¹³Righteousness will go before God,
  and will make a path
  for God's steps. ℛ

*Proper 10 [15] B and Proper 14 [19] A vs. 8–13; Advent 2
B omit vs. 3–7.*

# Psalm 86

Response
Antiphon: *Judy Hunnicutt, 1994*

O God, you a-bound in stead-fast love to all who call on you.

R

¹Incline your ear, O God,
and ánswer me,
for I am póor and needy.

²Preserve my life, for I am
devoted to you;
save your servant
who trusts in you.

You áre my God;
³be gracious to me, O God,
for to you do I cry áll day long.

⁴Gladden the soul óf your servant,
for to you, O God,
I lift úp my soul. R

⁵For you, O God, are good ánd
forgiving,
abounding in steadfast love to
all who call on you.

⁶Give ear, O God, to my prayer;
listen to my cry of supplication.

⁷In the day of my trouble
I call on you,
for you will ánswer me.

⁸There is none like you among
the gods, O God,
nor are there any wórks like yours.

R

⁹All the nations you have made
shall come and bow down
before you, O God,
and shall glorify your name.

¹⁰For you are great and do
wondrous things;
you alone are God.

¹¹Teach me your way, O God,
that I may walk in your truth;
give me an undivided heart to
revere your name.

¹²I give thanks to you, O God my God,
with áll my heart,
and I will glorify your name
forever. R

¹³For great is your steadfast love
toward me;
you have delivered my soul
from the depths of Sheol.

¹⁴O God, the insolent rise úp
against me;
a band of ruffians seeks my life,
and they do not set you
before them.

¹⁵But you, O God, are a God
merciful and gracious,
slow to anger and abounding
in steadfast love and faithfulness.

677

℟ *O God, you abound in steadfast love to all who call on you.*

¹⁶Turn to me and be gracious to me;
give your strength to your servant;
save the child óf your servant.

¹⁷Show me a sign of your favor, so
that those who hate me may see it

and be put to shame, because you,
O God, have helped me and
comforted me. ℟

*Proper 7 [12] A vs. 1–10, 16–17; Proper 11 [16] A vs. 11–17.*

# Psalm 89

℟esponse

Antiphon: Lee Dengler, 1994

Your stead - fast love is es-tab - lished for - ev - er.

℟

¹I will sing of your steadfast love,
O God, forever;
with my mouth I will proclaim
your faithfulness to all génerations.

²I declare that your steadfast love
is established forever;
your faithfulness is as firm
ás the heavens.

³You said, "I have made a
covenant with my chosen one,
I have sworn to my servant David:

⁴I will establish your descendants
forever,
and build your throne for all
génerations.'" ℟

¹⁵Happy are the people who know
the festal shout,
who walk, O God, in the light
óf your countenance;

¹⁶they exult in your name áll day long, and
extol your righteousness.

¹⁷For you are the glory
óf their strength;
by your favor our horn is exalted.

¹⁸For our shield belongs to God,
our ruler to the Holy One of Israel.
℟

¹⁹Then you spoke in a vision to
your faithful óne, and said:
"I have set the crown on one
who is mighty, I have exalted
one chosen from the people.

²⁰"I have found my servant David;
with my holy oil
I have anointed him;

²¹"my hand shall always remáin
with him;
my arm alśo shall strengthen him.

²²"The enemy shall not outwit him,
the wicked shall not humble him.

℟

²³"I will crush his foes before him
  and strike down those
  who hate him.

²⁴"My faithfulness and steadfast love
  shall be with him;
    and in my name his horn
    shall be exalted.

²⁵"I will set his hand on the sea
  and his right hand on the rivers.

²⁶"He shall cry to me, 'You are my
Father and Mother,
    my God, and the Rock
    of my salvation!' ℟

²⁷"I will make him the firstborn,
  the highest of the rulers
  of the earth.

²⁸"Forever I will keep my steadfast
love for him,
    and my covenant with him
    will stand firm.

²⁹"I will establish his line forever,
  and his throne as long as the
  heavens endure. ℟

³⁰"If his children forsake my law
  and do not walk according to
  my ordinances,

³¹"if they violate my statutes
  and do not keep my
  commandments,

³²"then I will punish their transgression
  with the rod
    and their iniquity with scourges;

³³"but I will not remove from him
  my steadfast love,
    or be false to my faithfulness. ℟

³⁴"I will not violate my covenant,
  or alter the word that went forth
  from my lips.

³⁵"Once and for all I have sworn
  by my holiness;
    I will not lie to David.

³⁶"His line shall continue forever,
  and his throne endure before me
  like the sun.

³⁷"It shall be established forever
like the moon,
    an enduring witness in the skies."
  ℟

*Proper 8 [13] A vs. 1–4, 15–18; Advent 4 B vs. 1–4, 19–26*
*(Alt.); Proper 11 [16] B vs. 20–37.*

# Psalm 90

Antiphon: Elaine Kirkland, 1994

**Response** *Unison*

From ev - er - last-ing to ev - er - last - ing, you are God.

℟

¹O God, you have been
our dwelling place
   in all generations.

²Before the mountains were brought
forth, or ever you had formed the earth
and the world,
   from everlasting to everlasting
   you are God.

³You turn us back to dust,
   and say, "Turn back, you mortals."

⁴For a thousand years in your sight are
like yesterday when it is past,
   or like a watch in the night. ℟

⁵You sweep them away;
they are like a dream,
   like grass that is renewed in
   the morning;

⁶in the morning it flourishes
and is renewed;
   in the evening it fades and withers.

⁷For we are consumed by your anger;
   by your wrath we are overwhelmed.

⁸You have set our iniquities
before you,
   our secret sins in the light of
   your countenance. ℟

⁹For all our days pass away
under your wrath;
   our years come to an end
   like a sigh.

¹⁰The days of our life are seventy years,
   or perhaps eighty, if we are strong;

even then their span is only toil
and trouble;
   they are soon gone,
   and we fly away.

¹¹Who considers the power
of your anger?
   Your wrath is as great as the
   fear that is due you.

¹²So teach us to count our days
   that we may gain a wise heart. ℟

¹³Turn, O God! How long?
   Have compassion on your servants!

¹⁴Satisfy us in the morning
with your steadfast love,
   so that we may rejoice
   and be glad all our days.

¹⁵Make us glad as many days as
you have afflicted us,
   and as many years as
   we have seen evil.

¹⁶Let your work be manifest
to your servants,
and your glorious power
to their children.

¹⁷Let the favor of the Sovereign our
God be upon us, and prosper for us
the work óf our hands —
O prosper the work óf our hands! ℛ

*Proper 25 [30] A vs. 1–6, 13–17; Proper 28 [33] A vs. 1–8,
(9–11), 12; Proper 23 [28] B vs. 12–17.*

# Psalm 91

ℛesponse                                                        Antiphon: David Hurd, 1994

My ref-uge and my for-tress, my God in whom I trust.

ℛ

¹You who live in the shelter of
the Most High,
who abide in the shadow of
the Almighty, ²will sáy to God,

"My refuge ánd my fortress;
my God, in whom I trust."

³For God will deliver you from
the snare óf the fowler
and from the deadly pestilence;

⁴God will cover you with God's
pinions, and under God's wings
you will find refuge;
God's faithfulness is a shield
and buckler. ℛ

⁵You will not fear the terror
óf the night,
or the arrow that flies by day,

⁶or the pestilence that stalks ín
the nighttime,
or the destruction that wastes
at noonday.

⁹Because you have made Gód
your refuge,
the Most High your dwelling place,

¹⁰no evil shall befall you,
no scourge come near your tent. ℛ

¹¹For God will command God's angels
concerning you
to guard you in áll your ways.

¹²On their hands they will bear you up,
so that you will not dash your foot
against a stone.

¹³You will tread on the lion
ánd the adder,
the young lion and the serpent
you will trample únder foot.

¹⁴Those who love me, I will deliver;
I will protect those who know
my name.

*R My refuge and my fortress, my God in whom I trust.*

<sup>15</sup>When they call to me,
 I will ánswer them;
  I will be with them in trouble,
  I will rescue them and hónor them.

<sup>16</sup>With long life I will satisfy them,
  and show them mý salvation. *R*

*Proper 24 [29] B omit vs. 1–8; Lent 1 C omit vs. 3–8;*
*Proper 21 [26] C omit vs. 7–13.*

# Psalm 92

*Response*

*Antiphon: Robert Train Adams, 1994*

The righ - teous flour - ish like the palm tree.

*R*

<sup>1</sup>It is good to give thanks to God,
 to sing praises to your name,
  Ó Most High;

<sup>2</sup>to declare your steadfast love ín
 the morning,
  and your faithfulness by night,

<sup>3</sup>to the music of the lute ánd the harp,
 to the melody óf the lyre.

<sup>4</sup>For you, O God, have made me glad
 by your work;
  at the works of your hands
  I síng for joy. *R*

<sup>12</sup>The righteous flourish líke the
 palm tree,
  and grow like a cedar in Lebanon.

<sup>13</sup>They are planted in the house of God;
 they flourish in the courts
  óf our God.

<sup>14</sup>In old age they still próduce fruit;
 they are always green
  and full of sap,

<sup>15</sup>showing that God is upright;
 God is my rock, and has
  no unrighteousness. *R*

*(May be sung with double tone.)*

# Psalm 93

*Antiphon: Emma Lou Diemer, 1994*

Response

Your throne, O God, is es-tab-lished from of old.

℟

¹God is ruler, God is robed in majesty;
   the Sovereign is robed,
    and is girded with strength.

God has established the world;
   it shall never be moved;

²your throne is established from
of old;
   you are from everlasting. ℟

³The floods have lifted up, O God,
  the floods have lifted up their voice;
   the floods lift up their roaring.

⁴More majestic than the thunders
  of mighty waters,
    more majestic than the waves
    of the sea, majestic on high is God!

⁵Your decrees are very sure;
   holiness befits your house,
   O God, forevermore. ℟

# Psalm 95

*Antiphon: Robert Fryson, 1994*

Response

Let us make a joy-ful noise to God with songs of praise.

℟

¹O come, let us sing to God;
   let us make a joyful noise to
    the rock of our salvation!

²Let us come into God's presence
with thanksgiving;

   let us make a joyful noise to
   God with songs of praise!

³For God is a great God,
   and a great Ruler above all gods.

⁴In God's hand are the depths of the
earth;

the heights of the mountains
are álso God's. ℟

⁵The sea is God's, for God made it,
and the dry land, which God's hands
have formed.

⁶O come, let us worship ánd bow
down,
let us kneel before God, our Maker!

⁷For God is our God,
and we are the people of God's
pasture, and the sheep óf God's hand.

O that today you would listen to
God's voice!

⁸Do not harden your hearts,
as at Meribah, as on the day at
Massah in the wilderness, ℟

⁹when your ancestors tested me,
and put me to the proof, though
they had seen my work.

¹⁰For forty years I loathed
that generation and said,
"They are a people whose hearts go
astray, and they do not regard my
ways."

¹¹Therefore in my anger I swore,
"They shall not enter my rest." ℟

*Proper 29 [34] A vs. 1–7a.*

# Psalm 96

℟esponse                                          Antiphon: Jane Marshall, 1994

Sing   to   God   and   bless   God's   name.

℟

¹O sing to God á new song;
sing to God, áll the earth.

²Sing to God, bless God's name;
tell of God's salvation
from day to day.

³Declare God's glory among
the nations,
God's marvelous works among
áll the peoples. ℟

⁴For great is God, and greatly
to be praised;

God is to be revered above all gods.

⁵For all the gods of the peoples
are idols,
but God made the heavens.

⁶Honor and majesty áre before God;
strength and beauty are in
God's sanctuary.

⁷Ascribe to God, O families óf
the peoples,
ascribe to God glorý and strength. ℟

⁸Ascribe to God the glory
due God's name;
bring an offering,
and come into God's courts.

⁹Worship God in holy splendor;
tremble before God, all the earth.

¹⁰Say among the nations, "God is ruler!
The world is firmly established;
it shall never be moved.

"God will judge the peoples;
God will judge the peoples
with equity." ℛ

¹¹Let the heavens be glad,
and let the earth rejoice;

let the sea roar, and all that fills it;

¹²let the field exult,
and everything in it.
Then shall all the trees of the forest
sing for joy ¹³before God;

for God is coming,
for God is coming
to judge the earth.

God will judge the world
with righteousness,
and the peoples with God's truth. ℛ

*Proper 24 [29] A vs. 1–9 (10–13); Epiphany 9 [9] C and*
*Proper 4 [9] C vs. 1–9.*

# Psalm 97

ℛesponse

Antiphon: *Vérne de la Peña, 1994*

Re-joice in God, O you righ-teous! Give thanks to God's ho - ly name!

ℛ

¹God is ruler! Let the earth rejoice;
let the many coastlands be glad!

²Clouds and thick darkness
are all around God;
righteousness and justice are
the foundation of God's throne.

³Fire goes before God,
and consumes God's adversaries
on every side.

⁴God's lightnings light up the world;
the earth sees and trembles. ℛ

⁵The mountains melt like wax
before God,
before the God of all the earth.

⁶The heavens proclaim
God's righteousness;
and all the peoples behold
God's glory.

⁷All worshipers of images are
put to shame, those who make their
boast in worthless idols;
all gods bow down before God.

⁸Zion hears ánd is glad,
and the towns of Judah rejoice,
because of your judgménts, O God.
℟

⁹For you, O God, are most high
over áll the earth;
you are exalted far abóve all gods.

¹⁰God loves those whó hate evil;
God guards the lives of God's

faithful; God rescues them
from the hand óf the wicked.

¹¹Light dawns fór the righteous,
and joy for the upríght in heart.

¹²Rejoice in God, Ó you righteous,
and give thanks to God's
hóly name! ℟

*(May be sung with double tone.)*

# Psalm 98

℟esponse
Antiphon: *Marty Haugen, 1994*

Make a joy-ful noise, a joy-ful noise, un-to God, all the earth.

℟

¹O sing to God á new song,
for God has done marvélous things.

God's strong hand and hóly arm
have given Gód the victory.

²God has made knówn God's victory,
and has revealed God's vindication
in the sight óf the nations.

³God has remembered having steadfast
love and faithfulness to the hóuse
of Israel.
All the ends of the earth have
seen the victory óf our God.

⁴Make a joyful noise to God,
áll the earth;
break forth into joyous song
ánd sing praises.

⁵Sing praises to God wíth the lyre,

with the lyre and the sóund
of melody. ℟

⁶With trumpets and the sound óf
the horn
make a joyful noise before the
Rúler, the Sovereign.

⁷Let the sea roar, and áll that fills it;
the world and thóse who live in it.

⁸Let the floods cláp their hands;
let the hills sing together for
joy ⁹at the presence of God;
for God is coming to júdge
the earth.

God will judge the wórld
with righteousness,
and the peóples with equity. ℟

*Holy Cross ABC vs. 1–5 (Alt.).*

# Psalm 99

Response
Antiphon: Carolyn Jennings, 1994

Ex-tol the Sov-ereign, our God, and wor-ship at God's ho-ly tem - ple.

*R*

¹God is ruler; let the peoples tremble!
  God sits enthroned upon the
  cherubim; let the earth quake!

²God is great in Zion;
  God is exalted over all the peoples.

³Let them praise your great and
  awesome name.
  Holy is God!

⁴Mighty Ruler, lover of justice,
you have established equity;
  you have executed justice and
  righteousness in Jacob.

⁵Extol the Sovereign our God;
worship at God's footstool.
  Holy is God!  *R*

⁶Moses and Aaron were
among God's priests,

Samuel also was among those
  who called on God's name.

They cried to God,
  and God answered them.

⁷God spoke to them
in the pillar of cloud;
  they kept God's decrees, and
  the statutes that God gave them.

⁸O Sovereign our God,
you answered them;
  you were a forgiving God to them,
  but an avenger of
  their wrongdoings.

⁹Extol the Sovereign our God, and
worship at God's holy mountain;
  for the Sovereign our God is holy.
  *R*

# Psalm 100

Antiphon: Peter Niedmann, 1994

It is God that made us, and we are God's peo - ple.

℟

¹Make a joyful noise to God,
  áll the earth.
    ²Worship God with gladness; come
    into God's preśence with singing.

³Know that the Sovereign is God. It
is God that made us,
    and we are God's; we are God's
    people, and the sheep óf God's
    pasture.

⁴Enter God's gates with thanksgiving,
  and enter God's courts with praise.
    Give thanks to God, and bless
    God's name.

⁵For God is good; God's steadfast love
  endures forever,
    and God's faithfulness to all
    génerations. ℟

*(May be sung with double tone.)*

# Psalm 103

Antiphon: Lee Dengler, 1994

(C7) F    C    Dm    Gm    C7sus4 C7    F

To you, O God, I will sing for - ev - er.

℟

¹Bless God, Ó my soul,
  and all that is within me, bless God's
  hóly name.

²Bless God, Ó my soul,
  and do not forget áll God's benefits —

³who forgives all ýour iniquity,
  who heals all ýour diseases,

⁴who redeems your life from the Pit,
  who crowns you with steadfast love
  and mercy,

⁵who satisfies you with good as long ás
  you live
    so that your youth is renewed líke
    the eagle's. ℟

⁶God works vindication and justice
  for all who áre oppressed.

⁷God made known God's wáys to Moses,
  and God's acts to the peóple of Israel.

⁸God is merciful and gracious,
  slow to anger and abounding in
  śteadfast love. ℟

⁹God will not alwáys accuse,
  nor will God be angry forever.

¹⁰God does not deal with us according to
  our sins,
    nor repay us according to óur
    iniquities.

¹¹For as the heavens are high abóve the
  earth,

so great is God's steadfast love
  toward those who fear God;

¹²as far as the east is from the west,
  so far God removes our
  transgreśsions from us. ℟

¹³As a father and mother have compassion
  for their children,
    so God has compassion for those
    who fear God.

²²Bless God, all God's works, in all places
  of God's dominion.
    Bless God, Ó my soul. ℟

*Proper 19 [24] A vs. (1–7), 8–13; Epiphany 8 [8] B vs.
1–13, 22; Proper 16 [21] C vs. 1–8.*

# Psalm 104

℟esponse

*Antiphon:  Judy Hunnicutt, 1994*

O    God,    how    man - i - fold    are    your    works!

℟

¹Bless God, Ó my soul.
  O God my God, you are véry great.

You are clothed with honor and majesty,
  ²wrapped in light as wíth a garment.

You stretch out the heavens líke a tent,
  ³you set the beams of your chambers
  ón the waters,

you make the clouds your chariot,
  you ride on the wings óf the wind, ℟

⁴you make the winds your messengers,
  fire and flame áre your ministers.

⁵You set the earth on íts foundations,
  so that it shall never be shaken.

⁶You cover it with the deep as wíth a
  garment;
    the waters stood abóve the
    mountains.

⁷At your rebuke they flee;
  at the sound of your thunder they
  take to flight. ℟

*R O God, how manifold are your works!*

⁸They rose up to the mountains;
they ran down to the valleys to the
place that you appointed for them.

⁹You set a boundary that they may not
pass,
so that they might not again cover
the earth.

²⁴O God, how manifold áre your works!
In wisdom you have made them all;
the earth is full óf your creatures.

³⁵ᶜBless God, Ó my soul.
Praise be to God! *R*

*Proper 24 [29] B. (May be sung with double tone.)*

# Psalm 104

*Response*

*Antiphon: Judy Hunnicutt, 1994*

O  God,  how  man - i - fold  are  your  works!

*(Selection for Pentecost Day)*

*R*

²⁴O God, how manifold áre your works!
In wisdom you have made them all;
the earth is full óf your creatures.

²⁵Yonder is the sea, great and wide;
it is teeming with countless
creatures, living things both small
and great.

²⁶There go the ships,
and Leviathan that you formed to
sport in it.

²⁷These all look to you
to give them their food in due
season; *R*

²⁸when you give to them, they gather it
up;
when you open your hand, they are
filled with good things.

²⁹When you hide your face, they áre
dismayed;
when you take away their breath,
they die and return to their dust.

³⁰When you send forth your spirit, they
áre created;
and you renew the face óf the ground.

³¹May the glory of God endure forever;
may God rejoice in God's works —

*R*

³²God who looks on the earth ánd it
trembles,
God who touches the mountains ánd
they smoke.

³³I will sing to God as long ás I live;
I will sing praise to my God while I
have being.

³⁴May my meditation be pleasing to God,
for in God do I rejoice.

³⁵Let sinners be consumed from the earth,
and let the wicked be no more.
Bless God, O my soul. Praise be to
God! *R*

*(May be sung with double tone.)*

# Psalm 105

Response
Unison

*Antiphon: Elaine Kirkland, 1994*

Let the hearts of those who seek God re - joice.

℟

¹O give thanks to God, call ón God's name,
>make known God's deeds among the peoples.

²Sing to God, sing praises to God;
>tell of all God's wonderful works.

³Glory in God's holy name;
>let the hearts of those who seek God rejoice.

⁴Seek God ánd God's strength;
>seek God's presence continually.

⁵Remember the wonderful works God has done,
>God's miracles, and the judgments God uttered,

⁶O offspring of God's servants Abraham and Sarah,
>children of Jacob, God's chosen ones. ℟

⁷God is the Sovereign our God,
>whose judgments are in áll the earth.

⁸God is mindful of the covenant forever,
>of the word that God commanded, for a thousand generations,

⁹the covenant made with Abraham,
>God's sworn promise to Isaac,

¹⁰which was confirmed to Jacob ás a statute,

to Israel as an everlasting covenant,

¹¹saying, "To you I will give the land of Canaan
>as your portion for án inheritance." ℟

¹⁶When God summoned famine against the land, and broke every staff of bread,
>¹⁷God had sent a man ahead of them, Joseph, who was sold ás a slave.

¹⁸His feet were hurt with fetters, his neck was put in a collar of iron;
>¹⁹until what he had said came to pass, the word of God kept testing him.

²⁰The king sent ánd released him;
>the ruler of the peoples set him free.

²¹He made Joseph lord of his house, and ruler of all his possessions,
>²²to instruct his officials at his pleasure, and to teach his elders wisdom. ℟

²³Then Israel came to Egypt,
>and Jacob lived as an alien in the land of Ham.

²⁴And God made the people very fruitful,
>and made them stronger than their foes,

²⁵whose hearts God then turned to hate God's people,
>to deal craftily with God's servants.

*℟ Let the hearts of those who seek God rejoice.*

²⁶God sent God's servant Moses,
and Aaron whom God had chosen. ℟

³⁷Then God brought Israel out with silver
and gold,
and there was no one among their
tribes who stumbled.

³⁸Egypt was glad when they departed,
for dread of them had fallen upon
Egypt.

³⁹God spread a cloud for a covering,
and fire to give light by night.

⁴⁰They asked, and God brought quails,
and gave them food from heaven in
abundance.

⁴¹God opened the rock, and water gushed
out;
it flowed through the desert like a
river.

⁴²For God remembered God's holy
promise,
and Abraham and Sarah, God's
servants. ℟

⁴³So God brought God's people out with
joy,
God's chosen ones with singing.

⁴⁴God gave them the lands of the nations,
and they took possession of the
wealth of the peoples,

⁴⁵that they might keep God's statutes and
observe God's laws.
Praise be to God! ℟

*Proper 12 [17] A vs. 1–11, 45b (Alt.); Proper 14 [19] A vs.*
*1–6, 16–22, 45b; Proper 17 [22] A vs. 1–6, 23–26, 45c;*
*Proper 20 [25] A vs. 1–6, 37–45.*

# Psalm 106

℟esponse                                    *Antiphon: David Hurd, 1994*

Re - mem-ber me, O God, when you show fa - vor to your peo-ple.

℟
¹Praise God! O give thanks to God, for
God is good;
for God's steadfast love endures
forever.

²Who can utter the mighty doings of
God,
or declare all God's praise?

³Happy are those who observe justice
always,
who do righteousness at all times.

⁴Remember me, O God, when you show
favor to your people;
help me when you deliver them;

⁵that I may see the prosperity of your
chosen ones,
> that I may rejoice in the gladness of
> your nation, and glory in your
> heritage. ℟

⁶Both we and our ancestors have sinned;
we have committed iniquity, and
have done wickedly.

¹⁹They made a calf at Horeb and
worshiped a cast image.
> ²⁰They exchanged the glory of God
> for the image of an ox that eats
> grass.

²¹They forgot God, their Savior, who had
done great things in Egypt,
> ²²wondrous works in the land of
> Ham, and awesome deeds by the Red
> Sea.

²³Therefore God said God would destroy
them —
> had not Moses, God's chosen one,
> stood in the breach before God,

to turn away God's wrath,
> that it not destroy them. ℟

# Psalm 107

℟esponse
*Antiphon: Marty Haugen, 1994*

Con - sid - er the stead - fast love of God.

℟

¹O give thanks to God, for God is good;
for God's steadfast love endures
forever.

²Let the redeemed of God say so,
those whom God redeemed from
trouble

³and gathered in from the lands,
from the east and the west, from the
north and the south. ℟

⁴Some wandered in desert wastes, finding
no way to an inhabited town;
> ⁵hungry and thirsty, their soul fainted
> within them.

⁶Then they cried to God in their trouble,
and God delivered them from their
distress;

⁷God led them by a straight way,
until they reached an inhabited town.

⁸Let them thank God for God's steadfast
love,
> for God's wonderful works to
> humankind.

⁹For God satisfies the thirsty,
and the hungry God fills with good
things. ℟

¹⁷Some were sick through their sinful
ways,

and because of their iniquities endured
affliction;

18they loathed any kind of food,
    and they drew near to the gates of
    death.

19Then they cried to God in their trouble,
    and God saved them from their
    distress;

20God sent out God's word and healed
them,
    and delivered them from destruction.

21Let them thank God for God's steadfast
love,
    for God's wonderful works to
    humankind.

22And let them offer sacrifices of
thanksgiving,
    and tell of God's deeds with songs of
    joy. ℟

23Some went down to the sea in ships,
    doing business on the mighty waters;

24they saw the deeds of God,
    God's wondrous works in the deep.

25For God commanded and raised the
stormy wind,
    which lifted up the waves of the sea.

26They mounted up to heaven, they went
down to the depths;
    their courage melted away in their
    calamity;

27they reeled and staggered like drunkards,
    and were at their wits' end. ℟

28Then they cried to God in their trouble,
    and God brought them out from their
    distress;

29God made the storm be still,
    and the waves of the sea were hushed.

30Then they were glad because they had
quiet,
    and God brought them to the haven
    they desired.

31Let them thank God for God's steadfast
love,
    for God's wonderful works to
    humankind.

32Let them extol God in the congregation
of the people,
    and praise God in the assembly of the
    elders. ℟

33God turns rivers into a desert,
    and springs of water into thirsty
    ground;

34God turns a fruitful land into a salty
waste,
    because of the wickedness of its
    inhabitants.

35God turns a desert into pools of water,
    a parched land into springs of water.

36And there God lets the hungry live,
    and they establish a town to live in;

37they sow fields, and plant vineyards,
    and they get a fruitful yield.

43Let those who are wise give heed to
these things,
    and consider the steadfast love of
    God. ℟

*Proper 26 [31] A vs. 1–7, 33–37; Lent 4 B vs. 1–3, 17–22;*
*Proper 7 [12] B vs. 1–3, 23–32; Proper 13 [18] C vs. 1–9, 43.*

# Psalm 110

*Antiphon: Emma Lou Diemer, 1994*

*Response*

God is at your right hand.

𝓡

¹God says to my sovereign,
  "Sit at my right hand until I
  make your enemies your
  footstool."

²God sends out from Zion your
mighty scepter.
  You shall rule in the midst óf
  your foes.

³Your people will offer themselves
willingly
  on the day you lead your forces on
  the holy mountains.

From the womb of the morning,
like dew,
  your youth will come to you. 𝓡

⁴God has sworn and will not regret it,
  "You are a priest forever according
  to the order óf Melchizedek."

⁵God is at your mighty hand;
  God will shatter rulers on the day
  óf God's wrath.

⁶God will execute judgment among the
nations, filling them with corpses;
  God will shatter heads over the
  wide earth.

⁷My sovereign will drink from the
stream by the path;
  and therefore will lift úp the head.
  𝓡

*(May be sung with double tone.)*

695

# Psalm 111

Antiphon: Marty Haugen, 1994

Response

Great, great, great are the works of God.

**R**

¹Praise God! I will give thanks to God with my whole heart,

in the company of the upright, in the congregation.

²Great are the works of God,
studied by all who delight in them.

³Full of honor and majesty is God's work,

and God's righteousness endures forever.

⁴God has gained renown by wonderful deeds;

God is gracious and merciful. **R**

⁵God provides food for those who fear God;

God is ever mindful of God's covenant.

⁶God has shown God's people the power of God's works,

in giving them the heritage of the nations.

⁷The works of God's hands are faithful and just;

all God's precepts are trustworthy.

⁸They are established forever and ever,
to be performed with faithfulness and uprightness. **R**

⁹God sent redemption to God's people;
God has commanded God's covenant forever. Holy and awesome is God's name.

¹⁰The fear of God is the beginning of wisdom;

all those who practice it have a good understanding. God's praise endures forever. **R**

# Psalm 112

Antiphon: *Jane Marshall, 1994*

*Response*

*Unison*

Hap - py are those who fear God.

*R*

¹Praise be to God!
  Happy are those who fear God, who
  greatly delight in God's
  commandments.

²Their descendants will be mighty in the
  land;
  the generation of the upright will be
  blessed.

³Wealth and riches are in their houses,
  and their righteousness endures
  forever.

⁴They rise in the night as a light for the
  upright;
  they are gracious, merciful, and
  righteous.

⁵It is well with those who deal
  generously and lend,
  who conduct their affairs with
  justice. *R*

⁶For the righteous will never be moved;
  they will be remembered forever.

⁷They are not afraid of evil tidings;
  their hearts are firm, secure in God.

⁸Their hearts are steady, they will not be
  afraid;
  in the end they will look in triumph
  on their foes.

⁹They have distributed freely, they have
  given to the poor;
  their righteousness endures forever;
  their horn is exalted in honor.

¹⁰The wicked see it and are angry; they
  gnash their teeth and melt away;
  the desire of the wicked comes to
  nothing. *R*

*Epiphany 5 [5] A vs. 1–9, (10).*

# Psalm 113

Response           *Antiphon: Vérne de la Peña, 1994*

Bless - ed be the name of God for - ev - er.

*R*

¹Praise be to God!
   Praise, O servants of God; praise the
   name of God.

²Blessed be the name of God from this
time on and forevermore.
   ³From the rising of the sun to its
   setting the name of God is to be
   praised.

⁴God is high above all nations,
   and God's glory above the heavens. *R*

⁵Who is like God our God, who is seated
on high,
   ⁶who looks far down on the heavens
   and the earth?

⁷God raises the poor from the dust, and
lifts the needy from the ash heap,
   ⁸to make them sit with nobles, with
   the leaders of God's people.

⁹God gives the childless woman a home,
   making her the joyous mother of
   children. Praise be to God! *R*

# Psalm 114

Response           *Antiphon: Hyeon Jeong, 1994*

trem - ble,
Trem - ble, O earth, at the pre - sence of God.

*R*

¹When Israel went out from Egypt,
   the house of Jacob from a people of
   strange language,

²Judah became God's sanctuary,
   Israel became God's dominion.

³The sea looked and fled; Jordan turned
back.
   ⁴The mountains skipped like rams,
   the hills like lambs. *R*

⁵Why is it, O sea, that you flee? O
Jordan, that you turn back?

⁶O mountains, that you skip like
rams? O hills, like lambs?

⁷Tremble, O earth, at the presence of
God,
　at the presence of the God of Jacob,

⁸who turns the rock into a pool of water,
　who turns the flint into a spring of
water. ℛ

# Psalm 116

Response

*Antiphon: Judy Hunnicutt, 1994*

I will call on God as long as I live (as long as I live).

ℛ

¹I love God, because God has heard my
voice
　and has heard my supplications.

²Because God inclined an ear to me,
　therefore I will call on God as long
ás I live. ℛ

³The snares of death encompassed me;
the pangs of Sheol laid hold on me;
　I suffered distress and anguish.

⁴Then I called on the name of God:
　"O God, I pray, save my life!"

⁵Gracious is God, and righteous;
　our God is merciful.

⁶God protects the simple;
　when I was brought low, God saved
me. ℛ

⁷Return, O my soul, to your rest,
　for God has dealt bountifully with
you.

⁸For you have delivered my soul from
death,
　and my eyes from tears, and my feet
from stumbling.

⁹I walk before God
　in the land of the living. ℛ

¹²What shall I return to God for all God's
bounty to me?
　¹³I will lift up the cup of salvation
　and call on the name of God,

¹⁴I will pay my vows to God,
　I will pay them in the presence of áll
God's people.

¹⁵Precious in the sight of God
　is the death of God's faithful ones.

¹⁶O God, I am your servant, and the child
of your servant.
　You have loosed my bonds.

*R͛ I will call on God as long as I live (as long as I live).*

¹⁷I will offer to you a thanksgíving
   sacrifice;
     I will call on the ñame of God.

¹⁸I will pay my vows to God
   in the presence of áll God's people,

¹⁹in the courts of the house of God,
   in your midst, O Jerusalem.  Praise
   be to God!  *R͛*

*Holy Thursday ABC and Proper 6 [11] A omit vs. 3–9;*
*Easter 3A omit vs. 5–9; Proper 19 [24] B vs. 1–9.*

# Psalm 118

*R͛esponse*

*Antiphon:   Carolyn Jennings, 1994*

*(Selection for Easter Sunday)*

*R͛*

¹O give thanks to God, for Gód is good;
   God's steadfast love endúres forever!

²Let all Isŕael say,
   "God's steadfast love endúres
   forever."

¹⁴God is my strength ánd my might;
   God has become mý salvation.

¹⁵There are glad songs of victory in the
 tents of the righteous: "The strong hand
 of Gód does valiantly;
   ¹⁶the mighty hand of Gód is exalted;
   the strong hand of Gód does valiantly."
*R͛*

¹⁷I shall not die, but Í shall live,
   and recount the déeds of God.

¹⁸God has punished mé severely,
   but God did not give me óver to
   death.

¹⁹Open to me the gátes of righteousness,
   that I may enter through them and
   give thanks to God.

²⁰This is the gáte of God;
   the righteous shall énter through it.
*R͛*

²¹I thank you that ýou have answered me
   and have become mý salvation.

²²The stone that the builders rejected
   has become the chief cornerstone.

²³This ís God's doing;
   it is marvelous ín our eyes.

²⁴This is the day that Gód has made;
   let us rejoice ánd be glad in it.  *R͛*

*Easter 2 C vs. 14–29 (Alt.); vs. 25–29 are on following page.*
*(May be sung with double tone.)*

*R The righteous shall enter the gate of God.*

*(Selection for Palm/Passion Sunday)*

R

¹O give thanks to God, for God is good;
God's steadfast love endures forever!

²Let all Israel say,
"God's steadfast love endures
forever."

¹⁹Open to me the gates of righteousness,
that I may enter through them and
give thanks to God.

²⁰This is the gate of God;
the righteous shall enter through it.
R

²¹I thank you that you have answered me
and have become my salvation.

²²The stone that the builders rejected has
become the chief cornerstone.
²³This is God's doing; it is
marvelous in our eyes.

²⁴This is the day that God has made;
let us rejoice and be glad in it.

²⁵Save us, we beseech you, O God!
O God, we beseech you, give us
success! R

²⁶Blessed is the one who comes in the
name of God.
We bless you from the house of God.

²⁷The Sovereign is God, and God has
given us light.
Bind the festal procession with
branches, up to the horns of the altar.

²⁸You are my God, and I will give thanks
to you;
you are my God, I will extol you.

²⁹O give thanks to God, for God is good,
for God's steadfast love endures
forever. R

*(May be sung with double tone.)*

# Psalm 119

Response

Antiphon: *Elaine Kirkland, 1994*

*(First selection)*

R

¹Happy are those whose way is
blameless,
who walk in the law of God.

²Happy are those who keep God's
decrees,
who seek God with their whole heart,

³who also do no wrong,
but walk in God's ways.

⁴You have commanded that all your
precepts
shall be kept with diligence. R

℟ *Teach me, O God, the way of your statutes.*

⁵O that my ways may be steadfast
    in keeping your statutes!

⁶Then I shall not be put to shame,
    having my eyes fixed on all your
    commandments.

⁷I will praise you with an upright heart,
    when I learn your righteous
    ordinances.

⁸I will observe your statutes;
    do not utterly forsake me. ℟

⁹How can young people keep their way
    pure?
    By guarding it according to your
    word.

¹⁰With my whole heart I seek you;
    do not let me stray from your
    commandments.

¹¹I treasure your word in my heart,
    so that I may not sin against you.

¹²Blessed are you, O God;
    teach me your statutes. ℟

¹³With my lips I shall declare
    all the ordinances of your mouth.

¹⁴I delight in the way of your decrees
    as much as in all riches.

¹⁵I will meditate on your precepts,
    and fix my eyes on your ways.

¹⁶I will delight in your statutes;
    I will not forget your word. ℟

³³Teach me, O God, the way of your
    statutes,
    and I will observe it to the end.

³⁴Give me understanding, that I may keep
    your law,
    and observe it with my whole heart.

³⁵Lead me in the path of your
    commandments,
    for I delight in your way.

³⁶Turn my heart to your decrees,
    and not to selfish gain. ℟

³⁷Turn my eyes from looking at vanities;
    give me life in your ways.

³⁸Confirm to your servant your promise,
    which is for those who fear you.

³⁹Turn away the disgrace that I dread,
    for your ordinances are good.

⁴⁰See, I have longed for your precepts;
    in your righteousness give me life.
℟

*Epiphany 6 [6] A vs. 1–8; Epiphany 7 [7] A vs. 33–40;*
*Proper 18 [23] A vs. 33–40; Lent 5 B vs. 9–16 (Alt.);*
*Proper 26 [31] B vs. 1–8. (May be sung with double tone.)*

℟ *Teach me, O God, the way of your statutes.*

*(Second selection)*
℟
⁹⁷O God, how I love your law!
    It is my meditation all day long.

⁹⁸Your commandment makes me wiser
    than my enemies,
    for it is always with me.

⁹⁹I have more understanding than all my
    teachers,
    for your decrees are my meditation.

¹⁰⁰I understand more than the aged,
    for I keep your precepts. ℟

¹⁰¹I hold back my feet from every évil
way,
    in order to kéep your word.

¹⁰²I do not turn away from your
ordinances,
    for ýou have taught me.

¹⁰³How sweet are your words tó my taste,
    sweeter than honey tó my mouth!

¹⁰⁴Through your precepts I get
únderstanding;
    therefore I hate every way thát is
false. ℛ

¹⁰⁵Your word is a lamp tó my feet,
    and a light tó my path.

¹⁰⁶I have sworn an oath ánd confirmed it,
    to observe your ríghteous ordinances.

¹⁰⁷I am severely afflicted;
    give me life, O God, according tó
    your word.

¹⁰⁸Accept my offerings of práise, O God,
    and teach mé your ordinances. ℛ

¹⁰⁹I hold my life in my hánd continually,
    but I do not forgét your law.

¹¹⁰The wicked have laid a snare for me,
    but I do not stray from your precepts.

¹¹¹Your decrees are my heritáge forever;
    they are the joy óf my heart.

¹¹²I incline my heart to perfórm your
statutes
    forever, tó the end. ℛ

*Proper 10 [15] A vs. 105–112; Proper 24 [29] C vs. 97–104.*
*(May be sung with double tone.)*

(Psalm 119)

ℛesponse                              *Antiphon: Elaine Kirkland, 1994*

*(Third selection)*

ℛ

¹²⁹Your decrees are wonderful;
    therefore mý soul keeps them.

¹³⁰The unfolding of your wórds gives
light;
    it imparts understanding tó the
simple.

¹³¹With open móuth I pant,
    because I long for ýour
commandments.

¹³²Turn to me and be grácious to me,
    as is your custom toward those who
love your name. ℛ

¹³³Keep my steps steady
    according tó your promise,
    and never let iniquity have domínion
over me.

¹³⁴Redeem me from human oppression,
    that I may kéep your precepts.

*R̩ Teach me, O God, the way of your statutes.*

¹³⁵Make your face shine upón your
  servant,
    and teach mé your statutes.

¹³⁶My eyes shed śtreams of tears
    because your law ís not kept. *R̩*

¹³⁷You are righteous, O God,
    and your judgménts are right.

¹³⁸You have appointed your decrees in
  righteousness
    and ín all faithfulness.

¹³⁹My źeal consumes me
    because my foes forget your words.

¹⁴⁰Your promise ís well tried,
    and your śervant loves it. *R̩*

¹⁴¹I am small ánd despised,
    yet I do not forget your precepts.

¹⁴²Your righteousness is an everlasting
  righteousness,
    and your law ís the truth.

¹⁴³Trouble and anguish have come upon
  me,
    but your commandments are mý
    delight.

¹⁴⁴Your decrees are righteous forever;
    give me understanding that I may
    live. *R̩*

*Proper 12 [17] A vs. 129–136; Proper 26 [31] C vs.*
*137–144. (May be sung with double tone.)*

# Psalm 121

Antiphon: David Hurd, 1994

*R̩esponse*

My help comes from God who made heav-en and earth.

*R̩*

¹I lift up my eyes ťo the hills —
    from where will mý help come?

²My help comes from God,
    who made heaven and earth.

³God will not let your foot be moved;
    God who keeps you will not
    slumber.

⁴God who keeps Israel
    will neither slumber nor sleep. *R̩*

⁵God ís your keeper;
    God is your shade át your side.

⁶The sun shall not strike ýou by day,
    nor the móon by night.

⁷God will keep you from all evil;
    God will keep your life.

⁸God will keep your going out and your
  coming in
    from this time on and forévermore. *R̩*

*(May be sung with double tone.)*

# Psalm 122

Antiphon: *Emma Lou Diemer, 1994*

May they pros - per who love you.

R

¹I was glad when they said to me,
  "Let us go to the house of God!"

²Our feet are standing within your gates,
O Jerusalem.
  ³Jerusalem — built as a city that is
  bound firmly together.

⁴To it the tribes go up, the tribes of God,
as was decreed for Israel,
  to give thanks to the name of God.

⁵For there the thrones for judgment were
set up,
  the thrones of the house of David. R

⁶Pray for the peace of Jerusalem:
  "May they prosper who love you.

⁷"Peace be within your walls,
  and security within your towers."

⁸For the sake of my relatives and friends
I will say,
  "Peace be within you."

⁹For the sake of the house of the
Sovereign our God,
  I will seek your good. R

*(May be sung with double tone.)*

# Psalm 123

Antiphon: *Robert Train Adams, 1994*

Have mer - cy on us, O God; have mer - cy on us, O God.

R

¹To you I lift up my eyes,
  O you who are enthroned in
  the heavens!

²As the eyes of subjects look to the hand
of their ruler,
  so our eyes look to the Sovereign
  our God, until God has mercy upon
  us.

*R  Have mercy on us, O God; have mercy on us, O God.*

³Have mercy upon us, O God, have
mercy upon us,
  for we have had more than enough óf
  contempt.

⁴Our soul has had more than its fill of
the scorn of those who áre at ease,
  and its fill of the contempt óf the
  proud. *R*

*(May be sung with double tone.)*

# Psalm 124

Antiphon:  Jane Marshall, 1994

*R*esponse

Our    help    is    in    the    name    of    God.

*R*

¹If it had not been God who was ón our
side
  — let Israél now say —

²if it had not been God who was ón our
side,
  when our enemies attacked us,

³then they would have swallowed us úp
alive,
  when their anger was kindled against
  us;

⁴then the flood would have swept ús
away,

the torrent would have gone over us;
⁵then over us would have gone the
raging waters. *R*

⁶Blessed be the Sovereign, our God,
  who has not given us as prey to their
  teeth.

⁷We have escaped like a bird from the
snare óf the fowlers;
  the snare is broken, and we have
  escaped.

⁸Our help is in the name of God,
  who made heaven and earth. *R*

# Psalm 125

Antiphon: *Vérne de la Peña, 1994*

Do good, O God, to those who are good.

𝑅

¹Those who trust in God are líke Mount Zion,

which cannot be moved, but abídes forever.

²As the mountains surróund Jerusalem, so God surrounds the people, from this time on and forévermore.

³For the scepter of wickedness shall not rest on the land allotted ío the righteous, so that the righteous might not stretch out their hands ío do wrong.

⁴Do good, O God, to those who are good, and to those who are upright ín their hearts.

⁵But those who turn aside to their own crooked ways, God will lead them away with evildoers. Peace be úpon Israel! 𝑅

# Psalm 126

Antiphon: *Martie McMane, 1994*

May those who sow in tears reap with shouts of joy.

𝑅

¹When God restored the fortunes of Zion, we were like íhose who dream.

²Then our mouth was filled with laughter, and our tongue with shouts of joy;

then it was said amóng the nations, "God has done great íhings for them."

³God has done great íhings for us, and we rejoiced. 𝑅

℟ *May those who sow in tears reap with shouts of joy.*

⁴Restore our fortunes, O God,
   like the watercourses in the Negeb.

⁵May those who sow in tears
   reap with shouts of joy.

⁶Those who go out weeping, bearing the
   seed for sowing,
      shall come home with shouts of joy,
      carrying their sheaves. ℟

## Psalm 127

*Antiphon:  Robert Fryson, 1994*

℟esponse

We   shall   not   be   put   to   shame.

℟

¹Unless God builds the house,
   those who build it labor in vain.

Unless God guards the city,
   the guard keeps watch in vain.

²It is in vain that you rise up early and
go late to rest, eating the bread of
ánxious toil;
   for God gives sleep to God's beloved.
℟

³Sons and daughters are indeed a heritage
from God,
   the fruit of the womb is á reward.

⁴Like arrows in the hand óf a warrior
   are the offspring óf one's youth.

⁵Happy is the person whose quiver is full
of them,
   who shall not be put to shame
   speaking with enemies in the gate.
℟

# Psalm 128

*Antiphon: Carolyn Jennings, 1994*

Bless - ed are they who fear God.

℞

¹Happy is everyone who fears God,
   and who walks in God's ways.

²You shall eat the fruit of the labor óf your hands;
   you shall be happy, and it shall go well with you.

³Your spouse will be like a fruitful vine within your house;
   your children will be like olive shoots around your table. ℞

⁴Thus shall the one be blessed who fears God.
   ⁵May God bless you from Zion.

May you see the prosperity of Jerusalem all the days óf your life.
   ⁶May you see your children's children. Peace be úpon Israel! ℞

# Psalm 130

*Antiphon: Judy Hunnicutt, 1994*

My soul waits for God.

℞

¹Out of the depths I cry to you, O God.
   ²O God, hear my voice!

Let your ears be attentive to the voice of my supplications!
   ³If you, O God, should mark iniquities, who could stand? ℞

⁴But there is forgiveness with you, so that you may be revered.
   ⁵I wait for God, my soul waits, and in God's word I hope;

⁶my soul waits for God more than those who watch for the morning,

more than those who watch for the
morning.

⁷O Israel, hope in God!
 For with God there is steadfast love.

With God is great power to redeem;
 ⁸It is God who will redeem Israel
 from all its iniquities. 𝓡

# Psalm 131

𝓡esponse

Antiphon: *Elaine Kirkland, 1994*

*May be sung as a round the last time.*

Hope in God, hope in God, hope in God for - ev - er-more.

𝓡

¹O God, my heart is not lifted up,
 my eyes are not raised too high;

I do not occupy myself with things too
great
 or things too marvelous for me.

²But I have calmed and quieted my soul,
 like a weaned child with its mother;

my soul is like the weaned child
 that stays with me.

³O Israel, hope in God
 from this time on and forevermore. 𝓡

# Psalm 132

Antiphon: David Hurd, 1994

**Response**

Let us go to God's dwell - ing place.

R

¹O God, remember in David's favor
all the hardships he endured;

²how David swore to God
and vowed to the Mighty One of Jacob,

³"I will not enter my house or get into my bed;
⁴I will not give sleep to my eyes or slumber to my eyelids,

⁵"until I find a place for God,
a dwelling place for the Mighty One of Jacob." R

⁶We heard of it in Ephrathah;
we found it in the fields of Jaar.

⁷"Let us go to God's dwelling place;
let us worship at God's footstool."

⁸Rise up, O God, and go to your resting place,
you and the ark of your might.

⁹Let your priests be clothed with righteousness,
and let your faithful shout for joy. R

¹⁰For your servant David's sake
do not turn away the face of your anointed one.

¹¹God swore to David a sure oath and will not turn back on it:
"One of the offspring of your body I will set on your throne.

¹²"If your offspring keep my covenant and my decrees that I shall teach them,
their offspring also shall sit on your throne forevermore." R

¹³For God has chosen Zion;
God has desired it for a habitation:

¹⁴"This is my resting place forever;
here I will reside, for I have desired it.

¹⁵"I will abundantly bless its provisions;
I will satisfy its poor with bread.

¹⁶"Its priests I will clothe with salvation,
and its faithful will shout for joy. R

¹⁷"There I will cause a horn to sprout up for David;
I have prepared a lamp for my anointed one,

¹⁸"whose enemies I will clothe with disgrace,
but upon my anointed a crown will gleam."

R

# Psalm 133

Antiphon: Hyeon Jeong, 1994

How plea - sant to live in u - ni - ty.

R

¹How very good and pleasant it is
　　when kindred live together in unity!

²It is like the precious oil on the head,
　　running down upon the beard,

upon the beard of Aaron,
　　running down over the collar of his
　　robes.

³It is like the dew of Hermon,
　　which falls on the mountains of
　　Zion.

For there God ordained the blessing,
　　the blessing of life forevermore. R

# Psalm 136

Antiphon: Emma Lou Diemer, 1994

Eb　　Gm　　AbM7　　Bb　　Eb

Stead - fast love sur - rounds those who trust in God.

R

¹O give thanks to God, for God is good,
　　for God's steadfast love endures
　　forever.

²O give thanks to the God of gods,
　　for God's steadfast love endures
　　forever.

³O give thanks to the Sovereign of
　sovereigns,
　　for God's steadfast love endures
　　forever;

⁴who alone does great wonders,
　　for God's steadfast love endures
　　forever; R

⁵who by understanding made the heavens,
　　for God's steadfast love endures
　　forever;

⁶who spread out the earth on the waters,
　　for God's steadfast love endures
　　forever;

⁷who made the great lights,
   for God's steadfast love endures
   forever;

⁸the sun to rule over the day,
   for God's steadfast love endures
   forever; ℛ

⁹the moon and stars to rule over the
night,
   for God's steadfast love endures
   forever.

²³It is God who remembered us in our low
   estate,

for God's steadfast love endures
forever;

²⁴and rescued us from our foes,
   for God's steadfast love endures
   forever;

²⁵who gives food to all flesh,
   for God's steadfast love endures
   forever;

²⁶O give thanks to the God of heaven,
   for God's steadfast love endures
   forever. ℛ

# Psalm 137

*Antiphon: Jonathan McNair, 1994*

ℛesponse

ℛ

¹By the rivers of Babylon — there we sat
down
   and we wept when we
   remembered Zion.

²And so we hung up our harps,
   there upon the willows.

³For there our captors asked us for songs,
and our tormentors asked for mirth,
   saying, "Sing us one of the songs of
   Zion!"

⁴How could we sing God's song in a
foreign land?
   ⁵If I forget you, O Jerusalem, let my
   right hand wither! ℛ

⁶Let my tongue cling to the roof of my
mouth, if I do not remember you,
   if I do not set Jerusalem above my
   highest joy.

⁷Remember, O God, against the
Edomites the day of Jerusalem's fall,
   how they said, "Tear it down!
   Tear it down to its foundations!"

⁸O city of Babylon, you devastator!
   Happy shall they be who pay you
   back what you have done to us!

⁹Happy shall they be who take your little
ones
   and dash them against the rock! ℛ

*(May be sung with double tone.)*

# Psalm 138

Antiphon: Emma Lou Diemer, 1994

℟esponse

Unison

Great is the glo - ry of God.

℟

¹I give you thanks, O God, with my whole heart;

 before the gods I sing your praise;

²I bow down toward your holy temple and give thanks to your name

 for your steadfast love and your faithfulness;

for you have exalted your name

 and your word above everything.

³On the day I called, you answered me,

 you increased my strength of soul. ℟

⁴All the rulers of the earth shall praise you, O God,

 for they have heard the words of your mouth.

⁵They shall sing of the ways of God,

 for great is the glory of God.

⁶For though God is high, God regards the lowly;

 but the haughty, God perceives from far away.

⁷Though I walk in the midst of trouble,

 you preserve me against the wrath of my enemies;

you stretch out your hand,

 and your right hand delivers me.

⁸God will fulfill God's purpose for me;

 your steadfast love, O God, endures forever. Do not forsake the work of your hands. ℟

# Psalm 139

*Antiphon: Jane Marshall, 1994*

Search me, O God, and know my heart.

𝑅

¹O God, you have searched me and known me.

²You know when I sit down and when I rise up; you discern my thoughts from far away.

³You search out my path and my lying down,
and are acquainted with áll my ways. 𝑅

⁴Even before a word is ón my tongue, O God, you know it completely.

⁵You hem me in, behind ánd before, and lay your hand upon me.

⁶Such knowledge is too wonderful for me;
it is so high that I cannót attain it. 𝑅

⁷Where can I go from your spirit? Or where can I flee from your presence?

⁸If I ascend to heaven, ýou are there; if I make my bed in Sheol, ýou are there. 𝑅

⁹If I take the wings óf the morning and settle at the farthest limits óf the sea,

¹⁰even there your hand shall lead me, and your right hand shall hold me fast.

¹¹If I say, "Surely the shadows shall cover me,
and the light around me become night,"

¹²even the night is not without light to you; the night is as bright ás the day, for the night is as light to you. 𝑅

¹³For it was you who formed my inward parts;
you knit me together in my mother's womb.

¹⁴I praise you, for I am fearfully and wonderfully made.
Wonderful are your works; that I know véry well. 𝑅

¹⁵My frame was not hidden from you, when I was being made in secret, intricately woven in the depths óf the earth.

¹⁶Your eyes beheld my únformed substance.
In your book were written all the days that were formed for me before they existed.

*℟ Search me, O God, and know my heart.*

¹⁷How weighty to me are your
thoughts, O God!
　　How vast is the sum of them!

¹⁸I try to count them — they are more
than the sand;
　　I come to the end — I am still
　　with you. ℟

²³Search me, O God, and know my
heart;
　　test me and know my thoughts.

²⁴See if there is in me any wicked way,
　　and lead me in the way everlasting. ℟

*Proper 11 [16] A vs. 1–12, 23–24; Epiphany 2 [2] B vs.
1–6, 13–18; Proper 4 [9] B and Proper 18 [23] C vs. 1–6,
13–18.*

# Psalm 141

℟esponse

Antiphon: Jonathan McNair, 1994

May the lift - ing of my hands be as an eve - ning sac - ri - fice.

℟

¹I call upon you, O God; come quickly
to me;
　　give ear to my voice when I call to
　　you.

²Let my prayer be counted as incense
before you,
　　and the lifting up of my hands as an
　　evening sacrifice.

³Set a guard over my mouth, O God;
　　keep watch over the door of my lips.

⁴Do not turn my heart to any evil, to
busy myself with wicked deeds with
those who work iniquity;
　　do not let me eat of their delicacies. ℟

⁵Let the righteous strike me;
　　let the faithful correct me.

Never let the oil of the wicked anoint
my head,
　　for my prayer is continually against
　　their wicked deeds.

⁶When they are given over to those who
shall condemn them,
　　then they shall learn that my words
　　were pleasant.

⁷Like a rock that one breaks apart and
shatters on the land,
　　so shall their bones be strewn at the
　　mouth of Sheol. ℟

⁸But my eyes are turned toward you, O
God, my God;
　　in you I seek refuge; do not leave me
　　defenseless.

⁹Keep me from the trap that they have laid for me,
    and from the snares of évildoers.

¹⁰Let the wicked fall into their own nets,
    while I alone escape. ℛ

## Psalm 143

*Response*

*Antiphon: Marty Haugen, 1994*

My soul thirsts for you, my soul thirsts for you like a parched land.

ℛ

¹Hear my prayer, O God; give ear to my supplications in your faithfulness;
    answer me in your righteousness.

²Do not enter into judgment with your servant,
    for no one living is righteous before you.

³For the enemy has pursued me, crushing my life to the ground,
    making me sit in the shadows like those long dead.

⁴Therefore my spirit faints within me;
    my heart within me is appalled. ℛ

⁵I remember the days of old, I think about all your deeds,
    I meditate on the works of your hands.

⁶I stretch out my hands to you;
    my soul thirsts for you like a parched land.

⁷Answer me quickly, O God; my spirit fails.

Do not hide your face from me, or I shall be like those who go down to the Pit.

⁸Let me hear of your steadfast love in the morning, for in you I put my trust.
    Teach me the way I should go, for to you I lift up my soul. ℛ

⁹Save me, O God, from my enemies;
    I have fled to you for refuge.

¹⁰Teach me to do your will, for you are my God.
    Let your good spirit lead me on a level path.

¹¹For your name's sake, O God, preserve my life.
    In your righteousness bring me out of trouble.

¹²In your steadfast love cut off my enemies, and destroy all my adversaries,
    for I am your servant. ℛ

*(May be sung with double tone.)*

# Psalm 145

Response

Antiphon: *Vérne de la Peña, 1994*

I will med - i - tate on your won - drous works.

R

¹I will extol you, my God and Ruler,
  and bless your name forever and ever.

²Every day I will bless you,
  and praise your name forever and
  ever.

³Great is God, and greatly to be praised;
  God's greatness is unsearchable.

⁴One generation shall laud your works to
  another,
  and shall declare your mighty acts. R

⁵On the glorious splendor of your
  majesty,
  and on your wondrous works, I will
  meditate.

⁶The might of your awesome deeds shall
  be proclaimed,
  and I will declare your greatness.

⁷They shall celebrate the fame of your
  abundant goodness,
  and shall sing aloud of your
  righteousness.

⁸God is gracious and merciful,
  slow to anger and abounding in
  steadfast love. R

⁹God is good to all,
  and God's compassion is over all that
  God has made.

¹⁰All your works shall give thanks to
  you, O God,
  and all your faithful shall bless you.

¹¹They shall speak of the glory of your
  dominion,
  and tell of your power,

¹²to make known to all people your
  mighty deeds,
  and the glorious splendor of your
  dominion. R

¹³Your reign is an everlasting reign,
  and your dominion endures
  throughout all generations.

God is faithful in every word,
  and gracious in every deed.

¹⁴God upholds all who are falling,
  and raises up all who are bowed
  down.

¹⁵The eyes of all look to you,
  and you give them their food in due
  season.

¹⁶You open your hand to all,
  satisfying the desire of every living
  thing. R

¹⁷In every way God is just,
  and kind in every action.

¹⁸God is near to all who call,
  to all who call on God in truth.

¹⁹God fulfills the desire of all who fear
God;
  God also hears their cry, and saves
  them.

²⁰God watches over all who love God,
  but will destroy all the wicked.

²¹My mouth will speak the praise of God,
  and all flesh will bless God's holy
  name forever and ever. ℛ

*Proper 9 [14] A vs. 8–14; Proper 13 [18] A vs. 8–9, 14–21;*

*Proper 20 [25] A vs. 1–8; Proper 12 [17] B vs. 10–18;*

*Proper 27 [32] C vs. 1–5, 17–21 (Alt.).*

# Psalm 146

Response

Antiphon: *Judy Hunnicutt, 1994*

I will praise God as long as I live.

ℛ

¹Praise be to God!
  Praise God, O my soul!

²I will praise God as long as I live;
  I will sing praises to my God all my
  life long.

³Do not put your trust in nobles, in
mortals,
  in whom there is no help.

⁴When their breath departs, they return to
the earth;
  on that very day their plans shall
  perish. ℛ

⁵Happy are those whose help is the God
of Jacob,
  whose hope is in the Sovereign their
  God,

⁶who made heaven and earth, the sea, and
all that is in them;
  who keeps faith forever;

⁷who executes justice for the oppressed;
  who gives food to the hungry. ℛ

God sets the prisoners free;
  ⁸God opens the eyes of those who
  cannot see.

God lifts up those who are bowed down;
  God loves those who are righteous.

⁹God watches over the strangers, and
upholds the orphan and the widow,
  but the way of the wicked God brings
  to ruin.

¹⁰The Sovereign will reign forever, your
  God, O Zion, for all generations.
  Praise be to God! ℛ

*Advent 3 A vs. 5–10 (Alt.).*

# Psalm 147

Response

*Antiphon: Elaine Kirkland, 1994*

Great is our God, and a - bun - dant in power.

℟

¹Praise God! How good it is to sing
praises to our God;
>
> for God is gracious, and a song of
> praise is fitting.

²God builds up Jerusalem;
> God gathers the outcasts of Israel.

³God heals the brokenhearted,
> and binds up their wounds.

⁴God determines the number of the stars;
> God gives to all of them their names.

⁵Great is our God, and abundant in
power,
>
> whose understanding is beyond
> measure. ℟

⁶God lifts up the downtrodden;
> God casts the wicked to the ground.

⁷Sing to God with thanksgiving;
> make melody to our God on the lyre.

⁸God covers the heavens with clouds,
prepares rain for the earth,
>
> and makes grass grow on the hills.

⁹God gives to the animals their food,
> and to the young ravens when they
> cry.

¹⁰God has no delight in the strength of the
horse,
>
> nor pleasure in the speed of a runner;

¹¹but God takes pleasure in those who
fear God,
>
> in those who hope in God's steadfast
> love. ℟

¹²Praise God, O Jerusalem!
> Praise your God, O Zion!

¹³For God strengthens the bars of your
gates;
>
> God blesses your children within
> you.

¹⁴God grants peace within your borders;
> God fills you with the finest of
> wheat.

¹⁵God sends out a command to the earth;
> God's word runs swiftly. ℟

¹⁶God gives snow like wool;
> God scatters frost like ashes.

¹⁷God hurls down hail like crumbs —
> who can stand before God's cold?

¹⁸God sends out a word, and melts them;
> God makes a wind blow, and the
> waters flow.

¹⁹God declares the word to Jacob,
 and declares God's statutes and
 ordinances to Israel.

²⁰God has not dealt thus with any other
 nation; they do not know God's
 ordinances.
  Praise be to God! ℟

*Christmas 2 ABC vs. 12–20 (Alt.); Epiphany 5 [5] B vs. 1–11, 20c.*

# Psalm 148

Antiphon: David Hurd, 1994

℟Response  Unison

Praise God from the heav - ens, praise God in the heights!

℟

¹Praise God! Praise God from the
heavens;
  praise God in the heights!

²Praise God, all you angels of God;
  praise God, all you host of heaven!

³Praise God, you sun and moon;
  praise God, all you shining stars!

⁴Praise God, you highest heavens,
  and you waters above the heavens! ℟

⁵Let them praise the name of God,
  for God commanded and they were
created.

⁶God established them forever and ever;
  God fixed their bounds, which cannot
be passed.

⁷Praise God from the earth, you sea
monsters and all deeps,

⁸fire and hail, snow and frost, stormy
wind fulfilling God's command!

⁹Mountains and all hills, fruit trees and
all cedars!
  ¹⁰Beasts of the forest and all cattle,
    crawling things and flying birds! ℟

¹¹Rulers of the earth and all peoples,
  nobles and all leaders of the earth!

¹²Young men and women alike,
  old and young together!

¹³Let them praise the name of the
Sovereign,
  whose name alone is exalted, whose
  glory is above earth and heaven.

¹⁴God has raised up a horn for the people,
  and praise for all the faithful,
    for the people of Israel who are close
    to God. Praise be to God! ℟

*(May be sung with double tone.)*

# Psalm 149

*Antiphon: Robert Train Adams, 1994*

Sing to God a new song.

R

¹Praise God! Sing to God á new song;
   sing God's praise in the assembly óf
   the faithful.

²Let Israel be glad ín its Maker;
   let the children of Zion rejoice ín
   their Ruler.

³Let them praise God's ńame with
dancing,
   making melody to God with
   tamboúrine and lyre.

⁴For God takes pleasure ín the people;
   God adorns the humbĺe with victory.  R

⁵Let the faithful exúlt in glory;
   let them sing for joy ón their
   couches.

⁶Let the high praises of God be ín their
throats,
   and two-edged swords ín their hands,

⁷to execute vengeance ón the nations
   and punishment ón the peoples,

⁸to bind their rulers with fetters and their
nobles with ćhains of iron,
   ⁹to execute on them the judgmént
   decreed.

This is glory for all God's faithful ones.
   Praise bé to God!  R

# Psalm 150

Antiphon: *Emma Lou Diemer, 1994*

Let ev - ery - thing that breathes praise God.

℟

¹Praise be to God! Praise God in God's
own sanctuary;
   praise God in the mighty firmament!

²Praise God for God's mighty deeds;
   praise God according to God's
   surpassing greatness! ℟

³Praise God with trumpet sound;
   praise God with lute and harp!

⁴Praise God with tambourine and dance;
   praise God with strings and pipe!

⁵Praise God with clanging cymbals;
   praise God with loud clashing
   cymbals!

⁶Let everything that breathes praise God!
   Praise be to God! ℟

# Psalm 51A

*Chant setting: Henry Purcell (1659–1695)*

1 Have mercy on me, O God, according to your stead-fast love; according to your abundant mercy blot out my trans-gressions.

2 Wash me thoroughly from my in - iquity, and cleanse me from my sin.

3 For I know 'my trans-'gressions, "and my 'sin is 'ever be - 'fore me.

4 Against you, you alone, have I sinned, and done what is e - vil in your sight,
so that you are justified 'in your 'sentence "and blame-less 'when you 'pass . . . 'judgment.

5 Indeed, I was born guilty, a sinner when my mother con - ceived me.

6 You desire truth in the 'in - ward 'being; "therefore teach me 'wisdom in my 'se - cret 'heart.

7 Purge me with hyssop, and I shall be clean; wash me, and I shall be purer than snow.

8 Let me hear 'joy and 'gladness; "let the bones that 'you have 'crushed re - 'joice.

9 Hide your face from my sins, and blot out all my in - iquities.

10 Create in me a clean 'heart, O 'God, "and put a 'new and right 'spirit with - 'in me.

11 Do not cast me a - way from your presence, and do not take your ho - ly spir - it from me.

12 Restore to me the 'joy of your sal-'vation, "and sus-'tain in me a 'will - ing 'spirit.

13 Then I will teach trans - gressors your ways, and sinners will re-turn to you.

14 Deliver me from bloodshed, "and my tongue
O God, O 'God of my sal-'vation, will sing a - 'loud of 'your de - 'liverance.

15 O God, open my lips, and my mouth will de-clare your praise.

16 For you have no de - 'light in 'sacrifice; "if I were to give a burnt offering, 'you would 'not be 'pleased.

17 The sacrifice acceptable to God is a trou - bled spirit; a broken and contrite heart, O God, you will not de - spise.

*(May be sung as a double chant. See next page.)*

# Psalm 63A

*Chant setting: Thomas Morley (c. 1557–1603)*

<sup>1</sup>O God, you are my God, I seek you, my soul . . . . thirsts for you;
my flesh faints for you, as in a dry and weary land where there is no water.

<sup>2</sup>So I have looked upon 'you in the 'sanctuary, "be - 'holding your 'power and 'glory.

<sup>3</sup>Because your steadfast love is better than life, my lips will praise . . . you.

<sup>4</sup>So I will bless you as 'long as I 'live; "I will lift up my 'hands and 'call on your 'name.

<sup>5</sup>My soul is satisfied as with a rich feast, and my mouth praises you with joy - ful lips

<sup>6</sup>when I think of 'you on my 'bed, "and meditate on 'you in the 'watches of the 'night;

<sup>7</sup>for you have been my help, and in the shadow of your wings I sing for joy.

<sup>8</sup>My soul 'clings to 'you; "your 'might - y 'hand up - 'holds me.

O God, you are my God, I seek you, my soul . . . . thirsts for you.

*(May be sung as a double chant. See below.)*

*Cambridge Chant*

*Daniel Hathaway, 1994*

# Psalm 67A

*Chant setting:  Vincent Novello (1781–1861)*

¹May God be
gracious to us    and bless us,
and make God's face to shine up - on us.

²That your
way may be known up-on earth,    your saving power a - mong    all nations.

³Let the
peoples    ᴵpraise you, O ᴵGod;    ᴵᴵlet    ᴵall the    ᴵpeo - ples ᴵpraise you.

⁴Let the nations
be glad and    sing    for joy,    for you judge the peoples with equity and guide the    nations upon earth.

⁵Let the
peoples    ᴵpraise you, O ᴵGod;    ᴵᴵlet    ᴵall the    ᴵpeo - ples ᴵpraise you.

⁶The earth has yielded    its increase; God, our    God, has    blessed . . .    us.

⁷May God con - ᴵtinue    to ᴵbless us; ᴵᴵlet all the    ᴵends of the ᴵearth re-vere ᴵGod.

*Joseph Barnby (1838–1896)*

*Jonathan McNair, 1994*

# Psalm 95A

*Chant setting: Richard Farrant (c. 1530–1580)*

<sup>1</sup>O come, let us sing to God; let us make a joyful noise to the rock of our sal - vation!

<sup>2</sup>Let us come into God's presence with thanks - giving; let us make a joyful noise to God with songs of praise!

<sup>3</sup>For God is a 'great . . . 'God, "and a great 'Ruler a - 'bove all 'gods.

<sup>4</sup>In God's hand are the depths of the earth; the heights of the mountains are al - so God's.

<sup>5</sup>The sea is 'God's, for God 'made it, "and the dry land, which 'God's . . . hands have 'formed.

<sup>6</sup>O come, let us worship and bow down, let us kneel before God, our Maker!

<sup>7</sup>For 'God is our 'God, "and we are the people of God's 'pasture, and the 'sheep of God's 'hand.

O that to - day you would lis - ten to God's voice!

*(May be sung as a double chant. See below.)*

*James Turle (1802–1882)*

*Daniel Hathaway, 1994*

# Psalm 100A

Chant setting: *William Byrd (1538–1623)*

<sup>2</sup>Worship
God with
<sup>1</sup>Make a joyful
noise to God,    all   the earth. gladness; come  into God's presence with singing.

<sup>3</sup>Know that the
Sovereign is
God. It is    God that made us, we are God's people

and we
are God's;   and   sheep
the   of   God's pasture.

<sup>4</sup>Enter God's gates
with thanksgiving,
and enter God's  <sup>|</sup>courts with <sup>|</sup>praise.

<sup>||</sup>Give
thanks to <sup>|</sup>God   and   <sup>|</sup>bless God's <sup>|</sup>name.

<sup>5</sup>For God is
good; God's
steadfast love en - dures for - ever,   and God's faithful-ness to  all  gene-rations.

*(May be sung as a single or double chant. See below.)*

*Daniel Hathaway, 1994*                    *Bruce Neswick, 1994*

*Bruce Neswick, 1994*

# Psalm 121A

*Chant setting: James Turle (1802–1882)*

¹ I lift up my eyes to the hills— from where will my help come?
² My help comes from God, the God who made heaven and earth.

³ God will
not let your ˡfoot be ˡmoved; ‖God who ˡkeeps you ˡwill not ˡslumber.
⁴ God who keeps Israel will nei - ther slumber nor sleep.
⁵ God ˡis your ˡkeeper; ‖God is your ˡshade . . . ˡat your ˡside.
⁶ The sun
shall not strike you by day, nor shall the moon by night.
⁷ God will ˡkeep you from all ˡevil; ‖and ˡGod will ˡkeep your ˡlife.
⁸ God will keep
your going
out and your com - ing in from this time on and for - ev - er - more.

*(May be sung as a double chant. See below.)*

*John Robinson (1682–1762)*

*Bruce Neswick, 1994*

# Psalm 141A

*Chant setting: William Croft (1678–1727)*

¹I call upon you,
O God; come quickly to me; give ear to my voice when I call to you.
²Let my prayer and the lifting
be counted as incense be - fore you, up of my hands as an eve - ning sacrifice.

³Set a guard
over my ᴵmouth, O ᴵGod; ‖keep ᴵwatch over the ᴵdoor of my ᴵlips.

⁴Do not
turn my heart to any evil, to busy my - self with wick - ed deeds;

with
those who work in - iquity, do not let me eat of their delicacies.

⁵Let the ᴵrigh - teous ᴵstrike me; ‖and ᴵlet the ᴵfaithful cor - ᴵrect me.

Never let for my
the oil of prayer is
the wicked a - noint my head, continually a - gainst their wick - ed deeds.

⁶When they are
then given over
to those who ᴵshall con-ᴵdemn them, ‖they shall ᴵlearn that my ᴵwords were ᴵpleasant.

⁷Like a rock
that one breaks so shall their
apart and shatters on the land, bones be strewn at the mouth of Sheol.

⁸But my eyes
are turned ‖in you I seek
toward you, O ᴵGod, my ᴵGod; refuge; ᴵdo not ᴵleave me de -ᴵfenseless.

⁹Keep me from laid and keep
the trap that they have for me, me from the snares of those who do evil.

¹⁰Let the
wicked fall into ᴵtheir own ᴵnets, ‖while ᴵI a - ᴵlone es - ᴵcape.

*(May be sung as a double chant. See below.)*

*Henry Purcell (1659–1695)*
*Arr. James Turle (1802–1882)*

# Psalm 141B
## Let My Prayer Rise Up

*Adaptation and musical setting by*
*Arthur G. Clyde, 1993*

*A leader may sing the refrain once, followed by the congregation. Following each verse, the congregation should sing the refrain.*

# Canticle of Mary
## (Magnificat)

Luke 1:46–55

℟

My soul magnifies the
Sovereign,
   and my spirit rejoices in God
   my Savior;

for God has looked with favor on
the lowliness óf God's servant.
   Surely, from now on all
   generations will c̀all me
   blessed;

for the Mighty One has done great
things for me,
   the Mighty One whose ńame is
   holy. ℟

God's mercy is for those who fear
God
   from generation to géneration.

God has shown great strength;
   and has scattered the proud in
   the thoughts óf their hearts.

God has brought down the
powerful from their thrones,
   and lifted úp the lowly;

God has filled the hungry with
good things,
   and sent the rich áway empty. ℟

God has helped God's servant
Israel,
   in remembrance óf God's
   mercy,

according to the promise made to
our ancestors,
   to Abraham and Sarah and to
   their descendants forever. ℟

# Canticle of Zechariah
## (Benedictus)

*Luke 1:68–79*

℟

Blessed be the Sovereign God of
Israel,
    who has looked favorably on
    the people ánd redeemed them.

God has raised up a mighty
savíor for us
    in the house of God's šervant
    David;

as God spoke through the mouth
of the holy prophets from of old,
    that we would be saved from our
    enemies and from the hand of
    áll who hate us. ℟

Thus God has šhown the mercy
    promised ťo our ancestors,

and has remembered God's hóly
covenant,
    the oath that God swore to our
    ancéstor Abraham,

to grant us that we, being rescued
from the hands óf our enemies,
    might serve God without fear,
    in holiness and righteousness
    before God áll our days. ℟

And you, child, will be called the
prophet of the Most High,
    for you will go before God
    to prepáre God's ways;

to give knowledge of salvation ťo
the people
    by the forgiveness óf their sins.

By the tender mercy óf our God,
    the dawn from on high will
    break upon us,

to give light to those who sit in
night and in the shadow of death,
    to guide our feet into the wáy
    of peace. ℟

# Canticle of Simeon
(Nunc Dimittis)

*Response*

*Antiphon: Arthur G. Clyde, 1994*

Your sal - va - tion is in the pres-ence of all peo - ples.

*Luke 2:29–32*

℟

O God, now you are dismissing
your servant in peace,
  according to your word;

for my eyes have seen your
salvation,

which you have prepared in the
presence of all peoples,

a light for revelation to the
Gentiles
  and for glory to your people
  Israel. ℟

# Second Canticle of Isaiah

*Response*

*Antiphon: Vérne de la Peña, 1994*

Re-turn to God  that God may have mer-cy, have mer-cy, have mer-cy.

*Isa. 55:6–11*

℟

Seek God while God may be
found,
  call upon God while God is
  near;

let the wicked forsake their way,
  and the unrighteous their
  thoughts;

let them return to God, that God
may have mercy on them,
  and to our God, for God will
  abundantly pardon. ℟

For my thoughts are not your
thoughts,
  nor are your ways my ways,
  says God.

734

For as the heavens are higher than the earth,
> so are my ways higher than your ways and my thoughts than your thoughts.

For as the rain and the snow come down from heaven,
> and do not return there until they have watered the earth,

making it bring forth and sprout,
> giving seed to the sower and bread to the eater,

so shall my word be that goes out from my mouth;
> it shall not return to me empty,

but it shall accomplish that which I purpose,
> and succeed in the thing for which I sent it. ℛ

# Canticle to the Lamb

*Antiphon: Robert Train Adams, 1994*

To the Lamb be bless-ing and hon - or.

*Rev. 4:11; 5:9–10, 12, 13*

ℛ

You are worthy, our Sovereign and God,
> to receive glory and honor and power,

for you created all things,
> and by your will they existed and were created. ℛ

You are worthy, O Christ, for you were slaughtered,
> and by your blood you ransomed saints for God

from every tribe and language
> and from every people and nation;

you have made them to be a dominion and priests serving our God,
> and they will reign on earth. ℛ

Worthy is the Lamb that was slaughtered to receive power and wealth and wisdom,
> and might and honor and glory and blessing!

To the one seated on the throne and to the Lamb be blessing and honor,
> and glory and might forever and ever! ℛ

# Canticle to Christ

*Antiphon: Marty Haugen, 1994*

Response
Unison

In Christ were all things cre - at-ed, in Christ were all things cre - at-ed.

*Col. 1:15–20*

𝓡

Christ is the image of the
invisible God,
   the firstborn of áll creation;

for in Christ all things in
heaven and on earth wére created,
  things visible ánd invisible,

whether thrones or dominions or
rulers or powers —
   all things have been created
   through Christ ánd for
   Christ.

Christ, indeed, is befóre all
things,
   and in Christ all things hóld
   together. 𝓡

Christ is the head óf the body,
   which ís the church;

Christ is the beginning, the
firstborn fróm the dead,
   so that Christ might come to
   have first pláce in everything.

For in Christ all the fullness of
God
   was pléased to dwell,

and through Christ God was
pleased to reconcile to God all
things,
   whether on earth or in heaven,
   by making peace through the
   blood óf the cross. 𝓡

# Canticle of the Mystery Revealed in Flesh

Response

Antiphon: *Hyeon Jeong, 1994*

The mys - tery of our faith is great.

1 Tim. 3:16; 6:15, 16

R

Christ was revealed in flesh,
vindicated in spirit,
   seen by angels, proclaimed
   among Gentiles,

believed in throughout the world,
   taken up in glory.

At the right time God will bring
about the manifestation of Christ—
   God who is the blessed and
   only Sovereign, the Ruler of

rulers and Sovereign of
   sovereigns.

It is God alone who has
immortality
   and dwells in unapproachable
   light,

whom no one has ever seen or can
see—
   to God be honor and
   eternal dominion. Amen. R

# Canticle of the Three
## (Benedicite omnia opera)

Response

Antiphon: Arthur G. Clyde, 1993

Praise and mag-ni-fy God for-ev-er!

*Prayer of Azariah 35–65*

℟

All you works of God, bless your
God;
    you angels of God, bless your
    God;

you heavens, bless your God;
    all the waters above the
    heavens, bless your God; ℟

You powers of God, bless your
God;
    you sun and moon, bless your
    God;

stars of the heaven, bless your
God;
    all rain and dew, bless your
    God; ℟

All the winds, bless your God;
    you fire and heat, bless your
    God;

you winter cold and summer
heat, bless your God;
    you dews and falling snow,
    bless your God; ℟

You ice and cold, bless your God;
    you frosts and snows, bless
    your God;

nights and days, bless your
God;
    you light and darkness, bless
    your God; ℟

Lightnings and clouds, bless
your God;
    let the earth bless God;

you mountains and hills, bless
your God;
    all that grows in the ground,
    bless your God; ℟

You running waters, bless your
God;
    you seas and rivers, bless
    your God;

you whales and all that move in
the waters, bless your God;
    all you birds of the air, bless
    your God; ℟

All you animals and cattle,
bless your God;
    all you people on earth, bless
    your God;

O Israel, bless your God;
    you priests of God, bless your
    God; ℟

all you who serve God, bless
your God;
    you spirits and souls of the
    righteous, bless your God;

you holy and humble in heart,
bless your God;
    Blessed are you, O God in the
    dome of heaven. ℟

*(May be sung with double tone.)*

# O Holy Radiance, Joyous Light
## (Phos Hilaron)

*Col. 3:16–17; Isa. 60:19–20; John 1:1–5*

*Greek, 2nd–4th century C.E.*
*Transl. The New Century Hymnal, 1994*

1 O ho - ly ra-diance, joy - ous light, O splen-did glo - ry shin-ing bright,
2 We see the sun-shine fade to night, and wel - com-ing the eve-ning light,
3 Un-ceas-ing - ly our tongues shall laud your worth, Be - got-ten One of God,

Im-mor - tal Fa - ther, heaven-ly One, O bless - ed Je - sus Christ, the Sun:
To Fa - ther, Son, and Spir - it raise our hymns of won-der, love, and praise.
O Breath of life; let all pro-claim the glo - ry of your won - drous name.

*Known as "The Candlelight Hymn" or "Phos Hilaron," this*
*hymn was sung in the ancient church at the Lighting of Lamps*
*for Vespers. St. Basil, who died in 379 C.E., referred to it as*
*being of uncertain date and authorship. Its original tune is also*
*unknown.*

Tune: CONDITOR ALME SIDERUM L.M.
*ancient Sarum plainsong, Mode IV*
*Harm. The New Century Hymnal, 1994*
*Alternate tune: TALLIS' CANON*

# O Wisdom, Breathed from God
## (O Sapientia)

*St. 1, 2, "O Antiphons," Latin, 6th–7th century,*
*Transl.* The New Century Hymnal, *1994*
*St. 3, The New Century Hymnal, 1994*

*Sir. 24:1–6; Wisd. 7:25, 8:1, 7; Luke 1:78–79;*
*John 8:12; Mal. 4:2*

1  O Wis-dom breathed from God, Most High, your depths all cos-mic bounds de - fy,
2  O Day-spring, ev - er shin - ing bright, O Sun of jus-tice, splen - did light,
3  All praise to you, great Mys - ter - y, the un - di-vid-ed Trin - i - ty,

Your might in gen-tle-ness holds sway; come forth and teach your pru-dent way.
Shine on each soul by sin held fast, break through the clouds of death at last.
Our con-stant aid, on you we call: one God, the Moth - er of us all.

*"Sophia" may be substituted for "O Wisdom" in stanza 1.*

*The first two stanzas of this hymn are a translation of two of the seven ancient "O Antiphons" used at vespers, one for each of the seven days before Christmas. The first of these is "O Sapientia" (O Wisdom). The third stanza includes ideas from the writings of Julian of Norwich and phrases from the early prayer services of the Western church.*

Tune: CONDITOR ALME SIDERUM  L.M.
*ancient Sarum plainsong, Mode IV*
*Harm.* The New Century Hymnal, *1994*
*Alternate tune:  TALLIS' CANON*

# SERVICE MUSIC

741

*Text and music: Robert Wooten, Sr., 1982; alt.*

I was glad when they said un-to me, I was glad when they said un-to
me: Let us go in-to the house of our God;
you'll find peace, joy, hap-pi-ness, a
great re-ward. Won't you come, come, come.

742

*Text and music: Phil Porter, 1990*

Gath-ered here in the mys-tery of this hour, gath-ered here in one strong
bod-y, gath-ered here in the strug-gle and the power, Spir-it draw near.

*This chant may be sung as a round.*

743

*Ps. 46:10*

*Music: Anon.*

Be still and know that I am God. Be still and know that
I am God. Be still and know that I am God.

744

Opening Sentence

*Ps. 70:1*

*Music: Thomas Tallis, c. 1564*

*Leader*    *Congregation*

O God, open my lips, and my mouth shall show forth your praise;

*Leader*    *Congregation*

Make haste, O God, to deliver me. Make haste to help me, O God.

# 745
## Trisagion

*Music:  Ronald A. Nelson, 1986*

Ho - ly God, Ho - ly and might - y One,

Ho - ly Im - mor - tal One, have mer - cy up - on us.

# 746
## Trisagion

*Music:  Alice Jordan, 1986*

Ho - ly God, Ho - ly and might - y,

Ho - ly Im - mor - tal One, have mer - cy up - on us.

# 747
## Agios O Theos (Trisagion)

*Text:  Ancient Greek*

*Music:  Russian Orthodox tradition*

A - gi - os O The - os, a - gi - os is - chi - ros,
Ho - ly, ho - ly, ho - ly God, ho - ly and might - y,

a - gi - os a - tha - na - tos, e - le - i - son i - mas.
ho - ly and e - ter - nal, have mer - cy on us.

## 748
### Trisagion

Music: *Francisco F. Feliciano*

Ho-ly God, ho-ly might-y, ho-ly Im-mor - tal, have mer-cy on us.

## 749
### Kyrie

Music: *John Merbecke, 1550*

*Unison*

Lord, have mer-cy up-on us; Christ, have mer-cy up-on us; Lord, have mer-cy up-on us.

## 750
### Kyrie

Text: *Traditional, 6th century*

Music: *The American Lutheran Hymnal*

*Congregation or choir*

*Leader*
Lord, have mercy upon us.

Lord, have mer - cy up - on us.

Christ, have mercy upon us.

Christ, have mer - cy up - on us.

Lord, have mercy upon us.

Lord, have mer - cy up - on us.

**751**
Kyrie

*Text:   Ancient Greek*

*Music:   Russian Orthodox tradition*

Ky - ri - e e - lei - son. Ky - ri - e e - lei - son.

Ky - ri - e e - lei - son.

**752**

*Music:   Leon Roberts, 1981*

Christ, have mer - cy, Christ, have mer - cy,

Christ, have mer - cy, have mer - cy on us.

**753**
Kyrie

*Music:   Emma Lou Diemer, 1995*

Sov - ereign have mer - cy. Christ have mer - cy.

Sov - ereign have mer - cy.

**754**

*Music: Ronald A. Nelson, 1986*

Glo-ry to God the Cre - a - tor, and to the Christ, and to the Ho - ly Spir - it: as it was in the be - gin-ning, is now, and will be for ev - er. A - men. A - men.

**755**

*Music: Alice Jordan, 1986*

Glo - ry to God the Cre - a - tor, and to the Christ, and to the Ho - ly Spir - it: as it was in the be-gin-ning, is now, and will be for ev - er. A - men.

**756**

*Music: Jacques Berthier, 1982*

1 Dm Gm C F 2 Dm Gm C F

Glo - ri - a, glo - ri - a, in ex - cel - sis De - o!
Glo-ry to God, glo-ry to God, glo-ry in the high - est!

3 Dm Gm C F 4 Dm Gm C F

Glo - ri - a, glo - ri - a, al - le - lu - ia, al - le - lu - ia!
Glo-ry to God, glo-ry to God, al - le - lu - ia, al - le - lu - ia!

*This Gloria may be sung as a round.*

*Music: Ancient Scottish chant*

1 Glory to God in the highest, and peace to God's
2 We praise you, we bless you, we worship you, ⎡ we glorify you,
⎣ we give thanks to you for

people on earth. 3 ⎡ Holy One,
your great glory, ⎣ heavenly God, the Cre-ator and the sov-ereign God.

4 O Jesus Christ, only Child of God, O Sovereign God, Lamb of God,
5 You take away the sin of the world: have mer - cy on us;
6 ⎡ You are seated
⎣ at the right hand of Majesty: re - ceive our prayer.

7 For you alone are the Mes-siah, you alone are the Ho-ly One,
8 ⎡ You alone are ⎡ with the Holy
⎣ the Most High, Je-sus Christ, ⎣ Spirit, in the glory of the tri-une God. A-men.

# 758

Music:   Pablo Sosa, 1988 (Cueca dance rhythm)

¡Glo - ria, glo - ria,   glo - ria   en las al - tu - ras  a   Dios!
Glo - ry, glo - ry,   glo - ry!   Glo - ry to God in the   high - est,

Y en   la  tie - rra   paz pa - ra a - que - llos   que   a - ma Dios. . . .
And   on earth  be   peace to all peo - ple   with whom God is   pleased.

# 759

Music:   Henry W. Greatorex, 1851

Glo - ry to  the Cre - a - tor,   the   Christ, the   Ho - ly Spir - it,

Three - in - One;   as  it  was  in   the  be - gin - ning,   is

now, and ev - er  shall be,   world with-out  end. A - men. A - men.

Or:
*Glo-ry be to the Fa-ther, and to the Son, and to the Ho-ly Ghost; . . .*

**760**

*S.C. Molefe, South Africa*
*Arr. Dave Dargie*
*From the* Lumko Songbook

(Ma - si - thi:) A - men, si - ya - ku - du - mi - sa. (Ma - si - thi:)
(Sing a - men:) A - men, we praise your name, O God. (Sing a - men:)

A - men, si - ya - ku - du - mi - sa. (Ma - si - thi:) A - men, Ba - wo,
A - men, we praise your name, O God. (Sing a - men:) A - men, a - men,

A - men, Ba - wo, A - men, si - ya - ku - du - mi - sa.
a - men, a - men, A - men, we praise your name, O God.

**SCRIPTURE RESPONSE**

**761**

*Music: John L. Playford (1674–1730)*

*Before the Gospel*    *After the Gospel*

Glo-ry be to you, O Christ.    Praise be to you, O Christ.

## 762

*Music:  Daniel L. Johnson, 1994*

*Before the Gospel* ... *After the Gospel*

Glo - ry to you, O Christ. Praise to you, O Christ.

## 763

*Music:  Jonathan McNair, 1994*

This is what the Spir-it is say-ing to the church-es: Thanks be to God!

## 764

*Music:  Emma Lou Diemer, 1994*

This is what the Spir-it is say-ing to the church-es: Thanks be to God!

## 765

*Text and music:  Jerry Sinclair, 1972; alt.*

1 Al-le - lu - ia, al-le - lu - ia, al-le - lu - ia, al-le - lu - ia,

Al - le - lu - ia, al - le - lu - ia, al - le - lu - ia, al - le - lu - ia!

2 You're my Sav-ior, al-le-lu-ia, . . .
3 You are wor-thy, al-le-lu-ia, . . .
4 I will praise you, al-le-lu-ia, . . .

**766**

*Music: Abraham Maraire, Zimbabwe*

Hal-le-lu - jah, hal-le-lu - jah, hal-le-lu - jah, hal-le-lu - jah!

Hal-le-lu - jah, hal-le-lu, hal-le-lu - jah, hal-le-lu - jah!

Hal-le-lu - jah, hal-le-lu - jah, hal-le-lu - jah, hal-le-lu - jah!

**767**

*Music: Jacques Berthier, 1978*

Al - le - lu - ia. Al - le - lu - ia, al - le - lu - ia.

Al - le - lu - ia, al - le - lu - ia!

## 768

*Music: Jacques Berthier, 1982*

Al-le - lu - ia, al-le - lu - ia, al-le - lu - ia. Al-le - lu - ia,

Cantor

(Psalm verses) Al-le-lu - ia!

al-le - lu - ia, al-le - lu - ia! *(Last time, end.)*

*This may be used as an alternative method of chanting psalms. A cantor chants the psalm verses as the congregation hums; at appropriate moments, the congregation repeats the "Alleluia."*

## PRAYER RESPONSE, MEDITATION

## 769

*Ps. 134:1*

*Music: George Whelpton, 1897*

Hear our prayer, O God, hear our prayer, O God; in -

cline your ear to us, and grant us your peace.

Ps. 19:4

770

Music: *Eli Wilson, Jr., 1989*

Let the words of my mouth and the med-i - ta-tion of my

heart be ac - cept-a-ble in your sight. Let the

heart be ac - cept - a - ble, God, to you.

Ps. 19:4

771

Music: *Joseph Barnby (1838–1896)*

[ Let the words of ]
my mouth and      of my heart
the meditation

[ be acceptable in ]
your sight, O God,   my Re - deem - er.
my strength and

772

Text: The Taizé Community, 1991;
based on the writings of St. Teresa of Avila, 16th century

Music: Jacques Berthier, 1991

773

Luke 23:42

Music: Traditional; harm. J. Jefferson Cleveland, 1981

*Ps. 5:8; 4:8*

**774**

*Text and music:   Samuel S. Wesley, 1861; alt.*

Shep - herd,   lead,   lead me in your righ-teous-ness,

make your way plain be - fore my   face.   For it is you, God,

you, God   on - ly, who makes me to   lie   down in   safe - ty.

*Text:   Exod. 19:4; paraphr. by Michael Joncas; alt.*

**775**

*Music:   Michael Joncas, 1979; arr. Carlton R. Young, 1988*

And God will raise you up   on   ea - gle's wings,

bear   you on   the   breath   of dawn,   make you to   shine   like the

sun,   and   hold you in   the   palm   of God's hand.

## 776

Text: Thomas Ken, 1674; adapt.

Music: Ronald A. Nelson, 1986

Praise God from whom all bless-ings flow; Praise Christ, all crea - tures

here be - low; Praise Ho - ly Spir - it, Com-fort-er; One God, Tri - une, whom

we a - dore. A - men, A - men.

## 777

Text: Thomas Ken, 1674; adapt.

Music: Alice Jordan, 1986

Praise God from whom all bless - ings flow;

Praise Christ, all crea - tures here be - low; Praise Ho - ly Spir - it, the

Com-fort-er; One God, Tri - une, whom we a - dore. A - men.

## 778

Text: Thomas Ken, 1674;
adapt. William B. Abernethy

*(This and other Doxology texts that follow may be sung to musical settings 776, 779, and 780)*

Praise God from whom all blessings flow;
Praise God, all creatures here below;
Praise God for all that love has done;
Creator, Christ, and Spirit, One.

779

*Text: Thomas Ken, 1674; alt.*

*Music: John Hatton (d. 1793);*
*adapt. George Coles; harm. Roberta Martin, 1968*

Praise God from whom all bless-ings flow; Praise Christ, all crea-tures here be-low; Praise Ho-ly Spir-it, Com-fort-er; One God, Tri-une, whom we a-dore. A-men.

780

*Text: Thomas Ken, 1674; alt.*

*Music: Louis Bourgeois, 1551*

Praise God from whom all bless-ings flow; Praise God, all crea-tures here be-low; Praise God a-bove, you heaven-ly host: Praise Fa-ther, Son, and Ho-ly Ghost.

781

*Text: Thomas Ken, 1674;*
*adapt. Book of Worship, United Church of Christ*

Praise God from whom all blessings flow;
Praise Christ the Word in flesh born low;
Praise Holy Spirit evermore;
One God, Triune, whom we adore.

# 782

*Text: Charles Coffin, 1736; transl. John Chandler, 1837; alt.*

*(May be used at Advent, Christmas, and other times)*

To God, all glorious heavenly Light,
to Christ revealed in earthly night,
to God the Spirit now we raise
our joyful songs of thankful praise.

# 783

*Text and music: Marty Haugen, 1990*

*Refrain*

As the grains of wheat once scat-tered on the hill were gath-ered in-to one to be - come our bread; so may all your peo-ple from all the ends of earth be gath-ered in-to one in you.

*to Stanzas*

you.

*Stanzas*

1 As this cup of bless-ing is shared with-in our midst, may we share the pres - ence of your love.

2 Let this be a fore-taste of all that is to come when all cre - a - tion shares this feast with you.

*to Refrain*

*Ps. 51:10–12*

**784**

*Music: Emma Lou Diemer, 1990*

Cre-ate in me a clean heart, O God, and re-new a right spir-it with-in me.

Cast me not a-way from your pres - ence, and

take not your Ho - ly Spir-it from me. Re-store in me the

joy of your sal - va - tion, and up - hold me with your free Spir - it.

*Text: William W. How, 1864; alt.*

**785**

*Music: Cantica Laudis, Lowell Mason and G. J. Webb, 1850*

We give you but your own, what - e'er the gift may be;

All that we have is yours a - lone, we give it grate-ful - ly.

## 786

*Music: Ronald A. Nelson, 1986*

This is the joy - ful feast of the peo - ple of God.

Men and wom - en, youth and chil - dren, come from the east and the

west, from the north and the south, and gath - er a-bout Christ's ta - ble.

## 787

*Music: Alice Jordan, 1986*

This is the joy - ful feast of the peo-ple of God.

Men and wom - en, youth and chil - dren, come from the east and the

west, from the north and the south, and gath - er a-bout Christ's ta - ble.

## 788

*Text: The Taizé Community, 1983*

*Music: Jacques Berthier, 1983*

Eat this bread, drink this cup, come to me and nev-er be hun - gry.

Eat this bread, drink this cup, trust in me and you will not thirst.

**HOLY, HOLY, HOLY (SANCTUS)**

**789**

*Music: Ronald A. Nelson, 1986*

Ho - ly, ho - ly, ho - ly God of love and maj - es - ty, the

whole u - ni - verse speaks of your glo - ry, O God Most High.

Bless - ed is the one who comes in the name of our

God! Ho - san - na! Ho - san - na in the high - est!

## 790

Music:   Alice Jordan, 1986

Ho - ly, ho - ly, ho - ly God of love and maj - es - ty,

the whole u - ni - verse speaks of your glo - ry, O God Most

High.   Bless - ed is the one who comes in the

name of our God! Ho - san - na in the high - est!

## 791

Music:   Healey Willan, 1928

Unison

Ho - ly, ho - ly, ho - - - ly, O God of hosts,

Heav - en and earth are full of your glo - ry: Glo - - ry be to

*Music: Martie McMane, 1991*

**792**

you, O God Most High. A - - - men.

Ho - ly, ho - ly, ho - ly God, Rul - er Al - might - y;

heaven and earth are full of your glo - ry. Glo - ry be to you, O God.

Bless - ed is the one who comes, who comes in the name of God.

Ho - san - na, ho - san - na, ho - san - na in the high - est!

## 793

*Text and music: Anon., Argentina*

¡San-to, san-to, san-to, mi cor-a-zón te_a-do-ra! Mi
Ho-ly, ho-ly, ho-ly, my heart, my heart a-dores you! My

cor-a-zón te sa-be de-cir: san-to e-res Dios.
heart is glad to say the words: you are ho-ly, God.

## 794

*Music: harm. Ronald A. Nelson, 1978;
melody twelfth-century plainsong, adapt. J. S. Bach, 1726*

Ho-ly, ho-ly, ho-ly God of all power and might:
Heaven and earth are full of your glo-ry. Ho-san-na in the
high-est! Blessed is the one who comes in the name
of our God! Ho-san-na in the high-est!

# 795

## Seraphic Hymn

*Music: Alonzo P. Howard (1838–1902)*

Ho - ly, ho - ly, ho - ly, God of the heaven-ly host;

Heav-en and earth are full, are full of the maj-es-ty of your glo - ry,

Ho - san - na, ho - san - na, ho - san - na in the high - est!

Bless-ed the one who comes in the name of our God,

Ho - san - na, ho - san - na, ho - san - na in the high - est!

**796**

Music: *Ronald A. Nelson, 1986*

Christ's death, O God, we pro - claim. Christ's
res - ur - rec - tion we de - clare. Christ's com - ing we a -
wait. Glo - ry be to you, O God.

**797**

Music: *Ronald A. Nelson, 1986*

Christ's death, O God, we pro - claim. Christ's
res - ur - rec - tion we de - clare. Christ's com - ing we a -
wait. Glo - ry be to you, O God.

**798**

Music: *Alice Jordan, 1986*

Christ's death, O God, we pro -
claim. Christ's res - ur - rec - tion we de - clare. Christ's

com-ing we a - wait.     Glo - ry be to you, O     God.

**799**

*Music: Timothy Gibson, 1987*

*Music: Ronald A. Nelson, 1986*

Christ has died.     Christ is ris - en.   Christ will come a - gain.

Je - sus,     Lamb of God:     have mer-cy on     us.

Je - sus, bear - er     of our sins:     have mer-cy on     us.

Je - sus, re - deem-er of the     world:     give us your     peace.

## 801

*Music:  Alice Jordan, 1986*

Je - sus, Lamb of God: have mer - cy on us.

Je - sus, bear - er of our sins: have mer - cy on us.

Je - sus, re - deem - er of the world: give us your peace.

## 802

*Music:  Vicente Bianchi, 1991*

1, 2 Cor - de - ro de Dios, Cor - de - ro de Dios, que
3 Cor - de - ro de Dios, Cor - de - ro de Dios, que
1, 2 O Lamb of God, O Lamb of God, who
3 O Lamb of God, O Lamb of God, who

qui - tas el pe - ca - do del mun - do, ten pie - dad de no -
qui - tas el pe - ca - do del mun - do, da - nos la
takes a - way the sin of the world, have mer - cy up -
takes a - way the sin of the world, O grant us your

so - tros, ten pie - dad de no - so - tros.
paz, . . . . da - nos la paz. . . . . .
on us, have mer - cy up - on us.
peace, . . . . O grant us your peace. . . . . . .

*Music:* Kirchenordnung, *Braunschweig, 1528*

O Christ, the Lamb of God, you take a - way the sin of the world; have mer - cy up - on us. O Christ, the Lamb of God, you take a - way the sin of the world; have mer - cy up - on us. O Christ, the Lamb of God, you take a - way the sin of the world; grant us your peace. A - - - men.

**LAMB OF GOD (AGNUS DEI)**

## 804

*Music: Grayson Warren Brown, 1987;*
*arr. Val Parker, 1987*

O Lamb of God, you take a - way the sin of the world; have mer - cy on us, have mer - cy on us.

*1, 2*

*3* Grant us peace.

**BLESSING, CLOSING SONG**

## 805

Song of Simeon (Nunc Dimittis)

*Music: Ronald A. Nelson, 1986*

Ho - ly One, now let your ser - vant go in peace; your word has been ful - filled: my own eyes have seen the sal - va - tion which you have pre-pared in the sight of ev - ery peo - ple: a light to re-veal you to the na-tions and the glo-ry of your peo-ple Is - ra - el.

# 806

*Music: Alice Jordan, 1986*

## Song of Simeon (Nunc Dimittis)

Ho - ly One, now let your ser-vant go in peace; your word has been ful - filled: my own eyes have seen the sal-va - tion which you have pre-pared in the sight of ev - ery peo-ple: a light to re-veal you to the na - tions and the glo - ry of your peo-ple Is - ra - el.

# 807

*Music: Richard Farrant (c. 1530–1580)*

## Song of Simeon (Nunc Dimittis)

1 Holy One, now let your servant go in peace:
2 My own eyes have seen
3 Which you have pre - pared
4 A light to reveal you to the nations

your word has been ful - filled.
the sal - va - tion
in the presence of all peo - ple:
and the glory of your peo - ple Is - ra - el.

# 808
## Song of Simeon (Nunc Dimittis)

*Music: Luis Olivieri, 1992*

A - ho - ra, oh Dios des - pi - de a tu sier - vo en paz con -
O God, now let your ser - vant go in peace, your

for - me a tu pa - la - bra; por - que han vis - to mis o - jos tu sal - va -
word has been ful - filled; my own eyes your sal - va - tion have

ción, la cual pre - pa - ras - te en pre - sen - cia de to - dos los
seen, pre - pared by you in the pres - ence of all

pue - blos, luz pa - ra re - ve - la - ción a los gen -
peo - ple: a light ... to re - veal you to the

ti - les, y la glo - ria de tu pue - blo Is - ra - el.
na - tions, and the glo - ry of your peo - ple Is - ra - el.

# 809

*Text and music: Thomas A. Dorsey and Artelia W. Hutchins, 1940*

*Slowly*

God be with you, God be with you,

God be with you till we meet a - gain. O

God be with you, God be with you,

God be with you till we meet a - gain.

## 810
### Twofold

*"Dresden"*

## 811

*Music: Vincent Persichetti, 1956*

A - men, a - men.

A - men, a - men.

## 812
### Threefold

*"Danish"*

A - men, a - men, a - men.

## 813
Fourfold

*Music: Roland M. Carter (b. 1942)*

A — men,

A - men, a - men, a — men.

## 814
Sevenfold

*John Stainer (1840–1901)*

a - men, a — men,

A - men, a - men, a — men,

a — men,

A — men, a — men, a - men.

. . . a - men,

## 815

*William Smith (d. 1645)*

A — men.

# WORSHIP RESOURCES

# Prayers before Worship

## 816

Gracious God, oil the hinges of our hearts' doors
that they may swing gently and easily to welcome your coming.

*Prayer from New Guinea*

## 817

Almighty God, who has given us grace at this time with one accord to make
our common supplications unto you, and does promise that where two or
three are gathered together in your name, you will grant their requests: fulfill
now the desires and petitions of your servants, as may be most expedient for
them, granting us in this world knowledge of your truth, and in the world to
come, life everlasting. Amen.

*John Chrysostom, Bishop of Constantinople*

## 818

O God, we give you hearty thanks for the rest of the past night and for the gift
of a new day, with its opportunities of pleasing you. Grant that we may so
pass its hours in the perfect freedom of your service, that at eventide we may
again give thanks unto you; through Jesus Christ our Sovereign. Amen.

*Daybreak Office of the Eastern Church*

# Opening Words

## 819

I lift up my eyes to the hills—from where will my help come?
My help comes from God, who made heaven and earth.

*from Psalm 121*

## 820

God is Spirit, and those who worship God
must worship in spirit and in truth.

*John 4:24*

## 821

LEADER:   This is the day that God has made;
PEOPLE:   **let us rejoice and be glad in it**.
LEADER:   O come, let us worship and bow down;
PEOPLE:   **let us kneel before God, our Maker.**

*from Psalms 118 and 95*

## 822

LEADER: Blessed be the name of God
from this time on and forevermore.
PEOPLE: **From the rising of the sun to its setting
the name of God is to be praised.**
LEADER: It is good to give thanks to God,
to sing praises to your name, O Most High;
PEOPLE: **to declare your steadfast love in the morning,
and your faithfulness by night.**

*from Psalms 113 and 92*

## 823

LEADER: ¡Mi corazón está listo, oh Dios, mi corazón listo está!
PEOPLE: **¡Cantaré, cantaré alabanzas! ¡Despierta mi alma!**
LEADER: ¡Despierta, oh arpa y lira! ¡Despertaré la aurora!
PEOPLE: **¡Te daré gracias a ti, oh Dios, entre todas las gentes!**
ALL: **¡Alabemos y adoremos al Dios de la creación!**

LEADER: My heart is ready, O God, my heart is ready!
PEOPLE: **I will sing, I will sing praises! Wake up, my soul!**
LEADER: Wake up, O harp and lyre! I will awake the dawn!
PEOPLE: **I will thank you, O God, among all people!**
ALL: **Let us praise and adore the God of Creation!**

*Vilma M. Machín; transl. by Rose M. Grijalva*

## 824

LEADER: Beautiful are the works of God!
PEOPLE: **Beautiful also are the skins of God's people!**
LEADER: Beautiful is the mind of God!
PEOPLE: **Beautiful also are the hopes of God's people!**
LEADER: Beautiful is the heart of God!
PEOPLE: **Beautiful also are the souls of God's people!**
LEADER: God made the heavens and the earth!
PEOPLE: **To God be the glory for the things God has done.**

*adapted, Trinity United Church of Christ, Chicago*

## 825

LEADER: Blessed is the One who spoke and the world came into being.
PEOPLE: **Blessed is the One who creates the world.**
LEADER: Blessed is the One who speaks and does.
PEOPLE: **Blessed is the One who decrees and fulfills.**
LEADER: Blessed is the One who has compassion for the earth.
PEOPLE: **Blessed is the One who has compassion for all creatures.**
LEADER: Blessed is the One who rewards those who fear God.

| | |
|---|---|
| PEOPLE: | **Blessed is the One who lives eternally and exists forever.** |
| LEADER: | Blessed is the One who redeems and saves. |
| ALL: | **Blessed is the Holy One.** |

*Congregation Beth El of the Sudbury River Valley*

# INVOCATIONS

## 826

Come, O Creator, O Immensity of love, O Eternity of mercy. Come, and be with us and in us and beside us and over us. Be as hands upon us, and fashion us for shining. Be as warmth within us, and fire us for caring. Be as strength beside us, and shape our lives for healing. Abide in our prayers, the spoken and the unspoken; and make your Word come true in our flesh; through Jesus Christ our Redeemer. Amen.

*Arnold Kenseth*

## 827

Spirit of Love, Spirit of Truth,
Guide us as we pray,
To think and wish and praise the best,
And mean the words we say.

Hushed is our quiet room,
Still is this place of prayer;
Silent, we bow our heads and feel
Your presence everywhere.

*from Children Worship*

## 828

Almighty and everlasting God, our Sovereign, who has safely brought us to the beginning of this day: defend us in the same with your mighty power; and grant that this day we fall into no sin, nor run into any kind of danger, but that all our doings, being ordered by your governance, may be righteous in your sight; through Jesus Christ our Savior. Amen.

## 829

O God of the morning and of the evening hours,
let your Spirit come on us here gathered.
This is the holy place where we, your people, call on you in faith,
joining heart and voice in thanksgiving and praise to your name. Amen.

*Book of Worship, United Church of Christ*

# 830

LEADER: O God, all-powerful, true and incomparable,
present in all things, yet limited by none,
untouched by place,
unaged by time,
unhurried by the years,
undeceived by words,
not subject to birth
nor in need of protection:
you are above all corruption,
you are beyond all change,
you are by nature immutable,
living in light that none can approach,
invisible, yet you make yourself known to me
and you are found by all who seek you with their whole heart;
you are the God of Israel
and of all who hope in Christ.
LEADER: You are our God.
PEOPLE: **We adore you.**

*The Joint Liturgical Group*

# 831

Holy God, we come before you with awe, for you are great in love and power.
Some of us come with reluctance and some with joy; some with sadness and
others full of fear, yet we know you receive us as we are. Mighty God, stay
with us always, as we worship and as we share the risk and challenge of living
our faith. By your powerful Spirit, turn our fear to courage and our confusion
to confidence. Touch us, God, with your healing fire. Speak to us through your
Word. Send us back into the world renewed and eager to do your will. We
pray in the name of Jesus the Christ. Amen.

*Ronald S. Beebe*

# CONFESSIONS

## Calls to Confession

# 832

The Word became flesh and dwelt among us, full of grace and truth; but we
esteemed it not and turned away. Let us confess our unfaithfulness and the
limits of our trust.

*Lavon Bayler*

# 833

Examinemos ahora nuestras vidas en frente a Dios, confesando humildemente nuestros pecados y abriendo nuestros corazones, no sea que engañándonos, hasta a nosotros mismos, nos excluyamos de tu presencia.

Let us examine our lives in the presence of God, humbly confessing our sins and opening our hearts, so that we do not deceive even ourselves, and exclude ourselves from your presence.

*Selva Lehman*

## Prayers of Confession

# 834

Almighty and everlasting God, always more ready to hear than we are to pray, always willing to give more than we either desire or deserve: pour upon us the abundance of your mercy; forgiving those things of which our conscience is afraid, and giving us those good things which we are not worthy to ask, except through the merits and mediation of Jesus Christ, your Begotten One, our Sovereign. Amen.

*A Book of Worship for Free Churches*

# 835

Gentle and holy God, we acknowledge to you, to one another, and to ourselves that we are not what you have called us to be. We have stifled our gifts and wasted our time. We have avoided opportunities to offer kindness, but have been quick to take offense. We have pretended that we could make no contribution to peace and justice in our world and have excused ourselves from risk-taking in our own community. Have mercy on us, forgive us our sins, and help us to live our lives differently, we pray in the name of Jesus Christ, whose call to follow haunts our every prayer. Amen.

*Maren Tirabassi*

# 836

God of love and justice, we long for peace within and peace without. We long for harmony in our families, for serenity in the midst of struggle, and for commitment to each other's growth. We long for the day when our homes will be a dwelling place for your love. Yet we confess that we are often anxious; we do not trust each other, and we harbor violence. We are not willing to take the risks and make the hard choices that love requires. Look upon us with kindness and grace. Rule in our homes and in all the world; show us how to walk in your paths, through the mercy of our Savior. Amen.

*Ruth Duck*

# 837

Almighty God,
>Whose breath quickened us,
>Whose tongue named us,
>Whose language we are:

Grant us grace to be true words—
>Not gentle when it is in anger that we live,
>Not smooth when it is desperation that we know,
>Not patient when time has narrowed down to now,
>Not wise, not neat, not all our fences mended,
>But words, broken yet honest words, and lost,
>Stumbling their way toward silence.

Take us back. Recall us. Then speak us once again.
>Set us in order. Mend our shattered syntax. Set all our commas straight.
>Imbue in us a power that keeps company with pain,
>Then march us across the pages of this beautiful, fragile, tormented,
>>and perishable earth to sing the songs of Zion.

In the name of the Word made flesh, made dead, and made alive again. Amen.

*Barbara Sargent*


# 838

LEADER: Help us, O God our Savior;
PEOPLE: **Deliver us and forgive us our sins.**
LEADER: Look upon your congregation;
PEOPLE: **Give to your people the blessing of peace;**
LEADER: Declare your glory among the nations;
PEOPLE: **And your wonders among all peoples.**
LEADER: Let not the oppressed be shamed and turned away;
PEOPLE: **Never forget the lives of the poor.**
LEADER: Continue your lovingkindness to those who know you;
PEOPLE: **And your favor to those who are true of heart.**
LEADER: Satisfy us by your lovingkindness in the morning;
PEOPLE: **So shall we rejoice and be glad all the days of our life.**

*Standing Liturgical Commission*


## Words of Assurance or Assurance of Pardon

# 839

One fact remains that does not change: God has loved you, loves you now,
and will love you always. This is the good news that brings us new life.

*Women and Worship*

## 840

Escucha estas palabras de la Escritura: la misericordia y el amor de Dios son inmensos, su ira lenta y su amor es eterno.

Listen to the words of the scriptures: the mercy and the love of God are endless; God's wrath is slow, and God's love is eternal.

*Vilma M. Machín; transl. by Rose M. Grijalva*

## 841

The almighty and merciful God grant us pardon and remission of all our sins, time for amendment of life, and the grace and comfort of the Holy Spirit. Amen.

*The Joint Liturgical Group*

# OFFERTORY SENTENCES AND PRAYERS

## 842

Having received new life through the generosity of God and the hope Christ brings, let us give thankfully and abundantly that we may be called God's generous people.

*June Christine Goudey*

## 843

LEADER:  Let us present with joy our offerings of commitment and support for the work of Christ's church.

PEOPLE:  **Let us prepare Christ's table with the offerings of our life and labor.**

*The United Congregational Church of South Africa*

## 844

All good gifts around us come from you, O God. You have given us life, and new life in Christ. As you have given us gifts, so we offer our gifts that we may be gifts to one another, even as Jesus so taught and lived. Amen.

## 845

O God, most merciful and gracious, of whose bounty we have all received: accept, we pray, this offering of your people. Remember in your love those who have brought it and those for whom it is given; and so follow it with your blessing that it may promote peace and goodwill among all people and advance the realm of our Savior Jesus Christ. Amen.

# Prayers

## Preparation

### 846

Almighty God, unto whom all hearts are open, all desires known, and from whom no secrets are hid: cleanse the thoughts of our hearts by the inspiration of your Holy Spirit, that we may perfectly love you and worthily magnify your holy name; through Christ our Sovereign. Amen.

### 847

Eternal One, Silence from whom my words come; Questioner from whom my questions arise; Lover of whom all my loves are hints; Disturber in whom alone I find my rest; Mystery in whose depths I find healing and myself: enfold me now in your presence; restore to me your peace; renew me through your power; and ground me in your grace. Amen.

*Ted Loder*

## Post Communion

### 848

Gracious and loving God, you have made us one in the body of Christ, and nourished us at your table with holy food and drink. Now send us forth to be your people in the world. Grant us strength to persevere in resisting evil, and to proclaim in all we say and do your Good News in Christ Jesus our Savior. Amen.

### 849

O God, who is eternal salvation and inestimable blessedness: grant to all your servants, we pray you, that we who have received things holy and blessed may be enabled to be holy and blessed evermore. Amen.

*Henry Harbaugh*

## Intercession

### 850

To God be glory;
To the angels honor;
To Satan confusion;

To the cross reverence;
To the church exaltation;
To the departed quickening;
To the penitent acceptance;
To the sick and infirm recovery and healing;
And to the four quarters of the world great peace and tranquillity;
And on us who are weak and sinful may the compassion and mercies of
our God come, and may they overshadow us continually. Amen.

*from the Old Syriac used by Christians in Turkey, Iran, and*
*South India*

## Guidance

# 851

My spirit is one with you, Great Spirit.
You strengthen me day and night to share my very best
with my brothers and sisters.
You, whom my people see in all of creation and in all people,
show your love for us.
Help me to know, like the soaring eagle, the heights of knowledge.
From the Four Directions, fill me with the four virtues of fortitude, generosity,
respect, and wisdom;
so that I will help my people walk in the path of understanding and peace.

*Lakota prayer*

## Serenity

# 852

God, give us
grace to accept with serenity the things that cannot be changed,
courage to change the things that should be changed,
and the wisdom to distinguish the one from the other.

*Reinhold Niebuhr -1943*

## Peace

# 853

O God, it is your will to hold both heaven and earth in a single peace. Let the
design of your great love shine on the waste of our wraths and sorrows, and
give peace to your church, peace among nations, peace in our homes, and
peace in our hearts. Amen.

## 854

O God of many names, Lover of all nations: we pray for peace in our hearts, in our homes, in our nation, in our world; the peace of your will; the peace of our need. Amen.

## For the Church

## 855

We beseech you, O God, for your church throughout the world. May it grow in the faith of the cross and the power of the resurrection. May your spirit minister to it continually the redemption and reconciliation of all things. Keep it in your eternal unity, in great humility, in godly fear, and in your own pure and peaceable wisdom so easy to be entreated. Make it swift and mighty in the cause of the dominion of heaven. Cover, establish, and enlighten it, that it may see through all that obscures the time, and that it may move in the shadow of your wing, with faith, obedience, sacrifice, and godly power, through Jesus Christ our Sovereign. Amen.

*P. T. Forsyth*

## Eternal Life

## 856

Bring us, O God, at our last awakening into the house and gate of heaven, to enter into that gate and dwell in that house, where there shall be no night nor burning sun, but one equal light; no voice nor silence, but one equal music; no fears nor hopes, but one equal possession; no ends nor beginnings, but one equal eternity in the habitation of your glory and dominion, world without end. Amen.

*John Donne*

## Renewal of Mission

## 857

Come, Holy Spirit, renew the whole creation. Send the wind and flame of your transforming life to lift up the church in this day. Give wisdom and faith that we may know the great hope to which we are called. Come, Holy Spirit, renew the whole creation. Amen.

# Providence of God

## 858

O God, giver of all good, who continually pours your benefits upon us, age after age the living wait upon you and find that of your faithfulness there is no end and that your care is unfailing. We praise you that the mystery of our life is a mystery of infinite goodness. We praise you for the order and constancy of nature; for the beauty and bounty of the earth; for day and night, summer and winter, seed time and harvest; for the varied gifts of loveliness and usefulness which every season brings. We give you thanks for all the comfort and joy of life, for our homes, for our friends, and for all the love and sympathy and goodwill of all people. Amen.

*A Book of Worship for Free Churches*

## Thankfulness and Hope

## 859

We thank you, for you are our God, and God of our fathers and mothers forever. You are the Refuge of our life, the Shield of our help. From generation to generation may we thank you and count your praises—evening, morning, and noon—for our lives which are committed into your hand, for our souls which are entrusted to you, for your miracles which are with us every day, for your wonders and goodness at all times. O Good One, your compassion does not fail. O Merciful One, your lovingkindness never ceases. Forever we hope in you.

*Congregation Beth El of the Sudbury River Valley*

## Those in Need

## 860

We bring before you, O God, the troubles and perils of people and nations, the sighing of prisoners and captives, the sorrows of the bereaved, the necessities of strangers, the helplessness of the weak, the despondency of the weary, the failing powers of the aged. O God, draw near to each, for the sake of Jesus Christ our Strength. Amen.

*Saint Anselm (1033–1109)*

# 861

Let us remember tonight those who are in the bonds of poverty, who have neither sufficient food nor drink, the beauty of home, or the love of beauty. Bring us the day, O God, when the world shall no longer know such poverty as stunts growth and feeds crime, and teach us to realize that such things are not necessary to earth but are the result of our greed and selfishness, our wastefulness and willful forgetting. Amen.

*W. E. B. DuBois*

# 862

Make us worthy, Blessed One, to serve those throughout the world who live and die in poverty or hunger. Give them, through our hands, this day their daily bread; and by our understanding love, give peace and joy. Amen.

*Mother Teresa of Calcutta*

## Justice

# 863

Show me the suffering of the most miserable
      so I will know my people's plight.
Free me to pray for others
      for you are present in every person.
Help me to take responsibility for my own life
      so that I can be free at last.
Grant me courage to serve others
      for in service there is true life.
Give me honesty and patience
      so that I can work with other workers.
Bring forth song and celebration
      so that the spirit will be alive among us.
Let the spirit flourish and grow
      so that we will never tire of the struggle.
Let us remember those who have died for justice
      for they have given us life.
Help us love even those who hate us,
      so that we can change the world. Amen.

*United Farm Workers*

## God's World

# 864

Almighty God, your word of creation caused the water to be filled with many kinds of living beings and the air to be filled with birds. With

those who live in this world's small islands we rejoice in the richness
of your creation, and we pray for your wisdom for all who live on this
earth, that we may wisely manage and not destroy what you have
made for us and for our descendants. In Jesus' name we pray. Amen.

*Prayer from Samoa*

## Endeavors of the Day

# 865

O God, we thank you for the sweet refreshment of sleep and for the glory and
vigor of the new day. As we set our faces once more toward our daily work,
we pray for the strength sufficient for our tasks. May Christ's spirit of duty
and service ennoble all we do. Uphold us by the consciousness that our work
is useful and a blessing to all. If there has been anything in our work harmful
to others and dishonorable to ourselves, reveal it to our inner eye with such
clearness that we shall hate it and put it away, though it be at a loss to ourselves. When we work with others, help us to regard them, not as servants to
our will, but as brothers and sisters equal to us in human dignity, and equally
worthy of their full reward. May there be nothing in this day's work of which
we shall be ashamed when the sun has set, nor in the eventide of life when our
task is done and we go to our eternal home to meet your face.

*Walter Rauschenbusch*

## Evening

# 866

At last, O God, the sun's heat has given way to the cool evening.
Take, we pray, the heat out of our desires and our tempers,
and in this evening hour calm us,
that we may experience the peace and serenity which come from you.
At last, O God, the sun's brightness has given way
to the rich colors of the evening.
Prevent us, we pray, from being dazzled by the apparent brilliance
of human achievement.
And, in this evening hour, help us to rediscover the varied beauty of your creation, and appreciate afresh, in the stillness, the value of your abiding presence.
For the sake of Jesus Christ. Amen.

*Prayers for Today, for African congregations*

# Prayers for Home Use

## Before a Meal

### 867

O God, you are the final source of all our comforts and to you we give thanks for this food. But we also remember in gratitude the many men and women whose labor was necessary to produce it, and who gathered it from the land and from the sea for our sustenance. Grant that they too may enjoy the fruit of their labor without want, and may be bound up with us in a communion of thankful hearts.

*Walter Rauschenbusch*

### 868

Jesus of the wedding feast, of breakfast by the lake,
(bless this food we have prepared for you and all our friends.)*
Be with us now and at all our meals give us appetite and joy in eating together.
Blessed be God for daily bread.

(*optional)

## Evening Prayer

### 869

We thank you, loving God, for the day you have given us, and for all the pleasure we have had. Guard us while we sleep, and bless all those we love, this night and forever.

## Evening Prayer with Young Children

### 870

Dear God, thank you for today. We are sorry if we have been unkind to anyone. Help us to forgive each other. Thank you for our family and for our friends. Please be with us tonight. Amen.

## Forgiveness

### 871

God of mercy, we are sorry that we have not always done what you wanted us to do. We have not loved you with all our heart, and we have not cared enough for other people. Forgive us, for Jesus' sake. Amen.

# Prayers of Benediction

## 872

May the God who shakes heaven and earth,
whom death could not contain,
who lives to disturb and heal us,
bless you with power to go forth
and proclaim the gospel. Amen.

*Janet Morley*

## 873

May the blessing of the God of Abraham and Sarah,
and of Jesus Christ born of our sister Mary,
and of the Holy Spirit, who broods over the world
            as a mother over her children,
be upon you and remain with you always. Amen.

## 874

May you love God so much that you love nothing else too much;
May you fear God enough that you need fear nothing else at all.

## 875

Jesus said, "You ought always to pray and not to faint."
Do not pray for easy lives;
            pray to be stronger women and men.
Do not pray for tasks equal to your powers,
            but for power equal to your tasks.
Then, the doing of your work will be no miracle—
            you will be the miracle.
Every day you will wonder at yourself and the richness of life
            which has come to you by the grace of God.

## 876

O Jesus,
Be the canoe that holds me up in the sea of life;
Be the rudder that keeps me in the straight road;
Be the outrigger that supports me in times of temptation.
Let your Spirit be my sail that carries me through each day.
Keep my body strong, so that I can paddle steadfastly on in the voyage of life.
Amen.

*An Islander's prayer from Melanesia*

# 877

May the great Ruler of all high places,
God of many names,
touch you with a wind that keeps you strong,
for all the days to come. Amen.

# LITANIES

## A Litany of Intercession

# 878

LEADER: Gracious God, who loves all and forgets none, we bring to you our prayers for all your children.
For all whom we love, watch over, and care for;

PEOPLE: **Hear us, O God.**

LEADER: For all prisoners and captives, and all who suffer from oppression, that you will manifest your mercy toward them, and make all hearts as merciful as your own;

PEOPLE: **Hear us, O God.**

LEADER: For all who bear the cross of suffering, the sick in body or mind;

PEOPLE: **Hear us, O God.**

LEADER: For all those who are troubled by the sin or suffering of those they love;

PEOPLE: **Hear us, O God.**

LEADER: For all who are absorbed in their own grief, that they may be raised to share the sorrows of others, and know the saving grace of the cross;

PEOPLE: **Hear us, O God.**

LEADER: For all perplexed by the deeper questions of life and overshadowed with doubt, that your light may guide them;

PEOPLE: **Hear us, O God.**

LEADER: For all who are tried by temptations or weakness, that your mercy may be their strength;

PEOPLE:     **Hear us, O God.**

LEADER:     For all who are lonely and sad in the midst of others' joy, that they may know you as their friend and comforter;

PEOPLE:     **Hear us, O God.**

LEADER:     For the infirm and aged and for all who are dying, that they may find their strength in you and light at evening time;

PEOPLE:     **Hear us, O God.**

LEADER:     For all forgotten by us, but dear to you;

PEOPLE:     **Hear us, O God.**

LEADER:     O compassionate God, hear our prayers, answer them according to your will, and make us channels of your infinite grace; through Jesus Christ we pray.

ALL:        **Amen.**

## A Litany for Evening

# 879

LEADER:     In faith let us offer our prayer, saying, "Christ, have mercy."
            For the peace of the whole world, and for our salvation, we pray to you, O Christ;

PEOPLE:     **Christ, have mercy.**

LEADER:     For your church, and for all who minister in it, we pray to you, O Christ;

PEOPLE:     **Christ, have mercy.**

LEADER:     For the leaders of nations, that they may ever seek justice and peace, we pray to you, O Christ;

PEOPLE:     **Christ, have mercy.**

LEADER:     For all who are traveling, and for those in danger, we pray to you, O Christ;

PEOPLE:     **Christ, have mercy.**

LEADER: For those who are in need, especially those who are hungry, sick, and dying, we pray to you, O Christ;

PEOPLE: **Christ, have mercy.**

LEADER: For those who are frightened and alone, we pray to you, O Christ;

PEOPLE: **Christ, have mercy.**

LEADER: For those who are oppressed and suffer injustice, we pray to you, O Christ;

PEOPLE: **Christ, have mercy.**

LEADER: For rest and refreshment for our minds and bodies, we pray to you, O Christ;

PEOPLE: **Christ, have mercy.**

LEADER: Remembering all who have died, (*especially <u>Name(s)</u>* ) and all the faithful saints, grant us eternal life with you, we pray to you, O Christ;

PEOPLE: **Christ, have mercy.**

LEADER: Grant us your protection as we sleep, and guide us in all that we do when we awaken. For all these things, and for whatever may be best for us, we pray in your holy name.

ALL: **Amen.**

## A Litany of Darkness and Light

# 880

I:* We wait in the darkness, expectantly, longingly, anxiously, thoughtfully.

II: The darkness is our friend. In the darkness of the womb, we have all been nurtured and protected. In the darkness of the womb, the Christ-child was made ready for the journey into light.

ALL: **You are with us, O God, in darkness and in light.**

I: It is only in the darkness that we can see the splendor of the universe—blankets of stars, the solitary glowings of distant planets.

II: It was the darkness that allowed the Magi to find the star that guided them to where the Christ-child lay.

ALL:    **You are with us, O God, in darkness and in light.**

I:      In the darkness of night, desert peoples find relief from the cruel, relentless heat of the sun.

II:     In the blessed desert darkness, Mary and Joseph were able to flee with the infant Jesus to safety in Egypt.

ALL:    **You are with us, O God, in darkness and in light.**

I:      In the darkness of sleep, we are soothed and restored, healed and renewed.

II:     In the darkness of sleep, dreams rise up. God spoke to Jacob and Joseph through dreams. God is speaking still.

ALL:    **You are with us, O God, in darkness and in light.**

I:      In the solitude of darkness, we sometimes remember those who need God's presence in a special way—the sick, the unemployed, the bereaved, the persecuted, the homeless, those who are demoralized and discouraged, those whose fear has turned to cynicism, those whose vulnerability has become bitterness.

II:     Sometimes in the darkness, we remember those who are near to our hearts—colleagues, partners, parents, children, neighbors, friends. We thank God for their presence and ask God to bless and protect them in all that they do—at home, at school, as they travel, as they work, as they play.

ALL    **You are with us, O God, in darkness and in light.**

I:      Sometimes, in the solitude of darkness, our fears and concerns, our hopes and our visions rise to the surface. We come face to face with ourselves and with the road that lies ahead of us. And in that same darkness, we find companionship for the journey.

II:     In that same darkness, we sometimes allow ourselves to wonder and worry whether the human race is going to survive.

ALL:    **We know you are with us, O God, yet we still await your coming. In the darkness that contains both our hopelessness and our expectancy, we watch for a sign of God's hope.**

*Department of Parish Development and Mission, New Zealand*

*This litany may be said in various ways: parts I and II may be spoken by individuals, by groups, or by a worship leader, with all responding.*

# CREEDS, AFFIRMATIONS OF FAITH

## 881

### The Apostles' Creed

I believe in God, the Father almighty,
  creator of heaven and earth.

I believe in Jesus Christ, God's only Son, our Lord,
  who was conceived by the Holy Spirit,
  born of the Virgin Mary,
  suffered under Pontius Pilate,
  was crucified, died, and was buried;
  he descended to the dead.
  On the third day he rose again;
  he ascended into heaven,
  he is seated at the right hand of the Father,
  and he will come to judge the living and the dead.

I believe in the Holy Spirit,
  the holy catholic Church,
  the communion of saints,
  the forgiveness of sins,
  the resurrection of the body,
  and the life everlasting. Amen.

## 882

### The Apostles' Creed,
### an alternate version

I believe in God
  the Father-Mother almighty,
  creator of heaven and earth.

I believe in Jesus Christ, God's only Child, our Sovereign,
  who was conceived by the Holy Spirit,
  born of the Virgin Mary,
  suffered under Pontius Pilate,
  was crucified, dead, and buried.
  Having descended to the dead and having risen on the third day,
  Christ ascended into heaven,
  sits at the right hand of the Father-Mother,
  and from there will come to judge the living and the dead.

I believe in the Holy Spirit,
  the holy catholic church,
  the communion of saints,
  the forgiveness of sins,
  the resurrection of the body,
  and the life everlasting. Amen.

## 883

### The Nicene Creed

We believe in one God,
    the Father, the Almighty,
    maker of heaven and earth,
    of all that is, seen and unseen.

We believe in one Lord, Jesus Christ,
    the only Son of God,
    eternally begotten of the Father,
    God from God, Light from Light,
    true God from true God,
    begotten, not made,
    of one Being with the Father;
    through him all things were made.
    For us and for our salvation
        he came down from heaven,
        was incarnate of the Holy Spirit and the Virgin Mary
        and became truly human.
        For our sake he was crucified under Pontius Pilate;
        he suffered death and was buried.
        On the third day he rose again
        in accordance with the Scriptures;
        he ascended into heaven
        and is seated at the right hand of the Father.
        He will come again in glory to judge the living and the dead,
        and his kingdom will have no end.

We believe in the Holy Spirit, the Lord, the giver of life,
    who proceeds from the Father and the Son,
    who with the Father and the Son is worshiped and glorified,
    who has spoken through the prophets.
    We believe in one holy catholic and apostolic Church.
    We acknowledge one baptism for the forgiveness of sins.
    We look for the resurrection of the dead,
        and the life of the world to come. Amen.

## The Nicene Creed,
## an alternate version

We believe in one God, the Father-Mother, the Almighty
maker of heaven and earth,
and of all things visible and invisible.

We believe in one Sovereign, Jesus Christ,
the only Child of God,
begotten from the Father-Mother before all worlds —
God from God, Light from Light, true God from true God;
begotten, not made;
of one Being with the Father-Mother;
through whom all things were made;
who because of us human beings and for our salvation,
came down from heaven,
being made flesh by the Holy Spirit and the Virgin Mary,
and became a human being;
who was crucified for us under Pontius Pilate,
and suffered and was buried,
and rose again the third day in accordance with the scriptures,
and ascended into heaven,
and sits at the right hand of the Father-Mother;
who will come again with glory to judge the living and the dead;
whose dominion will have no end.

We believe in the Holy Spirit, the Sovereign, the giver of life,
who proceeds from the Father-Mother, and from the Child;
who with the Father-Mother and the Child is worshiped and glorified;
who spoke by the prophets.
And we believe in one holy catholic and apostolic church;
we acknowledge one baptism for the forgiveness of sins;
we look for the resurrection of the dead,
and the life of the world to come. Amen.

# 885

## United Church of Christ Statement of Faith
## in the Form of a Doxology

We believe in you, O God, Eternal Spirit,
God of our Savior Jesus Christ and our God,
and to your deeds we testify:

You call the worlds into being,
create persons in your own image,
and set before each one the ways of life and death.

You seek in holy love to save all people from aimlessness
    and sin.

You judge people and nations by your righteous will
    declared through prophets and apostles.

In Jesus Christ, the man of Nazareth, our crucified and
    risen Savior,
    you have come to us
    and shared our common lot,
    conquering sin and death
    and reconciling the world to yourself.

You bestow upon us your Holy Spirit,
    creating and renewing the church of Jesus Christ,
    binding in covenant faithful people of all ages,
    tongues, and races.

You call us into your church
    to accept the cost and joy of discipleship,
    to be your servants in the service of others,
    to proclaim the gospel to all the world
    and resist the powers of evil,
    to share in Christ's baptism and eat at his table,
    to join him in his passion and victory.

You promise to all who trust you
    forgiveness of sins and fullness of grace,
    courage in the struggle for justice and peace,
    your presence in trial and rejoicing,
    and eternal life in your realm which has no end.

Blessing and honor, glory and power be unto you. Amen.

# 886

## Affirmation of Faith

You, O God, are supreme and holy.
You create our world and give us life.
Your purpose overarches everything we do.
You have always been with us.
You are God.
You, O God, are infinitely generous,
good beyond all measure.
You came to us before we came to you.

You have revealed and proved
your love for us in Jesus Christ,
who lived and died and rose again.
You are with us now.
You are God.

You, O God, are Holy Spirit.
You empower us to be your gospel in the world.
You reconcile and heal; you overcome death.

You are our God. We worship you.

*A New Zealand Prayer Book*

# 887

## A New Creed

LEADER: We are not alone, we live in God's world.

PEOPLE: **We believe in God:**
    **who has created and is creating,**
    **who has come in Jesus,**
      **the Word made flesh,**
      **to reconcile and make new,**
    **who works in us and others by the Spirit.**
**We trust in God.**
**We are called to be the Church:**
    **to celebrate God's presence,**
    **to love and serve others,**
    **to seek justice and resist evil,**
    **to proclaim Jesus,**
      **crucified and risen,**
      **our judge and our hope.**
**In life, in death, in life beyond death,**
    **God is with us.**
**We are not alone. Thanks be to God.**

*United Church of Canada, 1980*

# INDEXES

# COPYRIGHT ACKNOWLEDGMENTS

Divider page artwork by Joan Menocal Copyright © 1995 *The New Century Hymnal.*

## Orders for Worship

See acknowledgments following Orders for Worship.

## Hymns

2 Arrangement Copyright © 1992 The Pilgrim Press.
5 Words Copyright © 1983 Nobuaki Hanaoka. Harmonization Copyright © 1993 The Pilgrim Press.
6 Translation Copyright © 1993 by Madeleine Forell Marshall.
8 Words Copyright © 1966 by the Estate of Curtis Beach.
9 Words Copyright © 1992 by Gracia Grindal. Music Copyright © 1980 by G.I.A. Publications, Inc.
11 Copyright © 1989 by Hope Publishing Co., Carol Stream, IL 60188. All rights reserved. Used by permission.
12 Descant Copyright © 1993 The Pilgrim Press.
13 Words reprinted from "THE PRESBYTERIAN HYMNAL" Copyright © 1990 Westminster/John Knox Press. Alt.
14 Copyright © 1971 Bud John Songs, Inc.
15 Words Copyright © 1993 Medical Mission Sisters. Music Copyright © 1978 LUTHERAN BOOK OF WORSHIP. Reprinted by permission of Augsburg Fortress.
17 Word adaptations Copyright © 1993 Medical Mission Sisters. Harmonization Copyright © , Oxford University Press. From THE ENGLISH HYMNAL, 1906. Descant Copyright © 1993 The Pilgrim Press.
20 Copyright © 1986 James Gertmenian. Harmonization Copyright © 1986 Ronald Huntington. Used by permission.
21 Words Copyright © 1987 Jane Parker Huber from A SINGING FAITH. Used by permission of Westminster/John Knox Press.
22 Translation Copyright © 1993 Madeleine Forell Marshall.
26 Word alterations Copyright © 1993 The Pilgrim Press.
27 Harmonization Copyright © , Oxford University Press. From THE ENGLISH HYMNAL, 1906.
28 Words stanza 4 Copyright © 1993 Medical Mission Sisters.
29 Words and arrangement Copyright © 1991 The Iona Community. Used by permission of G.I.A. Publications, Inc. Music Copyright © 1989 Salvador T. Martinez.
30 Copyright © 1993 by Hope Publishing Co., Carol Stream, IL 60188. All rights reserved. Used by permission.
32 Words Copyright © 1983 Jaroslav J. Vajda. Music Copyright © 1983 by G.I.A. Publications, Inc.
33 Translation Copyright © 1983 Boris and Clare Anderson. Harmonization Copyright © 1983 I-to Loh.
34 Copyright © 1983 Discipleship Resources.
35 Translation and harmonization Copyright © 1994 The Pilgrim Press.
36 Words Copyright © 1986 by G.I.A. Publications, Inc.
37 Words Copyright © 1986 London Yearly Meeting of the Religious Society of Friends (Quakers).
38 Word alterations Copyright © 1993 The Pilgrim Press. Music Copyright © , Oxford University Press.
39 Words and music Copyright © 1976 by Resource Publications, Inc., 160 E. Virginia St., #290, San Jose, CA 95112. English translation Copyright © 1989 Augsburg Fortress. Reprinted by permission. Harmonization Copyright © 1993 The Pilgrim Press.
40 Word alterations Copyright © 1992 The Pilgrim Press.
41 Words and music by Kenneth Morris. Copyright © 1948 by Martin & Morris; Copyright renewed. All rights administered by UniChappell Music, Inc. International copyright secured. All rights reserved. Arrangement Copyright © 1992 The Pilgrim Press.
43 Word alterations Copyright © 1992 The Pilgrim Press.
44 Translation Copyright © 1993 Madeleine Forell Marshall.
45 Translation Copyright © 1993 The Pilgrim Press. Arrangement Copyright © 1993 Luis Olivieri.

46 Words Copyright © 1954, renewal 1982 by The Hymn Society, Texas Christian University, Fort Worth, TX 76129. All rights reserved. Used by permission.
47 Words Copyright © 1994 The Pilgrim Press.
48 Words Copyright © , Methodist Church Division of Education and Youth. Harmonization Copyright © , Oxford University Press.
50 Translation Copyright © 1993 Madeleine Forell Marshall.
51 Music arrangement and harmonization Copyright © , Oxford University Press. From THE ENGLISH HYMNAL, 1906.
52 Word alterations Copyright © 1993 The Pilgrim Press.
53 Copyright © 1982 Bob Jay Publishers.
54 Copyright © 1985, Oxford University Press, Inc. From NEW HYMNS FOR THE LECTIONARY.
55 Word adaptations Copyright © 1981 Ruth C. Duck.
56 Spanish Copyright © Osvaldo Catena. Translation Copyright © 1993 The Pilgrim Press. Arrangement Copyright © 1991 Concordia Publishing House.
57 Words Copyright © 1991 Jean Wiebe Janzen.
58 Words Copyright © 1992 by Hope Publishing Co., Carol Stream, IL 60188. All rights reserved. Used by permission.
59 Words Copyright © , The Community of Resurrection.
60 Translation Copyright © 1993 Madeleine Forell Marshall.
61 Music Copyright © 1985 by Hope Publishing Co., Carol Stream, IL 60188. All rights reserved. Used by permission.
62 Copyright © 1987 Vicki Vogel Schmidt.
64 Words Copyright © 1988, Oxford University Press.
65 Copyright © 1983 Pablo Sosa. English translation Copyright © 1983 Discipleship Resources. Arrangement Copyright ©1984 Roberto Milano.
66 Words stanza 3 Copyright © 1982 Charles P. Price. Words stanza 4 Copyright © 1982 The Church Pension Fund. Used by permission.
67 Translation Copyright © 1993 Madeleine Forell Marshall.
69 Copyright © 1992 Marion M. Meyer. Harmonization Copyright © 1994 The Pilgrim Press.
70 Words Copyright © 1979; Music Copyright © 1942, renewed 1970 by Hope Publishing Co., Carol Stream, IL 60188. All rights reserved. Used by permission.
71 Word adaptations Copyright © 1981 Ruth C. Duck. Music Copyright © 1974 by Shawnee Press, Inc. (ASCAP). All rights reserved. Used by permission.
72 Words Copyright © 1958; Phonetic transcription Copyright © 1989 The United Methodist Publishing House. Music: JASRAC; 1-7-13 Nishishimbashi, Minato-ku, Tokyo 105, Japan.
73 Words and music Copyright © 1992 Louise Ruspini. Harmonization Copyright © 1993 The Pilgrim Press.
74 Translation Copyright © 1993 Madeleine Forell Marshall.
76 Words Copyright © 1964 by World Library Publications (A Div. of J. S. Paluch Company, Inc.). All rights reserved. Used by permission. Music © 1972 CONTEMPORARY WORSHIP 4: Hymns for Baptism and Holy Communion. Reprinted by permission of Augsburg Fortress. Descant Copyright © 1993 The Pilgrim Press.
78 Harmonization Copyright © 1965 Abingdon Press.
79 Copyright © 1989 by Hope Publishing Co., Carol Stream, IL 60188. All rights reserved. Used by permission.
80 Word alterations Copyright © 1992 The Pilgrim Press.
82 Words stanza 1 and 3 Copyright © 1983; Words stanza 2 Copyright © 1990 Jaroslav J. Vajda.
83 Music Copyright © 1993, Selah Publishing Co., Inc. [Kingston, NY 12401. All rights reserved.]
84 Words stanza 1 and music Copyright © 1967, 1980, Scripture in Song. (Administered by MARANATHA! MUSIC c/o THE COPYRIGHT COMPANY, Nashville, TN.) All rights reserved. International Copyright Secured.
85 Arrangement Copyright © 1993 The Pilgrim Press.
86 Word alterations Copyright © 1992 The Pilgrim Press.

594    Word adaptations Copyright © 1993 Medical Mission Sisters.
595    Copyright © 1932 Albert E. Brumley & Sons c/o Integrated Copyright.
600, 601    Words Copyright © 1991 Jean Wiebe Janzen.
602    "Come Sunday" from BLACK, BROWN, AND BEIGE by Duke Ellington. Copyright © 1946 (renewed) by G. Schirmer, Inc. (ASCAP). International Copyright secured. All rights reserved. Used by permission.
604    Arrangement Copyright © 1993 The Pilgrim Press.
605    Words Copyright © 1993 The Pilgrim Press. Arrangement Copyright © 1940 The Church Pension Fund.
607    Words used by permission of the Estate of Purd E. Deitz. Music Copyright © Breitkopf and Härtel, Wiesbaden. Arrangement Copyright © 1933; renewed 1961 Presbyterian Board of Christian Education.
608    Copyright © 1989 by Hope Publishing Co., Carol Stream, IL 60188. All rights reserved. Used by permission.
611    Words Copyright © Emmanuel College, Toronto, Canada.
612    Copyright © 1991 Martha McMane. Harmonization Copyright © 1991 Don Brandon.
613    Arrangement Copyright © 1940 The Church Pension Fund.
614    Words and music Copyright © Oregon Catholic Press. Translation Copyright © 1989 United Methodist Publishing House. Harmonization Copyright © 1987 Juan Luis Garcia.
615    Words and arrangement Copyright © 1994 The Pilgrim Press.
616    Harmonization Copyright © 1981 Abingdon Press.

## Psalms and Canticles

The Scripture quotations included in the Psalms and Canticles section are adapted by *The New Century Hymnal*, The United Church Board for Homeland Ministries, United Church of Christ, from the *New Revised Standard Version of the Bible*, Copyright ©1989 by the Division of Christian Education of the National Council of Churches of Christ in the United States of America, and are used by permission. All rights reserved.

739    Translation and harmonization Copyright © 1994 The Pilgrim Press.
740    Words and harmonization Copyright © 1994 The Pilgrim Press.

## Service Music

741    Copyright © 1982 MAR-VEL.
742    Copyright © 1990 Elaine Kirkland and Phil Porter.
745    Reprinted from *Book of Worship*, Copyright © 1986. Used by permission of the United Church of Christ Office for Church Life and Leadership.
746    Reprinted from *Book of Worship*, Copyright © 1986. Used by permission of the United Church of Christ Office for Church Life and Leadership.
750    *American Lutheran Hymnal*, Copyright 1930, 1958 Augsburg Publishing House, Minneapolis, MN.
752    Copyright © 1981 Leon Roberts.
753    Copyright © 1995 The Pilgrim Press.
754    Reprinted from *Book of Worship*, Copyright © 1986. Used by permission of the United Church of Christ Office for Church Life and Leadership.
755    Reprinted from *Book of Worship*, Copyright ©1986. Used by permission of the United Church of Christ Office for Church Life and Leadership.
756    Music Copyright © 1978; rev. 1980, 1981 Les Presses de Taizé. G.I.A. Publications, Inc., U.S. agents.
758    Copyright © 1990 Pablo Sosa.
760    Used by permission of Lumko Institute, South Africa.
762    Music Copyright © 1994 The Pilgrim Press.
763    Music Copyright © 1994 The Pilgrim Press.
764    Music Copyright © 1994 The Pilgrim Press.

765    Copyright © 1972 Manna Music.
767    Music Copyright © 1978; rev. 1980; 1989 Les Presses de Taizé. G.I.A. Publications, Inc., U.S. agents.
768    Music Copyright © 1982; rev. 1983; 1984 Les Presses de Taizé. G.I.A. Publications, Inc., U.S. agents.
770    Copyright © 1989 Chenaniah Publications, Incorporated.
772    Copyright © 1991 Les Presses de Taizé. G.I.A. Publications, Inc., U.S. agents.
773    Harmonization Copyright © 1981 Abingdon Press.
775    Copyright © 1977, renewed 1979 North American Liturgy Resources.
776    Reprinted from *Book of Worship*, Copyright © 1986. Used by permission of the United Church of Christ Office for Church Life and Leadership.
777    Reprinted from *Book of Worship*, Copyright © 1986. Used by permission of the United Church of Christ Office for Church Life and Leadership.
778    Words Copyright © 1995 The Pilgrim Press.
779    Harmonization Copyright © 1968 Roberta Martin.
781    Word adaptations reprinted from *Book of Worship*, Copyright © 1986. Used by permission of the United Church of Christ Office for Church Life and Leadership.
783    Copyright © 1991 G.I.A. Publications, Inc.
784    Music Copyright © 1994 Emma Lou Diemer.
786    Reprinted from *Book of Worship*, Copyright © 1986. Used by permission of the United Church of Christ Office for Church Life and Leadership.
787    Reprinted from *Book of Worship*, Copyright © 1986. Used by permission of the United Church of Christ Office for Church Life and Leadership.
788    Copyright © 1989 Les Presses de Taizé. G.I.A. Publications, Inc., U.S. agents.
789    Reprinted from *Book of Worship*, Copyright © 1986. Used by permission of the United Church of Christ Office for Church Life and Leadership.
790    Reprinted from *Book of Worship*, Copyright © 1986. Used by permission of the United Church of Christ Office for Church Life and Leadership.
791    Music Copyright © , Oxford University Press.
792    Music Copyright © 1991 Martha McMane.
794    "Holy, Holy, Holy" reprinted from LUTHERAN BOOK OF WORSHIP. Music Copyright © 1978 by permission of Augsburg Fortress. Alt.
796    Reprinted from *Book of Worship*, Copyright © 1986. Used by permission of the United Church of Christ Office for Church Life and Leadership.
797    Reprinted from *Book of Worship*, Copyright © 1986. Used by permission of the United Church of Christ Office for Church Life and Leadership.
798    Reprinted from *Book of Worship*, Copyright © 1986. Used by permission of the United Church of Christ Office for Church Life and Leadership.
799    Music Copyright © 1987 Timothy Gibson.
800    Reprinted from *Book of Worship*, Copyright © 1986. Used by permission of the United Church of Christ Office for Church Life and Leadership.
801    Reprinted from *Book of Worship*, Copyright © 1986. Used by permission of the United Church of Christ Office for Church Life and Leadership.
802    Music Copyright © 1991 Concordia Publishing House.
804    Music and arrangement Copyright © 1987 Oregon Catholic Press.
805    Reprinted from *Book of Worship*, Copyright © 1986. Used by permission of the United Church of Christ Office for Church Life and Leadership.
806    Reprinted from *Book of Worship*, Copyright © 1986. Used by permission of the United Church of Christ Office for Church Life and Leadership.
808    Music Copyright © 1992 Luis Olivieri.

## Worship Resources

# Author, Composer, and Source Index

# METRICAL INDEX

# TUNE INDEX

# Scriptural Index

# LECTIONARY INDEX

(Based on the *Revised Common Lectionary*)

The relationship of a hymn to a specific reading from the lectionary is designated by the following letters: G = Gospel; E = Epistle, Other Early Christian Scripture (Other New Testament); P = Psalm; H = Hebrew Scripture (Old Testament); A = Apocrypha.

## Year A

### Advent 1
(*See also* ADVENT, 101–123)
G: Keep awake, be always    112
H: O God of love    571

### Advent 2
G: The Baptist shouts on    115
E: O Morning Star, how    158
H: Isaiah the prophet has    108
H: Now is the time    609
H: Return, my people    114
H: With joy draw water    109

### Advent 3
G: Canticle of Mary    p. 732
G: Mary, woman of the    123
G: My heart is overflowing    15
G: My heart sings out    106
G: My soul gives glory    119
H: Awake! Awake and    107
H: Strengthen all the weary    612

### Advent 4
G: "Gentle Joseph,    105
G: Hitsuji wa nemurei    137
G: Jesus, our brother, strong    138
G: O come, O come    116

### Christmas Day 1
(*See also* CHRISTMAS, 124–153)
G: Break forth,    140
G: Brightest and best    156, 157
G: "I am the light"    584
G: Love came down at    165
G: Now greet the swiftly    431
H: Now bless the God    110

### Christmas Day 2
(*See* Christmas Day 1)

### Christmas Day 3
(*See also* CHRISTMAS, 124–153)
G: Beautiful Jesus    44
G: Christ, mighty Savior    93
G: O holy radiance, joyous    739
G: O Holy Spirit, Root    57
G: O splendor of God's    87
G: O Wisdom breathed    740
P: To God compose a    36
H: God reigns o'er all    21

### Christmas 1
G: Amen, Amen    161
G: O sing a song    51
E: In a lowly manger    162
E: O love, how vast    209
E: What child is this    148

### Holy Name
G: Angels, from the realms    126
G: Pastores a Belén    149

### Christmas Day 2
E: A hymn of glory    259
E: All hail the power    304
E: Jesus—the very thought    507
E: O loving founder of    111

### New Year
G: Like a mother who    583
G: Standing at the future's    538
E: By gracious powers    413
E: For the healing of    576
E: I want to be    616
E: O holy city, seen    613
E: This is a day    417
H: In the bulb there    433

### Christmas 2
G: Born in the night    152
G: Christ, mighty Savior    93
G: Go tell it on    154
G: Manglakat na kita sa    142
G: O holy radiance, joyous    739
G: O splendor of God's    87
G: Of the Parent's heart    118
A: O Wisdom breathed    740

# TOPICAL INDEX

Immortal, invisible, God only wise 1
My heart is overflowing 15
Now thank we all our God 419
O God, how we have wandered 202
O God of all your people past 374
O my soul, bless your Creator 13
Por la mañana 88
Praise to God, your praises bring 430
Praise to the living God 8
Shadow and substance 398
'Tis winter now; the fallen snow 432
Unto the hills we lift our longing eyes 466
When minds and bodies meet as one 399
Why should I feel discouraged 475

**Realm of**
Come now, Almighty God 275
"Comfort, comfort O my people" 101
God reigns o'er all the earth! 21
Holy God, we praise your name 276
Isaiah the prophet has written of old 108
Keep awake, be always ready 112
Lead on eternal Sovereign 573
On River Jordan's banks I stand 598
We love your realm, O God 312
You are salt for the earth, O people 181

**Righteousness of**
God the Omnipotent! 577
In Egypt under Pharaoh 574
Let justice flow like streams 588
O God of earth and altar 582

**Shepherd, The**
God is my shepherd 479
My shepherd is the living God 247
Though falsely some revile or hate me 477

**Strength and Refuge of**
A mighty fortress is our God 439, 440
As pants the hart for cooling streams 481
Giver of life, where'er they be 603
How firm a foundation 407
How lovely is your dwelling 600
I look to you in every need 463
I will lift the cloud of night 482
Lift your heads, O martyrs, weeping 445
O God, our help in ages past 25
Rock of ages, let our song 10
Unto the hills we lift our longing eyes 466
We sing to you, O God 9

**Works in Creation**
All beautiful the march of days 434
All things bright and beautiful 31
Cantemos al Creador 39
Colorful Creator 30
Creating God, your fingers trace 462
De colores 402
God created heaven and earth 33
God of the sparrow God of the whale 32
God, who stretched the spangled 556
Golden breaks the dawn 470
Great Spirit God 341
How can I say thanks 14
I sing the mighty power of God 12
Let us with a joyful mind 16
"Lift up your hearts!" 38
O God, the Creator 291
O God, we bear the imprint of your face 585
O how glorious, full of wonder 558
Our God, to whom we turn 37
Praise to God 5

Praise to the living God 8
Sing praise to God, our highest good 6
Stars and planets flung in orbit 567
The weaver's shuttle swiftly flies 464
Wakantanka taku nitawa 3
When the morning stars together 453

**GOOD FRIDAY**
(*See also* JESUS CHRIST: Passion and Cross)
Ah, holy Jesus 218
Alas! and did my Savior bleed 200
Journey to Gethsemane 219
My song is love unknown 222
O sacred Head, now wounded 226
Sing, my tongue 220
Were you there 229
When I survey the wondrous cross 224

**GOSPEL CALL AND RESPONSE**
All my hope on God is founded 408
Before your cross, O Jesus 191
Christian, rise and act your creed 537
Come, labor on 532
Dear God, embracing humankind 502
God, who summons through all ages 356
"I am the light of the world!" 584
Jesus calls us, o'er the tumult 171, 172
Let us talents and tongues employ 347
Like a mother who has borne us 583
Mantos y ramos 214
Mary, woman of the promise 123
My eyes have seen the glory 610
"O come to me, you weary" 484
O Jesus, I have promised 493
Tú has venido a la orilla 173
We cannot own the sunlit sky 563
We gather together 421
You walk along our shoreline 504
Your ways are not our own 170

**GRACE** (*See* under GOD)

**GRATITUDE** (*See* THANKSGIVING)

**GRIEF**
(*See* COMFORT AND ASSURANCE; *see also* BURIAL AND MEMORIAL)

**GUIDANCE** (*See* under GOD; JESUS CHRIST: Guide and Leader; Presence)

**HARVEST**
(*See* SEASONS: Thanksgiving Day)

**HEALING (544–555)**
Ask me what great thing I know 49
Cristo es la peña de Horeb 45
For the healing of the nations 576
God, bless our homes 429
Immortal Love, forever full 166
Joys are flowing like a river 284
Lead us from death to life 581
Listen to your savior call 250
Now the green blade rises 238
O God of love, O God of peace 571
O Jesus Christ, may grateful hymns 212
O radiant Christ, incarnate Word 168
"Silence! Frenzied, unclean spirit" 176
We have the strength to lift and bear 178
We yearn, O Christ, for wholeness 179

**HEALTH AND WHOLENESS**
Christ will come again 608
O Christ, the healer, we have come 175
This is a day of new beginnings 417
We yearn, O Christ, for wholeness 179

**HEAVEN** (*See* ETERNAL LIFE)

**HERITAGE** (*See also* CHURCH: Anniversaries and Dedications, Communion of Saints; CITIZENSHIP)
God, creation's great designer 371
My eyes have seen the glory 610
This is my song 591
What gift can we bring 370

**HOLY NAME DAY**
O for a thousand tongues to sing 42

**HOLY SPIRIT**
(*See also* ADORATION AND PRAISE: Holy Spirit; PENTECOST)

**Baptism**
Soplo de Dios viviente 56
There's a sweet, sweet Spirit 293

**Comforter**
Come forth, O Love divine 289
Holy Spirit, come, confirm us 264
In solitude, in solitude 521
Joys are flowing like a river 284
Like the murmur of the dove's song 270
O holy Dove of God descending 285
O Holy Spirit, Root of life 57
O Spirit of God 60
Soplo de Dios viviente 56

**Fruits of**
God of change and glory 177
Gracious Spirit, Holy Ghost 61
O God in whom all life begins 401

**Illuminator**
Come forth, O Love divine 289
Come, O Spirit, with your sound 265
Come, teach us, Spirit of our God 287
Eternal Spirit of the living Christ 520
Holy Spirit, truth divine 63
O for a closer bond with God 450
O Spirit of God 60
O splendor of God's glory bright 87
Spirit of Jesus, if I love my neighbor 590

**Power of**
Come, O Spirit, dwell among us 267
Come, O Spirit, with your sound 265
Come, share the Spirit 62
Filled with the Spirit's power 266
Fire of God, undying Flame 64
God the Spirit, guide and guardian 355
Holy Spirit, ever dwelling 59
Holy Spirit, truth divine 63
Let every Christian pray 261
Like the murmur of the dove's song 270
Spirit, spirit of gentleness 286
There's a spirit in the air 294
Wind who makes all winds that blow 271

**Renewal of**
Come, Holy Spirit, heavenly Dove 281
Dust and ashes touch our face 186
Fire of God, undying Flame 64

Called as partners in Christ's service 495
Spirit of the living God 283
Tú has venido a la orilla 173

## PAIN AND SUFFERING
Be still, my soul 488
Here, Savior, in this quiet place 555
I love my God, who heard my cry 511
In Egypt under Pharaoh 574
Lead us from death to life 581
Mikotoba o kudasai 317
O Bread of life 333
O Christ, the healer, we have come 175
"O come to me, you weary" 484
O God in heaven 279
O God, my God 515
O Love that will not let me go 485
"Silence! Frenzied, unclean spirit" 176
Sweet hour of prayer! 505
Through all the world, a hungry 587
Where cross the crowded ways of life 543

## PALM SUNDAY
(See JESUS CHRIST: Triumphal Entry)

## PARDON (See FORGIVENESS OF SIN)

## PASSION SUNDAY (See JESUS CHRIST:
Passion and Cross; GOOD FRIDAY)

## PATRIOTISM (See CITIZENSHIP)

## PEACE (See also JUSTICE AND PEACE)

### Inner
Beams of heaven, as I go 447
Dear God, embracing humankind 502
Glorious is your name, O Jesus 53
Here, O my Lord, I see you face to face 336
How deep the silence of the soul 509
How like a gentle spirit 443
In the cross of Christ I glory 193 194
Jesus, priceless treasure 480
Let there be light, O God of hosts! 589
"O come to me, you weary" 484
Out of the depths, O God, we call 554
Peace I leave with you, my friends 249
Pues si vivimos 499
Savior, again to your dear name 80
What a covenant 471
When peace, like a river 438

### World
God of the ages, who with sure 592
Great God of earth and heaven 579
How beautiful, our spacious skies 594
It came upon the midnight clear 131
Let there be light, O God of hosts! 589
Now is the time approaching 609
O God of love, O God of peace 571
This is my song 591

## PENITENCE (See CONFESSION OF SIN;
FORGIVENESS OF SIN)

## PENTECOST (See also ADORATION AND
PRAISE: Holy Spirit; CHURCH:
Nature and Unity)

### Day of (261–272)
Come forth, O Love divine 289
Come, Holy Spirit, heavenly Dove 281

Come, share the Spirit 62
O holy Dove of God descending 285
Spirit, spirit of gentleness 286

### Hymns of the Spirit (281–294)
Creator Spirit, come, we pray 268
Hear the voice of God, so tender 174
Sweet delight, most lovely 269
Wind who makes all winds that blow 271

### Trinity Sunday (273–280)
(See also TRINITY, THE HOLY)

## PILGRIMAGE
At the font we start our journey 308
Awake, my soul, stretch every nerve 491
Behold the host all robed in light 296
For the faithful who have answered 384
Forward through the ages 377
Guide my feet 497
How firm a foundation 407
I sing as I arise today! 83
In the midst of new dimensions 391
It's the old ship of Zion 310
Jesus, Savior, pilot me 441
Jesus, still lead on 446
Lead on eternal Sovereign 573
Lift every voice and sing 593
My faith, it is an oaken staff 418
O Jesus, I have promised 493
Savior God above 602
Shall we gather at the river 597
Siyahamb' ekukhanyen' kwenkhos' 526
Somos pueblo que camina 340
We shall overcome 570
We who would valiant be 494
Won't you let me be your servant? 539

## PLURALISM (See also CHRISTIAN
UNITY; CHURCH: Nature and Unity;
JUSTICE AND PEACE)
Come, let us join with faithful souls 383
God of change and glory 177
O for a world 575
Praise with joy the world's Creator 273
We are your people 309

## PRAISE
(See ADORATION AND PRAISE)

## PRAYER (505–521)
(See also CHURCH: Worship and Prayer)
Every time I feel the Spirit 282
Give up your anxious pains 404
I am yours, O Lord 455
I must tell Jesus 486
Let there be light, O God of hosts! 589
More love to you, O Christ 456
Nearer, my God, to you 606
O kou aloha no 580
Out of the depths I call 483
Out of the depths, O God, we call 554
Por la mañana 88
Precious Lord, take my hand 472
Rising in darkness 90
Spirit of God, descend upon my heart 290
Wake, my soul 91

## PRESENTATION OF JESUS
(See JESUS CHRIST: Presentation of)

## PROCESSIONAL HYMNS
(See also OPENING OF WORSHIP)
All glory, laud, and honor 216, 217
All hail the power of Jesus' name! 304
Angels, from the realms of glory 126
As with gladness those of old 159
Crown with your richest crowns 301
For the beauty of the earth 28
From all that dwell below the skies 27
Glorious things of you are spoken 307
Hail O festal day! 262
Holy, holy, holy 277
Immortal, invisible, God only wise 1
Joyful, joyful, we adore you 4
Lift high the cross 198
"Lift up your hearts!" 38
Love divine, all loves excelling 43
Praise with joy the world's Creator 273
Rejoice, give thanks and sing 303
Rejoice, you pure in heart 55
The church's one foundation 386
The God of Abraham praise 24
The royal banners forward fly 221
To you, O God, all creatures sing 17
We worship you, God 26
When morning gilds the skies 86
You are salt for the earth, O people 181

## PROCLAMATION (See WITNESS)

## PROPHETS
"Comfort, comfort O my people" 101
God of the prophets 358
Little Bethlehem of Judah 113
Profetiza, Pueblo mío 578
Spirit, spirit of gentleness 286
The Baptist shouts on Jordan's shore 115
There's a voice in the wilderness 120

## PROVIDENCE (See under GOD)

## PSALM PARAPHRASES
(See also Psalter section (621–731))
A mighty fortress is our God 439 440
All people that on earth do dwell 7
As pants the hart for cooling streams 481
Creating God, your fingers trace 462
Enter, rejoice, and come in 73
Este es el día 65
From all that dwell below the skies 27
God is my shepherd 479
How lovely is your dwelling 600, 601
Let heaven your wonders proclaim 29
Let us with a joyful mind 16
My shepherd is the living God 247
O God, our help in ages past 25
O how glorious, full of wonder 558
O my soul, bless your Creator 13
Out of the depths I call 483
This is the day 84
To God compose a song of joy 36
To you, O God, all creatures sing 17
Unto the hills we lift our longing eyes 466
We worship you, God 26

## REALM OF GOD (607–617)
(See also GOD: Realm of)

## RECONCILIATION (See CHRISTIAN
UNITY; FORGIVENESS OF SIN)

God moves in a mysterious way 412
God of our life 366
God's actions, always good and just 415
I love my God, who heard my cry 511
I will trust in the Lord 416
If you but trust in God to guide you 410
I've got a feeling 458
Lead on eternal Sovereign 573
O God of love, O God of peace 571
Out of the depths I call 483
Por la mañana 88
Savior, like a shepherd lead us 252
Softly and tenderly 449
Such perfect love my Shepherd shows 248
Sweet hour of prayer! 505
We are often tossed and driven 444
We have the strength to lift and bear 178
Why should I feel discouraged 475

**TRUTH**
My eyes have seen the glory 610
O grant us light 469
We limit not the truth of God 316

**UNITY** (*See* CHRISTIAN UNITY;
   CHURCH: Nature and Unity)

**VISITATION OF MARY TO ELIZABETH**
Mary, woman of the promise 123
My heart sings out 106
My soul give glory 119

**VOCATION** (*See* WORK AND VOCA-
   TION; *See also* CONFIRMATION;
   STEWARDSHIP AND CREATION)

**WINTER** (*See* SEASONS: Changing)

**WITNESS (522–531)**
(*See also* CHURCH: Mission in the World)
Ask me what great thing I know 49
Faith of the martyrs 381
For all the saints 299
For the faithful who have answered 384
I sing a song of the saints of God 295
Lift your heads, O martyrs, weeping 445
Standing at the future's threshold 538
You are called to tell the story 357

**WORD OF GOD**
(*See* BIBLE, HYMNS ABOUT THE)

**WORK AND VOCATION**
O grant us, God, a little space 516
Take my gifts 562

**WORSHIP**
(*See* CHURCH: Worship and Prayer)

**WORSHIP RESOURCES (816–887)**
(*See Contents*)

**YOUTH** (*See also* CHILDREN; CONFIR-
   MATION; EDUCATION)
Come, teach us, Spirit of our God 287
Great work has God begun in you 353
I was there to hear your borning cry 351
I would be true 492
Now in the days of youth 350
Rejoice, you pure in heart 55
Take my life, God, let it be 448
We shall overcome 570
We would be building 607

**ZEAL**
Awake, awake to love and work! 89
Awake, my soul, stretch every nerve 491
Christian, rise and act your creed 537
Come, labor on 532
Come, we who love God's name 379, 382
Faith of the martyrs 381
Lead on eternal Sovereign 573
We who would valiant be 494

**ZION**
(*See also* CHURCH; CITY OF GOD)
Come, we who love God's name 379, 382
Glorious things of you are spoken 307

---

# First Line Index

Indentation and italics are used to indicate a first line or name by which a hymn is also known, or a translation.

A hymn of glory let us sing ...... 259
A mighty fortress is our God ...... 439, 440
A toi la gloire, ô Ressuscité! ...... 253
A woman came who did not count the cost ...... 206
Abide with me ...... 99
Adeste, fideles ...... 135
Adoro te devote ...... 339
Again we keep this solemn fast ...... 187
Ah, holy Jesus ...... 218
Ah, what shame I have to bear ...... 203
Alabanza ...... 34
Alas! and did my Savior bleed ...... 199, 200
All beautiful the march of days ...... 434
   *All creatures of our God and King* ...... 17
   *All earth is waiting* ...... 121
All glory, laud, and honor ...... 216, 217
All hail the power of Jesus' name! ...... 304
All my hope on God is founded ...... 408
All people that on earth do dwell ...... 7
All praise be yours, my God, this night ...... 100
All things bright and beautiful ...... 31
Alleluia! Alleluia! Hearts to heaven ...... 243
Alleluia! Gracious Jesus! ...... 257
   *Alleluia! Sing to Jesus!* ...... 257
Almighty God, your Word is cast ...... 318
Amazing grace, how sweet the sound ...... 547, 548
Amen, Amen ...... 161
An outcast among outcasts ...... 201
Angels, from the realms of glory ...... 126
Angels we have heard on high ...... 125

Arise, your light is come! ...... 164
As Moses raised the serpent up ...... 605
As pants the hart for cooling streams ...... 481
   *As shepherds filled with joy* ...... 149
   *As the rain is falling* ...... 34
As we gather at your table ...... 332
As with gladness those of old ...... 159
Ask me what great thing I know ...... 49
   *At early dawn* ...... 88
   *At the Cross* ...... 199
At the font we start our journey ...... 308
Awake! awake, and greet the new morn ...... 107
Awake, awake to love and work! ...... 89
Awake, my soul, stretch every nerve ...... 491
Away in a manger ...... 124

Baptized into your name most holy ...... 324
Be known to us in breaking bread ...... 342
Be not dismayed ...... 460
Be now my vision ...... 451
Be still, my soul ...... 488
   *Be thou my vision* ...... 451
Beams of heaven, as I go ...... 447
Beautiful Jesus ...... 44
   *Beautiful Savior* ...... 44
Because you live, O Christ ...... 231
   *Before the cross of Jesus* ...... 191
Before your cross, O Jesus ...... 191
   *Behold a host all robed in white* ...... 296
Behold the host all robed in light ...... 296

# Descant Index